THE ECONOMIC WAY OF THINKING

Fifth Edition

Paul Heyne

University of Washington

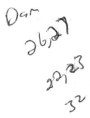

SCIENCE RESEARCH ASSOCIATES, INC.
Chicago, Henley-on-Thames, Sydney, Toronto

An IBM Company

Acquisition Editor	Robert F. Horan
Project Editor	Richard E. Myers
Copyediting	Timothy D. Loughman
Composition	Graphic World, Inc.
Illustrators	Pat Rogondino, Diana Hosier and George Robertson
Text Designer	Carol Harris and James A. Buddenbaum
Cover	James A. Buddenbaum

With gratitude to my joint authors, Wallie and Ruth

Acknowledgments

Photographs used by permission: *Chapter 1* © Erich Hartmann, Magnum Photos, Inc.; *Chapter 2* © Fernando Scianna, Magnum Photos, Inc.; *Chapter 3* © Katrina Thomas, Photo Researchers, Inc.; *Chapter 4* Bruce Davidson, Magnum Photos, Inc.; *Chapter 5* Richard Kalvar, © Magnum Photos, Inc.; *Chapter 6* © Richard Kalvar, Magnum Photos, Inc.; *Chapter 7* © 1978 Kosti Ruohomaa, from Black Star; *Chapter 8* © Sam C. Pierson, Jr., 1976, Photo Researchers, Inc.; *Chapter 9* Ingo Morath, © 1965 Magnum Photos Inc.; *Chapter 10* Elliott Erwitt, © 1966 Magnum Photos, Inc.; *Chapter 11* © Raymond Depardon, Magnum Photos, Inc.; *Chapter 12* Elliott Erwitt © 1970 Magnum Photos, Inc.; *Chapter 13* © Eugene Richards, Magnum Photos, Inc.; *Chapter 14* Kosti Ruohomaa, from Black Star; *Chapter 15* Kosti Ruohomaa, from Black Star; *Chapter 16* © 1978 Micheal Hayman, from Black Star; *Chapter 17* Dick Hanley, Photo Researchers, Inc.; *Chapter 18* © Norman Prince; *Chapter 19* Burt Glinn, © Magnum Photos, Inc.; *Chapter 20* Tom Hollyman, Photo Researchers, Inc.; *Chapter 21* © Arthur Tress, Magnum Photos, Inc.; *Chapter 22* © Norman Prince; *Chapter 23* Ingo Morath © 1963 Magnum Photos.

Library of Congress Cataloging-in-Publication Data

Heyne, Paul T.
  The economic way of thinking.

  1. Economics. I. Title.
HB171.5.H46 1987   330   86-20408
ISBN 0-574-19455-X

Printed in the United States of America

10 9 8 7 6 5 4 3 2

Contents

Preface   vii

1   **The Economic Way of Thinking**   **1**

    Questions for Discussion   12

2   **Substitutes Everywhere: The Concept of Demand**   **15**

    Questions for Discussion   35

3   **Opportunity Cost and the Supply of Goods**   **45**

    Questions for Discussion   60

4   **Supply and Demand: A Process of Coordination**   **67**

    Questions for Discussion   84

5   **Marginal Costs, Sunk Costs, and Economic Decisions**   **93**

    Questions for Discussion   111

6   **Efficiency, Exchange, and Comparative Advantage**   **119**

    Questions for Discussion   133

7   **Information, Middlemen, and Speculators**   **141**

    Questions for Discussion   154

8   **Price Setting and the Question of Monopoly**   **161**

    Questions for Discussion   171

9   **Price Searching**   **179**

    Questions for Discussion   193

10	**Competition and Government Policy**	**201**
	Questions for Discussion	214
11	**Profit**	**223**
	Questions for Discussion	247
12	**The Distribution of Income**	**257**
	Questions for Discussion	274
13	**Pollution and Conflicting Rights**	**287**
	Questions for Discussion	305
14	**Markets and Government**	**319**
	Questions for Discussion	337
15	**Inflation, Recession, Unemployment: An Introduction**	**349**
	Questions for Discussion	367
16	**Aggregate Supply and Aggregate Demand**	**373**
	Questions for Discussion	388
17	**The Supply of Money**	**393**
	Questions for Discussion	409
18	**Demand-Side Economics: Monetarist and Keynesian Perspectives**	**415**
	Questions for Discussion	432
19	**Fiscal and Monetary Policy**	**439**
	Questions for Discussion	458
20	**Supply-Side Perspectives**	**465**
	Questions for Discussion	482
21	**National Policies and International Exchange**	**489**
	Questions for Discussion	506
22	**Inflation, Recession, and Political Economy**	**511**
	Questions for Discussion	521
23	**The Limitations of Economics**	**527**
	Index	**530**

Preface

The Theory of Economics does not furnish a body of settled conclusions immediately applicable to policy. It is a method rather than a doctrine, an apparatus of the mind, a technique of thinking which helps its possessor to draw correct conclusions.

John Maynard Keynes

Introductory economics has long been an easy subject to teach. It's been a hard subject to *take*, but that's another matter. Moreover, the amount of learning that comes out of principles courses bears no reasonable relationship to the amount of teaching that goes in.

Principles of economics has been an easy course to teach because we have used it largely to regurgitate the bits of technique acquired during our own training in economics. There are so many such bits and pieces, and they are so hard for students to grasp, that principles teachers need never worry about what to do today. They can always introduce a new complication or spend the hour clarifying the complication introduced yesterday. And they don't even have to prepare the complications. A single phrase—elasticity, total-average-marginal revenue, long-run competitive equilibrium, marginal-value product, IS-LM, the multiplier—will serve as an adequate text for an entire class session.

What Are We After?

What should be the learning goal in the beginning economics course? It is clear from what has already been said that I have little use for what I take to be the usual learning goal: introducing the student to bits and pieces of technique. Why should we want a beginning student to be familiar with the concepts of average variable, average total, and marginal cost, their downward then upward shapes, the necessary intersection of marginal cost at the low point of average cost, and everything else contributing to the demonstration that in the long run, under perfectly competitive conditions, price will be equal to average total and marginal cost for all firms after quasi-rents have been capitalized? To ask the question is to answer it. We have no good reason for wanting a beginning student to know all this. Then why have we continued to teach it?

Part of the explanation lies in our commendable concern to teach *theory*. It is economic theory that gives to economics almost all its predictive or clarifying power. Without theory, we must grope our way blindly through economic problems, conflicting opinions, and opposing policy proposals.

But economic theory has proved itself unusually difficult to communicate. So those responsible for teaching undergraduate economics, struck by the apparent failure of theory-oriented principles courses, have sometimes opted instead for a problems and issues course. In such a course, students typically read and discuss statements by labor leaders, industry representatives, agricultural lobbyists, politicians, and a few domestic radicals or foreign socialists. They look at figures on income distribution, gross national product, employment, prices, and rates of economic growth. They read and discuss the arguments for guaranteed incomes and against planned obsolescence, for free enterprise and against unregulated competition, for nuclear power and against uncontrolled economic growth. And when it is all over, what have they learned? They have learned that opinions abound, with data to support every one of them, that "it's all relative," that every American is entitled to an opinion, and that economics is not a science and is probably a waste of time.

The insistence on teaching theory is correct insofar as it is a denial of the significance of facts without theories. Theory is essential! But what theory? Economic theory, of course. But that begs the real question. What *kind* of economic theory? And in what *context*? Before we can answer, we must know what we're after.

Concepts and Applications

I want beginning students to master a set of concepts that will help them think more coherently and consistently about the wide range of social problems that economic theory illuminates. The principles of economics make sense out of buzzing confusion. They clarify, systematize, and correct the daily assertions of newspapers, political figures, ax grinders, and barroom pontiffs. And the applicability of the economist's thought tools is practically unlimited. Students should come to appreciate all of this in a beginning course.

But they won't unless we, the teachers and textbook writers, persuade them. And we can persuade them only by showing them. *The principles of economics must therefore be taught as tools of analysis.* The teaching of a concept must take place in the context of application. Better, the potential application should be taught first, then the tool. There is so much evidence from pedagogy to support this approach that it's hard at first to understand how any other approach could ever have conquered the field.

"Here is a problem. You recognize it as a problem. What can we say about it?" That's step one.

"Here is how economists think about the problem. They employ the concept of such and such." Step two entails the exposition of some concept of economic theory.

After the applicability of the concept to the original problem has been demonstrated and some of the implications examined, the concept should be applied to additional problems. That's step three.

It isn't as easy as one-two-three, of course, and we don't mean to imply that it is. The teaching of economic principles requires imagination, insight, a knowledge of current events, and a sense of perspective, as well as familiarity with the formal techniques of economic analysis. Those are all scarce goods. And it presupposes a conviction on the part of the teacher that economic theory really is useful for something more than answering artificial questions and passing equally artificial examinations.

The Virtue of Restraint

Perhaps no one would disagree in principle with any of the foregoing statements. If so, our practice has been far out of step with our precept. One reason is undoubtedly the obsession with formal technique that characterizes so much teaching of economic theory at all levels. The disciple will very rarely rise above the master. And if the masters in our profession are more concerned with form than content, the effects will be felt at the principles level. We need not debate here the question of how much of the material taught in intermediate and advanced theory texts really belongs there, or what balance should be struck in graduate theory courses between the logic-mathematics and the economics of theory. For the question of what should go into a beginning course can be answered without resolving the other questions. And that answer is: *very little.*

For very little indeed of what might go into a complete and current compendium of economic theory is actually useful in enabling us to make sense of the real world and to evaluate policy proposals. Almost all the genuinely important things that economics has to teach are elementary concepts of relationship that people could almost figure out for themselves if they were willing to think carefully.[1]

The challenge is getting people to *appreciate* these few, simple concepts. To do that, we must practice the virtue of restraint. We must attempt less and thereby accomplish more. An introductory course should distinguish itself as much by what it excludes as by what it incorporates. Unless it is our aim to impress students with the esoteric quality of economists' knowledge, we should teach no theory in the introductory course that cannot be put to work immediately. Otherwise we drown beginning students; they are made to thrash about so desperately that they don't learn to swim a single stroke. Our aim should be to get them swimming and to instill in them the confidence that through practice they can learn to swim better.

Every introductory economics teacher ought to read a short essay by Noel McInnis, entitled "Teaching More with Less." Here are three excerpts:

> I dare say that all of us who teach have been guilty of telling our students much more than they cared—or needed—to know. In fact, I would theorize that we have probably been telling them more about our subjects than *we* care to know. That is one reason why we feel compelled to rely on notes to deliver lectures.

> Our present methods of communicating often obscure meaning rather than reveal it. . . . We often see the tragic results of this in our "best" students, who can repeat what we have told them but cannot apply it in a new context so that it means something. Their learning may have been comprehensive, but it has not been comprehend*ing*.

> Survey courses in almost all disciplines are becoming increasingly impractical because of their compulsive attempt to cover all relevant information. They could be made highly practical once again—or perhaps for the first time—if they were organized to convey the five or six most fundamental organizing and conceptual principles of the discipline, utilizing only the most immediately relevant information to bring the principles to life.[2]

I agree wholeheartedly with McInnis. Our implementation of this vision will undoubtedly be found far from perfect. But the teacher who wonders why this or that topic is not treated in the book, or why there is no complete exposition of

---

1. A compelling statement of this view was provided by Ely Devons in the first two of his *Essays in Economics* (London: George Allen and Unwin, 1961), pp. 13–46.
2. *Change: The Magazine of Higher Education* (January–February 1971), pp. 49, 50, 51.

some familiar portion of theory, should remember that knowledge is imparted by what is left out as well as by what is included. Judgments on relevance and relative importance will, of course, vary. But the argument of McInnis should be faced every time we are tempted to add another jot or tittle to the corpus of what we teach in beginning principles courses.

One Term or Two?

Every economics teacher, whether of graduates or undergraduates, knows how disconcertingly little most students bring with them from principles courses into subsequent studies. Sometimes they don't seem to remember anything except that they've "heard of it." Is the solution more credit hours of introduction? Should we detain them longer so that we can drill them more thoroughly in the fundamentals of our discipline? In my judgment the solution lies rather in the direction of fewer hours spent in the introductory course.

What is true and relevant tends to get lost when a beginning course is extended over two quarters or semesters. The student gets many fuzzy ideas of what the subject is *about*, but little grasp of what it *is*.

Moreover, there are too many pedagogical and administrative problems associated with the truncated unity of a two-term single course. Teachers change, textbooks change, micro comes before macro and then macro is put before micro, students drop out after the first term and return two years later for the second term. Why have we nonetheless persisted? It sometimes seems as if we're afraid to teach it all in one term for fear that we'll cut our demand in half. If we can persuade the curriculum makers, especially in the business schools, that two terms is the absolute minimum, we can better maintain the demand for our services.

But a single *worthwhile* term can leave the beginning student eager for more. And economic education doesn't have to end with the introductory course. It won't, at least for many of the students whom we want to continue, if we do a better job of getting them started. The demand for economic principles may even prove to be elastic: if we cut the hourly cost in half, the number of customers may more than double.

Some economists feel that, although a one-term course may be adequate for the general student, two terms are the essential minimum for economics or business majors. But isn't a brief and lively introduction to economics the best start for everyone, for those who plan never to take another course and for those who intend to go on to graduate school in economics? After all, a one-term principles course does not preclude subsequent courses in theory, courses that could be required or strongly recommended for majors. And more students might enroll in the theory courses if the introductory course managed to persuade them that economic theory is a worthwhile and occasionally even an exciting study.

Changes and Acknowledgments

Two significant changes will be found in the fifth edition. The quiet satisfaction I previously felt with the discussion questions at the end of the chapters has now become a case of sinful pride. Trivial questions have been weeded out; excellent new questions have been added; and a substantial number of graph questions have been included for those who find such exercises a valuable aid to learning economic theory.

I'm far less confident about the other major change: an extensive reorganization of the "macro" material (Chapters 15 to 22). After false starts, much agonizing, many delays, detours, and even some temper tantrums, all borne with commendable grace by my patient editor, Robert Horan, I have made the macroeconomic chapters tell a simpler but less decisive story. If it all turns out to be retrogression, I shall take comfort from the knowledge that enthusiasm for my handling of macroeconomics has probably never persuaded any economist to adopt the book.

My thinking continues to be challenged, clarified, and corrected by interactions with students, graduate assistants, and faculty at the University of Washington, and I am grateful to all of them. Among colleagues at other schools, I must single out for special thanks P.J. Hill of Montana State University, Charles Lave at the University of California, Irvine, and Howard Swaine of Northern Michigan University, three extremely thoughtful critics. I am also grateful for helpful suggestions from Eric Donohue, Martin Dermody, Wanda Morris, Southwestern Technical College; Ronald S. Fish, Northern Virginia Community College, J.S. Thompson, Seneca College (Toronto), and Peter Toumanoff, Marquette University. And I must not fail to acknowledge once again the pioneering role of Armen A. Alchian and William R. Allen, whose *University Economics* first showed me how to make introductory economics a useful and exciting course.

Special thanks are also due to Michelle Heyne for editorial assistance and to Marian Bolan for regularly bringing order out of chaos, often on short notice and always with good humor. For the forms and colors whose primacy I still too often forget, I am grateful to my wife, Juliana.

Paul Heyne

The Economic Way of Thinking

Good mechanics can locate the problem in your car because they know how your car functions when it *isn't having any problems*. A lot of people find economic problems baffling because they do not have a clear notion of how an economic system works when it's working well. They are like mechanics whose training has been limited entirely to the study of malfunctioning engines.

When we have long taken something for granted, it's hard even to see what it is that we've grown accustomed to. That's why we rarely notice the existence of order in society and cannot recognize the mechanisms of social coordination upon which we depend every day. A good way to begin the study of economics, therefore, might be with astonishment at the feats of social cooperation in which we daily engage. Rush-hour traffic is an excellent example.

Recognizing Order

You are supposed to gasp at that suggestion. "Rush-hour traffic as an example of social *cooperation?* Shouldn't that be used to illustrate the law of the jungle or the *breakdown* of social cooperation?" Not at all. If the association that pops into your mind when someone says "rush-hour traffic" is "traffic jam," you are neatly supporting the thesis that we notice only failures and take success so much for granted we aren't even aware of it. The dominant characteristic of rush-hour traffic is not jam but movement, which is why people venture into it day after day and almost always reach their destinations. It doesn't work perfectly, of course. (Name one thing that does.) But the remarkable fact at which we should learn to marvel is that it works at all.

Thousands of people leave their homes at about eight in the morning, slide into their automobiles, and head for work. They all choose their own routes without any consultation. They have diverse skills, differing attitudes toward risk, and varying degrees of courtesy. As these passenger automobiles in their wide assortment of sizes and shapes enter, move along, and exit from the intersecting corridors that make up the city's traffic veins and arteries, they are joined by an even more heterogeneous mixture of trucks, buses, motorcycles, and taxicabs. The drivers all pursue their separate objectives, with an almost single-minded devotion to their own interests, not necessarily because they are selfish but simply because none of them knows anything about the objectives of the others. What each one does know about the others is confined to a few observations on the position, direction, and velocity of a changing handful of vehicles in the immediate environment. To this they add the important assumption that other drivers are about as eager to avoid an accident as they themselves are. There are general rules, of course, which everyone is expected to obey, such as stopping for red lights and staying close to the speed limit. That's about it, however. The entire arrangement as just described could be a prescription for chaos. It ought to end in heaps of mangled steel.

What ensues instead is a smoothly coordinated flow, a flow so smooth, in fact, that an aerial view from a distance can almost be a source of aesthetic pleasure. There they are—all those independently operated vehicles down below, inserting themselves into the momentary spaces between other vehicles, staying so close and yet rarely touching, cutting across one another's paths with only a second or two separating a safe passage from a jarring collision, accelerating when space opens before them and slowing down when it contracts. The movement of rush-hour traffic, or indeed of urban traffic at any time of day, really is an astounding feat of social cooperation.

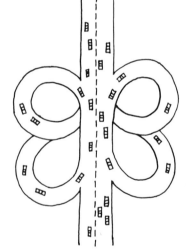

The Importance of Social Cooperation

The traffic example is particularly effective in making us see how much social cooperation we totally fail to notice, because everyone is familiar with traffic but almost no one thinks of it as a cooperative endeavor. But the example is also useful in making the point that we depend on mechanisms of coordination for far more than what we usually think of as "economic" goods. If we had no working procedures to induce cooperation, we could enjoy none of the benefits of civilization. "In such a condition," as Thomas Hobbes (1588-1679) observed in an often-quoted passage of his *Leviathan*:

> . . . there is no place for industry, because the fruit thereof is uncertain; and consequently no culture of the earth; no navigation, nor use of the commodities that may be imported by sea; no commodious building; no instruments of moving and removing such things as require much force; no knowledge of the face of the earth; no account of time; no arts; no letters; no society; and, which is worst of all, continual fear, and danger of violent death; and the life of man, solitary, poor, nasty, brutish, and short.[1]

Because Hobbes believed that people were so committed to self-preservation and personal satisfaction that only force (or the threat of it) could keep them from constantly assaulting one another, his writings emphasize only the most basic form of social cooperation: abstention from violence and robbery. He seems to have supposed that if people could be induced not to attack one another's persons or property, then positive cooperation—the kind that actually produces industry, agriculture, knowledge, and art—would develop of its own accord. But will it? Why should it?

How Does It Happen?

By what means do the members of a society induce one another to take precisely those complexly interconnected actions that will eventually produce the multitude of goods, tangible and intangible, that we all enjoy? Even a society of saints must use some procedures for inducing positive cooperation *of the right kind* if the life of each saint is to be more than "solitary, poor, nasty, brutish, and short." Saints must, after all, somehow find out exactly what ought to be done and when and where it ought to be done before they can play an effective part in helping others.

Hobbes probably failed to see the importance of this question for understanding life in the "commonwealth," because the society he knew was far simpler, more bound by custom and tradition, and less subject to rapid and disruptive change than the societies in which we have grown up. Not until late in the eighteenth century, as a matter of fact, did any significant number of thinkers begin to wonder why it was that society "worked"—that individuals pursuing their own interests on the basis of extremely limited information nonetheless managed to produce not chaos but a remarkably ordered society.

1. Hobbes, *Leviathan, or the Matter, Forme and Power of a Commonwealth Ecclesiastical and Civil*, 1651.

One of the most perceptive and surely the most influential of these eighteenth-century thinkers was Adam Smith (1723-1790). Smith lived in an age when most educated people believed that only the diligent attentions of political rulers could prevent a society from degenerating into disorder and poverty. Smith did not agree. But in order to refute the accepted opinion of his day, he had to describe the mechanism of social coordination that he saw operating in society—a mechanism that not only functioned, in his judgment, without the constant attention of government, but worked so power-fully that it often canceled the effects of contrary governmental policies. Adam Smith published his analysis in 1776 as *An Inquiry into the Nature and Causes of the Wealth of Nations*, and thereby established his claim to the title, Founder of Economics. He did not *invent* "the economic way of thinking." But he developed it more extensively than any of his predecessors had done, and he was the first writer to use it in a comprehensive analysis of social change and social cooperation.

An Apparatus of the Mind

What exactly do we mean by *the economic way of thinking?* To begin with, it is exactly what the term suggests: an approach, rather than a set of conclusions. John Maynard Keynes phrased it aptly in the statement quoted in the front of this book:

> The Theory of Economics does not furnish a body of settled conclusions immediately applicable to policy. It is a method rather than a doctrine, an apparatus of the mind, a technique of thinking which helps its possessor to draw correct conclusions.

But what is this "technique of thinking"? It is, most fundamentally, an assumption about what guides human behavior. The theories of economics, with surprisingly few exceptions, are simply extensions of the assumption that individuals take those actions they think will yield them the largest net advantage. Everyone, it is assumed, acts in accordance with that rule: miser or spendthrift, saint or sinner, consumer or seller, politician or business executive, cautious calculator or spontaneous improviser.

But don't misunderstand. Economic theory does not assume that people are selfish, or materialistic, or shortsighted, or irresponsible, or interested exclusively in money. None of these is implied by the statement that people try to secure for themselves the largest possible net advantage. Everything depends on what, in fact, people find in their own interest. As we know, some derive enormous satisfaction from helping people. A few, unfortunately, seem to derive satisfaction

Self-interested (not "selfish"!) actions

from actually hurting others. Some find their keenest pleasure in the sight of roses blooming. Others would far rather speculate on urban real estate.

But if people are all that different, how can economic theory explain or predict anything about their behavior merely by assuming that they all act in what they think will be their own best interests? What does the assumption imply except that people do what they want to do, whatever that is?

Matters aren't that hopeless, however, for people don't really seem to be as different in their interests as the preceding contrasts would suggest. All of us regularly and successfully predict the behavior of people whom we have never even met, and we could not function effectively in society without the ability to do so. Rush-hour traffic flow, for example, would be impossible if we could not predict the actions of others who are usually complete strangers. Moreover, in any society that uses money extensively, just about everybody prefers more money to less, because money offers a general command over the resources that can be used to advance one's interests, whatever they may be. This is a most useful fact to know when we are trying to predict the behavior of others.

Even Mother Teresa does better with more money.

It is also a useful piece of information when we want to *influence* the behavior of others. And that brings us back to the issue of social cooperation and to a second prominent characteristic of the economic way of thinking. Economic theory asserts that the actions people take in the pursuit of their own interests create the alternatives available to others, and that social coordination is a process of continuing mutual adjustment to the changing net advantages that their interactions generate. That is a very abstract argument. We can make it more concrete by referring once more to traffic flow.

Cooperation through Mutual Adjustment

Picture a freeway with four lanes in each direction and with all the entrances and exits on the right. Why don't all the drivers stay in the far-right lane? Why do some of them go to the trouble of driving all the way over to the far left when they know they'll have to come back to the right lane to exit? Anyone who has driven on a freeway knows the answer: the traffic flow is impeded in the far-right lane by slow-moving vehicles entering and exiting, so people in a hurry get out of the right lane as quickly as possible.

Which of the other lanes will they choose? Although we can't predict the action of any single driver, we know that the drivers will disperse themselves quite evenly among the three other lanes. But why does this happen? How does it

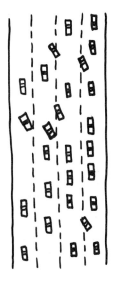

happen? The answer is also the explanation of what we meant just now by *a process of continuing mutual adjustment to the changing net advantages that their actions generate.* Drivers are alert to the net advantages of each lane and therefore try to move out of any lanes that are moving slowly and into those that are moving faster. This speeds up the slow lanes and slows down the fast lanes until all lanes are moving at the same rate, or, more accurately, until no driver perceives any net advantage to be gained by changing lanes. It all happens quickly, continuously, and far more effectively than if someone at the entrances passed out tickets *assigning* each vehicle to a particular lane.

That, according to the economic way of thinking, is how the social world works. Individuals choose their actions on the basis of the net advantages they expect. Their actions alter, however minutely, the relative benefits and costs of the options that others perceive. When the ratio of expected benefit to expected cost for any action increases, people do more of it. When the ratio falls, they do less. The fact that almost everyone prefers more money to less is an enormous aid in this process, an extremely important lubricant, if you will, in the mechanism of social coordination. Modest changes in the monetary cost and monetary benefit of particular options can induce large numbers of people to alter their behavior in directions more consistent with what other people are concurrently doing. And this is the primary system by which we obtain cooperation among the members of society in using what is available to provide what people want.

How Much Does Economic Theory Explain?

Some might object that the preceding paragraph claims too much. "You haven't given a description of 'how the social world works' but only of how the economic part of it works. You've described the market system. But that's not the whole of society. In addition to the market or economic sector, we have other institutions (such as the government sector) that operate by different principles and procedures."

That sounds like a reasonable objection, or at least one consistent with the traditional ways in which we've learned to divide up the world. But the economic way of thinking is subversive when it comes to those traditional distinctions. If it makes sense to explain the output of the Bethlehem Steel Company and the Chrysler Corporation as the product of competing interests mutually adjusted, why won't it make sense to explain the output of the United States Congress or the Department of Agriculture in the same way? Why draw a line between "the economy" and "the government"? Isn't

Is there actually a separate, distinguishable "economic sector" in our society? Where could one observe it?

every branch and agency of government made up, just like any other social group, of ordinary mortals with a wide variety of interests? The necessity of inducing others to cooperate doesn't stop when the capital city is reached! Or if it does, someone has failed to communicate that fact to the lobbyists, legislative leaders, staff assistants, and executive agents who struggle daily to shape the directions of government action.

To tell the embarrassing truth, economic theorists are highly imperialistic. They tend to think that their way of looking at society explains everything, or at least explains more occurrences more adequately than does any other approach. And so economists have been venturing out in recent years to raid territories traditionally occupied by sociologists, political scientists, historians, and others. Economists don't all agree (and representatives of the raided disciplines *surely* do not all agree) that these excursions have always captured valuable terrain. Some critics of the imperialistic ambitions of economics have even accused it of saying nothing about everything. We won't try to resolve those disputes at this point. But you should be aware in advance that this book will draw no clear lines to mark the boundaries of economics. Instead we shall fall back on the vague but sensible principle that economic theory should be used wherever it successfully explains or predicts and abandoned for something else whenever it sheds no light.

The Biases of Economic Theory

The admission that economics has imperialistic ambitions may not disturb you as much as our admission now that *the economic way of thinking is a biased perspective.* Economic theory does not offer an unprejudiced view of society, in which all the facts are presented and each is given the same weight. On the contrary, the economic way of thinking emphasizes a few facts out of a vast array of possibilities and discards most of what remains.

To begin with, economic theory focuses on the *choices* people make. Economic theory is so centrally concerned with choice, in fact, that some critics have accused it of assuming that people choose to be poor or choose to be unemployed. When we come to the issues of poverty and unemployment, you can decide for yourself whether this is a fair criticism or a misunderstanding. But there can be no doubt that economic theory attempts to explain the social world by assuming that events are the product of people's choices.

People choose.

Closely related to this focus on choice is the emphasis economic theory gives to the *individual.* Because only individuals actually choose, economists try to dissect the decisions

Only individuals choose!

Individuals choose rationally.

All social interactions can be viewed as market processes.

of such collectives as governments, universities, or corporations until they locate the choices of the individual persons who make them up. This analytical individualism looks suspiciously like certain other kinds of individualism that some people dislike, such as ethical individualism or "rugged" individualism. Does economic theory miss the significance of group action and social bonds by unduly emphasizing the individual? Whatever the merit or lack of merit in this charge, the economic way of thinking definitely does make the individual the ultimate unit of explanation.

Economic theory is also criticized by some as false or misleading because of its emphasis on *rationality*. Economists assume that people do not act capriciously, that they compare the expected costs and benefits of available opportunities before they act, and that they learn from and therefore do not repeat their mistakes. But are people really that rational? Aren't our actions guided more by unconscious urges and unexamined impulses than all this would admit? The question is again a hard one to answer, because it is a hard question even to pose in any clear and testable form. Although economists do not claim that people know everything or never make mistakes, the economic way of thinking does indeed assume that people's actions follow from calculations of costs and benefits.

Another charge often leveled against the economic way of thinking—or perhaps against the way in which it is sometimes used, as in this book—is that it harbors a *promarket* bias. This criticism, too, calls attention to a genuine and significant characteristic of economic theory, although a characteristic that may not be altogether what it seems to be. Economic theory does not really assume that markets work better than alternative institutions, notably government. Rather it assumes, as we have already indicated, that however poorly or well *any* institution functions, its functioning can best be understood as a consequence of market processes. Exaggerating somewhat for emphasis, we could say that economic theory does not find market solutions better (or worse) than government solutions, because it insists that government solutions *are* market solutions. The actions of government are the outcomes of market processes: individuals pursuing their own interests and mutually adjusting to one another's behavior, but doing so in the context of the special "rules of the game" that apply to the institutions that we call government.

Rules of the Game

That's a term you're going to meet repeatedly in this book: the *rules of the game*. Whether the "game" is business, govern-

ment, science, family, school, traffic, basketball, or chess, it can't be played satisfactorily unless the players know what the rules are and generally agree to follow them. Most social interaction is directed and coordinated by the rules that participants know and follow.

The rules of a game such as basketball or chess determine who gets to make what moves under which circumstances. So do the rules of the other "games" mentioned above. As we shall see, property rights form a large and important part of the rules governing most of the social interactions in which we regularly engage; by deciding *what is whose,* they determine, just as with games in the ordinary sense, who gets to make what moves under which circumstances. In this manner property rights and other rules of the game ultimately determine exactly what individuals will choose to do in the pursuit of their interests.

Biases or Conclusions?

Let's go back to those four prominent (and interrelated) biases inherent in the economic way of thinking. Are they really biases or prejudices? Why couldn't we call them convictions (or even conclusions), and simply say that economists explain social phenomena by postulating interaction among the rational choices of individuals, because this enables them to understand those phenomena? Do we say that astronomers are biased because they assume that all the light they observe has traveled toward them at 186,000 miles per second, or that biologists are biased because they assume that DNA molecules control the development of organisms?

The questions we're raising now are important and interesting.[2] But we cannot follow them further without pushing this chapter to an intolerable length. It has long seemed obvious to the author (a prejudice or a conclusion?) that the search for knowledge of any kind necessarily begins with some *commitments* on the part of the inquirer. We cannot approach the world with a completely open mind, because we weren't born yesterday. And completely open minds would in any event be completely empty minds, which can learn nothing at all. All discussion, every inquiry, and even each act of observation is rooted in and grows out of convictions. We cannot begin everywhere or with everything. We must begin somewhere with something. We proceed

---

2. The thoughtful student who would like to pursue these issues further should be sure to read *The Structure of Scientific Revolutions* by Thomas S. Kuhn (Chicago: University of Chicago Press, 1962). This highly readable essay on the history and philosophy of science has had an enormous influence in recent years on the thinking of social scientists about the respective roles of assumption and evidence in their investigations.

from where we find ourselves and on the basis of what we believe to be true, important, useful, or enlightening. We may, of course, be wrong in any of these judgments. Indeed, we are always wrong to some extent, since every "true" statement necessarily leaves out a great deal that is also true and thus errs by omission.

We cannot avoid this risk, as some people suppose, by steering clear of theory. People who sneer at "fancy theories" and prefer to rely on common sense and everyday experience are often in fact the victims of extremely vague and sweeping hypotheses. Consider this actual letter to a newspaper from a young person in Pennsylvania who was once "one of a group of teenage pot smokers. Then a girl in the crowd got pregnant. Her baby was premature and deformed and needed two operations." The newspaper's adviser to the teenage lovelorn printed that letter approvingly, as evidence that the price of smoking marijuana is high.

Perhaps it is. But suppose the writer of that letter had written: "Then the Pittsburgh Steelers won the Super Bowl, and the Philadelphia Flyers took the Stanley Cup." Everyone would object that those events had nothing to do with the group's pot smoking. *But how do we know that?* If the mere fact that the young girl's misfortunes followed her pot smoking is evidence of a causal relationship, why can't we also infer a causal relationship in the case of the Steelers and the Flyers?

No Theory Means *Poor* Theory

The point is a simple but important one. We cannot discover, prove, or even suspect any kind of causal relationship without having a theory in mind. Our observations of the world are in fact drenched with theory, which is why we usually can make sense out of the buzzing confusion that assaults our eyes and ears. Actually we observe only a small fraction of what we "know," a hint here and a suggestion there. The rest we fill in from the theories we hold: small ones and broad ones, vague and precise ones, well tested and poorly tested, widely held and sometimes peculiar, carefully reasoned and dimly recognized.

I.M.D. Little is a distinguished British economist who worked for a time as an adviser to the British treasury. He later wrote an article describing his experiences and discussing the usefulness of economic theory in the world of policymaking. Here is an interesting paragraph:

> Economic theory teaches one how economic magnitudes are related, and how very complex and involved these relationships are. Noneconomists tend to be too academic. They abstract

ingly few in number. But they are extraordinarily versatile. They unlock such mysteries as foreign exchange rates, business firms that make profits by accepting losses, the nature of money, and different prices charged for "identical" goods—mysteries that are generally conceded to be in the economist's province. But they also shed light on a wide range of issues that are not ordinarily thought of as economic at all—traffic congestion, environmental pollution, the workings of government, and the behavior of college administrators—to mention just a few that you will encounter in the chapters ahead.

The primary goal of this book is to start you thinking the way economists think, in the belief that once you start you will never stop. Economic thinking is addictive. Once you get inside some principle of economic reasoning and make it your own, opportunities to use it pop up everywhere. You begin to notice that much of what is said or written about economic and social issues is a mixture of sense and nonsense. You get in the habit of sorting the sense from the nonsense by applying the basic concepts of economic analysis. You may even, unfortunately, acquire the reputation of being a cynic, for people who habitually talk nonsense like to cry "cynic" at anyone who points out what they are doing.

QUESTIONS FOR DISCUSSION

1. What do you predict would happen if Los Angeles decided to reserve one lane on each of its freeways for "urgent vehicles," with an urgent vehicle defined as any vehicle whose driver might be late for an important event if the vehicle were to be delayed by congestion in the regular lanes? Do you think drivers would stay out of the urgent vehicle lane? Or would it become just as congested as all the other lanes? Would such an idea be more likely to succeed in practice if drivers were generally less selfish and more considerate?

2. When Mother Teresa accepted the Nobel Prize for Peace in October 1979 and decided to use the $190,000 award to construct a leprosarium, was she acting in her own interest? Was she behaving selfishly?

3. Freeway accidents typically produce traffic jams in the opposite-direction lanes, where the accident has created no obstruction at all, because motorists slow down to look. Assume that as a result each motorist going the opposite way is delayed ten minutes, and that all of them would gladly give up their quick peek at the accident in return for avoiding a ten-minute delay. Will the fact that no single motorist places a value of more than a one-minute delay on a chance to look at the accident mean that motorists won't slow down to look and so won't create the delay? What is wrong with the mechanism of social coordination in this case?

too much from the real world. No one can think about economic issues without some theory, for the facts and relationships are too involved to organize themselves: they do not simply fall into place. But if the theorist is untutored, he is apt to construct a very partial theory which blinds him to some of the possibilities. Or he falls back on some old and over-simple theory, picked up from somewhere or other. He is also, I believe, apt to interpret the past naively. *Post hoc ergo propter hoc*[3] is seldom an adequate economic explanation. I was sometimes shocked by the naive sureness with which very questionable bits of economic analysis were advanced in Whitehall. Of course, economists may be too academic in another sense: they may not appreciate administrative difficulties, or may lack a sense of political possibility. But, then, there is no danger of these things being overlooked.[4]

"*Noneconomists* tend to be too academic. They abstract too much from the real world." That isn't the way you usually hear it. But Little is probably correct. "I don't know anything about fancy economic theory," the confident amateur begins, "but what I do know this . . ." And what he says next demonstrates all too often that he was quite right in denying any knowledge of economic theory, but quite wrong in supposing that this preserved him from error. Those who try to reason about complex economic interrelationships without theory usually manage only to reason with very poor theory.

None of this should be interpreted as a wholesale defense of economists, who sometimes like to dazzle the public with complex theorems and exercises in pure logic instead of addressing the questions people are actually asking. Even in the teaching of economics, we have often behaved as if all the students enrolled in an introductory course were aiming at a Ph.D. in the subject, and that it was our duty to begin their preparation for the doctoral exams. That's probably why introductory courses typically offer so many more ideas than students can possibly digest.

This textbook developed out of a growing suspicion that when students found economic theory mystifying and tedious, it was largely because we economists were trying to teach them too much. This book very consciously sets out, therefore, to achieve more by attempting less. It is organized around a set of concepts that collectively make up the economist's basic kit of intellectual tools. The tools are all related to the fundamental assumptions we have discussed and are surpris-

---

3. Literally, "After this, therefore because of this"; the logical fallacy of assuming that A must have caused B if A preceded B in time. The argument of the penitent Pennsylvania pot smoker is an example.

4. I.M.D. Little, "The Economist in Whitehall," *Lloyds Bank Review* (April 1957).

too much from the real world. No one can think about economic issues without some theory for the facts and relationships are too involved to organize themselves: they do not simply fall into place. But if the theorist is untutored, he is apt to construct a very partial theory which blinds him to some of the possibilities. Or he falls back on some old and over-simple theory, picked up from somewhere or other. He is also, I believe, apt to interpret the past naively. *Post hoc ergo propter hoc*[3] is seldom checked by the naive sureness with which very sometimes bits of economic analysis were advanced in question. Of course, economists may be too academic in Whitehall: they may not appreciate administrative difficulties and may lack a sense of political possibility. But, then, there no danger of these things being overlooked.[4]

"...neconomists tend to be too academic. They abstract too ...from the real world." That isn't the way you usually ...it. But Little is probably correct. "I don't know anything ...ut fancy economic theory," the confident amateur begins, ...but I do know this. . . ." And what he says next demonstrates all too often that he was quite right in denying any knowledge of economic theory, but quite wrong in supposing that this preserved him from error. Those who try to reason about complex economic interrelationships without theory usually manage only to reason with very poor theory.

None of this should be interpreted as a wholesale defense of economists, who sometimes like to dazzle the public with complex theorems and exercises in pure logic instead of addressing the questions people are actually asking. Even in the teaching of economics, we have often behaved as if all the students enrolled in an introductory course were aiming at a Ph.D. in the subject, and that it was our duty to begin their preparation for the doctoral exams. That's probably why introductory courses typically offer so many more ideas than students can possibly digest.

This textbook developed out of a growing suspicion that when students found economic theory mystifying and tedio... it was largely because we economists were trying to teach them too much. This book very consciously sets out, the... to achieve more by attempting less. It is organized aro... set of concepts that collectively make up the economi... kit of intellectual tools. The tools are all related... fundamental assumptions we have discussed and...

3. Literally, "After this, therefore because of this"; the lo... assuming that A must have caused B if A preceded B in... of the penitent Pennsylvania pot smoker is an example...
4. I.M.D. Little, "The Economist in Whitehall," *Lloyds*... 1957).

ingly few in number. But they are extraordinarily versatile. They unlock such mysteries as foreign exchange rates, business firms that make profits by accepting losses, the nature of money, and different prices charged for "identical" goods— mysteries that are generally conceded to be in the economist's province. But they also shed light on a wide range of issues that are not ordinarily thought of as economic at all—traffic congestion, environmental pollution, the workings of govern- ment, and the behavior of college administrators—to mention just a few that you will encounter in the chapters ahead.

The primary goal of this book is to start you thinking the way economists think, in the belief that once you get started you will never stop. Economic thinking is addictive. Start inside some principle of economic reasoning and you get your own, opportunities to use it pop up everywhere. it begin to notice that much of what is said or written ou economic and social issues is a mixture of sense and . You get in the habit of sorting the sense from the non se. by applying the basic concepts of economic analysis. Yo even, unfortunately, acquire the reputation of being a cy. for people who habitually talk nonsense like to cry "cynic anyone who points out what they are doing.

ONS FOR DISCUSSION

1. What do you predict would happen if Los Angeles decided to reserve one lane on each of its freeways for "urgent vehicles," with an urgent vehicle defined as any vehicle whose driver might be late for an important event if the vehicle were to be delayed by congestion in the regular lanes? Do you think drivers would stay out of the urgent vehicle lane? Or would it become just as congested as all the other lanes? Would such an idea be more likely to succeed in practice if drivers were generally less selfish and more con- siderate?

2. When Mother Teresa accepted the Nobel Prize for Peace in October 1979 and decided to use the $190,000 award to construct a leprosarium, was she acting in her own interest? Was she behaving selfishly?

Freeway accidents typically produce traffic jams in the opposite-direction lanes, where the accident has created no obstruction at all, because motorists low down to look. Assume that as a result each motorist going the opposite ay is delayed ten minutes, and that all of them would gladly give up their ck peek at the accident in return for avoiding a ten-minute delay. Will fact that no single motorist places a value of more than a one-minute on a chance to look at the accident mean that motorists won't slow to look and so won't create the delay? What is wrong with the mech- of social coordination in this case?

4. What happens when the rules of the game (written or unwritten) decree that important meetings won't start until everyone is present and that late arrivals will incur no penalty? Is it in anyone's interest to be punctual? Are these rules of the game likely to prove satisfactory over time?

5. What are some of the more important rules that coordinate the actions of all those playing the "game" of this economics course? Who decided where and when the class would meet, who would teach it, who would enroll as students, what the textbook would be, when the exams would be given, and so on? Who decides where each student will sit? Do you find it odd that two students rarely try to occupy the same seat?

6. In the early 1980s, when the Polish people had to stand in long lines in order to purchase most consumer goods, the government ordered that every third place in line be reserved for pregnant women or disabled persons. This was presumably done to reduce their discomfort. Do you think it resulted in less standing in line by pregnant women? Do you suppose any women became pregnant in order to be able to cut into the long lines?

7. What do we mean when we say, "That's just a coincidence; it doesn't prove anything"? How does theory enable us to distinguish relevant evidence from mere coincidence?

8. Would you say that physicians who don't believe acupuncture works are biased if they reject it without trying it? If someone told you that you can get a perfect grade in this course without studying just by regularly chanting the mantra "invisible hand," would you believe him? Would it be a sign of bias or prejudice on your part if you totally ignored this advice even though you are extremely eager for a high grade in the course?

Substitutes Everywhere: The Concept of Demand

You must have heard or read statements like these many times in your life:

- Fire safety requires that there be two exits from each apartment unit.
- We need a new car.
- Our state will need large amounts of additional water in the coming decade.
- Traffic surveys have established the need for a new expressway.
- All citizens should be able to obtain the medical care they need regardless of ability to pay.
- There is no substitute for victory.

Fire safety, water, the smooth and rapid movement of traffic, medical care, victory, and even automobiles are all "goods." We say "even" automobiles because some doubts have begun to be expressed about the goodness of automobiles in our congested cities. But you can ask the man who owns one, and a lot of young people who don't. They will assure you that a new car is very much a good. Then what's wrong with those statements?

The element common to all six is the notion of *necessity*. And that is what makes each statement seriously misleading.

Take the first one. Will apartment dwellers who live with only one exit all be injured or killed by fires? Of course not. It's just that the risk is greater with one exit than with two. But then why not three exits? Or four? Why not go the whole route and make the outside walls nothing but doors? The answer is that, although fire safety is a good, it isn't the

only good apartment dwellers are interested in. Low rental costs and low heating and cooling costs are also goods, to say nothing of protection from burglars who notice that multiple exits are also multiple entrances. Moreover, there are other and perhaps better ways to increase fire safety. Extinguishers, alarm sprinklers, and large ashtrays also reduce the risk to apartment dwellers of injury or death from fire. If more than one exit is required, why not also require a fire extinguisher on every wall?

That sensible-sounding statement about apartment exits overlooks three interrelated facts: (1) Most goods are not free but can be obtained only by sacrificing something else that is also a good. (2) There are substitutes for anything. (3) Intelligent choice among substitutes requires a balancing of additional costs against additional benefits.

Costs and Substitutes

Now go back and look at the five other statements. "We need a new car." Who *needs* a new car? Obviously only those who value a new car more than what they must sacrifice to obtain one. That might be a vacation trip this year, new clothes, a lot of movies, and a stereo set. Is it worth it? There are, after all, plenty of substitutes for a new car: an overhaul of the present one, a used car, a bicycle, a car pool, public transportation, moving closer to work, or staying home more. Intelligent consumers determine their preferences after considering these various costs and benefits. (Of course, once a man has made up his mind, he might still want to say "We *need* a new car" in the hope that the definitive tone of his statement will dissuade his wife from making her own comparison of the costs and benefits of a new one.)

Consider the third statement: "Our state will need large amounts of additional water in the coming decade." Does any state really need large amounts of additional water? Dams and reservoirs, pipelines, and desalinization plants are ways of obtaining more water. But they have costs. Do the benefits justify the costs? If you think there are no substitutes for water, then you're thinking too academically. You have abstracted in a seriously misleading way from the real world. Probably you're assuming that water is used primarily for drinking, whereas in fact the overwhelming bulk of the water consumed in the United States goes for other uses. Since we shall use the case of water a bit later as an extended working exercise, we can pass this problem by for now. You might want to begin thinking, though, about the substitutes for water in such places of chronic scarcity as Arizona and southern California.

You'll be able to make much more sense out of the water problem and the expressway issue we take up next if you keep in mind that entities like *states* or *cities* never really want anything. Wants and goals are always attached ultimately to individuals. What does the person who says "The people want . . ." really mean? That all the people want it? A majority? Those who count? It is usually a good rule in analyzing statements like those opening this chapter to ask: *Who* wants more water, or more expressways, or more fire safety?

Only individuals choose!

> Things are seldom what they seem.
> Skim milk masquerades as cream.

The fourth of our misleading propositions—"Traffic surveys have established the need for a new expressway"— leads into one of the vexing issues in city planning. Perhaps it would never have become such a troublesome issue if we had admitted all along that expressways entail costs as well as benefits, that there are excellent substitutes for more expressways, and that intelligent city planning calls for the weighing of additional benefits against additional costs. Those who hope to derive most of the benefits from a new expressway while paying only a small percentage of the costs will not want others to notice the full costs of the expressway or how many substitutes there really are. That's why they pretend that a traffic survey can establish "needs." But a traffic survey only shows how many cars travel given routes *at existing costs to the drivers*, including such nonmonetary costs as delay, danger, and ulcers. Suppose that the cost of downtown parking increased 500%. What do you think would happen to rush-hour traffic? Commuters would form car pools and begin using public transportation. If the cost *to drivers* of commuting were made high enough, through parking charges, toll fees, or some other device, the need for a new expressway could turn overnight into a "need" for a rapid-transit system. It's a strange kind of need that can vanish so quickly in the face of a price change.

The fifth statement sounds humanitarian and liberal. "All citizens should be able to obtain the medical care they need regardless of ability to pay." But how much medical care does any person need? We might all agree that a woman with an inflamed appendix and no money should have an appendectomy completely at the taxpayers' expense if she is unable to meet any of the costs herself. But what of the man with a splinter in his finger? The services of physicians are not free goods, and they would not become free goods even if every physician treated patients without charging a fee. There just would not be enough physicians to go around if everyone consulted a doctor for every minor ill. The lower the

price of visiting a physician, the more frequently will people substitute a trip to the doctor for such other remedies as going to bed, taking it easy, or waiting and hoping. One could rather confidently predict that lower monetary fees would result in higher fees of other sorts, like waiting in line for many hours.

What about the sixth statement: "There is no substitute for victory"? It just isn't so. That may be a good battle cry, but it's unrealistic political analysis. Victory is usually obtained by making sacrifices. If the sacrifices reach a certain intensity, people choose compromise or even defeat, although they are then inclined to *say* that they have "no choice." Once again we notice that the intelligent formulation of policy, including foreign policy, flows from a careful balancing of additional expected costs and additional expected benefits.

The word *expected* should be stressed. We live in a world of uncertainty, forced to make choices that will affect our future without knowing for sure just how they will do so. A common mistake in reasoning about economic problems is to assume that there is no uncertainty or that economic decision makers are omniscient. At last report, omniscience was still a virtue denied to mortals. Condemned as we are to living with uncertainty, we can at least keep from making matters worse by pretending otherwise. Be alert for statements, in this book and elsewhere, which assume that completely adequate information is always available. You might even notice that information, too, is a good which has costs of acquisition and for which there are substitutes available.

The Concept of Demand

"Needs" turn out to be mere "wants" when we inspect them closely. That's an important difference, for in the case of wants we may ask: "How *urgently* are they wanted?" Economists get at this question through the concept of *demand*. Demand is a concept that *relates amounts that are purchased to the sacrifices that must be made to obtain these amounts.*

Ask yourself the following questions: How many records do you want to own? How many times do you want to go out to dinner in a year? What grade do you want from this course?

If you can answer any of those questions, it is because you have assumed some cost in each case. Suppose you said you want an A from this course and plan to get one. What difference would it make if the price of an A went up? The teacher isn't taking bribes; the price of an A *to you* (that's what counts) is the sacrifice you must make to obtain it. Would you still want an A if it required twenty hours of study a

Course grade	Cost of earning it
A	20 hours per week
B	1 hour per week
C	3/4 hour per week

week, whereas a B could be had for just one hour a week? You might still want it, but you would probably not be willing to buy it at such a high price when a fairly good substitute, a B, is so much cheaper. And that is what counts. Human wants seem to be insatiable. But when a want can only be satisfied at some cost—that is to say, by giving up the satisfying of some other wants to obtain it—we all moderate our desires and accept less than we would like to have.

The phenomenon of which we're speaking is so fundamental that some economists have been willing to assign it the status of a law: *the law of demand*. This law asserts that there is a negative relation between the amount of anything that people will purchase and the price (sacrifice) they must pay to obtain it. At higher prices, less will be purchased; at lower prices, more will be purchased.

Would you agree that this generalization can be called a law? Or can you think of exceptions? Genuine exceptions, if they exist at all, are rare. Why would people be indifferent to the sacrifices they must make? Or prefer more sacrifice to less? That is what a person would be doing who took *more* of something as the cost of obtaining it *increased*.

Alleged exceptions to the law of demand are usually based on a misinterpretation of the evidence. Consider the familiar case where the price of something rises and people increase their purchases in anticipation of further price rises. If you think about it carefully you will see that this is not an exception to the law of demand. The expectation of higher prices in the future, created by the initial price rise, has increased people's current demand for the item. They want to buy more now so they can buy less later. It isn't the higher price but the changed *expectations* that have caused people to buy more at the present time. We would observe something quite different if the initial price increase did *not* create those changed expectations. Moreover, those whose expectation of further price increases has prompted them to purchase sooner than they otherwise would have done will still consider the sacrifice they must make in deciding how much to buy.

It has sometimes been argued that certain prestige goods are exceptions to the law of demand. For example, people supposedly buy mink coats because the price is high, not low. No doubt there are people who buy some items largely to impress others with how much they can afford to pay. And people sometimes, in the absence of better information, judge quality by price, so that over a limited range at least, their willingness to purchase may be positively rather than negatively related to price. But these seeming exceptions can readily be explained in a way consistent with the law of demand. People are purchasing prestige rather than mere

"Let's stock up before the price goes even higher."

mink, or judging quality by price because they have no better information.

Cases such as these, however, are rare curiosities at most. Whether or not you are willing to call it a law, the fact is undeniable and extremely important: increases in the price of goods will characteristically be accompanied by decreases in the total amount purchased, and decreases in price will characteristically be accompanied by increases in the amount purchased. It is a serious mistake to overlook this relationship.

Misperceptions Caused by Inflation

One major reason why many people today think that the law of demand doesn't operate is that they have forgotten to take the effects of inflation into account. In an era of rapid inflation, such as the United States and much of the rest of the world experienced in the last two decades, most apparent price increases are not real price increases at all. The nature, causes, and consequences of inflation will be examined in detail later in this book (beginning with Chapter 15), but inflation so distorts our perceptions of relative price and cost changes that we'd better think about it before going any further. An ounce of anticipation may prevent a pound of confusion.

Inflation means an increase in the average *money* price of goods. But because we're accustomed to think of the price of anything as the quantity of money we have to sacrifice to get it, we easily conclude that twice as much money means twice as large a cost or sacrifice. That isn't the case, however, if twice as many dollars have only half as much purchasing power. If the money price of each and every good, including human labor and whatever else people sell or rent to obtain money, were to double, then *no* good would have changed in real price—except money, of course, which would have fallen by one-half. And so a doubling of the price of gasoline won't necessarily induce people to use any less gasoline— *if* at the same time their incomes and the prices of all the other goods they use have also doubled.

All money prices do not, in fact, change in equal proportion as a result of inflation—which is one of the reasons inflation is a problem. But they do tend to move together. Consequently, if we want to examine the effect of a particular price increase, we must first abstract from the effects of a general increase in prices. Suppose, for example, that a college which had been charging its students $2000 per year tuition in 1975 was charging $4000 in 1985. By how much had it raised tuition over this ten-year period? The answer is that it hadn't really raised its tuition at all. Because the purchasing

power of money was cut in half between 1975 and 1985, a $4000 tuition in 1985 was equivalent to a $2000 tuition in 1975.

Demand and Quantity Demanded

There is a general lesson to be drawn from all of this. In using the concept of demand, you must remain alert for the possibility that something else has changed in addition to the price. Your best protection is a clear grasp of the distinction between *demand* and *quantity demanded.* Commentators on economic events often use the word *demand* as a shorthand term for *quantity demanded.* That can and often does lead to error, as we shall see in a moment.

Demand in economic theory is a relationship between two specific variables: price and quantity demanded. You can't state the demand for any good simply as an amount. Demand is always a series of prices and a series of quantities (or amounts) that people would want to purchase at each of those prices. We express that fact by saying that demand is a schedule. A movement from one row of the schedule to another should always be called a change in the quantity demanded, not a change in the demand.

Demand is a <u>schedule</u>

Price	Quantity demanded
50¢	125,000
40¢	160,000
30¢	175,000

Making It Graphic

Many of the concepts economists use can be most easily expressed and understood by means of graphs. The troublesome but important distinction between demand and quantity demanded becomes clear immediately when it's presented on a graph. We can illustrate with the demand for water, as shown in Figure 2A.

(If you happen to be one of that considerable number of otherwise able people whose insides knot up at the sight of a graph, you ought to slow down at this point. Discover for yourself that graphs are not fatal by following carefully to see exactly what Figure 2A is asserting.)

The vertical axis shows possible prices that might be charged for water, in cents per 1000 gallons. The horizontal axis shows the quantity of water that would be demanded, or that people would want to purchase, at some of those prices.[1] The quantities are expressed in billions of gallons per year for whatever population the graph is summarizing.

---

1. It's unfortunate that economists ever chose the word "demand" to describe the desire to purchase; but they've been using it in this way for several centuries and it's too late to change now. The economist's concept of demand carries absolutely none of the word's ordinary connotations of authority or threat, as in "non-negotiable demand." Demand as the economist thinks of it is preeminently negotiable.

Figure 2A yields the following demand schedule:

Price per 1000 Gallons	Billions of Gallons per Year
74¢	9
50	13
36	18
28	29

If the price happened to be 74 cents per 1000 gallons to begin with, and was then lowered to 50 cents, the *quantity demanded* would increase from 9 to 13 billion gallons per year. At a price of 28 cents, the *quantity demanded* would be more than three times as great as at 74 cents. But the *demand* would be unchanged through all this, because the demand is the whole curve or schedule.

For the demand to increase, something would have to occur that made these people want to purchase more water

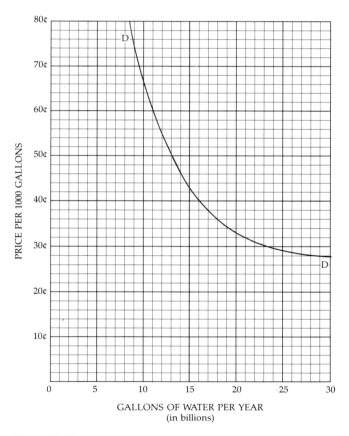

Figure 2A Demand curve for water

than before *at each price*. A drought, for example, might induce people to water their lawns more frequently. Population growth in the area would also be likely to increase the demand; that is, move the whole curve upward and to the right. A campaign to conserve water, if successful, would decrease the demand, causing the curve or schedule to shift downward and to the left to reflect the fact that, at unchanged prices, people now want to purchase less water than previously.

If you would like to graph an increase in the demand for water, plot the quantities in the second column below on Figure 2A. If you prefer to graph a decrease in demand, practice with the third column.

Price per 1000 Gallons	Billions of Gallons Demanded per Year	Billions of Gallons Demanded per Year
70¢	15	5
60	16	7
50	18	10
40	22	13

The Difference It Makes

A short editorial in the *Wall Street Journal* in November 1977 revealed the perils awaiting those who think such verbal distinctions are too trifling to bother with. The editorial writer wanted to chide an Agriculture Department economist for his ignorance of economics, an ignorance supposedly revealed by his stating that "the power of the U.S. consumer movement" had brought the price of coffee down again after it had hit a high of $4.42 a pound. Not so, said the *Journal's* editorial writer: "The coffee market is behaving the way the basic textbooks say a market behaves: Prices go up, demand falls, and prices come down."

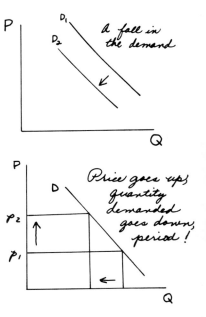

The basic textbooks say nothing of the sort. On the contrary, they say that the editorial writer has confused the quantity demanded and the demand. When the price of coffee went up, the quantity demanded fell. Period. If the consumer movement managed to change people's attitudes toward serving and drinking coffee (some people got so angry about the price rises that they wouldn't drink coffee for a while at *any* price), then the consumer movement did succeed in changing the demand. And if the demand falls, *then* the price comes down. The *Journal's* mistaken logic implies, if you think about it carefully, that the price will bob up and down indefinitely, since when the price comes down again, demand ought to increase once more, causing the price to go up, whereupon the demand will fall, causing the price to go down. . . .

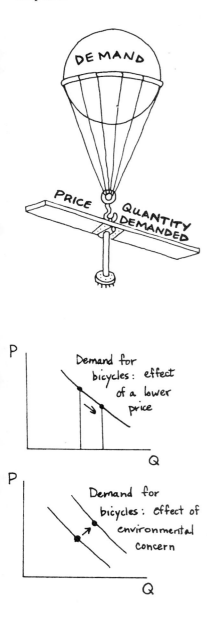

Demand for bicycles: effect of a lower price

Demand for bicycles: effect of environmental concern

But it's all just a confusion of thought introduced by a careless use of terms. Think of price and quantity demanded as objects on the opposite ends of a seesaw, and demand as a large, lighter-than-air balloon to which the seesaw is attached. When price goes one way, quantity demanded goes the opposite way. Changes in the demand (movements of the balloon up or down) will exert simultaneous pressure in the same direction on both the price and the quantity demanded. The demand for any good is the product of biological realities, social relationships, psychological factors, and a broad assortment of economic variables, such as income and the price, quality, and general availability of substitutes. All these forces combine to create the demand for a particular good, the relationship that will exist between changes in its money price and changes in the quantity people will decide to obtain. Unless the demand is changing (the balloon is ascending or descending), price and quantity demanded will always move in opposite directions.

To put it most simply: the one change that will *not* cause a change in the demand for bicycles is a change in the price of bicycles. If a combination of rising incomes, environmental concern, and new interest in outdoor exercise induces more people to want bicycles, the demand for them will increase. And both the price and quantity demanded may well increase as a consequence. Something like this happens frequently. You have grasped the distinction between demand and quantity demanded if you see clearly why this in no way contradicts the law of demand. An increase in demand may pull up both price and quantity demanded. But it will still be as true with the high demand as with the low demand that a smaller quantity will be demanded at higher than at lower prices. And this is what the law of demand asserts. Economic theory isolates the money price of goods for special attention because of the exceptionally important role that money prices play in adjusting and coordinating people's behavior.

Money Costs and Other Costs

None of this implies, however, that the price in money that must be paid for something is a complete measure of its cost to the purchaser. Indeed, sometimes it is a very inadequate measure (as in the case of the student who wanted an A). Economists know this at least as well as anyone else. The concept of demand definitely does not suggest that money is the only thing that matters to people. Confusion about this point has done so much to create misunderstanding that we might profitably take a moment to clarify the matter.

Consider the case of a woman buying soft drinks. Assume that she can purchase them in either returnable or throwaway bottles, and that a liter of her favorite drink is priced at $1.80 in the throwaway bottle, whereas a liter in a returnable bottle is $1.60 plus 40 cents deposit. Which will she buy? Which is cheaper? It depends on the cost to her, of which the retailer's price is only one element. If she doesn't mind saving and returning bottles—that is, if the cost to her of doing so is low—she will probably find the returnable bottles cheaper and will buy them. On the other hand, if she lives in an apartment with very limited storage space, gets to the store rarely, consumes large quantities of soft drinks, and has a waste-disposal chute a few steps from her door, she may well find the throwaway bottles cheaper and will purchase them in preference to returnable bottles.

Now suppose that our hypothetical apartment dweller with a passion for pop attends an ecology conference and comes away convinced that we must recycle to survive. The cost to her of using throwaway bottles suddenly jumps, for now she suffers pangs of guilt each time she tosses a bottle in the waste disposal chute. The added cost in moral regret may be sufficient to induce her to switch to returnable bottles.

Or it may not. Suppose that she is going on a camping trip and wants to take along a dozen bottles of pop. She must backpack them in to her campsite, and backpack the empties out again if she returns the bottles. The added cost of carrying a dozen empties may be enough to overcome the added cost of an uneasy conscience, so that in this case at least, she reverts to throwaway bottles. (Of course, she will throw them in a trash can.)

But let's change the last situation. Suppose the price of throwaways is not $1.80 per liter but $2.20, with the price of the returnable bottle still $1.60 but the deposit now raised to 80 cents. She can now save 60 cents, not just 20 cents, if she buys (and returns!) the returnable bottle. At *some* price we may confidently predict that the cost of transporting empties will become less than the combined cost of buying throwaway bottles and living with guilt.

There are several lessons to be drawn from this tale of the pop bottles. To assert that people purchase less of anything as the cost to them increases does *not* imply that people pay attention only to money, or that people are selfish, or that concern for social welfare does not influence economic behavior. It *does* imply that people respond to changes in cost and—a crucial implication—that a sufficiently large change in price can be counted on to tip almost any balance. Those who say that Americans won't give up the convenience of

Is a 20¢ saving worth the trouble?

Is a 60¢ saving worth the trouble?

throwaway bottles and cans unless the government outlaws them are overlooking several possibilities. A widespread change in attitude toward the environment could overcome the cost of being inconvenienced. And a sufficiently large tax on throwaway containers (call it a deposit if you wish) would make convenience a luxury too expensive to enjoy very frequently.

The essential point in all this is that the money price of obtaining something is only one part, and occasionally even a very small part, of its cost. What the law of demand asserts is that people will do less of what they want to do as the cost to them of doing it increases, and do more as the cost decreases. But at the same time we want to remember that money is a common denominator, and therefore a most useful device for securing widespread changes in behavior. That's why economists give it so much of their attention.

Who Needs Water?

People are creatures of habit, in what they think as well as what they do. Perhaps this also explains why so many have trouble recognizing the significance of substitutes and hence such difficulty appreciating the law of demand. Water provides an excellent example.

Back in the mid-sixties the first of a string of serious water shortages hit New York City. Several years of less than normal rainfall had depleted the city's reservoirs, and there was great fear that New York would run short of water during the summer unless consumption could be sharply reduced. A few brave souls suggested that the city should install more water meters and raise the price of water. The suggestion was not taken very seriously because, as everyone supposedly knows, water is a necessity. "People won't go thirsty just because the price of water goes up a little, or even a lot," said the critics. And so New York launched a massive campaign of education plus legal threat to try to get its citizens to be more sparing in their use of water.

Lawn sprinkling and car washing were condemned. Restaurants were told not to give customers a glass of water with their meals unless they specifically asked for it. The ornamental fountains of the city were turned off—largely as a symbolic gesture, since the water in the fountains is recirculated. Citizens were asked to refrain from keeping their beer cool by letting the shower drip on it. One of the more amusing aspects of the campaign was a set of ads for a particular Scotch whiskey that urged people to drink their Scotch with water. The word *water* was crossed out in the

advertisement and *soda* was written above it, with an appended admonition to save water by drinking soda.

The water shortage was relieved not by any of these trivial measures but by a providential end to the drought. New Yorkers thereupon went back to their old familiar habits to await the next drought. It came in 1980, and in January of 1981 the mayor of New York City, warning that "there will be a calamity" unless residents conserve water, signed a law imposing fines of up to $1000 on "water wasters." Fortunately, the rains came soon thereafter, enabling New Yorkers to return to their dangerous conviction that the forces of Nature, not human beings, cause water crises.

The best way to turn a drought into a calamity is to pretend that water is a necessity. The truth is that there are many substitutes for water, a fact which becomes glaringly obvious as soon as we break loose from the habit of assuming that people do nothing with water except drink it.

Here are just a few of the substitutes for water in New York City: dirty automobiles, brown lawns, plumbers, migration, deodorant, larger refrigerators (to hold the beer that would otherwise be cooled in the shower), plus a host of small inconveniences. The trick is to persuade people to *use* these substitutes: To call the plumber, for example, and have that leaky toilet repaired rather than allow it to continue wasting fifty gallons of water a day. To spend money on a larger refrigerator. To tolerate a dirty automobile. To put an ice cube in their glass of drinking water, rather than let the tap run for several minutes to cool it. In the case of industries using huge quantities of water, to sacrifice the advantages of a New York location in favor of locating near more plentiful water supplies. Or to install recycling equipment.

But what is the best way to induce the use of substitutes? Educational campaigns and moral exhortation can help. But how much? Most people are expert rationalizers when their own interest is involved, and it is all too easy to put off calling the plumber until the end of the month, or next month, or the month after that, always fully intending, of course, to do one's civic duty and get that leak repaired.

What about criminal penalties for wasting water? Enforcement becomes a problem here. Are the police to stage surprise raids to catch people cooling their beer in the shower? Shall we fine a person for rinsing a glass too many times before taking a drink? What constitutes *criminal* waste?

A quite different approach is available. Is there any way to enlist almost everyone in a conscientious effort to seek out and use substitutes for water? A sizable increase in the price of water just might do the job. Wouldn't the careless householder call the plumber more quickly if that leaky toilet

PLUMBER'S
BILL

$52.00

WATER
BILL

$74.00

cost more per month than the plumber would charge to fix it? Wouldn't people accept dirty automobiles more readily, or at least not let the hose run the whole time they were washing the car, if water became very expensive? There is some price for water at which it becomes cheaper to buy a new refrigerator than to use the shower as a cooler. Industries that use large quantities of water will tend to locate elsewhere if the price of water is high in their area of first choice.

And so it goes. There are substitutes for anything. A higher money price will induce some people to find and use some of those substitutes. And the higher the price, the more will substitutes be used.

Time Is on Our Side

If you are at all the suspicious sort of person, you will have wondered whether all these changes might not take too much time to be helpful. That is a healthy suspicion. Changes in the amount purchased will be greater for any given price change the longer the time period allowed for adjustment.

Check this out for yourself with a mental experiment. Suppose the price of water has been 30 cents per 1000 gallons for twenty years and it is raised overnight to 60 cents. What substitutions for water will be made *right away?* What substitutions would you expect to observe after a month or two had passed? What substitutions would you expect to observe over the next ten years—assuming that everyone expects the price to remain at the higher level?

But an even better example is gasoline. How high will the price of gasoline have to go before Americans reduce their consumption? Don't answer without first noting that the price hasn't gone up by nearly as much as the newspaper headlines suggest. It's the *relative* price that matters, and much of the increase in the price of gasoline since 1972 is merely an inflation-induced rise in its *money* price. The 1972 price of 38 cents per gallon for regular would have been 96 cents at the beginning of 1985 *if gasoline prices had merely gone up at the rate of inflation.* The question is nonetheless a good one: How large a relative price increase will it take to cut gasoline consumption by 10 percent or 25 percent or even 50 percent? The answer clearly depends on time: both the time allowed for adjustments and the time period over which these higher prices are expected to remain in force. People will buy cars that use less fuel, will move closer to work, and will arrange car pools if the price of gasoline rises far enough, but they won't do so at once. Moreover, they will delay such decisions longer the less sure they are that the higher price is going to stick. If every belligerent statement against OPEC by a

prominent political figure fans the hope for lower prices soon, it will induce some to live just a little longer with their much-loved gas guzzlers.

By taking our examples almost entirely from the area of household decisions, we may have obscured the important fact that customers include producers as well as consumers. Business firms use water and gasoline, too, and they sometimes use so much that they are exceptionally sensitive to price changes. You'll be neglecting some of the major factors that cause demand curves to slope downward if you overlook the contribution producers make to the demand for many goods. In the case of water, location decisions are often made on the basis of the expected price of water, and those decisions then affect the quantities demanded in different geographic areas.

But it takes time for customers to find and begin to use substitutes. It also takes time for producers to devise, produce, and publicize substitutes. As a result, the amount by which people increase or decrease their purchases when prices change depends very much on the time period over which we are observing the adjustment. Occasionally, even a rather large price increase (or decrease) will lead to no significant decrease (or increase) in consumption—*at first*. And this sometimes causes people to conclude that price has no effect on consumption. A very mistaken conclusion! Nothing in this world happens instantly. People, creatures of habit that they are, must be allowed time to prove that there are substitutes for anything.

Price Elasticity of Demand

It is extremely cumbersome to talk about "the amount by which people increase or decrease their purchases when the price changes." But this is an important relationship with many useful applications. So economists have invented a special phrase that summarizes the relationship. The formal title of the concept is *price elasticity of demand.*

That's an appropriate name. Elasticity means responsiveness. If the amount of any good that people purchase changes substantially in response to a small change in price, demand is said to be elastic. If even a very large price change results in little change in the amount purchased, demand is said to be inelastic.

Price elasticity of demand is defined precisely as *the percentage change in quantity demanded divided by the percentage change in price.* Thus, if a 10 percent increase in the price of eggs leads to a 5 percent reduction in the number of eggs sold, the elasticity of demand is 5 percent divided by 10

*Price elasticity
of demand:*

$$\frac{\% \text{ change in } Q}{\% \text{ change in } P}$$

percent, or 0.5. To be completely accurate, it is *minus* 0.5, since price and amount purchased vary inversely. But for simplicity we shall ignore the minus sign and treat all coefficients of elasticity as if they were positive.

Whenever the coefficient of elasticity is greater than 1.0 (ignoring the sign)—that is, whenever the percentage change in quantity purchased is *greater* than the percentage change in price—demand is said to be elastic. Whenever the coefficient of elasticity is less than 1.0, which means whenever the percentage change in quantity purchased is *less* than the percentage change in price, demand is said to be inelastic. Compulsive learners will want to know what is said when the percentage change in quantity is exactly equal to the percentage change in price, so that the coefficient of demand elasticity is exactly 1.0. You may file away the information that demand is then *unit elastic.* (Economics is a very systematic discipline.)

You can begin to familiarize yourself with the uses of this concept by asking whether demand is elastic or inelastic in each case below. Each case is discussed in the subsequent paragraphs.

- "People aren't going to buy much more no matter how far we cut the price."
- "This is a competitive business. We would lose half our customers if we raised our prices by as little as 2 percent."
- The demand for salt.
- The demand for Morton's salt.
- The demand for Morton's salt at the Kroger store at Fifth and Main.
- "The university's total receipts from tuition would actually increase if tuition rates were cut by 20 percent."
- "It's odd but true. Wheat farmers would gross more money if they all got together and burned one-quarter of this year's crop."

Thinking about Elasticity

"People aren't going to buy much more no matter how far we cut the price." If a businessman doubts that even a very large price decrease will do much to increase his sales, he believes that his demand is highly inelastic. He will obviously not want to lower his price under such circumstances, for he will lose more through the lower price than he will gain through the larger volume. But if people don't respond very much to a price cut, will they also be relatively insensitive to a price hike? If they are, a businessman out to increase his income will want to raise his price. Businessmen typically complain

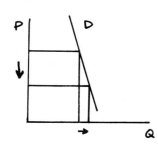

that prices are too low. Then why don't they raise their prices? It's a free country, isn't it? The answer, of course, is that they would usually lose too many customers if they did so. It is the elasticity of demand that determines whether or not a businessman can add to his money receipts by raising his prices.

"*This is a competitive business. We would lose half our customers if we raised our prices by as little as 2 percent.*" The business-woman making this statement is saying in effect that she faces a highly elastic demand: a 50 percent decline in quantity demanded would follow a mere 2 percent increase in price. The coefficient of elasticity is 25. The demand is very elastic indeed. Another way of putting it would be to say that her customers are extremely sensitive to any price change. And that makes it difficult for her to raise her prices, however eager she might be to do so.

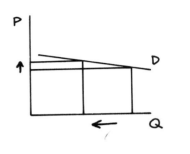

The demand for salt. What makes demand curves elastic or inelastic? The availability of good substitutes is clearly an important factor. Another is the importance of the item in the budget of purchasers. If the expenditure on some good is large relative to the income or wealth of purchasers, they will be more sensitive to any change in its price.

Apply this to table salt. One pound of salt lasts a long time and costs a penny or two an ounce. So who cares? Shoppers will be relatively insensitive to any change in the price of salt. Moreover, salt has few good substitutes. You would not be inclined to put sugar on your eggs if the price of salt rose dramatically, just as you would not cut the pepper and double the salt if the price of salt fell substantially.

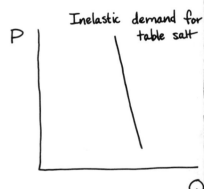

Adam Smith observed in *The Wealth of Nations* that "salt is a very ancient and very universal subject of taxation. . . . The quantity annually consumed by any individual is so small, and may be purchased so gradually, that nobody, it seems to have been thought, could feel very sensibly even a pretty heavy tax upon it." Moreover, salt was one of "the necessaries of life" in Smith's terminology. We can object to the term *necessary* and express Smith's meaning more accurately: salt has few good substitutes. The result is a highly inelastic demand and an apparently irresistible temptation to some governments to levy taxes on salt.

But it's possible to exaggerate the inelasticity of even the demand for salt. Householders in wintry regions sometimes sprinkle table salt on their sidewalks or porch steps to melt the ice. If salt were ten times as expensive, many would substitute chopping and scraping for salt.

The demand for Morton's salt. Why would the demand for Morton's salt be less inelastic than the demand for salt? Because there are substitutes—namely, other brands of salt.

The Morton Salt Company is not in the privileged position of ancient governments, which could raise the price of *all* salt. If someone in the marketing department at Morton chanced to read Adam Smith and was inspired by him to double the price, the grocery stores that are Morton's customers would tend to make their purchases from other salt manufacturers.

The demand for Morton's salt at the Kroger store at Fifth and Main. If there are more good substitutes for Morton's salt than for salt, there are even more good substitutes for Morton's salt sold at the local Kroger store. We have moved from a very inelastic to what is probably a highly elastic demand for the same quantity. And that is why you aren't victimized when you purchase salt. You might be willing to pay $5 a pound if salt were not available at a lower price. But fortunately for you, there are many options. Sellers who tried to take advantage of the fact that the total demand for salt is highly inelastic would lose customers. The demand for *the salt they sell* will be quite elastic.

People often make the mistake of assuming that those who sell "vital necessities" can get away with charging almost any price they choose. We have learned to be suspicious of the phrase *vital necessities*. Now we see again the grounds for this suspicion. Food has as good a claim as anything to the title "vital necessity." But the relevant fact is that *no one buys food*. Shoppers do not purchase a pound of "food"; they buy a pound of hamburger, or bacon, or calf's liver. And there are many sellers selling many kinds of food. All of which means that there are excellent substitutes for specific food commodities, and hence demand curves are highly elastic. So sellers are for the most part closely constrained in the prices they can charge.

Elasticity and Total Receipts

"The university's total receipts from tuition would actually increase if tuition rates were cut by 20 percent." The university's total receipts from tuition are the product of the tuition rate and the number of students who enroll. If a 20 percent decrease in the tuition rate results in an increase in tuition receipts, then there must have been a more than 20 percent increase in enrollment. The percentage change in quantity demanded is greater than the percentage change in price, so demand is elastic.

This suggests a simple way of thinking about elasticity. Keep in mind that the quantity demanded will always move in the opposite direction from the price. *If the price change causes total receipts to move in the* opposite *direction from the price change,* demand must be elastic. The change in the quantity purchased

P

Elastic demand for Morton's salt at a particular store

Q

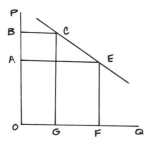

Demand is elastic between C and E, because OBCG < OAEF.

has to be larger in percentage terms than the price change because total receipts are nothing but the product of price and quantity. And that is the definition of an elastic demand. *If a price change causes total receipts to move in the* same *direction as the price change, demand must be inelastic.* The change in amount purchased was not large enough to outweigh the change in price. And that is the meaning of an inelastic demand.

Don't jump to the conclusion that the university will always be in a better financial position, given an elastic demand, if it lowers its tuition. True, lower tuition charges will mean larger receipts whenever demand is elastic; but a larger enrollment probably also means larger costs. The university must decide in such a case whether the addition to total receipts will be larger than the addition to total costs. (But problems of pricing strategy must be deferred until we reach Chapter 9.)

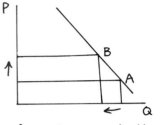

Demand is inelastic between points A and B.

"It's odd but true. Wheat farmers would gross more money if they all got together and burned one-quarter of this year's crop." The logic of the preceding case also applies here. Farmers can gross more money while selling less wheat only if the percentage change in price is greater than the percentage change in the amount sold. Demand would have to be inelastic. The only difference is that we have reversed the causal relationship assumed till now. We have been tacitly assuming that sellers set the price and buyers respond. This is not always the best way to look at the price-quantity relationship. In some industries, such as agriculture for the most part, it is more useful to assume that the quantity available for sale will determine the price. We'll be talking a lot about this later. For now it is only important to notice that the relationship between changes in total sales and changes in price depends on the elasticity of demand.

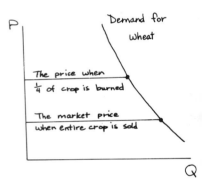

Farmers may never have heard about elastic or inelastic demands. But when they lobby for government controls on production, they are usually very much aware of the relation between price and the amount that is sold. Like Molière's famous Monsieur Jourdain, who spoke prose for forty years without knowing it, you can make good use of demand elasticities without ever having heard the term.

The Myth of Vertical Demand

Let's go back to the beginning. In the six statements with which we began this chapter, what was implicitly assumed about the elasticity of demand? Our objection to each statement, you recall, was that it ignored the fact that all goods have substitutes and that substitution does occur when prices

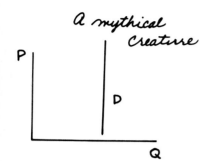

a mythical creature

change. In other words, demand curves are *not* completely inelastic. A completely inelastic demand curve would graph as a vertical line. You would be wise not to look for such demand curves in the real world.

The law of demand can now be expressed in the language of elasticity: *there is no such thing as a completely inelastic demand* over the entire range of possible prices. Most purchasers will respond at least a little to changes in the cost to them, and all purchasers will respond to a sufficiently large change. If this seems too obvious to bother mentioning, consult your daily newspaper for evidence that it is by no means obvious to everyone. Well-intentioned people and some not so well-intentioned talk constantly of basic needs, minimum requirements, and absolute necessities.

Demand curves are rarely as inelastic as orators suppose. This does not imply, of course, that they are always elastic. That is a more difficult question, to be answered by looking at each case. But as we shall subsequently discover, it is a very important question for anyone who wants to decide how well our economic system functions.

Once Over Lightly

Every good has substitutes: other goods that will be used in its stead when the cost of using the original good rises, goods for which the original good will become a substitute when their cost rises. Pork replaces beef when the price of beef goes up, and a restaurant beefsteak takes the place of a movie when theater tickets become more expensive.

By talking about "needs" we can sometimes win arguments we might otherwise lose. Needs are actually wants of many different urgencies.

People want more or less of a good as the cost those people must pay decreases or increases.

The concept of *demand* is preferable to the concept of *need*, because demand relates the amounts that are purchased to the sacrifices that must be made to obtain these amounts.

The "law of demand" asserts that more will be purchased at lower prices, less at higher prices—assuming that something in addition to the price has not changed to offset this consequence.

The money cost of a good is only one part of the cost that affects people's decisions.

A sufficiently large change in money cost (price) can usually overcome the effects that nonmoney costs exert on people's decisions.

A change in price will usually induce a larger change in amounts purchased when more time is allowed for consumers and producers to learn about and invent new substitutes.

Price elasticity of demand is a measure of the percentage change in the quantity of a good demanded relative to the percentage change in its price.

Demand is (price) elastic when the percentage change in quantity demanded is greater than the percentage change in price. Demand is inelastic when the percentage change in quantity demanded is smaller than the percentage change in price.

Price elasticity of demand depends on the importance of the price relative to one's income, but even more on the quality and price of available substitutes.

More separate sources of supply for a good imply better substitutes for any particular good and hence a more elastic demand.

Total receipts or expenditures move in the opposite direction from price when demand is elastic and in the same direction as price when it is inelastic.

The concept of "needs" implies a perfectly inelastic demand curve—an extremely rare phenomenon.

The demand for a good refers to the *schedule of relationships* between price and quantity demanded and must be distinguished from the quantity or amount that is demanded. The quantity of a good demanded changes with its price. But a true change in demand will alter both price and quantity demanded.

QUESTIONS FOR DISCUSSION

1. A Gallup Report in January 1985 found that the average U.S. family says it needs at least $252 per week after taxes "to get by." College graduates reportedly needed $301 a week on the average, but high-school graduates needed only $250 a week. While Democrats said they could get by on $251 a week, Republicans needed $298. Do you think college graduates and Republicans really have more needs, or more expensive needs, than high-school graduates and Democrats?

2. In 1978 dentists in the United States used 706,000 ounces of gold. In 1980 they used 341,000 ounces, or about 45 percent of the amount that they had been using just two years earlier. (Data are from a *Wall Street Journal* article of December 14, 1981.) The price of gold approximately tripled from 1978 to 1980. But why would dentists decide to use so much less gold when they can pass the higher cost along to their patients? Isn't it true that people who need gold fillings will pay whatever they are required to pay?

3. U.S. courts decided in 1977 that prohibitions on advertising by lawyers were illegal. Since that time many legal "clinics" have sprung up, advertising standard legal services at lower than ordinary fees. Would you agree with the results of a survey showing that about 60 percent of all middle-income Americans have "unmet legal needs"? Are "unmet legal needs" the reason

why lower prices have resulted in more people seeking the services of lawyers?

4. Most systems of hospitalization insurance substantially reduce the cost to the patient of hospitalization, sometimes to zero. How does this affect hospital use? Why? Evaluate the argument that it does not affect hospital use since "no one gets sick just because hospitals are cheap, or avoids getting sick because they're expensive."

5. In 1967 the president of the American Medical Association was quoted as saying that medical care was a privilege and not a right. Today the AMA officially proclaims that "health care is the right of everyone." What quantity and quality of health care do you suppose they're talking about?

6. The contention that certain goods are "basic human needs" carries a strong suggestion that access to those goods should be a matter of right, not of privilege. But the assertion of rights logically entails the assertion of obligations. Your right to vote, for example, entails the obligation of election officials to accept and count your ballot; your right to use your own umbrella implies an obligation on the part of others not to borrow it without your permission. If "health care is the right of everyone," who has the obligation to provide health care to everyone? Who currently accepts this obligation? How will the appropriate persons be persuaded to accept it?

7. According to a 1983 report by the American Planning Association, the average four-member household uses about 345 gallons of water daily. The report broke that down into 235 gallons for inside use and 110 for outside use. Of the "inside" water, about 95 gallons per day went to flush toilets. Drinking and cooking used 9 to 10 gallons per day. Water rates vary; but they are rarely higher than .1¢ (that's $.001) per gallon. Would a doubling or even a quadrupling of water rates work a serious hardship on poor people?

8. On June 18, 1985, the *Wall Street Journal* ran an article entitled "Denver Turns On to Xeriscape," describing efforts to persuade Denver residents to avoid "a consumer water crunch" by growing lawns that require little irrigation. (*Xeriscape* is the technique of gardening in dry climates.) The predominant grass in Denver lawns is currently Kentucky bluegrass, which requires about 18 gallons of added water per square foot each summer to thrive in the arid climate. Buffalo grass, by contrast, will do well on half as much water.

   (a) How much extra would a homeowner with a typical 5000 square-foot lawn pay in water costs to enjoy Kentucky blue rather than buffalo grass at a price of 60¢ per 1000 gallons? Is this likely to affect the decisions of many homeowners?

   (b) The schedule of water prices for Denver users with a ¾-inch main in June 1985 was actually 74¢ per 1000 gallons for the first 15,000 gallons per month, 60¢ per 1000 for the next 35,000, 46¢ per 1000 for the next 650,000, and 42¢ per 1000 gallons for all consumption beyond 700,000 gallons per month, with a minimum charge of $2.65 per month. How much does the first 4000 gallons cost under this pricing scheme?

   (c) What price would be taken into account by a manufacturer who was considering a move to the area and planning to use 1 million gallons of water per month?

   (d) Why, if Denver is facing the prospect of water shortages, does the pricing system grant lower rates to those who use *more* water?

9. A 1980 drought in the northeastern United States produced, early in 1981, numerous water-rationing schemes in the states, cities, and towns of the region. Evaluate the following bits of information, all gleaned from a *Wall Street Journal* feature of February 25, 1981:

   (a) Greenwich, Connecticut, limited users to 45 gallons of water per day. One resident predicted they would soon be drinking Perrier.

   (b) In Randolph, Massachusetts, people were paying 10 cents per gallon for deep-well water, because the low level of the town's reservoirs had given the water from them an offensive taste.

   (c) Many cities and towns banned "nonessential uses of water." Which of these uses, in your opinion, is nonessential: macaroni manufacture, beer brewing, lawn sprinkling, filling of swimming pools, ordinary household use (cooking, cleaning, showering, flushing)?

   (d) When New Jersey imposed rationing on about 200 communities, it limited each resident to 50 gallons per day. How many people have "essential uses" for 50 gallons of water per day?

   (e) Per-capita water use in New York City at the onset of the drought was 190 gallons. How much of that do you think went for "essential uses"?

10. Here is a question from a letter to the editor of a Seattle newspaper protesting a proposal to reduce gasoline consumption by imposing a tax of 50 cents per gallon. "How could you or anyone think that such a tax would reduce gas consumption when a doubling of the price, consisting of considerably more than 50 cents a gallon over the past two years, has not reduced consumption one iota?"

    (a) What does this letter writer think the demand curve for gasoline looks like?

    (b) Do we have any evidence on whether or not he is correct?

    (c) The writer recommends the elimination by law of nonessential uses and mentions as an example rural mail deliveries six days a week. Would we be eliminating a nonessential use of gasoline if all rural carriers took Saturdays off? Suppose they also took Tuesdays and Thursdays off?

11. A front-page article in the *Wall Street Journal* of May 13, 1980, was headlined: "Europe's Drivers Don't Reduce Gasoline Use Despite Soaring Prices." In the continuation of the story on a back page, the reporter revealed that pump prices had increased 120 percent in Great Britain from 1973 to 1979 while the general price level had risen by about 140 percent. How would you criticize that headline?

12. If the government forbids motorists to drive more than 55 miles per hour, does everyone stay within the 55-mile limit? What are the costs of going faster? What are some of the costs of going faster that do not fall on the speeding motorist? Do these latter costs affect motorists' decisions? Why might the fact that faster driving uses up more of the nation's scarce petroleum reduce the speed of some drivers but not others?

13. Why do people live in New York City if the costs of doing so—high rents, noise, dirt, congestion, the risks of being robbed or assaulted—are so high? Is it true that most of them "have no choice"? What do you think would happen if the costs mentioned were significantly reduced?

14. "Coffee Prices Sink as Demand Wanes." Does that newspaper headline use

the word *demand* correctly? Would you expect those falling prices to be associated with more or with less coffee consumption?

15. Higher prices for beef, automobiles, or television sets will lead to a reduction in the *amount of each demanded*. Think of some specific changes (such as in tastes, prices of substitutes, quality of complementary goods) that would cause the *demand* for each to increase so that more might actually be demanded at higher prices. Why is this completely consistent with the law of demand?

16. These were the prices per (U.S.) gallon of regular gasoline in U.S. dollar equivalents in selected countries in October 1975:

Italy	$1.65	Spain	$1.16
France	1.49	Canada	0.65
Japan	1.28	U.S.	0.59

Why would we *not* have a demand schedule if we obtained data on the gasoline purchased during October 1975 in each of those countries?

17. Does the graph below, employed by some medical organizations to predict a "doctor glut," use the concept of demand in the same way that economists use it?

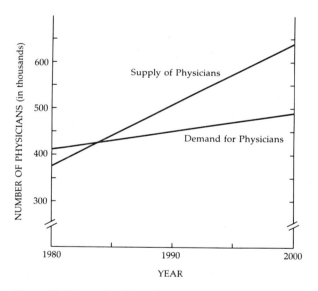

Figure 2B Demand and supply curves for physicians

18. Do the following statements use the word *demand* correctly? Or should the term *quantity demanded* be substituted?
    (a) When OPEC raised the price of oil in the 1970s, the demand for oil fell.
    (b) Inflation has increased the demand for oil.
    (c) When the Iran-Iraq war broke out, oil refiners panicked, and their panic increased the demand for oil and sharply raised its price.
    (d) The 55-mile-per-hour speed limit has reduced the demand for oil.
    (e) Price controls imposed by the U.S. in the 1970s on domestic oil pro-

ducers, by keeping down the price of U.S.-produced oil, increased our demand for OPEC oil.

19. A change in expectations can cause a change in demand. Explain how this could lead to a situation in which a price decline was followed by a decrease in the amount purchased.

20. Is it strictly true that a change in the price of a good causes a change in the quantity of that good demanded but *not* a shift in the demand curve for the good?
    (a) What effect did the large increases in the price of gasoline in the 1970s have on the demand (curve) for fuel-efficient cars?
    (b) What effect did this have after several years on the original demand (curve) for gasoline?
    (c) How did the increase in the price of heating oil in the 1970s affect the demand for housing insulation? How did this eventually shift the demand for heating oil?
    (d) Can you think of similar processes through which changes in the price of other goods would lead over time to shifts in the demand for those goods?
    (e) If the price of a good returned to its previous level after a time but the quantity demanded did not, would this be evidence that the demand had changed in the interim?

21. Although the combined population of Washington and Oregon was slightly less in 1975 than the population of Massachusetts, over three times as many kilowatt-hours were sold in Washington and Oregon during that year as in Massachusetts. How would you account for the enormous difference? (Hint: Over 92 percent of kilowatt-hours sold by electric utilities in Washington and Oregon were generated by falling water, in comparison with slightly more than 1 percent in Massachusetts.) What persuaded aluminum companies, who are very heavy users of electricity, to locate in the Pacific Northwest? How were so many home builders persuaded to install electric space heating?

22. Here is a classroom exercise that might be fun and also sharpen your ability to recognize substitution possibilities. Let one person come up with two goods that seem to have no connection and challenge others to construct a plausible set of circumstances in which one would be a substitute for the other. (Avoid the easy, though correct, answer that all goods are in the last analysis substitutes inasmuch as the acquisition of each uses up scarce time or income.)

23. John loves butter and thinks that margarine tastes like soap. George can't tell the difference. Whose demand for butter is likely to be more elastic?

24. Would the elasticity of a crowd's demand for cold lemonade be affected by the proximity of a drinking fountain?

25. How do you think the development of other copying machines affected the elasticity of demand for Xerox machines?

26. Is the demand for prescription drugs elastic or inelastic? Why? Do you agree with the statement sometimes made that the prices charged for prescription drugs can be freely set by the manufacturers, since people must buy whatever the doctor prescribes?

27. How does ignorance affect elasticities of demand?

28. How might the development of science and technology affect demand elasticities?

29. Does a society's transportation system in any way affect elasticities of demand? How?

30. The demand for aspirin at currently prevailing prices seems to be highly inelastic. What do you think would happen to the elasticity of demand if the price of aspirin relative to everything else were five times as high? Fifty times as high? Why?

31. In 1977 Brazil was supplying about a third of the world's coffee exports. When a frost wiped out about 75 percent of Brazil's 1976-77 crop, the price of green (unroasted) coffee rose 400 percent. What was the approximate price elasticity of demand for coffee? Why was it so low?

32. Harvest-time rains in California in the spring of 1978 destroyed a portion of the lettuce crop. As a result, the price for a 24-head carton loaded in California hit a record of $18 on May 1, 1978. On June 29, after new crops had come in, the price was $2.75. What does all this suggest about the demand for lettuce? What attitudes and practices on the part of households and restaurants contribute toward making the demand for lettuce very inelastic with respect to price?

33. In a January 1984 *Wall Street Journal* article on Chicago's attempt to attract more transit riders with lower fares, Joseph L. Schofer, research director at Northwestern University's Transportation Center, was quoted as saying that "lower fares never make up for loss of revenues. Even when losing riders by increasing fares, revenue usually goes up. It's a law of economics." What exactly is the "law of economics" Mr. Schofer seems to be defending? Would you agree in calling it a "law of economics"?

34. The Congressional Budget Office concluded in 1984 that adding access charges of $2 to $6 per month to the bills of phone subscribers would not induce many users to give up their phones—as some critics of the charges had maintained. "Demand for local telephone service is quite inelastic," according to the CBO report.

    (a) If the cost of local phone service rose from $12 to $18 per month, what percentage of telephone subscribers would have to give up their phones for the demand to be described as elastic?

    (b) What percentage do you estimate would actually do so? What is the coefficient of elasticity that you are estimating?

35. Price elasticity of demand can be calculated by dividing the percentage change in the quantity demanded by the percentage change in the price.

    (a) What is the coefficient of elasticity between the two points of the demand schedule in each of the cases shown below?

Price per Ticket	Tickets Demanded	Price per Cup of Coffee	Cups of Coffee Demanded
$2	200	35¢	600
$1	400	70¢	300

    (b) If you divided 100% by 50% in the ticket case, and 50% by 100% in the coffee case, you got very different coefficients—2 and .5 respectively—for what are actually identical relative changes. The different results

come from using the larger price and the smaller quantity as the base from which to calculate the percentage change in the first case, and using the smaller price and the larger quantity as the base in the second case. But the coefficient of elasticity should be the same between two points regardless of the direction in which the change is measured. How can this problem be handled?

(c) What is the coefficient of elasticity in each of these cases if you use the *average* of the prices and quantities between which the change is occurring as the base for calculating the percentage changes?

(d) In both cases, total expenditure (price times quantity) does not change when the price changes. What does this imply about the elasticity of demand between the prices given? Does this implication agree with your answer in (c)? (It should.)

36. Figure 2C shows a hypothetical demand curve for strawberries.

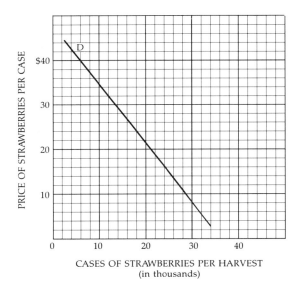

Figure 2C Demand curve for strawberries

(a) What price per case would maximize the gross receipts of strawberry growers? (Peek at part *d* of this question rather than waste too much time trying all sorts of different prices. The price that maximizes gross receipts will be found at the midpoint of a straight-line demand curve when the curve is extended to the axes. If you see why, good. If not, it's a bit of knowledge with only academic usefulness anyway.)

(b) If the price of strawberries is determined by the total quantity harvested in conjunction with the demand, what size crop will result in the price quoted in part *d?*

(c) What would the gross receipts of strawberry growers be if the crop turned out to be 30,000 cases?

    (d) Can you prove that the demand for strawberries is elastic above a price of $24 per case and inelastic below that price?

    (e) If strawberry growers can make more money by selling fewer than 30,000 cases, why would they ever market that much? Why wouldn't they destroy some of the crop rather than "spoil the market"?

37. See if you can clarify this analysis: "If half of our forests were destroyed in a fire, the value of the remaining lumber would be greater than the value of all the lumber in the country before the fire. This absurdity—that the whole is worth less than a half—shows that values are distorted in a market economy."

38. The advertising slogan of Maker's Mark whiskey is: "It tastes expensive . . . and is."

    (a) Isn't the seller foolish to advertise the high price? Or will people buy more at higher prices? Does this contradict the law of demand?

    (b) A waiter at Jean-Louis, a restaurant in Washington, D.C., often patronized by eminent politicians, says, "It is good to be known as expensive. People know they can impress their guests here." What does he think people are purchasing when they go to Jean-Louis for dinner?

39. Here's a question for those who wondered why price was graphed along the vertical axis in Figure 2A, which is the standard procedure in economics, rather than along the horizontal axis, where the independent variable usually goes. Is price in fact the independent and quantity the dependent variable? If quantity depends on price, on what does price depend? Who or what determines prices?

Opportunity Cost
and the Supply of Goods

You have already been introduced to the central concept of this chapter. If you failed to notice, that's because we didn't call it by its proper name. But several times in the preceding chapter, in talking about the relationship between price and quantity demanded, we pointed out that the amount of any good that a person will want to purchase is determined by the good's cost to that person, or the value of the sacrifice required to obtain it. That is the definition of *opportunity cost,* a concept that ties together the law of demand and the principles governing supply. We shall try to convince you in this chapter that it makes sense to think of cost as *the value of sacrificed opportunities.*

Costs Are Valuations

Everyone will concede that demand reflects people's values. But supply, many believe, is the material side of economics, governed by costs of production that are objective realities, in contrast with such subjective factors as people's values and preferences. That belief is in error. Supply and cost are also based on valuations. To help you see this, we shall detour through a college dormitory on a Monday night in the fall, where the following exchange takes place.

"Hey, Jack, do you want to go see the new Wim Wenders movie? It closes after tonight."

"I'd like to, but I can't. We've got a Russian test tomorrow, and I'll flunk if I don't cram some vocabulary."

"Forget it. You can borrow my vocabulary cards in your free period tomorrow. An hour with the cards right before class is a B for sure."

The cost of any action is the value of the opportunity foregone by taking that action.

"Well—trouble is, the Redskins and Miami are on TV tonight and I'd rather watch the game if I don't have to study."

"We'll go at six and be back for the kickoff."

"All right. Just let me see how much money I've got—five, six, seven, eight dollars—to last until I get paid on Thursday. And I'm out of meal tickets!"

"Eat peanut butter sandwiches! I thought you wanted to see the movie."

"I do. O.K., I'll let my stomach shrink until Thursday. Should we leave at quarter to six?"

The real cost of any action (going to a movie, buying a pair of jeans, manufacturing a lawnmower, moving to Halifax, raising beef cattle, building a hardware store, taking out an insurance policy) is the value of the alternative opportunity that must be sacrificed in order to take the action. The cost for Jack of going to the movie was at first calculated as a passing grade (given up!) in Russian. When his friend showed him how to reduce that cost, Jack looked at the next most valuable opportunity he would have to sacrifice if he went to the movie: watching the Monday night football game, a game he particularly wanted to see. His friend eliminated that cost for him, and Jack turned to the money cost. But money wasn't the real cost. The real cost that dollars and cents represent are the opportunities given up when the money is spent in one way rather than another. The three or four dollars Jack will spend for the movie represent some meals he would have liked to eat but is willing to sacrifice in order to see the film.

Producers' Costs as Opportunity Costs

The theory of supply in economics is not essentially different from the theory of demand. Both assume that decision makers face alternatives and choose among them, and that their choices reflect a comparison of the benefits anticipated from the alternatives. The logic of the economizing process is the same for producers as it is for consumers.

When we think about producers' costs—asking ourselves, for example, why it costs more to manufacture a ten-speed bicycle than a redwood picnic table—we tend to think first of what goes into the production of each. We think of the raw materials, of the labor time required, perhaps also of the machinery or tools that must be used. We express the value of the inputs in monetary terms and assume that the cost of the bicycle or the table is the sum of these values. That isn't wrong, but it leaves unanswered the question of why the inputs had those particular monetary values. The concept of opportunity cost asserts that those values reflect the value of the inputs in their next-best uses, or the value of the

opportunities forgone by using the inputs in the production of bicycles and picnic tables.

The manufacturer's cost of producing a bicycle will be determined by what he must pay to obtain the appropriate resources. And, because these resources have other opportunities for employment, he must pay a price that matches the "best opportunity" value. The value of forgone opportunities thus becomes the cost of manufacturing a bicycle. This makes excellent sense, for the meaningful cost of obtaining one more bicycle is the value of what must be given up or sacrificed or forgone in order to obtain that bicycle.

Consider the example of the picnic table. Part of its cost of production is the price of redwood. Assume that the demand for new housing has increased recently and that building contractors have consequently been purchasing a lot more redwood lumber. If this causes the price of lumber to rise, the cost of manufacturing a picnic table will go up. Nothing has happened to affect the physical inputs that go into the table, but its cost of production has risen. Because houses containing redwood lumber are now more valuable than formerly, the table manufacturer must pay a higher opportunity cost for the lumber he wants to put into his picnic tables.

The concept of opportunity cost also explains how labor enters into production costs. Workers must receive from their employers a wage that persuades them to turn down all other opportunities. A skilled worker will be paid more than an unskilled worker because and only insofar as those skills make the skilled worker more valuable somewhere else. Workers who can install wheel spokes while standing on their heads and whistling "Dixie" are marvelously skilled. But our bicycle manufacturer will not have to pay them additional compensation for that skill unless their unusual talent makes them more valuable somewhere else. That could happen. A circus might bid for their talents. If the circus offers them more than they can obtain as bicycle producers, their opportunity cost to the manufacturer rises. In that case the manufacturer will probably wish them goodbye and good luck and replace them with other workers whose opportunity cost is lower.

When the National Basketball Association and the American Basketball Association merged into one league, what happened to the opportunity cost of hiring physically coordinated seven-footers? With two leagues, each player had two teams bidding for his services. What either team was compelled to pay to get him was determined by what the other team was willing to pay, and both were willing to pay a lot if they thought he would make a big difference in ticket sales. When the leagues merged, however, the right to hire a

particular player was assigned to a single team, and the opportunity cost of a well-coordinated seven-footer fell. It's not surprising that owners of professional basketball teams prefer one league to two.

Let's take a more common case. If a large firm employing many people moves into a small town, the cost of hiring grocery clerks, bank tellers, secretaries, and gasoline station attendants in the town will tend to go up. Why? Because grocery stores, banks, offices, and gasoline stations must all pay the opportunity cost of the people they employ, and these people may now find better opportunities for employment in the new firm. Suppose the new firm is interested in hiring women exclusively; only the opportunity cost of hiring women will increase at first. But that will pull women out of some jobs, thereby creating additional opportunities for men and causing the opportunity cost of male workers to rise.

The resource that most clearly illustrates the opportunity-cost concept is probably land. Suppose you want to purchase an acre of land to build a house. What will you have to pay for the land? It will depend on the value of that land in alternative uses. Do other people view the acre as a choice residential site? Does it have commercial or industrial potentialities? Would it be used for pasture if you did not purchase it? The cost you pay for the land will be determined by the alternative opportunities that people perceive for its use.

Case Studies in Opportunity Cost

Let's examine some other cases of varying costs to see how the concept of opportunity cost explains familiar but often misunderstood phenomena.

Why, in the last fifty years, has the cost of getting a haircut gone up so much more than the cost of goods generally? It's because people who want barbers to cut their hair must be willing to pay them enough to keep them in the trade. If productivity in haircutting had kept pace over the last fifty years with productivity in manufacturing, barbers would have been able to maintain their incomes by trimming more heads per hour. But with productivity virtually unchanged, only a higher price per head could keep them working in the barber shop. We who want our hair cut by professionals have bid up the price of haircuts to meet the rising opportunity cost to barbers of working at a job in which productivity never increases.

Why is it often so much harder to find a teenage babysitter in a wealthy residential area than in a low-income area? The

If a barber can give two haircuts in an hour, what price must he charge to earn $7 an hour?

What price would yield $7 an hour if his productivity increased five-fold?

frustrated couple unable to find a babysitter may complain that all the kids in the neighborhood are lazy. But that is a needlessly harsh explanation. Teenage babysitters can be found by any couple willing to pay the opportunity cost. That means bidding the babysitters away from their otherwise most valued opportunity. If the demand for babysitters in the area is large because wealthy people go out more often, and if the local teenagers receive such generous allowances that they value a date or leisure more than the ordinary income from babysitting, why be surprised to find that the opportunity cost of hiring a babysitter is high?

Why did the cost of obtaining a college education rise so steeply during the 1960s? A very large part of the explanation lies in sharply increased instructional costs, made up partly of higher faculty salaries and partly of reduced teaching loads. But how did these developments come about? Ask your friendly neighborhood professor and he will probably tell you about the long years that must be spent getting a Ph.D. and the impossibility of doing research while teaching twelve hours. Any good member of the professorial guild will assent to the virtues of those arguments. But no good economics professor will be much impressed with their cogency as an explanation of why professors earned more and taught less at the end of the decade than at the beginning.

The rapidly rising demand for professors provides the explanation. State legislatures poured money into building new colleges and expanding old ones; the federal government responded to the fear of Soviet scientific superiority by appropriating vast sums for higher education and for research, which gave teachers new opportunities; the World War II baby boom became a college-student boom in the 1960s; and a larger percentage of the population became persuaded that a college degree was a passport to the good life. The government and private industry meanwhile increased their demand for the services of highly trained persons, widening the range of opportunities for people with extensive education. The net result was a vastly increased demand for the services of college professors. College professors, too, are scarce resources with opportunity costs. A larger number of them were obtained by bidding them away from alternative employments with the offer of higher salaries and reduced teaching loads. (All college professors know that it is easier to raise their incomes by finding a better opportunity elsewhere than by reciting their virtues to their current deans. Deans are more attentive to the recitals of professors with alternative opportunities.)

If you have grasped the argument, you should be ready to predict that the salaries of college professors will *decline*

through the 1980s. Inflation may conceal that decline; but once we have adjusted for changes in the value of the dollar, we will almost certainly see the same factors that pulled faculty salaries up in the 1960s pulling them down in the 1980s.

Why does the high-school dropout rate decrease during a recession? The opportunity cost of remaining in high school varies with the job market for teenagers. A decline in job opportunities reduces the opportunity cost of remaining in school for some young people; therefore fewer drop out.

Why are poor people more likely to travel between cities by bus and wealthy people more likely to travel by air? A simple answer would be that taking the bus is cheaper. But it isn't. It's a very expensive mode of transportation for people for whom the opportunity cost of time is high; and the opportunity cost of time is typically much lower for poor people than for those with a high income from working.

Do you have the idea? Figure out for yourself the cost of going to college. If you include in your calculations the value to yourself of whatever you would be doing if you were not in college, you have grasped the principle of opportunity cost.

A final example. Consider the case of a woman who runs a small grocery store all by herself. She says that she does pretty well because she has no labor costs. Is she right? The cost of her own labor is not a monetary outlay, but it certainly is a cost. And that cost can be measured by the value of the opportunities she forgoes by working for herself.

Costs and Actions

The economic way of thinking recognizes *no* objective costs. That offends common sense, which teaches that things do have "real" costs, costs that depend on the laws of physics rather than the vagaries of the human psyche. It's hard to win a battle against common sense, but we must try.

Perhaps we can disarm common sense most quickly by pointing out that "things" have no costs at all. We are talking about costs relevant to supply, of course—costs that have an effect on people's decisions to make goods available. "Things" cannot have costs in that sense. Only actions can. If you think that things do indeed have costs and are ready with an example to prove it, you are almost certainly smuggling in an unnoticed action to give your item a cost.

For example: What is the cost of a baseball? "Four dollars," you say. But you mean that the cost of *purchasing* a baseball at the local sporting goods store is four dollars. Since purchasing is an action, it can entail sacrificed opportunities and thereby have a cost. But note the smuggled-in action.

With other actions, the cost of a baseball changes. The cost of *manufacturing* a baseball is quite different. *Selling* one has yet another cost. And what about the cost of *catching* one at the ball park by spearing a line-drive foul with your bare hand, where the sacrifice may be the opportunity to wear an unbroken nose the rest of your life?

Let's return to the case of a college education. What does it cost? The answer is that "it" cannot have a cost. We must at least distinguish between the cost of *obtaining* a college education and the cost of *providing* one. As soon as we make that distinction, we should also notice something that has been implicit in everything we've said so far about costs, either in this or the preceding chapter; namely, that costs are always cost *to someone*. The cost of obtaining an education usually means the cost to the student. But it could mean the cost to the student's parents, which is not the same. Or, if that student's admission entailed the rejection of some other applicant, it could even mean the cost to John (who was refused admission) of Marsha's obtaining entrance to the first-year class. Those will all be different.

A great deal of fruitless argument about the "true cost" of things stems from a failure to recognize that only actions have costs, and that actions can entail different costs for different people. The ongoing debate about reinstituting the military draft is an excellent example. Let's take a look.

The Cost of a Volunteer Military Force

Selective service, as it is euphemistically called, has been around for a long time. Although almost everyone regards it as undesirable in itself, many Americans still seem to think of it as the only way to secure an adequate supply of military personnel at an acceptable cost.

There may be good arguments for the draft, but the familiar argument that an adequate volunteer army would cost too much is not one of them. The Department of Defense and others who worry about the relative costs of a conscripted and a volunteer military are conveniently bypassing the question, cost to whom? Are we talking about the cost to taxpayers, enlisted personnel, Congress, or the Pentagon? They are very different.

What is the cost to a young person of becoming a soldier? The best way to find out would be to offer a bribe and to keep raising it until it was accepted. If Marshall would enlist for $5000 per year, Carol for $8000, and Philip for no less than $60,000, these represent the opportunity costs of Marshall, Carol, and Philip. The cost of drafting all three, *to them*, would then be $73,000, even though the government can

conceal this fact by offering far less in wages and then compelling each to serve.

The opportunity cost is a function of forgone alternative employment opportunities and all sorts of other values: preferences with respect to life-style, attitude toward war, degrees of cowardice or bravery, and so on. When the government bids for military personnel, raising its offer until it can attract just the desired number of enlistments, the government in an important sense actually minimizes the cost of its program. For it pulls in those with the lowest opportunity costs of service—everyone like Marshall but no one like Philip. Under a draft, this could occur only through the most unlikely of coincidences. Figure 3A provides a simple way to grasp the argument.

There is a supply curve of military volunteers. The argument that people won't voluntarily risk their lives is refuted by the fact that people do—not only military volunteers but also police, steeplejacks, and even skiers. Whatever its precise position and slope, the supply curve will certainly incline upward to the right. Some people (those who assign low value to their available alternatives) will volunteer at a very low wage. But three million volunteers can be secured, on our assumptions, only if the wage offer is at least $8000 per year. That would mean a wage bill of $24 billion annually. But because taxpayers don't like to have their taxes raised, Congress is reluctant to approve such a huge appropriation.

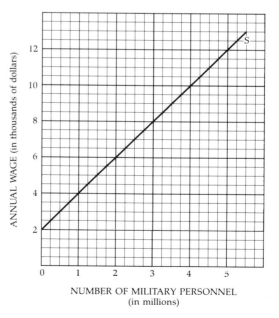

Figure 3A Supply curve of military volunteers

And the people in the Department of Defense care very much about the likes and dislikes of the people in Congress. They can cut that upsetting bill in half by offering only $4000 and compelling enlistments. The published cost will now be only $12 billion. Hurrah for cost savings!

But what of the costs to those who make up the armed forces? The cost of the *volunteer* army (to the volunteers) under our assumptions would be $15 billion. That is the value of the area under the supply curve up to three million men and women, or the sum of the values of the opportunities forgone by those who enlisted. The other $9 billion paid out by the government is a transfer of wealth from taxpayers to members of the military who would have enlisted at a lower wage but who nonetheless receive the higher wage that is required to induce the enlistment of the three-millionth volunteer.

What will be the cost to those who are drafted of a *conscripted* army? We can't say, except that it will certainly be larger. Only if the draft happened to hit exactly those and only those who would have enlisted under a volunteer system would the cost be as low as $15 billion. But that is most unlikely. The more draftees who are grabbed from the upper, rather than the lower, end of the supply curve, the higher will be the cost to the conscripts. For example, a man who would have volunteered at a wage of $4500 is offered $4000. He rejects the offer, and he is subsequently not drafted. Instead, a person who would only have volunteered at $12,000 is drafted. There was a saving of $500 annually to taxpayers but a loss of $8000 to the draftee.

The military draft does *not* reduce the cost of maintaining a military establishment. It rather transfers that cost from the shoulders of taxpayers to the shoulders of the draftees. That may in your judgment be one of the least of its faults, or it may be outweighed in your mind by presumed advantages. But at least it's a consequence that economists can point out.

Costs and Ownership

Everyone who has been in the armed forces knows horror stories about the inefficient ways the military makes use of its personnel. A highly skilled accountant is put to work painting barracks, and the commissary books are kept by someone who counts on his fingers. The stories are probably exaggerated. Nonetheless, we have grounds for predicting that personnel will tend to be used in such wasteful ways in the military more often than in civilian life.

Why? Because, in civilian life, those who employ people are usually compelled to pay them their opportunity cost.

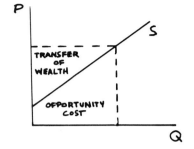

When you have to pay accountants the wages of accountants, you don't have them paint barracks—at least not if you're an employer with regard for the profitability of your enterprise. On the other hand, what is the cost to a sergeant of assigning a highly skilled recruit to a task that requires no skill at all? If the sergeant happens to resent the recruit for his air of superiority, real or imagined, then transferring him to a job more suited to his abilities might actually entail the sacrifice of a valuable opportunity for the sergeant—the opportunity to humiliate someone he dislikes.

Two conclusions emerge from the foregoing analysis. First, resources tend to be utilized thoughtlessly and carelessly when users don't have to pay the opportunity cost, or the value of the resources in their next-best use. Second, users are most often compelled to pay the opportunity cost of resources when those resources are clearly and definitely owned by someone. A man who is drafted does not "own his own labor," because the law has deprived him of the power to decide where and for whom and on what terms he will work. And so he can't insist upon receiving his opportunity cost when Uncle Sam beckons—as he can when United Soapchips wants his services.

The point also applies, of course, to nonhuman resources. If no one owns a resource, there is no one to insist that potential users of that resource pay the value of the opportunities sacrificed by their use. The resource will consequently tend to be underpriced. And underpriced resources, as we shall see time and again in a variety of situations, tend to be used with little care or thought for the consequences. The incentive to economize is weak when the cost of using is low.

A Note on Alternative Systems

Don't fail to notice that the concept of opportunity cost is fully applicable to a socialist society in which resources are allocated by government planners. To economic planners in the Soviet Union, the cost of building a railway from Lubny to Mirgorod is the value of whatever could otherwise have been done with the resources. But if government officials have the power to obtain valuable resources without having to bid for them, how will they discover the value of the resources in alternative uses? Recall the remarkable workers who could install spokes in bicycle wheels while standing on their heads and whistling "Dixie." In the absence of circus owners willing to bid for their services, how would central planners ever find out that they were too valuable to be assigned to bicycle production?

A distinguishing characteristic of different economic

systems is the way in which they assign costs to alternative actions. Where resources are privately owned, competing bids and offers generate prices that approximate opportunity costs to resource owners. Where resources are not clearly owned by anyone, this process cannot operate. What takes its place? Who determines the relative value of this railway line and that one, or of using steel for railroad tracks versus using it to build trucks, or of improving transportation versus improving the quality of what is transported, or of more and better consumer goods versus additional leisure? In the absence of the information that competing bids and offers create, the economic planners are fairly free to impose their own, private evaluations on the alternatives before them. Remember that intelligent choices presuppose good information. An effective economic system will be one that transmits reliable information to decision makers and gives them strong incentives to use the information so provided.

Do Costs Determine Prices?

When sellers announce a price increase to the public, they like to point out that the increase was compelled by rising costs. The business press publishes frequent announcements of this kind, and it's rare indeed when the announcement fails to include an expression of regret that higher costs made this unfortunate step necessary. In Chapter 9 we'll explore more fully the principles that guide sellers when they're setting prices. All we want to do now is use the concept of opportunity cost to examine critically the basic notion that prices are determined by costs. We want to show you that it makes as much sense to assert that costs are determined by prices. More accurately, we shall argue here that *costs always depend on demand*.

Demand and Cost

We can begin with an example discussed earlier in this chapter. Does it make sense to claim that the price of getting a haircut has gone up because barbers' wages have risen? If people weren't willing to pay high prices for haircuts, how could barbers' wages rise? The price people are willing to pay to have their hair cut professionally is one important factor that causes costs—that is, wages—to be what they are.

Plastic surgeons receive high wages for their services. Is this why it costs so much to have a face lift? Not exactly. The causal relationship also runs in the opposite direction. It's the fact that people are willing to pay a high price for cosmetic surgery that makes the cost of hiring a plastic surgeon

so high. Few people have the requisite skills, of course, and their acquisition is difficult and time consuming. That's why the demand for cosmetic surgery raises the income of the surgeons rather than merely increasing the number of people willing and able to provide the service. But the cost to any one person of the services of a plastic surgeon is obviously not independent of the demand of others for plastic surgery.

When the owners of professional football teams announce in the summer that ticket prices will be raised in the fall, they like to blame the increase on rising costs, especially the high wages that must be paid to the players. But why do the players receive such high wages? It can't be that their work is so dangerous and grueling, because it was just as dangerous and grueling in the days when players received only a few hundred dollars for the season. It's the demand, the willingness of many people to pay high prices to watch, that has made football players such valuable resources. Soccer players in the United States receive far less, not because they work less hard, but because soccer isn't that popular in this country.

One of the most interesting cases of the relationship we're stressing is found in agriculture. The average price per acre of farm real estate in the United States rose 267 percent from 1971 to 1981, more than twice as fast as the general price level increased over the same period. Consequently anyone who decided to go into farming in 1981 found that he had to pay a high price to obtain productive land. It would clearly be misleading to assert that the high cost of land is a cause of high food prices. It was the demand for land, determined in large part by the demand for agricultural products, that pulled up the cost of farming land. When farmers argue for higher government support prices for their crops because land costs so much, they are ignoring the fact that higher support prices will tend to pull up the price of the land on which those crops can be grown. It will do so by enhancing the value of the opportunities available to one who owns the land.

Similarly, the sharp declines in agricultural land prices in the 1980s have been the result, not the cause, of lower farm commodity prices.

Consider the case of a farmer whose land lies near a large city. As the suburbs expand, residential developers offer to buy the land for a price that is three or four times higher than the price it can command as agricultural property. If the farmer refuses to sell because he wants to stay in farming, it is very unlikely that he will complain about the rising cost of land. But farmers who *rent* land near large cities often do just that. The landowner will understandably want to sell

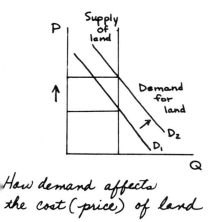

How demand affects the cost (price) of land

the land to developers unless the tenant farmer is willing to
pay three or four times more rent. We can certainly sympathize
with the tenant farmer dispossessed by the growth of the
suburbs. But it's important that we see why he's being asked
to pay a rent so much higher than before: it is the demand
for the land that is raising its cost.

Note that if *tax assessments* are based on what is called
"highest and best use," then the owner who wants to remain
in farming can legitimately complain that he can't afford *not*
to sell. In those circumstances he is required to pay taxes
based not on his own use of the land, but on the use to which
the land would be put by the highest bidder.

But let's push the analysis a bit further. Suppose the
farmer himself owns the land he's cultivating, and that the
county does not raise the assessed value of the land when
suburban developers bid up its price because public officials
want to keep the land in farming. Will the policy succeed?

The cost to the farmer of maintaining the land in agriculture
is the net value of the opportunities he thereby forgoes. By
rejecting an opportunity to sell, he gives up the income
he could obtain from investing the sales proceeds. If his annual
net income from the farming operation is $5000 per year, he
will be losing a large sum each year if he refuses to sell the
land for $300,000, since $300,000 can earn far more than
$5000 per year in such low-risk investments as U.S. govern-
ment bonds.

What about the value to the farmer of remaining a farmer?
Might he not, in selling his land, be giving up a valuable
opportunity to lead a good, simple, honest, and satisfying life?
Probably not. If he really does value farm living so highly,
he can buy a replacement farm in some location where subur-
banites aren't competing for the land. If he chooses not to
do this, we have evidence that he doesn't place all that high a
value on the agricultural life. In either event, the cost to him
of continuing to farm on the land that the developers want
goes up as soon as the developers bid up the price. That means
he is less likely to continue farming that land, which means
in turn that he is more likely to increase the supply of land
available for suburban development.

Consumer Prices as Opportunity Costs

In all these examples we've tried to show that the costs of
productive resources like labor and land are prices determined
by demand. That, in fact, is what's meant by calling them
opportunity costs. We can just as easily argue that the prices
of consumer goods are, in reality, costs—opportunity costs
that measure the value of the goods in alternative uses.

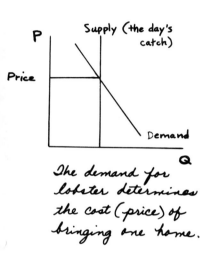

P

Price

Supply (the day's catch)

Demand

Q

The demand for lobster determines the cost (price) of bringing one home.

Take, for example, the case of lobster. Sad to relate, so few lobsters come to market that it just isn't possible for all of us to have as many as we could enjoy. More are brought to market as higher prices offer larger incentives to lobster fishermen; but the demand in recent years has increased considerably faster than the supply, and the price has consequently risen sharply.

The higher price can be viewed as the opportunity cost of the resources engaged in bringing lobsters to market. But when the lobsters have all been brought to market on a given day, so that the supply is, for that day at least, completely fixed, then the price should be viewed as the opportunity cost of the last potential purchaser who was persuaded by the high price to do without lobster. Think of it as follows: lobsters have many alternative uses, at least as many as there are potential lobster eaters. Lobsters have only one function, it is true, from the aggregate point of view. (We're notorious for ignoring the values and preferences of the lobster.) But the consumption of a lobster by one gourmet prevents its consumption by another. Lobster lovers in effect bid against one another for the limited supply. As the price rises, more and more potential consumers are reluctantly persuaded to do without. The price that clears the market, that makes the quantity demanded equal to the quantity supplied, will be the price that just barely persuades the most reluctant of the disappointed lobster lovers to go home from the seafood market with ocean perch or flounder fillets. It is *that person's* opportunity cost that is expressed by the market clearing price.

The point of all this is that people don't pay what lobster is worth to them, but rather what lobster is worth in its most valued alternative use: as food for the consumer who was just barely deterred by the price from making a purchase. It's the opportunity cost of this disappointed lobster lover that the price reflects, as well as the opportunity costs of the resources that might have been used to bring additional lobsters to market.

How many coffee drinkers realize that when the price of coffee soars because of a freeze in Brazil, they are continuing to pay a price based on cost? It's not the cost of *growing* the coffee that determines the new, much higher price; it's the opportunity cost of those coffee lovers who must be persuaded (by a rising price) to sacrifice the caffeine they covet to others who are less willing to give it up and therefore willing to pay more.

But now we have moved into the question of scarcity and its social management. That is the topic for Chapter 4.

Supply curves, as well as demand curves, reflect people's estimates of the value of alternative opportunities. Both the quantities of any good that are supplied and the quantities that are demanded depend on the choices people make after assessing the opportunities available to them.

Supply depends on cost. But the cost of supplying is the value of the opportunities forgone by the act of supplying. This concept of cost is expressed in economic theory by the assertion that all costs relevant to decisions are opportunity costs—the value of the opportunities forsaken in choosing one course of action rather than another.

Insofar as the resources utilized in producing goods can be obtained only through competitive bidding, costs of production will reflect the value to the resource owners of the alternative uses of those resources. This implies that producers will want to suppress competitive bidding for the resources they use, if they can find an effective way to do so.

The value of a human being may be infinite, but the wages of human beings in any task will be much closer to the value of their services in alternative employments than to infinity.

Many disagreements about what something or the other "really costs" could be resolved by the recognition that "things" cannot have costs. Only actions entail sacrificed opportunities, and therefore only actions can have costs.

Costs are always the value of the opportunities that particular people sacrifice. Conflicting assertions about the costs of alternative decisions can often be reconciled by agreement on whose costs are under consideration.

Prices rise to the level of opportunity costs insofar as the owners of resources insist on being paid their value in the next-best use. This discourages a careless use of resources, and assigns resources to those uses on which people place the highest monetary value.

Supply curves slope upward to the right because higher prices must be offered to resource owners to persuade them to transform a current activity into an opportunity they are willing to sacrifice.

Demand curves slope upward to the left because higher prices persuade resource users to sacrifice a current activity for their next-best opportunity.

Demand helps determine costs. Costs contribute to the determination of prices. The prices of goods affect the demand for other goods that they complement or for which they can substitute. From the perspective of opportunity cost, everything depends on everything else.

QUESTIONS FOR DISCUSSION

1. A prominent hospital in New England decided in 1980 to turn down a request by staff surgeons to perform heart transplants. The general director of the hospital objected to the statement that this decision was "based largely on cost considerations." On the contrary, he insisted, "the decision was based largely on the limited physical resources and highly trained personnel of the hospital. For each heart transplantation operation," he pointed out, the hospital "would have to turn away a number of other patients who receive less resource-draining open-heart surgery that is much more predictably beneficial to them than heart transplants currently are."

    Do you agree that the decision was not based on cost considerations?

2. Here is a statement from the economics textbook most widely used in American colleges before 1860: "The qualities and relations of natural agents are the *gift* of God, and, being His gift, they *cost us nothing*. Thus, in order to avail ourselves of the momentum produced by a water-fall, we have only to construct the water-wheel and its necessary appendages, and place them in a proper position. We then have the use of the falling water, without further expense. As, therefore, our only outlay is *the cost of the instrument* by which the natural agent is rendered available, *this* is the only expenditure which demands the attention of the political economist."

    Why do modern "political economists" disagree with Francis Wayland and pay attention to the cost of using "natural agents"?

3. The acres of grass surrounding the Taj Mahal in Agra, India, are often cut by young women who slice off handfuls with short kitchen blades. Is this a low- or high-cost way to keep a lawn mowed?

4. By taking an airplane one can go from D to H in one hour. The same trip takes five hours by bus. If the air fare is $30 and the bus fare is $10, which would be the cheaper mode of transportation for someone who could earn $2 an hour during this time? For someone who could earn $10 an hour? Five dollars an hour?

5. At a sufficiently high price for gasoline, almost everyone would choose to leave the car at home and use public transportation to commute to and from work. But that price will differ vastly from one person to another. Why might it be higher for self-employed than for salaried people? For executives than for clerks?

6. What would be the effect on the cost to students of completing high school if legislation denied drivers' licenses to anyone under the age of 18?

7. Why did the cost of hiring domestic servants increase dramatically during World War II? What would you have replied to people who said that servants "just weren't available"?

8. Explain the following statement by a military recruiter: "There's nothing like a good recession to cure our recruiting problems."

9. Are hand-carved redwood flamingos that sell for $150 valuable because they take so many hours to carve? Or do people spend many hours carving redwood flamingos because they are valuable? Does the value of an object ever depend on what people know about how it was produced? Would a

flamingo be more valuable if people thought it had been carved by Pope John XXIII than if they thought you had carved it?

10. Smith, Ricardo, Marx, and Keynes are potential tutors for students in introductory economics. Each wants to work 8 hours a day at his best available monetary opportunity. Students regard their services as perfect substitutes: as far as students are concerned, an hour of tutoring is equally valuable whichever of the four provides it.

   Marx is willing to tutor 8 hours a day for $4 an hour, because his next-best opportunity, fomenting revolution, currently pays only $3.99 an hour. Ricardo can work 4 hours a day at Merrill Lynch for $13.99 an hour; after that he's reduced to selling shoes for $4.99 an hour. Smith's best alternative is teaching moral philosophy at the local college for $7.99 an hour, 8 hours a day. Keynes has an 8-hour per day job, paying $11.99 an hour, raising money for the local symphony.
   (a) Construct the supply curve of tutoring services from these data on the graph below.
   (b) Show how the supply curve would change if Merrill Lynch hired Ricardo full time.
   (c) Show the change that would occur if someone offered Marx a job as a newspaper reporter at $9.99 an hour.
   (d) How would the supply curve change if the public suddenly became much more interested in learning something about moral philosophy?

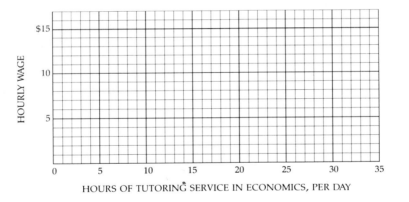

Figure 3B Supply of tutoring services

11. The supply curve on the graph below shows the wage rates that would have to be offered by business firms to obtain various quantities of hours of envelope stuffing on any given day.
   (a) What wage rate will firms have to offer if they want to hire 400 hours of envelope stuffing?
   (b) What will be the firms' total expenditure on the wages of envelope stuffers?
   (c) What will be the total opportunity cost to the envelope stuffers of stuffing envelopes? (Hint: Each square represents $20: 20 hours times $1.)

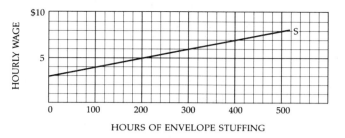

Figure 3C Supply curve for envelope stuffing

12. **(a)** It has been argued that a volunteer army would discriminate against poor people, because they tend to have the lowest-value alternatives to military service and hence would dominate the ranks of volunteers. Do you agree with the analysis and the objection?

   (b) Some critics have argued that if the military relied exclusively on volunteers, the armed forces would be filled with people of such low intelligence and skills that they could not operate sophisticated weapons. International Business Machines relies exclusively on "volunteers," and *its* employees are not predominantly people of low intelligence and skills. What's the difference between the armed forces and IBM? How would you reply to the argument of these critics?

   (c) Another frequent criticism of a volunteer military is that we don't want "an army of mercenaries." How high does the military wage have to be before the recipient becomes a mercenary? Are officers compelled to remain in the armed services? Why do they stay in? Are they mercenaries? Is your teacher a mercenary? Your physician? Your minister?

13. Why might a multinational corporation with identical plants in different countries pay different wage rates to workers in the two countries even though their skill levels are the same? Does this strike you as unjust? Why might the *higher-paid* workers object?

14. If people are offering to pay $100 for $10 (face-value) tickets to the Big Game, and someone gives you a ticket, what does it cost you to attend the game? Would you be more likely to attend if someone gave you a ticket than if you had to purchase one for $100? Would you be more likely to attend if someone gave you a ticket than if you had to purchase one that you could buy (through an inside source) for $10?

15. Rising commercial rents in San Francisco in recent years have induced many corporations to move their offices out of the city. Can a San Francisco firm that owns its own office building simply ignore rising rents?

16. Henrietta George bought her large, old house 48 years ago for $2000. She could get $200,000 for it today if she chose to sell it. About how much do you suppose it's costing her per month to continue living in her large, old house?

17. What is the cost per ticket to a professional baseball club that offers 50 free tickets to an orphanage? Does it matter for what game the tickets are offered? Why would it probably cost the ball club more to give the tickets to college students than to poor orphans?

18. Think about the cost of television commercials. What enters into the cost of a 30-second commercial plugging Friendly Fred's Ford Dealership? How do you explain the fact that the same commercial will cost $90 on Wednesday morning but $1600 right before a big football game? Local television stations are often asked to donate time for public-service spots. Does this cost the station anything? Do you think that station owners' religious beliefs make them more willing to donate time on Sunday mornings than on weekday mornings?

19. The network advertising fee per 30-second spot during Super Bowl XVIII was $484,000. Did that reflect the network's estimate of the cost of providing a 30-second advertising spot? What made the cost so high?

20. Why do parking lot fees vary so widely from city to city in the U.S.? The all-day rate in Manhattan, for example, is often $20. In Atlanta, it is likely to be less than $5. Does this difference reflect the greater greed of New York City parking-garage owners?

21. In 1977 a Seventh Day Adventist congregation in Manhattan purchased a former synagogue for $400,000. Several years later the congregation decided to sell it because the maintenance costs were running $100,000 per year, too much for the 80-family congregation to pay. In 1982 a developer paid the congregation $2.4 million in cash for the property. (The information is taken from a *Wall Street Journal* article of September 27, 1982.)
    (a) What would it have cost the congregation to continue using the building?
    (b) Would you say that it is greed that prompts congregations to sell large, old churches in downtown areas to commercial developers?

22. Most mobile-home owners own their homes but pay rent for the land on which the home sits. Some municipalities have recently begun to impose legal limits on the amount by which the owners of mobile-home parks can increase the rent they charge for their sites. One argument given in defense of such rent controls was that zoning regulations against mobile-home parks made it difficult for mobile-home owners to move to a new site when faced with a huge rent increase.
    (a) What determines the rent a mobile-home park owner can charge?
    (b) To what cost, if any, is this charge related?
    (c) How do zoning regulations against mobile-home parks affect the rents park owners can charge?
    (d) Do you agree with the mobile-home owner who, when faced with a large increase, protested indignantly, "My home gives value to that pad of dirt"?

23. A number of American cities have passed rent-control ordinances in recent years. These ordinances often try to restrict rent increases to the amount of the owners' cost increases. Use the analysis of this chapter in thinking about these questions:
    (a) What is the cost to a landlord of renting an apartment to you for $150 if someone else is willing to pay $250?
    (b) What determines the cost to a potential landlord of purchasing an apartment building?
    (c) What effect will a rent-control ordinance have on the cost of purchasing an apartment building?

(d) What effect will a rent-control ordinance have on the cost to landlords of letting an apartment unit stand idle, or of using it themselves, or of allowing relatives to live in it rent-free?

(e) What concept of cost do you think supporters of rent controls have in mind when they speak of basing maximum rents on landlords' costs?

24. "In the Middle Ages people believed in a just price for goods, not determined by supply and demand, but by the cost of raw material and labor." Assume that the author of that statement is accurate in his historical facts and correct his economic analysis.

Supply and Demand:
A Process of Coordination

In every functioning society, large or small, tasks must be assigned and benefits distributed.

"Who takes out the garbage?"

"Who gets the last slice of pumpkin pie?"

The above questions represent two common kinds of allocation issues that arise in the family, the smallest functioning society we know.

"Who will live in the White House?"

This is a recurring allocation question in the largest functioning society in which we participate, the nation. The answer we give simultaneously assigns some very important tasks and distributes some intensely coveted benefits.

One way for a society to assign tasks and distribute benefits is by the principle: "from each according to ability, to each according to need." That seems to be a sensible principle; but in order for it to become workable, it must be attached to an acceptable system for assessing both abilities and needs. That's where the problems begin.

Allocating Tasks and Benefits

In one sense, individuals are the best judges of their own abilities and needs: I know better than anyone else what I can and cannot do and what will satisfy my particular wants. But in another sense, I am the person *least* qualified to judge, because of my obvious partiality toward my own interests. It is well and wisely established that people ought not to be judges in their own cases. Societies commonly compromise, therefore, by making the allocation of tasks and benefits a matter for negotiation among the interested parties.

The negotiations we're talking about rarely take the form of committee meetings. They are rather the daily bids and offers that we make in the many societies in which we participate, bids and offers that are based upon well-defined rules of the game, and in which 99 percent of the relevant rights and obligations are taken for granted. "Will you do this for me, if I agree to do that for you?" Usually we don't even have to ask. We just walk uninvited into the pizzeria and tell an attendant to prepare us a medium pizza with green peppers, black olives, and extra cheese. The attendant doesn't ask what we're willing to do in return, but simply assumes we will pay the posted money price.

The Coordinating Role of Prices

These continual negotiations are what the economist refers to as supply and demand. Money prices play a crucial role in the process.

It is nowhere decreed in the laws of nature that tasks and benefits have to be allocated on the basis of monetary bids and offers. But it is undeniably the case that a whole lot of allocation and reallocation will have to occur before most goods get where they're going. Consider a gallon of gasoline. People and machinery have to be precisely assigned to explore, drill, pump, pipe, refine, truck, and store before we can fill our tanks at the self-service island. That intricate system is coordinated by means of adjustments in money prices. The right number of people, equipped with the necessary knowledge and skills and accompanied by the appropriate tools, showed up at the correct times and places, so that we could eventually buy our fifteen gallons of unleaded regular. They did not accomplish this spectacular feat of coordination because they love us and know how much we need gasoline. They did it to further their own interests. Their efforts meshed because those efforts were coordinated by the ever-changing signals emitted by money prices.

We must insist again that the crucial importance of money prices to the working of our society implies nothing about the character or morality of our citizens. People pay attention to money prices insofar as they want to economize, that is, to get as much as possible of what they value from the resources they command. They don't pay attention *exclusively* to money prices, of course; that wouldn't make sense. They do, however, change their behavior when prices change, in order to "take advantage" of the new situation signaled by the new prices. This is what causes markets to clear and self-interested behavior to become cooperative action.

Try thinking of supply and demand as a process of mutual accommodation. When any good becomes more scarce—less

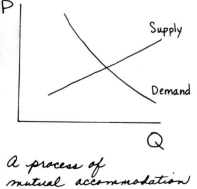

a process of mutual accommodation

is supplied relative to how much is demanded—its price rises. The higher price persuades demanders to take less, thus leaving more for others, and persuades suppliers to produce more. A lower price signals that a good has become less scarce than before; the lower price induces demanders to substitute this good for other goods and prompts suppliers to shift their efforts toward the production of alternative, more highly valued goods.

In a society as wealthy and specialized as ours—and it is wealthy *because* it is so extensively specialized—the coordination of activities is an enormously complex task. Its successful performance requires, above all else, a social system that facilitates the rapid exchange of accurate information about relative scarcities and induces people to act appropriately on the basis of that information. If economists are obsessed with money prices, it's because they see that prices provide such indispensable information and incentives.

The Urge to Fix Prices

To a demander, the price of a good is its cost. Demanders consequently tend to look on rising prices as an imposition. To a supplier, prices represent income. So suppliers see falling prices as a threat. That's probably why so many people don't appreciate the coordinating role that price changes play and why they often try to get government to prevent the changes from occurring. The consequences will usually be quite different from what was intended, however, because price fixing amounts to suspending the mechanism of social coordination.

Figure 4A presents a hypothetical demand curve for gasoline in the United States, labeled DD, with the price per gallon on the vertical axis and the number of gallons demanded per month on the horizontal axis. The demand is very inelastic within the range shown: a large percentage increase in the price will lead to a much smaller percentage decrease in the quantity demanded. That's a reasonable assumption, well supported by experience. The substitutes for gasoline are not very attractive to most of the people who use it.

But there *are* substitutes for gasoline: joining a car pool, moving closer to work, buying a smaller car, taking the bus, planning ahead, getting more frequent tune-ups, or staying at home. As the price of gasoline rises, so do the sacrifices people must make in order to buy it. As a result, although a few may choose not to reduce their consumption at all, most people will find ways to economize at least a little, and some will decide to curtail their purchases substantially as the price goes up. The demand for gasoline is not totally inelastic.

Figure 4A also shows a relatively inelastic supply curve of

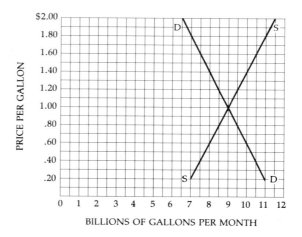

Figure 4A Hypothetical demand and supply curve for gasoline

gasoline, labeled SS.[1] The element of time, which plays such a large role in determining the responses of users to price changes, performs an even larger part in determining the responses of suppliers. Gasoline in storage can be quickly released for sale if a higher price makes selling more attractive than storing. But time is required to import gasoline from abroad in response to a higher price. Still more time is required to increase the flow of gasoline from the refineries by switching over from the production of other refined products, such as heating oil. And far more time will necessarily elapse before additional refinery capacity can be created in response to the higher price of gasoline.

What about the availability of crude oil? Weren't the gasoline shortages of 1973-74 and 1979 the result of inadequate supplies of the basic raw material? We must answer carefully if we are to avoid begging the question. Iran's political turmoil in 1978 and 1979 certainly disrupted the flow of oil imports into the United States. But other OPEC countries had the capacity to step up their rate of production and thereby compensate for the Iranian cutbacks. They did not do so, because they wanted the price of crude oil to rise. But that is precisely our point. More than enough oil could have been supplied in 1979 to keep the refineries running at 100 percent of capacity if the refineries—and ultimately the consumers of refined products—had been willing and able to pay the price. We must add the word *able,* because the ability of

---

1. Price elasticity of supply is analogous to price elasticity of demand: the percentage change in quantity supplied divided by the percentage change in price.

consumers and refiners to offer more money for gasoline and
for crude petroleum was deliberately restricted by law in
the United States.

Why was it restricted? Why did the U.S. government
impose ceiling prices on the sale of petroleum and petroleum
products in the 1970s? Judging by the statements made at
the time, the price controls were designed to prevent "oil
companies" from obtaining large, unearned profits at the
expense of low-income consumers. Proponents of the controls
failed to point out, however, perhaps because they didn't
realize, that by freezing prices the government was discon-
necting a crucial link in society's system of mutual adjustment
and cooperation.

What Causes Shortages?

Go back to Figure 4A. If the price of gasoline in this situation
is $1 per gallon, demanders will want to purchase precisely
as much as suppliers want to sell. The market clears at a price
of $1.

Now suppose that the price of gasoline is fixed by law so
that it cannot exceed 80 cents a gallon. At 80 cents the
quantity demanded per month will be 9.5 billion gallons. But
the quantity supplied will be only 8.5 billion gallons. That
is what we mean by a shortage: the quantity demanded exceeds
the quantity supplied, in this case by 1 billion gallons per
month.

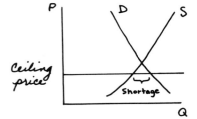

On the graph of Figure 4A, the shortage appears as a gap
between the demand curve and the supply curve at the
80-cents-per-gallon price. People cannot obtain as much as
they want even though they are willing to pay the money price
that's being asked. The price fixing is the *cause* of the
shortage.

Scarcity and Competition

No one blames the thermometer for low temperatures or
seriously proposes to warm up the house on a cold day by
holding a candle under the furnace thermostat. People do,
however, often blame high prices for the scarcity of certain
goods and act as if scarcity could be eliminated by enforcing
price controls. That just isn't so.

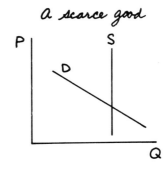

Scarcity is a relationship between desirability and availability, or between demand and supply. In a society where
everyone is terrified of snakes, snakes may be rare but they
cannot be scarce. In another society, where snakes are valued
as food, they could be quite common but nonetheless scarce.
A good is scarce whenever people cannot obtain as much of it

as they would like without being required to sacrifice something else of value.

Now it follows immediately that if a good is scarce, it must be rationed. In other words, a criterion of some kind must be established for discriminating among claimants to determine who will get how much. The criterion could be age, eloquence, swiftness, public esteem, willingness to pay money, or almost anything else. We characteristically ration scarce goods in our society on the basis of willingness to pay money. But sometimes we use other criteria in order to discriminate.

Harvard University each year has many more applicants than it can place in the freshman class, so Harvard must ration the scarce places. It discriminates on the basis of high-school grades, test scores, recommendations, and other criteria.

Only one person at a time can be president of the United States. Since many more people than one want the position, we have evolved an elaborate system of discrimination in the form of conventions and elections. Although there is considerable doubt about just what the criteria for discrimination are, the system does discriminate. We end up every fourth year with only one satisfied candidate.

Joe College is the most popular man on campus and has young women clamoring for his favor. He must therefore ration his attentions. Whether he employs the criterion of beauty, intelligence, geniality, or something else, he must and will discriminate in some fashion.

But the other side of discrimination is competition. Once Harvard announces its criteria for discrimination, freshman applicants will compete to meet them. The criteria for selecting a president are studied carefully by the hopefuls who begin competing to satisfy those criteria long before the election year. If the women eager to date Joe College believe that beauty is his main criterion, they will compete with one another to seem more beautiful.

Competition is obviously not peculiar to capitalist societies or to societies that use money. The point is of fundamental importance: *competition results from scarcity* and can be eliminated only with the elimination of scarcity. Whenever there is scarcity, there must be rationing. Rationing is allocation in accord with some criteria for discrimination. Competition is merely what occurs when people strive to meet the criteria that are being used.

Of course, the criteria used do make a difference. If a society rations on the basis of willingness to pay money, members of that society will strive to make money. If it uses physical strength as a primary criterion, members of the

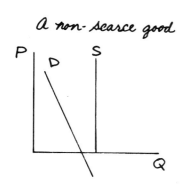

a non-scarce good

society will do body-building exercises. And if the better colleges and universities use high-school grades as an important criterion for selection, high-school students will compete for grades. They might be competing for grades to acquire other goods as well (status among classmates, compliments from teachers, use of the family car), but it is odd for colleges to complain of grade grubbers when their own rationing criteria promote grade grubbing.

Competition When Prices Are Fixed

What is going to happen, then, when a good like gasoline becomes more scarce but its money price is not allowed to rise? We will certainly see increases in the nonmonetary costs of purchasing it, for gasoline is scarce and therefore *must* be rationed. If by law we suppress the rationing device of monetary price, other rationing criteria will have to be used, whether by drift or by design. Potential purchasers of gasoline will attempt to discover the new criteria being used to discriminate among buyers, and they will compete against one another in trying to satisfy those criteria. Their competition will raise the total cost—price plus nonmonetary costs— and will continue raising it until the quantity demanded no longer exceeds the quantity supplied.

   The gas line is probably the best example. When people think they may be unable to purchase as much gasoline as they would like to buy at 80 cents a gallon, they try to get to the station early before the stocks have all been sold. But others have the same idea, so that the lines form earlier and grow longer. Waiting in line is unquestionably a cost. As this cost rises, the law of demand comes into play: consumers drive less when they expect to have to pay $12 plus half an hour's wait for a fill-up than when they can fill their tanks for a straight $12.

   Some drivers may decide to hunt around rather than wait in line. They will pay their additional cost in time and gasoline spent on searching. Others will strike deals: a fill-up out of reserved supplies in return for a tip to the station operator, or the payment of a special fee for parking at the station, or an agreement to have service work performed there, or maybe tickets to the theater for the station owner. All these ways of competing for gasoline raise the cost of obtaining it. And the cost will continue rising until it finally reduces the quantity demanded to match the quantity supplied.

   Competition among people—whose combined desires to purchase a good cannot all be fully satisfied at the prevailing money price—will bid up the cost of purchasing it. Usually it is the money price that rises in such a situation. Whenever

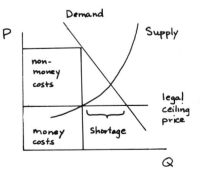

other components of the cost of purchasing a good start to climb, we can be fairly certain that some kind of social pressure (such as legislated price controls) is holding down the money price. And when that occurs—that is, when lengthening lines, longer searching, or special arrangements come into play to ration a good (because the quantity demanded is greater than the quantity supplied *at the prevailing money price*) we have a shortage of that good.

The economist's concept of shortage zeroes in on the money price. Shortages exist only when money prices are not able to perform the function of rationing scarce goods to competing demanders. *We spot a shortage in real life whenever we find nonmoney costs rising to ration scarce goods.*

The Supplier's Role in Rationing

We aren't surprised to see the money price of a good rise when the good becomes scarcer. Why? Because it is almost always in the interest of suppliers to raise the money price rather than see some other component of the acquisition cost increase. What does the owner of a gas station gain, after all, when customers wait in line for 30 minutes? Nothing (and maybe less than nothing if they are all less pleasant people by the time they get to the pump). But an increase of 20 cents in the money price of a gallon of gasoline is simultaneously an addition of 20 cents per gallon to the station owner's wealth. An increase in nonmoney costs usually entails an increase in what the economist calls *deadweight costs.* These are *costs to the purchaser that are not simultaneously benefits to the seller.* The cost of waiting in line is a perfect example.

If sellers have it in their power to transform a deadweight cost into a benefit for themselves, they will want to do so. And whenever sellers are free to raise the money price of the good they are supplying, they have ready at hand a simple tool for making that transformation. Notice what a handy and versatile tool it is. Everyone values money because its possession confers command over a whole universe of other goods. Everyone is accustomed to paying money for goods. The seller is usually the owner or agent of the owner with an acknowledged right to change the money price. The money price can be minutely adjusted, up or down, in a search for the price that most completely converts the buyer's cost of acquisition into the seller's benefit from supplying.

All of this explains why changes in money prices are the usual response to changes in relative scarcities, and why economists view changing money prices as such a crucial

means for securing social coordination. No doubt there are goods that *cannot* and other goods—most people would agree—that *should not* be rationed by means of changing money prices.[2] But it is a fact well worth noting that where this mechanism for achieving social coordination is not available, cooperation on any extensive scale becomes much more difficult to achieve.

Appropriate and Inappropriate Signals

What will suppliers do if the law prevents them from raising their prices in a situation of obvious shortage? They will probably look for alternative ways to turn the situation to their advantage. Gasoline retailers may decide to lower the cost *to themselves* of selling by reducing their daily hours of operation and closing altogether on weekends. If they can sell their entire weekly allocations in 20 hours, why should they bother to stay open for 120 hours a week? This response to the shortage will tend further to increase the cost *to buyers* of purchasing gasoline: they will face even longer lines, will be forced to cancel or curtail weekend traveling, will more frequently find themselves stranded because of the inability to obtain fuel, and will pay additional costs through searching, worrying, and even endangering their lives by improperly siphoning and storing gasoline.

FRED'S FRIENDLY SERVICE
Open for ~~your~~ my convenience
~~24~~ 3 hours daily

Those who supply or demand gasoline are not peculiarly selfish or inconsiderate. The costly chaos that we have actually witnessed in recent years at the gasoline pumps simply demonstrates how dependent we are on changing money prices to secure effective cooperation in our complex, interdependent society and economy. When prices are not permitted to signal a change in relative scarcities, suppliers and demanders receive inappropriate signals. They do not find, because they have no incentive to look for, ways to accommodate one another more effectively. It is important that people receive some such incentive, because there are so many little ways and big ways in which people *can* accommodate— ways that no central planner can possibly anticipate, but which in their combined effect make the difference between chaos and coordination. Changing money prices, continuously responding to changing conditions of demand or supply, provide just such an incentive.

---

2. It would be difficult to assign all residents on a city block the precise amount of street illumination for which each is willing to pay. And we apply a variety of derogatory terms to people who ration their affections by the criterion of money price.

Is There a *Better* System?

To say that money prices perform this function is not to say that they perform it perfectly. They certainly don't. In subsequent chapters we'll be looking at the limitations of social coordination through a price system as well as at its accomplishments. We'll ask under what circumstances money prices are less likely to reflect people's preferences in an adequate way, and we'll discover that ignorance, market power, collusive arrangements, disagreements about property rights, and inequalities in society all interfere with the "ideal" operation of the price system. But we do not discard the first law of motion (which says that bodies in motion tend to remain in motion) just because there is friction in the actual world. It would be a similar mistake to overlook the achievements of the price system just because it fails to coordinate flawlessly.

A system that rations scarce goods by means of money prices will, of course, allocate the goods to those who are willing to pay. Consequently, when rationing occurs by means of price, poor people tend to get less than rich people. That, in fact, is the very meaning of *rich* and *poor* when used in an economic context. But it is not the whole picture. Price rationing accommodates all sorts of other differences among people as well, differences that will prove extremely difficult to handle fairly under any other form of rationing.

Suppose we decide to ration gasoline by means of specially issued coupons. How will the government allocate those coupons? It would not be fair to allocate the same number to a single person as to a family of seven but neither would it be fair to give seven times as many coupons to the family. It wouldn't be fair to allocate an equal number of coupons to each licensed driver, and it wouldn't be fair to assign coupons to each owner of an automobile. (This would encourage people to stock their driveways with clunkers.) People who live in dense metropolitan areas probably travel shorter distances on average and also are more likely to have access to public transportation. Fairness therefore suggests that they should receive fewer coupons than those who live in thinly populated regions of the country. But some people in New York City regularly drive farther than some people in Silverton, Colorado. Would a system that ignored the special circumstances of individuals be fair? How could coupons be awarded fairly to a traveling sales representative in west Texas and an elderly woman in Cedar Rapids who drives only to church? Should the person who hates to drive receive as many coupons as someone who enjoys driving?

And what about business users? (An adequate rationing system must take account of the fact that diesel fuel and gasoline compete for scarce petroleum and scarce refinery

capacity.) If farmers, taxicab companies, commercial fishermen, and trucking firms—to mention just a handful of businesses that use large amounts of motor fuel—are allotted "all that they need," they will turn out to "need" more than anyone had anticipated. If we therefore create a government agency charged with determining the specific quantities to which each individual firm is entitled, what criteria will it use to make its decisions? Past consumption? Probably. But in an economy where new firms are continually born and old ones die, where some businesses expand and others decline, where technology is constantly changing and so is demand, how can past consumption be an adequate guide to current allocation?

The unfairness of its decisions might be the least of the agency's worries. Because business firms supply inputs to other business firms, as well as final goods to consumers, mistakes that were not quickly caught and corrected could have a domino effect. An error in allocation could close down an entire industry by inadvertently preventing the manufacture or transportation of some seemingly minor but actually indispensable input. The intricate interdependence of a modern, industrialized economy could not long be maintained in the face of arbitrary allocations of motor fuel among business firms.

Inflation and Rent Controls

Popular hostility to rationing by means of money prices grows in periods of inflation, because people mistakenly assume that an increase in money prices means a decline in their level of living. It's hard for most of us to see that our money incomes tend to rise right along with the prices of the goods we buy. When expenditures on a particular good take up a large percentage of our monthly budget, we become especially sensitive to increases in that good's price. If in addition the price of the good changes infrequently, and therefore by large jumps when it does change, we grow even more indignant about increases in its price. And popular indignation is fertile ground for the growth of legislative interference in the movement of money prices.

Rent controls are far and away the best example. Although grocery and clothing prices creep slowly upward in a period of inflation and are therefore commonly ignored, rents tend to remain fixed for longer periods of time—and then to do their advancing with a bound. A rent increase from $150 to $225 makes a big dent in the budget and seems unreasonably steep, even when the average prices of the other goods we buy have increased by more than 50 percent since the last rent

increase. People look for scapegoats in such circumstances, and landlords (the word itself stirs resentment) are prime candidates.

There is an unusual irony in the case of residential rents, an irony that greatly aggravates the problem. Because residential rents are exceptionally "sticky" prices, tending to lag behind the rate of change in other prices, the average level of rents tends actually to fall during rapid inflations. Thus whereas the average level of prices paid by consumers more than doubled from 1967 to the end of 1978, rents increased slightly less than 70 percent. That means that rents actually declined by about 15 percent.[3]

But this fall in rental prices was caused by a malfunction of the price system, not by any change in underlying conditions of demand or supply. The result in one American city after another was *declining vacancy rates*. These low vacancy rates, themselves a result of underpriced housing, then became a further argument for rent controls. "We cannot permit rent gouging when the vacancy rate is less than 1 percent." Or even better: "We must impose rent controls until the vacancy rate rises to an acceptable 3 percent." Since the low vacancy rate is the product of low rents, that is an argument, whether recognized or not, for permanent rent controls. Note that the suppliers who are thus singled out and specifically forbidden to raise their prices are suppliers whose prices are already failing to keep pace with inflation.

When law or custom keeps money rents below the level at which the quantity demanded equals the quantity supplied, other ways of rationing will evolve. Landlords might discriminate on the basis of age, sexual preference, personal habits, family size, letters of reference, pet ownership, length of residence in the community, or willingness to abide by petty regulations. Tenants who were lucky enough to be in a rent-controlled apartment when the controls were imposed will hang on to as much space as possible for as long as they can and will try to pass the unit on to a friend or to sublease when they do vacate. Landlords will lower the quality of the services they provide, since they know that there is a long line of tenants waiting to move in if any current tenant becomes dissatisfied.

All of these responses will lead to demands for costly administrative review boards and for additional legislation prohibiting particular landlord responses. The long-term result

---

3. The ratio of rents to all consumer prices, which by definition was 100/100 in 1967, had become 170/200 in 1978; so rents in 1978 were at only 85 percent of their 1967 levels when measured in relative prices. That constitutes a 15 percent decline.

may be the eventual disappearance of landlords, as existing buildings are allowed to deteriorate or are turned into condominiums, and new rental units are not constructed. But even the most unrelenting foe of landlords must concede that it will be hard to find an apartment to rent when none is being offered.

Surpluses and Scarcity

Many people use the word *surplus* to suggest that a particular good is not scarce. But this doesn't make a lot of sense. Let's consider the much discussed problem of farm surpluses.

Agricultural surpluses have been a continuing concern in the United States for many years. Farmers and their supporters maintain that the prices of agricultural products should go up at about the same rate as the prices of other goods. They have persuaded Congress to establish parity prices: prices that preserve the ratio that farmers had enjoyed from 1910 to 1914 (prosperous years for farmers generally) between the prices they received for their crops and the prices they paid for the goods they bought. A common policy goal was 90 percent of parity.

Through the Commodity Credit Corporation, an agency of the Department of Agriculture, the federal government offers to store for farmers, free of charge, any crops for which they cannot find a market at the established parity price, meanwhile lending the farmers the value of the crops they choose to store. These are nonrecourse loans, which means that farmers can simply pocket the loan and let the Commodity Credit Corporation keep the stored produce. In effect farmers use the government as a buyer of last resort in order to be sure of receiving the target price for any "supported" crop. The resulting surpluses do not mean that wheat, corn, cotton, and other supported crops are not scarce. They simply mean that Congress is unwilling to let key farm prices fall to the level at which the quantity demanded for current consumption will match the quantity farmers want to produce.

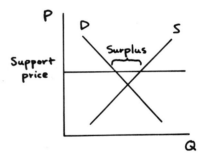

The American Medical Association has begun to warn us about an imminent surplus of physicians. There were 149 doctors for every 100,000 people in the United States in 1966 and 189 per 100,000 in 1976. By 1990, according to the AMA, there will be 242 physicians for every 100,000 Americans, or 25,000 to 50,000 more than will be "needed." But how many physicians do people "need"? San Francisco reportedly had 525 doctors per 10,000 population already in 1978. Do you suppose that physicians are not scarce in San Francisco? When members of a profession talk about the number "needed," they almost always mean the quantity that would be demanded

at the present price. They would rather not contemplate any reduction in the price of their services, of course.

Surpluses of teachers have also become a problem in recent years, at least for the teachers. From the standpoint of school boards and local taxpayers, the problem often looks more like an opportunity. At lower wage rates, school districts would be willing to hire more teachers. And at lower wage rates, some of those now offering to teach would decide to seek careers elsewhere. If salary scales cannot be reduced, either because of union contracts or just because it "wouldn't be right" to lower the pay of those to whom we entrust the hearts and minds of our youth, other ways will be found to balance the quantity supplied and the quantity demanded. Salary scale increases that are less than the rate of inflation reduce the real wage. School boards can also add to the duties of teachers, lowering the wage per unit of product by getting more product for a given salary.

If these measures are insufficient to balance quantity supplied with quantity demanded, other criteria will of necessity be used to ration out the scarce supply of teaching positions. (A surplus of teachers is a shortage of teaching positions.) Seniority is an obvious and common rationing criterion. It's one that appeals to long-established teachers, but not one that younger or prospective teachers find very attractive. And certainly it does little to promote a situation in which those most eager to teach are also most likely to end up in the classroom.

Suppliers Who Don't Care About the Price

When a good becomes more scarce, competition from demanders tends to bid up its price. Suppliers are usually happy to cooperate in letting this occur, because they benefit from higher prices. What will happen, however, when a good becomes more scarce but those who supply the good have nothing to gain from letting its price rise?

A good example is landing space at some of the nation's busiest airports. The Federal Aviation Administration predicts that 23 U.S. airports will face serious congestion problems by the end of the 1980s, and that twice this number will have major problems by the end of the century. Why is this occurring?

An increase in demand, even a huge, rapid increase in demand, won't necessarily create a shortage. There is no current shortage of personal computers, to take a dramatic example. And, when more people want to fly, the airlines simply offer more flights. They hire more people and buy

more airplanes, if they have to. That costs them money, of course, but those are expenses the airlines are happy to incur, because they expect their additional revenue to exceed their additional costs.

The bottleneck appears at the airports because the airports and the airspace surrounding them are not privately owned and hence are not priced to earn a profit. The additional travelers who bring joy to the heart of the airline managers are a pain in the neck to those who manage the airports, because those who "own" the airports and the airspace around them don't charge higher prices when the goods they supply become more scarce.

Your Very Own Airport

The easiest way to grasp the essential point might be to suppose that you owned National Airport in Washington, D.C., one of the most crowded in the country, and that you were free to operate as you saw fit. The "congestion problem" would disappear immediately, transformed into "full-capacity operation." (Do theater owners worry about congestion when they've sold all the tickets?)

The various airlines would still be eager to schedule more flights into National, because it's just a few minutes from the Capitol and hence the airport preferred by most travelers to Washington. But you would make them bid for the scarce landing slots, because you (money-grubbing rascal that you are) want to squeeze as much revenue as you can out of the landing fees. In the resulting competition, the price would rise to reflect the opportunity cost of the first *excluded* bidder. You would make a mint. But you would also have allocated the available landing slots to those who valued them most highly, as measured by their willingness to pay a landing fee that clears the market.

Won't travelers suffer, however, from your mercenary maneuver? It's quite likely that the airlines would tack a little extra onto the ticket price under this system for flights into National Airport. But that would in effect ration the scarce landing space at National to those passengers who placed a high value on the convenience of landing close to downtown rather than an hour away at Dulles Airport far out in Virginia.

In fact, many passengers would be better off if passengers flying into National had to pay a premium. That would induce the airlines to divert more flights to the uncrowded, almost deserted runways of Dulles. As a result, many passengers who didn't want to go to downtown Washington in the first place, or who were merely making a connection in

Washington, would be able to enjoy the convenience and greater safety of Dulles Airport.

Moreover, if there is any way for you to expand the capacity of your airport, you will investigate it carefully. And if the cost of the expansion is less than the value of the expansion, as measured by the willingness of the airlines and ultimately of travelers to pay for landing, you will quickly and expeditiously carry through the expansion. You won't behave like the FAA, which cries "crisis" but announces a program to upgrade air-traffic-control equipment only *over a ten-year period.*[4]

Flight delays, near misses, and other evidence of a shortage of airspace can be traced rather directly to our system of airspace ownership. The rules of the game make it next to impossible for those who value scarce airspace most highly to bid it away from those who value it far less. A slow, small, propeller-driven plane carrying half a dozen passengers will be allowed to land at Washington's National Airport or Chicago's O'Hare at a peak hour, thereby delaying two jumbo jets with 600 passengers, because the rules of the game make it almost impossible for the 600 passengers to bid the landing slot away from the six. Supply and demand are still at work, but they don't produce a great deal of mutual accommodation in cases like this.

Prices, Committees, and Dictators

The central economic problem is the challenge to secure cooperation among people in using what is available to obtain what is wanted. Effective cooperation among large numbers of people who barely know each other requires that the terms of exchange be clear, simple, and standardized.

Money prices are a device of extraordinary effectiveness for simplifying, clarifying, and standardizing. Have you ever wondered why committees achieve so little while consuming so much of their members' time and energy? It's because committees are such poor devices for simplifying, clarifying, and standardizing the available options. If a committee does manage to evolve procedures for performing these tasks, it ceases to behave like a committee—instead it becomes a cooperative venture.

There's another method for getting work done through committees, of course: by letting one person make all the decisions. Dictators do get things done quickly. And dictatorial decision-making can also perform, in the larger society, many

Information about Scarcity

4. Data in this case study were taken largely from a *Wall Street Journal* article of April 5, 1985.

of the simplifying, clarifying, and standardizing functions of the price system.

The other side of the coin is that the price system makes social cooperation possible in the absence of dictators. That's a definite plus for all those who don't care much for dictators.

Once Over Lightly

Scarcity is a relationship between availability and desirability, or between supply and demand. A good ceases to be scarce only when people can obtain all that they want at no cost.

Money prices provide information about relative scarcities.

Changes in relative prices create incentives to change behavior: to use less and provide more when prices have risen, to use more and provide less when prices have fallen.

Supply and demand is the process of interaction through which relative prices are determined. It is a process of mutual adjustment and coordination.

A system of money prices that change readily in response to changing conditions of demand and supply is an essential mechanism for coordinating behavior in highly specialized economic systems.

Scarce goods must be rationed in some fashion. Rationing entails the use of discriminatory criteria to determine who gets how much. Competition is the attempt to satisfy whatever discriminatory criteria are being used to ration scarce goods.

When a good becomes more scarce, but prices are prevented from rising, a shortage develops: the quantity demanded at the prevailing price is greater than the quantity supplied.

A surplus is a situation in which the quantity of a good supplied exceeds the quantity demanded at the prevailing money price. Any good, whatever its scarcity, will exist in surplus supply if its price is fixed at a high enough level.

When competition is prevented from raising prices, it will raise other components of the cost of acquisition. These are often deadweight costs: costs to demanders that, unlike money payments, are not benefits to suppliers.

Suppliers usually have an incentive to convert deadweight costs into benefits for themselves by raising money prices when a shortage appears.

When suppliers do not benefit from higher prices, perhaps because the scarce resources are not privately owned, money prices will be less responsive to changing conditions of scarcity, and cooperation in the use of scarce resources will be more difficult to secure.

Allocating rights and obligations by means of monetary

prices discriminates in favor of those with high monetary incomes. But it also allows individuals to obtain special consideration for their particular wants and abilities in social assignments of benefits and tasks.

QUESTIONS FOR DISCUSSION

1. Here is a problem of social coordination you might want to think about. Millions of Americans change their residences each year, many moving long distances to new and strange areas. How do they all find places to live? Who sees to it that almost every individual or family moving to a new state finds someone in that state willing to sell or rent them a house or apartment that suits their tastes and circumstances? Who oversees new construction so that those states which are growing most rapidly manage to expand their stock of housing at a rate that matches their population growth?

2. Should parents with one television set and three children allocate program choice to the sibling who submits the highest bid? How do parents ration scarce strawberries, served as dessert at dinner, among competing children? If it is better for parents to allocate these scarce goods according to their sense of justice and fairness, wouldn't it also be better if the Department of Energy allocated scarce energy resources among competing citizens according to the Department's sense of justice and fairness? What is the difference between the two cases?

3. The text maintains that the price system is an institution that secures social cooperation in large part by simplifying options. Another institution that does this effectively is the traffic light. Are traffic lights fair? How much attention do they pay to the special circumstances of the drivers who approach them? Would you prefer a system of traffic control that always gave the right of way to the motorist on the more urgent errand?

4. If the distribution of income were completely equalized, would everyone purchase the same quality automobile? Against whom do automobile prices discriminate? Under an equal income distribution, would all families of the same size want to own or rent the same quantity and quality of housing space? Against whom do rental prices discriminate?

5. When federal environmental rulings forced stricter limits on street parking in midtown New York, parking-garage rates rose. Why? New York's consumer affairs commissioner called for a crackdown on parking-garage "gougers." What would happen if parking-garage rates were held down by law?

6. The city of Seattle decided to "give downtown parkers a break" on Monday, February 22, 1982, because so many had put money into the parking meters when they didn't legally have to on the previous Monday, a legal holiday. Did downtown parkers really benefit from not having to pay the meters on February 22? Who benefited from this decision, and who was made worse off?

7. Many ceiling prices were fixed by law in World War II. How were scarce goods rationed?

8. State colleges and universities set very low tuition. How do they ration scarce facilities? Who do you think gains from this system? Why might professors and administrators of state schools prefer *not* to have scarce facilities rationed by means of higher prices (tuition)?

9. There are no toll charges for driving on many urban expressways during the rush hour. How is the scarce space rationed?

10. Parking space is often sold on college campuses at a zero price. How is the scarce space rationed? If all students who bring cars onto the campus are charged $100 a year by the college as an automobile registration fee, is that fee a rationing device?

11. A letter to the editor recommends: "Gasoline should be rationed, if it becomes necessary, according to need—real need." How will the rationing authorities determine *real need?*

12. Evaluate for their fairness toward single-car and multiple-car families the following proposed systems for rationing gasoline:
    (a) People whose license plates end in odd numerals can buy only on odd-numbered days; people whose plates end in even numbers buy on even-numbered days.
    (b) People are required to choose one day of the week on which each car will *not* be driven. They are assigned numbers (1 through 7) that they must display. Any car being driven on the prohibited day is ticketed by police.
    (c) No one may buy gas on Sundays.
    (d) No one may buy less than $10 worth of gasoline.

13. If you travel through the western states in the summer, you are much more likely to encounter a shortage of camping spaces than of motel rooms. Why?

14. When motels raise their rates "during the season" and reduce them "off season," are they exploiting customers or promoting a better allocation of resources?

15. The government did not impose controls on sugar prices in 1974, and the price per pound rose about 600 percent. Did the high price cause any more sugar to be available in 1974 than would have been available at a lower, controlled price? Do you think there would have been any refined sugar available on grocers' shelves if the government had frozen the price near its original level? Where would it have gone?

16. What do you think would have happened had the government imposed price ceilings in 1977 when the price of coffee increased about 400 percent? What do you think would have happened had the government imposed price controls in 1978 when lettuce prices increased by about the same percentage?

17. If a ceiling of $1 per pound were placed on lobster sold at retail, where could you go to eat a lobster?

18. A May 1979 wire-service story reported that a San Diego Chargers' football player got so upset waiting in line to buy gasoline for his Rolls Royce that he purchased a gas station. "I bought it for my friends' convenience, too," Johnny Rodgers said. Do price controls keep the wealthy from obtaining more than the poor?

19. One reason that local governments sometimes impose rent controls is pre-

cisely to prevent money prices from rationing scarce residential space. Do the controls succeed in doing this? How has it happened, do you suppose, that most of New York City's rent-controlled apartments are occupied by relatively wealthy people?

20. Suppose the Department of Defense decides to close a military base along the seashore and to turn the land over to private citizens. The land is close to heavily populated areas and offers choice view lots.
    (a) If the lots are allocated by means of a lottery, who will end up building on them?
    (b) Some lots are clearly more desirable than others. Will more expensive houses tend to be constructed on the more desirable lots if the lots are allocated by lottery?
    (c) Were you assuming in the answers above that the government places no restrictions on reselling? What difference will it make if the rules of the lottery declare that lottery winners cannot sell their lots for 5 years after acquisition, on penalty of forfeiture?
    (d) Is it fairer to allocate the lots by a lottery than on the basis of willingness to pay?

21. Help the Federal Communications Commission decide how to award scarce broadcast licenses for low-power television stations among the 5000 competing applicants by indicating the principal advantages and disadvantages of the following systems. Award the licenses:
    (a) to the highest bidders.
    (b) to the most qualified applicants.
    (c) by lottery.
    (d) by a lottery that favors groups currently underrepresented in the ranks of broadcast license holders as long as the lottery winners are qualified.
    Can you understand why the FCC, when instructed by Congress to use method (d) above, replied that it lacked the ability to devise a system that would withstand lawsuits from disappointed applicants?

22. Utah annually sells 27 licenses to hunt buffalo in a 1500-square-mile area of the state. The fee is $200 for residents and $1000 for nonresidents. Because the state receives more than a thousand applications each year, it holds a lottery to decide who will get the 27 licenses.
    (a) Why do you suppose Utah doesn't sell the licenses to the highest bidder?
    (b) Do you think people who receive a license should be allowed to sell it to someone else?
    (c) What effects do you think a lottery system *with freely transferable licenses* would have?

23. A well-known college basketball coach has urged high school stars not to accept summer jobs, jobs for family members, or cash payments from college recruiters because this would violate National Collegiate Athletic Association rules that narrowly limit what a college can offer a star athlete by way of inducement to enroll. The famous coach urges high school stars not to "sell their souls."
    (a) Are the high school stars selling their souls or their bodies?
    (b) Why do college recruiters secretly offer larger monetary inducements than the NCAA rules allow?
    (c) If recruiters are prevented from offering high school athletes as much

money as the recruiters think the athletes are worth to the college, how will competition among colleges for the athletes' services nonetheless raise the cost to colleges of acquiring the athletes?

24. Far fewer babies are currently offered for adoption in the United States than couples want to adopt. Would you call this a shortage? Why doesn't the price of an adopted baby rise? By what criteria are the scarce babies rationed to prospective buyers?

25. If the supply of turkeys in a particular November turned out to be unusually small, do you think a turkey shortage would result? Why or why not?

26. (a) There is currently much concern about a growing surplus of college teachers. How could the surplus be reduced or eliminated? Do you think this will happen? Why or why not?

    (b) Note that a surplus of college teachers can be viewed as a shortage of college teaching positions. How will the scarce supply of positions be rationed if price (salary of teachers) is not allowed to perform this function?

27. How do you account for the fact that so many people were concerned about world food shortages in 1974 when only five years earlier the governments of Australia, Canada, and the United States had been worrying about surpluses? (As this is written, the concern is once again about surpluses.)

28. The state with the highest ratio of physicians to population in 1985 was Massachusetts, with 277 physicians per 100,000 people. Idaho had the lowest ratio: 107 physicians for every 100,000 people. Does Massachusetts have a surplus of physicians? Does Idaho have a shortage? Or do people in Massachusetts need more doctors than people in Idaho? Why might people receive more medical services relative to the population of the state in Massachusetts than in Idaho even if people in Idaho were to receive exactly as much medical care per capita as people in Massachusetts?

29. Think about a registration scheme under which students would have to pay tuition for 10 o'clock classes and would receive discounts for taking 8 o'clock classes. Would you favor such a plan? Why do colleges *not* charge higher prices for the hours in greater demand? A student willing to pay a friend $5 to stand in line for him and grab a 10 o'clock section might protest vigorously if he were charged an extra $3 to take a 10 o'clock class—even though the $3 fee gets rid of the line that he was willing to pay $5 to avoid. If you think these apparently inconsistent responses are plausible, how would you explain the contradiction?

30. In an article in *Energy* (Vol. 8, No. 8-9, 1983) economist Charles Lave has written:

> Perhaps a virtue of price-oriented solutions (in the energy sector) is that people already know how to solve problems that way; there is continuity with the past. And perhaps the drawback of bureaucratic solutions is that they lack this continuity and instead require people to learn and understand a new set of behaviors.
>
> We vastly underestimate the complexity of the familiar. The distribution and sale of gasoline seemed a trivial thing until the government tried to manage it in 1973 and 1979.

    (a) Does this explain in any way the "contradiction" pointed out in the

preceding question—that we are *familiar* with bureaucratic solutions in school systems?

(b) Does Lave's suggestion explain why something like the system discussed in the text for allocating scarce airspace is unlikely to be implemented? Would such a system require a sharp break with familiar patterns of behavior?

(c) How do complex systems ever become familiar? Who introduces them? Why does anyone ever try to introduce a new and complex system to replace an old and familiar but less "efficient" one?

(d) How did the absurd arrangement of the keys on typewriters ever get established? In view of the demonstrated inferiority of the existing system (QWERTY) to the Dvorak Simplified Keyboard, why has QWERTY survived? Why is it perpetuating itself on computer keyboards? (For an illuminating discussion of this issue, see "Clio and the Economics of QWERTY" by Paul David in the May 1985 *American Economic Review*.)

31. The sign in the cafeteria says: "Please conserve napkins during the paper strike." Suggest some ways in which the cafeteria could ration paper napkins to its customers by raising the cost of taking one (in addition to charging for them). Who will conserve if the cafeteria does nothing except post the above sign?

32. Why do restaurants have such different pricing policies for different items? With napkins, for example, the policy usually is to charge no price and let customers have as many as they want. With beverages, a price may be charged with additional servings available at no fee or a reduced fee. With other items, customers pay a set price for each unit consumed. If your answer is that napkins don't cost very much, how do you account for the fact that grocery stores don't let their customers take as many napkins as they want free of charge? And why do cafeterias typically charge per pat of butter while sit-down restaurants will usually provide additional butter at no extra charge if the customer requests it? What accounts for these differences?

33. All the customers of Myrtle's Diner say that they place more value on a cup of coffee in the morning than on a cinnamon roll. Myrtle nonetheless manages to sell lots of cinnamon rolls every morning at 80 cents apiece, but her coffee sells for only 35 cents a cup. Does this prove that her customers aren't telling the truth?

34. According to an article by economist Terry Anderson in the *Wall Street Journal* of September 30, 1983, farmers in the Imperial Irrigation District of California are required to pay only $6.50 an acre-foot for water that may cost taxpayers as much as $300 an acre-foot to deliver.

(a) At which number—$6.50 or $300—will Imperial Valley farmers look when deciding whether to irrigate a little more or a little less?

(b) Do these figures demonstrate that irrigation is not really worthwhile in the Imperial Valley?

(c) Why would anyone pay $300 to supply an acre-foot of water that is worth only $6.50 to the demander?

(d) What do you think the demand curve for water in the IID looks like? What about the opportunity cost of supplying water to the IID?

35. In many cities, tennis players can reserve municipal courts by phoning early

in the week for a reservation. What will occur if there is no charge for reservations? If you think you might want to play later in the week, will you make a reservation? What will you do if you later change your mind and decide not to play? Why do people "waste" free goods? Who bears the cost of such waste?

36. The graph below reproduces the original data of question 10 in Chapter 3 in the form of an opportunity cost curve, or supply curve. It adds to those data a demand curve, showing how many hours of tutoring students would want to buy at various prices.

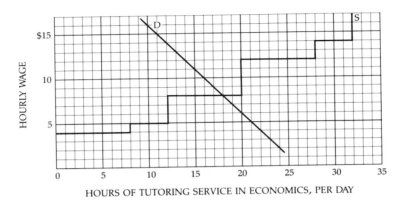

Figure 4B Hypothetical demand and supply curves for economics tutoring

(a) What will students have to pay for an hour of tutoring in economics? How many hours will they buy?

(b) The opportunity cost to Marx of tutoring was given as $3.99—the wage he could get for fomenting revolution. If you know this fact and consequently ask Marx to tutor you for $5 an hour, he will tell you that the opportunity cost to himself of tutoring you is $8. Is he right? Or is he just trying to exploit you?

(c) If Merrill Lynch offers Ricardo full-time work at $13.99 an hour, he will no longer be willing to supply 4 hours of tutoring per day for $5 an hour. What will happen to the price of tutoring service as a result?

(d) If the demand for tutoring service doubled (i.e., twice as many hours were demanded at each price as previously), what would happen to the price of tutoring services and to the number of hours supplied?

(e) If the demand tripled, what would be the price and the number of hours supplied?

37. The graph below presents a hypothetical demand curve for wheat labeled D, and the aggregated opportunity-cost curves of all wheat farmers, labeled S for supply.

(a) Why will the price of wheat move toward $2.50? What would occur if the price were $2.75? If it were $2.25?

(b) Suppose wheat farmers persuade the government to "support" the price

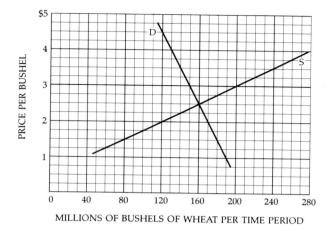

Figure 4C Hypothetical demand and supply curves for wheat

of wheat at a "fair" price of $3.75 per bushel, by itself purchasing for $3.75 a bushel any wheat farmers can't sell at that price or higher. What will this do to the total demand for wheat?

(c) How many bushels of wheat will the government have to buy and store? (Why can't the government simply buy the wheat and then resell it?) Is this properly called a *surplus?*

(d) What would happen, under the supply and demand conditions depicted, if the government told wheat farmers they should sell their wheat for whatever they can get on the market, and then collect from the government a subsidy of $1.25 for every bushel sold? What will be the price of wheat? How many bushels will be exchanged?

(e) What will be the cost to the taxpayer of the support program? Of the subsidy system? Are there any other advantages that one method of aiding wheat farmers has over the other?

38. The U.S. Mint responded to complaints about a shortage of pennies several years ago by saying that there would be plenty of pennies for exchange purposes if people who were hoarding pennies would put them back into circulation. Some banks and other businesses tried to lure pennies out of hoards and into circulation by offering premiums, such as $1.15 for two rolls. (There are 50 pennies in a roll.)

What effect do you think such offers of a higher price for pennies had on the quantity of pennies demanded? On the quantity supplied? Are such schemes likely to alleviate a penny shortage? (Word of caution: Demanded *by whom?* Supplied *to whom?*)

39. Contemporary homes and workplaces are full of time-saving devices that our grandparents did not own. Have all these devices, which enable us to do what our grandparents did in a fraction of the time it took them, made time less scarce for us than it was for them? What determines the value of time for anyone? What do we mean when we say, "I can't afford to take the time"?

40. Is smallpox virus rare today? Is it scarce? What's the difference?

41. The last question for discussion invites you to return to the problem raised by the first question.

A *Wall Street Journal* article (January 3, 1983) was headed: "Moving House Isn't Easy to Do in China, Where Government Is the Only Landlord."

(a) Is the problem government ownership? Or the fact that the government keeps rents very low—equal to about 3% of an average worker's monthly income?

(b) If the government owned all residential property in the U.S. and kept rents at $50 per month, do you think it would be easy for you to find a place to live in a new city to which you were moving?

(c) The Chinese government maintains housing-exchange stations in all the major cities. Why is a housing exchange less effective than a system of changing prices in facilitating trades among millions of people who want to change residences in any given year?

Marginal Costs, Sunk Costs, and Economic Decisions

Supply is the more interesting side of the demand and supply interaction. It is on the supply side that farmers rotate crops, wildcatters drill for oil, electricians wire houses, pharmacists compound prescriptions, semiconductor companies design digital circuits, and colleges hire faculty to teach economics.

Supply is limited by cost. In order to obtain a larger quantity of any good, we must offer potential suppliers some inducement to move resources from their current use into the production of the good we want. We must make the benefit of doing so greater than the cost—that is, greater than the value to potential suppliers of the opportunities they will have to forgo.

But what counts as cost? More precisely, what are the costs that influence the decisions of suppliers? The theme of this chapter is that the costs that influence supply are always *marginal* costs, or *expected additions* to the potential suppliers' costs. That turns out to have a lot of interesting implications that aren't always seen by people who haven't yet learned the marginal way of thinking.

Decisions at the Margin

Economic analysis is basically marginal analysis. Many economists even use the word *marginalism* to refer to what we have called "the economic way of thinking." *Marginal* means *additional*. Economic theory is marginal analysis because it assumes that decisions are always reached by weighing additional costs against additional benefits. Nothing matters in decision making except marginal costs and marginal benefits.

Suppose that the love of your life phones you at 9 p.m., while you're studying desperately for your physics exam the next day. He wants to come over for a couple of hours. You tell him you have to study. He pleads. You say no. He asks plaintively, "Is physics more important than me?" And if you've grasped the economic way of thinking, you respond without hesitation: "Only at the margin."

If that doesn't stop his whining, tell him to enroll next term in an economics class, and go back to your studies. The issue of *his value* versus the *value of physics* just doesn't arise in this situation. The question, rather, is whether an additional two hours with him is worth more than an additional two hours with your physics text.

Since you don't want to alienate him, you might explain a little further. Ask him which is more important to him, water or toothpaste. If he answers, "Water," you've got him. For he undoubtedly *uses* water as if it had no value at all. And he would probably refuse indignantly to pay as little as 5 cents for a drink of water if someone tried to charge him that price in a restaurant. Why? Because it is the value and importance of *additional* water in his actual situation that affects his behavior, not the value of water in the abstract. What he and you are each willing to give up to obtain a drink of water is *not* what you would be willing to pay if you were dying of thirst in a desert; it is what you are willing to pay when you're surrounded by faucets and fountains that offer virtually unlimited quantities of water at the turn of your wrist.

He is thinking in terms of "all or nothing." But that just isn't the choice when he phones on the evening before your exam. In fact, that is rarely the choice we face when we're called upon to make decisions. It's usually more of this and less of that versus more of that and less of this. The economic way of thinking rejects the all-or-nothing approach in favor of attention to marginal costs and marginal benefits.

The Irrelevance of "Sunk Costs"

When you pass through the cafeteria line, pick up the tuna lasagna, and pay the cashier $1.90, you incur a cost: the value of whatever opportunity you will have to forgo because you've spent $1.90. Then you take your first bite and suddenly wish you hadn't selected this item. What will be the cost to you of leaving the lasagna on your plate?

It will *not* be $1.90—or $1.80 if we assume your first bite consumed about ten cents worth of tuna lasagna. That cost is history. The cost of leaving the lasagna on your plate will be the value of whatever opportunity you forgo by doing so. Do you have a dog that would enjoy pasta with tuna, cheese,

and spicy tomato sauce? If so, the cost of leaving the lasagna is the opportunity you forgo (by not asking for a doggie bag) to see your dog's eyes light up and its tail wag.

The price you paid is what economists dismiss as a *sunk cost*. Sunk costs are irrelevant to economic decisions. Bygones are bygones.

> The Moving Finger writes; and, having writ,
> Moves on; nor all your Piety nor Wit
> Shall lure it back to cancel half a Line,
> Nor all your Tears wash out a Word of it.

Of course, we must be certain that a cost is really sunk, or fully sunk, before we decide to regard it as irrelevant to decision making. If you were to purchase a new motorcycle and immediately afterward regret your decision, what would be the cost to you of continuing to own the motorcycle? Clearly, you would not be forced to say, "I did it and now I'm stuck." You could resell the motorcycle. By not doing so you would incur a cost (a benefit forgone) equal to its resale value. The genuine sunk cost would therefore be only the difference between what you paid for it and what you can get by selling it. That is the irrelevant part of your cost. *In the economist's way of thinking it is no cost at all, for it represents no opportunity for choice.* It may be cause for bitter regret and the occasion of some education in the dangers of impulse buying, but it is no longer a cost in any sense relevant to the economics of present decisions.

Yet we all know that people do not consistently reason things out in this way. Many people who made such a purchase and then regretted it would be tempted to retain possession of the motorcycle rather than sell it for substantially less than the original price. They might justify this action by saying "I can't afford to take the loss." But they already took the loss! They made a mistake, and their full loss occurred when they made it. If they nonetheless choose to keep the motorcycle, they are probably practicing self-deception. They persuade themselves that a motorcycle gathering cobwebs in the garage has the same value as the money they paid to put it there, and more value than the opportunities forgone by keeping it there. But the only relevant cost now is the opportunity forgone *by not selling*.

The Case of the Las Vegas Caper

Let's practice this approach. Suppose you own a television retail store, and one of your suppliers is sponsoring a gigantic Dealers Contest. For every television set you buy (no returns allowed), you receive one day in Las Vegas with all expenses

$ 1960.00   Wholesale Costs
   19.60   Interest for 1 month
  200.00   Handling Costs
   80.00   Advertising costs
  140.00   Display space
$ 2399.60 Total cost ?

paid. You gleefully order 28 sets, and your wife starts planning your two-week holiday together.

Upon your return from Las Vegas you begin wondering how you will sell all those television sets. One month later you're still wondering. It seems that none of your customers is interested in that brand or model. You are about ready to give up and store the whole lot in the back workroom.

Then you get an offer from an orphanage in some distant city to take all those sets off your hands for $2000. You know that a businessman can't make money by selling below cost, so you sit down to figure out the cost of the sets. You paid $70 apiece to the supplier. Moreover, you have had them in your store for a month tying up valuable floor space. You borrowed the money to buy them at 12 percent annual interest. You also had various handling costs that you estimate at $200. And you spent $80 on advertising in a vain effort to move the sets. By estimating $140 as the cost of display space tied up for a month, you arrive at a figure of $2400. You write back to the orphanage that you would be willing to sell the lot at cost for $2400, forgoing any profit on the transaction in the interest of charity. The orphanage replies that $2000 is their top price, since they can get the sets they want somewhere else for that price. But you are a good businessman, you know that losses don't make profits, and you refuse.

You were actually a rather poor businessman. Every one of the "costs" you enumerated in arriving at your total of $2400 was a *past expenditure* and hence no cost at all. *The proper stance for making cost calculations is not looking back to the past, but forward to the future.* Your costs, if you sell, will be the opportunities thereby forgone, or what you can get for the sets if you do not sell to the orphanage. You know the market fairly well and you estimate you could get $560 by selling them for junk. The marginal cost of selling to the orphanage is therefore $560. Your gain from selling to the orphanage is consequently $1440. Any loss that you're worrying about should be assigned to experience and the glorious memories of Las Vegas. It is irrelevant for decision-making purposes.

Marginal Effects Guide Decisions

The word *marginal* means in economics exactly what it means in everyday speech: situated on the border or edge. The concept is of fundamental importance in economic thinking, because economic decisions, like all effective decisions, always involve *marginal* comparisons. That is to say, they always have to do with movements at the border, with positive or negative *additions*. What will be the *additional*, or *marginal*, cost that results from this decision? And how does it compare

with the marginal cost of alternative decisions? If you think about it for a moment, you will discover that opportunity costs are always expected marginal costs. The term *marginal cost* does no more than bring into strong relief an aspect of opportunity-cost thinking.

It's important not to get the marginal concept mixed up with the notion of *average*. You may have no intention of confusing marginal with average; if so, what follows may only plant in your head the seeds of a bad idea. Let's hope it doesn't. A simple production schedule of a hypothetical zerc manufacturer will illustrate the distinction.

Number of Zercs Produced	Total Cost of Producing Zercs
42	$4200
43	4257
44	4312
45	4365

A little long division reveals that 42 zercs can be produced at an average cost (total cost per unit) of $100; the average cost is $99 for 43 zercs, $98 for 44, and $97 for 45. A little subtraction reveals, however, that the cost of producing the 43d zerc is not $99 but $57. The incremental expenditure, or the extra cost, incurred by producing the 43d zerc, is its marginal cost. The marginal costs of the 44th and 45th zercs are $55 and $53, respectively. It is clear that marginal cost can be more or less than average cost and can even differ substantially from average cost. It should also be clear that for a zerc manufacturer trying to make production decisions, it is the marginal costs that should guide him. Shall we produce more? Or less? Marginal cost is the consequence of action; it should therefore be the guide to action.

Are business people then not interested in average costs? Unless they receive sufficient revenue to cover all their costs they will sustain a loss. They won't willingly commit themselves to any course of action unless they anticipate being able to cover their total costs. They might therefore set up the problem in terms of anticipated production cost per unit against anticipated selling price per unit. But notice that the *anticipated* costs of any decision are really *marginal* costs. Marginal cost need not refer to the additional cost of a single unit of output. It could also refer to the additional cost of a batch of output, or the addition to cost expected from a decision regarding an entire process. Decisions are often made in this "lumpy" way.

For example, no one plans to build a soda-bottling factory expecting to bottle only one case of soda. There are important

Average costs:

$$\frac{\$4200}{42} = \$100 \qquad \frac{\$4257}{43} = \$99$$

Marginal cost:

$$\begin{array}{r} \$4257 \\ -\ 4200 \\ \hline \$57 \end{array}$$

economies of size in most business operations, so that unless business people see their way clear to producing a large number of units, they won't produce any. They won't enter the business. They won't build the bottling factory at all. The entire decision—build or don't build, build this size plant or that, build in this way or some other way— is a *marginal* decision at the time it is made. Remember that additions can be very large as well as very small.

Whether or not business people cast their thinking in terms of averages, it is expected marginal costs that guide their decisions. Averages can be looked at after the fact to see how well or poorly things went, and maybe even to learn something about the future if the future can be expected to resemble the past. But this is history again—admittedly an instructive study—whereas economic decisions are always made in the present with an eye to the future.

The Cost of Driving

The Hertz Corporation conducts an annual study of automobile operating costs to determine how much it costs motorists per mile to drive the cars they own. Hertz takes into account depreciation over the life of the car, license fees, insurance premiums, interest on the automobile loan, maintenance, and of course gas and oil. They then announce that it costs so many cents per mile to drive an intermediate-size car if the car is owned four years and driven 10,000 miles per year.

But what does this really tell us? Does it offer any guidance to someone who is trying to decide whether to drive or to take the bus to work each day? Or to someone weighing a commercial airplane against the family car for a vacation trip? Let's suppose you have been asked by your college to drive your car to a conference. You plan to attend the conference whether you drive your own car or not. The college offers you 25 cents a mile. Will it pay you to drive, or should you say no and hitch a ride with someone else? If you go about deciding by trying to calculate whether the cost to you of owning and operating a car is less than 25 cents a mile, you're being foolish. It makes no more sense to speak of the cost per mile of owning a car than to speak of the cost per mile of owning a house. Neither houses nor cars are *owned per mile*. They're owned per month or per year, but not per mile. If you nonetheless decide to divide the cost of owning by the miles driven, you will come up with numbers that tell you the more you drive, the less it costs. That just isn't so. Each time you drive, you *add* something to your costs. In order to decide whether or not to drive, you must know the marginal cost of driving.

Costs of purchase, license, insurance, borrowing, plus maintenance and depreciation not due to operation are all unrelated to your decision whether or not to drive. That is why they are irrelevant. The relevant cost is the marginal cost: How much extra will you be out of pocket if you drive? Be sure to include not only the cost of gas but also the costs of oil, tire wear, and mileage-induced repairs. Insofar as cost can be expected to vary proportionately with mileage driven, it can properly be expressed as so many cents per mile. If it is less than 25 cents, as it probably would be, you make money by driving your car. As long as the marginal cost remains less than the price paid by the college, you gain from every additional mile "produced" and "sold."

Are the costs of purchase, license, insurance, borrowing, and time-related depreciation *completely* irrelevant? Shouldn't you be allowed to cover these costs, too? After all, you have to pay them even if they are not related to the trip you've been asked to undertake.

You are certainly free to ask the college for as high a mileage rate as you choose. And if you have no scruples, you are even free to trot out all your sunk costs and wave them righteously. There is ample precedent for such action. But the one person you don't want to confuse is yourself. Only marginal costs are relevant to your decision, whatever price the college finally agrees to pay you.

Perhaps you've begun to suspect that it's our example that is irrelevant. We're interested, after all, in ordinary business decisions, and whatever may be true of the student driver as entrepreneur, businesses surely have to cover *all* their costs, not just marginal costs. It would seem so. But it isn't so. There is no more necessity to cover sunk costs in the business world than there is in our case study.

The plain fact is that each year many businesses fail to cover sunk costs. But most of them don't stop operating. We can illustrate by supposing that you bought your car with the intention of driving it for the college. When you made up your mind to become a sort of taxi operator, you hoped to make enough money to pay your way through college. So you purchased a car, the license, and insurance. You probably would not have done so had you expected the college to offer only 25 cents a mile. Maybe you had reason to believe they would pay you 50 cents. Your calculations in these circumstances might have run as follows:

Purchase price: $8000.00
License: $200.00
Insurance: $500.00
Gas and oil: $0.08 per mile

Maintenance: $0.04 per mile
Chauffeur service: $6.00 per hour

Your problem now is the familiar one of adding apples and oranges. Or even worse, adding apples and velocity. How can you add $8000 to 8 cents per mile and $6 per hour? Obviously you can't.

You could, however, turn all these figures into costs per year, much as Hertz does. The license and insurance are annual costs. The purchase price could be converted into an annual figure by estimating annual depreciation and adding the annual interest charge on your initial outlay of $8000. But you can't state the other costs on an annual basis without knowing how far and how long you'll be driving. You must anticipate. Remember what we said earlier: the significant costs and benefits in economics are *expected* costs and benefits. That means they're uncertain. But uncertainty is a fact of life, and if you want to be a student entrepreneur, you'll have to live with it. So you estimate that you'll obtain so many miles and so many hours of business per year. You can then plug in your estimate and obtain numbers for gas and oil, maintenance, and chauffeur services per year.

Now you can do your addition and come up with a figure for the annual cost of doing business. You can then take your estimate of miles used in calculating gas, oil, and charges for wear and tear, multiply by the rate you expect to be paid, and thereby calculate prospective revenue per year. If the anticipated annual revenue exceeds the anticipated annual cost, you take the plunge and buy a car. If it doesn't, you don't.

So sunk costs are relevant? Of course not. Until you take the plunge they aren't sunk. They are marginal. They are additions to cost that you are thinking about incurring. That's the essence of being marginal. And as long as they're marginal, they are relevant. But only that long! Until you commit yourself in some way to a business operation, *all* your costs are marginal. Once you have committed yourself, the situation has obviously changed. If you want to maximize your profits (or minimize your losses, which comes to the same thing), you must produce and sell all those units of output whose anticipated marginal cost is less than the anticipated price to be set by the college.

Who Pays Sunk Costs?

But if a business firm doesn't cover its sunk costs, who does? Who pays the bill for mistaken decisions in the past? The general answer is *investors:* those who provided the means by

which the mistakes were made. They had hoped to profit; but matters failed to turn out as expected, and so they take a loss.

Consider a simple case. Amber Crombie and her husband Fitch pay $250,000 to buy a lot and build a home overlooking beautiful Lake Lilypad. They expect to receive more than $250,000 worth of benefits from living in their comfortable new home with its breathtaking view. Soon after moving in, however, they notice that Lake Lilypad supplies an odor as well as a view. The smell gets progressively worse. Finally Amber and Fitch decide they can't stand it any longer and will have to move. When they put their house on the market, however, the best offer they get is $60,000, from a couple with chronic nasal congestion. What will happen next?

Amber and Fitch must weigh the odor-reduced benefits from continuing to live in their house against the cost of doing so, which is $60,000 forgone. In other words, would they choose to buy this house, knowing what they now know, if the total price were $60,000? If not, they should sell.

What about the other $190,000 they've invested? That's the loss they incurred by paying $250,000 for something that has turned out to be worth only $60,000. They can't avoid that loss by staying in the house, at least not if they themselves place a lower value on the house than what the congested couple is willing to pay. They have sustained a $190,000 reduction in their wealth. And their loss will be even greater, under our assumptions, if they try to avoid the loss by not selling.

Suppose, however, that the Crombies had put up only $75,000 of the original cost, and had taken out a bank mortgage for the remaining $175,000. Who bears the loss in this case? The bank will want the mortgage paid off when the sale goes through; but the sale proceeds of $60,000 won't come close to meeting the Crombies' indebtedness. If they have no other assets with which to satisfy the bank, the bank might decide to prevent the sale. But what is there then to stop the Crombies from defaulting on the mortgage and turning the house over to the bank? Whereupon the bank will sell the house to recover its investment, and get . . . $60,000 from the non-smelling couple. In that case the Crombies will have lost $75,000, their original investment, and the bank will have lost $115,000, the difference between what it loaned and what it recovered by foreclosing on the mortgage and selling the property.

$75,000	down payment
+ 175,000	bank loan
$250,000	purchase price
− 60,000	resale price
$190,000	total loss
− 75,000	Crombies' loss
$115,000	bank's loss

There are other possibilities, of course. The Crombies may decide that the (expected future!) loss of honor and credit worthiness is a cost too high to accept, in which case they won't default, but will faithfully continue to pay the bank long

after they have abandoned the house on Lake Lilypad. There is a good chance that the Crombies or the bank will try to shift the loss to whoever can be found responsible for the odor, or, if no villain can be located, whoever should have warned the Crombies about the fumes from Lake Lilypad.

Whatever ultimately occurs, the cost of buying the lot and building the house was incurred when these steps were taken. All but $60,000 of that is a sunk cost and a loss. Mortgage payments in this case are the marginal cost of retaining possession, or, if the Crombies sell but continue paying, the marginal cost of retaining their credit rating and their honor.

The Rising Cost of Medical Care

Let's use this way of looking at costs and decisions to see if it can clarify the controversy over rising medical costs and how to contain them. We will look first at physicians' fees.

People often assert that physicians charge high prices in order to recover the cost of their education. Could this be true? The argument implies that dullards who take an extra year to finish medical school will set higher-than-average fees, and geniuses who breeze through in less than the normal time will set lower-than-average fees. We don't see that occurring. The argument also implies that physicians who went through college and medical school on full scholarships will establish lower fee schedules than those who had to pay their own way. That implication is not confirmed by observation either. Suppose a recent medical school graduate learns that she has only two years to live. Could she raise her fees enough to recover the full cost of her education in her two remaining years of practice? The argument makes no sense. To a practicing physician, the cost of a medical education is entirely in the past and consequently irrelevant to current decisions.

Does the cost of acquiring a medical education have no effect, then, on physicians' fees? The answer is that it affects fees indirectly by influencing the supply of physicians' services. The prospect of many arduous years in preparation deters people from premedical programs. The necessity of forgoing income for all those years and of borrowing money to live and to pay tuition decreases the anticipated attractiveness of a physician's life. The expected future cost of going through medical school thus restricts the number that will eventually supply physicians' services. (This restriction is in addition to others, of course: not everyone who wants to graduate from medical school is able to.) All of this ultimately affects the prices physicians charge. But to see exactly how it does so, we must push our analysis further.

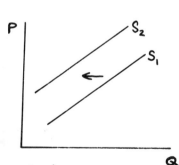

a higher expected cost of acquiring a medical education eventually reduces the supply of physicians' services (shifts the supply curve to the left).

The fees that physicians charge for seeing patients are indeed related to costs, but the relevant costs are *the costs of seeing patients*. What is the cost to physician X of seeing patient A? What opportunity does physician X thereby sacrifice? In the common case today it will probably be an opportunity to care for patient B. What determines the value to the physician of that opportunity? It will be the fee that patient B is prepared to pay.

In other words, people bid for the scarce time of physicians on the basis of their demand for physician care. This demand interacts with the supply of physicians' services to determine the cost of a visit to the doctor, or the price that physicians will be able to charge. The more that physician X can get from seeing other patients, the higher is the cost of tending patient A. Note that this is not determined by the value of the time the physician spent in school, but by the value of the physician's time *to patients*. The point is a most important one. If the demand for physicians' services increases but there is no increase in the amount of such services supplied, demanders will simply raise the cost of medical care, essentially by trying to bid it away from other people. In short, we who call for appointments determine the cost of physicians' services.

Physicians are not required to raise their fees when demand increases faster than supply, and many do not. They can instead allow other elements of the cost to rise. "I can't get you in before Thursday." "You can come into the office and wait, if you want to, but the doctor may not be able to see you." The less that fees rise in response to increased demand, the more will queuing costs tend to rise. As a result, those who would have been willing to pay more money will tend to surrender some portion of available medical services to those willing to sit for hours reading old magazines.

The reasons for the large increases in recent years in the demand for physicians' services are many. People are living longer, and older people have more ailments. Our expectations of what physicians are able to do have gone up, and so we consult them more often. And increasingly, the people who visit physicians are not required to pay the marginal cost of that visit. The last reason is an especially important one, because it contains a warning against a popular "solution" to the problem of rising medical costs that is really no solution at all.

Costs and Insurance

Any system of medical insurance that pays for physicians' services lowers the cost to patients of obtaining those services—and thereby increases the amount people will want to

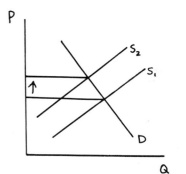

with a reduced supply of medical services, demanders bid up their price.

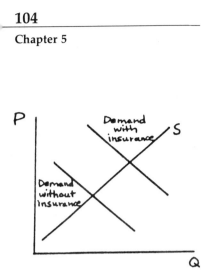

purchase. It doesn't much matter for the present argument whether the insurance system is a public one financed wholly out of taxes or a private system under which the beneficiary pays all of the premiums. So long as patient A's decision to visit the doctor has no discernible effect on the amount patient A must pay, the relevant price is zero. It's true enough that if beneficiaries go to the doctor more often, premiums (or taxes) will have to be increased. But those additional payments will be made by the policyholders (or taxpayers) whether they decide to see their physicians or, alternatively, to stay at home, get plenty of rest, and drink lots of liquids. The additional payments are sunk costs, and so they cannot affect decisions.

Here is the catch in the insurance approach to the problem of medical costs. If we respond to higher costs by offering larger insurance benefits, we subsidize the use of these scarce services. But that increases the demand, bids up the cost, and necessitates yet another increase in benefits. It also makes people ask why we don't do something to keep medical costs down! We will certainly not keep them down as long as our response to the problem is one that pulls them up by increasing the demand for medical services faster than the supply is increasing.

Hospital Costs

The question of *who pays* is also important in the case of another, even more important, contributor to rising medical care costs—hospital services. The average cost of a hospital room in 1985 was more than seven times what it was in 1965. It is almost certain that an increase this large would not have happened if the people using the rooms had been the ones who paid the bills. But under a system in which patients' payments for medical service are exactly the same whether they enter the hospital or receive only out-patient care, patients are much more likely to enter the hospital. The care is usually better in the hospital than outside it, and physicians can more easily monitor patients' progress in the hospital. On top of that, insurance often covers the full cost of hospital care, while paying only a part of outpatient care. That's a direct invitation to people to increase the demand for scarce hospital services, and it quite predictably produces a steadily mounting level of room charges.

Hospital administration also demonstrates that sunk costs do have their uses. Suppose a particular hospital adds a 200-bed wing and purchases a lot of sophisticated new laboratory equipment. Once these decisions have been taken, the costs associated with them are sunk costs. But that doesn't mean they can't be useful to the hospital's administrators. If the

government and private insurance companies have agreed to make payments to the hospital based on the hospital's cost of providing service to patients, and if the hospital gets to decide what counts as cost, every dollar of those sunk costs will be used. The sunk costs will be "spread over" each patient, according to whatever formula enables the hospital to recover them as quickly as possible without unduly antagonizing those who must pay.

Cost *to whom?* Benefit *to whom?* That's always the best way to pose the question of costs and benefits if you want to find out why some policy is being followed. If the benefits from a hospital's ownership of all the most modern equipment accrue largely to its medical staff, if the cost of not pleasing the medical staff falls primarily on the hospital's administrators, if the cost of acquiring that equipment is borne entirely and uncomplainingly by government, insurance companies, or philanthropists, then hospital administrators will purchase expensive equipment even if it is rarely used—and the cost of hospital-care services will soar. In recent years insurers and government have started to pay hospitals a fixed fee for particular services rather than just reimburse the hospitals for whatever costs they claim to have incurred. Hospital administrators as a consequence now have more reason to control costs and less reason to pretend that sunk costs are costs of providing particular services.

Cost as Justification

The economic analysis of costs is an especially treacherous enterprise for the unwary, because costs often have an ethical and political as well as an economic dimension. Many people seem to believe that sellers have a right to cover their costs, have no right to any price that is significantly above their costs, and are almost surely pursuing some unfair advantage if they price below cost. This way of thinking, in which cost functions as *justification,* has even infiltrated our laws. Legislated price controls, for example, usually allow for price increases when costs go up but refuse to permit any price hikes that are not justified by higher costs. And foreign firms selling in the United States can be penalized for "dumping," if a government agency determines that they sold in this country at prices "below cost." In circumstances such as these, when costs become a rationalization rather than a genuine reason for decisions, all statements about costs must be inspected for evidence of special pleading.

Prices *ought* to be closely related to costs, in popular thought, because costs supposedly represent something real and unavoidable. The most enthusiastic advocates of rent control will agree, at least in principle, that landlords should

be allowed to increase their rents when the cost of heating fuel goes up. They will never agree—if they did, they wouldn't advocate rent controls—that landlords should be allowed to raise rents merely because the demand for apartments has increased faster than the supply. That would be "gouging," "profiteering," or "a rip-off," because it is unrelated to cost. But such a rental increase is just as surely related to cost as is an increase in response to higher heating bills. When the demand for rental apartments increases, tenants bid against one another for available space, thereby raising the cost to the landlord of renting to any particular tenant. What another tenant would be willing to pay for the third-floor corner apartment in the Hillcrest Arms is the landlord's marginal cost of continuing to rent to the present occupant. The case seems to be different with higher heating-fuel prices but really is not. The cost of fuel oil is also determined ultimately by the bids of competing users in relationship to the offers of suppliers. Cost is always the product of demand and supply.

When you grumble to your butcher about the high price of hamburger, the butcher will deny all responsibility. "They keep raising the cost to me," he will say. If you were to investigate further to find out who "they" are and why "they" keep raising the butcher's cost, you would eventually discover that "they" are "we"—we who like hamburger and bid against one another for it. To see exactly how this works, imagine a sudden and unexpected increase in the demand for hamburger, occasioned perhaps by splendid summer weather and a surge of backyard cookouts. The first effect will be a depletion of butchers' hamburger inventories. When butchers find their hamburger inventories low and the demand continuing strong, they will increase their orders for beef suitable for grinding. With this happening all over the country, meat packers will in turn find their inventories of beef reduced and will try to buy more cattle. But the increased demand for cattle will encounter a relatively inelastic supply curve, and the price of cattle will rise. The packers who must consequently pay more for cattle will increase the price to the butcher, who can then honestly say "they raised the cost," without for a moment suspecting that "they" are in front of the checkout stand, not back at the wholesale meat market. The cost of hamburger in the supermarket is determined by the interactions of demanders and suppliers.

Price, Cost, and Suppliers' Responses

We can easily imagine circumstances under which such a surge in the demand for hamburger would *not* increase its cost

to the butcher. Suppose that the increased demand for hamburger is accompanied by a *decreased* demand for round steak, chuck roast, and other beef cuts that can be used to make hamburger. The meat packers and the butchers may be able, under those circumstances, to produce the additional hamburger being demanded without increasing their demand for cattle. In that case, there would be no additional bidding for cattle to raise their price, create higher costs for the butcher, and hence produce a higher price for hamburger at the meat counter.

The passage of time can have a similar effect. Suppose the increased demand for hamburger is part of a general, widespread increase in the demand for beef. The demand for cattle will increase at the livestock market, the price per pound will rise, and consumers will end up paying more for beef.[1] The competitive bidding of consumers will have increased the price.

But that will trigger a new kind of competitive bidding, some of which will go on within the mind of single livestock growers. The higher price for cattle will make resources more valuable in cattle production than they were previously and will consequently "bid" some resources away from other uses—growing hogs, raising soybeans, feeding chickens, or working less at the business of feeding cattle. The more effective the higher price is in pulling additional resources into cattle growing, the less will the price of cattle (and hence the price of beef) increase as a result of the original increase in its demand. But the supply adjustments that we're now describing take time. That's why supply curves are typically more elastic in the long run than in the short run.

Let's summarize what we've been trying to say in this section. An increase in the demand for any good (hamburger, medical care, rental apartments) will bid up the cost of acquiring the good (its price) to the extent that it does *not* cause a larger quantity to be supplied. Or looked at from the other side, an increased demand for any good will *not* raise its price to the extent that suppliers respond by making larger quantities available. The responses of suppliers will depend on the marginal cost of transferring resources out of their current uses into the production of the good for which the demand has increased.

If resources can be shifted at marginal costs only slightly above those already prevailing, the increased demand will

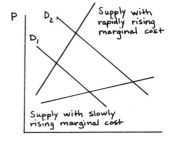

The effect on price of a change in demand depends on the marginal cost to suppliers of responding.

---

1. Don't forget that this higher price will also have the effect of decreasing the quantity demanded. Consumers will end up increasing their monthly beef consumption by less than they had originally intended—before their increased demand raised the price.

lead to a larger output rather than a higher price. But as the supply of such resources is used up, progressively higher prices will have to be offered to cover the rising marginal cost of shifting less suitable resources. Since resources are more mobile, or less rigidly specialized to one use, in the long run than in the short run, the marginal cost of additional output will usually rise less when adequate time has been allowed for adjustments than when suppliers are restricted entirely to those responses that are immediately available to them.

Summaries tend to be both abstract and obscure. You can make the preceding paragraph more concrete and thus more comprehensible by testing each step of the argument against some real-life situation with which you're familiar. (The case of rental housing in the vicinity of your college might be an excellent example on which to practice.)

Another Note on Alternative Systems

Is all this just the economics of capitalist societies? Or does it also apply to communist and socialist societies? The principles we have described are the general principles of economizing, applicable wherever resources are scarce. The central planners in a socialist state also operate within the constraints imposed by scarcity: the resources available to them have alternative uses; substitution possibilities are pervasive; one good can usually be achieved only by giving up some other good. Rational planners will calculate the opportunity cost of contemplated actions, treating sunk costs as irrelevant and paying attention only to marginal costs.

There will nonetheless be important differences. Suppose that the minister of coal production in a socialist state is trying to decide how much coal should be mined this month. He can increase coal production by using more workers or employing them for longer hours, or by using more machinery or better machinery. The relevant cost to the society of doing so is the value of whatever is given up through his decision, or the marginal (opportunity) cost. If he obtains new machinery in order to increase coal output, society loses what could otherwise have been produced with the aid of that machinery, or what could have been produced with the resources employed in the construction of the new machinery. The real cost to the larger society of increased coal production is therefore decreased production of locomotives, or cement, or farm tractors.

If the minister can expand coal production by using machinery already in place that would otherwise stand idle, the opportunity cost is much lower and may even be zero. The sunk cost of the equipment is irrelevant. Notice, though,

that the marginal cost will be greater than zero if the machinery has any alternative use, including use as scrap metal.

The differences emerge when we ask how all these costs are calculated. In a society where workers own their own labor and must therefore be induced through monetary bribes (wages) to work in particular ways, the wage measures the opportunity cost to workers. The wage must be sufficient to attract them from their (subjectively) next-best alternative. But if workers can be compelled to do what the state dictates, the wage need not bear any relation to the opportunity cost as determined by the workers. (We saw in Chapter 3 how that occurs under a military draft.) In moving from an eight- to a ten-hour day, the miners might be sacrificing two hours of leisure. Whether this is worthwhile would depend on the *planners'* valuation of the extra coal produced in relation to the *planners'* valuation of the leisure forgone.

It would be clearly wrong under any circumstances to suppose that the cost of producing the extra coal can be determined from the *average* cost of coal production. This is worth mentioning because some socialists have argued in the past that marginal cost considerations were relevant only in an economy guided by the pursuit of private profit. It is true that in a capitalist society entrepreneurs will not choose to produce anything whose marginal cost of production to them exceeds its value to the consumer as measured by its price. But it is just as true that in a socialist society the central planners and enterprise directors will produce nothing whose marginal cost exceeds its value.

The major difference lies in the different rules of the game under which opportunity costs and prices are calculated. One of the distinct advantages of a system characterized by substantial private ownership and control of resources is its pricing mechanism. Under such a system, competitive offers to buy and sell resources interact to establish scarcity prices and opportunity costs expressed in monetary units. An enormous quantity of information summarizing a vast range of alternatives is thus distilled into the prices that in turn guide the choices of decision makers.

In no economic system past or present have prices ever summarized perfectly the available range of opportunities. And under certain circumstances, as we shall see later, they may do so in a fashion so inadequate as to be politically unacceptable. The relevance of all this for making a choice between alternative economic systems is a complex issue that cannot be resolved exclusively by economic arguments.

In any economic system, however, the following general principles will be applicable:

- Real costs are opportunity costs, the value of opportunities forgone.
- Sunk costs are irrelevant, because they are costs that the decision cannot affect.
- Opportunity costs are always additional or marginal costs, the costs expected to result from the decision under consideration.
- Some method of assigning indexes of value to alternative opportunities must be used in any economic system, or decision makers will be operating blindly.
- Supply and demand, or the market process of competing bids and offers, creates indexes of value for decision makers by placing price tags on available resources.

The supply and demand process also operates in socialist societies. But where the rules of the game do not clearly assign to particular persons rights to control and exchange specific resources, this process will not generate indexes of scarcity to guide allocation and coordinate activity.

Once Over Lightly

Supply curves reflect costs. All costs capable of influencing supply will have three interrelated characteristics that should be watched for: they will belong to actions, not to things; they will be opportunities forgone by particular decision makers; and they will be the expected, not-yet incurred consequences of decisions at the margin.

Past expenditures cannot be affected by present decisions: they are sunk costs and hence irrelevant to decision making.

Opportunity costs are necessarily marginal costs: they are the additional costs that a decision entails.

If costs per unit are to be used in making supply decisions, the units must be related to the decisions. The cost per mile of owning a car or the cost per bushel of owning a farm are both meaningless, because "owning" is not a decision that produces either miles or bushels (although it may be a precondition for such decisions).

Because economic decisions are based on future or expected consequences, they always entail some degree of uncertainty. The expectation that future revenue will cover future costs is often frustrated in experience.

The common notion that prices ought to be related to costs generates a substantial amount of confusing rhetoric among suppliers who want to justify (or others who want to condemn) a particular price.

Costs are not something independent of demand. The demand for goods helps to determine the cost of supplying them.

Increases in demand for a good will result in higher prices, rather than additional output, to the extent that resources cannot be shifted into production of that good. To the extent that resources can be shifted with no significant rise in marginal cost, the increased demand will result in additional output rather than higher prices.

Under a system characterized by private ownership and control of resources, the forces of supply and demand will establish relative prices that function as indexes of scarcity. It will ordinarily be in the interest of private decision makers to be guided by these indexes in their decisions to demand or to supply.

QUESTIONS FOR DISCUSSION

1. A cost specialist for AT&T estimated the cost of a daytime telephone call from New York to Los Angeles in 1981 at 68.9 cents for the initial period and 33 cents for each additional minute. The 68.9 cents included 11.3 cents for maintenance, 3.3 cents for operator services, 4.4 cents for business services such as sales and advertising, 2.7 cents for pricing and billing, 8.2 cents for depreciation and amortization, 10.6 cents for general purposes, 12.9 cents for taxes, and 15.5 cents for earnings.
   (a) When these calculations were made, AT&T was charging less than 25 cents for a one-minute call from New York to Los Angeles. Was the phone company losing money at that rate? Or don't some of those costs have to be met at night and on weekends?
   (b) AT&T presented these data to the Federal Communications Commission, which oversees long-distance rates, and asked for permission to set a fee of 74 cents. Does that fact help explain which items the cost specialist included?
   (c) Does it actually cost the phone company less when people place long-distance calls at night or on weekends? What is the marginal cost to the phone company of a call from New York to Los Angeles? Why might it differ with time of day and day of the week?
2. The *Wall Street Journal* headlined a story in January 1982: "Ford Offers Incentives on Subcompacts That Are Unprofitable Despite Hot Sales."
   (a) Why would a company offer incentives that were unprofitable?
   (b) The story reveals that Ford executives, convinced the subcompacts would be a big success, had spent $2 billion to convert four assembly plants that would be capable of producing 950,000 of these models per year. Sales were running at a rate below 400,000 when the "unprofitable" promotion was announced. Use the concept of *expected marginal cost* to explain both Ford's decision to invest $2 billion and its decision to cut prices "below cost."
3. How long will you search for a $20 bill that you lost if you value your time at $5 an hour? Suppose you know that you lost it somewhere in your

bedroom. Would it ever be rational for you to search more than four hours? Use the concepts of sunk cost and expected marginal cost to explain how a rational person who values time at $5 an hour could *search indefinitely* for a lost $20 bill.

4. A news report from London stated that British doctors, although dissatisfied with some aspects of their country's National Health Service, generally appreciated the fact that they could treat patients under this system "without regard to cost." Correct those last four words.

5. A study of the New York City housing situation revealed that many landlords are abandoning apartment buildings they own because, under rent controls, they cannot get enough revenue to cover their costs. What costs are relevant to such a decision?

6. An airline is thinking about adding a daily flight from Denver to Billings. It has estimates of the number of passengers who would use the flight. What costs should and should not be considered in deciding whether the anticipated revenue is sufficient to make the flight profitable?

7. The city of Seattle owns a marina and rents space to boat owners. City officials decided in 1981 to set rental rates that would yield a 5 percent profit on the estimated cost of replacing the facility. They said this would call for an approximate doubling of moorage fees over the next three years.
    (a) What does the estimated cost of replacing the facility have to do with the cost of renting out moorage space?
    (b) The most important part of the facility is the ocean water that fills Puget Sound, on which the marina was constructed. Should the estimated cost of replacing the ocean be included in the price? (If you argue that it should *not* be included because the ocean is a free gift of nature, go back and check your answer to question 2 at the end of Chapter 3.)
    (c) At the time they announced their intention to raise the fees, city officials estimated the waiting time for a space at 17 to 20 years. What does this have to do with the cost of renting out moorage space?

8. Suppose that taxicabs raised their fares during rainstorms and lowered them again when the sun came out. How would these different prices be related to cost? Whose cost? Of doing what?

9. The Public Utility Regulatory Policies Act of 1978 requires electric utilities to purchase electricity from small power producers. They are required to pay a price based on "avoided cost," which is what the utilities would have had to spend to generate the purchased electricity themselves.
    (a) How is "avoided cost" related to marginal cost?
    (b) The owners of a large office building burn fuel to create steam to heat the building. When they learn that the local electrical utility will pay them 8 cents per kilowatt-hour for electricity, they attach a generator turbine to the steam boiler. How should they decide on the respective costs of heating the building and generating electricity when it is the same steam that does both jobs?

10. "Tuition covers only 43 percent of the cost of educating your son or daughter. We're counting on your annual gift to sustain operations that are fundamental to the kind of education for which our university is noted." Those sentences are from a letter sent to parents by a prestigious university whose tuition is currently close to $10,000. Do you think that a student paying

$10,000 per year in tuition is really paying only 43 percent of the education's cost? Would the university find its total costs reduced by $23,256 if the student dropped out?

11. In order to decide whether or not to drop intercollegiate football, your school undertakes a study of the program's cost. To what extent do you think the following budget items represent genuine costs?
    (a) Tuition scholarships to players
    (b) Payments on the stadium mortgage
    (c) Free tickets to all full-time students
    (d) Salaries of the athletic director, ticket manager, and trainer

12. What determines the cost to a university of providing parking spaces on campus for faculty, staff, and students? Why would a parking facility probably cost an urban university more than it would cost a university located in a small town? If monthly parking fees are higher for students than for faculty, does this mean it costs the university more to provide parking for students?

13. The American Society of Internal Medicine is not happy with the schedule of relative fees that insurers use to compensate for different kinds of medical service. The ASIM maintains that internists are grossly underpaid relative to surgeons. It wants fees set by taking into account the time and effort required to learn the particular skill (e.g., cardiac surgery or diagnosis of an infection) and the time it takes to perform the service. (See "Doctors Debate How to Split the Fees" by Harry Schwartz, the *Wall Street Journal*, January 15, 1985.)
    (a) Does the ASIM proposal violate the maxim that sunk costs are irrelevant?
    (b) What consequences would you predict from implementation of this proposal? If surgeons' fees fell and internists' fees rose, would a shortage of surgeons and a surplus of internists develop?
    (c) If an internist and a surgeon are both necessary to the successful completion of a particular medical procedure, how can the relative importance of each one's contribution be assessed?

14. Pan American Airways has complained to the British government that flights between the U.S. and Britain on the supersonic Concorde are priced too low. The Concorde flies for British Airways, which is subsidized by the British government. That enables Concorde fares to be set below cost, according to Pan Am.
    (a) Is the cost of developing the Concorde supersonic plane part of the cost of flying it from New York to London?
    (b) If there are empty seats on a Concorde flight, what is the cost to British Airways of carrying an additional passenger?

15. What does it cost you to sleep through one of 30 lectures in a course for which you paid $300 in tuition?

16. Do students put more effort into courses when they have to pay higher tuition to take the courses?

17. Do hot dogs taste better at the ball park where they cost twice as much as they ordinarily cost? Do they taste better *because* they cost more?

18. Would you expect to find any people who don't particularly like Ingmar Bergman's movies attending a Bergman film festival if the price of the festival ticket is $5 for 10 movies? Would you expect to find many people who aren't

enthusiastic about Bergman attending a Bergman festival where the price is $50 for 10 movies? Does your answer to this question change your answer to the preceding question about hot dogs at the ball park?

19. "We regret that rising costs have compelled us to raise our prices." That's a very common statement made by sellers who are raising their prices. But is it true? Do increases in suppliers' costs always compel them (or even allow them) to raise their prices? Think carefully about each of the following cost-increase scenarios. In which cases would you expect higher prices to follow from the higher costs? In which cases would you expect to see the sellers absorb the cost increases rather than raise their prices?

(a) Physicians are forced to pay higher malpractice insurance premiums.

(b) Only some physicians—those with poor records or credentials—have their malpractice insurance premiums raised.

(c) A taxi driver pays high insurance rates because he has a poor driving record.

(d) A grocery store in a high crime area must pay extra for store security. (Would its customers pay higher prices rather than shift their patronage to stores in low-crime areas?)

(e) Landlords' expenses rise due to a general increase in property taxes.

20. When the price of coffee quadrupled in 1977, many cafés and restaurants doubled the price they charged for a cup of coffee. Sometimes they accompanied the price increase with a statement to the effect that, although they were willing to absorb most of the price increase, harsh reality compelled them to pass along a portion of the increase to their valued customers. How many cents worth of ground coffee goes into a restaurant cupful? Why do restaurants and other businesses make such statements?

21. (a) What differences would you expect to observe in the fees set by three young physicians just setting up practice if one financed her education by borrowing and must now make payments of $4000 per year for 15 years, another had his entire education paid for by his parents, and the third went all the way through on government-provided scholarships and grants?

(b) Evaluate the argument, put forward in a *Newsweek* column of March 19, 1979, that the government could lower our doctor bills by paying for the entire education of physicians, thus making it unnecessary for physicians to recover the costs of their education (plus interest) by raising their fees.

(c) The author of the *Newsweek* article asserts that "you and I" will have to cover the cost of the doctors' loan repayments in our fees because these payments "are a legitimate cost of doing business." What difference does it make whether particular payments are or are not "a legitimate cost of doing business"? Suppose all physicians practicing in an area were required to pay $5000 a year to the local crime syndicate as protection money. Would these payments be "a legitimate cost of doing business"? Would they affect doctors' fees?

22. The Department of Defense awards you a cost-plus-10% contract to build missiles in your garage. Which of the following may you legitimately include in your costs?

(a) Original cost of constructing the garage, adjusted for inflation and depreciation.

(b) Weather damage to your car from parking it outside because your garage is full of missile-making machinery.

(c) Cost of lengthening the garage by four feet so the missiles don't extend into your driveway where neighborhood children might accidentally set one off.

(d) Cost of the course you took at the community college to qualify as a missile maker so you could win the government contract.

(e) Cost of the math courses you took years ago which turned out to be prerequisites for the course on missile making.

(f) Cost of your elementary school education, since you wouldn't be able to manufacture missiles if you didn't know how to read.

(g) Cost of the tetanus shot you received when you were three years old, which saved your life and thereby enabled you to become a successful defense contractor.

(h) Cost of psychological counseling whereby you seek to overcome depression when your children scorn you as a member of the military-industrial complex.

23. Your boss tells you in an angry voice, "I don't care what you learned in economics. If you don't include all our sunk costs in your report and recommendation, I'll fire you." Are the sunk costs now irrelevant to your decision making?

24. Should the casualties already incurred in a war be taken into account by a government in deciding whether it is in the national interest to continue the war? This is obviously not a trivial question. And it is a much more difficult question than you might at first suppose, especially for a government depending on popular support.

25. The economist's rule, "sunk costs are irrelevant," is like a string around your finger. It reminds you to consider only marginal costs, but it cannot identify the marginal costs. That requires informed judgment. You could sharpen your judgment by trying to enumerate and assess the marginal costs of retaining or not retaining your college apartment over the summer vacation. Try to calculate the minimum rental from subleasing that would persuade you to retain it for fall reoccupancy.

26. Here is what it would cost you to fulfill your long-time ambition to own and operate a small ski resort:

• To acquire the land	$200,000
• To acquire the ski lift	100,000
• To acquire a shelter	20,000
• To operate the lift and sell tickets	50 per hour

You plan to be open 50 hours a week for 20 weeks in the year. You therefore anticipate operating costs of $50,000 per year. You will be able to borrow the $320,000 you need to get started under a 20-year loan. Your annual payments on the loan (principal and interest) will come to $43,000 per year.

(a) What is the minimum amount of annual revenue from the sale of lift tickets that you will have to anticipate in order to take the plunge and invest $320,000?

(b) Suppose your actual revenue in the first year of operation turns out to be $60,000. Should you go out of business?

(c) You can occasionally earn $600 by opening your resort for 8 hours on weekdays (when you would ordinarily be closed) for the benefit of special charter groups. This revenue will cover your operating costs of $400 for the day; but since your operating costs are only 54 percent of your total costs, you would need about $750 in revenue to make it worth your while to open. Or would you?

(d) If you spend $10,000 a year on advertising in your second year, and as a result increase your total revenue to $75,000, was the decision to advertise a good one?

(e) What are your options if it turns out after several years that you cannot do any better financially than you did in your second year of operation? Should you go out of business? If you decide you can't afford to lose $28,000 a year on a ski resort, what are your options? Suppose the best offer you get when you put the facility up for sale is $100,000 for land, lift, and shelter. Should you sell?

(f) If the lender forecloses because you default on your payments, what will he do with the property? Should the lender foreclose or allow you to spread out the length of your loan so that your payments are reduced to an amount you can meet out of your revenue?

27. New York City announced a plan in 1980 to determine the value of all its fixed assets: city-owned buildings, subway cars, sewers, water lines, garbage trucks, police cars, fire engines, even the courthouse and—presumably—the Brooklyn Bridge. If you were an investor considering lending money to New York City, would you care about the value of the city's assets? Would you determine the value of the Brooklyn Bridge by its cost of construction? If not, how would you do it?

28. The graph on the opposite page shows the demand for and supply of residential rental space in an imaginary city. The market-clearing rent is $300 per month.

    Then two events occur: (1) Inflation causes the value of money to fall by one-third; (2) The city and state dramatically lower the property-tax rate, so that landlords' net income from residential rental property rises by one-third.

    (a) How would you expect these two events to affect the demand for and supply of residential rentals? What would happen to rents? Distinguish between short-run and long-run effects.

    (b) What difference would it make if the property-tax reduction were confined exclusively to residential property?

    (c) If rents rise in the short run as a consequence of these occurrences and the city responds by imposing rent controls, what will be the longer-run effect?

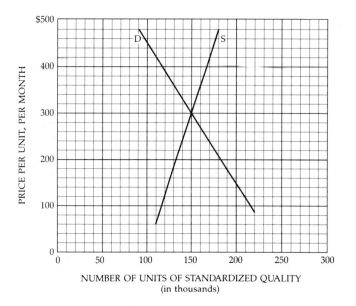

Figure 5A Hypothetical demand and supply curves for residential rental space

Efficiency, Exchange, and Comparative Advantage

Efficiency is the virtue most consistently praised by economists. That should occasion no surprise, since efficiency and economy are practically synonyms. Both terms refer to the effectiveness with which means are used to achieve ends. Getting as much as possible out of the scarce resources available—that's what we mean by efficiency and by economy.

Voices have begun to appear in our society in recent years suggesting that we place too high a value on efficiency; that we sometimes sacrifice more valuable goals to achieve an efficiency that isn't worth what it costs us. Could this be true? Anyone who thinks about it carefully will discover that there is something logically odd about this critique of efficiency. While the critics may have valid and important points to make, it cannot be true that we are paying too high a price for efficiency.

Technological Efficiency?

If efficiency is to have any useful meaning, it must be understood as a ratio of one thing to another. Engineers use a definition of efficiency that seems to satisfy this test. They define efficiency as the ratio of the work done by a machine to the energy supplied to it, and that ratio is usually expressed as a percentage. From the engineering standpoint, a diesel locomotive is more efficient than a steam locomotive because, per unit of potential energy contained in its fuel, the diesel does more work.

This definition is unsatisfactory, however, when we think about it more critically. Efficiency cannot be measured by

$$\frac{Energy\ output}{Energy\ input} = One$$

$$\frac{Value\ of\ output}{Value\ of\ input} = \begin{array}{c} Measure \\ of \\ Efficiency \end{array}$$

the ratio of energy output to energy input because, by the laws of thermodynamics, that ratio is always unity for any process. The engineer's efficiency is rather a measure of *work done* in relation to energy input. But what constitutes "work done"? Doesn't that depend on what is wanted? What qualifies as "work"? Engineers actually call a steam engine less efficient than a diesel because with a steam engine a higher percentage of the energy input is *wasted*. Strictly speaking, however, even wasted energy does work. It just doesn't do any *useful* work. That means it doesn't do work that anybody wants done. All of which implies that efficiency is not a purely objective or technological matter, but depends inevitably on valuations.

Efficiency and Values

Efficiency is inescapably an evaluative term. That's the first point to be grasped. It always has to do with the ratio of the *value* of output to the *value* of input. Efficiency will always have an objective component, of course; our likes and dislikes don't determine the potential heat in a pound of fuel. But physical facts by themselves can never determine efficiency. It follows that the efficiency of any process can change with changes in valuations, and because everything depends on everything else, any change at all in any subjective preference is in principle capable of altering the efficiency of any process.

Let's go back to the question of the relative efficiency of diesel and steam locomotives. Each can be put into operation only with the use of a large number of inputs; not only coal or oil and locomotive operators but also all the inputs used in manufacturing the locomotives, the inputs that went into the fabrication of these inputs, the inputs that went into the fabrication of the products that were inputs in the process of producing the products that were inputs in the manufacture of the locomotives, and so on, without any discernible limit. Anything that changes the value of anything that contributes to a locomotive's operation can in principle alter its efficiency.

We don't need any farfetched illustrations to make the essential point. An increase in the value of oil relative to coal, if it is large enough, can by itself transform their relative efficiencies so that a coal-fired steam locomotive becomes more efficient than a diesel. It follows that these relative efficiencies depend on the demand for and supply of oil and coal, and hence on such factors as the motoring habits of the general public, the political situation in oil-producing countries, and the value placed on the environmental effects of strip-mining coal. Perhaps it never occurred to you that the relative

efficiency of the old steam locomotive was affected by the efforts of the United Mine Workers!

"Wait a minute," says a voice from the rear of the room. "Aren't you talking now about something other than efficiency? I'll grant you that it costs a railroad less per ton-mile of freight to use diesels than to use coal-fired steam locomotives. But that's not the same as being more efficient. If coal became cheap enough, some railroads might go back to using their old steam locomotives. But that would be because the old locomotives were cheaper, not because they had become more efficient."

From the standpoint of the railroad, however, cheaper *is* more efficient, because the relevant values are monetary values. The illusion of a purely technological efficiency dies hard, but it deserves to be stomped until it's dead. No machine, no process, no arrangement is so efficient that it cannot be rendered inefficient (or so inefficient that it cannot be made efficient) by an appropriate change in values.

The Myth of Material Wealth

In emphasizing the essential role of valuations in any measure of efficiency, we are also rejecting the common belief that economics has to do peculiarly with the "material": with material wealth, material well-being, or material pursuits. It just isn't so, and the word *material* actually makes no sense when attached to such words as *wealth* or *well-being*.

What does wealth consist of? What constitutes your own wealth? Many people have drifted into the habit of supposing that an economic system produces "material wealth," like cars, houses, basketballs, breakfast cereals, and ball-point pens. But none of these things is wealth unless it is available to someone who values it. Additional water is additional wealth to a farmer who wants to irrigate; it is not wealth to a farmer caught in a Mississippi River flood. A food freezer may be wealth to an American housewife but not to an Eskimo. The crate in which the freezer was delivered is trash to the housewife but a treasure to her small son, who sees it as a playhouse.

Economic growth consists not in increasing the production of *things* but in the production of *wealth*. And wealth is whatever people value. Material things can contribute to wealth, obviously, and are in some sense essential to the production of wealth. (Even such "nonmaterial" goods as love and peace of mind do, after all, have some material embodiment.) But there is no necessary relation between the growth of wealth and an increase in the volume or weight or quantity

of material objects. The indefensible identification of wealth with material objects must be rejected at root. It makes no sense. And it blocks understanding of many aspects of economic life. Trade (or exchange) is the best example.

Trade Creates Wealth

Trading has long had an unsavory reputation in the Western world. This is probably the result of a deep-seated human conviction that nothing can *really* be gained through mere exchange. Agriculture and manufacturing are believed to be genuinely productive: they seem to create something genuinely new, something additional. But trade only exchanges one thing for another. It follows that the merchant, who profits from trading, must be imposing some kind of tax on the community. The wages or other profit of the farmer and artisan can be obtained from the alleged real product of their efforts, so that they are entitled in some sense to their income; they reap what they have sown. But merchants seem to reap without sowing; their activity does not appear to create anything and yet they are rewarded for their efforts. Trading, some have thought, is therefore social waste, the epitome of inefficiency.

This line of argument strikes a deeply responsive chord in many people who still retain the old hostility toward the merchant in the form of a distrust of the "middleman." Everybody wants to bypass the middleman, who is pictured as a kind of legal bandit on the highways of trade, authorized to exact a percentage from everyone foolish or unlucky enough to come his way.

However ancient or deep-seated this conviction of the unproductiveness of trade, it is completely erroneous. There is no defensible sense of the word *productive* that can be applied to agriculture or manufacturing but not to trading. Exchange is productive! It is productive because it promotes greater efficiency in resource use.

Many have taken a fatal wrong turn at the very beginning in considering this question by assuming that exchange, unless it is fraudulent or coerced, is always the exchange of *equal values*. The exact reverse is true: exchange is never an exchange of equal values. *If it were, it would not occur.* In an informed and uncoerced exchange (and this is what we mean by genuine exchange), both parties gain by giving up something of lesser for something of greater value. If Jack swaps his basketball for Jim's baseball glove, Jack values the glove more than the ball, and Jim values the ball more than the glove. Viewed from either side, the exchange was unequal. And that is precisely the source of its productivity. Jack now

has greater wealth than he had before, and so does Jim. The exchange was productive because it increased the wealth of both parties.

"Not really," says that contentious voice from the rear. "There was no real increase in wealth. Jack and Jim feel better off, it's true; they may be happier and all that. But the exchange didn't really produce anything. There is still just one baseball glove and one basketball."

But the manufacturers of the baseball glove and the basketball didn't "really" produce anything either; they just rearranged materials into more valuable patterns. And isn't that essentially what occurs when people trade? Our suspicion of exchange is evidence of our material bias, a bias obviously shared by that voice from the rear. Both Jack and Jim do have greater wealth after their exchange.

Recall what we concluded earlier about efficiency: it is measured by the ratio of one *value* to another, not by physical ratios of any sort. You can think of Jack and Jim's exchange as an act of production. Jack used the basketball as an input to obtain the output of a baseball glove. For Jim the glove was the input and the ball the output. The result of the productive process (the exchange) was an output value greater than input value for both parties. Nothing further is required to make an activity productive. The exchange expanded real output.

$$\text{For Jack:} \quad \frac{\text{Value of glove}}{\text{Value of ball}} > \text{One}$$

$$\text{For Jim:} \quad \frac{\text{Value of ball}}{\text{Value of glove}} > \text{One}$$

Efficiency and Opportunity Cost

Perhaps we can clarify all this and link it up with earlier chapters if we work our way through a simplified case study. Imagine a society with only two goods and three producers. We shall call the goods M and S, which you may think of, if you wish, as material goods and spiritual goods respectively. The producers we'll call Ann, Ben, and Cal. In a given period of time (a day, for example), each is capable of producing the following quantities of M or S:

- Ann can produce 8 Ms or 4 Ss or any linear combination between, such as 6 Ms plus 1 S, or 5 Ms plus 1½ Ss, or 2 Ms plus 3 Ss, and so on.
- Ben can produce 3 Ms or 3 Ss or any linear combination in between.
- Cal can produce 1 M or 2 Ss or any intermediate linear combination.

Ready for the question? Who would you say is the most efficient producer of spiritual goods in this drastically simplified economy? Check the data before answering.

Do you agree that it's Cal? Or did you mistakenly suppose

Cost of Producing One Unit
of Spiritual Good

Cal   ½ unit of material goods

Ben   1   "   "   "   "

Ann   2 units "   "   "

it was Ann, who is in fact the *least* efficient producer of Ss in this society? If you failed to identify Cal correctly as the most efficient producer of Ss, you weren't using the concept of opportunity cost in your calculations.

What does it cost when Cal produces an S? The cost of an action is the sacrifice that action entails. Since Ms and Ss are the only goods in this society, the only way we can state the cost of producing an S is in terms of forgone Ms. Now look at the data. Cal forgoes the production of ½ M to make an S. Ben sacrifices 1 M when he makes an S. And Ann, who is such a prolific maker of Ms, gives up 2 Ms for each S she produces. The conclusion is obvious. Cal is the lowest-cost producer of Ss, and Ann is the highest-cost producer of Ss.

Suppose you are the commissar of production in this little society, and you want to produce the maximum quantity of Ss that can be obtained consistent with producing the minimum quantity of Ms required to keep the society going. Let's further assume that 1 M per day is enough to keep everyone alive and functioning; your production plan therefore calls for 1 M plus as many Ss as can be turned out with the resources that remain.

If you order Cal to produce that required 1 M, in the mistaken belief that he's an inefficient S producer, while instructing Ann and Ben to concentrate exclusively on Ss, you'll find yourself at the end of the day with the 1 M you ordered plus 7 Ss: 4 from Ann and 3 from Ben.

If, however, you recognize that Cal is your most efficient S producer, who must therefore be kept exclusively on S production, and that Ann should produce the single M you want because she's your most *in*efficient S producer—then you'll end up with 2 Ss from Cal, 3 from Ben, and 3½ from Ann, for a total of 8½ Ss, along with the required single unit of M. If more is better than less, you're better off by 1½ Ss per day when you assign Ann rather than Cal to M production.

What would the output have been if you had told Ben to produce the 1 M? Then you would have gotten 4 Ss from Ann, 2 from Ben, and 2 from Cal, for a total of only 8 (plus the 1 M).

What's going on here? Nothing at all strange if you remember to wear the spectacles of opportunity cost. What it costs you, as commissar, to have any person produce an M or an S is the value of what you thereby forgo. When Ann produces an S, you give up 2 Ms. When Ben produces an S, you lose 1 M. But when Cal produces an S, only ½ M is sacrificed. From your point of view, therefore, Cal is clearly the lowest-cost producer of Ss and Ann is the highest-cost producer.

Cost of Producing One Unit
of Material Good

Ann   ½ unit of spiritual good

Ben   1   "   "   "   "

Cal   2 units "   "   "

When we look at the costs of M production, we see that it costs you ½ S when Ann produces an M, 1 S when Ben produces an M, and 2 Ss when Cal produces an M. Ann is therefore the lowest-cost producer of Ms, which is why you got the most of what you wanted by assigning Ann to M production.

Efficiency and the Gains from Trade

Does this counterintuitive result—namely, that fumble-fingered Cal, who can't turn out much of anything, is nonetheless the most efficient producer of spiritual goods—does this affront to common sense perhaps arise from the fact that we put a dictator in charge? Not at all. It is entirely a result of the logic of opportunity cost.

Let's stage a coup, get rid of the commissar of production, and allow Ann, Ben, and Cal to decide individually what they want to produce.

They would presumably begin by deciding what each preferred to consume. Let's suppose that Cal, a well-balanced person, wants 1 M and 1 S. He's got a problem. There's no way he can produce that much. If he produces the M he wants, he'll have to go without S altogether. If he produces the 1 S he wants, he'll have to get along with only ½ M.

Now let's further suppose that Ben is an equally well-balanced person and wants to consume 1½ Ms and 1½ Ss, which is exactly what he's capable of producing. If Ben and Cal know and trust one another well enough, they can arrange an exchange that will be advantageous to Cal without making Ben any worse off. Cal could agree to specialize exclusively in S production. He would then keep one of his Ss for his own use and give the other to Ben. That would enable Ben to produce 2½ Ms, since he would now have to produce only ½ S for his own use. Keeping 1½ Ms for himself and giving the other to Cal would leave Ben no worse off than before. But Cal would now have obtained, through specialization and trade, the greater wealth that he wanted but hadn't been able to achieve on his own.

Does it look like a trick? Perhaps it is, but not in the sense of an illusion or something deceptive. It's the trick that all of us perform every day in order to supply ourselves with the goods that we want but can't even begin to produce for ourselves. We all specialize in the production of those goods in which we think we have the greatest *comparative advantage*, and then exchange our products for the goods we really want. Just as Jack found that he could use a basketball as an input to produce a baseball glove that he wanted more

How much food can be produced on a basketball court ?!

than the basketball, so Cal found he could use an extra S as an input to obtain the M he wanted. That in essence is what we all do.

In a world where people can arrange and carry out exchanges with one another at low cost, people will find it in their interest to specialize and trade. They'll discover that specialization can bring them more of what they want, whether they want material goods, spiritual goods, leisure, or even a chance to make more of everything available to others. If Julius Erving, a basketball player of extraordinary ability, had decided it was his primary aim in life to make more food and more prayer books available to the destitute in Philadelphia, he would still have worked as a professional basketball player. That's where his comparative advantage lay. He could "grow" far more food by playing basketball for pay and using the proceeds to "hire" farmers than he could ever have grown by sitting on a tractor. And the truck farmers of New Jersey "grew" entertainment for themselves by specializing in vegetable production and using the proceeds to buy a color television set on which to watch Julius Erving play.

You don't have to be "better than others" to pull this trick off. Cal can benefit from trading with Ben even though he's less productive than Ben in both spiritual and material goods. He can even gain from trade with Ann, who has the ability to turn out in a day twice as many Ss and eight times as many Ms as Cal. The important fact is that Ann has a *greater* advantage over Cal in Ms than in Ss. That means Cal has a *lesser disadvantage* with respect to Ann in Ss than in Ms. And that in turn implies that both Ann and Cal may be able to benefit from trading with each other after specializing in that good in which each has the *comparative advantage*.

Comparative Advantage in International Trade

Popular thinking hangs on tenaciously to the notion that some countries may be able to produce almost everything at a lower cost. If wages in Mexico or Italy are lower than in the United States, won't Mexican and Italian manufacturers be able to produce just about anything more cheaply than U.S. manufacturers can do it? How can the United States compete with countries that tolerate wage rates, even for skilled workers, below our legal minimum? In Mexico and Italy, however, you could find workers arguing that they can't compete with America's low-cost techniques of mass production. And the suspicion would properly arise that something is wrong with the argument.

The basic flaw in such arguments is their neglect of opportunity cost. It is *logically* impossible for one country to

be more efficient than another in the production of everything. And that becomes apparent as soon as you remember to calculate efficiency as a ratio between what is produced and what is consequently *not* produced. The real cost of producing anything is the value of what is given up in order to produce it. Calculations in dollars, yen, pesos, and francs (or working hours) all too easily obscure these real costs of production.

Suppose that Japan and the United States each produced only three goods: grain, textiles, and radios. Suppose further that competition had moved prices in both countries to levels that reflected the opportunity costs of each good, with these results:

Prices per unit of good (identical quantity and quality)

	United States	Japan
Grain	30 dollars	9,000 yen
Textiles	20 dollars	4,500 yen
Radios	50 dollars	13,500 yen

Which country is the more efficient or lower-cost producer of these goods? Before we can answer, we must find some way of comparing costs. What measure is available?

Dollars and yen clearly won't do. It's obviously absurd to suggest that the United States is more efficient in producing all three goods simply because the dollar prices are lower than the yen prices. That would be true only if a yen had the same value as a dollar. We shall see in the later chapter on international exchange how the relative values of national currencies are established. It's enough for now to note that this is a blind alley because currency exchange rates only reflect the value of currencies; they indicate nothing about costs of production.

Some people might want to use the labor time invested in the production of these goods as the ultimate measure of their relative costs. To do that we would first have to find some common denominator for labor of different skill and effectiveness plus some way of translating such other inputs as machinery and land into units of labor time. And even if we could find a satisfactory way to do this, we would still be forced to adopt the arbitrary assumption that an hour of labor in Japan is as valuable as an hour of labor in the United States. But is it? Attitudes toward work and leisure are culturally determined, and there is no good reason to assume that an hour of working time is exactly as "costly" in one country as in another.

Then how can we decide which country is the lower-cost

In the U.S.,

    1 unit of radios costs:

        1⅔ units of grain, or

        2½ units of textiles

In Japan,

    1 unit of radios costs:

        1½ units of grain, or

        3 units of textiles

producer of these goods? The answer is: *There is no way at all to do so.* All we can do is determine that one country or the other is the more efficient producer of a particular good *relative to some other good or goods.* This is the meaning of comparative advantage.

Take radios, for example. The price ratios show that in the United States, a unit of radios costs either 1⅔ units of grain or 2½ units of textiles. It costs that much because that's what is given up in obtaining one unit of radios. In Japan, a unit of radios costs 1½ units of grain or 3 units of textiles. Those are the quantities of grain and textiles that are given up in Japan when additional radios are produced. It follows, then, that Japan is more efficient than the United States in producing radios *relative to grain,* but less efficient *relative to textiles.*

Which country is the more efficient textile producer? If you've gotten the idea by now, you will immediately ask: relative to what? A unit of textiles costs ⅔ unit of grain and ⅖ unit of radios in the United States, and ½ unit of grain and ⅓ unit of radios in Japan. So Japan is the more efficient (lower-cost) producer of textiles relative to both grain and radios.

The United States in turn is the lower-cost producer of grain relative to textiles: 1½ units of textiles are given up to produce a unit of grain, versus 2 units of textiles given up in Japan. The United States is also the lower-cost producer of grain relative to radios: ⅗ unit of radios is the cost of a U.S. unit of grain; ⅔ unit of radios is the Japanese cost.

Don't lose the point in all the fractions. *A nation can become an inefficient producer of good X simply by becoming a fabulously prolific producer of good Y.* When you become extraordinarily good at one thing, it is costly for you to do anything else. If Japan starts to produce radios and television sets at a lower cost than they can be produced in the United States, that does not imply that U.S. radio and TV manufacturers have failed in some fashion. It could just as well mean that U.S. productivity has been increasing rapidly in other industries.

The Pursuit of Comparative Advantage

No one except economists ever goes through these kinds of calculations, and even economists do it only in order to explain to students the logic of comparative advantage. In the real world people pursue comparative advantage, as distinct from merely talking about it, simply by choosing the option that seems most advantageous to them. Cal produces spiritual goods, Julius Erving plays basketball, American apparel makers buy Japanese textiles, and Japanese millers

purchase grain from the United States because, in each case, they believe that is the best way to obtain what they want. In all of these decisions relative prices provide fundamental information. Given his various abilities and the price his work commands, Cal discovers that he can earn more income producing Ss than producing Ms. Americans looking for textiles find Japanese products less expensive than domestically produced textiles of similar quality. Japanese farmers choose not to raise wheat because they know that they could not raise enough to earn a satisfactory living, given the fact that they could not sell it above the price at which U.S.-grown wheat was available to Japanese millers. In short, they all behave as if the least costly way to achieve a given objective was the most efficient way. And in doing so they continuously coordinate these processes of cooperative interaction and mutual accommodation that comprise the economy.

None of this implies that they pay attention exclusively to prices, which would be an absurd and impossible way to behave. It means rather that relative prices guide their decisions when other things are equal. The other things that must be equal—or to be quite accurate, must be *thought* to be equal—include an enormous array of factors from the technological to the psychological. Consider a homeowner, for example, who wants to eliminate broad-leaved weeds from a lawn. Would it be more efficient to dig them out with a hand tool or to spray them with a herbicide? The homeowner's decision will reflect a judgment on the effectiveness of each procedure in killing the root, on likely damage to ornamental shrubs, on the desirability of exercise, and on the joys of yard work, and not just the relative prices of herbicide and hand tools. But those relative prices play a crucial coordinating role.

Disagreements on Values

If efficiency is finally an evaluative concept, expressing the ratio of output value to input value, anything at all can be inefficient to a person who holds the appropriate values. There are people to whom exercise is a total waste of energy. There are also people to whom a grassy knoll by the side of the road is a waste of space unless it displays a billboard. A person who neither visits wilderness areas nor derives satisfaction from knowing that they exist will correctly condemn as inefficient every legislative decision to create new wilderness preserves. Flying between cities rather than driving is a much more efficient travel arrangement for someone who gets car sickness than for someone who enjoys the scenery. And someone somewhere may even believe that Rembrandt wasted time by not painting with a six-inch-wide brush.

We could multiply such examples indefinitely, but the point is surely clear. *What we value determines what we will consider efficient or inefficient.* It follows that disagreements in society about the relative efficiency of particular projects will usually be disagreements about the relative value to be assigned to particular goods—or the relative disvalue of particular nongoods. Knowing this won't settle any controversial issue. But failing even to recognize what we're arguing about surely makes the resolution of controversy more difficult.

The question is not, "What is *really* more efficient?" but rather, "Who has the *right* to make particular decisions?" Crawling out of a sleeping bag to climb a mountain is atrociously inefficient to someone who plans to crawl back into that sleeping bag in the evening and is merely looking for the shortest distance between those two points. Fans of mountain climbing strenuously disagree, of course. But that creates no social conflict, because we all agree that individuals should have the right to decide for themselves whether it's more valuable to put their bodies on mountain peaks or to keep them in bed during vacations. When we do *not* agree on who has which rights, that's when we get into vehement arguments about whether it is "really" efficient, for example, to clear-cut forests or to strip-mine coal.

Efficiency, Values, and Property Rights

You should be able to see now why we insisted at the beginning of this chapter that the common critique of efficiency is logically confused. A society that placed "too high a value on efficiency" would be one that placed too high a value on using its resources in the most valuable way. That's an odd notion at best. The real target of the critics has to be either the values people hold or the rights they exercise.

Suppose a mineral exploration company came to the conclusion that there were large quantities of chrome, vanadium, and manganese under the ground in Yellowstone National Park and requested permission from Congress to search for them. Can you imagine the cries of outrage that would greet such a request? "Profiteers with no respect for nature!" "Greedy materialists willing to destroy an irreplaceable national heritage!" And someone would surely say: "Efficiency and economic growth are not worth pursuing if they deprive us of everything that makes life worth living."

The issue in such a case, however, would not be efficiency and economic growth versus nature, wilderness, or anything else that makes life worth living. The issue would rather be *what is efficient,* or what constitutes genuine economic

growth. There is nothing intrinsically more efficient about mining than about meditating. It is not necessarily the case that economic growth proceeds faster when manganese is extracted from a mountain than when trout are extracted from a stream. To decide whether it would be efficient to mine in Yellowstone Park, we must set the expected value of what would be obtained from mining against the expected value of what would thereby be lost. Chrome, vanadium, and manganese have no value that we can talk about apart from the purposes to which people intend to put them. And the same is true of the vistas, the tranquility, or the unblemished land and water that mining would destroy.

The issue comes down to this: *By what process should the prospective benefits and costs of mining in Yellowstone Park be evaluated?*

When the rules of the game establish clear and secure property rights, they implicitly decide by what process prospective benefits and costs are to be evaluated for decision-making purposes. If I decide to open my windows and turn up the thermostat on a cold winter day, I am using resources efficiently as long as I have an uncontested right to allocate all the resources I'm using. If, on the other hand, I am cooling off someone else's living space, or if someone else is paying the heating bills, my property rights are likely to be challenged. Then the issue becomes *not* the efficiency of my preferred arrangements but rather my exclusive right to value the inputs and the outputs in what I am doing.

When property rights are clear, stable, and exchangeable, scarce resources tend to acquire money prices that reflect their relative scarcity. Decision makers then pursue efficiency by using these prices as information. To say that the prices are "wrong" because they don't reflect the *real* value of certain costs or benefits amounts to rejecting the process by which those prices were determined. It is a critique not of efficiency but of the existing system of property rights, and of the rules of the game of which they form a part.

Comparative Advantage: The Economist's Umbrella

The term with which economists summarize almost everything we have been discussing in this chapter is *comparative advantage*. It might even be thought of as a term to summarize the entire collection of concepts presented thus far. To pursue comparative advantage means simply to sacrifice that which is less valuable for the sake of something more valuable.

Why do demand curves slope downward to the right? Because people pursue their comparative advantage. A rise in the price of any good means that its users will now be able

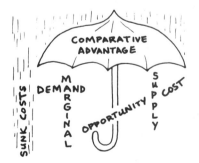

to obtain the satisfaction it provides at a *relatively lower cost* by using some substitute.

How is the opportunity cost of any resource established? Through the pursuit of comparative advantage. People bid for a resource after estimating the potentiality of that resource *relative to other resources* for providing whatever they're after.

Why are only expected marginal costs and not sunk costs relevant to decision making? Because expected marginal costs reflect the *comparative advantages of alternative decisions,* whereas sunk costs can never do more than reflect the comparative advantages of past decisions. But no one makes decisions with the hope of affecting what happened yesterday.

It is comparative advantage—the advantage resources have over other resources in particular uses relative to other uses—that determines the most efficient way to employ one's resources.

The economic way of thinking may at root be nothing more than the ability to think consistently in terms of comparative advantage.

Once Over Lightly

Efficiency depends on valuations. Although physical or technological facts are certainly relevant to the determination of efficiency, they can never by themselves determine the relative efficiency of alternative processes. Efficiency depends on the ratio of output *value* to input *value.*

Exchange creates wealth, because voluntary exchange always involves the sacrifice of what is less valued (input) for what is more valued (output). Exchange is as much a wealth-creating transformation as is manufacturing or agriculture.

People specialize in order to exchange and thereby increase their wealth. They specialize in activities in which they believe themselves to have a comparative advantage.

Comparative advantage is determined by opportunity costs. No person, no group, no nation can be more efficient than another in every activity, for even the most highly productive agents must have some activities in which they are less highly productive. If you're four times as intelligent, three times as strong, and twice as beautiful as another person, then that person has a comparative advantage in beauty—and you, handsome as you are, have a comparative disadvantage in beauty.

A social system with clear property rights and few restrictions on exchange generates money prices that help people who are pursuing their comparative advantage to discover in exactly which direction their advantage lies.

Disagreements about whether some process or arrangement is or is not efficient are at root disagreements about

the relative weights that should be given to different people's evaluations. They are therefore disagreements about the rules of the game, or about who should have what rights over which resources.

133

Efficiency, Exchange, and
Comparative Advantage

QUESTIONS FOR DISCUSSION

1. Many people enjoy the sight and sounds of a steam locomotive.
   (a) Should these aesthetic pleasures be included in the valuable output of a steam locomotive, right along with the value of the freight that is hauled?
   (b) If the owners of railroads could somehow collect a fee from all those who enjoyed seeing and hearing steam locomotives, would they include aesthetic pleasures in the value of a steam locomotive's output?
   (c) Would the efficiency of steam locomotives increase if a low-cost way were found to extract from steam-locomotive buffs a fee proportioned to the pleasure they derive from seeing and hearing them?

2. Is it efficient to feed a family using large quantities of frozen "convenience" foods? Under what circumstances could these expensive grocery items provide the lowest-cost inputs for producing the output of family dinner? What questionable premise is being used by someone who says that shoppers are wasting money by paying twice as much for convenience foods as they would have to pay for dinner items they prepare themselves?

3. The United States used wood as a fuel in metallurgy long after the British had changed to coal. Was this evidence of technological backwardness in the United States? If the United States was technologically backward, how would you explain the fact that all sorts of machines for woodworking were perfected in the United States in the first half of the nineteenth century? Fireplaces are often said to be inefficient ways to heat a room. Why then were they so widely used in the United States in the nineteenth century in preference to stoves? (Hint: Larger logs can be used in fireplaces.) Why did stoves become more popular as wood prices increased?

4. Is it more efficient to build dams with lots of direct labor and little machinery or with lots of machinery and little labor? Why will the answer vary from one country to another?

5. Which is more efficient: Japanese agriculture with its carefully terraced hillsides or American agriculture with its far more "wasteful" use of land? How have relative prices in the two countries brought about these different methods of farming? How have opportunity costs entered into the formation of these relative prices?

6. Attorney Fudd is the most highly sought-after lawyer in the state. He is also a phenomenal typist who can do 120 words per minute. Should Fudd do his own typing if the fastest secretary he can obtain does only 60 words per minute? Prove that Fudd is *not* twice as efficient as his secretary at typing, that he is in fact *less* efficient at typing, and that he should therefore retain a secretary.

7. The dean knows that Professor Svelte is the most capable administrator in

his department, far more capable than Professor Klunk. Can you think of any reasons (related to efficiency rather than nepotism) for nonetheless appointing Klunk over Svelte as department chairman?

8. The Boeing 767 uses less than 110 pounds of jet fuel per seat per 1000 miles. The older 727 uses about 155 pounds of jet fuel per seat per 1000 miles. But the 767 costs far more per seat to purchase. Which of the planes should an airline purchase if it is interested in efficiency? Does the price of jet fuel affect the answer? How might the decision to purchase a used 727 rather than a new 767 turn out to be not only more economical but also more conserving of natural resources?

9. It has often been claimed that under a capitalist system business firms will sometimes continue to use obsolete equipment rather than the new, "most efficient" equipment because they have a lot of money tied up in the old equipment. Does this make sense? What is the relevance to such decisions of "money tied up"? When would an airline that has "money tied up" in 727s elect to replace them with 767s?

10. You own and occupy a large brick house in an old residential neighborhood. The area is being rezoned to allow multiple-family occupancy and apartment buildings. How would you go about deciding whether to (a) continue to occupy the house as a single-family dwelling, (b) divide the house into several apartments, or (c) tear down the house and erect a new apartment complex? If you were to choose (b), could you be accused of retarding the economy by failing to adopt the most up-to-date equipment because of your vested interest in obsolete equipment? Does this differ from question 9?

11. A May 1979 letter to the editor of the *Wall Street Journal* wondered why, in view of the gasoline shortage, such "utterly wasteful uses of gasoline" as auto racing were still permitted. The writer also urged that such "obvious waste" be curtailed in the public interest. Is auto racing an utter and obvious waste of gasoline? Try to construct a clear and defensible definition of *waste* that would indict auto racing but exonerate other uses of automotive gasoline at a time when there might be a gasoline shortage.

12. Grain farmers have many options when it comes to preparing the soil. They can plow and then thoroughly harrow a field before planting, they can practice minimum tillage, or they can go so far as to plant without preparing the ground at all. Heavy tilling buries and thus kills weeds and insects. No-till farming requires careful and extensive use of herbicides and pesticides and also produces slightly lower yields. Explain how each of the following will affect the relative efficiency of maximum tillage and no-till farming:
    (a) Higher prices for diesel fuel
    (b) Improved herbicides and pesticides
    (c) Tougher government controls on stream and lake pollution caused by chemicals used in agriculture (Note: Untilled ground is more likely to retain the chemicals put into it.)
    (d) Farmers adopt the same attitude toward their fields that some suburban homeowners have toward their lawns: they find satisfaction in looking at a broad, well-tended expanse of land
    (e) Higher prices for land

13. Some critics of U.S. agriculture argue that highly mechanized production

techniques in farming are inefficient because the energy consumed by the machinery used to grow food exceeds the amount of potential energy available in the food that is grown. Does this argument make any sense? Is energy the ultimate measure of value?

14. In recent years millions of acres of barley- and rye-growing land have been kept out of production in the Soviet Union to save scarce fertilizer. Nonetheless, Soviet farmers sometimes burn fertilizer to conceal the fact that they haven't spread it on the soil, and there are regions in which it is common to see huge mounds of unused, years-old, and now thoroughly hardened fertilizer. Can you account for this anomaly: the deliberate nonuse of a critically scarce resource? Why would U.S. farmers not behave in this way?

15. The Sevier River in Utah has been used for about a century to irrigate farm land in central Utah. Recently a 3000-megawatt, coal-fired electrical generating plant was proposed for this area. The generating plant would require about 40,000 acre-feet of water per year from the Sevier River. Operation of the generating plant would mean less water for agriculture.
   (a) Is the water of the Sevier River used more efficiently when it grows food or when it generates electricity?
   (b) Can you answer this question by comparing the value of food with the value of electricity? (Hint: Value is determined at the margin.)
   (c) If farmers who own rights to Sevier River water sell their rights to the power company, is the water allocated to its most valuable use?
   (d) Who are some of the parties who might be adversely affected by the farmers' decision to sell their water rights?

16. Have you ever noticed how few gasoline stations are found in the center of large cities? With such heavy traffic one ought to be able to do an excellent business. Why then are there so few?

17. The key to question 16 is the high price of land in the center of large cities. Would it make sense for the city government, which has the right of eminent domain, to take over some of this land in order to provide "vitally needed service stations"?

18. Land has become so expensive in Beverly Hills and Westwood, California, that developers estimate it would require more than $25 million to construct a supermarket with adequate parking space in these communities, according to *Parade Magazine*, January 20, 1985.
   (a) Why has the land become so expensive?
   (b) There is only one supermarket in all of Beverly Hills and central Westwood. Why?
   (c) At these land prices, supermarket construction is not a profitable investment project. Might it nonetheless be efficient to have another supermarket or two in the area?

19. In a June 6, 1985 article titled "On the Waterfront: Tugs, Barges Battling Quiche and Fern Bars," the *Wall Street Journal* discussed the gentrification of waterfront property.
   (a) A Seattle land-use specialist who wants to halt this development said, "A condominium can be built anywhere, but the shipyard it replaces can't move two miles inland." Why is that not a convincing argument?
   (b) Maritime interests in Boston have objected to a plan to turn unused

piers into housing and parkland on the grounds that the now vacant piers may be needed someday. Why is this an unconvincing argument?

(c) Marine businesses complain that they cannot outbid developers for waterfront land, and so need zoning help and other protection from local government in order to keep down the price of goods that move by water. Why should the cost of water carriage be kept down by government action?

20. Is it efficient for cars to have bumpers so strong and heavy that the car will sustain no damage in collisions at speeds up to 5 miles per hour? How would you answer such a question if you were a car buyer? If you were an automobile manufacturer? If you were a federal official charged with setting minimum standards for automobile bumpers?

21. In view of the high cost of transporting milk from the mainland U.S., is it efficient for Hawaii to produce within its own borders all the milk its citizens consume? What difference does it make to your answer to know that Hawaiian dairy farmers import all their cattle feed? If it is inefficient to import milk into Hawaii, why does the state's Milk Control Board receive requests to import milk from other states? Is it efficient for the Milk Control Board to deny these requests, as it has regularly done?

22. A 1984 study issued by the Congressional Office of Technology Assessment concluded that a high-speed rail system capable of moving passengers between U.S. cities would probably not be able to attract enough riders to stay in the black. Does this imply that it would be inefficient to construct such a system?

23. Bonneville Dam is the oldest dam on the Columbia River, and its navigation lock is much smaller than the locks on the seven dams farther up the river. As a result Bonneville is a bottleneck for Columbia River barge traffic, with barges sometimes compelled to wait 10 hours for passage.

(a) By what process could the federal government, which owns and operates the dam, decide whether it would be efficient to construct a new lock at Bonneville?

(b) The Burlington Northern and Union Pacific railroads operate tracks along the northern and southern banks of the Columbia River. They argue that a new lock should be constructed only if barge owners and towboat operators are willing to pay for it. Barge and towboat people respond that the benefits of the lock would extend far beyond themselves, and that this justifies a government subsidy for the proposed new lock. Would other beneficiaries be able to avoid paying for the benefits they receive if the federal government financed the new lock through a fee paid by the towboats and barges that use it?

24. Should the government build a $520-million network of dams, reservoirs, and irrigation canals near Durango, Colorado, to capture the spring run-off in the Animas and La Plata rivers? Would this be an efficient use of taxpayer funds? How could we decide?

25. Chapter 4 discussed the problem of increasing airport congestion, using Washington, D.C.'s crowded National Airport and the near-deserted Dulles Airport as a case study. Airlines prefer to fly into National because it's only 10 minutes from downtown Washington; Dulles is almost an hour away.

(a) Is it efficient for airlines to choose National over Dulles when scheduling their flights? Would that efficiency change if the government charged a higher landing fee at National?

(b) Is it efficient for passengers to choose a flight into National over one into Dulles? Would their relative efficiencies change if ticket prices for flights landing at National rose by twice the price of a cab from Dulles to the Capitol?

(c) In 1966 the FAA decreed that flights coming into Washington from any city more than 650 miles away had to land at Dulles. Was this an efficient order? What effects do you think it had?

(d) The Transportation Department has been floating proposals recently to buy and sell landing rights at National and other busy airports. Some critics of this proposal object that the larger airlines would buy all the slots. Do you think this would occur? What sort of factors would determine how much any airline was willing to pay for a particular landing slot?

26. Airlines are willing to overbook flights because they know that some people who make reservations will not show up. Sometimes, however, this results in more people holding reservations at the gate than there are seats on the flight.

(a) Is overbooking efficient from the airlines' standpoint?

(b) If the airlines are required by law to pay huge sums as compensation to passengers who are "bumped" because of overbooking, does this change the efficiency of overbooking?

(c) Is overbooking efficient from the standpoint of passengers?

(d) How would you recommend that airlines handle situations in which, because of overbooking, they are required to deny boarding to some passengers? Which passengers should be "bumped"?

(e) In recent years airlines have adopted the practice of "bumping" volunteers from overbooked flights. Volunteers are obtained by offers of money or free trips as inducements to surrender confirmed reservations. Who gets "bumped" under this system? Does the system discriminate against poorer people?

(f) If passengers can sell their confirmed reservations when a seat shortage arises, why can't passengers sell their right to land at a crowded airport when a shortage of landing slots arises?

(g) Compare your analysis here with your analysis in the question that follows, especially part (b).

27. Bent Grasz spent $100,000 to plant grass, flowers, shrubs, and trees and make his home a landscaping showplace. The city is suffering from a drought this summer and has prohibited all watering of lawns and gardens. Bent would be willing to pay several thousand dollars if necessary to obtain the water he needs to irrigate adequately. Many of Bent's fellow citizens would be willing to conserve the amount of water Bent wants in return for a payment far less than Bent is willing to offer.

(a) Is there room here for everyone to become better off through exchange?

(b) Why can't people ordinarily sell the water they conserve in a drought to someone else who wants it more than they do?

(c) Suppose the city responded to the drought not by prohibiting watering

but by tripling the price of water. Would this make Bent happy?

(d) If the city distributed the extra revenue from higher water prices to water users, an equal amount going to each customer, would this cancel out the effect of the price increase? Who would be better off and who would be worse off under such a system (better or worse than under the system of restrictions on use but no price increase)?

28. During the 1970s the federal government maintained extensive and complex controls on the prices of petroleum and petroleum products.

(a) Why would you expect these controls to lead eventually to greater scarcity of petroleum products in some areas than in others, or to what were called "supply imbalances"?

(b) When the U.S. Department of Energy authorized oil companies to move as much as 5 percent of their supply among and within the states to "relieve imbalances," the companies generally declined to do so. How could the oil companies know where to move oil and how much to reallocate with prices fixed by law?

(c) The Department of Energy authorized the governors of states to move this 5 percent of supply when the oil companies declined the invitation. How were the governors able to allocate petroleum products efficiently when the oil companies could not do so?

(d) In a March 16, 1981, letter to the editor of the *Wall Street Journal*, the Commissioner of the New Jersey Department of Energy argued that the oil companies' refusal to accept the authority granted to them and their decision to hide "timidly behind government controls" demonstrates the inadequacy of "the free-market philosophy." Is this a sound argument?

29. Is it possible to assess the efficiency of the federal government's 55-mile-per-hour speed limit?

(a) What is the output or desired result whose value would go in the numerator of the efficiency ratio? What is the input or cost or forgone opportunity whose value would go in the denominator? How would you choose appropriate values once you had decided on the appropriate output and input?

(b) Suppose we use fuel saved as the output of the 55-mph limit and time lost as the input. What might we use as appropriate value weights so that we can decide whether the value of the output is greater than the value of the input?

(c) If we include in the output not only fuel saved but also the lives saved, won't our assessment inevitably conclude that the 55-mph speed limit is efficient? How can we set a finite value on a human life?

(d) Economist Charles Lave has calculated that the 55-mph speed limit causes Americans to spend 102 extra years driving in order to "save one life," and suggests that 102 years traveling in an automobile rather closely fits his personal notion of hell (*Newsweek*, October 23, 1978). List a few ways in which 102 years could be used to "save" far more lives than one.

(e) Far more lives would be saved if we required that all motorists be preceded by a person on foot carrying an orange flag. Would such an

arrangement consequently be even more efficient than a 55-mph speed limit?

   (f) Who gains from the 55-mph speed limit? Who loses the most?

30. In 1977 the Environmental Protection Agency ordered eight Ohio utilities to meet federal sulfur-dioxide emission standards. The utilities could satisfy these standards either by installing "scrubbers" or by shifting to low-sulfur coal.

   (a) They chose the second alternative because it was cheaper. Was it also the more efficient choice?

   (b) Ohio coal mines produce high-sulfur coal that cannot be burned without exceeding EPA emissions standards unless expensive scrubbers are installed. The utilities therefore reduced their purchases of Ohio coal and began buying low-sulfur coals from Kentucky and West Virginia. This caused disruption and unemployment in Ohio coalfields. Does that fact change your answer to question (a)?

   (c) Special legislation enacted by Congress gave the EPA authority to *compel* utilities to buy "regionally available coal" when this was necessary to prevent significant disruption or unemployment in nearby coalfields—even though it would necessitate the installation of expensive scrubbers. Does this legislation compel inefficient decisions?

   (d) Is it more efficient to relax EPA emissions standards for electrical utilities so they can burn high-sulfur coal, to permit strip-mining in order to obtain low-sulfur western coal for electricity generation, to generate electricity by nuclear reaction, or to maintain clean-air standards without strip-mining or an expansion of nuclear power by raising electricity prices so high that people cut their consumption to one-third of its previous level?

31. A pumped-storage reservoir is a reservoir that an electrical utility drains during hours of peak demand in order to generate electricity, then refills during hours of slack demand by pumping water back up into it.

   (a) The electricity generated by the falling water is inevitably far less than the electricity used to refill the reservoir. Does this mean the practice of using pumped-storage reservoirs is inefficient?

   (b) If you think it's inefficient or wasteful to use two watts of electricity to create one watt, why do you suppose the utilities do it? Can it be profitable to behave inefficiently?

   (c) If you believe that inefficient behavior can sometimes be profitable, would you ever want to condemn such behavior as not in the general or long-term interest of society? Why or why not? Under what circumstances?

32. If you saw a bumper sticker that said "Eliminate Government Waste—At Any Cost," would you laugh, cry, or cheer?

33. Construct the supply curve of Ms from the data in the text on Ann, Ben, and Cal. The quantity of Ms will go on the horizontal axis. What will you put on the vertical axis? Then construct the supply curve of Ss.

Information, Middlemen, and Speculators

The costs and benefits that affect decisions to demand or to supply are always *expected* costs and benefits. Producers decide to supply so many units of X because they expect to pay no more than a certain amount for the required resources and to receive at least some larger amount than that from selling X. Consumers decide to purchase a product because they expect to receive some benefit from its possession greater than what they expect to pay for it. But the future is uncertain, so expectations are often frustrated by events. Decisions turn out to be mistaken. And mistakes are costly.

Because of all the interdependencies that characterize our highly specialized economic system, mistaken decisions will often have costly consequences for many more people than the ones who made the decision. If refiners don't build up adequate inventories of crude oil, motorists may have to wait in line for gasoline. If physicians don't anticipate the adverse side effects of a drug, a patient may die. And if manufacturers overestimate the demand for their product, employees who sacrificed other opportunities to work for those manufacturers may find themselves unemployed.

Since mistakes are costly, people try to avoid making them. Unfortunately, avoiding mistakes is costly, too. The way to eliminate mistakes is to acquire more information before acting. But information is a scarce good with its own costs of acquisition. It may be less costly, as a result, to accept some mistakes than to acquire the information that could have prevented them. One mistake we can all avoid is the mistake of assuming that information is a free good. We shall see as we proceed through this chapter just how often that

mistaken assumption seems to influence our attitudes and actions.

Real-Estate Agents Are Information Producers

"How to save about $900 and lose $3000 . . . right on your own home."

That was the headline under which the National Association of Real Estate Boards ran an advertisement urging people to use the services of a realtor in selling their homes. The ad continued:

> Don't laugh. It could happen. For instance, suppose you decide to sell your house. Yourself. You decide it's worth $15,000, and you sell it for $15,000. Great. But how did you arrive at that price? By guesswork. It takes a lot more than that to determine a property's value. It takes a Realtor who knows houses and what they're worth. Suppose he said your house was worth $3000 more. A fair price to buyer and seller. It could happen. Of course, you'd save the Realtor's fee. But at quite a cost.
>
> So when you decide to sell a house, use your Realtor. He's not just anyone in real estate. He's the professional who is pledged to a strict code of ethics. That's good. Especially if you want to make the best sale you can. Or for that matter, the best buy.

That ad is eloquent testimony to something mentioned in Chapter 6: the public's deep-rooted suspicion of middlemen.[1] The fact that the realtors' association thought the ad worth running is strong evidence that such a suspicion exists, and the argument used in the ad is further evidence. For the ad seems designed to obscure the realtor's function while defending it, almost as if the truth is more than the public would tolerate.

Suppose, we might ask, that the realtor said your house was worth $3000 *less:* "A fair price to buyer and seller." Isn't it just as likely that homeowners selling their own houses will guess too high as too low? Or even more likely in view of the hopeful optimism typical of so many homeowners? Then the use of a realtor will cost the owner twice over. And just what constitutes a "fair price"? Moreover, if the realtors obtain higher prices for sellers, how can they simultaneously obtain better buys for purchasers, as the last paragraph asserts? Something is wrong with the argument.

Don't criticize the realtors' association too harshly. The plight of middlemen forced to explain their function is not an

---

1. It is also testimony to the inflation that has occurred since the early 1970s. $15,000 today may buy a garage; it wouldn't buy much of a house.

easy one, because most people don't see that *information is a scarce good* or what this fact implies. If you want to sell your house for as much as you can get, the appropriate buyer is the one person in the world willing to pay the highest price. That seems obvious. What isn't obvious is how you find that person. You presumably are not omniscient, so you will never even discover the existence of many potential purchasers. It is almost a certainty, therefore, that when you finally do sell, you will not have found that one buyer willing to pay the very top price. Does this imply that you should keep searching indefinitely?

Information is a scarce good with its own costs of production, including all the costs of postponing action. It simply does not pay to go on acquiring information forever before acting. A rational seller will continue acquiring information, therefore, only so long as the anticipated marginal gain from doing so is greater than the anticipated marginal cost of acquiring information. A rational buyer will behave in the same way. The reason that both can gain from using the services of a realtor is that the realtor enables each to obtain additional information at low cost. When you think about it, this seems in fact to be the primary function of middlemen: they promote efficiency and hence increase wealth by acting as low-cost producers of valuable information. Realtors provide sellers and buyers with better opportunities than they would otherwise have by putting them in possession of additional information. That is a valuable service. Although it's true that only the seller actually "hires" the realtor, the fact that buyers go to them and make use of their multiple-listing services shows that realtors provide a service to buyers, too.

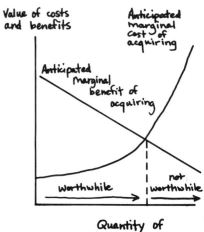

Reducing Search Costs

Suppose you own ten shares of General Electric stock and want to sell. You could go around to your friends and try to peddle it or you could put an ad in the newspaper. But it is very likely that you would obtain a higher price by using the services of a middleman, in this case a stockbroker. No doubt if you advertised long enough you could find a buyer willing to pay the price the stockbroker obtained for you. But it is most improbable that the cost of your search would be less than the broker's fee.

"Getting it wholesale" is a popular pastime for many people who think that they're economizing. Perhaps they are. If they enjoy searching for bargains (and many people do), then they may well gain from their activities. But for most people, retailers are an important low-cost source of valuable

information. The retailer's inventory reveals something of the range of opportunities available, information that is often difficult to obtain in any other fashion. How many times have you gone shopping without knowing what you were looking for, hoping to discover what you want by finding out what retailers have for sale?

Much the same is true of job-placement agencies. Many people resent the fee charged by private agencies for finding them a job. But unless they expected the information obtained through the agency to be worth more than the fee, they presumably would not have used the agency's service. Employers are also willing to pay for such services, and for exactly the same reason.

A large part of the middleman's bad press stems from our habit of comparing actual situations with better but nonexistent ones. The exchanges we make are rarely as advantageous as the exchanges we could make if we were omniscient. So we conclude that the middleman takes advantage of our ignorance. But why look at it in that way? Using the same argument, one could say that doctors take advantage of your illnesses, and that they should receive no return for their services because they would be unable to obtain a return if you were always healthy. That is both true and irrelevant. We are neither always healthy nor omniscient. Physicians and middlemen are consequently producers of real wealth. Other prestigious persons performing similar services are lawyers, teachers, preachers, and corporation executives.

Markets Create Information

One of the continuing themes of this book is that supply and demand, or the market process of competing bids and offers, creates indexes of value for decision makers by placing price tags on available resources. The capacity of the market to generate high-quality information at low cost is one of its most important but least appreciated virtues. Middlemen are important participants in this process.

But what, you may ask, is "the market"? That's a good question and not an easy one to answer. The market is clearly not a place, though it may sometimes be closely identified with a particular place. Nor is it anything one can observe in the usual sense of observation. It is finally just a set of interrelationships, or what we have called a "process of competing bids and offers."

Markets are not peculiar to capitalism. They also exist in the most thoroughly socialist of societies. They aren't uniquely associated with business firms or the "private sector" either.

Interrelationships characterized by competing bids and offers are also, as we shall see in Chapter 14, important characteristics of the political process and of government organizations. Nor must money change hands for markets to function, even though the use of money enormously facilitates their working. Rush-hour drivers who look for space, fill it up, and thereby continuously shift the relative value of the options that they all perceive exemplify a market. College students looking for courses to take and departments thinking of courses to offer are participating in a market process, too.

Some markets, like stock markets and commodity markets, are "well organized," which means that the bids and offers of prospective buyers and sellers are rather comprehensively assembled, so that a single price for a fairly uniform good tends to be established for all transactions over a wide geographic area. Other markets, like the market that even the least practiced eye can see operating in a singles bar, are much less well organized: the precise good to be exchanged and the terms of the exchange have to be negotiated for each separate transaction. The market for used furniture is relatively unorganized: transactions take place at prices that vary greatly, because buyers and sellers are not in extensive contact. The market for retail groceries, on the other hand, is far along toward the well-organized end of the spectrum, so that hamburger prices will vary much less over a given area than will used furniture prices.

It is sometimes said that stock markets and commodity markets are more nearly "perfect" than retail grocery markets and used furniture markets. This is a misleading way to describe the difference, because it implies that the latter markets ought to be changed (perfection is better than imperfection). Such a recommendation makes sense, however, only if the costs of improving the markets are less than the gains from more efficient exchange made possible by the improvement. It is often the case, however, that we simply don't know of any way to improve a particular market except at costs too high to make it worthwhile. Moreover, some efforts to "improve" markets through government action look suspiciously like efforts to promote special interests.

But in every case the relationships between buyers and sellers, whether constant and extensive or sporadic and scattered, generate prices of some sort: terms of trade. Each such price is a piece of potentially valuable information to other people about available opportunities. The more such prices there are, the more clearly and precisely they are stated, and the more widely they are known, the greater will be the range of opportunities available to people in the society.

The range of available opportunities expands when restaurants pos[t] their menus outside.

Information and Wealth

Because markets exist, the range of opportunities available to decision makers expands. And that is a way of saying that wealth increases or that economic growth occurs. Is that not what we finally mean by an increase in wealth? A wider range of available opportunities? The freedom and the power to do more of what we want to do? Once again we urge you not to confine your understanding and application of all this to what most people rather arbitrarily call "the economic area" of life. Information about what others are willing to do and under what circumstances is important in any area of life where social cooperation is desired. Clear and precise information does not guarantee effective cooperation, but it does make cooperation far easier to achieve. "I didn't realize that you were willing . . ." is the opening line in the often-repeated story of opportunities missed, a story that we would hear even more frequently were it not for the fact that we *never* find out about most of the opportunities that we lose through lack of information.

Summing up: information about available opportunities is valuable. Good information is often hard to come by. Markets generate vast quantities of clear and accurate information about available opportunities. Middlemen, brokers, and professional traders are specialists in the organization of markets and hence in the creation of valuable information. They presumably specialize in this way because they think they have a comparative advantage in information production. Whatever their motives, however, they provide services on which we all depend for our well-being far more than we realize.

That is one side of the coin. The other side is that we don't realize how important these functions are, largely because we have trouble seeing that information really is scarce. This blind spot frequently leads us to impose legal restrictions on traders whenever we don't like the information they're providing. It's a version of the old tale about the king who punishes the messengers who bring him unpleasant news. Kings who behave in this way deny themselves useful information. So do citizens who use the law to prohibit exchange or harass traders in ignorance of their functions.

What remedy would we prescribe for someone who has noticed that fire trucks are always present when buildings burn and therefore proposes to prevent fires by banning fire trucks from the streets? We would probably recommend a closer attention to cause and effect. Speculators are frequent victims of just this kind of public misunderstanding. We'll try to make the analysis of the preceding paragraphs more

concrete by examining the functions of speculators in
our society.

Varieties of Speculation

The dictionary defines speculation as "trading in the hope of
profit from changes in the market price." That's good enough
for our purposes. The most celebrated (or, more accurately,
the most vilified) speculator is the "bear" of Wall Street, who
"sells short"—that is, sells for future delivery shares of
stock not actually owned at the time of sale. This speculator
believes that the stock will go down in price, so that when the
time comes for delivery of the shares, they can be purchased
at a low price and sold at the previously agreed-upon
higher price.

A more important speculator is probably the commodity
speculator, who may trade in such items as wheat, soybeans,
hogs, lumber, sugar, cocoa, or copper. This kind of speculator
buys and sells "futures." These are agreements to deliver,
at some specified date in the future, amounts of a commodity
at a price determined now.

These are the spectacular speculators whose feats make
the financial pages. A less-publicized speculator is you
yourself. You are buying education now, partly in the hope
that it will increase the value of the labor services you'll be
selling in the future. But the future price of your services
could turn out to be too low to justify your present
investment.

Another familiar speculator is the consumer who reads
that the price of sugar is expected to rise and responds by
loading the pantry with a two-year supply. If the price of sugar
rises far enough, these sugar hoarders gain. If it does not,
they lose. Their wealth has been tied up in sugar, cluttering
the pantry shelves and blocking the opportunity to purchase
more valuable assets—an interest-bearing savings account,
for example.

The motorist who fills the gas tank at the sight of a sign
advertising gasoline at two cents a gallon less than the usual
price is speculating; the price may be four cents lower two
blocks ahead. The motorist who drives on an almost empty
tank in hope of lower prices up ahead is a notorious speculator.
And the motorists who continually "top" their tanks when
gasoline supplies are rumored to be short are surely
speculators.

But many people overlook that they themselves are
speculators, heaping blame on the "profiteers" who allegedly
"take advantage" of special situations and innocent people

in pursuit of their own unprincipled profit. Are speculators really the enemies of the people they are so often alleged to be?

Consequences of Speculation

It is often said that speculators exploit natural disasters by
driving up prices before the disaster occurs. And sometimes
the expected disaster never even materializes. That is true.
But it is only one small and misleading part of the truth.
Suppose evidence begins to accumulate in early summer
that corn-leaf blight is spreading to major corn-producing areas
of the Midwest. A significant percentage of the year's corn
crop could be wiped out as a result. People who think this is
likely to occur will consequently expect a higher price for
corn next year. This expectation will induce some people to
pull some corn away from current consumption in order
to carry it over into the next crop period when, they believe,
the price will be higher. That is speculation.

Many different parties engage in such speculation: farmers
substitute other livestock feed for corn in order to maintain
their corn stocks at a higher level, either to avoid having
to buy corn next year at a higher price or to sell it then at the
higher price; industrial users increase their inventories now
while the price is relatively low; and traders who might
not know a bushel of corn from a peck of soybeans try to
make a profit from buying cheap now and selling dear later.
There are well-organized commodity markets to facilitate
this kind of transaction, in which people can buy or sell
"futures"—contracts for future delivery of commodities at
prices agreed upon now. The effect of all these activities is to
reduce the current supply of corn; the price consequently
rises. And just as the critic protested, it rises before the disaster
occurs.

But that is only a part of the picture. These speculative
activities cause corn to be transported *over time* from a period
of relative abundance to one of greater scarcity. The price
next year, when the blight is expected to have its effects, will
therefore be lower than it otherwise would be. Speculators
thus even out the flow of commodities into consumption and
diminish price fluctuations over time. Since price fluctuations
create risks for those who grow or use corn, speculators are
actually reducing risk to others. More accurately, they are
purchasing risk, in hope of a profit, from others less willing to
take risk and willing to pay something in the form of reduced
expected returns to avoid it. (Those who choose to sell risk
are called *hedgers*.)

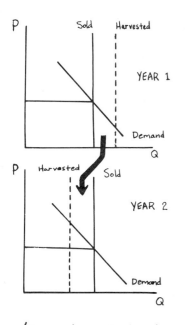

Storage in good year for sale
in bad year stabilizes the
price.

All this assumes, however, that the speculators are correct in
their anticipations. What if an unusually large crop appears
instead? Then the speculators are transporting corn from
a period of lesser to a period of greater abundance and thereby
magnifying price fluctuations. This is clearly a misallocation
of resources, involving as it does the giving up now of some
high-priced corn for the sake of obtaining later an equal
amount of low-priced corn. That doesn't help other people.

But neither is it profitable for the speculators! They will
sustain losses where they had hoped for gains. We should
not expect them, consequently, to behave in this fashion *except
as a result of ignorance.* Are speculators likely to be ignorant?

No one is omniscient. And speculators make mistakes.
(Why would they otherwise be called speculators?) But
living as we do in an uncertain world, we have no option but
to act in the presence of uncertainty. We can't escape
uncertainty and the consequences of ignorance by refusing to
act or to think about the future. And if we think we know
more than the speculators, we can counter them at a profit by
betting against them. It is interesting and somewhat revealing
to note that those who criticize speculators for misreading
the future rarely give effective expression to their own supposedly greater insight by entering the market against them.
Hindsight, of course, is always in copious supply—and the
price is appropriately low.

As we have repeatedly tried to show, information is a
scarce good. Better information means greater efficiency because it provides a wider range of opportunities and hence
expanded scope for the exploitation of comparative advantage.
Speculators provide information. Their offers to buy and sell
express their judgments concerning the future in relation
to the present. The prices generated by their activities are, like
all prices, indexes of value: information for decision makers
on present and future opportunity costs. This information is at
least as important to conservatives as it is to gamblers. It is
true that the information they provide is "bad" information
whenever the speculators are wrong. But harping on this
is again a case of comparing one situation with a better but
unattainable situation. If we think we can read the future
better than the speculators, we are free to express our
convictions with money, profit from our insight, and benefit
other people in the process.

Meanwhile, those whose ordinary business activities
involve them in the use of commodities that are speculatively
traded do make effective use of the information generated
by the speculators. Farmers consult the prices predicted in the

A farmer who sells September corn futures when he plants in May is hedging -- transferring the risk of price changes to speculators.

A corn chip maker hedges by buying corn futures.

commodity exchanges and so do industrial users. And those who use goods not ordinarily thought of as speculative commodities also take advantage of the information generated by speculators. For we all use prices as information, and prices reflect competing bids and offers inevitably based to a large extent on a (speculative!) reading of the future.

A substantial part of the public's distrust and dislike of speculators is probably grounded in a suspicion that speculators take advantage of information from which they have no right to profit. The problems created by scarce information and consequent uncertainty are often complicated by this sort of disagreement about specific rights and obligations. What do buyers have a right to know? What do suppliers have an obligation to reveal? What constitutes an unfair advantage with respect to information? And who ought to be responsible for acquiring and disseminating important information about products? We can't begin to answer all these questions. But we may be able to clarify some of the issues and options by thinking through a few specific problems created by the scarcity of information.

The Decline of *Caveat Emptor*

Let's look first at the decline of the *caveat emptor* doctrine and the rise of an increasingly comprehensive law of seller's liability. *Caveat emptor* means: let the buyer beware. It is a legal principle, once widely accepted by the courts, which holds that sellers can be liable only for those qualities of a product that they specifically guarantee. Beyond that, the buyer must pay the consequences of a mistaken purchase. That doctrine has now been almost totally eclipsed by *caveat venditor*: let the seller beware. Buyers increasingly are receiving the legal right to demand compensation from sellers for any deficiency in the product, including deficiencies of which the seller is not aware and even some deficiencies created by improper buyer use of the product. The buyer of a rotary lawnmower who cuts off a finger by pulling grass from the mower while it is running may be able to extract financial compensation from the manufacturer by arguing that there wasn't an adequate warning, or that the mower should have been designed so that its user couldn't do such a foolish thing.

What consequences can we predict from an evolution of the law in this direction? People respond to the costs that they expect to bear. If sellers must pay for foolish actions by buyers, they will attempt to prevent foolish actions. How? By selling only foolproof products. Should we applaud? The trouble is that foolproof products will be very expensive products. When mattress manufacturers are allowed to sell

only mattresses that cannot be ignited by a lighted cigarette, everyone who buys a new mattress must pay for a quality that is useful only to the small minority that falls asleep while holding lit cigarettes. That helps a few, but harms many more.

Sellers have a cost advantage in the generation of a great deal of information about products and in the creation of many product safeguards; but with other kinds of information and safeguards the comparative advantage will lie with buyers. If *caveat emptor* once compelled buyers to take high-cost actions to protect themselves, *caveat venditor* is now compelling sellers to take some precautions for which buyers could undoubtedly find much less costly substitutes.

Physicians and Malpractice Suits

The furor over malpractice suits against physicians and the rise in the cost of malpractice insurance raises similar questions. Malpractice once meant negligent or improper action by a physician that resulted in death or injury to the patient. Increasingly today it means making a mistake, any mistake at all that results in harm to the patient, even if the physician's diagnosis and treatment satisfied the highest standards of currently acceptable medical procedures. Where will this take us?

If physicians are held liable for malpractice whenever they make a mistake, they will try even harder to avoid making mistakes. Isn't that what we want? Not altogether. We actually *want* physicians to accept the risk of making mistakes when the cost to the patient of avoiding mistakes becomes greater than the cost of committing them. Forget about money costs, which tend to introduce irrelevant emotions into the discussion, and simply set pain against pain and death against death. How many tests should a physician perform before settling on a diagnosis? Each additional test reduces the probability of pain or death from a particular disease but also entails pain and risk of its own. Would you want to submit to a spinal tap to be certain you don't have an obscure but fatal disease never yet found outside the island of Madura in the Java Sea?

The common contention that even the smallest risk of death is too great to accept simply makes no sense. It might make sense if risk could always be avoided without incurring new risks. That isn't the case, however. It only appears to be the case to those who concentrate on just one risk at a time. The harsh-sounding truth is that some ways of prolonging life are not worth the cost. The apparent harshness of that statement disappears when we recall that resources used

Using resources to prevent premature death in one way makes those resources unavailable to prevent premature death in other ways.

in one way to reduce the number of probable deaths are not available for use in other ways that could possibly prevent even more premature deaths.

It also helps to remember that we're dealing with probabilities and uncertainty. If the highway department uses the rest of its budget to straighten out Deadman's Curve, where five people die each year, and consequently leaves uncorrected the Lake Road grade crossing, where three people die each year, the department does *not* thereby "sentence three people to death." No particular persons must die because of the highway department's decision. And any driver who wants to get through that crossing safely has the option to stop, look, and listen. It may in fact be much more productive of "saved lives" in this case to take dollars out of highway improvements and put them into warning signs, thereby increasing the responsibility of buyers (drivers) for their own safety and reducing the responsibility of suppliers (highway builders).

We shall venture into one more issue to conclude this discussion of efficiency in the production of information: the question of advertising.

Is Full Disclosure Possible?

Some advertising disseminates valuable information. Even the most fervent foe of advertising will concede that at least the Yellow Pages provide people with information that extends the range of their opportunities. Some advertising is a deliberate attempt to deceive and succeeds in its purpose. The most fervent fan of advertising will concede that there are a few bad apples in the barrel. But what about most advertising? Does it inform? Persuade? Manipulate? Misinform? Where does it fit on the continuum from informative (and therefore wealth-creating) to deceptive (and therefore wealth-reducing)?

A lot of people's lives would be simpler, although perhaps less interesting, if a thick, dark line could always be drawn between informative and deceptive advertising. One reason that such a line cannot be drawn is that information is not a simple matter of words. Telling people doesn't necessarily inform them. They can fail to understand, not believe, not be listening, not care, or not remember. In addressing any large group you will always find that some have forgotten what you said before others have understood, and that some still won't care enough to listen when others have stopped listening out of boredom. Moreover, what is valuable information to one person will often be mere noise to another, and if you try to tell everybody what they want to know, you may generate so much static that no one learns anything from

Is "full disclosure" possible if some are not paying attention?

your communication. If you try to avoid deceiving some, you will in the process fail to provide others with information they wanted to have.

"Full disclosure," consequently, is an illusion. It may be a useful ideal. On the other hand, it could be a dangerous delusion if it encourages us to believe that someone or some procedure can infallibly protect us from misinformation.

Once Over Lightly

An opportunity of which you're unaware is not a real opportunity. Information is therefore a valuable resource, whose possession enables people to increase their wealth.

Information is a scarce good whose production usually entails costs. The efficient decision maker accumulates additional information only so long as the anticipated marginal benefit is greater than the marginal cost.

A great deal of economic activity is best understood as a response to the fact that information is a scarce good. The much-abused "middleman" is in large part a specialist in information production. Just as the real-estate broker enables prospective buyers and sellers to locate one another, so the typical retailer provides customers with knowledge of the goods sellers are offering and brings sellers into contact with those who want the sellers' offerings.

The common habit of viewing the middleman as an unproductive bandit on the highway of trade stems from the erroneous assumption that information is a free good.

Everyone who makes a decision in the absence of complete information about the future consequences of all available opportunities is a speculator. So everyone is a speculator.

People who think they know more than others about the relationship between present and future scarcities will want to buy in one time period for sale in the other. If they are correct, they make a profit on their superior insight and also transport goods through time from periods of lesser to greater scarcity. If they're wrong in their predictions, they perversely move goods from periods of greater to lesser scarcity and suffer the penalty of a personal loss on their transactions.

Because prices are summary indicators of scarcity, they are valuable information. Those whose buying and selling activities create prices are generating information that is useful to others.

The cost of producing information is not the same for everyone. People will specialize in the production of those kinds of information in which they have a comparative advantage.

A person who is able to shift the full cost of mistakes onto others has little incentive to gather information before acting. A person who is compelled to bear the full cost of mistakes committed by others will attempt to keep them from committing mistakes. Avoiding mistakes is also costly, but people will tend to slight the costs that they themselves don't have to bear.

QUESTIONS FOR DISCUSSION

1. Here is a criticism of shopkeepers and other middlemen written several centuries ago that still finds echoes today. "Their meer handing of Goods one to another, no more increases any Wealth in the Province, than Persons at a Fire increase the Water in a Pail, by passing it thro' Twenty or Forty hands."
   (a) Why would persons at a fire bother to pass a pail of water through forty hands if doing so increased no one's wealth?
   (b) It's true that the physical quantity of water is not increased when the water changes hands (some will even be spilled), just as the physical quantity of goods is not increased by the transactions of middlemen. But what about the *value* of the water and of the middleman's goods?
   (c) Does wealth depend on physical quantities or on valuations?
2. Evaluate the following paragraph from a newspaper article:

   One sure way to save money on groceries is to eliminate the middleman by buying directly from farmers and other suppliers. This is what a group of socially motivated and normally hungry people have decided to do by forming a grocery cooperative.

3. If you found that you could reduce your bills for new clothing 10 percent by buying exclusively from catalogs, would you do it? Why would some people be unwilling to take advantage of this "saving"? What do people do when they "go shopping"?
4. You find out in late December that you can probably make $1000 on a business deal if you can gain the goodwill of a client by getting him two tickets to the Super Bowl game. You manage to buy two well-located seats from a scalper for $250. Were you cheated by the scalper? Or are you glad that scalpers exist? Why do so many people intensely dislike scalpers?
5. Students frequently complain about the low prices the campus bookstore pays for used texts. Why then do they sell to the bookstore? Is it true that they cannot find a buyer on their own? Or is it more true that they are unwilling to go to the trouble (incur the cost) of finding a buyer on their own? What useful service does the college bookstore perform in handling used texts? Can you be sure it's a genuine service and not just a "rip-off"?
6. Would you expect prices for goods of similar quality offered in garage sales to vary more than prices for goods offered in regular retail outlets? Why? Do the differences in prices mean that someone is being cheated, or that someone is taking unfair advantage of someone else?

7. A man approaches you in a busy airport terminal, shows you a handsome wristwatch, which he says is worth $135, and offers to let you have it for $25. Would you buy it? Would you be more willing to buy it if you had better information? What do you "know" when you buy a watch from an established local jeweler that you do not know in this situation?

8. Have you ever tested your butcher's scales to be sure they are accurate? How do you know you aren't being consistently short-weighted?

9. Why does a new car lose so much of its value in the first year? Is it because Americans have an irrational attachment to cars that are new rather than used?

    (a) Which year-old car is more likely to be on the used-car market: one that performed handsomely for its owner or one that had to be taken in regularly for repairs during its first year?

    (b) Which set of vehicles being offered for sale will contain a larger percentage of vehicles with defects known to the seller but unknown to the buyer: new cars or year-old cars?

    (c) What does all this imply about the prices sellers are willing to accept and that buyers are willing to offer for year-old cars, relative to what they would be if all buyers and sellers had complete information?

10. Suppose that you are leaving tomorrow for a two-week combined business and vacation trip to a distant location. You'll be traveling by plane.

    (a) In what way are you speculating as you pack your suitcase?

    (b) On which side would you be more inclined to err—taking too many clothes and having to haul heavy suitcases around, or taking too few and finding yourself without an item you want?

    (c) Would your answer to the previous question differ according to whether you were planning to be in a large city or a remote resort?

    (d) Suppose you take only a single pair of dress shoes and accidentally spill ink on one of them just before an important business meeting. You dash out quickly and buy a new pair of shoes. Explain how the shoe seller's willingness to take a risk reduced your risk in taking only a single pair of dress shoes.

11. The June 18, 1979, issue of *Time* magazine contained an article on hoarding in the United States in which a number of social scientists were quoted. A sociologist said that gasoline hoarding was not rational but rather a result of Americans' emotional stake in their cars. A historian said hoarding was an absolutely typical American trait. Some attributed hoarding to a "shortage psychosis," and others spoke of "panic buying." Another sociologist said that strong leadership was required to stop such "competitive behavior."

    (a) How could we decide whether hoarding is irrational, psychotic, a national character trait, a product of emotion and panic, *or* an intelligent response to uncertainty?

    (b) What is the difference between hoarding and maintaining an appropriate level of inventory?

    (c) Why do both business firms and households maintain inventories? How do they decide on the proper level of inventories for particular goods?

12. Are you speculating when you buy fire insurance on your home? Could you save money by getting together with your friends to form an insurance cooperative, thereby eliminating the necessity of paying something to a

middleman (the insurance company)? What kinds of useful information do insurance companies provide?

13. Does a policy of protecting people against losses due to their own mistakes make those mistakes more frequent and the losses consequently greater?
    (a) Will insured houses have more fires than uninsured houses, other things being equal? Why?
    (b) Would people take more effective precautions against theft of their automobiles if insurance companies stopped selling policies that offered compensation for losses due to theft?
    (c) Why is it so much easier to purchase insurance against loss due to fire than against loss due to being laid off or discharged from one's job?
    (d) People who work in jobs covered by unemployment compensation do have some of the benefits of insurance against job loss. Do you think that this causes people to be laid off or discharged more often?

14. You decide in May that the coming summer's corn crop will be much larger and the fall corn price consequently much lower than most people expect.
    (a) To act on your beliefs, should you buy or should you sell December corn futures? (*Futures* are contracts to buy or sell at a future date at a price established now.)
    (b) If a substantial number of knowledgeable people come to share your opinion about the size of this summer's crop, what will happen to the price of December corn futures?
    (c) What information will this change in the price of corn futures convey to current holders and users of corn?
    (d) How will this information affect their decisions about holding corn for future sale or use?
    (e) How will these decisions, based on the information provided by the change in the price of December corn futures, affect June consumption?
    (f) Can speculators carry a bumper crop *backward in time* from a period of lesser to a period of greater scarcity?

15. The *Wall Street Journal* published two articles in the winter of 1985 on food and famine in Sudan and Ethiopia. One was titled "The Tragedy of Sudan's Spreading Starvation Is That It's Caused by Man's Errors, Not Nature's" (January 22, 1985); the other was headed "Getting Excess U.S. Food to World's Hungry Is Complicated by Politics and Bureaucracy" (March 14, 1985).
    (a) The former article said that the government in Sudan "has had to impose credit restrictions to stop banks from financing speculators hoping to profit from the misery." It also quoted a relief specialist working in the Sudan who claimed that assistance always came too late and who called for "a system of advance warning and standby funds." Don't speculators provide a system of advance warning? Do speculators who "profit from . . . misery" create the misery from which they profit or add to it? Or do they alleviate the misery from which they profit?
    (b) The article also described wasteful crosshauling of food: trucks taking food from A to B passed other trucks hauling food from B to A. It also said that the U.S. stopped selling food and began giving it away when British charitable organizations protested that the policy of selling the

food was depriving those who needed it most. A U.S. official said that the selling policy was instituted at the urging of local governments "who didn't want local markets disrupted," but the U.S. agreed nonetheless to change the policy. Do you see a connection between disruption of local markets and wasteful crosshauling or other delays in getting contributed food from dockside to hungry mouths?

(c) Suppose that the U.S. government and all other contributors to famine relief were to distribute among the starving people the money that had been contributed, and let these people purchase food for themselves. Do you think food would more quickly and surely get into the hands of hungry people under such a system than under one in which Western relief organizations try to handle the distribution of the food itself?

(d) Those who condemn shopkeepers and other middlemen as worthless, wasteful, and wicked seem to be saying that the physical distribution of valuable goods is not a difficult social problem to handle once the goods have been produced. The African nations that have instituted capital punishment for those who speculate in food supplies seem to be saying the same thing. The two articles cited suggest otherwise. But would you want to be a merchant participating in a food distribution system when a charge of speculating or profiteering could result in the death penalty?

16. A construction company signs a contract in January with a developer calling for the completion of 100 houses by the end of October at a price fixed in the contract. The construction company wants to protect itself against the possibility of sizeable increases in the price of lumber that could wipe out any profit on the transaction. The Chicago Mercantile Exchange offers an opportunity to buy or sell lumber futures, which are contracts calling for the delivery in specified future months of 130,000 board feet of spruce, pine, or fir at a price agreed upon now. A lumber futures contract is available that calls for July delivery.

(a) Would the construction company want to buy or to sell July lumber futures when it signs the construction contract in January?

(b) Suppose that July lumber futures are trading in January at $150 per 1000 board feet. When July arrives, construction lumber has risen in price to $165 per 1000 board feet. As a result, the construction company will have to pay 10 percent more for lumber than it expected to pay. How will it use its futures contracts to offset this loss?

(c) Suppose the price of lumber had fallen to $135 instead of rising to $165. Why will this not result in an unexpectedly large profit for the construction company on its contract with the developer?

17. Suppose you are in your car trying to make a left turn across heavy traffic on a busy highway. You plan to turn as soon as the large truck coming toward you has passed. But then you notice that there is a long line of cars following the truck. You make an instant decision and turn in front of the truck.

Assume you saved 2 minutes by turning at that time rather than waiting for the whole line of traffic to clear, that you value your time at $6 an hour, and there was a probability of .0001 that your car would stall and the truck

would be unable to stop so that you would be killed. What was the implicit value that you placed on avoiding the collision when you decided to turn? Would it be correct to say that this is the implicit maximum value you assign to your own life?

18. A letter to the editor of an urban newspaper, criticizing as "foolhardy" a fatal attempt by a Japanese mountain climber to make a solo ascent of Mt. McKinley in the winter, concluded with this sentence: "Safe mountaineering is and always should be the bottom line." What is "safe mountaineering"?

19. My neighbor is an orthopedic surgeon who enjoys building things out of wood. He purchased a power saw to reduce the time he had to spend cutting lumber. But he subsequently decided that he didn't want to risk an accident and sold the saw to me. Since he is a more careful worker than I am, the probability that he would have severed a finger using the saw is less than the probability that I will do so. Nonetheless, I am willing to take the risk while he is not. Use the concept of opportunity cost to explain the difference in our attitudes toward the hazards of using power saws.

20. When a manufacturing firm cuts costs in an overseas plant by adopting occupational safety standards that are more lax than the standards governing its domestic operations, is it exploiting its foreign employees? Why might potential workers in a very poor country be willing, even eager, to accept workplace hazards that workers would not accept in a wealthier country? Who is harmed and therefore most likely to protest the adoption of less-strict workplace safety standards in the operation of overseas plants?

21. If the Food and Drug Administration prolongs the testing period for new drugs in order to protect consumers against threats to their life and health from the premature introduction of drugs with unknown but dangerous side effects, will it actually succeed in protecting consumers? What is the threat to life and health that the FDA thereby increases?

22. A commissioner of the Food and Drug Administration said that, although he was willing to weigh health risks against health benefits in formulating commission rulings, he was absolutely opposed to weighing health risks against economic factors. Evaluate this statement.

23. We can reduce the probability that children will die from accidentally swallowing large quantities of drugs by requiring drug dispensers to provide containers with child-resistant caps on request. Can we further reduce that probability by prohibiting the dispensation of drugs except in containers with child-resistant caps? What will drug purchasers do who have difficulty opening these caps, such as people with arthritis, if they are not allowed to purchase prescription drugs in containers with caps that are easy to open?

24. Should commercial air travel be 100 percent safe? If this is impossible, how safe should we try to make it? What are some of the costs of making air travel safer? Who will bear these costs? If passengers must pay higher ticket prices to cover additional airline safety procedures, and as a result some choose to drive rather than fly, have we actually increased the safety of travelers?

25. In the autumn of 1981 authorities in the Soviet Union raised the price of vodka in an attempt to reduce alcoholism. Two years later they lowered the price again, reportedly in order to stop the increase in the incidence of alcohol

poisoning. What general rule is illustrated by this case, the case of the child-resistant medicine caps, and the case of overly safe airplane travel?

26. The Securities and Exchange Commission prohibits "insider trading" in the stocks of corporations. This is defined as trading on the basis of information that has not yet been made public but is only available to those who are "inside" the corporation. The basic argument in support of the insider-trading rule is that it isn't fair for insiders to take advantage of information others don't yet have.

    (a) Why is this unfair? Who is harmed by insider trading? How are they harmed?

    (b) One approach to this issue is to define insiders as agents of others whose interests the insiders are supposed to promote. "Insider-trading" by this definition amounts to a betrayal of trust. Would this cover the case of a government official who purchased land along a new highway that the state was going to construct, if he learned about the state's plans through his job and bought before the information became public?

    (c) How would you regard the case of a research scientist who buys shares in the corporation for which he works because he thinks his research is about to yield a very profitable product for the company?

27. Walter Wriston, former chairman of Citicorp, argued in an address to the American Society of Newspaper Editors that the government was suppressing information or censoring the news when it tried to prohibit firms from posting higher prices. He argued that firms don't so much raise prices as announce that prices have gone up. In what sense are price controls a form of censorship?

28. Since the Bill of Rights in the U.S. Constitution prohibits government from censoring the promises of political candidates, however absurd or irresponsible, why doesn't it afford the same protection to commercial advertisements? Is it because deceptive commercial claims do more damage to the society and its members than do deceptive political claims? Is it because citizens can more easily and effectively evaluate political claims on their own, but need considerable protection against deceptive claims for commercial products? If neither of these seems an adequate explanation for the difference, what explanation would you suggest?

Price Setting and the Question of Monopoly

The term *administered prices* was first introduced to public discussion in the 1930s in order to make a distinction between prices that were set by supply and demand and prices supposedly set unilaterally by sellers. Since that time the term has been widely used, especially by those who believe that the U.S. economic system is dominated by large corporations. Some critics have accused professional economists of ignoring the role of administered prices in the American economy, and of pretending that prices are all set by supply and demand. According to most of these critics, the American economy is today largely controlled by monopolists and oligopolists, who pay no attention to supply and demand, but instead use their market power to manipulate prices according to their own selfish and narrow interests.

It is impossible to evaluate any of these claims without first obtaining a clearer notion of what is meant by such terms as *administered prices* and *monopolist*. We have consciously steered around these issues as much as we could in the preceding chapters. The tactic that usually enabled us to do so was the implicit assumption that there were so many buyers and sellers in any market at which we were looking that none of them had any power to affect the price through individual action. It is now time to look more closely at issues that have been bypassed.

Who Qualifies as a Monopolist?

We begin with the word *monopoly*, the product of two Greek words meaning "sole seller." Are there any monopolists in

that strict sense of the word? Try to think of something that is sold exclusively by one seller.

Local telephone service suggests itself as a good example. But is it an accurate example? There were many independent sellers of telephone service in the United States, as a matter of fact, even before the breakup of AT&T in 1984. Still, that may be beside the point. For any given buyer there is typically only one seller, since telephone companies usually enjoy exclusive selling privileges in particular areas. On the other hand, buyers don't have to live in a given area; they can move to another franchise area if they prefer the product there. Back comes a justifiably impatient snort: "That's irrelevant." But it's not completely irrelevant. Moving your residence may be a prohibitively expensive way to shift your telephone patronage, and it's hard to imagine people actually moving just because they resent the local phone company. But that *is* a way of obtaining a substitute product. And by its absurdity, our example calls attention to the crux of the problem: the availability of substitutes.

Suppose we redefine the commodity sold by telephone companies and call it "communication services." There would be nothing intrinsically misleading about that. After all, that is why anyone wants a telephone: to obtain communication services. But if this is the product being sold, the telephone company is clearly *not* a monopolist, but rather a seller in competition with Western Union, the post office, various messenger and delivery services, loud shouting, fast running, and all sorts of computer communication techniques. The point of all this is simply that, if we define the commodity broadly enough, not a single commodity in the country is sold by a monopolist.

Now let's look at the other side of the coin. Suppose we define the commodity very narrowly. If telegrams are not the same thing as telephone calls, neither is a gallon of milk at the little store next door the same thing as a gallon of milk three blocks away at the supermarket. If you have no car, are rocking a screaming baby who won't stop until fed, and have no one to leave the baby with, the milk three blocks away is a vividly different commodity from the milk at the store next door. Ask any parent of a small baby. Thus we are forced to conclude that, when the commodity is defined narrowly enough, every seller is a monopolist, since no two sellers will ever be offering completely identical products.

We're trying to convince you that the word *monopoly* is extraordinarily ambiguous. For everyone or no one is a sole seller depending on how we define the commodity being sold. Furthermore, there is no satisfactory way to decide in all cases just how broadly or narrowly the concept of a commodity ought to be defined. The Supreme Court of the United

States has sometimes listened to persuasive arguments on both sides of a contested definition and then divided in its decision. Take cellophane, for example. Is it a separate commodity or should it be put in the category "flexible wrapping materials"? The answer given in cases such as this may determine whether a manufacturer is convicted under federal antimonopoly laws.

Alternatives, Elasticity, and Market Power

So let's try another approach. What would be so bad about a sole seller if we found one? The telephone company hints at the answer when it advertises: "We may be the only phone company in town, but we try not to act like it." If we find a case where there really is a sole seller, the customer will have no alternatives. No one wants to be without alternatives. The poorer our alternatives, the weaker our position and the more easily we can be taken advantage of.

But we learned in Chapter 2 that there are always some alternatives. There is a substitute for anything, even the services of the local telephone company. After all, no one "needs" a telephone. On the other hand, a phone is a valued convenience for many families and business firms. The concept from economics that suggests itself is price elasticity of demand.

No seller is a monopolist in the strictest sense of the word because there is no such thing as a *perfectly* inelastic demand. No seller has any buyer totally over the barrel. On the other hand, very few sellers of anything face perfectly elastic demand curves. Anything less than complete elasticity means that sellers will retain some business when they raise their price, which in turn implies that sellers have at least a morsel of market power. Where is the line between a morsel and monopoly?

There is no clear line of demarcation unless we decide to draw one arbitrarily. Elasticities of demand reflect the availability of substitutes; other things remaining equal, the more good substitutes there are for anything, the more elastic will be the demand for it. Market power is thus seen to be a matter of degree and to be inversely related to elasticity of demand. Defined in this way, the term *market power* has a meaning that we can talk about and use. But we have not yet found a useful definition for the word *monopoly*.

Privileges and Restrictions

Let's try another approach. In the early nineteenth century there was often no distinction made in the United States between a monopoly and a corporation. The reason was

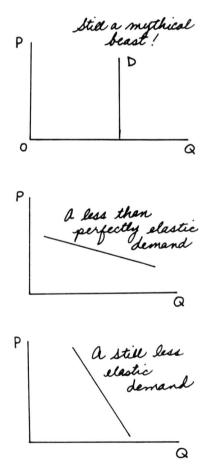

that corporations had always been created by special governmental acts. They received, whether from Crown and Parliament before the Revolution or from state and national legislatures afterward, special "patents," as they were called: official documents granting rights and privileges not available to others. Corporate charters were therefore called "grants of monopoly," since they gave to one party a power that was withheld from others. The East India Company was such a "monopoly," and the special privilege of selling tea in the colonies, given to it in 1773, helped bring on the American Revolution.

Here is another and quite different meaning of monopoly, one related to acts of the state. If the state allows some to engage in an activity but prosecutes others for doing so, or if it taxes or restricts some sellers but not others, or if it grants protection or assistance to some while compelling others to make their own way unaided, the state is creating exclusive privileges. This meaning for the word *monopoly* has contemporary relevance as well as historical significance.

Many business organizations operate with monopoly grants of this kind. In the name of all sorts of commendable-sounding goals—public safety, fair competition, stability, national security, efficiency—governments at all levels have imposed restrictions upon entry into various industries or trades. The beneficiaries of these restrictions always include the parties who can escape them. These parties will rarely admit that they enjoy a grant of monopoly power. But the effect of the restrictions nonetheless is to prevent some from competing who would otherwise do so.

We are not saying that restrictions on entry into a market are always to be condemned, or that the businesses which benefit necessarily behave badly afterward, or that consumers can never be better off as a consequence of restrictions on competition. We are only concerned that the restrictions be noted so that their consequences can be evaluated. They will often turn out to be different from what most people assume. We could, if we wished, use the word *monopolist* to describe any individual or organization operating with the advantage of special privileges granted by the government. The trouble is that most people no longer use the word in this way. By such a definition, the postal service is a monopolist, as are most public utilities, many liquor stores, morticians, and crop dusters; the American Medical Association, state bar associations, and labor unions; farmers with acreage allotments, licensed barbers, and most taxicab firms. The list is long indeed.

And so we are going to take the heroic step of dropping the word *monopoly* from our working vocabulary. Its meanings are too many and too vague. "'When I use a word,' Humpty

Dumpty said in a rather scornful tone, 'it means just what I choose it to mean—neither more nor less.'" *Monopoly* is a favorite word of contemporary Humpty Dumpties. And that's why we are not going to employ it. We shall try to use alternative terms that are more likely to communicate the precise situation we have in mind.

Price Takers and Price Searchers

Let's go back now to the phrase with which this chapter began: administered prices. Is there a distinction between administered prices and prices that are set by supply and demand?

It's a free country, as they say, and businesses are usually free to set their own prices. The USX Corporation (formerly United States Steel) has substantial discretion when it prints its price lists, and a wheat farmer from Kansas can feel quite safe from the threat of prosecution if he decides to offer his crop at $5.00 per bushel. But there is obviously an important difference that helps to explain why USX hires people to decide what its prices should be and wheat farmers do not. The difference, we shall nonetheless insist, is a difference of degree, not kind.

Take the case of the wheat farmer first. If he consults the financial pages of his newspaper or tunes in for the noonday market reports, he will find that number 2 ordinary hard Kansas City wheat opened at $3.43¾ a bushel. That news may disappoint or delight him, but there is almost nothing he can do to change it. If he decides that the price is an excellent one, and sells his entire crop for immediate delivery, the market will feel scarcely a ripple. Even if he is one of the biggest wheat farmers in the state, he is still such a small part of the total number of those offering to buy or sell wheat that he cannot affect the price. The difference between what the closing price will be if he sells all his crop, and what it will be if he sells only half of it, will not be as much as ¼ cent.

Economists therefore call the wheat farmer a *price taker*. He cannot affect the price by his own actions. The price at the local grain elevator is determined by the actions of many buyers and sellers all over the country. If the farmer exercises his legal right to put a price tag on his wheat 2 cents higher than the market decrees, he will sell no wheat. And since he can sell all the wheat he has at the going price, he has no incentive to offer to sell any wheat at less than the going price. Price takers face perfectly elastic demand curves, or what for all practical purposes amount to perfectly elastic demand curves. The demand curves are horizontal at the going price.

Most sellers are not in this position. They can raise their

The Demand Schedule Faced by Each Wheat Farmer

Price	Quantity Demanded (of <u>that farmer's</u> wheat)
$3.45	None at all
$3.43	All he has
$3.41	All he has

(when the market price is $3.43¾)

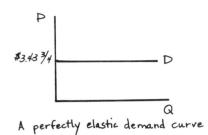

A perfectly elastic demand curve

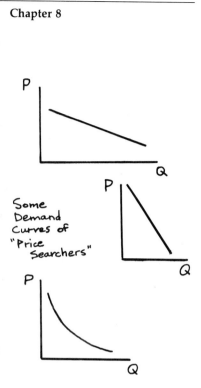

Some
Demand
Curves of
"Price
Searchers"

prices if they choose, without losing all their sales. And, unlike the farmer, they can't always sell everything they're capable of producing without lowering their prices. At higher prices they will sell less; at lower prices they will be able to sell more. They must choose a price or set of prices. Economists therefore call them *price searchers.* Torn between the desire for higher prices and the desire for larger sales, they must search out the price or set of prices most advantageous to them.

Price searchers include USX, the trustees of a private university weighing a tuition increase, the proprietor of a local grocery store, and the little boy selling lemonade on a hot afternoon. There is a long tradition in economics of referring to all price searchers as monopolists. But this is a technical use of the word that is confusing to everyone except professional economists. Since the little boy selling lemonade does not face a perfectly elastic demand curve, he is not a price taker but a price searcher. It seems silly to anyone not steeped in the history of economics to call him a monopolist. So we shall not do it. The term *price searcher* captures the situation in which we're interested. Price searchers all have some market power, but it is a matter of degree inversely related to the elasticity of the demand the seller faces.

Price Takers' Markets and "Optimal" Resource Allocation

Economists applied the disapproving term *monopolist* to what we shall call *price searcher* in large part because they wanted to emphasize the different consequences of these two types of price setting. Markets in which all buyers and sellers were price takers were graced with the approving term *competitive markets.* We want to point out the advantages they saw in price takers' markets without adopting the misleading monopolistic-competitive distinction, which erroneously implies that price searchers face no competition. To do so we shall use the graph of Figure 8A, which shows the demand and supply curves for house painters during a particular summer in the town of Pratte Falls.

The number of house-painting hours that will be demanded and supplied depends on the price per hour of house painters' services. Since people's skills in this area differ considerably, we shall simplify our exposition by assuming that each hour of service shown on the horizontal axis has been adjusted for quality. If Freddie Fumblefingers is only 40 percent as productive in an hour as the average Pratte Falls painter, he will take 2½ hours to supply "one hour" of the good shown on the graph. Betsy Brightbrush, who is three times as good as the average, supplies "one hour" of house painting every 20 minutes.

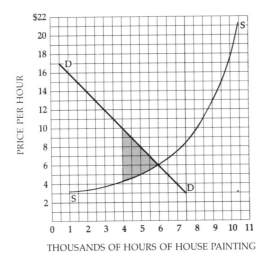

Figure 8A Demand and supply curves for house painting in Pratte Falls

The first point to remember is that supply curves are
marginal opportunity-cost curves. The curve labeled SS in
Figure 8A shows the value of all the opportunities given up as
Pratte Fallers provide progressively larger amounts of house-
painting services. The people who contribute to the lower-
left portions of the curve are people with large comparative
advantages in house painting, because they are either
extremely adept painters or extraordinarily inept at everything
else. The upper-right portion of the curve, including sections
not even shown, depicts the supply responses of those who
would have to give up a lucrative law practice to paint, who
are subject to attacks of dizziness at heights above seven feet,
or who for any other reason must sacrifice a highly valued
opportunity in order to supply an hour of house painting. Keep
in mind that the marginal-cost curve of any single individual
will also eventually slope upward to the right. The value
of the opportunities forgone as one devotes more and more
time to any particular activity is bound to increase as that
activity crowds out alternative activities, simply because people
sacrifice their least-valued opportunities first and give up
more highly valued opportunities only in response to a stronger
inducement.[1]

---

1. This hypothetical example also illustrates the fundamental similarity of
supply and demand. The people who are willing to pay up to $20 per hour to
have someone else paint their houses, and who thereby create that portion
of the demand curve below $20, may well be among the people who create the
supply curve at prices above $20. Example: "I'll pay up to $20 per hour to
get my house painted this summer. But if I have to pay more than that, I'll
do it myself." Such a person, who stops demanding and starts supplying
to himself at some high enough price may, at an even higher price, also begin
supplying to others.

If the price now settles down at $6 an hour, so that 6000 hours of the good are exchanged over the summer, the heart of many economists will leap with a special kind of joy. Why? Because at the price of $6, given the demand and supply curves, no unit of the good is being produced whose marginal opportunity cost, as represented by the supply curve, exceeds its marginal benefit, as represented by the demand curve. Moreover, every unit of the good whose marginal benefit exceeds its marginal cost is being produced. And how could we do better than that? Economists have traditionally gone so far as to call such an arrangement an *optimal allocation of resources. Optimal* means best, which is surely excessive praise; but let's look a little more closely to see exactly what's happening here.

Suppose that the people supplying those 6000 hours at $6 an hour decide that they deserve larger incomes, and somehow persuade the town council to pass a law setting $10 an hour as the minimum price for an hour of house-painting services. We'll suppose further that the law is effectively enforced. What will happen? Only 4000 hours will now be demanded. And since that's all that can be sold, that's all that will *actually* be supplied, even though, as the graph shows, painters will *want* to supply about twice that amount at a price of $10.

Establishment and enforcement of the $10 price will make some people better off and others worse off. Note that some of those who are worse off may be former house painters forced into less desirable occupations by the legislated price increase. Economists have no satisfactory way of balancing one person's gain against another person's loss to decide whether net social well-being will go up or down as the result of such a change. About all they can really do is point out that the Pratte Falls law prevents mutually advantageous exchange. The area under the demand curve between 4000 and 6000 hours represents the dollar value of what demanders are willing to give up to obtain those units of the good. The area under the supply curve represents the dollar value of what suppliers are willing to give up to provide those units of service. The difference between the two areas, shaded in Figure 8A, is a potential gain from trade that the ordinance effectively removes by prohibiting any exchanges at less than $10 per hour.

What does all this have to do with price takers' markets and their superiority, in traditional economic analysis, over price searchers' markets? It comes to this: prices that are fixed above marginal cost rule out some mutually advantageous exchange opportunities. In price takers' markets, sellers don't have the power to set and keep the price above marginal cost. In price searchers' markets, they do.

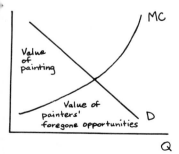

How serious that problem is and how high the costs of correcting it might be are two of the questions that will run through Chapters 9 and 10.

Administered Prices Once Again

It would seem then that price searchers set their own prices, whereas price takers accept what the market sets. Is this the distinction between administered prices and those prices that are set by supply and demand? Not if one thinks about it carefully. Every seller in the last analysis sets the final price, though some sellers can do so with little or no real searching, because they in effect accept the prevailing price (price takers). A more serious objection is that price searchers are by no means free from the constraints imposed by supply and demand.

"Big oil" is a favorite target of those who decry administered prices, but whatever the faults or failings of corporations in the oil industry, their decisions are surely conditioned by supply and demand. Supply depends on cost, and cost is taken into account by every price searcher. Demand curves are never completely inelastic, so demand must also be taken into account if price searchers hope to find what they are looking for, which is presumably the most profitable price to set. Firms in the oil industry may have excessive market power. Whether or not they do, or which ones do and which ones do not, or how much market power any firm has—all these questions can best be investigated by looking at marginal-cost curves and demand curves and how they change over time in response to the pressures of competition. We will discover nothing useful if we pretend that there are firms that "administer" prices *in total disregard of supply and demand.*

So we end up with no usable meaning for the term *administered prices* either. *All* prices are administered and *all* prices are set by supply and demand. The term *administered prices* consequently will not be used in subsequent chapters. An examination of its history would reveal that it has more often been used as a polite "bad word" than as a concept to aid analysis or critical discussion. Economic problems are sufficiently complex without complicating them further by using terms that generate much heat and no light.

One other term appeared in the introductory paragraph: *oligopolist.* The dictionary suggests that an oligopolist is "one of a few sellers." The Big Three in automobiles and the major cigarette manufacturers are commonly cited as examples of oligopoly situations. But what about the daily newspapers in a large city? Or do they compete with other newspapers that can be trucked or flown in, with news magazines, billboards, television, the Yellow Pages? What is the commodity

that allegedly has only a few sellers? Should it be broadly or narrowly defined? What about gasoline stations? Hardware stores? Automobile dealers? Shops that restring tennis rackets? How few is few? We don't have to multiply examples to discover that all the problems associated with defining a monopolist as a sole seller return to haunt us when we define an oligopolist as one of a few sellers.

There is a special market situation to which many economists have chosen to apply the term *oligopoly*. We'll examine and analyze that situation in Chapter 10. But we shall not use the word *oligopoly*, on the grounds that, like administered prices and monopoly, it creates confusion rather than clarity and understanding.

Once Over Lightly

The word *monopoly* means literally a sole seller. But whether any seller is the sole seller depends on how narrowly or broadly we define the product. Under a sufficiently broad definition, there are innumerable sellers of every product. Under a sufficiently narrow definition, however, every seller's product differs from every other's, and all sellers are monopolists. The word *monopoly* is therefore inherently ambiguous and will not be used in subsequent chapters.

The antisocial connotations of the word *monopoly* stem from the belief that the customers of a sole seller have no alternatives and are therefore at the mercy of the seller. Since there are in fact alternatives to every course of action and substitutes for every good, no seller ever has unlimited power over buyers. Market power is always a matter of degree.

The concept of price elasticity of demand provides a useful way of thinking and talking about the degree of market power. Demand elasticities, which can vary between zero and infinity, reflect the availability of substitutes. The more good alternatives buyers have, the more elastic are the demand curves sellers face and the more limited is the power of sellers to establish terms of sale strongly advantageous to themselves.

In the early years of the United States, a monopoly usually meant an organization to which the government had granted some exclusive privilege. The monopolist was thus the sole legal seller. Although this meaning of the term is no longer common, it does have contemporary relevance since federal, state, and local governments are extensively involved in the granting of special privileges that restrict competition.

A useful distinction to make in trying to understand how prices are established is the distinction between *price takers* and *price searchers*. Price takers must accept the price decreed by the market. Buyers have such excellent substitutes for

the product that any attempt to raise the price or otherwise shift the terms of sale will leave the seller with no customers at all. The price searcher, on the other hand, can sell different quantities at different prices and must therefore search for the most advantageous price.

When price is greater than marginal cost, some goods are not going to be produced and sold despite the fact that the monetary value buyers place on acquiring them is higher than the monetary cost to suppliers of making them available. Competition tends to push production in price takers' markets to the point where price and marginal cost are equal.

The concept of *administered prices* is misleading inasmuch as almost all prices are "administered" by sellers—within the constraints imposed by their situation. The important question is whether competition imposes adequate constraints in particular circumstances.

The word *oligopoly* is at least as ambiguous as *monopoly*; whether there are just a few or very many sellers depends on how we choose to define the product. And so the word *oligopoly* will also be discarded in favor of terms that are more precisely descriptive.

QUESTIONS FOR DISCUSSION

1. List some commodities or services that are sold by only one seller. Then list some of the close substitutes for these goods. How much market power is possessed by the sole sellers you listed?
2. Does a firm have a monopoly if it publishes the only morning newspaper in a particular city? If it publishes the only daily newspaper, morning or afternoon? If it publishes the only daily newspaper and owns the only television channel in the city? What are the various goods that a daily newspaper supplies? With what other goods do they compete?
3. Electric utilities are usually given exclusive franchises by the government to sell electricity in a particular area. Are they in competition with sellers of anything else? Do they compete for sales in any way with electric-utility companies franchised to operate in other areas?
4. Is the U.S. Postal Service a monopoly?
   (a) With whom does the Postal Service compete in its first-class mail service (for correspondence)? Its second-class mail service (for publishers of newspapers and magazines)? Its third-class mail service (for advertisers)? Its parcel service? Its express mail service (guaranteed next-day delivery)?
   (b) If the Postal Service has the power to set its prices without regard to supply and demand, why does it usually operate at a loss? Why doesn't it raise its prices and eliminate those troublesome losses?
   (c) When the Postal Service raised the first-class postage rate by 10 percent in 1985 (from 20¢ to 22¢), do you think its revenue from first-class mail

also rose by 10 percent? What would a 10-percent increase in revenue have implied about the elasticity of demand for first-class mail service?

5. Is AMTRAK a monopolist? If you want to travel by train between cities in the U.S., you are likely to find that AMTRAK provides the only such service. Why is it nonetheless misleading to refer to AMTRAK as a monopolist? Is "intercity rail passenger service" a commodity for which there are no good substitutes?

6. The good that the public school systems in American cities supply is one that many persons are required by law to consume. Moreover, competing suppliers, because they are denied the right to finance their activities through taxation, must ordinarily charge much higher prices than the public schools charge. Are public school systems monopolists?

7. It is illegal to market certain agricultural commodities, such as tobacco and hops, unless the product was grown on land which the federal government has licensed for the growing of these commodities. Does this mean tobacco and hops farmers are monopolists? Are they price takers or are they price searchers?

8. If monopolies are undesirable, as almost everyone seems to assume, why do governments so often try to protect particular sellers against the competition that additional entrants to the industry would provide?
   (a) Why does the U.S. government prohibit people from competing with the Postal Service in the delivery of first-class mail?
   (b) Why do cities almost always impose stringent restrictions on those who would like to provide a transportation service to compete directly with the city-owned or -licensed urban bus service?

9. Which are the biggest big businesses in the United States? Here are the ten industrial corporations with the largest sales in 1984, as listed by *Fortune* magazine in its issue of April 29, 1985:

(1) Exxon	(6) International Business Machines
(2) General Motors	
(3) Mobil	(7) E.I. duPont de Nemours
(4) Ford Motor	(8) American Telephone and Telegraph
(5) Texaco	
	(9) General Electric
	(10) Standard Oil of Indiana

Is sales volume really the best measure of a corporation's size? Which were the ten largest in terms of the value of assets owned? Here is the *Fortune* ranking for 1984:

(1) General Motors	(6) United Technologies
(2) International Business Machines	(7) Mobil
(3) Ford Motor	(8) E.I. duPont de Nemours
(4) American Telephone and Telegraph	(9) Exxon
(5) ITT	(10) PepsiCo

For some purposes the net income earned might be a truer indication of corporate size. Here is the *Fortune* list of the ten biggest income earners in 1984:

(1) International Business Machines
(2) Exxon
(3) General Motors
(4) Ford Motor
(5) Chrysler
(6) General Electric
(7) Standard Oil of Indiana
(8) Shell Oil
(9) Chevron
(10) Standard Oil of Ohio

A quite different ranking emerges if we measure the size of a corporation by the number of its employees:

(1) General Motors
(2) International Business Machines
(3) Ford Motor
(4) American Telephone and Telegraph
(5) ITT
(6) United Technologies
(7) Mobil
(8) E.I. duPont de Nemours
(9) Exxon
(10) PepsiCo

(a) Which of the above measures of size is the best indicator of market power, or the ability to take advantage of consumers because they have few good substitutes available?

(b) How much market power does Exxon have, considering that 5 of the 10 largest corporations measured by value of assets (and 12 of the largest 20) are oil companies?

(c) Of the five top income earners in 1984, three were automobile manufacturers. Do they comprise an oligopoly? From what source, not included in the *Fortune* 500 largest industrial corporations, did they receive some of their most troubling competition? What special protection did the U.S. government grant them that helps to account for their splendid 1984 earnings record?

10. It has been argued by some that we can measure the extent to which "monopolists and oligopolists" control the U.S. economy by looking at *concentration ratios* in various industries. These ratios, calculated by the Bureau of the Census, show the percent of the total shipments in various industries that are accounted for by the 4 largest, 8 largest, 20 largest, and 50 largest companies in each industry. The table below shows the ratios for selected industries as calculated from the 1977 Census of Manufacturers, the most current data available.

(a) Why does the concentration ratio in motor vehicles and car bodies provide a seriously exaggerated indication of the market power of U.S. automobile manufacturers?

(b) The concentration ratios in meatpacking plants and fluid milk are similar. It is much more costly, however, to ship fluid milk long distances than it is to ship processed meat. What difference does this make if we're trying to infer the degree of market power from an industry's concentration ratio?

Table 8A Percent of shipments accounted for by large manufacturing companies in the United States

Industry	4 Largest	8 Largest	20 Largest	50 Largest
1. Petroleum refining	30%	53%	81%	94%
2. Motor vehicles and car bodies	93	99	99+	99+
3. Blast furnaces and steel mills	45	65	84	95
4. Aircraft	59	81	99	99+
5. Meatpacking plants	19	37	49	62
6. Fluid milk	18	28	43	60
7. Newspapers	19	31	45	62
8. Sawmills and planing mills	17	23	36	49
9. Plastic materials and resins	22	37	60	87
10. Soap and other detergents	59	71	82	89

(c) Why is the similarity of the concentration ratio in newspapers to that in meatpacking plants probably not very significant?

(d) Do the progressively higher concentration ratios in lumber, plastics, and then soap (the 8th, 9th, and 10th industries listed) indicate a progressively greater degree of market power? How large geographically are the markets for the lumber, plastics, or soap shipped from a particular manufacturing plant?

11. It has been argued that the development of the railroad in the middle of the nineteenth century substantially reduced the market power of many American manufacturing firms. Explain.

12. One often reads that there are "only three firms in the industry" (or five firms, or eight firms), and that this is too few for competition to be effective. How would you define an industry? Do firms in different industries (however defined) compete with one another? Are all the firms within a single industry (however defined) in competition with one another?

13. Do steel girders for bridge construction produced in Utah compete at all with girders produced in Maryland? (The phrase "at all" will usually make a statement true.) Can you think of ways in which wood products compete with steel girders?

14. Is the college you're attending a price searcher? How much freedom does it have in setting the tuition rate you will pay? Might a just-enrolled freshman answer the above differently from an about-to-graduate senior? Does your college enjoy any special grants of legal privilege?

15. Those who use the term *administered prices* do not include in this classification the prices charged by grocery stores. Nonetheless, grocers stamping prices on products seem clearly to be "administering" prices. Can you suggest criteria that would enable us to distinguish "administered" from "nonadministered" prices?

16. Adam Smith wrote the following in *The Wealth of Nations:* "The price of monopoly is upon every occasion the highest which can be got . . . the highest which can be squeezed out of the buyers, or which, it is supposed, they will consent to give." Does this assertion have any clear and defensible meaning, or must we conclude that even the founder of economics sometimes reasoned carelessly?

17. The number of moorage sites for houseboats in Seattle has been limited by law to 440 since the city adopted a Shoreline Management Plan in 1975. All sites are currently occupied by houseboats. Some houseboat owners who do not own their moorage sites asked the city to impose controls on the rents that owners could legally charge. They claimed that, with the vacancy rate at zero, owners had acquired a monopoly and could consequently set rents as high as they pleased.

(a) The graph below shows an imaginary demand curve for moorage sites, labeled DD. Construct the supply curve from the data provided above. (Assume throughout this problem, until part (i), that the sites are owned by 440 different people.)

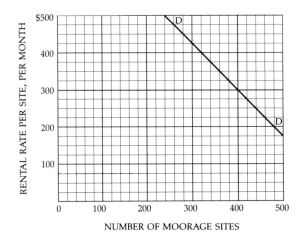

Figure 8B Hypothetical demand and supply curves for houseboat moorage sites in Seattle

(b) What will happen if owners set the rental rate at $275 per month?

(c) What will happen if owners set the rental rate at $225 per month?

(d) Is it true that a zero vacancy rate enables owners to set any rental rate they please? What does a low vacancy rate in residential or office space usually indicate?

(e) What effect on the rental rate would you predict if houseboat living became much more popular in Seattle? What would happen if houseboat living declined in popularity? What are some factors that might cause such an increase or decrease in the demand for houseboat living?

(f) What would be the effect on the rental rate if 40 additional moorage sites became available through a modification of the Shoreline Management Plan?

(g) What would be the effect on rental rates of a $50-per-month increase in the property tax that site owners must pay? Demonstrate your result graphically.

(h) What would be the effect of a $50-per-month tax on houseboat occupants? Use the graph to answer.

(i) Does a zero vacancy rate indicate monopoly power? Suppose all 440 moorage sites were acquired by one party who consequently became the only supplier of moorage sites for houseboats in Seattle. Would this owner now be able to set rents as high as she pleased? What do you think would happen to the vacancy rate if one party became the sole seller of moorage space?

(j) Why do you suppose the houseboat owners chose to use the word "monopoly" in asking the city council to regulate rental rates?

18. Market power is not the only kind of power that business firms might have and exercise. Neither market power nor any of these other types of power is necessarily correlated closely with the size of business firms. You might want to think about the nature, sources, and consequences of some of the powers listed below and how they are linked (or not linked) with market power. Power:

(a) as capability, the ability to achieve desired results

(b) to influence the outcome of elections

(c) to influence legislation

(d) to influence regulatory agencies of government

(e) to manipulate people through advertising

(f) to pollute the environment; to reduce pollution

(g) to pursue sexist and racist hiring policies; to institute affirmative action programs

(h) to intervene in the affairs of other nations

(i) to shape the basic attitudes and beliefs of people

What about the power that we sometimes assume others must have simply because we ourselves feel *powerless*? Is it true that someone always has power to cause or to prevent undesirable events?

Price Searching

How do price searchers find what they're looking for, and what happens when they find it? We're going to argue in this chapter that price searchers estimate marginal costs and marginal revenues and then try to set prices that will enable them to sell all those units of their product—and only those units—for which marginal revenue is expected to be greater than marginal cost. Does that sound complicated? It's just the logic of the process by which net revenue is maximized. But is it the procedure business firms actually use? It sounds much too theoretical, like something an economist might dream up but few real-world sellers would even recognize.

The Popular Theory of Price Setting

It certainly is not the way most people assume that prices get set. The everyday explanation is a simple cost-plus-markup theory: business firms calculate their unit costs and add on a percentage markup. A large number of price searchers will themselves describe their price-setting practices in terms of the cost-plus-markup theory. Their testimony deserves to be taken seriously, but it isn't conclusive evidence. A lot of people cannot correctly describe a process in which they themselves regularly and successfully engage. Most people who ride bicycles, for example, don't know how they keep the bicycle balanced. And if asked to think about it, they'll conclude that they keep the bicycle from tipping by leaning or shifting their weight slightly each time the bicycle inclines in one direction. If that were the way they actually balanced, they wouldn't make it to the end of the block. In reality they balance by steering, not leaning; they turn the front wheel imperceptibly and allow centrifugal force to counter any tendency to tip. The fact that they don't know what they're

Why are percentage markups so much larger in furniture stores than in grocery stores?

Why do furniture stores often lower their percentage markups for a few days (during sales)?

Why do furniture stores sometimes go bankrupt if their percentage markups are typically so large?

doing doesn't keep them from doing it. Although they can balance successfully only by winding along a series of curves whose precise curvature will be inversely proportional to the square of the speed at which they're proceeding, many mathematical illiterates are skillful cyclists.

There are excellent reasons for doubting the cost-plus-markup theory. One is that it tells us nothing about the size of the markup. Why choose a 25 rather than a 50 percent markup? Why do different firms mark up their prices by different percentages? Why will the same firm vary its percentage markup at different times, on different products, and even when selling to different people? Why do sellers sometimes set their prices *below* their average unit cost?

Moreover, if firms can always mark up their prices proportionately when their costs rise, why don't they raise their prices *before* their costs rise? Why are they satisfied with a smaller net revenue when they could be earning more? That doesn't square with the perennial complaints of many price setters that they aren't making adequate profits. We all know, too, that firms are sometimes forced out of business by rising costs. That couldn't happen if every firm were able to mark up its prices to cover any increase in costs.

The popular cost-plus-markup theory is obviously inadequate. It just doesn't explain the phenomena with which we're all familiar. We'll return to the question of why so many people, including price searchers themselves, nevertheless hold to the theory. But we can't do that until we've gone through the economist's explanation of the price-searching process.

Introducing Ed Sike

Simple cases are best for illuminating basic principles. We're going to examine the imaginary case of Ed Sike, a sophomore who is supporting himself at Ivy College by working as special-events manager for the College Student Association. One of Ed's tasks is to run a Friday night feature-film series that is open to the college community, and a large part of that job is setting ticket prices.

Let's suppose that Ed has to pay the following bills each time he shows a movie:

Film rental	$1800
Auditorium rental	250
Operator	50
Ticket takers	100
Total:	$2200

Ed's budget receives all the revenue from ticket sales. The auditorium seats 700 people. And Ed has somehow discovered the precise demand for the films he shows. (We'll relax that heroic assumption later on.) The demand, which (quite remarkably) doesn't change from film to film, is graphed in Figure 9A. Given this information, what will Ed want to charge for tickets?

We can't answer that question until we know Ed's objectives. If his aim is to fill all the seats without having to turn anyone away, $3 would be the best price to set. That's the price at which the quantity of tickets demanded would equal the number of seats available in the auditorium. One possible objection to a $3 price, however, is that each film showing would lose money. Total costs would be $2200, but total revenue would be only $2100.

That isn't necessarily a compelling objection. The student association may be willing to subsidize the films, perhaps because someone thinks movies make an important contribution to liberal education. If Ed doesn't have to cover costs out of ticket revenue, all sorts of possibilities open up. For example, he might set the price at $2.50. That would cause the quantity demanded to exceed the quantity supplied, but it might also make Ed a very popular man on campus—someone who can get you tickets to a Friday night film even though the film is already "sold out."

Price	Quantity Demanded	Total Revenue	Net Revenue
$3.00	700	$2100	−$100
2.50	750	1750*	−$450

*Remember — there are only 700 seats.

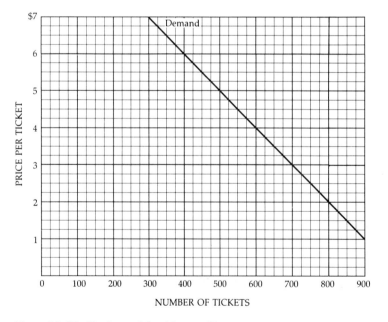

Figure 9A Weekly demand for tickets to films

We'll come back to that possibility in a later chapter when we look more closely at how "nonprofit" institutions work. Let's assume for now that Ed not only has to get enough revenue from ticket sales to cover all costs, but that he's under orders to earn as much *net* revenue from the series as he can. Under these circumstances, what price will Ed want to charge for a ticket?

The Basic Rule for Maximizing Net Revenue

Look again at the basic rule presented in the first paragraph of this chapter, the rule we said all price searchers try to follow if their goal is to maximize net revenue: Set the price or prices that will enable you to sell all those units and only those units for which marginal revenue is expected to be greater than marginal cost.

Marginal cost you've met before. That's the additional cost a seller expects to incur as a result of a contemplated action. In this case the action is *selling another ticket*. Look at the data on Ed Sike's costs. What is the additional cost to him of selling another ticket? Since all $2200 of his costs have to be paid no matter how many tickets he sells, the marginal cost of selling another ticket is zero, under the assumptions we've adopted. If you wanted to draw the marginal cost curve on Figure 9A, it would be a horizontal line running across the graph at $0.

The Concept of Marginal Revenue

But what's marginal revenue? *Marginal revenue is the additional revenue expected from an action under consideration.* For Ed Sike, marginal revenue is the extra revenue received from selling one more ticket.

If you look at the demand curve in Figure 9A, you can see at a glance that Ed Sike's net revenue is going to depend on the price he decides to set. At $3 total revenue would be $2100, and so net revenue would be *minus* $100. At $6 net revenue would be $200: $2400 in total revenue minus $2200 in costs. It would also be $200 if the ticket price was set at $4. At what price would net revenue be maximized, given the data with which we're working?

The answer is $5. If the price is set at $5, then 500 tickets will be sold. Total revenue will be $2500, and net revenue will be $300. Ed can't do any better than that.

How do we know? One way to find the answer is to try out every possible price. A better way, because it clarifies the logic of the process we're trying to explain, is to locate the quantity at which marginal revenue equals marginal cost

Price	Quantity Demanded	Total Revenue
$ 7	300	$ 2100
6	400	2400
5	500	2500
4	600	2400
3	700	2100

and then find the price at which exactly that quantity can be sold.

The logic is extremely simple. Each of the first 500 tickets that Ed sells adds more to his revenue than it adds to his costs. (Remember that in this particular case it adds *nothing* to his costs; marginal cost is zero no matter how many tickets are being sold.) But each ticket sold beyond 500 adds more to costs than to revenue. It adds nothing to costs, but it adds *less than nothing* to total revenue, because marginal revenue becomes negative after 500 tickets have been sold.

Why Marginal Revenue Is Less Than Price

It seems at first that this can't be correct. Since Ed is still taking in money for each ticket he sells beyond 500, the additional revenue from selling another ticket, or marginal revenue, looks as if it ought to be positive. But that appearance is in fact false. It ignores something very important. In order to sell additional tickets, Ed has to lower the price. And when he does so, he lowers the price not only to the additional customers he's trying to capture with the price decrease, but also to all those customers who would have purchased tickets at the higher price. The additional revenue he gains from the new customers is offset by revenue lost, or given up, from the old customers. After he has sold 500 tickets, the revenue lost becomes greater than the revenue gained, and so marginal revenue becomes negative.

Let's check it out by looking carefully at the graph. Suppose Ed set the price at $5. At that price he would sell 500 tickets, and total revenue would be $2500.

What would happen if he decided to sell 550 tickets? To do so, he would have to lower the price to $4.50. That would bring him an additional $4.50 from each of the 50 "new" customers, for a total of $225 extra. But it would cost him 50 cents *not* paid now by each of the 500 "old" customers who were willing to pay $5 until Ed offered to sell them tickets at $4.50: 500 times 50 cents is $250. That more than offsets the $225 gained. Ed Sike actually reduced his total revenue by $25 when he decided to expand his ticket sales from 500 to 550. Marginal revenue is *negative* over this range.

We can be even more precise. Since the additional revenue from the 50 additional tickets sold is minus $25, we can say that marginal revenue per ticket is minus 50 cents when Ed tries to expand sales from 500 to 550. If we want to show that on Figure 9A, we can plot marginal revenue as minus 50 cents at 525 tickets, the midpoint between 500 and 550.

Check your understanding of the basic idea by asking what happens when Ed expands his sales from 450 to 500

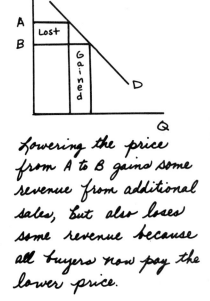

Lowering the price from A to B gains some revenue from additional sales, but also loses some revenue because all buyers now pay the lower price.

tickets. The demand curve shows he could sell 450 tickets for $5.50 each. To sell 500 tickets, he must lower the price to $5. So his total revenue will be $2475 when he sells 450 tickets, and $2500 when he sells 500 tickets. The additional or marginal revenue is 50 cents per extra ticket sold when Ed expands his sales from 450 to 500 tickets. We would therefore plot plus 50 cents as the marginal revenue at 475 tickets.

If we connected these two points with a straight line, the resulting marginal-revenue curve would intersect the marginal-cost curve at precisely 500 tickets. Consequently, we can say that if Ed is content to sell fewer than 500 tickets, he sacrifices potential net revenue by failing to sell some tickets for which marginal revenue is greater than marginal cost. If he sells more than 500 tickets, Ed sacrifices potential net revenue by selling some tickets for which marginal revenue is less than marginal cost. He therefore maximizes net revenue by selling exactly 500 tickets: the quantity at which marginal revenue equals marginal cost. And the demand curve tells us that 500 tickets can be sold by setting the ticket price at $5.

Setting Marginal Revenue to Equal Marginal Cost

You can be sure you've grasped the idea if you're able to figure out what would happen if the film distributor changed the rental fee from a flat $1800 to $800 plus $2 for every ticket sold.

The key difference is that Ed's marginal costs would now rise from zero to $2. Each additional ticket sold would now add $2 to total cost; the marginal-cost curve is a horizontal line at $2. Since to maximize net revenue, Ed must sell all those tickets for which marginal revenue is greater than marginal cost, and no tickets for which marginal cost is greater than marginal revenue, Ed wants to find the price and quantity at which marginal revenue will exactly equal $2.

The marginal-revenue curve has been drawn in Figure 9B. This curve shows by how much the sale of one additional ticket increases total revenue at the various volumes possible. Marginal revenue is $4 when 300 tickets are being sold and falls rapidly as sales increase, becoming negative after 500 tickets are sold. We now see at once that, given the film distributor's new policy, Ed will want to sell 400 tickets. This is the quantity that equates marginal revenue and marginal cost. To sell 400 tickets, Ed should set the price at $6. It turns out that Ed does somewhat better under the film distributor's new policy than he did under the old one. Total revenue is now $2400 and total cost is $2000, for a net revenue of $400.

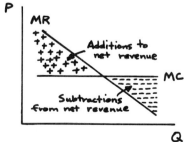

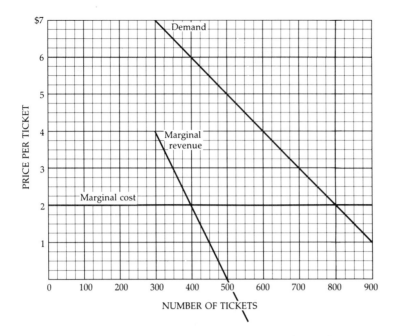

Figure 9B Weekly demand for tickets to films and marginal cost of selling tickets

What About Those Empty Seats?

Under both the old and the new policy, seats were "going to waste." That phrase is in quotation marks because waste, you should recall from Chapter 6, is an evaluative concept. What constitutes waste from the point of view of moviegoers may be efficiency from the point of view of exhibitors like Ed. Still, there does seem to be something wasteful about this situation from everyone's perspective. There are people who want to see the movies, who are willing to pay Ed an amount greater than his marginal cost if he will let them in, but to whom Ed nonetheless denies admission. Movie fans are missing an opportunity for which they're willing to pay the marginal cost; and Ed isn't getting any revenue from those empty seats for which people are willing to pay more than his marginal cost. There seems to be a substantial gain from exchange that isn't being realized. (The situation matches the case of the house painters under a legal minimum wage, as discussed in Chapter 8; it's not an "optimal" arrangement of resources.)

Situations like this are extremely common, of course. At almost every major-league baseball game there will be empty seats inside the stadium, and people outside the stadium who would be happy to pay the team owner for the chance to sit in them. Since letting in another spectator adds nothing

to the cost of playing the game, the owner would gain extra net revenue from each additional fan admitted at any ticket price greater than zero. But this will be the case only if the owner can reduce the ticket price to the "new" customers without also reducing the price to those who are willing to pay more to see the game.

The Price Discriminator's Dilemma

There's the catch. It is in fact efficient (from his point of view) for Ed to leave 200 or 300 seats empty, as long as the cost of discriminating among potential ticket buyers is greater than the additional revenue that can be gained through discrimination. Let's see what this means.

Suppose Ed is paying a flat $1800 rental fee, charging $5, selling 500 tickets, and earning $300 per week. One Friday night he looks over the house and says to himself: "I could increase my net revenue by filling those 200 empty seats. All I'd have to do is lower the price to $3, but *only* for those who won't attend if I charge them more than that. I'd get an extra $600 each week, and 200 additional people could enjoy these fine movies."

A brilliant idea? The following week Ed hangs up a new sign at the campus ticket outlet: "$5 per ticket," it says; and then it adds in smaller print: "$3 for those unwilling to pay more." What's going to happen? Almost all the ticket buyers will pay $3, of course, because they're all "unwilling to pay more" if they can get their tickets for $3. Ed will end up with only $2100 in revenue and a loss of $100 from that week's program. It wasn't such a brilliant idea after all.

The flaw, however, was more in the execution than in the idea itself. What Ed must do if he wants to eliminate the "waste" of empty seats and lost revenue is find a sufficiently low-cost procedure for distinguishing among potential buyers. He has to be able to offer low prices to those who otherwise won't buy, without making those low prices available to customers who are willing to purchase tickets at higher prices. Ed might be able to pick up a few hints from the Ivy College administration.

The College as Price Searcher

College administrators often talk about the high costs of providing an education and the need for charitable contributions to make up that 50 percent or so of the cost not covered by tuition. Have you ever wondered why it is, then, that privately owned colleges grant tuition scholarships to needy students? If colleges are so poor that they must ask for charity, why do they simultaneously *dispense* charity? The answer is

that they probably don't. Tuition scholarships for needy students may be a partially successful attempt to do what Ed Sike failed to do.

Figure 9C is the demand for admission to Ivy College as estimated by the college administration. We shall assume that the marginal cost of enrolling another student is zero. That isn't accurate, but it's realistic enough for our purposes and it doesn't affect the logic of the argument in any event. Ivy College wants to find the tuition rate that will maximize its receipts.

If Ivy restricts itself to a uniform price for all, it will set the tuition at $3000 per year, enroll 3000 students (the enrollment at which marginal revenue equals marginal cost), and gross $9,000,000. But some students whom it would be profitable to enroll are excluded by this tuition rate, and some students who would have been willing to pay more are admitted for only $3000. Ivy's administrators wish they could charge what each student is willing to pay. If they could find out the maximum each student (or the parents) would pay rather than be denied admission to Ivy, they could set the annual tuition at $6000 and then give scholarships (price rebates) to each student. The scholarship would equal the

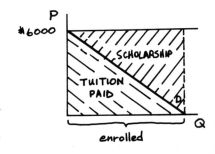

Figure 9C Demand curve for enrollment at Ivy College

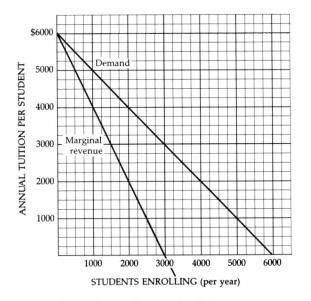

Note: There is a simple gimmick you can use to obtain quickly the marginal-revenue curve corresponding to any straight-line demand curve. Draw perpendiculars to the price axis from the demand curve; bisect the perpendiculars; extend a straight line through these midpoints. The marginal revenue corresponding to any point on the demand curve will then be the point on this line (the marginal-revenue curve) directly below the point on the demand curve in which you're interested. Thus the marginal revenue is zero when the price is $3000.

difference between $6000 and the maximum each student is willing to pay.

The problem is how to get information on willingness to pay. Students or their parents will not reveal the full value of Ivy to them if they know that candor will cause them to pay a higher price. But if willingness to pay is correlated with wealth, a partial solution lies at hand. Ivy announces that scholarships are available to needy students. Need must be established by filling out a statement on family wealth and income. Families will complete the forms in order to qualify for scholarship aid and will thereby provide the college with information it can use to discriminate. If the correlation were perfect between income and willingness to pay, and if families filled out the forms honestly, Ivy could discriminate with precision and increase its gross receipts to $18,000,000 (the area under the entire demand curve). Marginal revenue would be equal to price despite the fact that Ivy is a price searcher.

Be careful about condemning Ivy College! Notice some of the consequences of this discriminatory pricing policy. First of all, Ivy earns more income. If you approve of Ivy, why begrudge it a larger income from tuition? Is it better for philanthropists and taxpayers to cover Ivy's annual deficit than for students (or their parents) to do so through being charged the maximum they're willing to pay? Notice, too, that under a perfectly discriminating system of tuition charges, 3000 students who would otherwise be turned away are enabled to enroll at Ivy. They aren't complaining.

Some Strategies for Price Discrimination

Sellers have developed a wide variety of strategies for doing what Ivy College does through its tuition scholarship program. The goal is to find low-cost techniques for distinguishing high-price from low-price buyers and then to offer reduced prices exclusively to those who otherwise won't purchase the product.

For example, grocery stores often offer discounts to customers who present special coupons clipped from newspaper advertisements. Why do they do this? The discounts are designed to attract bargain-hunting shoppers who otherwise wouldn't patronize the store. Customers who fail to present coupons at the checkout counter thereby identify themselves as people who aren't price-conscious bargain-seekers. So they pay higher prices.

If airlines lower their ticket prices, they can fill some empty seats with vacation travelers who would otherwise go by car. But the airlines don't want to lower their prices for business travelers who are willing to pay high fares to save time, and for whom the cost of travel is a tax-deductible

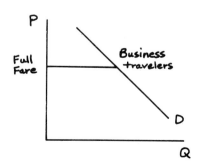

expense anyway. How can the airlines distinguish these two classes of travelers and give discounts only to those who won't fly without them? One way is to confine the discount prices to those who buy round-trip tickets and stay more than a week or over a weekend. Business travelers usually can't afford to stay away that long. It's far from an infallible way to discriminate, but it's a low-cost system and it works surprisingly well.

Discount prices are commonly offered for all kinds of entertainment events to children, students, and senior citizens. Is this an act of generosity on the part of those who sponsor the events? It's more likely that they want to attract some additional business from groups that are more sensitive to prices, but without lowering the price to everyone. Potential customers with more elastic demands for the good are prime targets for special price reductions, *if* the seller has a low-cost way to identify the people with more elastic demand curves *and* can prevent them from reselling to people with less elastic demand curves.

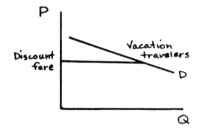

Ed Sike Finds a Way

Let's return to the case of Ed Sike. Suppose his data on the demand for tickets enable him to distinguish the student demand from the staff and faculty demand. In Figure 9D we've drawn two demand curves to show these separate student

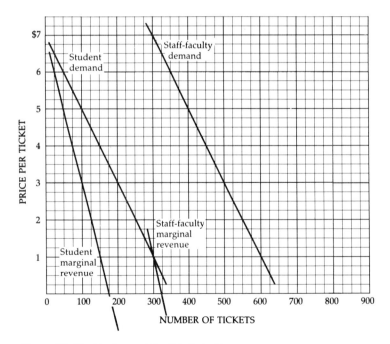

Figure 9D Weekly demand for tickets to films

and staff-faculty demands for tickets to the Friday film series. (If you add the curves together—summing the quantities demanded by each group at various prices—you'll get the demand curve presented in Figure 9A.) Our question is: Can Ed, knowing these separate demand curves, increase his net revenue by setting different prices for students and for staff or faculty?

Intuition suggests it might work. The typical student doesn't have a lot of income and so tends to pay attention to prices. Staff and faculty members who want to see the films are less likely to change their minds because of a modest price increase. It might be that Ed could do better by lowering the price he charges students and raising the price to staff and faculty.

Recall that when marginal cost was zero, Ed maximized net revenue by charging $5 per ticket and selling 500 tickets. Now he wants to set marginal revenue equal to marginal cost *for each group separately.*

Marginal revenue from sales to the students equals zero (marginal cost) at 175 tickets. To sell 175 tickets to students, Ed should charge them $3.50.

Marginal revenue from sales to staff and faculty equals zero at 325 tickets. To sell that number to staff and faculty, Ed should charge them $6.50.

He'll still be selling 500 tickets. But his total revenue will now be $2725 rather than $2500, and his net revenue will increase from $300 to $525.

Why did it work? It worked because the student demand for tickets was much more elastic than was the staff and faculty demand at the common price of $5. By lowering the price to the students, who are more responsive to price changes, and raising the price to staff and faculty members, who are less responsive, Ed does a more effective job of extracting from each group what it's willing to pay.

Note carefully, however, that the entire scheme is crucially dependent on Ed's ability to identify members of each group and prevent them from reselling tickets. It won't do to let students buy tickets for $3.50 and then sell them to members of the staff or faculty. Ed's price-discrimination system would probably work because he could, at low cost, print the tickets in different colors and require that official college I.D. cards be shown when the tickets are presented at the door.

Resentment and Rationale

Of course, Ed would also have to justify his "exploitation" of staff and faculty. That's not likely to be a problem in this case. He could say that $6.50 is what each ticket "really" costs and that the $3.50 price to students is the result of a special

subsidy to promote liberal education. Don't underestimate the importance of "justification." Price discrimination of this type increases Ed's net revenue and doesn't compel anyone to pay more than they're willing to pay. But it can arouse fierce indignation on the part of those who aren't offered the discount prices.

As an example, consider the bitter complaints of all those cross-country air travelers who found a few years ago that they had to pay more per mile than people flying between Los Angeles and New York. Why should a round-trip ticket from Seattle to New York, for example, cost more than a similar ticket from Los Angeles to New York, especially when Seattle is closer to New York? The explanation was the fierce competition among the numerous carriers operating between the nation's two largest cities. This competition created excellent substitutes for any one airline's tickets, made the demand curve that each airline faced very elastic, and kept prices close to marginal cost. To Seattle–New York travelers, however, it looked as if they were subsidizing Los Angeles–New York passengers, and they didn't like it.

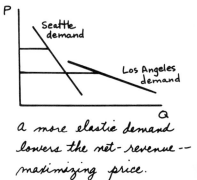

a more elastic demand lowers the net-revenue --maximizing price.

Lunch and Dinner Prices

Everything we've been talking about is nicely illustrated in the common restaurant practice of charging more for the same food in the evening than at lunch.

Why do restaurants catering to both a luncheon and a dinner trade mark up their prices so much more on dinners than on lunches? The theory we've presented looks for the answer in different elasticities of demand. Lunch customers as a class are much more responsive to price increases or decreases than are dinner customers. A 10 percent increase in the price of a luncheon entrée will often lose the restaurant more customers than would a 30 percent increase in the price of the same item on the dinner menu. There are several reasons for this.

One is the fact that lunch customers eat out so much more frequently. People who buy lunch five times a week have many opportunities to gather information on relative prices. And because 50 cents less or more adds up over the course of a month, they have a strong incentive to shop around for the best deal, to stick to it when they think they've found it, and to shift when something better comes along. A dinner out, by contrast, is a much more rare event for most people; they have, as a consequence, less opportunity and less incentive to gather information on relative prices.

Another major reason for the lower price elasticity of demand among dinner patrons is the fact that what they pay for their food is typically only a fraction of what they are

paying for the entire event or experience of "dinner out." A couple going out for dinner may pay $8 for a babysitter, $2 for parking, and $10 for cocktails or wine. If they pay $10 each for their dinners, the food is only half of their costs for the evening. And so a 40 percent hike in the menu price comes through to them as only a 20 percent increase in the cost of their evening out.

We should therefore expect to see restaurant managers following low-markup policies at lunch and high-markup policies at dinner. To reduce the chance of indignation and resentment, they will do a little more than merely raise the price of the London broil from $8 at lunch to $12 at dinner. They will also offer the dinner patron both soup *and* salad (the luncheon customers must choose one or the other) and perhaps include coffee in the price of the dinner (but not the lunch). A $4 increase is thus "justified" by an increase in marginal food cost of perhaps 40 cents. The real reason for the different markups, however, is found in the different elasticities of demand characteristic of luncheon and dinner patrons.

Cost Plus Markup Reconsidered

So how do price searchers find what they're looking for? By (1) estimating the marginal cost and marginal revenue, (2) determining the level of output that will enable them to sell all those units of output and only those units for which marginal revenue is greater than marginal cost, and (3) setting this price or prices so that they can just manage to sell the output produced. That sounds complicated, and it is. The logic is simple enough. But the estimates of marginal cost and especially the estimates of demand and marginal revenue are hard to make accurately. That's why price searchers are called "searchers." And why they could sometimes be called price "gropers."

The complexity and uncertainty of the price searcher's task helps explain the popularity of the cost-plus-markup theory. Every search has to begin somewhere. Why not begin with the wholesale cost of an item plus a percentage markup adequate to cover overhead costs and yield a reasonable profit? If costs increase, why not assume that competitors' costs have also increased and try passing the higher cost on to customers? Why not begin with the assumption that the future will be like the past and that the procedures which have previously yielded good results will continue to do so? In that case one would try to increase prices roughly in proportion to any cost increases experienced, and one would expect eventually to be forced by competition to lower one's prices roughly in proportion to any lowering of costs.

The cost-plus-markup procedure is in general a rule of thumb for price searchers, offering a place from which to begin looking, a first approximation in the continuing search for an elusive and shifting target. But price searchers engage in cost-plus-markup pricing only as a search technique and only until they discover they are making a mistake. The marginal-cost/marginal-revenue analysis of this chapter explains how price searchers recognize mistakes and what criteria they use in moving from rules of thumb and first approximations toward the most profitable pricing policy.

Once Over Lightly

Price searchers are looking for pricing structures that will enable them to sell all units for which marginal revenue exceeds marginal cost.

The popularity of the cost-plus-markup theory of pricing rests on its usefulness as a search technique and the fact that people often cannot correctly explain processes in which they regularly and successfully engage.

A crucial factor for the price searcher is the ability or inability to discriminate: to charge high prices for units that are in high demand and low prices for units that would not otherwise be purchased, without allowing the sales at lower prices to "spoil the market" for high-price sales.

A rule for successful price searching often quoted by economists is: set marginal revenue equal to marginal cost. This means: continue selling as long as the additional revenue from a sale exceeds the additional cost. Skillful price searchers are people who know this rule (even when they don't fully realize they're using it) and who also have a knack for distinguishing the relevant marginal possibilities. The possibilities are endless, which helps to make price theory a fascinating exploration for people with a penchant for puzzle solving.

Sellers in the real world don't have precisely defined demand curves from which they can derive marginal-revenue curves to compare with marginal-cost curves. Working with such curves is nonetheless good exercise for a student who wants to begin thinking systematically about the ways in which competition affects the choices people make and the choices they confront.

QUESTIONS FOR DISCUSSION

1. If you're still uncertain about the meaning of marginal revenue, here is some additional practice.

Price per Unit	Quantity Demanded
$12	1
$11	2
$10	3
$ 9	4

Assume that all sales take place at a single price. What is the *addition to total revenue* from selling the second unit, the third, the fourth? Why is marginal revenue less than price?

2. "A price searcher should set marginal revenue as far above marginal cost as possible." Explain why this statement is wrong. What is being erroneously assumed by someone who thinks that net receipts will be zero at an output where marginal revenue equals marginal cost?

3. Locate the most profitable uniform price for sellers to set in each of the situations graphed below and the quantity they will want to produce and sell. Then shade the area that represents the net income from that pricing policy. What will happen to net income in each case if the price is raised? If it's lowered? (Caution: What happens if a seller whose marginal revenue curve is the same as the demand curve raises the price?)

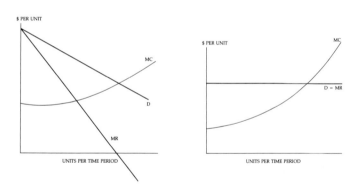

Figure 9E Finding the most profitable selling price

4. The marginal cost curves of the Anchorage Aardvark Breeding Company and the Houston Aardvark Breeding Company are identical, but the demand curves they face differ, as shown in Figure 9F.
   (a) What price will each firm want to set?
   (b) Suppose something happens to raise marginal cost for each firm to $20 while nothing else changes. What price will each now set?
   (c) What is the relationship between elasticity of demand and the profit maximizing percentage markup?

5. Have you ever wondered why otherwise identical books usually sell for so much more in hard-cover than in soft-cover editions?
   (a) Is it because publishers must pay so much more to produce books with hard covers?

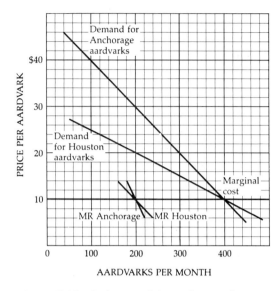

Figure 9F Marginal cost and demand curves for two companies

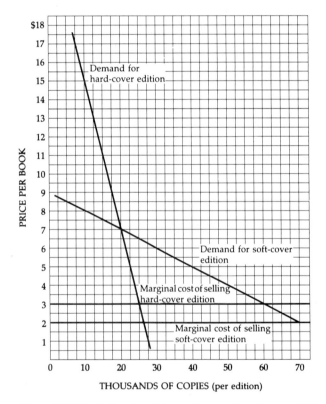

Figure 9G Marginal cost and demand curves for a book publisher

(b) Some potential buyers will have a strong preference for a hard-cover edition. They include libraries, purchasers who intend to use the book intensively, and people looking for gift items. Would you expect the price elasticity of demand at any particular price to be greater or less for the hard-cover than for the soft-cover edition?

(c) Figure 9G shows the marginal cost to a publisher of producing and selling hard-cover and soft-cover editions of a particular book and the demand curve for each edition. What prices will the publisher want to set? How much of this reflects cost differences?

6. The graph below presents the daily demand for round-trip tickets on Transcontinental Airlines' flights between Seattle and New York City and between Los Angeles and New York City. Assume that the cost to Transcontinental of carrying an additional passenger is $25 one way, for a round-trip marginal cost of $50.

(a) What specific expenses would enter into Transcontinental's marginal cost (of selling an additional round-trip ticket)?

(b) Construct the marginal revenue curves that correspond to each of the demand curves shown, using the technique described in Figure 9C.

(c) How many tickets of each kind would Transcontinental want to sell to maximize its net revenue?

(d) What price would it want to set on each route?

(e) Are Seattle customers subsidizing Los Angeles customers? What price would Transcontinental want to set for its Seattle flights if it terminated its Los Angeles operation? For its Los Angeles flights if it terminated its Seattle operation? Are Seattle prices higher *because* Los Angeles prices are lower?

(f) Are Seattle prices perhaps *lower* because of Transcontinental's Los Angeles operation? Since Transcontinental is adding to its net revenue by flying Los Angeles passengers, it could well be the case that the Los

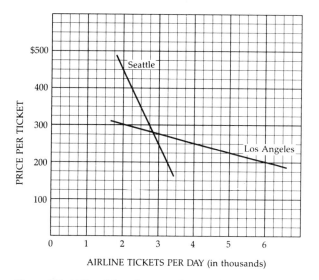

Figure 9H Airline tickets between Seattle and Los Angeles

Angeles operation is enabling it to stay in business. How would this contribute to lower prices for Seattle customers?

7. Many firms use a technique called *target pricing* in trying to decide what prices to set for new products they're introducing. The target price is a price that enables the firm to recover a certain percentage of the product's development and production costs. What, in addition to costs, must the seller know in order to calculate the return a particular price will yield? If earnings from the sale of the product turn out to fall short of the target, should the firm raise the price? If earnings exceed the firm's expectations, should it lower the price?

8. How should the British and French manufacturers of the Concorde supersonic commercial airliner take account of the plane's development costs in determining the prices to charge airline companies? Should they suspend production if they can't obtain a price that will cover development costs?

9. When the university's athletic director announces that football ticket prices are being raised for next year, he is likely to say this unfortunate step has been made necessary by rising costs—perhaps the rising cost of the women's sports program. How does the cost of the women's sports program affect the marginal cost of selling a football ticket? If you are unable to think of any answer to that question, ask yourself how the prospect of a winning season affects the cost of selling a football ticket. Which plays a larger role in determining the most profitable price at which to sell football tickets: the athletic department's budget for women's sports or an excellent team?

10. In 1980 Heublein Inc. raised the price of its Popov brand vodka by 8 percent, in what it called a move to "reposition" the brand. Sales fell only 1 percent in response to the 8 percent price increase.
    (a) Since vodka is colorless, odorless, and tasteless, why do you suppose consumers are willing to pay substantially more for some brands of vodka?
    (b) What do you suppose Heublein was trying to do when it "repositioned" its Popov brand?
    (c) Marketing people refer to certain goods which are kept on display as "ego-sensitive" merchandise, and point out that consumers show a preference for higher prices when it comes to ego-sensitive goods. Does that mean that sellers of such goods can always earn more by raising prices?

11. Do beer drinkers have to pay more for the beer they drink because the brewery pays a huge sum of money to advertise it on network television? In what manner are advertising costs capable of affecting the net-revenue-maximizing price for the product advertised?

12. Do small convenience stores charge higher prices (on average) than large supermarkets charge because the small stores have higher overhead costs per unit of sales? How can a seller induce customers to pay a higher price for a product than they would have to pay elsewhere?

13. Can hog owners raise the prices at which they sell when feed costs go up?
    (a) A rise in the price of hog feed increases the cost to hog farmers of continuing to feed the hogs they have. What is the alternative to continuing to feed and fatten hogs? Why might an increase in the price of hog feed lead to a short-run decline in the price of hogs?

(b) By what process will an increase in the price of hog feed eventually produce an increase in the price of hogs?

(c) A news item in the summer of 1985 stated that refiners were raising the price of gasoline, despite lower oil prices, to help cover the higher cost of removing lead. Can they get away with something like that?

14. In 1985 Missouri began assessing commercial property for tax purposes at a higher percentage of "fair market value" than residential property. For purposes of this reassessment, apartment buildings of 5 or more units were classified as commercial property; property taxes on such buildings increased sharply, while taxes on apartment buildings with 4 units or fewer did not change.

    (a) Would you expect this change to increase the rents paid by people living in large apartment buildings relative to the rents paid by tenants in buildings with fewer than 5 units? Does the tax increase affect either the marginal cost to the landlord of renting or the demand for apartments on the part of tenants?

    (b) What effect do you think this tax change will have on the average size of apartment units in existing buildings? What effect will it have on the average size of apartment buildings constructed in the future?

    (c) What effect would you predict from this change in assessment methods on the demand for units in buildings of fewer than 5 units and hence on the rental rates tenants will pay for such units?

    (d) The president of the St. Louis Apartment Association was quoted as saying that no apartment owners would pay those tax increases, but rather would pass them along in the form of rent increases. If owners can raise rents in this fashion after property taxes rise, why don't they raise them *before* the taxes rise and increase their income? If owners can pass on tax increases, why did some Missouri apartment owners go to the expense of filing a suit to overturn the reassessment?

15. One store sells Wilson Championship extra-duty felt optic-yellow tennis balls at $3.49 for a can of three. Another store in the same shopping center sells Wilson Championship extra-duty felt optic-yellow tennis balls at $2.89 for a can of three. How is this possible? Why would anyone buy balls from the first store? Why do you think we repeated the long description in the second sentence instead of just saying "identical tennis balls"?

16. Information is a scarce good and its acquisition has a cost. How does this fact explain the frequent willingness of small firms to charge whatever prices are set by much larger firms?

17. If a surgeon charges $1500 to remove the gallbladder of a wealthy patient and $500 to remove another patient's gallbladder, is she exploiting the first patient or giving a discount to the second? How does she prevent the second patient from buying several operations at the lower price and reselling them for a profit to wealthy patients?

18. You want to sell at auction an antique dining-room suite. There are three people who want it, and they're willing to pay $8000, $6000, and $4000, respectively. Your reservation price (the price above which the bidding must go before you sell) is $5000. No one in the room has any information about the value of the suite to anyone else.

    (a) At about what price will the suite be sold?

(b) Suppose you run a Dutch auction. The auctioneer announces a price well above what anyone would be willing to pay and then gradually lowers the price until a bid is received. At about what price will the suite be sold?

(c) Why do stores sometimes add to their advertisements: "Available only while supplies last"?

19. You and your fiancée are shopping for wedding rings. After showing you a sample of his wares, the jeweler asks, "What price did you have in mind?"

(a) Why does he ask this question?

(b) If you tell him you don't plan to spend more than $200 on each ring, are you helping him find the rings to sell you or the price to charge for the rings you prefer?

(c) What might be a good technique for finding out the lowest price at which the jeweler is willing to sell the rings you like?

20. Why do camera retailers so often sell the cameras themselves at prices very close to their own wholesale cost, while marking up the price of accessories (carrying cases, extra lenses, filters, and so on) by 100 percent or more?

21. Some Manhattan restaurants have experimented with using two breakfast menus. One, with higher printed prices, is handed to entering customers who look like tourists. The other menu, with lower prices, is given to customers in business clothing who look like people on their way to work. How might this two-menu policy raise net revenue for the restaurants using it?

22. A *Wall Street Journal* story (July 25, 1980) reports that tourists in China are charged more than double the price that Chinese pay for movies, taxicabs, and airline or train tickets, and that many manufactured items offered for sale in "friendship" stores can actually be purchased for half as much in retail stores in Hong Kong. Can you explain this?

   The Chinese also charge foreign diplomats very high prices for apartments, but often charge lower "friendship" rents to representatives from poor Third World nations. Do the lower rents charged Third World diplomats represent a foreign-policy decision or an attempt to maximize net revenue?

23. Professional sports teams have long sponsored "Ladies' Days," occasions on which women are admitted at reduced prices. Is this a case of discrimination against males, since the teams never have a "Gentlemen's Day"? How would you explain "Ladies' Day"?

24. An August 1981 newspaper story reported what it called "a mystery." Representatives of the manufacturer and the regional distributor of a well-known brand of skis tried to buy the entire stock of their own skis being offered for sale at very low prices by a chain of discount stores. At one store the purchasers immediately went outside and broke all the skis in the store parking lot. Can you explain this mystery?

25. Suppose you're willing to pay 60 cents for one doughnut with your morning coffee and 30 cents for a second doughnut. The owner of the doughnut shop knows this and also knows that his cost of selling an additional doughnut is 20 cents. Should he charge you 60 cents or 30 cents if he wants to maximize his net revenue? How about 60 cents and two for 90 cents?

26. Why will sellers make offers like this one? "Buy two giant pizzas at regular price and get a third one for only a dollar."

Competition and Government Policy

Will economic competition disappear unless the government has an active program to preserve it? Or does competition preserve itself, sometimes in the face of diligent efforts by the government to restrict it?

Is the government promoting competition when it prevents larger, more efficient, or perhaps more unscrupulous firms from driving other firms out of business? Or does the protection of competitors entail the suppression of competition?

When the government prohibits mergers, is it preventing competitors from eliminating rivals? Or is it stifling the development of more competitive and efficient organizational forms?

What do we mean by competition and how are we to decide whether the economy or some sector of it is adequately competitive? Is competition in an industry to be measured by the number of competitors, by the practices in which they engage, or by the behavior of prices, costs, and profits and the industry's record with respect to innovation?

Those questions will not be answered conclusively in this chapter. But we hope that, when you've finished thinking about the sources and consequences of competition as well as the origins and effects of government policies, you will have a better sense of what the issues are.

The Pressures of Competition

Every seller facing a demand curve that is less than perfectly elastic—tilted downward to the right rather than horizontal—will maximize net revenue by restricting sales or output

and keeping the selling price above marginal cost. How and why that occurs was the theme of the preceding chapter.

One problem from the seller's viewpoint with prices higher than marginal cost is that they are a standing invitation to competition. If a piece of apple pie that costs the cafeteria owner 30 cents is selling for 90 cents, the owner is likely to insist that the 60-cent difference isn't profit; it's only a contribution toward meeting all the other costs of running the cafeteria: labor, taxes, rent, equipment maintenance, breakage, theft, and so on. That may be completely true. Nonetheless, each additional piece of pie that is sold for 90 cents contributes a net 60 cents toward the owner's wealth. If the same is true for all the other cafés and cafeterias in town, each owner will be earnestly wishing that more hungry people would abandon the other eating places and buy their apple pie from him.

Wishes like this often prompt action. Pie prices might be slightly reduced after three o'clock to induce some afternoon coffee-break customers to allow themselves a little treat. Or a sign could be put up after 3 P.M. announcing free coffee with pie purchases. There are dangers inherent in this strategy. Some lunch customers may simply postpone their dessert at noon and have it at three when it's cheaper. And competing restaurants may undermine the promotional effort by offering their own inducements, so that instead of capturing additional customers each owner ends up selling only as much pie as previously but at lower prices.

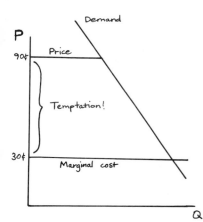

We assumed in the last chapter that Ed Sike and some of the other sellers whose policies we were examining somehow knew exactly what the demand was for their product. That assumption was useful in enabling us to present the logic of the simple price-searching process. In reality, of course, sellers must usually probe for information on the demand for their product and try to stimulate and maintain it by advertising and by offering reliable service. Moreover, when there are several sellers of a product in the market, each seller's demand curve is going to depend on the policies, including the price policies, of those competing sellers. The demand for Ed Sike's film series will shift downward to the left if neighboring theaters show better movies or cut their prices, or if sororities and fraternities pick Friday night to sponsor parties, or if the college basketball team plays home games on Friday nights and hits a winning streak.

The price that any one cafeteria in the downtown area sets for apple pie will affect the demand (curve or schedule) for apple pie at other restaurants. Since each of the restaurants will be using estimates of its own demand to set prices that will, in turn, affect the demand that all other restaurants

encounter, we have a situation more closely resembling chess or poker than a technical maximization problem. The best price for anyone to set *next* may depend on the price set *last*, as in a game of chess. The neat little world of Chapter 9, with its clearly defined curves, becomes blurry. Unfortunately from an analytic standpoint, though perhaps fortunately from an aesthetic one, the real world is not as neatly outlined as the pages in a coloring book.

Chapter 8 introduced the word *oligopoly*, meaning "few sellers." We decided there that the concept of a few sellers shared all the ambiguities of the concept of a sole seller, ambiguities inherent in the problem of deciding just how broadly or narrowly to define the commodity being sold. Some economists have retained the slippery word oligopoly and have assigned it a very special meaning: a situation in which the demand curve of one seller depends on the reactions of identifiable other sellers, sometimes called *rivals*. Whether or not we choose to call this oligopoly—the usage is certainly misleading—situations of that sort, where the demand curves of different sellers are significantly interdependent, are obviously both common and important. It all adds to the competitive pressures of which sellers so commonly complain.

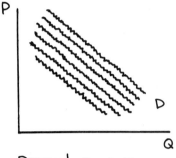

Demand curve as
seller perceives it

Controlling Competition

Then why don't sellers agree not to compete, or to compete less, or to share the market among themselves in some mutually satisfactory way? The answer is that they would very much like to do so and often try, but it isn't as easy as it might seem at first. Agreements between competing sellers to maintain prices and share markets are usually unenforceable in court and are, moreover, illegal under the laws of many states and under federal law where it is applicable. In addition, it's very difficult to devise agreements that everyone will accept, that will cover all the possibilities, and that can be effectively enforced. The incentives to compete are so persistent that soon one or the other party will seek to circumvent the terms of the agreement. On top of all this, successful collusion by the members of a cartel[1] will attract the attention of outsiders, who will begin trying to enter the business in order to enjoy some of the profits that collusion has created.

Cartels consequently reveal a fragility that often surprises people who don't realize on how many margins competition

---

1. A cartel is an agreement among a group of sellers to regulate prices or output. There are also buyers' cartels, such as the owners of professional basketball teams mentioned in Chapter 3 who want a single league to keep down the cost of hiring players.

can occur. To be successful in increasing the wealth of its members, a cartel must solve two problems. It must first prevent competition among its own members from dissipating the profits of collusion, whether through a fall in actual selling prices or a rise in selling costs. And then the cartel must find some way to keep new competitors from spoiling the whole operation by trying to enter the act.

That is why price searchers and even price takers yearn so ardently for *legal* restrictions on competition. Sellers are sometimes extraordinarily imaginative in devising reasons why the government ought to outlaw price cutting or prevent new sellers from entering the market. Here are a few actual items culled from a number of newspapers, with identities sometimes altered slightly to protect the guilty. It's a very good idea to ask in each case exactly who stands to gain and who is most likely to lose.

"The Washington, D.C. Medical Society launched a major lobbying campaign over the weekend against proposed legislation that would encourage granting of hospital privileges to qualified nurse midwives, psychologists, podiatrists and other nonphysician health professionals. The medical society envisioned erosion of standards, speculating in its newsletter that 'pretty soon a boy scout with a rusty knife will be permitted to perform brain surgery.' "

"All plumbers must spend a minimum of 140 hours a year for five years learning higher mathematics, physics, hydraulics, and isometric drawing."

"Woolen makers are arguing that since woolen worsted fabric is essential to national defense, the government should impose quotas on imports from abroad."

"By saying barbers don't need to be licensed you want to put someone across the street or next door to me who can't tell the difference between alopecia areata and acne vulgaris. What am I to think? That I should not have loved my country so much and gone to New Zealand?" (From a letter to the editor written by a barber who had thought of migrating to New Zealand after visiting that country during his World War II service in the merchant marine.)

"The president of the Airline Pilots' Association said the industry needs 'a minimum of deregulation' and a 'zone of reasonableness' that would put a floor under airline fares. He claimed that the new airlines spawned by deregulation were waging suicidal fare wars that are driving some older, unionized airlines to bankruptcy."

"The prominent owner of a local television sales and service center said today that he welcomed the state's investigation of the television repair business and he demanded regulation of the industry. 'We must eliminate janitors, fire

fighters, messengers, and similar amateurs who defraud the public by providing poor-quality service at cut-rate prices,' he argued."

"The Senate Public Health Committee yesterday rejected a bill to allow use of multiple offices and trade names in the diagnosis of eye problems and fitting of glasses. Single-office optometrists contend that optometrists who have private offices are in effect employed by their patients. If optometrists work under a trade name, their boss is their company."

"The owner of the Piney Woods Nursing Home and secretary of the State Association of Licensed Nursing Homes accused the state health department last night of approving new nursing-home construction without proper investigation of the need for additional facilities or the qualifications of the applicants. 'Unqualified people, including speculators from other parts of the country, are hoping to reap big profits,' he said. 'A great surplus of beds will bring about cutthroat competition, which means nursing homes will have to curtail many needed services, resulting in lower standards detrimental to patients and the community.' "

And once again, the plumbers, who aren't any worse than many others but seem to draw better press coverage:

"Changes proposed in the plumbing section of the city building code would require that a plumber serve as an apprentice for five years, instead of the present three, before becoming a journeyman. In addition, apprentices would have to register annually with the city and could not become apprentices after reaching the age of 25. For a plumber to become a master plumber, that is, one contracting plumbing work, an examination would be required. The code now requires only that a plumber seeking master plumber status furnish bond."

The Ambivalence of Government Policies

An old proverb wisely asserts that the wolf should not be sent to guard the sheep. Should the government be relied on to preserve competition in the economy? The history of government intervention in economic life reveals a pattern of concern for the special interests of competitors at least as strong as concern for competition. And the two are not identical, even though our rhetoric so often and easily uses them interchangeably.

The cases cited above show government taking or being urged to take a variety of actions designed to prevent potential sellers from offering more favorable terms or more attractive opportunities to buyers. These actions constitute restrictions on competition, regardless of the arguments used to defend

them. The ultimate effect of a particular restriction on competition may be to preserve competition, by protecting a substantial number of competitors who would otherwise be forced out of business. But whether or not that is the long-term effect in certain cases, it is important to begin any evaluation of government policy toward competition by acknowledging one principle: *A law that restricts competitors restricts competition.*

One extremely common justification for such laws is that they preserve competition by preventing "predatory" practices.

Selling Below Cost

Do you agree with the following paragraph?

"In order to preserve our competitive economic system, we need laws that prohibit unfair practices such as sales below cost. Large firms can often afford to sell products below cost until their rivals are driven out of business. If they are not restrained by law, we could easily wind up with an economy dominated by just a few huge corporations."

Most Americans apparently accept this argument. For our laws, at the federal, state, and local level, abound with provisions designed to prevent or inhibit price cutting. Until recently many states enforced resale-price-maintenance laws, laws that permitted (and in fact assisted) manufacturers and retailers to work together to establish minimum prices and to prosecute retailers who sold below these prices. A special federal law passed in 1937 to exempt such practices from prosecution under the Sherman Act was finally repealed in 1976. But many states still have statutes prohibiting sales below cost, statutes that usually go by some such name as Unfair Practices Act. And regulatory commissions, ostensibly created to hold down the prices that may be charged by public utilities, often wind up enforcing minimum rather than maximum rates. This is true, for example, of the grandfather of all such commissions in the United States, the Interstate Commerce Commission (created by Congress in 1887).

It's fairly obvious why some business firms would approve that kind of legislation: they want protection against competition. But why do consumers and the general public go along? The public seems to have accepted the argument that price cutting can create "monopolies" by driving competitors out of business. And monopolies, of course, are Bad Things.

The paragraph with which this section began states the essential argument. How valid is it? Is it possible to construct a defensible case for laws that prohibit "sales below cost"? A lot of questions should immediately arise in your mind.

What Is the Appropriate Cost?

What is the cost below which prices should not be set? Does anyone actually sell below cost? Why would anyone interested in increasing his wealth ever want to?

Case: Matilda Mudge, proprietor of the Thrifty Supermarket, orders 1000 pounds of ripe bananas. She gets them for 5 cents a pound, because the produce distributor is eager to move them before they become too ripe. Mudge advertises a weekend special on bananas: 10 cents a pound. But Monday morning finds her with 500 pounds of bananas, now beginning to turn brown. How low can Mudge cut her price without selling below cost? The answer is *not* 5 cents a pound. That is sunk cost and hence no cost at all. If Mudge will have to pay someone to haul the unsold bananas away on Tuesday morning, her cost on Monday could be less than zero. In that case it might be to her advantage to give the bananas away. If a zero price is to her advantage, how can it be "below cost"? (By the way, did Mudge *buy* the bananas below cost?)

Or suppose Mudge bought a truckload of coffee: 1000 one-pound cans for $750. It was an unknown brand on which a local distributor offered her an attractive price. But it turns out that her customers aren't interested. She cuts the price down to 80 cents a pound, but still can't move it successfully. Four weeks after her purchase she still has 987 cans of coffee cluttering her shelves and storage room. If she now cuts the price below 75 cents, is she selling below cost? She is not. She has no intention of replacing the cans she sells, so each sale is that many additional cents in the till and one less can in the way. The relevant cost of a pound of coffee could well be zero. The relevant cost is, of course, the marginal cost.

Let's try a different kind of example and then return to Matilda Mudge. It might make sense to estimate the cost of producing a steer, but does it make any sense to estimate separately the cost of producing hindquarters and forequarters? Should the price of steaks, which come from the hindquarter of a beef carcass, cover the cost of producing the hindquarter, leaving it to pot-roast prices to cover the cost of the forequarters from which they derive? The question is nonsensical. Unless it is possible to produce hindquarters separately from forequarters, one cannot speak of the cost of producing one and the cost of producing the other. Hindquarters and forequarters, or steaks and pot roasts, are joint products with joint costs. There is no way to determine the specific costs of joint products or to allocate joint costs "correctly."[2]

---

2. If there are techniques for growing steers with relatively larger hindquarters than forequarters, or vice versa, then it may be possible partially to distinguish the costs under appropriate circumstances.

Back to Matilda Mudge. Can we legitimately segregate the costs of each item sold in her grocery store? Think of her frozen-food items, for example. How much of the cost of owning and operating the freezer case should be allocated to vegetables, how much to Chinese dinners, and how much to orange juice? It's true that she could not carry frozen cauliflower without a freezer case. But if she finds it profitable to own and operate a freezer case just for the sake of the frozen juices she can sell, and if she then has some extra room in which she decides to display boxes of frozen cauliflower, it might make sense for her to assign *none* of the freezer cost to the cauliflower.

A successful businesswoman (or businessman) is not concerned with questions of cost allocation that have no relevance to decision making. She knows that production—and a merchant is a producer just as certainly as is a manufacturer—is usually a process with joint products and joint costs. The businesswoman is interested in the additional costs associated with a decision and the additional revenue to be expected from it, not in such meaningless problems as the allocation of joint costs to particular items for sale. If there is room for a magazine rack near the checkout counter, the question is: How much will its installation *add* to total costs and how much will it *add* to total revenue? If the latter is larger, the rack makes sense; and the magazines sold need not have a price that covers utilities, rent, depreciation on cash registers, *or even the wholesale prices of the magazines.*

Mark well the italicized phrase. It may be profitable to sell a magazine for 5 cents even if it costs 10 cents to obtain it from the distributor. Why? Because the magazine display may bring in new customers who add to net revenue through the purchases of other items. Matilda Mudge is interested not in the net revenue on any one item she sells but in the difference between total revenue and total costs. Retailers have often carried cigarettes not for the sake of the profit they make on the sale of cigarettes but for the sake of the profitable sales of other items that are made possible by carrying cigarettes. Similarly, hardware stores that sell odd-lot bolts, screws, and nuts lose money on each sale but (or so their owners hope) more than make it up through the goodwill they thereby create.

"Predators" and Competition

There would be little point in stressing all this were it not for the popular mythology of "selling below cost." Our argument suggests that many allegations of sales below cost are based on an arbitrary assignment of sunk costs or joint costs.

Below cost?

Cost to whom?

Cost of doing what?

Business firms often complain about below-cost sales, of course; but that is because they dislike competition and want government to protect them from its rigors by prohibiting price cutting.

But aren't there dangers to competition in allowing firms to cut prices as low as they wish? It is odd, but not really surprising, how often people identify the protection of competitors with the preservation of competition. In reality they are more like opposites. Competitors are usually protected by laws inhibiting competition, laws that benefit privileged producers by restricting consumers and nonprivileged producers. The hobgoblin hauled out to justify this is "predatory price cutting" backed up by a "long purse."

Predatory price cutting means reducing prices below cost in order to drive a rival out of business or prevent new rivals from emerging *with the intention of raising prices afterward to recoup all losses.* It is supposedly a favorite tactic of larger firms who can stand prolonged losses, or temporary losses on some lines, because of their larger financial resources—the so-called "long purse." Economic theory does not deny the possibility of predatory price cutting. But it does raise a long list of skeptical questions, headed by all the questions we have been discussing regarding the proper definition of an item's cost.

How long will it take for such a policy to accomplish its end? The longer it takes, the larger will be the short-run losses accepted by the predator firm and, consequently, the larger must be the long-term benefits if the policy is to justify itself.

What will happen to the physical assets and human resources of the firms forced out of business? That's an important question, because if those assets remain in existence, what is to prevent someone from bringing them back into production when the predator firm raises its prices to reap the rewards of its villainy? And if this occurs, how can the firm hope to benefit from its predatory policy? On the other hand, the human resources may scatter into alternative employments and be costly to reassemble.

Is it likely that the predator firm will be able to destroy enough of its rivals to secure the degree of market power that it must have to make the long-run profits justify the short-run losses? Charges of predatory pricing have most frequently been leveled against large discount houses, drug chains, and grocery supermarkets. But these sellers are not pitted exclusively against small independent competitors: they must tangle with other large discount houses, other drug chains, and other supermarkets. Perhaps A&P could cut its prices far enough and keep them low enough to drive Matilda Mudge out of business, but that wouldn't work on Safeway.

Protecting competitors is not the same as preserving competition.

And it's Safeway, not Matilda Mudge, that keeps A&P executives awake at night.

We are not denying the possibility of predatory pricing in business. Well-documented examples are hard to find, but it is surely possible. Minimum-price laws, however, offer the *certainty* of higher prices in order to eliminate the *possibility* of higher prices: a case of accepting a known and certain evil as a way of avoiding an uncertain evil of unknown dimensions. That may or may not be a good social bargain. But since it is so often advocated by business firms that clearly stand to gain from it, we should at least approach their arguments skeptically.

"Antitrust" Policy

We shall see in Chapter 14 why it is that governments so often intervene in ways that harm consumers by *reducing* competition, despite the fact that consumers and competition always win easily in the rhetorical battles. But local and state governments and especially the federal government also have adopted specific policies to *promote* competition, policies that are ordinarily justified on the ground that competition is an effective coordinator of economic activity but requires some government maintenance if it is to be adequately preserved. The assessment of these laws, their applications, and their consequences forms an interesting study in history and judicial interpretation as well as economic analysis. All we shall try to do here, however, is raise a few fundamental questions.

The most important such law is the Sherman Act, often called the Sherman Antitrust Act, enacted by Congress with almost no debate or opposition in 1890. (The name reflects the attempts of nineteenth-century businessmen to use legal trusteeships as a device to prevent competition.) Its sweeping language has caused some to call it the constitution of the competitive system. It forbids all contracts, combinations, or conspiracies in restraint of interstate trade and all attempts to monopolize any part of interstate trade. The language is so sweeping, in fact, that it was bound to be qualified in its application. After all, any two partners entering into business together could be deemed to have combined with the intention of making trade more difficult for their competitors and thus gaining an ever-larger share of trade for themselves. The federal courts consequently came to hold that combinations or other attempts to monopolize had to be "unreasonable" or major threats to public welfare before they could be prohibited under the Sherman Act.

To help the courts in their efforts to apply the policies of the Sherman Act, Congress has passed additional legislation such as the Clayton Act and the Federal Trade Commission Act, both of which became law in 1914. The latter act created the Federal Trade Commission as a supposedly expert body and authorized it to promote competition by prohibiting a wide range of "unfair" practices. A principal provision of the Clayton Act (and subsequent amendments) aims specifically at the question of mergers, prohibiting all mergers that might "substantially" lessen competition. But difficult and important questions remain unresolved.

When does a merger substantially lessen competition? And do mergers ever increase competition? Suppose two steel firms want to merge. This is usually referred to as a *horizontal merger*. At first glance we would be inclined to say that the merger will substantially lessen competition in an industry already made up of a relatively few very large firms. But suppose they sell in different geographic areas? Suppose they each specialize in a different line of steel products? Suppose each is on the edge of failure and that the merger will lead to economies that may enable both to survive?

A great deal of dispute has arisen in recent years regarding so-called *conglomerate mergers:* mergers between firms producing widely divergent goods. Does the acquisition of a car-rental firm by an electrical-machinery manufacturer enable the rental firm to compete more effectively against Hertz and Avis? Does it lead to special arrangements between the machinery manufacturer, its suppliers, and the rental firm that tie up a portion of the car-rental business and thus reduce competition? Do conglomerate mergers lead to concentrations of financial power that are dangerous and undesirable regardless of their effects on competition?

What about *vertical mergers,* mergers between firms that previously existed in a supplier-buyer relationship, as when a supermarket chain acquires a food processor? Is this more likely to increase efficiency or to reduce competition by depriving other food processors of opportunities to sell?

What constitutes an illegally unfair trade practice? Is it unfair for a large firm to demand discounts from its suppliers? Is it unfair for suppliers to offer discounts to some purchasers but not to others? What about the whole question of advertising? Do large firms have unfair advantages in advertising, advantages that advertising increases? Must advertising be truthful in order to be fair? Of course it must, almost by definition. But what is the truth, the whole truth, and nothing but the truth? Anyone who thinks about this issue seriously

Horizontal merger
Two oil-refining
companies

Conglomerate merger:
An oil-refining
company and
a steel maker

Vertical merger:
An oil-refining
company and a
gasoline-retailing
chain

or for very long is forced to admit that the regulation of "deceptive" advertising by the Federal Trade Commission inevitably involves the commission in complex questions of purpose and effect and in a large number of judgments that appear quite arbitrary.

And always we return to the root problem: restrictions on competitors will reduce their ability to compete. Competition is essentially the offering of additional opportunities, and additional opportunities mean a wider range of choices and hence greater wealth. But the manner in which a firm expands the set of opportunities it offers may diminish, over a short or a longer period, the set of opportunities other firms are able to offer. Under what circumstances do we want the government to restrict one firm's competitive efforts for the sake of the larger or long-run competitive situation? It is important to remember that many of the most effective pressures on government policies stem not from consumer but from producer interests. And those policies will too often be shaped by the desire of producers to protect themselves against the rigors of the competitive life.

The Range of Opinion

Is the whole body of "antitrust" law perhaps more of a hindrance than a help to competition? There are some who come to that conclusion. There are others—heavily concentrated, it often seems, in the economics profession—who would retain the Sherman Act and the antimerger provisions of the Clayton Act and junk the rest. Some of these defenders claim that the Sherman and Clayton acts have made important contributions to the maintenance of a competitive economy. Others claim that they could make a much larger contribution if they were seriously enforced. But still others view them at best as harmless rhetoric, at worst as weapons that, in the hands of ignorant political appointees, may do a lot of damage to the economy.

The author is firmly convinced that he doesn't know who is right. "Antitrust" policy is certainly full of contradictions, of cases where the right hand is doing what the left hand is undoing. State laws rarely promote competition; more often they promote the interests of the competitor protectors rather than the competition protectors. Federal enforcement of the Sherman Act and the antimerger provisions of the Clayton Act often seems to strain at gnats while swallowing camels. Firms unable to compete effectively by offering their customers lower prices and better quality sometimes file complaints under the antitrust laws to see if they can persuade the courts to raise the prices or reduce the quality of their competitors'

offerings. On the other hand, the existence of the Sherman Act, with its ringing denunciation of price-fixing conspiracies, may have retarded the development in this country of the cartel arrangements that have so often appeared in Western Europe and Japan. The economist George Stigler once suggested that "the ghost of Senator Sherman is an ex officio member of the board of directors of every large company." That statement will never meet the minimum criteria for empirical scientific truths, but good history is still a long way from being a pure science.

Toward Evaluation

The conclusions that we shall offer at the end are far more modest than the questions with which we began. They are only two in number.

Restrictions on potential competitors reduce the range and diminish the availability of substitute goods, and allow sellers more room to increase their own wealth by denying opportunities to others. Competition is a process, not a state of affairs. To put it another way, competition can be recognized only in motion pictures, not in still photographs. The fact, for example, that the price of some good is exactly the same, no matter from which seller you buy, establishes absolutely nothing about whether the industry producing that good is adequately competitive. The important question is how those prices all came to be identical. It happens with surprising frequency that even public figures, who ought to know better, will infer an absence of competition from the uniformity of price. The quickest antidote to this error is the recollection that wheat farmers all charge the same price.

The other observation is that an inadequate situation must be compared with more desirable situations that are actually attainable. It is a mistake to contrast a less-than-ideal situation with an ideal-but-unattainable situation. There are costs involved in changing market structures, such as the cost of an investigation, prosecution, court order, and compliance under antitrust statutes. Only if these marginal costs are less than the marginal benefits can one maintain that we would be "better off" if we took legal action to reduce the market power of price searchers, to prevent business mergers, or to prohibit practices that might eventually lessen competition.

Once Over Lightly

A gap between the price of a good and the marginal cost of making it available is a source of potential advantage to someone. Competition occurs in the economy as people locate

such differentials and try to exploit them by filling that gap with additional goods.

Competition takes more forms than we can list and usually more forms than competitors can anticipate and head off.

Because competition tends to transfer the gains from providing a good to purchasers and to other suppliers, firms frequently try to obtain government assistance in excluding competitors, often displaying remarkable ingenuity and stunning sophistry.

Firms often charge that their competitors, whether domestic or foreign, are "selling below cost" and call for the government to prevent such "predatory" practices. Most such charges make sense only if they include some expenses in per-unit cost that are irrelevant to the particular decisions under attack. They make a different kind of sense when we remember that sellers characteristically prefer less competition.

The notion that government is the Defender of Competition Against Rapacious Monopolists is probably more a hope than a reality. Federal, state, and local governments have created and preserved numerous positions of special privilege whose effect is to restrict competition and reduce the options available to consumers.

An adequate and balanced evaluation of the substantial body of statutes, commission decrees, and judicial holdings that makes up federal antitrust policy has not yet been published.

Competition is a process in which competitors engage. We obviously cannot have competition without competitors. It does not seem as obvious to people that we also cannot have competition if we prohibit competitors from taking actions intended to increase their share of the market.

QUESTIONS FOR DISCUSSION

1. How would you account for the fact that although some observers claim competition is declining in the American economy, every business firm insists that it faces strenuous competition?

2. Consult the technical definition of *oligopoly* presented in the text. Are the manufacturers of cigarettes oligopolists by that definition? Are the owners of the gasoline stations in a small town oligopolists? Name some other sellers who are and are not oligopolists by that definition.

3. The attempt by sellers to make their product more attractive to consumers is sometimes called *product differentiation.*
   (a) Is product differentiation a wasteful process, imposing costs on sellers that are greater than the benefits conferred on buyers? Think of cases

where it probably is wasteful in this sense and other cases where it is not.

(b) Evaluate the following argument: "New practices initiated by sellers to differentiate their products are liable to be wasteful from the social point of view because they are liable to entail high marginal costs and low marginal benefits. But this only means that producers have already made use of the low-cost/high-benefit techniques of product differentiation; it does not show that the whole process of product differentiation is wasteful."

4. A 1982 survey by a New York advertising agency found that many consumers thought there were too many different brands available for sale in several product categories. For example, 72 percent of the consumers surveyed thought there were too many brands of dry cereal, and 60 percent thought there were too many brands of bar soap. How many is "too many" from your point of view if you know exactly what you want? How many is "too few" if you can't find what you're looking for? (The survey by Batten, Barton, Durstine, and Osborn was described in the April 22, 1982, issue of the *Wall Street Journal*.)

5. Why must an effective price-fixing agreement between sellers include such restrictions on sales as output limitations or geographic divisions of sales territory?

6. This problem is designed to help you appreciate the joys and tribulations of cartels.

   Let D in Figure 10A be the demand for oil and MC the sum of the marginal cost curves of all oil producers. (Ignore the line labeled H for now.)

(a) If oil producers are price takers because there are thousands of them and they have no effective cartel, why will the price of oil move toward $9 per barrel? What will occur if the price is much above or below $9?

(b) Now assume that one party acquires control over all producing oil wells and hence the power to control the price by controlling output. How many millions of barrels per day (mb/d) will be produced if the goal is to maximize net revenue? What price will be set?

(c) Change the above assumption slightly. The oil wells remain under the ownership and control of the thousands of original owners, but each owner agrees to sell only at the price determined by the Organizer of Prices to Exploit Consumers (OPEC). This is an agent hired by the oil producers to determine and announce the price for oil that will be most advantageous to oil producers collectively. OPEC announces that the price shall be $29 per barrel. What must occur if this price is to hold?

(d) Why will the individual oil producers want to sell individually a quantity of oil that sums in aggregate to far more than 13 mb/d?

(e) How can OPEC prevent output from expanding way beyond 13 mb/d and thereby bringing down the price of oil? If OPEC assigns production quotas to each individual oil producer, how can it make sure that all the producers will be satisfied that their quotas are "fair"? How can it make sure that individual producers don't exceed their quotas?

(f) Is the demand curve for oil that obtains when oil has long been selling at $9 per barrel and is expected to remain at about that level likely to

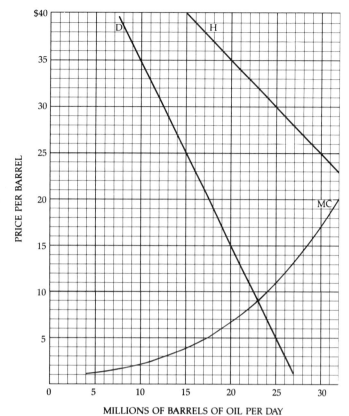

Figure 10A Market demand for oil and combined marginal cost curves of producers

remain unchanged when the price of oil rises to $29 per barrel and is expected to stay at that much higher level for a number of years? What sort of developments are likely to *shift the demand* over time? What effect will this have on the oil producers who created OPEC?

(g) A serious threat to the wealth of the OPEC oil producers is likely to come from *new* producers who are attracted into the industry by OPEC's success in raising the price of oil. In the case of the real-world OPEC (Organization of Petroleum Exporting Countries), the 13 member nations saw their sales decline between 1980 and 1985 from over 30 mb/d to fewer than 15 mb/d, with some of the difference reflecting a reduced total demand but most of it a result of increased production by non-OPEC members. Suppose that H had been the demand for OPEC oil in the happy days when the cartel began operating. Compare the price, output, and total revenue of OPEC's members when the demand is H with the price, output, and total revenue when the demand is D—even assuming no "cheating" by cartel members.

7. The analysis in the preceding question raises an interesting issue: Why did the Organization of Petroleum Exporting Countries succeed so well for so

long in raising the world price of oil? A major part of any answer is contained in the concept of the marginal cost of producing and selling oil. The cost of extracting oil from an established field can be very low indeed, so low as to be almost negligible. But the relevant marginal cost is the cost of extracting *and selling*. In the 1970s, many respected parties were predicting that, because the demand for petroleum products was highly inelastic and the world's reserves were quickly running out, the price per barrel might rise by the end of the century as high as $1000 a barrel. How do expectations of such dramatically higher future prices affect the opportunity cost of selling oil currently? How would such expectations solve OPEC's "cheating" problem? Why did those extravagant expectations, so common in the 1970s, disappear by the mid-1980s?

8. Some states have established legal minimum prices for liquor sold at retail. Do you think this eliminates competition among retail liquor stores? Why do you think retailers in such states often lend glassware without charge to customers planning parties?

9. All the real-estate brokers in an area will generally charge the same fee for selling a house, a certain percentage of the sales price established by some association and adhered to by all real-estate agents as a matter of "ethical practice."
   (a) Why would it be unethical if a broker offered to accept 5 rather than 6 percent for selling your house? Toward whom would it be unethical?
   (b) How do real-estate agents compete with one another?
   (c) Is an industry likely to become overcrowded if it's successful in fixing a high minimum price for its product? Is the real-estate profession overcrowded in your judgment? What evidence might be used to answer this question?

10. A survey reported in the *Harvard Business Review* asked businessmen to describe the unethical practices in their own industry that they would most like to see eliminated. Of those responding, 62 percent mentioned "unfair pricing," "dishonest advertising," "unfair competitive practices," or "cheating customers." How would you interpret these responses? How would you define the practices they condemn?

11. Examine the paragraph in the text recounting the complaint of the nursing-home operator. How many wrong or misleading assertions can you locate in that paragraph?

12. The legislature of a large state recently considered a bill that would require all grocery stores and drugstores selling package liquor to provide separate entrances to their liquor departments. It was maintained by supporters of the bill that this was necessary to prevent minors from entering the liquor department. Who do you think lobbied for this bill? Why?

13. A study several years ago pointed out that 73 percent of the professions licensed by a populous midwestern state required entrants to have "good character." Why? How can good character be determined? Who is best able to determine whether a mortician's character is sufficiently blameless to entitle him to a license?

14. The Seattle City Council stopped setting taxicab rates in May 1979. Since that time there have been several efforts to compel the city to resume reg-

ulation. Are you surprised to learn that these efforts are being financed and promoted by the owners of taxicabs? Do you believe their statement: "We're doing it to keep people from being ripped off"?

15. A former chief executive officer of AT&T testified in August 1981, in an antitrust suit, that AT&T had tried to forestall competition to the Bell system in order to safeguard its quality of service rather than to protect its profit. Does that claim surprise you? Do you think it's true?

16. A March 10, 1982, letter to the *Wall Street Journal* argued that "continued economic regulation of the motor carrier industry . . . is in the public interest." The letter, signed by the president of the American Trucking Association, argued that collective rate making and restrictions on entry were necessary to prevent unstable service, industry concentration, loss of service to small communities, predatory pricing, and discrimination against small shippers and small communities. Are you surprised to learn that members of the American Trucking Association *want* to be regulated by government so that they don't act contrary to the public interest?

17. The president of a county medical society in Florida warned doctors there that if they took out even a small ad in the Yellow Pages, they would be "summarily called before the executive committee of the county association to explain their actions." He added his opinion that using bold-face type in a standard Yellow Pages listing constituted "unprofessional conduct."
    (a) What kind of doctor is least likely to want to advertise? Which doctors are most likely to want to advertise?
    (b) What is the consumer interest in this matter? Is advertising by physicians likely to lead to better or poorer service for patients?

18. An advocate of state regulation of cosmetologists and barbers in Washington State argued that the state cosmetology agency had taken in $756,805 in revenue in the preceding year while spending only $589,014, thus providing a net benefit to the state. Where would you look to locate some additional costs created by the agency?

19. When the Washington State legislature was debating a bill in 1981 that would allow optometrists to administer certain eyedrops during eye exams, 50 ophthalmologists descended on the Capitol to lobby against the bill. The chairman of the state Academy of Ophthalmology told a reporter: "There is no economic advantage one way or the other." The ophthalmologists' sole concern was that, if the bill became law, "more people will be harmed through inappropriate use of drugs." Do you believe that 50 medical specialists all took a day off from their practices to lobby the legislature exclusively out of concern for the public's health?

20. In January 1983 a U.S. appeals court rejected a lower-court finding that AT&T had engaged in "predatory pricing" against MCI Communications Inc. by setting rates "below cost" on some of its long-distance services. Go back to question 1 in Chapter 5 and examine AT&T's explanation of what a long-distance call "costs." Would you be willing to argue that any price under 68.9 cents for the initial minute is evidence of below-cost pricing? How would you determine whether particular long-distance rates are above or below cost?

21. In June 1983 the U.S. Justice Department agreed to drop a consent decree that it had extracted from Safeway 25 years earlier, under which Safeway had been prohibited from selling at prices below its cost of acquiring grocery products or at "unreasonably low prices" that might be above cost. The decree stemmed from a government suit that had accused Safeway of selling below cost in an effort to monopolize the market for retail food in Texas and New Mexico.

   (a) How likely is it that Safeway or anyone else would be able to monopolize the market for retail food in two states?

   (b) The alleged attempt to monopolize led Safeway to reduce prices to customers. Who do you suppose complained to the Justice Department about Safeway's behavior?

   (c) What is the appropriate way to determine the cost of specific grocery items? Is a retailer selling paper bags below cost when it makes them available to customers at no charge? Is the retailer cross-subsidizing paper bags? (For more on cross-subsidies, see question 24 below, especially part (d).)

22. Which of the following products are being sold below cost? With what other products are they competing? Is the competition "unfair"?

   (a) Coffee offered by a bank to its customers without charge

   (b) As many cups of coffee after dinner as the diner in an expensive restaurant requests, at no extra charge

   (c) Commercial television programs

   (d) Soft drinks on an airline flight

   (e) A roll of film given to each adult customer during a pizza shop's first week of operation

23. Three elements that must be present for a firm to be engaged in predatory pricing are pricing (1) below cost, (2) in order to eliminate rivals, and (3) with the intention of raising prices afterward to recoup. What factors would make the last step of the process difficult to complete? Under what kinds of circumstances would it be relatively easy? Can you cite any actual examples?

24. Here is a simplified problem on "predatory pricing" to help you get a clearer grasp of some of the issues.

   The demand for the shipping services of the Midwestern Railroad Company is shown as D in Figure 10B. The marginal cost to Midwestern of carrying freight is $1 per ton-mile. In addition to its marginal costs, Midwestern has monthly expenses of $480,000 covering all those costs that are not affected by the amount of freight the railroad carries: property taxes, mortgage payments on equipment, most wages and salaries, etc.

   (a) If Midwestern sets marginal cost equal to marginal revenue to maximize its net revenue from operation of the railroad, what rate will it set per ton-mile? How many ton-miles of freight will it carry per month? What will be its monthly loss?

   (b) Now assume that the demand curve above $2.00 is entirely the demand from coal producers, and that the demand below $2.00 comes entirely from grain shippers. If Midwestern sets different rates for coal and for

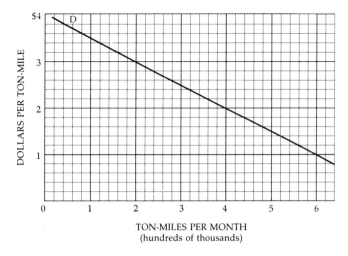

Figure 10B Demand for shipping services of the Midwestern Railroad Company

grain, what rate will it want to set in each case to maximize net revenue? How many ton-miles of coal and of grain respectively will Midwestern carry each month? What will now be its total costs and its total revenue?

(c) Suppose that prior to the institution of a separate and lower price for grain, barge companies on the Ohio, Illinois, and Mississippi rivers had been charging $2.00 per ton-mile to carry grain. Why will they be unhappy about Midwestern's two-price policy? If they want to protest that Midwestern is charging a price "below cost," what evidence can they come up with to support their complaint? What is Midwestern's "total cost" per unit for carrying a ton-mile of freight?

(d) If Midwestern is carrying grain "below cost," is it "cross-subsidizing" by using the "excess profits" earned from "exploiting" coal producers? Or is it also carrying coal "below cost"? How can Midwestern earn a positive net revenue by charging rates "below cost" on all the freight it carries? (To clarify the picture, you might want to plot Midwestern's total cost per unit on the graph, and then note the relationship between price and cost under first a single-price and then a dual-price policy.)

(e) If you were a member of a regulatory commission charged with preventing exploitation of shippers as well as predatory pricing aimed at competitors while also preserving the profits of the railroad, would you approve or disapprove Midwestern's dual-price policy?

25. The Staggers Rail Act of 1980 substantially reduced the power of the Interstate Commerce Commission to control the rates that railroads charge shippers.

(a) The president of the National Coal Association has denounced the system of "letting the railroads charge what the traffic will bear" and has called for renewed rate regulation. Many other shippers, however, applaud the extensive deregulation of the railroads. Why might the coal industry favor rate regulation while most other shippers oppose it?

(b) One 1983 study of the price elasticity of demand for rail transport of grain in the Corn Belt states calculated an elasticity coefficient of 3.75. What is the nature of the competition that makes the demand elasticity so high?

(c) If the railroads, barge lines, and trucking firms of this country were allowed to set their rates free from government regulation, what do you think would follow: "gouging of customers" (higher prices) or "ruinous price cutting" (lower prices)? Does this happen in other areas of the economy where prices are not regulated by commissions—for example, in the grocery or automobile industries?

26. What is the difference between reducing prices to attract more customers and reducing prices in order to monopolize?

27. The Federal Trade Commission staff sought (unsuccessfully) in 1980 to secure approval for "no-fault" antitrust cases. The government would not have to prove, under this approach, that a large firm had acted anticompetitively, only that the firm in fact commands a dominant share of the market. Would this promote or retard competition?

28. Think about this assertion put forward by the economist M.A. Adelman: "A useful if not very precise index of the strength of competition . . . is the resentment of unsuccessful competitors." How would you evaluate the argument by other firms in the office equipment industry that IBM engages in unfair competition?

Profit

"Perhaps no term or concept in economic discussion is used with a more bewildering variety of well-established meanings than *profit*." That sentence was written about fifty years ago by Frank Knight, a distinguished student of the subject, to introduce an encyclopedia article on profit. The situation has not changed greatly since then. A few years ago the *Wall Street Journal* ran a feature article entitled "Some Plain Truth about Profit." The author listed no fewer than seven distinct definitions of the word *profit* that have been employed by "economic experts," decided none of them was very helpful, and then offered his own. A month later the *Journal* published seven letters of response from its readers; their verdicts on the new definition and accompanying exposition ran from excellent through misleading to ridiculous.

So what shall we do? We shall take the coward's course and assert that *there is no correct definition of profit*. The meaning of any word depends, after all, on the way people use it; and it is an incontrovertible fact that people (including economists) use *profit* in many different senses. We certainly don't want to quibble about mere definitions. But attitudes toward profit and such closely related concepts as cost of production and interest affect economic legislation, and those attitudes depend in large part on what people have in mind when they use the terms. So we're going to expend an unusual amount of effort in this chapter trying to decide what things ought to be called, but only insofar as we must do so to avoid both misleading distinctions and misleading identifications. We don't want to ignore important realities. But neither do we want to be misled by language into seeing things that don't exist.

Profit as "Total Revenue Minus Total Cost"

The most common definition of profit is simply *total revenue minus total cost*. That's almost everyone's intuitive definition of the term and that's how we've used it until now. A synonym would be *net revenue*. When a business firm has paid all of its costs, what it has left over is profit, or net revenue. But before we can agree on the size of profits, defined in this way, we have to agree on what counts as costs.

What Should Be Included in Costs?

Monetary outlays are not the same as costs, at least not from the opportunity-cost perspective. This is clear in the case of an owner-operated business: part of the cost of doing business is the owner's own labor, even though owners may not figure their salaries as part of their regular costs and write no weekly payroll check to themselves. If owners pay rent for the building they use, they'll count the rental payments as part of their costs; but they may fail to do so if they themselves own the building. They ought to do so, however, because they're losing the amount that could be obtained from renting the building to someone else. There is a genuine cost in not having the building available for alternative uses.

Business proprietors may also be using equipment that they bought and now own. If they bought the equipment with a bank loan, they will include the interest on their bank payments in their costs. But suppose they bought the equipment out of previously accumulated savings? Then they gave up interest income that they could have obtained from letting someone else use their savings, and this is certainly part of the opportunity cost of doing business. But they may or may not decide to include the forgone income in their costs. The point is that they should. The income forgone represents a genuine cost for the business.

Corporate profits have a legal definition because corporations must pay taxes on their profits. But the legal definition is unsatisfactory from an opportunity-cost point of view. It begins with the commonsense definition of profit as revenue minus costs. But it excludes from cost the dividend payments made to stockholders of the corporation while including the interest payments made to bondholders. Are these payments that different? Both seem to be payments for the use of borrowed funds. The principal difference is that payments to bondholders are a contractual obligation of a fixed amount, whereas the dividends paid to stockholders are a kind of residual that may vary from year to year or quarter to quarter. Still, the funds loaned by the stockholders are funds not earning income somewhere else, and those funds were loaned only because the stockholders expected to receive a return

The total cost of operating an enterprise is the value of all the opportunities that must be given up in order to operate it.

at least equal in value to their next best opportunity. Surely some portion of the dividends paid by corporations represents a cost of doing business, no matter how dividends are regarded for purposes of taxation.

Why Is Interest Paid?

But why is interest paid in the first place? For what is it a payment?

The notion that interest is a payment for the use of money, the way that a Hertz or Avis fee is a payment for the use of a car, is quite mistaken. My employer offers me money in return for my services; I hand that money over to grocers, utility companies, and others to secure goods that they supply and I want; they in turn use the money I provide them to pay their employees, and so on. None of us pays any interest for the use of the money that changes hands in this way. Moreover, if I choose to put a pair of $20 bills into my sugar bowl for a rainy day and it doesn't rain for several years, the Federal Reserve Bank that issued those bills doesn't charge me for their use during this period. Contrast that with the probable reaction of Hertz or Avis if I stored one of their cars in my garage for a rainy day.

We don't pay any rent to Federal Reserve Banks for use of the paper money they have produced and put into circulation.

The usual way to obtain money is to earn it by selling a service to someone. We only pay interest when we *borrow* money. Borrowing is a matter of obtaining money that we have not earned—*yet*. Borrowers want money *now* though they currently have no valuable service to offer in exchange for it. They persuade lenders to give them money now by promising to pay later. The ratio between what is given back later and what is obtained now determines the interest rate.

Interest is thus the price that people pay to obtain resources now rather than wait until they have earned the money with which to buy the resources. The best way to think about interest is to view it as *the premium paid to obtain current command of resources.*

People pay interest in order to obtain current command over resources.

To explain why interest is paid, then, we must explain why present resources are generally more valuable than future resources. That isn't too hard to understand. Having resources now expands one's opportunities. Present command of resources will often enable us to do things that cause our earning capacity to increase over time, so that we will have more resources at some future date than we would otherwise have had. When we see such a prospect, we want to borrow. And we are willing to pay, if we have to, a premium—interest—as long as the interest is less than what we expect to gain as a result of borrowing.

Present command of resources is generally worth more than future command of the same resources.

Suppose that Robinson Crusoe, long a useful character in economists' arguments, keeps himself alive from day to day

by digging for clams with his fingernails. Five clams a day is the most he can obtain by digging with his hands during every available hour. And five clams per day is just enough to keep body and soul together, so that Robinson is living on the edge of bare subsistence. If he had a shovel, however, he could triple his daily output to fifteen clams. Unfortunately for Robinson, it would require a month's work to manufacture a suitable shovel, during which time he could not dig for clams and would consequently starve.

How many clams would Robinson Crusoe be willing to give up later in return for 150 clams now, or more accurately, in return for five clams a day on each of the next thirty days while he is all tied up in shovel making? He could *afford* to give up as many as 300 clams at the end of the second month and each month thereafter, because that is how much the loan of 150 clams now would increase his productivity in future months. Presumably he would be *willing* to give up any amount less than that if he had no other way of obtaining a shovel.

Clams now are worth more than clams later if, as in this case, present command of clams enables one to increase the future production of clams. The rate of exchange between present and future clams would be the rate of interest in Robinson Crusoe's world. And it would have no relationship at all to money.

There are very few tasks that cannot be performed more effectively with the appropriate tools, which is to say, with the assistance of *capital*. Capital in economics means *produced goods used to increase the production of future goods*. Examples include Crusoe's shovel, cash registers in retail stores, drill presses in a sheet-metal fabricating shop, the card catalogue in libraries, and all the skills embodied in human beings that enable them to produce more goods than they could produce before they acquired those skills. As long as people believe that they can increase their future productivity by acquiring present command of resources and creating capital from them, they will be willing to pay a premium to obtain resources now rather than wait until they have "earned" them.

Interest is consequently not something unique to capitalist economies, much less a result of the avarice and power of bankers and other moneylenders. Above all, it is not something that could be eliminated just by making more money available. Interest rates are generally talked about as if they were the cost of borrowing money simply because money is the usual means by which people acquire possession of present goods. But interest would exist in an economy that functioned without money, since it's fundamentally the difference in value between present and future goods.

We don't want to leave the impression that it's only the

Cost of producing a shovel: 30 days' labor, or 150 clams.

Value of owning a shovel: 300 clams per month.

productivity of capital that makes resources now generally more valuable than resources at some future date. Consumers also seem to display what the economist calls *a positive rate of time preference;* that is, people tend to place a higher subjective value on consumption in the near future than on consumption in the more distant future. Some critics have interpreted this as evidence of shortsightedness, or of inability to imagine the distant future with as much vividness and force as one contemplates the immediate future, or of an innate human tendency to view the future through rose-tinted glasses. Each of these interpretations casts suspicion on the ultimate "rationality" of time preference. Given the facts of human mortality, however, and all the contingencies of life, it isn't necessarily irrational or shortsighted to prefer a bird in the hand to two in the bush. Moreover, if people have reason to believe that their income will increase over time, they could very logically conclude that giving up something now entails a larger subjective sacrifice than giving up quite a bit more of the same thing at a future date when they expect their income to be larger.

Whatever the relative importance of each factor, it is clear that people's beliefs about the productivity of capital goods and their preferences for consuming sooner rather than later have combined to produce a premium on present goods over future goods and thus a positive rate of interest in every known society. Interest is paid, then—to answer the question with which we began this section—to induce people to give up present command of resources. It is a payment for the value of the opportunity that lenders forgo, a payment that borrowers are willing to make because of the opportunities that borrowing opens up for them.

The Risk Factor in Interest Rates

The rates charged by banks to corporate borrowers, by department stores to customers with revolving charge accounts, or by individuals lending to savings-and-loan institutions all reflect the net rate of time preference in a particular society. But they also include risk premiums of various sizes plus differences in the cost of negotiating loans. It will ordinarily cost you more per dollar to borrow from a commercial bank than it will cost a large and successful corporation. This doesn't really mean that you're paying a higher rate of interest, however. You are paying for the costs incurred by the bank in investigating your credit standing and doing the bookkeeping entailed by your loan, as well as a kind of insurance premium that the bank collects from the borrower in anticipation of losses through costs of collection and defaults. If the bank could not charge this premium, it would not find it

advantageous to make loans to customers in higher-risk categories. So when legislators impose ceilings on the "annual interest" that lenders may legally charge, they don't reduce interest rates so much as they exclude certain categories of borrowers from contracting for loans. Since the borrowers wouldn't contract for the loans unless they deemed them advantageous, it's difficult to discover in what way maximum interest-rate laws benefit low-income borrowers.

This is an important point, and not only because it corrects certain popular but mistaken notions about interest-rate legislation. The return that any lender will demand as a condition of lending depends on what the lender could obtain by lending to a different borrower *plus* the risk assigned to that particular loan. Commercial lenders aren't unique in that respect. Imagine the bonds of two corporations, one of them Exxon and the other a shaky corporation teetering on the edge of bankruptcy. Both sets of bonds have a maturity value of $1000 and are scheduled to mature one year from now. At what prices will these bonds be bought and sold on the market?

$$\$1000 \div 1.12 = \$892.96$$

Suppose the Exxon issue sells at $893. That $893 now is worth $1000 at maturity (in one year) at a 12 percent rate of interest. The $893 price would mean, in effect, that people are willing to hold Exxon bonds for a 12 percent annual return, because $893 times 1.12, the principal plus the interest, is $1000.

But the bonds of the shaky corporation would sell for far less even if they were bought by the same people who purchased the Exxon bonds. The probability of default is so much higher in the second case that buyers could be persuaded to take the risk only if they were offered the possibility of a very high return. If the second issue sold for $714, buyers would be demanding the possibility of a 40 percent annual return.

$$\$1000 \div \$714 = 1.40$$

If all works out well, they'll receive $179 more than they would have earned from holding an Exxon bond. But that outcome is highly uncertain, and there is also the possibility they'll lose most or all of the principal. The higher "interest rate" on the latter bonds should therefore be interpreted as a risk premium, rather than as pure interest. Perhaps when legislators contemplate interest-rate ceilings, they should ask themselves whether they have ever purchased bonds at a heavy discount.

$$
\begin{array}{r}
\$1000 \\
-\ 893 \\
\hline
\$\ 107
\end{array}
\qquad
\begin{array}{r}
\$1000 \\
-\ 714 \\
\hline
\$\ 286
\end{array}
$$

Uncertainty as the Source of Profit

Let's summarize the argument now. Total cost is opportunity cost, and so it includes not only a firm's payments to others for commodities and services used, but also the implicit value

of any goods—labor, land, capital—that the firm itself
supplies. Interest payments are part of the firm's costs,
including the portion of its dividends that is about equal
to the interest return its shareholders could have received by
lending their money elsewhere. When we include all these
opportunity costs in our calculations of total costs, there seems
to be no reason why any firm would have to earn revenues
in excess of costs. Firms could make zero profits and continue
in business. They could even be considered successful firms
and be able to borrow new funds for expansion—so long
as their revenues were adequate to cover all their costs.

In fact, if there were some way for a firm to get into a
line of business that *guaranteed* more in revenue than it entailed
in cost, wouldn't so many people move into that line of
business that competition would reduce the difference between
revenue and cost to zero? Remember that cost means all
costs, including an actual or implicit payment for getting the
business organized and keeping it in operation. The certainty
of a return greater than this would surely attract new
business firms. Their entry would increase output, reduce the
price of the product consistently with the law of demand,
and thus reduce the gap between total revenue and total cost.
The gap might simultaneously be reduced from the other
direction as the new entrants increased the demand and raised
the cost for the inputs used in turning out the product. Only
when the gap between total revenue and total cost had
disappeared, or when profits had been reduced to zero, would
there no longer be any incentive for new firms to enter.

In the actual, continually changing, and always uncertain
world, it doesn't work that way. People see profits being
made in particular lines of business but they aren't sure how
to go about cutting themselves in on the profits. In a world
of scarce information, the existence of such profits might not
even be widely known. And so *profits do exist and continue
to exist* without being reduced to zero by competition. But this
happens *because of uncertainty,* in the absence of which
everything relevant to profit making would be generally
known, all opportunities for profit making fully exploited, and
profits everywhere consequently equal to zero.

The same argument applies to losses. No one would
embark on a business enterprise knowing that the total revenue
was going to fall short of the total cost. But the future is
uncertain; events don't always work out as investors hope;
decisions are made and actions taken that prove to be mistakes;
and so losses do occur.

Since there would be no profits or losses in a world
without uncertainty, we conclude that profit (or loss) is the
consequence of uncertainty. Profit is thus not a payment that
has to be made to obtain some resource or another. It is a

residual; it is what's left over out of revenue when costs have all been met; it is the result of predicting the future more accurately than most others have predicted it.

The Pursuit of Profit

Let's consider a simple example. Suppose you read an advertisement urging you to invest in Florida real estate because its value increases by 30 percent each year. A 30 percent annual return is more than you can expect to receive from alternative investments, so you sink $30,000 into an undeveloped lot near Orlando. You plan to sell it in a year for $39,000. But you will probably be disappointed.

If Florida real estate really can be expected to increase in value by 30 percent per year, many people will be eager to buy Florida lots. Their eagerness to purchase will bid up the price of the lots, until the lots are no longer better buys than other available investment opportunities. If there happen to be many investors who uncritically accept the claims of the advertisement, their eagerness to benefit from the promised appreciation in real-estate prices could even bid the present price of lots so high that price decreases—rather than increases—will subsequently occur.

No one can make a profit by putting money into an asset or an operation that is *generally expected* to return more than the going rate of interest. For that would be a "good deal." And the demand for a "good deal" bids up the cost of getting in on it, until it's no longer a better deal than other assets or opportunities.

Every investor knows this. The time to buy Xerox or Polaroid was before the word got around. Those who bought stock in these companies after it became widely known that they were going to earn large net revenues from their new products received no profits. About the best they could hope for was the going rate of interest as a return on their investment. The market price of Xerox and Polaroid stock was bid up by people eager to share in those companies' future earnings, until the earnings relative to what had to be paid to share in them were no more attractive than earnings generally available in the market.

The common notion that one can accumulate wealth by investing in profitable companies is therefore seriously misleading. International Business Machines is rightly regarded as a highly profitable corporation, because it has consistently earned large returns for many years on its original investment. But the market value of IBM stock long ago increased to take full account of its expected high future earnings. Consequently, IBM stock is not necessarily a better buy than the stock of many companies with dismal earning records.

The way to accumulate a fortune is to supply something that can be sold for much more than it costs to produce, or to invest in someone else's enterprises that are going to generate huge net revenues by doing this. But it's essential that this outcome be uncertain. And there's the rub. You must know more than others—or be able to read the uncertain future more accurately—if you hope to make large profits. Or else you rely solely on luck. But if you rely on luck, you have an equal probability of being unlucky and sustaining a large loss. The significant thing about pure luck is that it's pure. Any investors who consistently make profits, defined as net income *beyond the common rate of return from readily available investment opportunities,* must be predicting the uncertain future more successfully than others.

We ought to pause a moment to clear the concept of profit (and loss) from the narrow connotations that it may have acquired in the course of this discussion. Profits and losses appear everywhere, for everyone, and not just for business firms or those who invest in financial assets.

Everyone Is Doing It

Consider the sad case of Giuseppe Vibrato, who attends a music conservatory for three years, planning on a career in opera. At about the time of Vibrato's graduation, the public abandons all interest in opera. So Vibrato sustains a loss. We mustn't exaggerate the loss, for Vibrato may receive a generous return on his educational investment in the form of many years of listening to himself sing Verdi and Wagner. (Education can prepare people to enjoy life as well as provide them with marketable skills.) But to the extent that Vibrato paid tuition and sacrificed earnings for three years in order to earn an income in opera, the unexpected change in public tastes caused him to sustain a loss.

In the same way aerospace engineers suffer losses when the federal government cuts back on the space program, college professors receive profits when the federal government decides to spend huge sums on higher education, authors make a profit when they hit on a book that captivates the public, and highly trained astrologers took a loss when people abandoned the belief that the stars shape individual destiny. (But note also that in the last case some of their intellectual descendants have recently made profits from an unexpected return to older persuasions.)

All these examples involve monetary income. But profits and losses don't have to entail changes in monetary wealth. The skier who goes to the slopes and finds rain incurs a loss. If he heads for the lodge to drown his sorrows and there meets his future wife, he makes a profit. If she turns out after

several years of marriage to be even more pleasant and intelligent than he had thought, his profit increases. And the profit from that rain-drenched ski trip becomes almost exorbitant if they jointly produce a cherubic child who fills their days with cheer. These examples may be frivolous. However, they serve to remind us that undeserved profits occur in all aspects of life and—equally important—that they also depend most of the time on the exercise of some discretion. This last point has considerable political importance.

"Windfall" Profits and Losses

One term that's often used to describe these differences between expected and realized outcomes is *windfalls*. Because the differences can be positive or negative, we should speak of *windfall profits* and *windfall losses*. We don't often encounter the term *windfall losses*, however, and it's worthwhile to think about why we don't. The word *windfall* originally referred to fruit that was blown down from a tree. The fruit was not earned through the effort of climbing and picking but was a gift of the wind, which blows unpredictably and beyond anyone's control. The term *windfall profit* implies an origin in luck rather than merit. Windfall profits are thus undeserved profits, because no one *deserves* good luck.

Of course, no one deserves bad luck either. So why don't we speak of windfall losses? The reason would appear to be that people don't go about claiming a *right* to losses, or insisting that society is violating their rights in compensating them for losses sustained. The adjective *windfall* is only attached to *profit* because only in the case of profit do people frequently want to counter the claim that the recipient earned or otherwise deserved what happened.

When we talk about what people do or do not deserve, we're talking about ethics rather than economics. Ethics is such a difficult subject that we would much prefer to go around it. But economists are once again beginning to discover (Adam Smith was fully aware of it two centuries ago!) that supply curves and demand curves—the most basic building blocks of economic analysis—depend on convictions and commitments that are fundamentally ethical in nature. This fact will be dogging our steps throughout this and the next three chapters. We had better turn now and face it squarely.

Property Rights: An Introduction to the Concept

The heart of the matter from the standpoint of the economic analyst is that the decisions people make in any economic system depend in a crucial way on the property rights that are established and accepted in that society. The term *property*

rights—as we're now using it and will continue to use it in subsequent chapters—has a much broader connotation than what is usually conjured up in people's minds. Perhaps when you hear the term you picture a rancher with a shotgun saying, "Git off my land," or someone indignantly announcing, "It belongs to me and I can do what I want with it!" We must enlarge the concept far beyond those pictures if it's to help us understand how economic systems function, how income is distributed, why pollution occurs, or what we can reasonably expect from government. When economists speak of property rights, they have in mind something closely akin to what we have called "the rules of the game." *Property rights are rights to control the way in which particular resources will be used and to assign the resulting costs and benefits.* It is property rights—or what people believe to be the relevant rules of the game—that determine how the processes of supply and demand will work themselves out in a society.

Perhaps the best way to explain is to illustrate, using the notion of "windfall" profits and losses.

Property rights create expectations.

Expectations guide actions.

How Shall We Treat "Windfalls"?

Oil refiners maintain sizable inventories of crude oil in order to assure a smooth and continuous operation of the refinery. If forces beyond their control increase the demand for or reduce the supply of crude petroleum, its price will rise. The value of the refiners' inventories will therefore rise, too. An increase in the value of a firm's inventories is an addition to its wealth, and additions to wealth are what we call income. Any income of business firms in excess of costs we call profit. So oil refiners, in this case, receive a profit from the occurrence of events beyond their control. Almost everyone will (and did) call that a windfall profit. Some go further and argue that it ought to be taxed away, because the refiners have no right to receive windfall profits. They belong by right to . . . whom?

This case illustrates the dependence of actions upon expectations and of expectations upon established property rights, as well as the significance of ethical convictions in the shaping or reshaping of property rights. The managers of a refinery accumulate inventories in the first place because they expect to be able to use them when and how they please. (That's not quite accurate; the managers know that they would not be allowed to use the inventories as they pleased if it pleased them to pump some onto the city's sidewalks for the fun of seeing pedestrians slip and slide. But they did expect to be allowed to use the inventories for accepted business purposes.) This expectation reflects existing property rights. Under a different set of rights, the managers of the refinery might have chosen to accumulate less inventory or

even none at all. They would have chosen to accumulate very little if, according to the accepted rules of the society, anyone who wants some crude is entitled to draw freely on the inventories of anyone else who happens to have some in stock. The refinery managers would also have chosen to carry smaller levels of inventory had they thought that the taxing authorities would appropriate any increase in inventory value due to price increases, without compensating the firm for losses due to price declines and a consequent fall in the value of inventory. People don't normally accept wagers of the form, "Heads I break even, tails I lose." The accepted rules of the society—customs and moral principles as well as laws— affect people's behavior by defining their property rights.

Expectations and Actions

We're focusing on property rights related to the oil inventories of refiners. But you should notice that everything else associated with the operation of the refineries, including the actions of employees, stockholders, motorists, or legislators, can also be viewed as a response to prevailing property rights. People act as they do because of the expectations created by existing property rights. Employees show up for work because they confidently expect to claim a paycheck on Friday. Stockholders purchase and retain shares because they expect to be cut in, as a matter of legal right, for a percentage of the firm's earnings proportionate to the number of shares they own. Motorists buy automobiles because they expect to be able to obtain suitable fuel at acceptable prices. And legislators draft laws that may alter the expectations of everyone else because they themselves expect to be able to win reelection by doing so.

Expectations are always much more complex than any of the capsule summaries above suggest. Oil refiners don't accumulate inventories exclusively in order to smooth the flow of production or to fulfill their contracts with customers. They also look ahead, try to anticipate changes in supply or demand, add to inventories if they predict higher prices in the future, and reduce inventories to some minimum level if they expect prices to fall. To some degree, in short, the inventory managers of an oil refinery function like the speculators described in Chapter 7. *They cannot choose not to speculate,* since both holding and not holding large inventories are speculative decisions, either of which could lead to a substantial gain or loss. Which of these eventually appears will depend on the relationship between what the managers expect to happen and what actually happens.

The windfalls that result from the inventory decisions of oil-refinery managers turn out now to be not altogether

windfalls after all. Windfalls are, by definition, the product of pure luck. It follows that managers who obtain them for their firms by predicting the future a little bit or a whole lot better than others are not really obtaining windfalls. They *are* obtaining increased profits—of that much we can be sure. The source of these profits is the fact that the managers' decisions predicted the future more accurately than did the predictions of others. That's also clear. Were the profits deserved? That is not as clear. It's at least in part an ethical question, and one on which opinions differ sharply.

Although economic analysis cannot by itself resolve such ethical issues, it can contribute to a resolution of the debate by clarifying the consequences of alternative answers. If people expect to have the profits from correct decisions taken away from them, on the grounds that such profits are undeserved, and if they also expect that the losses that accrue from incorrect decisions will not be fully subsidized, they will attempt to minimize risk. Decisions will converge toward the average. Only short-range projects will be undertaken. Fewer resources will be invested in research. Innovative projects will be explored less often. Problems that could have been avoided through better foresight will be encountered more frequently. Coordination failures will occur more often as individuals try to reduce their private risks.

If profits are confiscated but losses lie where they fall...

If both the profits and the losses that arise from the inescapable necessity of making decisions in the presence of uncertainty are removed from those who made the decisions and shared by everyone in society, less care will be invested in the making of decisions. Taking care is costly whenever it means, as it usually does, the forgoing of valuable opportunities. That is why people behave "care-lessly" when they themselves have nothing to gain or lose. It is also why students usually read more "care-fully" in a course taken for grade credit than in one they're only auditing. And it explains why people without theft insurance on their automobiles more often take the trouble to roll up all the windows and lock the doors.

If profits are confiscated and losses are fully compensated...

The significance of these consequences can, of course, be debated. To what extent do progress, achievement, creativity, wealth, harmony, happiness, or any other of these hard-to-define goods depend on the willingness to take risks or to take care? But the consequences themselves could be denied only by someone who was prepared to argue that superior knowledge of a legitimate kind does not exist, that everyone is equally well informed or equally ignorant—except insofar as some have unfair advantages. That, too, could probably be argued. All advantages become unfair advantages if one begins with the assumption that no one *ought* to have any kind of advantage over another. But does anyone seriously maintain

this? Are we prepared to restrict the game of basketball to people who are 5 feet, 9 inches tall and require Van Cliburn to wear mittens while playing the piano? The issue of merit, of what people deserve, does without question influence our convictions about the rights that people ought to have. But the rights that people believe themselves to have also entail consequences. In order to secure certain consequences that we want, we may be required to concede rights to people without regard to their personal merit. To take an extreme example: if rewards to criminal informants produce very large benefits for the rest of us, then probably such rewards ought to be paid, even though the informants obviously don't deserve them in any moral sense.

The term *windfall profit* is dangerous, because it suggests that such profits ought to be taxed or otherwise taken away. The difficulty with this is that no one knows how to distinguish the profits that are produced by astute forecasting from those profits that are purely the product of luck. Moreover, the potential of profit is an important, perhaps indispensable stimulus to action. The potential of a profit prompts people to search for more efficient ways of combining resources, new products for which there may be a demand, and organizational innovations that promise to increase effectiveness. The potential of profit often persuades people to take pains when they would otherwise prefer not to and to take chances in which the possible benefits to others are associated with the possibility of substantial losses for the one taking the chance. The potential of profit persuades some people (the unusually courageous, or foolhardy, or adventurous, or greedy, or perceptive, or knowledgeable, or public-spirited—who among us is competent to judge?) to increase the security of others by accepting risks themselves.

Restrictions on Competition

Something important seems to be missing from this analysis of profit. If profit is always the consequence of uncertainty, what were all those special interest groups pursuing in the preceding chapter? When associations of physicians, plumbers, farmers, airline pilots, nursing home operators, or automobile manufacturers urge the government to restrict competition in their trade, what are they after? They surely aren't pursuing uncertainty. On the contrary, they are trying to reduce uncertainty, at least for themselves, by preventing price cutting and keeping out competitors. If they succeed in their efforts, don't they secure for themselves something close to a guaranteed profit? And a guarantee is at the opposite pole from uncertainty.

As we said at the beginning of this chapter, there is little

to be gained by arguing about definitions. We do want to take a closer look, however, to see whether restrictions on the ability to compete really do give rise to something we can call a guaranteed profit.

Suppose that you accidentally—with no investment of time, effort, or other resources—discover the way to build a better mousetrap. You snagged the blueprints, let's say, while out fishing. Recognizing the value of your find, you immediately obtain a patent from the government and make plans to go into production. Since the world will beat a path to the door of anyone who builds a better mousetrap, and since the patent prohibits any competitor from duplicating your product for 17 years, you are going to become rich. It's a virtual certainty. And the first year's results confirm your happy prediction: net revenue is $100,000. You can confidently expect another $100,000 for each of the next 16 years. It looks like an annual *and fairly certain* profit of $100,000. But let's pursue the story further.

What is the source of this "profit"? It's your patent, of course, which prevents competition from eroding the difference between your total revenue and your total costs. But have you accurately calculated the cost of producing these superior mousetraps?

Competition on Other Fronts

If ownership of the patent generates a virtually certain $100,000 per year for you in net revenue, wouldn't its ownership generate just as much income for somebody else? In fact, wouldn't the patent be even more valuable—generate more than $100,000 annually—in the hands of someone who had specialized in mousetraps and knew more than you about their production and distribution? So some of those who beat a path to your door when you build a better mousetrap are going to be established mousetrap manufacturers who want to purchase or rent your patent. You will consequently discover that the cost to you of continuing as the exclusive producer of these superior mousetraps has gone up by the value of the opportunity you spurn if you decline to sell or lease your patent.

Suppose a long-established maker of mousetraps offers to buy your patent for $1.5 million. How might the firm arrive at such a figure? It could estimate that your patent will produce at least a $200,000 annual increase in its net revenue. If the going rate of return on relatively risk-free investments, such as U.S. government bonds, is currently 10 percent, your patent is a good investment at a purchase price of $1.5 million; it promises to yield more than 13 percent per year. Of course, the firm would prefer to get that patent for less. At a price of $1.2 million, $200,000 becomes a 16.5 percent annual return

$200,000 per year from a $1.5 million investment is an annual return of 13.3%

Refusal to sell the patent will deprive you of an annual income of $150,000: the interest on $1.5 million

on investment. But there are other mousetrap manufacturers, 16.5 percent is too good a deal for them to pass by, and so the winning bid rises to $1.5 million. That's the process by which the market price of your patent would be determined.

What does all this do to your annual "profit" of $100,000? It wipes it out entirely and turns your "profit" into an actual loss. Do you see why and how? When competition among mousetrap makers sets a price of $1.5 million on your patent, the cost to you of continuing to manufacture mouse-traps increases by about $150,000 per year, which is the income you will forgo if you decide not to sell your patent and invest the proceeds in government bonds. What has happened is this: When the word got out that ownership of your patent was a virtual guarantee of profit—an annual revenue greater than cost—potential owners began bidding for the patent. Their bids transformed your "profit" into a cost of production: the value of the opportunity you forgo by not selling.

What about the firm that buys your patent? Will it make a profit afterwards? It might. If events turn out as the firm had hoped and its net revenue does increase by $200,000 a year, acquisition of the patent will prove to have been a smart move. Of course, $150,000 of that $200,000 will be a cost of production: the income forgone by investing $1.5 million in the patent rather than in government bonds. The remaining $50,000 could be viewed as a genuine profit, the result of prior uncertainty about the actual value of the patent to the acquiring firm.

Notice, though, that the process of competition just described will resume once the $50,000 becomes relatively "certain." Other firms might renew the bidding for the patent, raising its price above $1.5 million. Should the patent be worth more than $1.5 million *only to this firm*, that would suggest this firm controls some unique complementary resources—a marketing manager, perhaps, with a special talent for designing ads that arouse the fear of mice. In that case, the price of the complementary resources will be bid up as other firms discover what's going on and try to obtain these "profitable" resources for their own use. If the firm is forced to pay the marketing manager a higher salary to retain his services, a part of the "profit" will turn into an addition to its wage and salary costs.

You can watch this happening in all sorts of places once you have learned where to look.

Competition for the Key Resource

When the government tries to increase the income of wheat farmers by guaranteeing them a higher price for their product,

land suitable for wheat production becomes more valuable and so its price rises. Tenant farmers subsequently have to pay more for the land they rent and farmers who try to buy land must pay more to get it. The increased "profit" for wheat farmers at which the government policy was aimed produces, as soon as the policy becomes known, an increase in the cost of producing wheat, through a rise in the cost of land. The beneficiaries will be those who owned land suitable for growing wheat before it became generally known that the government was going to raise the support price of wheat.

When taxicab operators secure legislation restricting the number of cabs that are licensed to operate in a city, ownership of a license becomes more valuable. Competition for the licenses then bids up their price until the cost of operating a cab—including the opportunity cost of acquiring or of retaining ownership of the license—is equal to the revenue from its operation. That doesn't mean taxicab operators don't get any benefit from their lobbying campaign. Those who owned licenses before the legal restrictions were generally anticipated benefit from an increase in the value of their licenses. That increase is their profit, and it's what they were hoping for when they launched their lobbying efforts. But after the lobbying efforts have succeeded it will cost more to operate a cab, because each cab operator will now have to own a costly license in order to do so.

The right to broadcast on a VHF television channel in a large city is a very valuable property right. If the Federal Communications Commission were to assign these rights to the highest bidder, the government would receive a tidy sum and the "profit" from use of the channel would become a cost of doing business to the broadcaster. In fact, however, the FCC has always assigned the right to use a particular channel, without charge, on the basis of obscure criteria having to do with the merit of competing applicants and the promises they make regarding future public service. As a result, applicants compete by hiring lawyers, accountants, and assorted public-relations specialists to influence the FCC's assignment. In this case the critical resource that creates a "profit" is the FCC's decision, and competition consequently aims at acquiring control of that decision. The "profit" from receipt of the channel is transformed along the way into the cost of exerting political influence.

Competition and Property Rights

Profits and losses arise from uncertainty and cannot exist in the absence of uncertainty. Where everything relevant to the making of a profit is known for certain, competition to obtain the profit will eliminate it, either by reducing revenue

Could anyone obtain a profit from any activity in the absence of some uncertainty?

or by raising cost. There's nothing very surprising about that conclusion; it follows logically from the way we have defined cost and profit. What matters, and what this chapter was intended to clarify, are the forms that competition takes in response to the lure of a possible profit and the social consequences that emerge.

Will the pursuit of profit lead people to produce better mousetraps or to prevent others from selling better mousetraps in their territory? Will it yield more wheat or higher-priced wheat land? Better taxi service or an increase in the cost of licenses? Lower prices for consumers or higher incomes for the owners of critical resources? Exploration or retrenchment? Innovations in technology or in social organization? A wider range of choices or more restrictions on choice? The answers will depend upon the rules of the game and the system of property rights that they create.

AN APPENDIX: DISCOUNTING AND PRESENT VALUES

If the prevailing annual interest rate reflects the greater value that people assign to goods now over goods one year from now, it follows that the value of goods expected to be received a year from now must be discounted by the rate of interest to determine their *present value*. The process of discounting to determine the present value of future goods plays a large part in economic decision making. Mastering this process will equip you better to understand the analysis of subsequent chapters and will acquaint you with procedures widely employed in the business and financial world.

Suppose that Ivy College, that well-managed institution of higher learning introduced in Chapter 9, offers the parents of entering students a Tuition Stabilization Plan. Tuition, currently at $2000, is almost sure to rise each year, they point out, because of continuing inflation. Ivy even announces in advance its intention to increase the annual tuition charge by $200 in each of the next three years. But parents who subscribe to the TSP receive a special deal. They pay $8000 in September of the first year and nothing thereafter. In effect, says Ivy's multicolored brochure, parents who sign up for TSP save $1200 on the cost of their child's education. Ivy may go so far as to call it a 15 percent saving.

But is $8000 paid now really less than $2000 now plus $2200 one year from now, $2400 two years from now, and $2600 three years from now? The last three amounts are amounts due in the future, and future dollars, like any other future goods, must be discounted if we want to assess their present value. What interest rate should we use? The best

answer is provided by the opportunity cost to the parents of lending money to Ivy College, since that is in effect what they are doing. They are lending Ivy money by paying the tuition before it is due. Thus $2000 of the sophomore year tuition is lent for one year, $2000 of the junior year tuition is lent for two years, and $2000 of the senior year tuition is lent for three years. What's the alternative opportunity for those amounts?

What a Present Amount Grows To

Suppose the parents sell stock to obtain the money, and their stock investments ordinarily earn an annual return, in dividends plus increased market price, of 12 percent a year. Then the opportunity cost of lending $2000 to Ivy College for one year is $240. That's $240 expended to avoid $200 in increased tuition—not an attractive arrangement. The junior-year loan is an even poorer investment: $2000 grows in two years, at 12 percent per year, to $2000 × 1.12 × 1.12 or $2508.80. The phenomenon of compound interest is at work, and it makes the three-year loan still less appealing. To avoid the $600 in additional tuition due for the senior year, the parents give up $809.86 that they might otherwise have earned from the ownership of stock, since $2000 × 1.12^3 is $2809.86.

Present Value of Future Amounts

We've assessed Ivy's proposal by calculating what a dollar now will grow to, at the appropriate rate of return, in one year, two years, and three years, and comparing those amounts with the tuition that would ordinarily be due in one year, in two years, and in three years. We can reach the same conclusion by working in the other direction. What is the *present value* of the $2200 that will be due in one year? That amounts to asking: What present sum would grow to exactly $2200 in one year if invested at 12 percent? The answer is $2200 divided by 1.12, or $1964.29, which means that in prepaying the sophomore year tuition the parents give up $2000 now to save $36 less than that in present value. The $2400 that would be due in two years has a present value of $2400 divided by (1.12 × 1.12), or $1913.27, which is $87 less than what the parents actually pay. The $2600, when divided by 1.12^3, turns out to have a present value of only $1850.63.

People who make these computations in the course of their everyday business decisions use tables that enable them to calculate quickly the sum to which a present amount will grow or the present value of future amounts. Three such tables are provided on the succeeding pages. You can use the

first two, Tables 11A and 11B, to check the conclusions just presented, which is a subtle way of suggesting that you practice with the tables until you're able to obtain the above results. One more problem will be presented to introduce you to the third table, Table 11C.

Present Value of Annuities

What should a maker of mousetraps be willing to pay for a patent that is expected to produce an additional $200,000 per year for the next 17 years? It is certainly less than 17 times $200,000 or $3.4 million.

If U.S. government bonds are available that pay 10 percent per year, $3.4 million invested in them will yield $340,000 a year, which is considerably more than $200,000 a year. Moreover, that $340,000 will continue indefinitely, while the $200,000 will end after 17 years. So the mousetrap maker clearly won't be willing to pay $3.4 million for the patent.

The maximum that the firm will be willing to pay is the present value of $200,000 to be received at the end of each of the next 17 years. (We assume that all the income becomes available at the end of the year to simplify our calculations.) We could calculate that by summing the first 17 amounts in the appropriate column of Table 11B and multiplying by $200,000. Table 11C saves us that effort. The row for 17 years shows the present value of $1 received at the end of *each* of the next 17 years at various interest rates.

But what interest rate should we choose? If a less risky investment, like government bonds, pays 10 percent, then we wouldn't want to choose a rate lower than 10 percent. On the other hand, that 10 percent rate on government bonds is the return on a *fixed dollar* amount. It is therefore a nominal, not a real rate of return: a return expressed in dollars that can change in value rather than a return expressed in real purchasing power. If the value of the dollar were to fall 4 percent each year, which is to say, if inflation occurred at a 4 percent annual rate, then the real return from a nominal interest rate of 10 percent would be only 6 percent. The basic reason government bonds were yielding 10 percent or more in 1985, when these words were written, was the expectation of future inflation. Investors were not willing to hold long-term government bonds in 1985 unless they were promised a nominal rate of return sufficient to compensate for the infla-tion they feared would take place over the life of the bonds.

The net revenue from manufacturing mousetraps can reasonably be expected to vary right along with the rate of inflation. If the price of everything doubles, the net revenue from mousetrap manufacturing ought to double, too—if other things are equal, as we're assuming. In that case, we

Table 11A Amount to Which $1 Will Grow in the Designated Number of Years When Compounded Annually at Various Interest Rates

Year	0.01	0.02	0.04	0.06	0.09	0.12	0.18	0.24
1	1.0100	1.0200	1.0400	1.0600	1.0900	1.1200	1.1800	1.2400
2	1.0201	1.0404	1.0816	1.1236	1.1881	1.2544	1.3924	1.5376
3	1.0303	1.0612	1.1249	1.1910	1.2950	1.4049	1.6430	1.9066
4	1.0406	1.0824	1.1699	1.2625	1.4116	1.5735	1.9388	2.3642
5	1.0510	1.1041	1.2167	1.3382	1.5386	1.7623	2.2878	2.9316
6	1.0615	1.1262	1.2653	1.4185	1.6771	1.9738	2.6996	3.6352
7	1.0721	1.1487	1.3159	1.5036	1.8280	2.2107	3.1855	4.5077
8	1.0829	1.1717	1.3686	1.5938	1.9926	2.4760	3.7589	5.5895
9	1.0937	1.1951	1.4233	1.6895	2.1719	2.7731	4.4355	6.9310
10	1.1046	1.2190	1.4802	1.7908	2.3674	3.1059	5.2338	8.5944
11	1.1157	1.2434	1.5395	1.8983	2.5804	3.4786	6.1759	10.6571
12	1.1268	1.2682	1.6010	2.0122	2.8127	3.8960	7.2876	13.2148
13	1.1381	1.2936	1.6651	2.1329	3.0658	4.3635	8.5994	16.3863
14	1.1495	1.3195	1.7317	2.2609	3.3417	4.8871	10.1473	20.3191
15	1.1610	1.3459	1.8009	2.3966	3.6425	5.4736	11.9738	25.1956
16	1.1726	1.3728	1.8730	2.5403	3.9703	6.1304	14.1290	31.2426
17	1.1843	1.4002	1.9479	2.6928	4.3276	6.8661	16.6723	38.7408
18	1.1961	1.4282	2.0258	2.8543	4.7171	7.6900	19.6733	48.0386
19	1.2081	1.4568	2.1068	3.0256	5.1417	8.6128	23.2145	59.5679
20	1.2202	1.4859	2.1911	3.2071	5.6044	9.6463	27.3931	73.8642
21	1.2324	1.5157	2.2788	3.3996	6.1088	10.8039	32.3238	91.5916
22	1.2447	1.5460	2.3699	3.6035	6.6586	12.1003	38.1421	113.5735
23	1.2572	1.5769	2.4647	3.8197	7.2579	13.5524	45.0077	140.8312
24	1.2697	1.6084	2.5633	4.0489	7.9111	15.1787	53.1091	174.6307
25	1.2824	1.6406	2.6658	4.2919	8.6231	17.0001	62.6688	216.5421
26	1.2953	1.6734	2.7725	4.5494	9.3991	19.0401	73.9491	268.5121
27	1.3082	1.7069	2.8834	4.8223	10.2451	21.3249	87.2600	332.9551
28	1.3213	1.7410	2.9987	5.1117	11.1671	23.8839	102.9668	412.8643
29	1.3345	1.7758	3.1186	5.4184	12.1722	26.7500	121.5008	511.9517
30	1.3478	1.8114	3.2434	5.7435	13.2677	29.9600	143.3710	634.8201
31	1.3613	1.8476	3.3731	6.0881	14.4617	33.5552	169.1777	787.1770
32	1.3749	1.8845	3.5081	6.4534	15.7633	37.5818	199.6298	976.0994
33	1.3887	1.9222	3.6484	6.8406	17.1820	42.0917	235.5631	1210.3633
34	1.4026	1.9607	3.7943	7.2510	18.7284	47.1427	277.9645	1500.8503
35	1.4166	1.9999	3.9461	7.6861	20.4139	52.7998	327.9982	1861.0544
36	1.4308	2.0399	4.1039	8.1472	22.2512	59.1358	387.0378	2307.7075
37	1.4451	2.0807	4.2681	8.6361	24.2538	66.2321	456.7048	2861.5576
38	1.4595	2.1223	4.4388	9.1542	26.4366	74.1799	538.9116	3548.3315
39	1.4741	2.1647	4.6164	9.7035	28.8159	83.0815	635.9156	4399.9316
40	1.4889	2.2080	4.8010	10.2857	31.4094	93.0513	750.3806	5455.9140
41	1.5038	2.2522	4.9931	10.9028	34.2362	104.2175	885.4492	6765.3339
42	1.5188	2.2972	5.1928	11.5570	37.3175	116.7326	1044.8303	8389.0155
43	1.5340	2.3432	5.4005	12.2504	40.6760	130.7304	1232.8996	10402.3788
44	1.5493	2.3901	5.6165	12.9854	44.3369	146.4181	1454.8218	12898.9491
45	1.5648	2.4379	5.8412	13.7645	48.3272	163.9883	1716.6899	15994.6971
46	1.5805	2.4866	6.0748	14.5904	52.6766	183.6669	2025.6941	19833.4217
47	1.5963	2.5363	6.3178	15.4658	57.4175	205.7069	2390.3188	24593.4490
48	1.6122	2.5871	6.5705	16.3938	62.5851	230.3918	2820.5766	30495.8707
49	1.6283	2.6388	6.8333	17.3774	68.2177	258.0388	3328.2807	37814.8746
50	1.6446	2.6916	7.1067	18.4201	74.3573	289.0035	3927.3720	46890.4526

Table 11B Present Value of $1 at the End of the Designated Number of Years When Discounted at Various Interest Rates

Year	0.01	0.02	0.04	0.06	0.09	0.12	0.18	0.24
1	0.9901	0.9804	0.9615	0.9434	0.9174	0.8929	0.8475	0.8065
2	0.9803	0.9612	0.9246	0.8900	0.8417	0.7972	0.7182	0.6504
3	0.9706	0.9423	0.8890	0.8396	0.7722	0.7118	0.6086	0.5245
4	0.9610	0.9238	0.8548	0.7921	0.7084	0.6355	0.5158	0.4230
5	0.9515	0.9057	0.8219	0.7473	0.6499	0.5674	0.4371	0.3411
6	0.9420	0.8880	0.7903	0.7050	0.5963	0.5066	0.3704	0.2751
7	0.9327	0.8706	0.7599	0.6651	0.5470	0.4523	0.3139	0.2218
8	0.9235	0.8535	0.7307	0.6274	0.5019	0.4039	0.2660	0.1789
9	0.9143	0.8368	0.7026	0.5919	0.4604	0.3606	0.2255	0.1443
10	0.9053	0.8203	0.6756	0.5584	0.4224	0.3220	0.1911	0.1164
11	0.8963	0.8043	0.6496	0.5268	0.3875	0.2875	0.1619	0.0938
12	0.8874	0.7885	0.6246	0.4970	0.3555	0.2567	0.1372	0.0757
13	0.8787	0.7730	0.6006	0.4688	0.3262	0.2292	0.1163	0.0610
14	0.8700	0.7579	0.5775	0.4423	0.2992	0.2046	0.0985	0.0492
15	0.8613	0.7430	0.5553	0.4173	0.2745	0.1827	0.0835	0.0397
16	0.8528	0.7284	0.5339	0.3936	0.2519	0.1631	0.0708	0.0320
17	0.8444	0.7142	0.5134	0.3714	0.2311	0.1456	0.0600	0.0258
18	0.8360	0.7002	0.4936	0.3503	0.2120	0.1300	0.0508	0.0208
19	0.8277	0.6864	0.4746	0.3305	0.1945	0.1161	0.0431	0.0168
20	0.8195	0.6730	0.4564	0.3118	0.1784	0.1037	0.0365	0.0135
21	0.8114	0.6598	0.4388	0.2942	0.1637	0.0926	0.0309	0.0109
22	0.8034	0.6468	0.4220	0.2775	0.1502	0.0826	0.0262	0.0088
23	0.7954	0.6342	0.4057	0.2618	0.1378	0.0738	0.0222	0.0071
24	0.7876	0.6217	0.3901	0.2470	0.1264	0.0659	0.0188	0.0057
25	0.7798	0.6095	0.3751	0.2330	0.1160	0.0588	0.0160	0.0046
26	0.7720	0.5976	0.3607	0.2198	0.1064	0.0525	0.0135	0.0037
27	0.7644	0.5859	0.3468	0.2074	0.0976	0.0469	0.0115	0.0030
28	0.7568	0.5744	0.3335	0.1956	0.0895	0.0419	0.0097	0.0024
29	0.7493	0.5631	0.3207	0.1846	0.0822	0.0374	0.0082	0.0020
30	0.7419	0.5521	0.3083	0.1741	0.0754	0.0334	0.0070	0.0016
31	0.7346	0.5412	0.2965	0.1643	0.0691	0.0298	0.0059	0.0013
32	0.7273	0.5306	0.2851	0.1550	0.0634	0.0266	0.0050	0.0010
33	0.7201	0.5202	0.2741	0.1462	0.0582	0.0238	0.0042	0.0008
34	0.7130	0.5100	0.2636	0.1379	0.0534	0.0212	0.0036	0.0007
35	0.7059	0.5000	0.2534	0.1301	0.0490	0.0189	0.0030	0.0005
36	0.6989	0.4902	0.2437	0.1227	0.0449	0.0169	0.0026	0.0004
37	0.6920	0.4806	0.2343	0.1158	0.0412	0.0151	0.0022	0.0003
38	0.6852	0.4712	0.2253	0.1092	0.0378	0.0135	0.0019	0.0003
39	0.6784	0.4619	0.2166	0.1031	0.0347	0.0120	0.0016	0.0002
40	0.6717	0.4529	0.2083	0.0972	0.0318	0.0107	0.0013	0.0002
41	0.6650	0.4440	0.2003	0.0917	0.0292	0.0096	0.0011	0.0001
42	0.6584	0.4353	0.1926	0.0865	0.0268	0.0086	0.0010	0.0001
43	0.6519	0.4268	0.1852	0.0816	0.0246	0.0076	0.0008	0.0001
44	0.6454	0.4184	0.1780	0.0770	0.0226	0.0068	0.0007	0.0001
45	0.6391	0.4102	0.1712	0.0727	0.0207	0.0061	0.0006	0.0001
46	0.6327	0.4022	0.1646	0.0685	0.0190	0.0054	0.0005	0.0001
47	0.6265	0.3943	0.1583	0.0647	0.0174	0.0049	0.0004	0.0000
48	0.6203	0.3865	0.1522	0.0610	0.0160	0.0043	0.0004	0.0000
49	0.6141	0.3790	0.1463	0.0575	0.0147	0.0039	0.0003	0.0000
50	0.6080	0.3715	0.1407	0.0543	0.0134	0.0035	0.0003	0.0000

Table 11C Annuity Table: Present Value of $1 Received at the End of Each Year for the Designated Number of Years When Discounted at Various Interest Rates

Year	0.01	0.02	0.04	0.06	0.09	0.12	0.18	0.24
1	0.9901	0.9804	0.9615	0.9434	0.9174	0.8929	0.8475	0.8065
2	1.9704	1.9416	1.8861	1.8334	1.7591	1.6901	1.5656	1.4568
3	2.9410	2.8839	2.7751	2.6730	2.5313	2.4018	2.1743	1.9813
4	3.9020	3.8077	3.6299	3.4651	3.2397	3.0374	2.6901	2.4043
5	4.8534	4.7135	4.4518	4.2124	3.8896	3.6048	3.1272	2.7454
6	5.7955	5.6014	5.2421	4.9173	4.4859	4.1114	3.4976	3.0205
7	6.7282	6.4720	6.0021	5.5824	5.0329	4.5638	3.8115	3.2423
8	7.6517	7.3255	6.7327	6.2098	5.5348	4.9676	4.0776	3.4212
9	8.5660	8.1622	7.4353	6.8017	5.9952	5.3283	4.3030	3.5655
10	9.4713	8.9826	8.1109	7.3601	6.4177	5.6502	4.4941	3.6819
11	10.3676	9.7869	8.7605	7.8869	6.8052	5.9377	4.6560	3.7757
12	11.2550	10.5754	9.3851	8.3838	7.1607	6.1944	4.7932	3.8514
13	12.1337	11.3484	9.9856	8.8527	7.4869	6.4236	4.9095	3.9124
14	13.0037	12.1063	10.5631	9.2950	7.7861	6.6282	5.0081	3.9616
15	13.8650	12.8493	11.1184	9.7122	8.0607	6.8109	5.0916	4.0013
16	14.7178	13.5777	11.6523	10.1059	8.3126	6.9740	5.1624	4.0333
17	15.5622	14.2919	12.1657	10.4772	8.5436	7.1196	5.2223	4.0591
18	16.3982	14.9921	12.6593	10.8276	8.7556	7.2497	5.2732	4.0799
19	17.2260	15.6785	13.1339	11.1581	8.9501	7.3658	5.3162	4.0967
20	18.0455	16.3515	13.5903	11.4699	9.1285	7.4694	5.3527	4.1103
21	18.8569	17.0112	14.0292	11.7641	9.2922	7.5620	5.3837	4.1212
22	19.6603	17.6581	14.4511	12.0416	9.4424	7.6446	5.4099	4.1300
23	20.4558	18.2922	14.8568	12.3034	9.5802	7.7184	5.4321	4.1371
24	21.2433	18.9140	15.2470	12.5503	9.7066	7.7843	5.4509	4.1428
25	22.0231	19.5235	15.6221	12.7833	9.8226	7.8431	5.4669	4.1474
26	22.7951	20.1211	15.9828	13.0032	9.9290	7.8957	5.4804	4.1511
27	23.5595	20.7069	16.3296	13.2105	10.0266	7.9426	5.4919	4.1542
28	24.3164	21.2813	16.6631	13.4062	10.1161	7.9844	5.5016	4.1566
29	25.0657	21.8444	16.9837	13.5907	10.1983	8.0218	5.5098	4.1585
30	25.8076	22.3965	17.2920	13.7648	10.2737	8.0552	5.5168	4.1601
31	26.5422	22.9377	17.5885	13.9291	10.3428	8.0850	5.5227	4.1614
32	27.2695	23.4684	17.8736	14.0840	10.4062	8.1116	5.5277	4.1624
33	27.9896	23.9886	18.1476	14.2302	10.4644	8.1354	5.5320	4.1632
34	28.7026	24.4986	18.4112	14.3681	10.5178	8.1566	5.5356	4.1639
35	29.4085	24.9986	18.6646	14.4982	10.5668	8.1755	5.5386	1.1644
36	30.1074	25.4889	18.9083	14.6210	10.6118	8.1924	5.5412	4.1649
37	30.7994	25.9695	19.1426	14.7368	10.6530	8.2075	5.5434	4.1652
38	31.4846	26.4407	19.3679	14.8460	10.6908	8.2210	5.5452	4.1655
39	32.1629	26.9026	19.5845	14.9491	10.7255	8.2230	5.5468	4.1657
40	32.8346	27.3555	19.7928	15.0463	10.7574	8.2438	5.5482	4.1659
41	33.4996	27.7995	19.9930	15.1380	10.7866	8.2534	5.5493	4.1661
42	34.1580	28.2348	20.1856	15.2245	10.8134	8.2619	5.5502	4.1662
43	34.8099	28.6616	20.3708	15.3062	10.8379	8.2696	5.5510	4.1663
44	35.4554	29.0800	20.5488	15.3832	10.8605	8.2764	5.5517	4.1663
45	36.0944	29.4902	20.7200	15.4558	10.8812	8.2825	5.5523	4.1664
46	36.7271	29.8923	20.8847	15.5244	10.9002	8.2880	5.5528	4.1665
47	37.3536	30.2866	21.0429	15.5890	10.9176	8.2928	5.5532	4.1665
48	37.9739	30.6732	21.1951	15.6500	10.9336	8.2972	5.5536	4.1665
49	38.5880	31.0521	21.3415	15.7076	10.9482	8.3010	5.5539	4.1666
50	39.1960	31.4236	21.4822	15.7619	10.9617	8.3045	5.5541	4.1666

would be taking account twice of the effects of inflation if we discounted the expected net revenue from acquiring the patent at a rate of interest incorporating expectations of inflation. A 6 percent or even a 4 percent discount rate seems more appropriate.

Let's try 4 percent. What is the present value of $200,000 to be received at the end of each of the next 17 years when discounted at 4 percent? Table 11C says that $1 for 17 years has a present value of $12.1657. The present value of a $200,000 annuity (an annuity is an annual amount) is therefore $2,433,140.

That's a good bit higher than the $1.5 million estimated in the chapter. Unless that $200,000 is highly certain, however, it's surely too much to offer for the patent. If the mousetrap manufacturer plays it safe and offers only $2,095,440, it would be discounting the expected future income at 6 percent.

At a discount rate of 9 percent, $200,000 a year for each of the next 17 years has a present value of $1,708,720.

Use Table 11C to check these results for yourself. The appropriate interest rate will be one that takes account of the patent purchaser's subjective estimate of the risks entailed in the purchase. Will the patent stand up to legal challenges? Will someone else invent an even better mousetrap? Will new technologies for the eradication of mice turn mousetraps into museum relics? The more uncertain the expected income whose present value we want to determine, the higher the interest rate at which we will want to discount it.

One last question: What happens to the present value of the patent if we assume it can be renewed upon expiration for an additional 17 years? If we discount at 9 percent, $200,000 for each of the next 34 years if $2,103,560. Notice that this is only $400,000 more than the value of a 17-year income stream. That shouldn't surprise you. A dollar that isn't due until 18 years from now has a present value of only 21¢ when discounted at 9 percent. And a dollar in 34 years has a present value of only 5⅓¢.

Once Over Lightly

Profit is a term with many meanings. The meanings must be sorted out if we want to understand the way in which economic systems function.

Profit can be usefully defined as total revenue minus total cost if we include all opportunity costs in our calculation of total cost.

Interest, which is often confused with profit, is a cost for anyone who pays it. It is the cost of obtaining present command of resources, or the difference in value between present and future goods. It is usually attached to money

loans simply because money represents general command over present or future goods.

The rate of interest in a society is typically positive because people generally find present goods more valuable than future goods.

Profit arises from uncertainty. In the absence of uncertainty, any differences between total revenue and total cost would be competed away and profits would become zero.

The possibility of a profit encourages risk taking, innovation, and special effort on the part of those who expect to appropriate the difference between generally anticipated and actual outcomes.

The forms that competition takes in any society are determined by the relevant rules of the game, or by the property rights that assign the ability to allocate resources and to appropriate the benefits from their use.

QUESTIONS FOR DISCUSSION

1. Chuck Waggin owns and operates a small tax-accounting firm, which he runs out of the basement of his home.
   (a) The basement was just wasted space until Chuck turned it into an office for his business. He says his firm is more profitable than most tax-accounting businesses because he doesn't have to pay any rent. Do you agree that rent is not a cost of production for Chuck?
   (b) Chuck recently turned down an offer to go to work for a larger firm at a salary of $45,000 a year. Chuck's net income from his business runs about $35,000 a year. Would you say that Chuck's firm is profitable?
   (c) Chuck says he likes being his own boss, and that he would be willing to sacrifice at least $25,000 a year in income to avoid working for someone else. Does that information change your answer to part (b)?
   (d) Chuck recently invested $10,000 of his savings in an office computer. How would you include the effects of this investment in his costs?
   (e) Chuck could have earned 12 percent per year on his savings had he not used them to buy the personal computer. If he had not had these savings, he still would have bought the computer, using a loan from the bank at 18 percent annual interest to finance the purchase. Is the opportunity cost of owning the computer really less for Chuck because he had savings of his own from which to buy it? If Chuck had been required to pay 18 percent interest to the bank rather than giving up 12 percent interest, for what would the additional 6 percent have been a payment? Does Chuck reduce his costs by financing the computer purchase himself?
2. Here are the first three sentences from a booklet on "The Arithmetic of Interest Rates" published by the Federal Reserve Bank of New York: "Everything has a price. And money is no exception. Its price—the interest rate—is determined in the marketplace where money is borrowed and lent." Is it correct to speak of interest as the price of money?

(a) If interest is the price of money in the same way in which 35¢ is the price of an orange, then we should expect an increase in the quantity of money to lead to lower interest rates just as an increase in the quantity of oranges leads to a reduced price for oranges. Why then are interest rates very high in nations that allow their money supplies to increase very rapidly?

(b) A large increase in the supply of money will indeed have an effect on "the price of money" similar to the effect of a large increase in the supply of oranges on the price of oranges—*if* by "price" we mean value relative to other goods. The term we use to describe a fall in the value of money relative to other goods is *inflation*. If an increase in the supply of money creates expectations of inflation, what will happen to interest rates?

(c) Interest is the price of something, but not of money. What is the good whose price has gone up when the interest rate rises?

(d) The law of demand says that a higher price for a good causes less of that good to be demanded. What is the good for which the quantity demanded declines when the interest rate rises?

3. What form would the rate of interest take in a society that used no money but depended entirely on barter for the exchange of goods?

4. You purchase for $900 a $1000 government bond maturing one year from the date of purchase. Will you make a profit if you hold the bond to maturity? Will you make a profit if there is a sharp, general increase in prevailing interest rates a week after your purchase? What effect will this have on the price you can obtain from selling your bond in the market?

5. Humbert and Ambler are very different personalities. Humbert likes to eat, drink, be merry, and let the future care for itself. He suspects that the world is going to disintegrate in a few years anyway. Ambler is only 21 but is already planning conscientiously for his retirement years. What would you predict about their respective rates of time preference? How do people of Humbert's type benefit from the existence of people like Ambler, and vice versa?

6. What effect would you expect the rate of technological innovation in a society to have on the level of interest rates? Why?

7. "When lenders extend credit to high-risk borrowers, they must raise the interest rates they charge low-risk borrowers in order to cover their losses from defaults." Do you agree?

8. Suppose that Congress imposes a 12 percent ceiling on the interest rate that may be charged for federally guaranteed mortgages. Lending institutions, meanwhile, find themselves able to obtain all the mortgage business they want at 15 percent interest. Will they lend at 12 percent? How might the interest ceiling be circumvented? If you wanted to purchase a house and were eligible for a federally guaranteed mortgage, would you want Congress to set an interest-rate ceiling on such loans?

9. "A wealthy society has little difficulty paying interest. But in a poor country with almost no capital, economic planners cannot afford to take interest charges into account in their calculations." What's wrong with that argument?

10. Oil producers immediately objected when President Carter proposed in 1979

that the decontrol of oil prices be accompanied by a "windfall-profits" tax.

(a) The oil producers claimed that the tax would reduce companies' incentives for new exploration and drilling. The press secretary for the late Senator Henry Jackson, then chairman of the Senate Energy Committee, denied this claim in the following words: "As far as increased production is concerned, the oil companies have an enormous cash flow right now. The incentives are already there." Do profits earned in the past (or current cash flow) provide incentives to explore and drill for oil?

(b) The reported net income after taxes in 1978 of 94 leading companies in the petroleum production and refining industry was $14,971 million. Is $15 billion dollars enough money to finance extensive exploration and drilling for new oil? Were those $15 billion dollars an incentive to explore and drill?

(c) The nine largest manufacturers of tobacco products in the United States earned a net income after taxes of $1,313 million in 1978. Would $1.3 billion pay for much oil exploration? Under what circumstances might the profits earned in the tobacco industry be used to explore for oil?

(d) Much of the exploration and drilling for oil that occurred in the United States in the past was financed by borrowing, not out of the net income from previous production or refining. Under what circumstances can money be borrowed to finance the search for new oil?

(e) Why would any firm in the business of producing or refining oil choose to invest some of its profits in shopping-center development (or anything else) rather than in exploration for oil?

(f) Does the news that the 94 largest firms in the petroleum production and refining industry earned $15 billion in 1978 make *you* eager to (1) explore and drill for oil, or (2) buy stock in oil companies?

(g) What difference would it make to your answers in the preceding part of this question to know any of the following (which all happen to be true)? (1) Oil industry profits rose 12 percent from 1977 to 1978. (2) The average return on stockholders' equity in the oil industry in 1978 was 14.3 percent compared with 14.0 percent in 1977. (3) The average percentage return of leading manufacturing corporations in 1978 was 15.9 percent; it was 14.9 percent in 1977.

(h) Suppose the government imposes a windfall-profits tax on all net income received from the sale of oil already discovered and flowing, but exempts from the tax all oil that is found after the tax is imposed. Will this maintain incentives to explore and drill for oil?

(i) Why do critics of the oil industry rarely distinguish between producers (who bring oil out of the ground) and refiners (who turn it into useful products)?

(j) Senator Jackson popularized the term "obscene profits" in discussing the profits of the oil industry during and immediately after the original OPEC price increases of 1973-74. Assuming that he intended *obscene* to mean repulsive or disgusting, rather than lewd or sexually exciting, explain the circumstances under which one might reasonably describe profits as obscene.

11. You ask your college for permission to set up a lemonade stand at the annual

spring commencement, and the college grants permission. After paying your bills for materials (lemons, sugar, cups, and so forth), you clear $250 for an afternoon's work.

(a) Did you make a $250 profit?

(b) Are you likely to be given the lemonade concession again next year? What difference does it make whether or not word gets around about how much you cleared?

(c) If the college next year auctions off the franchise, how much would you be willing to bid? Who will then get the profit from the lemonade stand?

12. If a district-court judge enters a $300-million judgment against a corporation for violation of antitrust statutes, do the owners of that corporation sustain a loss? What form will it take? If you believe that the judge was in error and that his decision will eventually be reversed on appeal, how could you profit from your knowledge?

13. You buy shares of common stock in two corporations. Over the next six months, the price of one falls and the price of the other rises. Which was a better buy? Which would be the better one to sell if you want cash?

14. Evaluate the following argument: "General Motors has taken advantage of its dominant position in the automobile industry and made huge profits year after year. It would be perfectly just, therefore, to impose a special tax on General Motors as a way of recovering for society some of the exorbitant profits earned in the past." Who would pay that tax?

15. In June 1979 the provincial legislature of Quebec gave final approval to legislation authorizing the expropriation of Asbestos Corporation, a mining concern with headquarters in Montreal. Asbestos Corporation was at the time a 55 percent-owned subsidiary of General Dynamics Corporation.

(a) General Dynamics had repeatedly insisted that it did not want to sell to the province of Quebec. What do the officers of a corporation usually mean when they say they do not want to sell a subsidiary?

(b) In a voluntary sale the price is set by mutual agreement. In a forced sale some other method must be used to determine the price or compensation to be received for the expropriated property. A study commissioned by the province put the value of Asbestos Corporation at about $42 a share. A valuation done for General Dynamics set the value at almost $100 a share. If you were the arbitrator asked to decide on the *true value*, what data would you consult to find the answer?

(c) Suppose someone suggests that the fair value of the corporation be determined by the going market price of Asbestos Corporation stock. If the stock were widely held by the public, investors would determine the value of a share by what they were willing to pay to own it or had to be paid to surrender ownership. What is the flaw in this proposal? What determines the price of a corporation's stock when that corporation faces imminent nationalization?

(d) Could General Dynamics benefit from nationalization if the compensation received was less than the sum of what was originally paid to purchase the assets of Asbestos Corporation, plus the cost of all subsequent additions and improvements to those assets?

(e) General Dynamics finally agreed to sell in late 1981, under the threat of expropriation. Soon thereafter, mounting concern over the health effects

of exposure to asbestos particles led to a massive decline in the demand for asbestos, and the government-owned firm began to incur losses. By the end of 1983, the stock had fallen to $10 a share from $37 a share just prior to its acquisition by the Quebec government. Did General Dynamics profit from the nationalization?

16. The average price of farmland in the U.S. tripled during the 1970s. How would you account for this?

17. In June 1985 the U.S. Department of Agriculture announced its decision to end controls on hops production. In 1966 each hops grower in business at the time had been assigned a share of the total amount of hops that could be sold. Ever since, new hops farmers have had to purchase or lease allotments from existing growers, at a considerable price. The Agriculture Department, in announcing its decision to terminate the system, objected to the fact that new growers had to pay for an allotment that had been given to the original growers at no charge. Does the Agriculture Department's objection make any sense? If the allotments had *not* acquired any value after 1966, what would this imply about the original decision to restrict hops production?

18. Prior to 1980, the Interstate Commerce Commission rarely granted new permits to trucking firms to haul goods interstate, and operating rights were often extremely valuable. They were listed as assets on the books of trucking companies and made up a significant part of the purchase price whenever such companies were sold.
    (a) What factors established the market value of such operating rights?
    (b) When the Motor Carrier Act of 1980 took effect, allowing much easier entry into interstate trucking, the market value of operating rights fell. Why?
    (c) Was this fall a loss?
    (d) Losses as well as profits are the consequence of uncertainty. What was the uncertainty that produced this loss for trucking companies in 1980?
    (e) What would have happened to the value of operating rights in the 1970s if everyone had known 10 years in advance that Congress was going to ease restrictions on entry into interstate trucking after 1980?
    (f) The Motor Carrier Act of 1980 was a change in the rules of the game. Which were the principal property rights affected, and with what consequences?

19. Seats on the New York Stock Exchange have sold in recent years for about $400,000. Why would anyone pay that much to be allowed to trade stocks on the New York Stock Exchange? Does that price prove that one can make large profits by trading on the floor of the NYSE?

20. In March 1980, 157 farmers filed a suit against the federal government asking for $18 million in damages incurred as a result of an erroneous prediction by the Bureau of Reclamation. The bureau had estimated that water for irrigation in 1977 would be only 6 percent of normal because of a severe drought the previous winter. As a result, the 157 suing farmers had dug expensive wells, planted less valuable crops, and in some cases had planted no crops at all. The actual runoff proved to be much higher than the bureau's predictions, but the truth came too late to do these farmers any good. What caused the farmers' loss? How do they want that loss to be allocated? Do

you think they had a legitimate case? Should a carnival operator be able to sue the weather bureau if almost no one comes to the carnival on a fine, sunny day because the weather forecast erroneously predicted thundershowers?

21. In the spring of 1963 Fidel Castro announced a sugar-production goal for 1970 of 10 million tons. As the target date approached and it began to appear that this much-publicized target might not be attained, the Cuban government transferred labor and other resources in large amounts from the production of alternative goods into the production of sugar. The goal was still missed by a large margin. How do you suppose the consequent loss was distributed? How would the profit have been distributed had this decision turned out better than anticipated?

22. Why do corporate officers sometimes make illegal election contributions? Are those contributions "investments" subject to profit or loss?

23. When the government takes over privately owned land for a highway and pays compensation to the owners, should that compensation be based on its value in its present use, on its value in the use to which the government will put it, or on the value of the adjoining land that will increase (or decrease) in value because of the highway? What is unfair about each option?

24. Does ownership of gold or silver enable people to protect themselves against the hazards of uncertainty?

25. It has been proposed that state and local governments abolish property taxes for homeowners and turn to sales or income taxes for revenue. What effects on home prices would you predict from such a step? Who would be most likely to benefit?

26. In June 1972 the National Coalition for Land Reform asked the secretary of the interior to reclaim land given to the Southern Pacific Railroad in the nineteenth century. The coalition claims the railroad was supposed to sell this land for family-sized plots at $2.50 an acre or less, or forfeit the land. What do you think would happen if the federal government now required that all such land be sold within the next year in family-sized plots and at prices not to exceed $2.50 an acre? Who would lose and who would gain?

27. Suppose it costs $100,000 a year just to maintain a large, old church building on Manhattan Island in New York City. Membership has declined to about 100, and so the congregation discusses whether it can afford to keep the church open any longer.

    (a) What is it costing per member to continue using the building as a church? What major cost component have you left out if your answer is $1000?

    (b) If a developer offers $2 million for the site (not an unreasonable price in Manhattan), what is the annual cost to the congregation of continuing to use the building?

    (c) If the congregation had 400 members and was quite capable of meeting the regular maintenance costs, could it afford to ignore the developer's offer of $2 million? What would be the real cost, as distinct from the nominal or money cost, of rejecting the offer?

    (d) In 1977, a Manhattan synagogue with declining membership sold its building to a Seventh-Day Adventist congregation for $400,000. The rabbi said he was "happy to get rid of it" because of dwindling attendance and high operating costs. But the new owners soon encountered

the same problems. When they then put the building up for sale, it was purchased for $2.4 million. Who, if anyone, made a profit from these transactions?

(e) The people who live near an old, attractive church building would usually much prefer to see the building remain than to have it torn down and replaced by an office tower or condominium complex. In New York City, neighbors have sometimes been able to lobby the Landmarks Preservation Commission and have the building officially declared a "landmark." Once that occurs, the building cannot be torn down or substantially altered. How does such an official landmark designation alter property rights? Would a congregation that wants to sell its building profit from removal of a landmark designation?

(f) The executive director of the NYC landmarks commission, when asked to comment on a suit filed by a congregation whose church building had been declared a landmark, said that "a church should be forever." Do you think this is or should be part of the established rules of the game in society: that church buildings are forever?

(g) A former director for the arts of the National Council of Churches commented as follows on the demolition of church buildings in favor of commercial structures: "I don't give a damn what others think. It's a perversion that property is more important than beauty." Has he accurately described the issue in depicting it as a choice between "property" and "beauty"? (This entire question draws extensively upon a *Wall Street Journal* article of September 27, 1982, written by Luis Ubinas.)

28. A *Wall Street Journal* article on fire safety in high-rise buildings contained this argument: "Sprinklers can save on insurance rates by providing added protection. By one estimate the savings over 30 years would pay for the system, but high-rise buildings are often built by speculators who plan to sell them far sooner than that."

    (a) Why is the fact that builders typically sell high-rise buildings within a few years irrelevant to the decision about installing sprinkler systems?

    (b) If you don't see that it's irrelevant, ask yourself why contractors who build homes that they plan to sell within a year often put on roofing material with a fifteen-year warranty.

    (c) Suppose a sprinkler system costs $30,000 to install and produces savings in insurance premiums of $1000 per year. How many years of such savings would be required to justify the expenditure if the interest rate is 1 percent per year? 2 percent? Are you surprised that builders aren't impressed by savings on insurance that takes 30 years to equal the amount spent to obtain those savings?

29. The Army Corps of Engineers estimates that a canal between Tussle and Big Stone would save shippers $500,000 per year. The canal would cost $20 million to construct and $200,000 per year to maintain.

    (a) Is it correct to say that the canal is a good investment in the long run because it will save society a net $300,000 per year and eventually that will come to more than the $20 million construction cost?

    (b) About how low would the interest rate have to be to make the canal a profitable investment? (The canal would not be profitable if the interest payments plus maintenance costs ate up the saving to shippers.)

(c) "The advantage of having the government build the canal is that government can do things that are in the public interest whereas private enterprise is constrained by narrow considerations of profitability." Evaluate that argument.

30. A company offers retiring employees an option on their pension benefits. They may choose either to receive a designated sum each month for as long as they live or a lump sum at the time of retirement.
    (a) How could the firm go about determining the present value of a certain amount each month for life?
    (b) How will a rise in interest rates affect the size of the lump-sum option?
    (c) What is the present value of a $10,000 annual pension to be received at the end of each of the next 15 years when discounted at 9 percent? When discounted at 12 percent?
    (d) Does a rise in interest rates make the lump-sum option less attractive to retiring employees?

31. Many mortgage contracts on residences include a due-on-sale clause, which says that the full amount of the unpaid balance falls due when the residence is sold. This prevents the new buyer from taking over or "assuming" the mortgage of the seller.
    (a) If in 1985 the seller still owed $20,000 on a 30-year mortgage taken out in 1965 at 6 percent interest, and current mortgage rates are 12 percent, why will the lending institution *not* want the buyer to assume the existing mortgage?
    (b) If the buyer assumes the existing mortgage, he will have to make monthly payments of about $225 to pay off the $20,000 still due to the lending institution. If the buyer has to secure a new loan at 12 percent, the monthly payments would come to about $295 if the $20,000 balance is to be paid off in 10 years. By assuming the mortgage, the borrower is able to save about $840 a year for 10 years. How will the seller be able to capture that saving for himself?
    (c) In recent years some state legislatures and occasionally even state courts have decided that due-on-sale clauses in mortgage contracts should not be enforced. This was a change in the rules of the game. How did it affect property rights, and with what consequences for these parties: lending institutions; sellers of houses with low-rate mortgages containing due-on-sale clauses; buyers of such houses; sellers of houses without low-rate mortgages?

32. The state lottery claims that its grand prize is $1 million. The lucky winner will receive $50,000 upon presentation of the winning ticket plus $50,000 at the end of each of the next 19 years. Is that really a $1 million prize? What is it actually worth? Will you want to use a real or a nominal interest rate to discount these future amounts? Why? Suppose the 19 future payments were all to be adjusted for any intervening changes in the value of money. What interest rate would you use then to calculate the present value of the "$1 million" prize? What effect does the decision to "index" future payments to changes in the value of money have on the present value of the prize?

33. "Save it," somebody says. "Don't sell it. It's not worth much now, but in 20 years it will probably be worth five times as much." Should you save it

or sell it? What will $1 now be worth in 20 years if invested at the rate of interest currently obtainable from relatively risk-free loans?

34. What is the present value of each of the following when discounted at interest rates of 4 and 18 percent?
    (a) A $10,000 prize in a limerick-writing contest, to be received one year from now.
    (b) A $10,000 cash legacy from your Aunt Mehitabel, to be received when you reach your 25th birthday. (If you have already passed it, choose some other birthday.)
    (c) $10,000 per year for each of the next ten years, beginning one year from now, as first prize for telling in 25 words or less why you like a detergent.
    (d) Ownership of an office building from which you expect to receive an annual net income of $10,000 per year for each of the next 30 years, at the end of which time you expect to sell the building and land for $100,000. Assume the annual amounts are all received at the end of each year.
    (e) $10,000 in additional income per year from age 25 to age 65 if you're willing to go to school for an extra 5 years when you reach the age of 20.

35. If a gallon of gasoline currently costs $1, and if the price increases in future years at exactly the rate of inflation, what will be the price of gasoline 5 years, 10 years, and 20 years from now if inflation occurs at an annual rate of 2 percent? If it occurs at a 6 percent annual rate? If it occurs at a 12% annual rate?

36. Marxists often used to argue that the owners of capital were not entitled to any income from that ownership because labor produced all value. Today they are more likely to admit that capital contributes to the production of value, but they still deny the right of capitalists to receive a profit on the grounds that the *ownership* of capital is not productive.
    (a) Would you be willing to argue that those who own capital *have a right* to whatever income they can obtain from that capital? Is this the same as arguing that they *deserve* the income? Is it the same as saying that they *ought to be allowed* to receive the income?
    (b) Does the productivity of resources depend at all on those who manage those resources, or are all individuals and all organizations equally good at managing resources efficiently? Does the ownership of resources have anything to do with who manages those resources? Is it true that the ownership of capital is not productive?

37. Are the profits of U.S. corporations currently earned more through coercion or through persuasion? (Definition of terms: *coercion*—inducing people to cooperate by reducing their options; *persuasion*—inducing people to cooperate by expanding their options.) If you don't know how to answer the question, try thinking about the adequacy in this context of the proposed definitions for coercion and persuasion.

The Distribution of Income

Have you ever reflected on the fact that we all obtain our incomes by inducing other people to provide them? We also produce some goods for ourselves directly, of course, and there may even be a few hermits in the country who never use money and never have to depend on other people's cooperation. Except for counterfeiters, however, we all get our money incomes from other people.

We persuade them to hire us, to buy from us, to lend to us, or simply to recognize that our status entitles us to income. That last technique is the one employed by children to extract income from their parents, by retired people to get social-security benefits, by people who qualify for unemployment compensation, and by the lucky holders of winning lottery tickets, to mention just a few. Another way to put it is that we supply what other people are willing to pay for. In short, the distribution of income results from supply and demand.

Suppliers and Demanders

We took this roundabout route to get to that very orthodox conclusion in order to underline the fact that income isn't really distributed—regardless of what the title of this chapter asserts. No one actually distributes income in our society in the sense of parceling it out. People's incomes are rather the outcome of many interacting decisions, decisions ultimately made by different individuals on the basis of the benefits and the costs they expect from their decisions.

Individuals aren't free to decide just anything they please, of course. Few of us can decide to obtain $300,000 per year by getting others to watch us play basketball. People make *constrained* choices. But they do choose. Income is not a fact of nature. Unlike height and (natural) hair color, choice can change it. Income may be more like place of residence.

Although few of us can choose to live anywhere, most of us have substantial discretion about where we're going to live, whether Iowa or California, city or suburb, apartment or house. The decisions of other people, from relatives through employers to housing developers, interact with our own preferences to determine the relative costs and advantages of living in one place or another. Places of residence, like incomes, are the outcome of millions of interrelated decisions.

Those decisions, it should be noted, can even be unfair—and often are. Racial prejudices limit people's options with respect both to choosing residence and to securing money income. Suppliers and demanders sometimes perpetrate frauds. People are the victims of poor schooling or destructive environments that limit their options in later life. Sometimes what matters is who you know rather than what you can do. Thus the claim that income accrues to people as a result of supply and demand is not an endorsement of existing income patterns, but a way of thinking about the question.

Economic theory explains the distribution of income as the product of the supply of and demand for *productive services.* The word *productive* means no more than *demanded;* an activity is productive if it enables people to obtain something for which they're willing to pay. All sorts of thoroughly disreputable persons (you may provide your own list) are thus suppliers of productive services. Nor does the word *service* necessarily mean that effort has been expended. A man who lives entirely on his inheritance is supplying a productive service, in our sense of the term, by giving up some command over current resources. No one would dream of commending him for effort, since he makes none. But a playboy heir who lives off dividends still contributes to current production by the activity of not consuming his capital. The relevant fact for economic analysis is not the merit of the playboy but the demand for the resources whose ownership provides him with regular income.

The demand for productive services will generate no income for a person who owns no resources capable of supplying those services. The distribution of income among individuals or families depends fundamentally, therefore, on the ownership of productive resources.

Sometimes this is expressed by saying that the distribution of income depends on the prior distribution of wealth. That's an acceptable restatement, as long as we don't define wealth too narrowly. The trouble is that most empirical studies of personal wealthholdings, as well as the ordinary connotation of the word, restrict wealth to such assets as cash, stocks, bonds, and real estate. However, most of the income that Americans receive annually does not derive from ownership of

wealth in these forms but rather from the ownership of *human capital.*

Capital and Human Resources

We defined the term *capital* in Chapter 11. As economists use the word, it means *produced means of production,* or *goods that can be used to produce future goods.* Machinery is capital, as are industrial and commercial buildings. But so are the knowledge and skills that people accumulate through education, training, or experience and that enable them to supply valuable productive services to others. Only when we include human capital in our definition of wealth is it at all adequate to say that the distribution of income depends on the distribution of wealth.

Most income in the U.S derived from the ownership of human capital.

Total employee compensation, for example, regularly dwarfs corporate profits in the government's annual calculations of the national income. Through the first half of the 1980s, "compensation of employees" came to 14 times the total of dividends plus retained corporation earnings.

This does not mean that factory operatives and office workers take home the bulk of the nation's income. The human services that produce most of the nation's income include the services of physicians, corporate executives, athletes, actors, and rock stars as well as teachers, typists, and technicians. The point is that, contrary to popular belief, inequality in the distribution of income in the United States today arises primarily from unequal abilities to supply valuable human services. Human capital has to be included in our definition of wealth, because most income is earned in the United States by supplying the services of human resources.

Human Capital and Investment

Is it misleading, though, to refer to these resources as *capital?* Capital means *produced resources.* To what extent are the abilities that enable people to command high incomes *produced* rather than inherited or just stumbled upon? It seems impossible to generalize safely or usefully in response to this question. Perhaps the word *capabilities* would therefore be a more neutral and consequently more satisfactory term.

On the other hand, the implication that these capabilities are *produced* does call attention to a fact of some importance. People can and do choose to acquire additional capabilities in the expectation of earning additional income. They invest in themselves by going to school, acquiring special job training, practicing certain skills, or otherwise adding to the value of the services they can supply to others. It makes sense to refer

to such investments in oneself as the acquisition of human capital.

We must once again beware of confusing the question of function with the question of merit, a confusion to which we referred earlier in discussing profits—and which seems to crop up in conjunction with any issue of income distribution. The value of a tax accountant's services doesn't depend on the extent to which his or her skills were acquired rather than inherited. But it does depend on the level of those skills, and that level can usually be raised through diligent effort. The expectation of an increased income from the sale of their services induces tax accountants to pore over tedious tax-court rulings, when they would rather be playing golf. Pride and a sense of craftsmanship may also be at work. But the prospect of a greater income exercises a constant and steady pressure on people to acquire capabilities that will permit them to supply more valuable services to others. That's a useful social function, even if we were to decide that all differences between people are ultimately matters of good or evil fortune, so that people are never authorized to say that they *deserve* the incomes they receive.

Property Rights and Income

Who then owns productive resources? They're owned by many different people, individually and jointly, through partnerships, corporations, and informal arrangements. The owners acquired these resources by many different means, most of which we can never hope to untangle in retrospect. The resources themselves have an enormous variety of forms, running all the way from ideas and skills to turret lathes and fertile fields. Do not assume, however, that the people who own productive resources are the ones who happen to have possession or who have the title deed in their safe-deposit box. Property rights depend upon the reigning rules of the game, not upon more physical facts.

Ownership is a bundle of rights; some sticks may be missing from the bundle.

Suppose you "own" your driveway but are unable to prevent people from parking on the street in a way that blocks your entrance. Since you can't expect to park in it yourself or to receive income from renting the space to others, you don't have an effective property right and consequently don't own a parking space. Perhaps what you own is a shuffleboard court or a splendid place to play hopscotch.

Consider the case of a woman who has been expertly trained as a physician but can't obtain a license to practice because she was educated in a foreign country. She owns a human resource of limited value; the only services she can supply will be to her own family and friends.

The owner of an apartment building under rent controls may be unable to set rents high enough to cover taxes and maintenance. In that case, he doesn't actually own the units. The services that the units provide are appropriated by the tenants occupying the apartments, who are thus the effective owners. The proof of the nominal owner's actual nonownership in such a case would be his inability to sell the units at any price and his willingness simply to abandon them by surrendering legal ownership to the taxing authorities.

Federal law says that the airwaves belong to the public. But the Federal Communications Commission allows the owners of television stations to use assigned channels at no charge. Since the owners of the stations can appropriate the income from supplying television services, they are the actual owners of the channels. A proof of this will be their ability to sell the physical plant and facilities at a price many times greater than the cost of the facilities' reproduction—*if* the purchaser can expect to obtain, along with the station, the right to use the assigned channel.

The mayor of a city doesn't legally own any of the city's facilities. But if she can expect to enjoy the benefits supplied by a spacious office, a large staff, motorcycle escorts for her limousine, and a place at the head table for just about any banquet she chooses to attend, her wealth is much greater than it seems. She cannot sell these property rights, it's true; so they're limited in that respect. But *all* property rights are limited in one respect or another. The ability to sell is an important part of property rights; but it is only one stick in a larger bundle, and its absence limits but doesn't eliminate property rights.

Actual, Legal, and Moral Rights

A useful distinction that can often help us agree on what we're talking about is the distinction between actual and legal or moral property rights. It is people's actual rights that govern their expectations and consequently determine how they will behave. If the city council decrees that dog owners must keep their pets on a leash while they are in city parks and clean up all mementoes that the dogs leave behind, the council thereby grants city residents the *legal* right to stroll barefoot through the parks without fear or trembling. If the police cannot enforce the ordinance, however, and many dog owners simply ignore it, resident's *actual* rights will diverge from their legal rights. What park users see as their actual rights will determine whether or not they take off their shoes. If they leave their shoes on while indignantly insisting that they "have a right" to a park free of dog feces, they are

asserting a *moral* right, a right that they believe they *ought* to enjoy.

Because rights are social facts, they depend upon acceptance by others of the appropriate obligations. Until dog owners accept the obligation to monitor their pets' behavior—either to avoid legal penalties or to show consideration for others—park users will not enjoy the actual right to frolic fearlessly and will consequently keep their shoes on while strolling in the park.

Expectations and Investment

Every decision about the use of resources is based finally on the expectations of the decision maker. Families and individuals decide whether to consume or to invest their income by assessing the relative values of the benefits they expect to receive from each option. And they choose among alternative investments by considering not only the expected rates of return, but also the confidence with which those returns can be expected. People who fear confiscation of their investments will opt for investments that are difficult to confiscate, even though they promise a lower return than more vulnerable investment projects. Dictators who suspect their control is slipping shift into Swiss bank accounts, and ethnic minorities encountering native hostility invest in jewelry or other readily portable wealth. The most readily portable form of wealth is human capital, which may explain why prospering ethnic minorities have so often obtained unusually high levels of education. Of course, even human capital *can* be confiscated; people who are barred from practicing a profession for which they were trained have been effectively deprived of the human resource which that training created.

When you reflect upon the fact that the returns from investment decisions are *future* returns, you realize that a person's rate of time preference also affects consumption or investment decisions. Someone who discounts future events at a high rate will be present-oriented, will prefer consumption to investment, and will thereby choose in effect to receive a lower income in future years. On the other hand, people who discount at a low rate of interest will be more willing to give up present consumption for the sake of greater consumption in the future and will consequently invest more heavily while they're young, thereby securing for themselves a higher expected income in later years. The interesting implication of all this is that people choose, to some extent, their lifetime income profiles.

A further implication is that we can't always tell from a simple comparison of two people's current incomes which of

them has the higher income. A promising student in the last year of medical school probably has a large *negative* income. But would we really want to say that he or she is poorer than someone the same age who is earning $10,000 a year from a semiskilled job? The relevant comparison is *lifetime* incomes. That was the comparison relevant to the medical student's decision to become a physician, and it's probably the more relevant comparison for anyone who wants to evaluate the equity of a particular income distribution.

Data on lifetime incomes are hard to obtain, of course, except long after the fact. That's probably why we continue to exaggerate the poverty of many people who are students and the wealth of many who were students long ago. The two errors don't necessarily cancel out, however. If public policy responds to these opposite exaggerations by transferring income from the older to the younger group, it lowers the expected rate of return and hence the amount of investment that will occur during people's younger years.

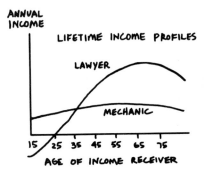

The Law of Demand and Productive Services

The demand for the services of productive resources is like all other demand curves: it slopes downward to the right. Other things remaining equal, a larger quantity will be demanded at lower prices and a smaller quantity at higher prices. In the case of productive resources, this relationship may be so well disguised that people won't see it or will refuse to believe it. But the relationship will hold whether it's recognized or not.

The best example is probably the case of labor services demanded by an employer. Employers purchase labor services after estimating the probable contribution those services will make toward the creation of income. They hire when they expect the additional revenue from a hiring decision to be greater than the additional cost which the decision entails. They use the simple rule of Chapter 9: take those actions and only those actions whose expected marginal revenue is greater than their expected marginal cost. The higher the wage rate, the higher the marginal cost of purchasing labor services. Other things remaining equal, therefore, a smaller quantity of labor services will be demanded as the price that must be paid to obtain them goes up.

Why is this so widely and frequently denied? It's denied, for example, by those who insist that opposition to legal minimum wages is evidence of indifference toward the plight of the poor. But do poor people really benefit from legislated increases in the minimum wage? If the legal minimum is no higher than what employers are already paying, it has no

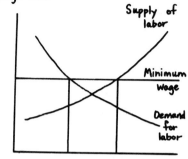

effect. It will have an impact only if some covered employers are paying less than the legal minimum. But won't these employers lay some workers off if they're compelled to pay a higher wage, or at least not replace workers who quit?

"They wouldn't have to" isn't a good answer. It's a common answer, because so many people believe that employers pay wages "out of profits" and can therefore refrain from laying workers off when wage rates rise, so long as profits are adequate to cover the increased wages. This seems to imply that the quantity of labor services demanded is a constant, dictated perhaps by technology, so that the only options before employers are either to pay the higher wage rates or to close down the operation. But the demand for labor services is not perfectly inelastic and will at times be highly elastic, because employers can almost always find substitutes, within some range, for labor services of any particular type.

What might the owners of a fast-food franchise do if an increase in the legal minimum wage forced them to pay a 25 percent higher hourly wage to the teenagers they employ? It simply is not true that it takes a fixed number of workers to operate the franchise; there are many margins on which adjustments might be made that would reduce the number of employees. One is hours of operation; at a low wage rate it might be profitable to open during less busy times of the day, but not at a higher wage rate. Another is quality of service; quick service can be offered at peak times by having surplus employees during slack times; when wage rates rise, economies can be achieved by reducing that surplus and making customers wait a bit longer during peak periods. Of course, that will raise the effective price to customers and so turn some away; but no sensible business firm wants to serve customers regardless of the cost of doing so. There are all sorts of ways to economize on labor of a particular kind, ways that an outsider won't be able to think of. Some of them will be ways to economize that the owners didn't think of either, until a rise in their labor costs gave them a strong incentive to think harder and longer.

It's true but largely irrelevant that the present legal minimum wage ($3.35 at this writing) won't provide a weekly income sufficient to support a family at the level to which most Americans are accustomed. For one thing, many wage earners don't have families to support or are not the principal source of support for the families to whose incomes they contribute. (Almost 60 percent of married-couple families in the U.S. now contain two workers or more.) More crucially, if $134 a week isn't an adequate income, nothing per week is even less adequate. A large increase in the legal minimum

wage would produce more income for some; but it would mean less income for a substantial number who could not obtain employment at a significantly higher wage.

People or Machines?

The strange notion that the demand for labor services of any type is completely inelastic with respect to the wage rate also seems to underlie the widespread belief (or fear) that machines "destroy" jobs because they are so much more productive than people. But what could it mean to say that machines are "more productive" than people? Employers aren't interested in mere physical or technical capabilities; they're interested in the relation between marginal revenues and marginal costs. A machine is more efficient than a person, and hence will be substituted for a person, only if the marginal revenue from the machine's use *relative to its marginal cost* is greater than the same ratio for a person. That implies, among other things, that wage rates play an important part in shaping the speed and direction of technological change in the economy.

Automatic elevators didn't replace elevator operators in the United States in recent years merely because of improvements in technology. Time, money, and energy were spent to develop automatic elevators—and building owners subsequently installed them—because of benefit-cost estimates they made, not because automatic elevators were new and shiny. In some other society where the wage rates (opportunity costs) of elevator operators are quite low, elevators run by trained operators could still be more efficient than automatic elevators.

The fear that our society or any society may run out of jobs is an odd kind of fear. A job, after all, represents an obstacle to be overcome. A society that has run out of jobs for people to do has come very close to overcoming scarcity; and that would be something to cheer, not fear. We're not in any such fortunate situation. Technological innovations release labor resources from some employments to make them available for others. The automatic or self-service elevator made it possible for people who were formerly employed in transporting passengers up and down to do something else, to make some other and additional contribution to our total output of commodities and services.

The reallocation of labor in response to changed circumstances does lead to a loss of wealth for some people. A rising demand for labor attracted some elevator operators into more remunerative employments and pulled up the wages of the rest; automatic elevators were in part a response to this situa-

tion. But as they were introduced, some elevator operators found themselves pushed rather than pulled: deprived of their present jobs and compelled to accept less desirable alternatives, rather than attracted away from their present positions by better opportunities. Such people suffered, at least temporarily, a loss of wealth. They were forced to incur the cost of searching for new employment, and they were not guaranteed that the new job would be better than the old. Resistance to technological change and fear of automation are therefore quite understandable. Even college professors have been known to speak harshly about the introduction of such technological innovations as videotaped lectures and teaching machines.

The Derived Demand for Productive Services

Another factor that may help to conceal the downward-sloping character of the demand curve for productive services is the derived nature of that demand. The demand for productive services is derived from the demand for the goods they produce. When firms announce that they're expanding their hiring or laying some workers off, they almost never attribute the decision to a change in wage rates. Instead they credit (or blame) the market for their product: "Sales have increased beyond our expectations" or "Inventories of finished goods have grown to unacceptable levels because of disappointing sales." Thus the quantity of services demanded at any time from carpenters or automobile assemblers will seem to depend on conditions in the housing or automobile market, rather than on the wages of carpenters or automobile assemblers.

But they actually depend on both. The point to be noted is that the prices of houses and of automobiles and the way they are produced have been influenced by the wage rates that had to be paid to obtain the services of carpenters and of automobile assemblers. In the case of carpenters, fewer new houses are purchased, and hence fewer carpenters are employed, insofar as the cost of obtaining carpenters' services has raised the price of new construction. Moreover, houses are increasingly constructed in ways that economize on carpenters' services, with less elaborate woodwork, for example, and with factory-built cabinets.

Demand Creates Income

Our discussion of the demand for productive services has emphasized the demand as a *constraint:* the income that owners

of productive resources can obtain by supplying the services of the resources they own is limited by the demand for those services. The corollary also deserves emphasis: the income that resource owners can receive is *created* by the demand for the services of those resources. Any sheik who owns an oil well provides a vivid illustration.

Whether a country like Kuwait, which each year produces about a thousand barrels of oil per inhabitant, is fabulously wealthy or almost desperately poor depends on the demand for the services of a thick and flammable liquid hydrocarbon that seemed both ugly and useless when it was first discovered. In the absence of that demand, the Organization of Petroleum Exporting Countries (OPEC) would have had less influence over world affairs during the 1970s than the Audubon Society. But given the enormous demand that had developed in this century for the services of petroleum, OPEC became a household word.

Who Competes against Whom?

When owners of productive resources form organizations like OPEC in an effort to increase their incomes, they often argue that their association will enable them to compete more effectively against the buyers of whatever service they're supplying. Whether we call this argument confused or devious depends on how we want to assess the motives of those who make it. The plain fact is that buyers don't compete against sellers. Buyers compete against one another to obtain what sellers are supplying. Sellers compete against sellers to obtain the custom of buyers. The competition that OPEC was designed to eliminate was competition among the petroleum-exporting countries. OPEC succeeded insofar as it was able to restrict production.

Buyers may try to play the same game. We can refer at this point to an example used earlier: the agreement among owners of professional sports teams not to compete for the services of athletes. To make this agreement effective they had to assign the exclusive right to each athlete's services to a single owner. This is the purpose of the "draft," as developed by owners' associations in major professional sports. When buyers present this kind of unified position, organization on the part of sellers may be an effective way of countering their power. But the objective of the sellers' association in such circumstances would be to *reactivate competition* among the buyers or to *reduce competition* among the sellers, and could not be correctly described as an attempt to compete more effectively against the buyers.

Buyers prefer that sellers have 12 players on the field rather than 11 — because buyers don't compete against sellers.

Unions and Competition

In the case of labor unions, the basic federal statute regulating union organization and collective bargaining makes the mistake of asserting in its preamble that unorganized workers need unions to help them compete against corporations. But workers compete against workers, corporate employers against corporate employers. And this is the competition that affects wage rates.

Employers can't pay their workers whatever wage their callous hearts suggest for the same reason that Exxon was never able to buy oil from Saudi Arabia for whatever price it chose. Workers have alternative opportunities in the form of other employers, and Saudi Arabia always had alternative opportunities in the form of other refiners. The services of workers are valuable to employers, and so they're willing to bid for them, even though that may raise the going wage. The services of crude oil are valuable to refiners, and so they too are willing to bid, raising its price above $3 a barrel in 1972 before OPEC learned how to restrict production, above $30 a barrel when OPEC mastered the art, and keeping it for a while above $20 a barrel even when OPEC began to disintegrate in the 1980s.

Similarly, workers cannot successfully insist on the wage they think they deserve if other workers are willing to supply very similar services at lower wage rates. Workers compete against other workers, and unions are in part attempts to control *this* competition. The implication is that unions improve the position of the members they represent by finding ways to restrict competition from those who are not members of the union. They may do this directly, for example, by securing contracts with employers that make union member-ship a prior condition of employment and then limiting membership. Or they may do it indirectly. Just as a legal minimum wage excludes some people from employment opportunities, so a high wage secured by union contract (perhaps under the threat of a strike or total withdrawal of labor services) excludes those who would be willing to work for less.

The belief that unions arose in the United States to counter the power of large corporations is unsupported by history. Unions first became powerful in this country in industries characterized by small-scale firms: construction, printing, textiles, mining. The railroads are an exception that supports the rule: it was special legislation that enabled unions to become powerful in the railroad industry. The unions that today bargain with the large corporations in steel, automobiles, and electrical machinery were originally missionary projects of the unions that bargained mostly with small employers.

WAGE RATE

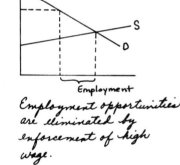

Employment

Employment opportunities are eliminated by enforcement of high wage.

What does it all come to? What's the pattern of the income distribution among people in the United States?

There are many ways to summarize and present the data on income distribution that the Bureau of the Census gathers. The most common is the quintile (by fifths) distribution of family income. The Census Bureau counted almost 62,000,000 families in the United States in 1983. This includes everyone except individuals living alone or living with persons to whom they were not related by kinship or marriage. Table 12A shows the percentage of total family income received in 1983 and in three earlier years by the 20 percent of these families with the lowest incomes, by the second-lowest fifth, and so on up to the 20 percent who received the highest incomes. If family income were equally distributed, each fifth would receive 20 percent of the total. That obviously isn't the case. The percentage received by the highest 5 percent is also shown in the table.

People who encounter these data for the first time are usually quite surprised. The figures seem to indicate that the distribution of income in the United States hasn't changed significantly since World War II, despite progressive income taxes and vastly expanded government programs for transferring income to low-income families and individuals. The data don't agree with "what everyone knows."

In this case, however, "what everyone knows" may be more accurate than what the percentages seem to show. To begin with, these percentages refer to income before the payment of personal taxes. Second, the data take no account of *in-kind transfers*. They do reflect *money transfers*. Thus they include income from private pensions, veterans' benefits, social-security benefits, the program of Aid to Families with Dependent Children (AFDC), and all other welfare assistance—*when paid in money*. But they don't include the value of such in-kind transfers as medical assistance, rent subsidies, or food stamps—all of which are income even though they don't

Table 12A Money income of families—percent of aggregate income received by each fifth and highest 5 percent

	1950	1960	1970	1983
Lowest fifth	4.5	4.8	5.4	4.7
Second fifth	12.0	12.2	12.2	11.1
Middle fifth	17.4	17.8	17.6	17.1
Fourth fifth	23.4	24.0	23.8	24.4
Highest fifth	42.7	41.3	40.9	42.7
Highest 5 percent	17.3	15.9	15.6	15.8

Source: U.S. Bureau of the Census, *Current Population Reports*, series P-60, No. 145.

Table 12B Percentage of aggregate family money income received by each fifth of families, adjusted to reflect personal taxes and in-kind transfers and calculated on a per capita basis

	1952	1962	1972
Lowest fifth	8.1	8.8	11.7
Second fifth	14.2	14.4	15.0
Middle fifth	17.8	18.2	18.2
Fourth fifth	23.2	23.1	22.3
Highest fifth	36.7	35.4	32.8

Source: Edgar K. Browning, "The Trend Toward Equality in the Distribution of Net Income," *Southern Economic Journal* (July 1976).

involve the exchange of money. Third, these data are not adjusted to take account of differing family sizes. When these three adjustments are made, the percentages going to each quintile change over time in precisely the direction we would expect. The share of lower-income groups rises, and that of upper-income groups falls. One careful attempt to make these adjustments produced the results shown in Table 12B—results that are far more consistent with common sense than are the unadjusted data of Table 12A.

A Spurious Rigidity

A more fundamental difficulty with data of this sort is that they don't actually mean what they seem to say. Even the adjusted data of Table 12B give a misleading picture of the actual inequality and rigidity of the U.S. family-income distribution since World War II. We're inclined to assume without thinking about it that the families in the second or fourth quintile in a current year are the same families (or an earlier generation of the same families) who occupied those fifths in some preceding year. This isn't necessarily the case. In fact, it's quite unlikely to be the case for one simple reason: the relative income position of a family depends very much on the age of the family's principal earner.

The data of Table 12C illustrate what we're talking about. They show the mean income of all families in 1982 by the age of the householder. (The Bureau was embarrassed by its use of the term *head* and so it recently substituted the term *householder*, defined as the owner of the residence or, in the case of joint ownership, the person whose name appears first on the survey form.) The table demonstrates unmistakably that a substantial amount of the inequality that shows up in a still picture would disappear if we were able to take a moving picture—that is, to compare the incomes of families over the lifetimes of the householders.

Age of Householder	Mean Income
15 to 24 years	$15,831
25 to 34 years	24,040
35 to 44 years	30,363
45 to 54 years	34,298
55 to 64 years	30,971
65 years and over	20,990

Source: U.S. Bureau of the Census, *Current Population Reports,* series P-60, No. 142.

When we compare the data of Table 12C with the upper limits of the various family-income quintiles in 1983, we find that "an average family" would move in its lifetime from the second fifth through the middle fifth into the fourth fifth and descend again to near the bottom of the middle fifth when the householder retires.[1]

On Redistributing Income

Interest in issues of this sort usually grows out of a belief that too much inequality in the distribution of income is undesirable. Few people pause to think their way carefully through the questions of why inequality is undesirable, how much inequality is acceptable, or why income inequality should be of so much more concern than inequalities of other kinds.

Regardless of how these important questions are answered, programs to reduce the income inequality among U.S. families and individuals will run up against a fundamental difficulty: since income isn't really distributed, it can't actually be redistributed. No one is in a position to apportion shares of the social product. The most that even government can do is alter the rules of the game in the hope of securing a preferred outcome. What happens next will not be exactly what was intended and may be something altogether different.

The simplest and most direct way to reduce income inequality would appear to be a program of taxes on high incomes and cash transfers to people with low incomes. But nothing about economic systems is ever as simple and direct as it seems at first glance. To raise taxes on high incomes, the government must change the rules that relate taxes owed to particular kinds of income received. When it does so, people don't merely pay the higher taxes; they also try to adjust their behavior to minimize the impact of the new rules. Some of these adjustments will be legal tax avoidance; others may

1. The upper limits of the lowest through the fourth fifth in 1983 were, respectively, $11,629; $20,060; $29,204; and $41,824.

be illegal tax evasion; but they all combine to drive a wedge between what was intended when the rules were rewritten and what actually emerges. The revenue that results from the tax increase will be less, and may be much less, than what was hoped for.

In order to supplement the incomes of poor people, government must write new rules controlling eligibility for grants. These rule revisions will also have undesired effects as people adjust their behavior to fit the new criteria. Once again the adjustments will be both legal and illegal; but their combined effect can be substantial, because there are so many margins along which adjustments can be made. The number of people classified as poor may actually increase as a result of efforts to reduce poverty.

Consider the hypothetical but unfortunately not implausible case of a single-parent family with three small children. Suppose the mother is currently receiving $400 a month in cash grants, food stamps worth $100 per month, and subsidized medical care for herself and the children worth $50 a month. Then she obtains a job offer promising $1,000 per month. Will she take the job and go off welfare? Would she be better off if she did so?

Her income from welfare is not taxed; but she will have to pay social security and income taxes on her earnings. She will also have to secure day care for the children, buy some additional clothing, and incur transportation expenses if she takes the job. Moreover, she will lose her monthly cash grant and her family's eligibility for food stamps and medicaid. When she adds up all these costs of taking the job, she may find that her earnings are going to be taxed at a marginal rate of 90 percent or more.

Plug in some plausible numbers and check the results for yourself. If the income and social security taxes plus day care, transportation, and clothing expenses take $350 a month from her paycheck, and the loss of welfare reduces her monthly income by $550, she would be giving up $900 in order to earn $1,000. That amounts to a 90 percent marginal tax rate, or a 90 percent tax on *additions* to her welfare income— which isn't terribly attractive. No one could accuse a mother in such a situation of laziness or irresponsibility if she decided to turn down the job offer, stay on welfare, and care for her children.

People with yachts are wealthy; people who scrounge through trash barrels and garbage cans are poor. But if we write new rules that obligate every yacht owner to contribute $10,000 a year to a fund for trash and garbage scroungers and grant each scrounger a right to $2,000 a year from the fund, the number of recorded yacht owners will rapidly

Marginal tax rate: the percentage of additional earnings taken from the worker by the system.

decline and the number of people claiming to be scroungers will show a surprising increase. That may be an overly dramatic way to summarize the problem, but it makes the essential point. A large society such as the United States cannot allocate tasks and benefits to its citizens the way that loving parents do it in a family: on the basis of abilities and needs. Tasks and benefits will inevitably be allocated in response to people's pursuit of their own interests under the perceived rules of the game. What government can achieve by way of income redistribution is pretty well confined to what can be achieved by changing the rules. That will almost certainly turn out to be something less satisfactory than what was hoped for when the rules were changed.

Changing Rules and Social Cooperation

It might be thought that the solution is to change the rules again when the initial change doesn't yield the desired results, and to keep on modifying the rules until the target has been attained. But who has the knowledge that would be required to choose these fine adjustments? Even if the knowledge were available, would anyone have the power to put them into effect in a democratic society? Most important of all, what happens to the complex cooperative processes upon which a highly specialized economic system depends if the society is subjected to continuous changes in the rules of the game?

People invest, make sacrifices, and otherwise commit themselves in the belief that established property rights will be respected, that the rules will *not* be changed "in the middle of the game." A rule that says the rules can be changed at any time would destroy the foundation for most social cooperation. Property rights must be reasonably clear and stable if people are to plan for the future and to take long-run consequences into account.

It's also worth observing that when expectations are regularly frustrated by unanticipated changes in the rules of the game, participants stop playing the ordinary game and shift their attention to the game that matters: making the rules.

Once Over Lightly

The distribution of income is the result of the supply of and demand for productive services.

The production of productive resources is investment, or the creation of capital. One important form of capital is human capital, or productive capabilities embodied in human beings. The production of human capital is an important consideration, because monetary income is primarily earned

in the United States, even by the wealthy, by supplying the services of human resources.

The amount and nature of the investment that will occur in a society depends on established and accepted property rights, because property rights determine what people can expect from the actions that are open to them.

Lower rates of time preference encourage investment over consumption. Greater uncertainty about future returns from investment will prompt the discounting of future income at higher rates and consequently will lead to less investment.

The demand for productive services of any kind will not be perfectly inelastic. A greater quantity will be demanded at lower prices and a lesser quantity at higher prices, because there are substitutes for any productive service.

Potential users of productive services decide on the amount they will demand by comparing the marginal-benefit/marginal-cost ratios of alternative procedures for achieving their purposes.

The demand for productive services and hence their price is partly dependent on the demand for the goods they produce. But the price of productive services also reacts back on the cost and price of producing particular goods and thus on the quantity that will be produced and sold.

Suppliers of productive services don't compete against buyers of those services. Suppliers compete against other suppliers, buyers against other buyers. The quest for higher incomes produces attempts to suppress competition, because what a seller can obtain and what a buyer must pay will depend on the alternative opportunities that competitors are providing.

Census Bureau data on the distribution of family money incomes exaggerate the inequality of income in the United States by neglecting in-kind transfers, personal taxes, and differences in family size. They also give an erroneous impression of rigidity by ignoring the extensive circulation of individual families throughout the overall distribution.

Social cooperation on any extensive scale requires relatively stable property rights because it presupposes the ability to predict the consequences of decisions.

QUESTIONS FOR DISCUSSION

1. *Income* is a flow of receipts per unit of time: $240 per week, or $30,000 a year. *Wealth* is a stock of assets: cash, shares of stock, buildings, tools, and so on. How are income and wealth related?
   (a) If you own an annuity that will pay you a $10,000 income for each of the next 20 years, what is the present value of that annuity? How much does the annuity contribute to your wealth?

(b) Suppose you own 100 shares of stock in a promising new company that has not yet begun to pay dividends and probably won't do so for several years. The stock is currently exchanging on the New York Stock Exchange for $50 a share. What is your wealth from ownership of this stock? If you wanted to convert this wealth into income, how could you do so? About how much income could you obtain without reducing the amount of your wealth?

(c) Why would the stock referred to above be bought for $50 a share if the company isn't expected to pay any dividends for several years?

(d) A privately owned automobile is wealth. Does it yield income to its owner? In what form?

(e) What determines the market value of a house and thus its contribution to the wealth of the owner? Do the expected benefits from living in the house (income) determine the value of the house (wealth)? Or does the price of the house determine the income received by living in it? Suppose someone happens to detest the house which he owns and occupies because it has such distracting views of the bay and the mountains from every window. Would this idiosyncratic attitude reduce his income from living in the house? Would it reduce his wealth from owning the house? What behavior would this inconsistency between his income and his wealth probably induce?

(f) Is an engineering degree wealth? What determines the value of such a degree? How could an engineer with a freshly minted degree who is just beginning her first job convert some of her wealth into current income in order to buy furniture for her apartment?

(g) A successful and popular physician decides to retire and "sell his practice." What is he actually selling? What will determine its value to a potential buyer?

(h) Is the expectation of future retirement benefits a part of one's wealth? Is the expectation of social security benefits a major part of the wealth of someone 65 years of age?

2. In a widely publicized 1983 case, the ex-wife of a doctor sued to obtain half the value of his medical degree, on the grounds that she had helped put him through medical school and was entitled to half of everything they owned under California's community property law.

(a) The attorney for the doctor insisted that education was not property and so could not be shared because it had no value at the time it was acquired. If the doctor had dropped dead upon receiving his diploma, his wife would not have gotten one cent, the attorney claimed. Do you agree?

(b) Suppose the couple had owned a house which burned down at the time of their divorce. What steps do people take to protect themselves against the accidental destruction or other loss of valuable physical assets? What steps do young physicians usually take to assure their families a large income even if the physician drops dead?

(c) The wife's attorneys asked for $250,000 as her share of the value of her ex-husband's medical training. Suppose the medical degree could be conservatively expected to add $30,000 per year for 30 years to what the doctor would have earned without the degree. Since this amount will presumably rise with any inflation that occurs over the period, a real

rather than nominal interest rate should be used to calculate its present value. Would you support the ex-wife's attorneys in their estimate of what she was entitled to? What is one-half the present value of a $30,000 annuity for 30 years when discounted at 4 percent?

(d) The doctor said: "I don't think she is entitled to half of my future." His ex-wife said: "I should get a return on my investment in the partnership." The couple separated after ten years of marriage during which she worked as an accountant while he completed medical school, an internship, and a residency. How would you decide the issue?

3. As this is written the New York Knicks professional basketball team is negotiating a contract with Patrick Ewing, the first player chosen in the 1985 draft of college players. If the signing of Ewing induces twice as many people to buy season tickets, Ewing will add $3 million to the Knicks' revenue in ticket sales alone. What is Ewing's value to the Knicks? Is this value *human capital?*

4. If a male with a high school diploma will on average earn $900,000 over his lifetime, while a male with a college diploma will average $1,200,000 in lifetime earnings, what is the value to an average male of going on after high school to earn a college diploma? (It is less than $300,000, because future income must be discounted to obtain its present value.)

5. If a female with a high school diploma earns an average of $400,000 over her lifetime, and earns $550,000 if she obtains a college diploma, what is the value of a college diploma to the average female?

6. A fifth year of college will on average increase the lifetime earnings of a man by 9 percent; but it will increase the lifetime earnings of the average woman by 34 percent. Can you suggest a plausible explanation for this difference in the effect of a fifth year of college? (Data in this and the preceding two questions are approximations of Census Bureau estimates.)

7. Alpha and Beta are identical twins. Alpha takes a job right after high school, because she thinks four years of college would be an eternity and she wants a sporty car. Beta believes her sister is foolish; she intends to go to college, take an additonal two years to earn an MBA, and make far more money than Alpha will ever see.

(a) Why does the fact that Beta's income will be far larger than Alpha's after six years not necessarily mean that Alpha made a foolish decision from the standpoint of monetary income?

(b) Use the tables of Chapter 11 to compare (1) the present value at age 17 of $20,000 per year to age 65, with (2) the present value of $40,000 per year to age 65 when the latter income doesn't start until age 23. Compare these amounts at discount rates of 18 percent and again at discount rates of 6 percent.

(c) Would it be irrational for Alpha to discount future income at a rate of 18 percent? For Beta to discount at 6 percent?

8. Should college students be required to pay the full cost of their own education?

(a) Who benefits from a person's obtaining a college education?

(b) If only low-income students are to receive educational subsidies, where would you place the ceiling on low incomes?

(c) If education is an investment designed to secure a higher future income, why don't people who want to acquire years of expensive education simply borrow the money—the way business firms borrow to finance investment?

9. If television channels belong to the public, not to the owners of the television stations who are allowed to use them, why will the sale price of a television station often be more than ten times the cost of replacing all the physical facilities that change hands after the sale? What is the previous owner selling?

10. Who owns national parks? The government? The people? Park Service officials in the Interior Department? What are the implications of a sign that reads: "U.S. Government Property: No Trespassing"?

11. Your airplane boarding pass assigns you seat A, by the window. When you come to your row you find a six-year-old child sitting in your seat. His boarding pass says C. You ask him to move, but he says he wants to look out the window and tells you to take his seat on the aisle. Since you also want to look at the scenery, you call the cabin attendant and explain the situation. The cabin attendant says, "Do you *really* want me to make that little child move away from the window?"

At this point, who owns seat A? Sort out the actual, legal, and moral property rights in this case.

12. A Santa Monica apartment owner decided to tear down his six-unit apartment building rather than operate under rent controls. The city refused him permission to tear down the building, however, claiming that its interest in preserving rental housing took precedence over his right to demolish his property. The California Supreme Court sustained Santa Monica's refusal to allow the demolition.

Who owns the building? Sort out the actual, legal, and moral rights in this case.

13. "Entitlement programs" of the federal government are defined as "programs that provide benefit payments for individuals whose eligibility is determined by law." Because the criteria for eligibility are established by existing law, expenditures are not controlled by the process of congressional appropriation.

(a) Would you say that the beneficiaries of entitlement programs receive income because of certain property rights?

(b) The criteria for some entitlement programs are outside the range of the beneficiaries' choice: payments based on age are an example, or veterans' benefits. Other programs use criteria that persons can more or less choose to satisfy. Would you expect the law of demand to affect the rate at which expenditures increase in this second category?

14. Prior to 1977, the national food stamp program gave each participating household a monthly stamp allotment sufficient to purchase a minimally adequate diet. The allotment varied with family size but not with family income. What varied with income was the price the family had to pay for the stamps. This ranged from nothing for the poorest families to about 85 percent of the stamps' value for the eligible families with the highest incomes. This system was changed in 1977 to one in which allotments did vary with family income but stamps were given away rather than sold. The

1977 reform received strong support from the argument that it was absurd if not downright immoral to make poor people pay for food stamps. Was it absurd? What were the consequences of this policy?

(a) Suppose a family earning $300 a month chooses to spend $150 on housing, $100 on food, and $50 on other goods. Then it is given $100 in food stamps. Why can't we predict how much the family will subsequently spend per month on housing, food, and other goods? What is the range of possibilities?

(b) If government officials want to be sure that the poor family uses its food stamp allotment to double its monthly expenditure on food, how can they constrain the family's choice to the outcome desired by the officials? (Assume that the family does not sell the stamps for money, something that does occur but is illegal.)

(c) Is a family better off if it chooses to use food stamps as a substitute for income previously spent on food, so that it can increase its consumption of other goods? Or should the family be constrained to follow an expenditure pattern dictated by government officials (and presumably based on the recommendations of nutritionists)?

(d) If the government makes large grants to church-owned colleges to support instruction in science but provides no funds to support religious instruction, does the government in reality support science but not religion?

(e) If a donor to a united charity appeal earmarks her contribution for alcoholism counseling, does she thereby increase the funds that will be available for alcoholism counseling in her community?

15. The claim is often made—and also often ridiculed—that taxes on income reduce people's incentives to earn income.

(a) If you were required to pay the government 50 percent of all money income you earn during the summer, would you choose to work more or fewer hours than if your income was not subject to tax? Would you look for ways to raise your income without raising your money income or taxable income?

(b) How does a 50 percent marginal tax rate (additional taxes divided by additional income) affect the cost to a physician of building his own home rather than hiring a contractor?

(c) An unmarried woman with three preschool children has no earned income but is receiving $400 a month in cash welfare assistance, plus food stamps worth $200 a month and government-financed medical care worth $100 a month. She is offered a job that will pay $1000 a month. If she takes the job, she will no longer be eligible for any of the cash or in-kind assistance. What is the marginal tax rate to which her earnings are subject? Would you take the job in her situation?

16. Teachers began encountering serious job shortages in the 1970s after many years of rising demand for their services. An intensified interest in unionization followed. What can unionization accomplish for teachers in a highly unfavorable job market? Who is likely to benefit? Who will be harmed?

17. "Farmers complaining that they can't get field hands now that the bracero program has been curtailed aren't sincere," said an official of the United

Packinghouse Workers Union. "About one-third of the unemployed in Los Angeles are former farm workers, and the farmers could get them back if they'd make wages and working conditions attractive enough." Do you think farmers are insincere? Could California farmers get enough workers if they tried harder? Explain.

18. Under a closed-shop arrangement, employers may hire only workers who are already union members. Under a union-shop arrangement, employers may hire whomever they please but the employees must then join the union. What different effects would you expect these alternative arrangements to have on wages? On employment? On discrimination by the union against members of minority races? Why?

19. College professors in the United States have never had an effective union. Then why did their average wage rise spectacularly in the 1960s? How might college professors have used unionization to obtain even larger salary increases over this period? Why might some professors be interested in a law that prohibited anyone without an earned doctorate from teaching in colleges? What consequences would you predict if a few states passed such a law?

20. Do the relative salaries of humanities professors and football coaches at major state universities reflect the relative value of football and humanities? Do they reflect the number of years that professors and coaches must spend acquiring an education? The number of hours they work? The difficulty or unpleasantness of their work? Why do the football coaches usually receive salaries that are so much higher?

21. In Holland the government pays about $50 million per year to purchase the work of artists who can't find other buyers. Much of the art winds up in warehouses—close to 500,000 pieces in 1982.
    (a) Do you think a program like this raises the average income of artists?
    (b) How might it actually lower the average income of artists?

22. There has been a growing trend in recent years toward two-tier contracts in wage negotiations between employers and unions. Current employees receive one wage; new employees are hired at a much lower wage rate.
    (a) How might such an arrangement benefit each of the following four parties: employers; current employees; union leaders; new employees.
    (b) For which of the above four groups would such a two-tier contract tend to become less satisfactory as time went by?

23. Do high wage rates in such strongly unionized industries as steel and automobiles pull up the general level of wages in nonunionized, lower-wage industries? If you think they do, what is the process by which this occurs? If contracts that call for high wages reduce employment opportunities in the industries that must pay these wages, where do the excluded workers find employment?

24. A plumbers' local in Fort Lauderdale, Florida, some years ago voluntarily lowered by 45 percent the hourly rate for union workers on low-rise construction projects. The higher rate continued to apply to high-rise construction. The business manager of the union said this was being done to curb inflation and help homeowners. Do you think it might also have been done because nonunion plumbers were available in the area at less than half of

union scale? Why do you suppose the union didn't lower the rate on high-rise construction work as well?

25. "If we had no unions with their united strength we would have unlimited hours of work, low wages, child labor wherever possible, speed-up and unsafe and dangerous working conditions. All these evils of the industrial system have been eliminated by workers united into unions and withholding their labor."

   (a) Do you agree with that statement from a newspaper letter?

   (b) Can you think of a way to test the statement or any part of it?

26. A letter to a magazine wonders "how [we will] cope with the growing number of unemployed put out of work on corporate capital-intensive high technology," and asks: "To what end these corporate methodologies that actually impoverish more than they enrich most of us?"

   (a) Can you help the writer find an answer?

   (b) The percentage of Americans over 16 who were *employed* through the year averaged 56.4 percent in 1964, 58.3 percent in 1974, and 59.9 percent in 1984. Does this trend support the letter writer's argument?

27. A nationally syndicated columnist, in attacking a proposal to reduce the federal minimum wage from $3.35 to $2.50 an hour for teenagers, stated: "Any employer with an eye to the bottom line, would prefer to hire help at 85 cents an hour less, given a choice."

   (a) If the minimum wage for teenagers were lowered by 85¢, why would some employers "with an eye to the bottom line" choose *not* to reduce the wage rate paid their teenage employees?

   (b) Why do so many employers pay teenagers (and others) wages that are far above the legal minimum wage—even in the absence of a union contract or any apparent threat of unionization?

   (c) The same columnist denies that lowering the minimum wage for teenagers would increase the number of jobs available to teenagers. "It takes McDonald's X amount of workers to offer its products to the public and that is probably going to be the amount of help hired, regardless of wages." Do you agree? What do you think would happen if McDonald's had to pay $7.70 an hour to its employees? Would X turn out to be a constant?

28. How would each of the following groups be affected by a large increase in the legal minimum wage?

   (a) Unionized workers

   (b) Teenagers

   (c) Unskilled workers

29. "Comparable worth" is the name of a movement that began in the 1980s to determine the worth of different jobs and then to adjust relative wage rates to the relative worth of those jobs. The movement gains most of its support from the belief that women are unfairly discriminated against in the labor market. The jobs at which most of them work (secretaries and nurses, for example) are regarded as "women's jobs" and so are allegedly paid less than their "comparable worth." The comparison is with jobs traditionally held by men.

   (a) Can a job have an inherent worth? Can you think of any situation where

the worth of a job is not its value to some particular party in a specific situation?

(b) Imagine a medical clinic with 20 medical doctors, one nurse, and one laboratory technician. Is it plausible to suppose that an additional nurse or lab technician could have more worth to the clinic in such a situation than an additional doctor?

(c) The worth or value that influences decisions is always *marginal* worth or value. Why is a secretary worth more to the economics department if it employs only one than if it employs eight? Describe a situation in which the worth of a secretary to the economics department would likely be greater than the worth of an economist fully armed with a Ph.D.

(d) Why will an employer who follows the maximizing rule of Chapter 9— Do more if marginal revenue exceeds marginal cost, less if marginal cost exceeds marginal revenue—want to pay each employee a wage equal to his or her marginal worth? What would be implied by the assertion that an employer was paying employees less than their marginal worth?

30. The graph below depicts the marginal value of nurses and of custodians to the Community General Hospital.

(a) Why might a nurse be worth as much as $80 an hour to the hospital?

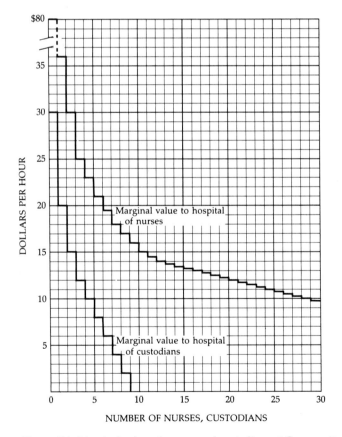

Figure 12A Marginal value of nurses and custodians at Community General Hospital

Why might a custodian be worth as much as $30 an hour? Do you think a hospital forced to pay $75 an hour for the services of a nurse would ever put the nurse to work emptying bedpans, taking temperatures, or serving meals to patients?

(b) Now suppose that the custodians are unionized and that the hospital must pay its custodians $19 an hour. How many custodians will the hospital hire? What will be the marginal worth of a custodian?

(c) Assume that the nurses are not unionized and that the hospital is able to obtain as many nurses as it wants to hire at an hourly wage of $10. How many nurses would it want to hire? What would be the marginal worth of a nurse?

(d) What would be the relative worth in this situation of a custodian and a nurse? Would their relative worth reflect the intrinsic importance of their work?

(e) Will hospitals use nurses to empty bedpans if it can hire them for $10 an hour? Will it ask nurses or will it ask custodians to empty wastebaskets if custodians must be paid twice as much as nurses? What hospital tasks do you suppose would be performed by custodians if they had to be paid $29 an hour? Would a custodian's services become worth three times as much as a nurse's services?

31. Why would nurses be willing to work for as little as $10 an hour, as in the preceding question?

(a) What factors determine the supply curve of nurses' services?

(b) Until fairly recently one could become a registered nurse by completing a three-year nurses' training program at a certified hospital. The general rule now is that nurses must acquire a bachelor of science degree, and will not be admitted to nursing curricula until they have successfully completed courses in inorganic and organic chemistry, microbiology, mathematics, social science, and language. Do these tougher requirements increase the value of registered nurses to prospective employers? Do they shift the supply curve of nurses? Are they likely to affect the wage rate that must be paid for nurses? Will this affect the marginal worth of nurses?

32. Question 30 above assumed that the custodians' union was able to enforce a wage rate of $19 an hour.

(a) Is this likely, given what you know about supply and demand for custodians' services?

(b) What would the union have to do to maintain the wage rate for custodians at $19 an hour?

(c) Why is it easier for a union of electricians than for a union of custodians to establish a wage of $19 an hour for members?

(d) Why are so few typists and clerical workers organized into unions?

(e) Why have skilled workers, who tend to receive higher wages anyway, generally been more successful in forming unions and raising their wages than unskilled workers?

33. Should high school history and English teachers be paid as much as science and math teachers?

(a) Suppose that a school district pays all high school teachers with the same years of experience the same salary, regardless of teaching field,

and that this produces a surplus of history and English teachers and a shortage of science and math teachers. Would this create a case for salary differentials?

(b) How could the problem of concurrent surplus and shortage be solved without paying science and math teachers more than history and English teachers?

(c) Why has the policy of identical wages in fact produced shortages of science and math teachers along with surpluses of history and English teachers in many school districts? What factors have contributed on the demand side? On the supply side?

34. According to the American Medical Association, physicians in family practice have experienced a decline in their average incomes in recent years while medical specialists' incomes were rising. Surgical specialists have been doing best of all, and their average incomes are now about twice what generalists earn.

(a) Much of this difference in income arises from long-established differences in the fees paid by insurers for various medical services. The American Society of Internal Medicine claims that insurers' fee schedules are unfair. How would you decide on the validity of such a claim? What is a fair way to determine the relative worth of a successful surgical procedure against that of an accurate diagnosis followed by an effective prescription?

(b) Surgeons justify their higher incomes by claiming that they spend four more years in school than do general practitioners. Do four additional years in school justify higher fees because it's costly to attend school, or because those extra years in school improve knowledge and skill levels?

35. A survey conducted during the 1980 recession revealed that 118,000 households were dissolved in one month.

(a) Why would a recession cause households to disappear? What happens to them?

(b) What happened to average family income as a result?

36. In each of the cases described below, an increase in the family's monetary income puts all members of the original family into families with lower incomes. Explain how this occurs. Does it imply that the individuals involved are worse off? What important questions does it raise about the interpretation of family-income data?

(a) An elderly couple living with their married son receive an increase in social-security benefits that permits the couple to obtain their own apartment.

(b) Two married people who fight constantly, and stay together only because they can't afford to maintain two homes, separate with great relief when both receive promotions and raises, each taking one of the children.

(c) The husband of an orthopedic surgeon quits his job to stay home, tend the house, and give the children better care when his wife's practice begins to earn a very large income.

37. How should in-kind transfers be treated in calculating the incomes of people on welfare?

(a) Does it make sense to count the monetary value of food stamps, rent subsidies, and free school lunches in the income of a family on welfare?

(b) How would this lead to an overstatement of their income? (Hint: Would you rather have a shopping cart full of items that someone else selected or the money equivalent of those items?)

(c) Medicare benefits are a major contribution to the well-being of many elderly Americans. If an elderly person receives a $5000 operation, should we calculate that person's income as $5000 higher?

38. We often encounter the phrase "the low-income elderly." How poor are elderly people in the United States?

(a) Why does the figure in Table 12C seriously understate the average relative income of people over 65?

(b) In 1982 only 8.5 percent of all elderly persons in families lived below the official poverty line, as compared with 27 percent in 1959. How do you suppose this change came about?

(c) How many benefits can you think of that accrue to people over 65 but don't affect their money incomes?

39. A substantial number of government programs are specifically intended to improve the relative position of lower-income groups. In addition, government economic policies in other areas are often formulated in ways designed to avoid harming lower-income groups. Such policies are usually defended on the grounds that they promote greater justice in the distribution of income.

(a) Can you defend the assertion that the distribution of income that emerges from the interactions of demand and supply is just? Can you defend the assertion that it is unjust?

(b) How would you define a just distribution (or an unjust distribution) of income?

(c) If the preceding question is too difficult, perhaps you can define a *more* just (or less unjust) distribution of income.

(d) Two common but very different ways to define justice are in terms of *rules* and in terms of *results*. We usually define a just (or fair) game of any sort in terms of rules: Were the rules clearly stated, known and accepted in advance, and impartially enforced? We do not use the game's final score as a test of its fairness. On the other hand, we are likely to assess the justice with which food, clothing, and other goods are distributed among children in a family in terms of results: Does each child receive an equal share except insofar as differences among the children clearly call for unequal shares? Few would want to define a just distribution of income among children in terms of impartial rules regarding competition for goods.

Which of these provides better criteria for assessing the justice or injustice of the income distribution in a society such as the United States?

40. Suppose you have an irrational prejudice against non-Polish pickle packers and refuse to purchase any pickles that haven't been packed by Polish people.

(a) How will this prejudice affect the price you must pay for pickles of a given quality?

(b) How does an employer pay for any decision to discriminate in hiring on the basis of criteria unrelated to job performance?

(c) Do employers in general benefit from employment discrimination directed against nonwhites and women? Who does benefit?

Pollution and Conflicting Rights

Many people have concluded in recent years that the growing problem of pollution demonstrates the inadequacy of a purely economic point of view. That position is vigorously rejected in this chapter. Ecology and economics are very closely related, as a matter of fact, and in more than the common Greek stem of the words. Ecology in the narrow sense is a branch of biology that deals with the interrelations between organisms and their environment. In the broader meaning of the word, it's a point of view, an informing conviction that everything ultimately depends on everything else. Actions prompt reactions, and the reactions set the stage for all future actions. That is also the point of view of economic theory. Economics and ecology are allies, not competitors or antagonists.

The economist maintains that, if pollution is a growing problem in our society, it's because we have allowed or even encouraged people to neglect certain important costs. The problem requires for its solution that we find ways to correct this neglect. If, like Stephen Leacock's Lord Ronald, we fling ourselves upon a horse and ride madly off in all directions, we're not likely to find acceptable solutions.

Our first task is to agree on exactly what we mean by pollution. Unfortunately, that's not quite as easy as it might seem.

A Definition of Pollution

It won't do at all to define pollution as damage to the environment. That's much too broad. Everything we do, including walking and breathing, damages some part of the environment. Nor can we salvage this definition by inserting the word *irreversible* before "damage to the environment." That dramatizes the problem but does nothing to clarify it.

Most of the damage we do to our environment in the ordinary course of living will in fact never be reversed; but very little damage is irreversible in the sense that it cannot be reversed no matter what people do.

We must begin by recognizing that pollution is a cost, a cost of engaging in valued, productive activities. It is a cost, however, with one distinctive feature: it is borne by people who have not agreed to do so. *Pollution*, in short, refers to *costs imposed on others without their consent.*

Disagreements and Property Rights

The core of the pollution problem is what the economist calls *externalities* or *spillovers*. These are consequences of action that the actors don't take into account and that therefore don't influence their decisions.

Individuals who behave according to the economic way of thinking engage in activities for the sake of the benefits they expect to receive, after taking into account the associated costs they expect to bear. Most of our costs in obtaining the goods we want are monetary payments to others to induce them to bear the costs of providing what we're after. The costs we bear in the pursuit of our goals turn out to be largely the prices we have to pay to obtain the cooperation of other people.

We all benefit, however, from a great deal of valuable cooperation for which we don't have to pay a cent. The reasons vary. Our collaborators may be generous people who are glad to be of assistance. They may not have noticed how much they're helping us and how large a sum we would be willing to pay if we had to. The cost they bear in cooperating may just be too small for them to bother about. Or they might know that they're providing valuable assistance at considerable cost to themselves but also that there is nothing they can really do about it. It is this last case that presents the problem of externalities, or pollution.

Pollution is not a fact of physical nature. It is rather a judgment put forward by particular people. It is a complaint: "You are obtaining your good by imposing this cost on me (or us), and you have no right to do that." Pollution therefore represents a disagreement about property rights. Pollution is eliminated *not* by eliminating environmental damage, which is an impossibility anyway, but by resolving disagreements over property rights.

Soot on the Windowsills

Does this make sense? Let's try it out. Why does almost everyone agree that the soot that falls on their windowsills

from a nearby factory's smokestacks is pollution? Because they all agree that the factory's managers *have no right* to impose the costs of waste disposal on neighboring home owners.

Why does almost everyone agree that the oil that washes up on an ocean beach is pollution? Because they all believe that whoever is responsible *had no right* to let an oil spill occur. Somebody chose a method of drilling for oil or flushing tanks or whatever that imposed a large part of the costs on users of the beach who had not agreed to bear it.

Does this seem clear? It shouldn't, because it really isn't.

Suppose the offending smokestack is a low one that drops all its soot within a 500-yard radius. Suppose further that all the land within reach of the smokestack's emissions belongs to the corporation that owns the factory, and that this corporation rents out the houses it built on its own land only after informing prospective tenants that they would have to live with soot on their windowsills. If the home seekers nonetheless decide to move in, the lower rent or other advantages that these houses offer must have been enough, in their eyes, to compensate them for the expected cost of living with the factory's soot. They have consented to the soot on their windowsills, and so it is *not* pollution. The soot is still as dark and dirty as it ever was; but it is no longer a cost imposed on others without their consent.

The tenants were paid to consent and they did so. Consequently, the soot that begrimes them is not pollution, any more than the dirt that gets on the hands of the employees who work inside the factory is pollution. Just as the employees are offered a wage to secure their agreement to bear certain costs, of which a dirty working environment may be one, so the tenants in the situation described were offered a lower rent (or some other advantage) to secure their agreement to bear part of the costs of the factory's system of waste disposal. If everyone agrees that all parties are acting within their rights, there can be no pollution.

Oil on the Beach

If you find this argument troubling, try to withhold your judgment long enough to see where it takes us. The important challenge at the moment is to understand exactly what the argument entails. Let's use the second case above—the oil-fouled beach—to draw out some more implications of this property-rights approach to the pollution issue.

Suppose that the beach in question is a public one near a major port, and that the oil on the beach is a long-term accumulation from the ordinary and legal operations of a multitude of ocean going ships. Of course, the whole operation *could* be cleaner. If someone were willing to

incur the cost, a port operation could be made as antiseptic as a surgical operation. But would the benefit be worth the cost?

To someone who loves the beach but doesn't give a fig for ocean commerce and doesn't care one whit for the advantages he and others derive from international trade, the benefit would be greater than the cost—because the cost *to this single-minded individual* would be nothing. The opportunities that would have to be forgone if the port were closed (and no one could afford to operate it with zero contamination of the beach) are opportunities that he does not value. He can logically continue, therefore, to call that oil on the beach *pollution.* In doing so he is asserting that the relevant property rights are wrongly assigned: that he ought to be protected in the enjoyment of an oil-free beach even though that would infringe on the property rights of all those who benefit from continued operation of the port.

It would be a mistake, though, for someone who approved the existing assignment of property rights to call that oil on the beach *pollution.* To do so would be to concede that our fanatical beach lover should have the right to stop the entire port operation by withholding his consent. But that is precisely the point at issue. The oil on the beach is pollution only for someone who claims that those who put it there had no right to do so.

An Analysis of Airport Noise

Let's try this argument out on noise pollution. Commercial jets make a lot of noise. Is the noise pollution? It isn't pollution to airport baggage handlers, because they consent to be subjected to the noise. Their consent is secured by the payment of a wage. Is the noise pollution to families who live near the airport? It is if they bought their house before the airport was contemplated. The noise of the jets deprives them of peace and quiet without their consent.

Now change the situation. Suppose the airport authorities buy all the adjacent land at prices that reflect the land's value before the planning of the airport. Then, after the airport is finished, the airport authorities resell the land for whatever price buyers consent to pay. Those who build or buy homes on this land will hear the noise of the jets, but the noise will not be pollution, because they have consented to bear it. They knew about the noise when they bought, but presumably decided that the lower price for the land was adequate compensation for the noise of the jets.

Let's introduce a further change in the situation. The people who bought their houses after the airport had been constructed, fully knowing about the noise, may now decide to lobby the city council for noise-abatement restrictions. If

they succeed and the airlines are required to eliminate all flights before 7 A.M. and after 10 P.M., the airlines then become, in an important sense, the victims of pollution. The new noise-abatement rules deprive the airlines of valuable opportunities. The restrictions may impose costs on the airlines without securing their consent. The homeowners are obtaining benefits for themselves and letting the costs be borne by others.

Conflicting Rights

But should those costs be called pollution? There is little point in arguing about what we're going to call something. It is important, however, that we see clearly what's happening, and that we not suppose we have solved a problem when we've only created a new one to take its place. The characteristic of jet noise that we must not overlook is its association with valuable opportunities. Jet noise isn't created around airports in order to bedevil the neighbors, but is a by-product in the production of the valuable service of rapid transportation. We could without doubt eliminate jet noise by eliminating jet airplanes. But would the gain in peace and quiet be enough to outweigh the loss to all those who want to travel quickly between distant points? That's the question.

We pointed out way back in Chapter 2 that the demand is never completely inelastic for *any* good, not even for the good of clean air. With clean air, as with peace and quiet, we must decide exactly how much we want—in view of the fact that more can be obtained only by giving up increasing amounts of other goods that we also want. The problem is compounded when, as in the present case, those who receive the benefits and those who pay the costs are different people. It would all be much simpler if we had to choose only between the wicked polluters and the virtuous citizens. This kind of choice is so easy and appealing, in fact, that we often succumb to the temptation of defining the problem in exclusively moral terms. *Industry* and *corporations* and *vested interests* want to foul our streams, darken our air, cut down our forests, strip-mine our land, and destroy our heritage for the sake of "their" profits. Who would hesitate a moment in deciding between the conflicting claims of greedy exploiters and "the American people"? But those who pose the issues in this way are either engaging in propaganda or deceiving themselves. Our actual choices are almost always choices between the legitimate expectations of some and the legitimate expectations of others.

Moreover, we have confused the issue for ourselves by identifying pollution with environmental damage. The flaw in this identification is that it fails to indicate when and why pollution is a problem. Everything, including the simple act of breathing, damages the environment, whereas many polluting

acts do not damage the biological environment in any accepted sense of that term. Actions that alter the environment don't become problems until they infringe on someone's rights. The infallible sign of pollution is the statement, "You have no right to do that, because it interferes with my right to do this." Pollution exists when people's expectations about what they can and may do come into conflict. Pollution is eliminated when disagreements about property rights are resolved—when those who formerly protested the actions of others consent to those actions.

An Impossible Goal

"That's absurd," says the voice from the rear which has been silent through several chapters. "People's expectations will always conflict to some extent. People in a large society like ours are bound to disagree about who has which rights. We can't expect everybody to consent to absolutely everything that other people want to do. With your definition of pollution, pollution would be impossible to get rid of."

Precisely. There may be no more important lesson for us to learn about pollution than that pollution so thoroughly permeates our society that we cannot realistically hope to eliminate it. Pollution exists when teenagers play their transistor radios and thereby infringe on the right of other bus passengers to enjoy peace and quiet; pollution still exists, though in a changed form, when the other bus passengers infringe on the teenagers' right to hear music by enforcing their own desire for peace and quiet. Pollution exists when a rose lover cultivates his bushes and thereby infringes on the right of rose-fever victims to breathe easily; the pollution does not disappear but only changes its form when the rose-fever sufferers infringe on the right of the rose lover by uprooting his rose bushes.

Traffic on a residential street imposes costs on the homeowners that they would like to eliminate. But sealing off one end of the street imposes costs on the drivers who are now compelled to take a less satisfactory route. A coal-burning utility pumping sulfur dioxide into the air is imposing costs on people in the vicinity of the plant. But if those people compel the utility to burn more expensive low-sulfur coal, they are imposing costs on consumers of the utility's electricity. Pollution means that rights are in conflict and poses the question: Whose rights ought to prevail?

Reducing Pollution: The First Steps

We want to turn our attention in the rest of this chapter to four procedures for reducing pollution or maintaining it within

acceptable bounds. The first is the cultivation of the civic virtues of empathy, courtesy, humility, and tolerance among the members of a society. Civilization will simply be impossible among a people who don't possess substantial amounts of these virtues. If people insist on obtaining absolutely everything to which they think they have a right, civilization will give way to warfare. But how to cultivate or renew these virtues where they have withered—that is a question far beyond the scope of this book. We would do well to remember, however, that the other procedures for controlling pollution that we're now going to examine—negotiation, adjudication, and legislation—presuppose these virtues to some extent, because they presuppose an established society, and they work more effectively the more widely these virtues are practiced.

Reducing Pollution by Negotiation

Our everyday garden-variety procedure for minimizing pollution is *negotiation*. We strike bargains with one another. People consent to bear the costs associated with the production of particular goods because other people who want those goods offer compensation that makes it worth their while. That's why baggage handlers don't complain about jet noise, why the grease on the clothes of an automobile mechanic is not pollution, and why the owner of a dog kennel will cheerfully let other people's dogs perform the same act that arouses an urban lawn fancier to fury.

"Work it out for yourselves" is sound advice. Because people differ so widely in their tastes, talents, and other circumstances, they will often be able to negotiate an exchange of costs that makes everyone involved better off than before. Moreover, the necessity of working it out for themselves encourages cooperation among those who are in the best position to know the possibilities. When people aren't required to negotiate, they often adopt positions that are costly to others. For example, they demand legislation that would prohibit smoking in restaurants, rather than ask for a table where no smoke will blow. And they point indignantly to minute traces of tobacco smoke in the air, while ignoring the dangerous emissions that they themselves put into the atmosphere by driving to the restaurant.

Negotiation produces mutual gains from exchange.

We would probably have a much greater respect for negotiation as a social procedure for reducing pollution if we learned to recognize the myriad ways in which we actually use it. People who hate the noise and dirt of the city move to outlying areas. People who detest the culture of suburbia live in small towns. People who despise the isolation of rural life choose to live in the city. The hard-of-hearing get residential real-estate bargains under airport approach lanes.

Surfboard riders seek out companions and thereby voluntarily segregate themselves from swimmers who hate to dodge surfboards. The afternoon naptaker pays $1.59 for a box of wax earstoppers and thereafter lives in peace with the neighboring teenager's mufflerless motorcycle. Not everyone is completely satisfied. But voluntary exchange does reduce the total of costs imposed on reluctant bystanders.

Negotiation cannot be effective, however, unless property rights are clearly defined. Voluntary exchange of any sort works well only when all involved parties agree on who owns what. In some cases, a clarification of property rights may be all that stands in the way of a mutually satisfactory agreement.

Suppose, for example, that Smith and Brown disagree by two feet on the location of the boundary line dividing their properties. It wouldn't matter much, since both want to plant flowers in the disputed strip, except for the fact that Smith wants to plant zinnias and Brown has his heart set on petunias. Until the question of who has a right to do what is settled, neither one will plant flowers, and both will be living with the inferior alternative of crabgrass.

If they then hire a surveyor who proves that Smith in fact owns the disputed strip, flowers can finally bloom. Nor will the flowers necessarily be zinnias! Once it's clearly established that Smith is the owner and hence has the right to decide what will grow in the boundary strip, Brown may be able to purchase that right. Brown's passion for petunias could be so powerful that he offers Smith $25 a year for the right to grow them between their lots. And if Smith prefers petunias *with $25* to zinnias without $25, the flowers that bloom will be petunias.

Reducing Pollution by Adjudication

In introducing the boundary surveyor, we introduced another important social procedure for reducing pollution: *adjudication,* by which we mean a process for deciding who actually has which rights. People will not be able to improve their positions through the exchange of rights if they aren't sure what rights anyone has to begin with. Clearly defined property rights are not a sufficient condition for successful negotiations, but they do seem to be a necessary condition.

Property rights that might once have been clearly and adequately defined can become vague and uncertain when surrounding circumstances change. The development of low-cost photocopying techniques, to take one example, created an enormous amount of uncertainty about what copyright holders could realistically expect to sell in view of the new capability that photocopy machines gave to every possessor of

Clearly established property rights provide the basis for negotiations.

a book. When evolving circumstances make previously compatible property rights incompatible, adjudication is one way of settling the conflict.

We are using the term *adjudication* to refer specifically to the kind of resolution that the surveyor provided: a resolution that *discovers* who has which rights. The surveyor answered the question of ownership by investigating, not by choosing. If Smith and Brown had agreed to flip a coin, they would have relied on a procedure that does not discover but rather *creates* property rights. The distinction between the discovery and the creation of property rights is an important one, because *discovery or adjudication aims at maintaining the continuity of expectations.* At the end of Chapter 12 we emphasized the importance of stable expectations in securing effective cooperation among the members of a society. When expectations change radically, supply and demand decisions also change radically. That, in turn, alters in unpredicted ways the relative costs and benefits of all kinds of actions and so induces additional changes in supply and demand. In short, if no one knows what to expect, no one knows what to do or what others will do. The result is chaos. Stable expectations are another of those realities whose importance we haven't learned to recognize, because we don't notice how society is working when it's working well.

Adjudication clarifies property rights.

The Case of the Complaining Homeowner

We can use the airport once more to bring out the importance of adjudication, or the discovery rather than creation of rights, in resolving disputes over property rights. Polly Sigh, who owns a house ten miles from a major airport but directly under the principal approach route, may decide one morning—when her sleep has been interrupted by commercial jets—that she deserves compensation. The airport or the airlines ought to pay her something, she decides, for depriving her of the opportunity to use her bedroom as a place of rest and renewal. She is the victim of pollution, of costs imposed on her without her consent. So she files suit demanding compensation.

Ought she to get it? Is she *likely* to get it? Assume that Polly bought the house before the airport was even thought about, so that no one can say she knew the situation when she bought and has already received her compensation in the form of a lower purchase price. She is consequently, by our definition, the victim of pollution. The noise pollution to which she is subject could be eliminated if she were paid the amount by which the airport reduces the market price of her house. But *should* she be compensated?

The trouble is that there are thousands of homeowners

with equally valid claims. If one receives compensation, all ought to receive compensation. But if all receive compensation, a heavy cost will be imposed on the airport and the airlines, who will pass that cost along to airline passengers in the form of higher ticket prices.

At first glance that might seem fair enough. The higher prices will compel airline passengers to pay the costs of the noise that is created as a by-product of their travel. But now a new problem forces itself upon our attention. Externalities run throughout society. Shall we correct for them *all*? Shall homeowners receive compensation for the automobile traffic that goes past, the dandelions that their neighbors let go to seed, the passing gifts of dog-walkers and their pets, the noise of the neighborhood children, the sound of power mowers, the spreading chestnut tree next door that blocks their view, or the loss of the shade if their neighbor cuts down the spreading chestnut tree because it blocks *his* view? When we are through with homeowners, we would have to start ordering the compensation of pedestrians, many of whom suffer from the same sorts of uncompensated costs that afflict homeowners. Perhaps we could, in the final stages of our effort to make the world perfect, impose fines on especially dull people in order to compensate those whom they bore.

We just can't do that. There are too many spillovers; the appropriate compensations would be too difficult to determine. Even the direction in which compensation ought to be paid will often be unclear. Wouldn't it be just as much in order, for example, to levy fines on inattentive people to compensate the bores whose sensitivities they offend? Who says bores are worse than boors?

The Importance of Precedents

We are ready for the question: *Should* Polly Sigh, the homeowner ten miles from the airport, be compensated by airline passengers for the inconvenience she suffers as a result of the flights from which they benefit? Our answer: It would be extraordinarily difficult and probably impossible to do so in a way that was both practical and fair.

We originally asked *two* questions, however. The second question asked whether homeowners in such circumstances were *likely* to receive compensation. The answer to this question is almost certainly *no*. The courts would attempt to decide the issue by *discovering* what rights the contending parties have, and homeowners would end up with very little to show on their behalf. The ruling consideration would almost surely be this: that homeowners and those in the business of providing airline transportation have proceeded for a long time

on the expectation that no such compensation must be paid. *These expectations indicate the respective property rights of home-owners and airlines.*

We could even prove that homeowners ten miles from the airport don't have a legal right to be compensated for the noise, simply by showing that the market price of homes under the approach route would jump sharply if the court decision held in favor of the homeowner. This would be an *unexpected event* that would create profits for homeowners and losses for holders of airline stock. The appearance of these unexpected changes in values would be conclusive evidence that the affected parties did not believe such compensation was owed, and that the court decision had consequently *created* property rights that had not existed previously.

Where do the rights of a homeowner end?

There's a qualification to this conclusion that further establishes the point we're making. If a judge held for the homeowner in such a case, the price of affected houses might rise very little, because prospective home buyers would probably be advised that the judge had erred and was likely to be reversed on appeal. The concept of error is instructive. There can be no error when the decision *creates* the rights. Error is possible only when the decision seeks to *discover* what the rights are that actually prevail and therefore ought to govern the outcome of the case.

Adjudication, or the attempt to resolve conflicting claims by seeking to discover existing rights, always tries to avoid unexpected decisions or outcomes. It tries to settle disagreements over property rights by supporting and reinforcing *the expectations that are most widely and confidently held.* Adjudication is thus an effort to maintain the continuity of expectations in the presence of changing circumstances. And stable expectations, we remind you once more, are the foundation of effective cooperation in any large, complex society.

The Problem of Radical Change

Adjudication is an evolutionary approach to the problem of pollution. But sometimes changes don't occur at an evolutionary pace. When we're overtaken by events so novel that established principles and practices furnish little guidance in dealing with them, adjudication cannot work very well. Technological innovations often force rapid changes upon us in a wide variety of situations. Snowmobiles, pesticides, radar-assisted whaling ships, antibiotics, and nuclear reactors are just a few of the many examples that could be cited from recent years. When technological innovation radically expands our capacity to inflict costs upon others without obtaining

their consent, new rules may be required to maintain the level of pollution within tolerable limits.

The demand for new definitions of property rights has also been created by rising incomes. Not too many years ago Americans seemed to have had a working consensus that the social advantages from allowing the atmosphere to be used as an industrial dump were greater than the disadvantages. Our laws and customs decreed that the atmosphere belonged to everyone and therefore to no one, so that factory owners were free to use it as a receptacle for industrial wastes. People could move away from factories, or purchase residential space near the factories at a low price if they preferred that saving to the delights of clean air. Meanwhile factories held their costs down by discharging wastes into the atmosphere, and this meant a greater availability of the goods that factories produced. But the situation has changed. The goods that factories produce are now available in much larger quantities, and many people have begun to place a lower relative valuation on them. When we begin to place a higher relative value on blue skies and clean air, we start to think of them as our *right*. We start to claim a property right in these environmental goods and demand that others stop putting them to uses that are incompatible with our ability to enjoy them. That requires new rules, not just an application of the old rules to new situations.

Reducing Pollution by Legislation

We call the creation of new rules *legislation*. The line between adjudication and legislation is not as clear in practice as all this pretends. But the distinction is important in principle, because legislation creates changes in prevailing property rights, and changing the rules of the game always raises the question of fairness and often compels major adjustments in behavior. The challenge for a society that wants to reduce pollution is to legislate in ways that avoid gross injustices and that minimize the cost of achieving the objectives. We shall focus on the second of those criteria, not because it's more important, but because economic theory has more to say about minimizing costs than about maximizing justice.

Physical Restrictions on Polluters

The legislation of uniform physical restrictions is a popular approach to the problem of pollution. "Command and control" it's called. After some date, no one is allowed to discharge more than so many particles of this or that into the air or the water system. This approach will usually fail to minimize

the cost per unit of pollution reduction. It ignores the variety of ways in which a given objective can usually be achieved, and therefore offers few incentives to people to search for and implement the least costly alternative. We're going to use a very simplified example to illustrate some principles of pollution control that deserve to be better understood and more widely appreciated.

Suppose that everything that fouls the air over the city of Springfield comes from three sources: automobiles, utilities, and factories. The following table shows the quantities of polluting material put into the air of Springfield monthly by each source. It also shows the cost to each polluter of eliminating the objectionable emissions. (You will notice that the analysis treats each of the three sources as a *single decision-making unit*, to keep the analysis simple enough to be useful.)

	Units of Obnoxious Material Emitted Monthly	Cost of Eliminating Emissions, per Unit
Automobiles	20,000	$ 5
Utilities	30,000	10
Factories	40,000	20

Now let's suppose that the Environmental Protection Agency (EPA) decides to improve the air quality over Springfield by securing a reduction of monthly emissions from the present total of 90,000 to a tolerable total of 60,000. (We'll pass by the question for now of how the EPA decides that 60,000 is the tolerable level.) There are many ways to reach that objective. The EPA could set 20,000 as the maximum allowable emissions from each source, or require each source to reduce its emissions by 10,000, or order a one-third reduction in emissions by each source. Let's compare the costs of each approach.

Setting a 20,000 unit ceiling on each source would achieve the goal at a total cost of $500,000. Utilities would pay $10 for each of the 10,000 units by which they reduce their emissions, factories would pay $20 for each of the 20,000 units by which they reduce their emissions, and automobiles would escape all costs, because they're already at the target level.

Requiring each source to reduce emissions by 10,000 units would achieve the goal at a total cost of $350,000. Automobiles would pay $50,000, utilities $100,000, and factories $200,000. This is clearly a less costly way to reach the goal.

Ordering a one-third reduction by all sources would result in total costs of $400,000: $33,333 to the automobiles, $100,000 to the utilities, and $266,667 to the factories. From the

Cost of uniform ceiling:
To utilities: 10,000 x $10 = $100,000
To factories: 20,000 x $20 = $400,000
    $500,000

Cost of uniform quantity reduction:
To automobiles: 10,000 x $5 = $50,000
To utilities: 10,000 x $10 = $100,000
To factories: 10,000 x $20 = $200,000
    $350,000

Cost of uniform percentage reduction:
To automobiles: 1/3 (20,000) x $5 = $33,333
To utilities: 1/3 (30,000) x $10 = $100,000
To factories: 1/3 (40,000) x $20 = $266,667
    $400,000

Least-cost solution:

To automobiles: 20,000 x $5 = $100,000
To utilities: 10,000 x $10 = $100,000
                              ───────────
                               $200,000

standpoint of cost minimization, that's better than the first solution but not as good as the second.

There's an even less costly way to go, however. The EPA would minimize the cost of achieving its objective if it ordered a 20,000-unit reduction by automobiles and a 10,000-unit reduction by utilities and left the factories alone. The total cost of getting pollution down from 90,000 to 60,000 units by this method would be $200,000: $100,000 paid by the automobiles and $100,000 paid by the utilities. Would the EPA be likely to choose this approach?

Another Approach: Taxing Emissions

Let's defer that question and examine the problem further. Suppose that the EPA doesn't actually know how much it will cost per unit to reduce pollution from each source. That's much more plausible than our original assumption, for several reasons. The polluters themselves will be in the best position to know the actual costs, but they will also have an incentive to exaggerate their costs in pleadings before the EPA or the public. Moreover, exaggeration will not be wholly dishonest, because one never knows for certain the costs of something that hasn't yet been tried, and it's just ordinary prudence to estimate them high, especially if higher estimates mean the costs are less likely to be imposed. Finally, though costs can usually be reduced through research and experiment, no one can predict the results that research and experiment will produce. What is the least costly solution when the EPA is faced with this kind of information scarcity?

The EPA would gain the applause of many economists if it responded to this situation by imposing a tax per unit of pollution and then allowing each polluter to respond as it thought best. If you're willing to grant that pollution is a spillover cost, a cost not borne by its producer, placing a tax on polluting activities makes good sense. If the tax per unit of pollutant can somehow be set equal to the spillover cost per unit, the creator and presumed beneficiary of the costs is made to bear them.

If that makes the polluting activity too costly to continue, it will cease, as it should if its costs are greater than its benefits. If the benefits still outweigh the costs when the tax is being paid, then the polluting activity will continue, though at a lesser rate because it's now more costly. But in that case the tax revenue will be available to compensate—to buy the consent of—those upon whom the spillover costs are falling.

In the Springfield case, any tax rate between $5 and $10 will reduce pollution by 20,000 units per month. It will induce

the automobiles to avoid the tax by choosing the lesser-cost-alternative of eliminating their obnoxious emissions. Utilities will choose to avoid the tax when it rises above $10 per unit of pollution, so that a tax rate of $11 would reduce pollution by 50,000 units per month, while simultaneously garnering $440,000 in revenue with which to compensate the suffering citizens of Springfield for the continuing pollution from the factories.

As we have set up the problem, there is no tax rate that achieves a reduction to exactly 60,000 units: $9.99 would lower pollution to only 70,000 units, and $10.01 would lower it all the way to 40,000 units. In the real world, costs would not be the same for all levels of pollution reduction, but would be relatively low for small percentage reductions from each source and extremely high as we approached 100 percent. The pursuit of perfection is almost always prohibitively expensive.

But the inability of *any* tax rate to achieve some particular physical target is not so much a criticism of the tax approach to pollution control as a criticism of physical targets. Why aim at 60,000 units? *Every* unit is a bad, so why not eliminate them all? The answer, as you know by this time, is that there are costs of eliminating those costs that we call pollution. The task for the EPA is to compare the marginal costs of reducing pollution with the marginal costs that are avoided by reducing pollution, or the marginal benefits. The use of taxes enables the EPA to acquire information about these costs and benefits by observing what happens when variously estimated pollution costs are assessed against the polluters. It's an approach that lends itself to learning by experimentation. And obtaining reliable information about costs and benefits is essential to any program of environmental protection that is concerned with human well-being.

The Issue of Fairness

Let's go back now to a question that we asked but deferred answering. After comparing the costs of four different ways of reducing Springfield air pollution to 60,000 units per month, we asked whether the EPA was likely in such a situation to choose the least costly approach. We put off answering in order to argue that physical directives of any sort—the command-and-control method—were generally inferior to taxes as a way of controlling pollution. By taxing emissions, we enlist the aid of the price system in solving our problem. But the tax approach isn't popular with the public for a reason that would also make it difficult for the EPA to issue the least costly set of physical directives. *It doesn't seem fair.* Taxes on pollution have acquired the derogatory label of "licenses

to pollute," and they're widely rejected because they supposedly place the whole burden of reducing pollution on the poor while allowing the rich to go right on fouling the environment. Choosing the people who must reduce their pollution on the basis of the cost to them of doing so, which is required by the least-cost solution, also seems arbitrary and unjust to many people.

The "license to pollute" argument, however, is confused from the outset. If pollution is a cost inflicted on others without their consent, people who secure consent by paying the cost are no longer polluting. It's true enough that they will still be imposing costs on others. But there's nothing at all wrong with that as long as they compensate them adequately. If people object that the tax they pay isn't enough to make up for the costs they create, they are really saying that the tax rate should be increased, not that such taxes are a "license to pollute."

Exchange and Efficiency in Pollution Control

An important part of any reply to those who raise the fairness issue, however, is to show that the *efficient* solution can be achieved while settling the *fairness* issue in different ways. In other words, we don't necessarily commit ourselves to place the costs on any particular parties when we select the most efficient solution. The Springfield case can again provide our illustration.

Suppose that the EPA wants to impose the entire cost of pollution reduction on the factories, whether because the factories can best afford it, or because they have long been the heaviest polluters, or because everyone in Springfield dislikes them, or for some reason more closely related to fairness. Whatever the reason, all the EPA need do is tell the factories that they will have to pay a tax of $10.05 for each unit of pollution emitted monthly in excess of 60,000, regardless of the pollution's source. The factories will then look for the least costly way to deal with this situation. If they have all the information that we have, they will offer the automobiles $100,000 to eliminate all their pollution and offer the utilities $100,000 to reduce their pollution by 10,000 units.

The factories will thus reduce the level of pollution in Springfield to 60,000 units. They'll do so to avoid a tax of $303,000. But rather than reduce their own emissions by 30,000 units, which would cost the factories $600,000 they'll pay the most efficient pollution reducers in the city $200,000 to do the job for them.

Pollution reduction is a lot like any other useful activity in that some are more efficient at it than others. Just as we gain

from having our food, toys, and cosmetics produced by those with a comparative advantage in their production, so we gain by having additional clean air produced by those with the greatest comparative advantage at the job. But comparative advantages are exploited through exchange. That's why the tax approach to pollution reduction is in general superior to an approach that assigns physical restrictions to particular firms. The tax approach tries to alter relative money costs to reflect new decisions about who has which rights. But it then leaves all parties free to trade on the basis of their own comparative advantages and to secure the new social goals in the most efficient manner.

Progress and Regress at the EPA

In December 1978 the Environmental Protection Agency took a step in the direction suggested by this analysis when it proposed new regulations that would permit more trade-offs among pollution sources. Rather than set rigid limits on allowable emissions from particular production processes, enforcement agencies would permit firms to exceed the limits in one process if they could compensate by reducing emissions from another process. Under this policy, firms could lower the cost of achieving a target level of environmental quality by allowing emissions to rise where their control is most costly and reducing them where reductions are possible at the least cost. Some EPA officials have also suggested that firms be allowed to buy and sell rights to pollute the air, a proposal that neatly incorporates the principles outlined in this chapter. This has already been done, in effect, where companies desiring to build plants in an area have satisfied air-quality standards by paying other companies to reduce their emissions. It makes good sense. Why should an oil company pay $150 million for pollution-control equipment in a refinery it wants to build if it can obtain the same results in air quality by building the refinery without the pollution-control equipment and purchasing $75 million of pollution-control equipment for a neighboring power plant?

EPA reports unfortunately don't always show the firm grasp of economic principles demonstrated by the above proposals to encourage trade-offs and exchange in pollution-control programs. In March 1979 the EPA released a report that claimed to show that the total economic benefits of cleaning up air pollution from factory smokestacks outweigh the total costs. The report was a response to complaints, coming from other government officials and agencies, that the EPA often issued regulations without paying sufficient attention to their cost.

Costs and Benefits

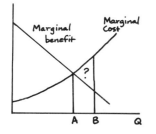

Total benefits are greater than total costs at B, but benefits would exceed costs by even more at A.

But the nature of the EPA's response showed that the point had been missed. We learn nothing of significance if we discover that the cost of controlling air pollution from plants in 1977 was $6.7 billion, and that the subsequent benefits in higher productivity and lower medical bills were worth $10 billion. It is *marginal* costs and *marginal* benefits that matter, the additional costs and additional benefits *expected to be associated with a specific regulatory decision.* A new EPA decision that added $3 billion to costs and $1 billion to benefits would be a wrong decision, even though it left total benefits higher than total costs. Totals and averages are simply irrelevant to economic decisions. A person with sunburn should get out of the sun, even if benefit-cost studies show that the benefits of sunshine to human beings far exceed its costs.

Rights and Efficiency

We don't want to conclude this chapter with an endorsement of efficiency, because inefficiency is not the fundamental problem. Pollution is a problem because people disagree about rights. When people agree on who owns what rights, they begin exchanging rights in ways that expand mutual benefits and reduce mutual costs. If property rights can be clearly established, efficiency will take care of itself.

Once Over Lightly

Pollution is a spillover cost created in the process of producing goods but paid by people who have not consented to do so.

The first condition for the reduction of pollution is that people understand clearly who has which rights. The existence of pollution entails disagreements over property rights, and disagreements must be clarified before they can be resolved.

Pollution can be entirely eliminated only if everyone consents freely to everything that others want to do. Perfection is consequently impossible. But the degree to which it can be approached in any society will depend crucially on the extent to which very traditional civic virtues are honored and practiced.

Negotiation is the standard procedure used by members of a society, to secure the cooperation and consent of others and thereby achieve their purposes while holding down the level of pollution. Negotiation is easier and more effective when property rights are more clearly specified.

Conflicting claims of right can often be resolved by examining established principles and practices. Adjudication in this manner preserves the continuity of people's expectations. Unexpected changes in effective property rights are

in general not desirable, because they arbitrarily transfer wealth from one party to another and also make social coordination more difficult by making it harder for anyone to plan with confidence.

Rapid or radical social change may make it so difficult to resolve conflicting claims through adjudication that legislation is called for. Legislation means the creation of new rules to establish and define what people may do with the resources at their command.

New rules are more likely to produce efficient solutions to pollution problems if they make it easier rather than more difficult for parties to employ their comparative advantages by exchanging rights and obligations.

Rules that place taxes on undesired emissions are usually more effective than detailed physical regulations in reducing pollution, because they make greater use of people's detailed knowledge of relevant differences.

Fairness and efficiency can often be partially reconciled in the creation of new rules by allowing those to whom the costs of change are assigned to negotiate an exchange with others who can realize the same objectives at a lower cost.

QUESTIONS FOR DISCUSSION

1. Does it make sense to define pollution as "damage to the environment"?
   (a) Sunshine changes the environment, and the changes are sometimes damaging or even fatal to various living organisms, including human beings. Is sunshine therefore pollution?
   (b) If you are unwilling to think of sunshine as pollution, *why* do you reject the designation? Is it because sunshine cannot be controlled by humans? (It can.) Is it because sunshine occurs naturally? (Do you, I, or the manufacturers of aerosol sprays occur *un*naturally?)
   (c) Why do some people try to acquire dark suntans every summer, despite evidence that extensive exposure to sunshine often causes sunburn, sunstroke, and skin cancer?
   (d) If you love sunshine, are the clouds that cover the sun pollution? Is a new high-rise building pollution if it casts a shadow on your home and yard?
2. No one who genuinely cares about the environment would be a litterer. Which of these would you want to call *littering?*
   (a) Dumping trash in a farmer's field rather than hauling it to the county dump.
   (b) Paying one dollar and then dumping trash in the field of a farmer who has erected a sign: "Dump Site Open to the Public—$1 Per Vehicle." What is the difference?
   (c) Tossing a candy wrapper on the sidewalk.

    (d) Tossing a candy wrapper under your seat at a major league baseball game. (Why do people who would never toss peanut shells on the sidewalk often toss them on the floor when attending sports events?)

    (e) Throwing confetti from an office building during a downtown parade.

3. A Connecticut state legislator proposed a bill in 1985 that would ban the throwing of rice at weddings on the grounds that uncooked rice is unhealthful for birds. Is this an antilittering ordinance?

4. Does the practice of clearcutting forests damage the environment? Why do you suppose timber companies engage in clearcutting on lands they own if it damages the environment? If the practice of clearcutting results in lower prices for construction lumber, whose environment is improved by clearcutting?

5. Are Western ranchers damaging the environment when they kill coyotes? The environment for whom? Whose environment is improved when the coyote population is reduced? Do mousetraps damage the environment?

6. Officials in the suburb of River Edge, New Jersey, passed an ordinance in November 1982 making it illegal for residents to park vehicles with commercial license plates or with signs on the doors in their driveways overnight.

    (a) Does this ordinance reduce "visual pollution"?

    (b) Does it "protect property values"? Which property values?

7. Do cigarette smokers pollute the environment? Do they pollute the environment if they only smoke in their own homes?

8. Why do people disturb others by talking during movies? Do the talkers and those whom they're disturbing agree about the rights one acquires by purchasing a movie ticket?

9. What are the property rights claims that are in conflict in each of the cases below? What is the resolution that would best "protect the environment"?

    (a) Owners of motorcycles want to remove their mufflers to obtain more efficient engine performance, but the law limits the noise that any motorcycle may emit.

    (b) A group wants to prohibit billboards along rural highways, but farmers claim they have a right to erect any kind of sign they want on their own property.

    (c) A Missouri state legislator introduced a bill in 1984 making it a crime to blow your nose in a loud or offensive manner in a restaurant.

    (d) Restaurant owners want to exclude people whose dress doesn't satisfy certain standards. (Should this be legal?)

    (e) People who never bathe want to use city buses. People who never brush or comb their hair want to sit and stroll in public parks. (Should the unwashed be barred from the buses? The unkempt, from the parks?)

10. Do we need laws to prevent cropland erosion?

    (a) How will farming practices that cause soil erosion affect the present value of farmland?

    (b) How will an owner of farmland who wants to maximize the present value of the land decide whether or not to adopt particular soil conservation measures?

    (c) Why will a tenant farmer ordinarily adopt fewer and less-effective soil conservation techniques?

    (d) Why would land owners ever permit farm tenants to reduce the present

value of the land through practices that raise current yields but increase the vulnerability of the land to erosion?

(e) What are some of the consequences of soil erosion that impose costs on people other than landowners? Will even an owner-operator take these costs fully into account in making decisions about whether and how to plow and plant land that is particularly subject to wind or water erosion?

(f) Suppose that people who are farming their own land have trouble earning enough income to pay their mortgages and begin to fear that they will lose ownership of the land to lending institutions. How will this fear affect their decisions about the trade-off between increased yields and reduced soil erosion?

(g) A Montana farmer buys hundreds of thousands of acres of grazing land from longtime ranch operators, then plows up the land and plants wheat. Why did the ranchers sell? Why did the purchasing farmer convert the land from livestock to wheat production? If the farmer knew he would be required to compensate residents of the county for the dust storms that will result when the land is shifted from livestock to wheat, might he find raising livestock more profitable than growing wheat?

(h) Should farmers whose practices aggravate the problem of dust storms be required to compensate others for the additional dust they put into the air? How could such a compensation system be administered?

11. When you bought your house, only 5 commercial planes passed over it daily, on the average. That number has grown slowly and almost imperceptibly over the intervening years and now numbers 150. Is the change from 5 to 150 a drastic or radical change? Is your situation with 150 planes flying over your house each day more tolerable because the number increased slowly and imperceptibly? Would you be more likely to receive compensation of some sort if the changes had occurred over a very short period of time? Does the fact that we can't tell which straw broke the camel's back mean that the addition of more straw to the camel's burden was not the cause of its broken back?

12. Many large urban airports have established programs for buying out those homeowners most seriously affected by airport noise.

(a) Do people who own houses directly under an approach route and within 3000 feet of the runway deserve compensation for the noise made by planes landing or taking off? If you think they do, ask yourself where you will draw the line. What about people whose homes are 5000 feet from the beginning of the runway or who live very close to but not quite under the approach route?

(b) If the owner is renting the house out, should it be the owner or the tenants who receive compensation? Why?

(c) Are current owners the appropriate people to compensate? Wasn't a current owner compensated in the purchase price if the house was bought within the past 10 years?

(d) What difference does it make in your answer to the previous question whether it was generally believed when the house changed hands that the airport would buy out those homeowners most severely affected by the noise?

13. If airlines are required to pay landing fees that are adjusted to take account

of the level of particular aircraft's noise emissions, the time of day or night when they land, and the density of the residential population in the vicinity of the airport, how will airlines take steps to reduce the impact of their operations on homeowners who live near airports?

(a) A government agency in 1977 calculated for each of 23 airports the decline in the annual rental value of surrounding property due to noise and divided this total by the number of takeoffs and landings during the year. The highest average was $196.67 for New York's La Guardia; the lowest was the Portland, Oregon airport with a cost of $.82 per takeoff or landing. This means that each takeoff or landing imposed a combined cost of almost $200 on La Guardia's neighbors, but less then a $1 cost on all those living around the Portland airport. Will airlines find it in their interest to use some airports more than they now do and others less if their landing and takeoff fees are increased by these amounts?

(b) Will airlines be more likely to install retrofitted noise-control gear or buy new and quieter planes if they must pay higher fees for noisier aircraft? Respond to the argument that "no airline is going to scrap an expensive 707 just to save a few $400 airport surcharges." Is this critic of surcharges thinking marginally?

(c) How would such a system of surcharges induce airlines to fly their noisier planes to Portland and their quieter ones to New York City, or to use Dulles Airport rather than National when flying into Washington, D.C.? (Dulles, which is far out in the Virginia countryside, showed a cost of $5.64 per operation in the 1977 study.)

14. The beautiful beach in Seaside City is municipally owned and no fee is charged for its use.

(a) There are nonetheless costs of using the beach that beach users incur. What are some of these costs that potential beach users would consider when they're deciding whether or not to go to the "free" beach?

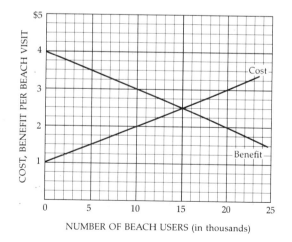

Figure 13A Costs and benefits of using Seaside City Beach

(b) One important cost is the cost of getting to the beach. This cost rises on a hot summer day as more people head for the beach, creating traffic congestion enroute and in the beach area. The beach is also a less pleasant place to be as it becomes more crowded. The graph on the opposite page shows, in dollar equivalents, the value of a trip to the beach and the cost of getting there on an average summer day for an average citizen of Seaside City. Both the value and the cost are functions of the total number of people visiting the beach on that day. Why should you expect to find 15,000 people using the beach on a "typical" day? (The question assumes Seaside is a large city.)

(c) How much satisfaction will these 15,000 derive from their visit to the beach if each one is exactly "average"? Remember that each one pays the marginal cost of getting there and each one receives the benefit that accrues when there are 14,999 others at the beach.

(d) What will happen if some Seaside City people eventually conclude that "it's not worth it" and stop considering a trip to the beach on pleasant summer days?

(e) What would happen to the number of people visiting the beach if Seaside City charged each of them a fee of $1.50 per visit?

(f) How much satisfaction will the beach users now obtain?

(g) Does a fee for use of the beach always make beach users worse off? What does the introduction of a fee for using the beach accomplish?

15. Each additional vehicle that enters the freeway during the morning rush hour slows all the other automobiles using the freeway. What are the costs considered by each motorist as he or she decides whether or not to use the freeway? What are the costs created for others by this decision? Why is it true—not a joke—that "cars multiply to congest the expressways constructed to eliminate congestion."

16. What would be the consequences of making the freeway into a tollway? Why might you, as a regular user of the expressway, prefer a toll during the rush hour to not paying any toll? When is it better for a limited-access highway to be a freeway, and when is it better for it to be a tollway?

17. If a tax on downtown parking is used to subsidize and improve the city's bus system, are drivers being taxed to provide benefits that accrue only to nondrivers? If you commuted to work each day in your own car because you had to use the car in your work, why might you want to vote in favor of an increased tax on downtown parking to finance subsidies for bus commuters?

18. History books often lament the destruction of the great herds of bison that roamed the western prairies prior to the arrival of white men.

(a) Why were so many white men willing to shoot these animals and leave their meat and hide to rot? Wasn't this highly wasteful? Why did so many people apparently place such a high value on a moment of sport as to kill these animals for no other reason than the excitement of it?

(b) Who bore the costs when a hunter shot a bison or "buffalo" from the window of a passing train?

(c) Was the near extinction of the buffalo an irreversible act? Or could we bring those huge herds of buffalo back within a few years if the proper incentives existed?

(d) What is the animal that has replaced the buffalo on the western prairies? Why do the numerous vast herds of cattle that cover the country not suffer the fate of the buffalo? What do you think would happen to the relative size of cattle and buffalo herds if Americans lost their taste for beef and acquired an intense love of buffalo meat?

19. What difference does ownership make?

(a) What response would you predict from the Sierra Club if an oil company requested a permit to extract natural gas from a wilderness area owned by the federal government?

(b) What difference do you think it would make to the Sierra Club's decision if the oil company was willing to pay an enormous royalty to the federal government because there was a great deal of natural gas available in that wilderness area?

(c) What difference do you think it would make if the oil company promised to extract the natural gas in ways that had a very small impact on the environment?

(d) What difference do you think it would make if the wilderness area, instead of belonging to the federal government, was the property of the Sierra Club?

(e) Why do you suppose the Audubon Society allows three oil companies to extract natural gas from its 26,800-acre Rainey Wildlife Sanctuary in Louisiana?

(f) The oil companies in the Rainey Sanctuary pay almost a million dollars per year in royalties to the Audubon Society. Do you think this arrangement promotes the purposes of the Audubon Society? Do you think it promotes the well-being of natural-gas consumers? (The instructive story of the Rainey Sanctuary was told by economists John Baden and Richard Stroup in the July 1981 issue of *Reason* magazine.)

(g) Is it rational for the Audubon Society to allow extraction of natural gas from its own land while opposing it elsewhere?

20. Major construction projects often cannot be undertaken today until an environmental impact statement (EIS) has been filed. Groups that oppose a project can delay its approval by showing that the EIS is incomplete. Is it possible to produce a *complete* description of the impact that any construction project will have on its environment? What effects should the drafters of an EIS be allowed to omit? What effects will opponents of a project agree are irrelevant to the EIS?

21. Four major American cement companies filed environmental lawsuits in 1980 to block the construction of a terminal to receive foreign cement in the small port of Redwood City, California. They claimed that the unloading of cement would put dust into the air that would endanger pelicans, fish, and marine ecosystems. Cement companies also used environmental laws in an effort to block the construction of cement terminals at three other California ports between 1978 and 1983, according to a *Wall Street Journal* article of December 28, 1984. Why do you suppose these companies were willing to spend money

in defense of brown pelicans? How can we determine whether someone claiming to defend the environment is sincere? How can we prevent persons from using environmental legislation to advance their own, much narrower interests?

22. Should the socioeconomic effects of a construction project be included in the environmental impact statement written by its promoters? If the effect of a project will be to raise property values in the neighborhood, is this a positive environmental impact? For whom would it be a negative impact on the environment? What methods or criteria should be used to decide whether to authorize a project that improves the environment for some people and worsens it for others?

23. Many towns have begun passing laws that set a limit on the amount of new housing that can be constructed each year. They defend these laws as attempts to protect the environment. What are the effects of such laws? Do they really protect the environment? Do you think they have an effect on the average income of the new people who move to the towns?

24. Should states pass "solar access" laws to prevent people from putting structures on their property that would block solar devices on other buildings? Would this protect property rights or deprive people of property rights? Why are rights to solar access generally poorly defined and uncertain at the present time? How does this uncertainty inhibit the development of solar energy devices?

25. A large mulberry tree in your neighbor's yard provides you with welcome shade but gives her only a lot of inedible and messy mulberries. She wants to cut the tree down.
    (a) Does she have the legal right to do so?
    (b) You say to her: "I know you hate those messy mulberries, but not nearly as much as I would hate losing the shade." Can you prove your statement? If you can't prove that you value continued shade more than she values a clean yard, can you induce *her* to place a higher value on *her* benefits from leaving the tree than on *her* benefits from cutting it down? (Hint: How do you induce the sewer cleaner to decide he would rather clear your sewer line on a Sunday afternoon than watch his favorite football team?)
    (c) An alternative route for you is to challenge her legal right to cut down the tree. You might try to have the tree declared a historic landmark, or go to court to demand that she file an environmental impact statement before being allowed to remove the tree. What is the danger to you in this tactic? (Hint: If you think you may be prevented in the future from exercising a right you now possess, will you wait to see what becomes of your right or will you exercise it while you still clearly have it?)

26. Two children are quarreling about who gets to choose the program that will be watched on the family's single television set. This is a case of conflicting property rights.
    (a) Should the parents tell them to work it out for themselves? Under what circumstances is this likely to produce a satisfactory resolution of the conflict?

(b) How do poorly defined property rights make it more difficult in such a case to achieve a satisfactory resolution through negotiation?

(c) Show how the parents might contribute to a resolution of the conflict first by offering adjudication, then by providing legislation.

27. "I'd pay almost anything if I could get all my classes scheduled before 11:30 so that I can take this great job I've got lined up for the afternoons." Why will it be difficult for the speaker to get what he wants despite his willingness to pay a high price for it?

28. A *Wall Street Journal* article (September 16, 1981) on business attitudes toward regulatory standards under the Reagan administration reported that many corporate executives say that they have adjusted quite well to existing regulations and see no big need for a rollback.

(a) Why might a company that has been compelled by law to reduce its emission of air pollutants *not* want to see the law relaxed?

(b) Why is it important that regulations governing air pollution by industry not be changed frequently?

29. Here is a quotation from *A Treatise of Human Nature* by David Hume. The words were written around 1740.

> Our property is nothing but those goods, whose constant possession is established by the laws of society; that is, by the laws of justice. . . .
>   No one can doubt, that the convention for the distinction of property, and for the stability of possession, is of all circumstances the most necessary to the establishment of human society, and that after the agreement for the fixing and observing of this rule, there remains little or nothing to be done towards settling a perfect harmony and concord.

Has Hume exaggerated the importance of clearly defined and stable property rights?

30. Surveys by the Michigan Highway Department showed that beverage-container litter decreased 82 percent and total litter decreased 32 percent when the state adopted a mandatory-deposit law for beer and soft-drink containers. According to one estimate of the effect of the law on prices, Michigan consumers were paying an extra $300 million per year for beer and soft drinks as a result of the law.

(a) If these figures are correct, is the mandatory-deposit law "cost-effective" in your judgment? How could you decide?

(b) Suppose we knew that Michigan citizens actually value the reduction in litter at more than $300 million per year. Would this demonstrate the cost-effectiveness of the mandatory-deposit law?

(c) How many people could be hired full time to walk around picking up litter for $300 million per year? Assume that litter-lifters receive $5 an hour, which works out to $10,000 a year for 50 weeks of 40 hours each. Do you think such an army of full-time litter-lifters could reduce total litter by considerably more than 32 percent?

31. In 1981 the Boeing Company "deposited" 5 tons of volatile organic compounds and 137 tons of fugitive dust in a "bank" operated by the Puget

Sound Air Pollution Control Agency. Boeing was "credited" with this quantity of air pollutants because it had reduced emissions by that amount in excess of legislated requirements.

Boeing will be able to sell its credits in the future to new industries that want to add pollutants to the air. However, it will be able to sell only 100 units for each 130 deposited.
  (a) Will air quality be better or worse, in your judgment, if Boeing is allowed to sell other companies the right to pollute?
  (b) Wouldn't the people of the Puget Sound area be better off if other companies were not allowed to increase pollutants in the air just because Boeing had reduced its emissions by more than the law requires?
32. The Times Mirror Company recently completed a $120-million expansion of a paper-making plant near Portland, Oregon, after purchasing for $50,000 the right to emit 150 tons of extra hydrocarbons into the air each year. The right was purchased from a dry-cleaning firm and the owners of a wood-coating plant that had gone out of business. Without those rights, Times Mirror could not have secured permission to expand. Are the people of Portland better or worse off as a result of this arrangement?
33. Suppose that government environmental agencies decide exactly how much of each kind of pollutant they will allow within a given airshed, and sell the rights to discharge these quantities of pollutants to the highest bidder.
  (a) Which firms would offer the highest bids?
  (b) How could citizens interested in cleaner air than the environmental agency had ordered use this system to obtain what they want?
34. "Taxes can't control pollution. They'll just drive the little firms out of business while the big firms, who can afford to pay, go right on polluting." Do you agree?
35. Assume that the graph below shows how much it costs per year per car to reduce undesirable automobile emissions by various percentages through mandatory exhaust-control devices.

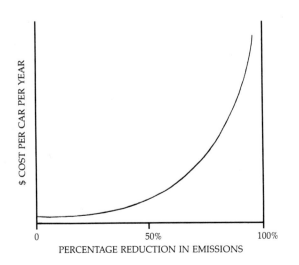

Figure 13B Costs of reducing automobile emissions

(a) Why does the curve rise slowly at first and increase more rapidly as emission levels decline? Is this a peculiar characteristic of automobile exhaust-control systems, or is it a more general relationship?

(b) Does this curve tell us how much emissions ought to be reduced? Does it provide any guidance at all to those who make public policy in this area?

(c) If you think of this curve as the marginal cost of supplying cleaner air, what kind of data would you want in order to construct the demand for cleaner air? What would be the significance of the intersection between these two curves?

(d) Suppose you want to find out how much people in your area value cleaner air. So you commission a survey in which people are asked how much they *would be willing to pay* in order to obtain various levels of reduction in the amount of noxious automobile emissions in their community. Can you generally count on them to tell the truth? Remember that they know they won't be held to their valuation—that is, they won't actually be required to pay what they say they would be willing to pay. What are the major sources of bias in such a survey procedure?

(e) Suppose that your survey is done for the government and that the people whom you ask know they will actually be required to pay an annual tax equal to the amount they say they are willing to pay for whatever level of reductions is finally decided upon and enforced. What sort of bias will this introduce into your measurement of the community demand for cleaner air?

(f) "No cost is too great to pay to reduce the smog level." Do you think that people who make such statements expect to be among those who actually pay the costs of reducing the smog level?

36. Here is a paragraph from a letter to the *Wall Street Journal* (September 20, 1982) written by the Chairman of the House Subcommittee on Health and the Environment:

> The cheapest and best way to clean air is to make sure that new industrial facilities are built clean. It is far easier to build a new coke oven or blast furnace clean than to try to retrofit an old facility with pollution controls. Just as replacing old, dirty cars with new, clean cars will lessen automotive pollution, so too will turning over America's capital stock clean the air.

A law that requires new cars or new industrial facilities to be "clean" raises the cost of producing new cars or new facilities and hence their price. How will that encourage longer use of old and "dirty" cars and facilities? Show how a law could result in *dirtier* air by setting excessively stringent and costly controls on new cars or industrial facilities.

37. Milk trucks traveling from the dairy farms of Pushpin to the bottling plants in Poetrie must travel an additional 18 miles each day because the bridge is out over the Bentham River. The county road commissioners ask you to do a benefit-cost study to determine whether a new bridge should be built.

(a) What would you want to include in benefits and in costs?

(b) Would you want to know the total benefits from milk drinking in the county or the total cost of driving milk trucks?

(c) How is this related to comparisons of the total benefits and total costs of pollution-control programs?

(d) If appendectomies have saved far move lives than they have cost over the years, should you have your healthy appendix removed by a welder? (The point of this absurd question is that the net benefits from appendectomies do not justify removing *every* appendix by *any* means.)

38. A political cartoon shows a man in a gas mask wheezing and gasping his way to the bank to deposit a sack of money. The caption reads: "News item: The Environmental Protection Agency has decided federal smog standards are too costly for cities and industry."

(a) How does the use of the money sack in the cartoon misrepresent the issue? What are some of the *real* costs of strict smog standards?

(b) Why does the assertion that current smog standards are too costly *not* necessarily mean that smog should be allowed to increase? (Hint: There are many different ways to improve air quality. Current standards actually require specific actions; they do not simply establish a target in terms of air quality.)

39. Bombast City allows motor vehicles to be operated without mufflers if they carry a current noise license, which costs $20 per month. In Tranquil Heights it is illegal to operate a motor vehicle without a muffler, and the fine for violation is $100. Motorists who choose to violate the ordinance are caught and fined about once every 5 months. In other words, Bombast City permits noisy vehicles upon payment of a fee and Tranquil Heights prohibits them and fines violators. The fee and the fine are monetarily equivalent when we multiply the fine by the probability of .2 that it will have to be paid in any month.

(a) Given this monetary equivalence, what is the difference between the approaches of Bombast City and Tranquil Heights to the problem of mufflers and noisy motor vehicles?

(b) It's clear that people who drive without mufflers in Bombast City are licensed to make noise. Do the people who drive without mufflers in Tranquil Heights acquire a license when they pay their fines? Would the legislators of Tranquil Heights agree that payment of the fine authorizes one to drive without a muffler?

(c) One difference between "you may make noise if you pay" and "you may not make noise and you'll pay if you do" is that in the latter case but not the former the party who makes noise does something that the society condemns as *wrong*. Does this fact exercise its own effect on behavior? How do societies usually respond when individuals *persist* in behavior that has been legally condemned as wrong? Does the penalty remain constant, as it does in the case of a fee for permitted behavior?

(d) Does this distinction aid us in understanding what lies behind some of the objections to pollution fees? When people protest that fees based on emissions into the air or water constitute a "license to pollute," are they perhaps objecting to the law's *authorization* of the emissions? Do they want the emitters to bear moral blame as well as higher monetary costs? Why might people who are intensely interested in cleaner air or water want the issue to be a moral one?

(e) When would it be desirable to treat discharges into the air or the water

as costs imposed on others that will be allowed upon payment of a fee, and when would it be better to treat them as crimes punishable by fines?

40. Why do people sometimes provide valuable services without asking for or even being willing to accept payment, whereas at other times they will insist upon being paid for a service that costs them nothing to provide?

(a) Why do managers of urban skyscrapers sometimes charge a fee just for letting people look out the windows on the top floor?

(b) Why do managers of department stores never charge a fee to let people who have no intention of buying anything walk through their stores before Christmas to enjoy the displays?

(c) Why don't people who landscape their premises in a beautiful way charge a fee to those who pass by and enjoy it? Are there ways of collecting benefits from passing spectators other than charging them a fee for looking?

(d) Why don't city residents ask for a contribution to defray expenses when they are stopped by tourists seeking directions? Are such tourists imposing costs on the people whom they stop?

(e) If you were flagged down on a highway by a motorist with a flat tire who said that his jack was broken and asked to borrow yours, would you cooperate? Would you ask to be paid for your services? Would you accept a payment of $5 afterwards if the motorist insisted strenuously? If you would absolutely refuse the money, might you nonetheless accept his offer to buy you dinner at a pleasant restaurant a few miles up the road? Assume that you've found him good company, that you do want to have dinner, and that the dinner will cost considerably more than $5.

(f) Suppose your elderly neighbor injures his back so that he cannot mow his lawn. You know this and so you quickly mow his lawn while doing your own. How would you react if your neighbor, grateful for your kindness, came over that evening and offered you a $10 bill? Would you be less surprised and affronted and more likely to accept if the gift he offered was a $15 bottle of wine? Why?

41. The industrialized nations of Europe and North America have been eager in recent years to secure international agreements to restrict industrial practices that threaten to cause deterioration in the quality of the environment. The less-industrialized countries of the world have been far less eager for such agreements. How would you explain this? Why are people more likely to become concerned about the quality of the environment as their incomes rise?

Markets and Government

What should we leave to the market and what are appropriate tasks for government? It's difficult to answer that question unless we know what we mean by *the market* and by *government*. To choose intelligently we must know what the options are, and the choice between market and government is by no means as clear as our public-policy debates often make it seem.

Private versus Public?

Most of the standard contrasts between the market system and government don't hold up very well under close examination. To begin with, the market is usually characterized as the *private* sector, with government agencies and officials occupying the *public* sector. But what can this possibly mean? It surely doesn't mean that consumers and the managers of business firms pursue private interests, whereas everyone who works for government pursues the public interest. The senator who claims that "the public interest" guides all his decisions is in fact guided by a personal interpretation of the public interest, filtered through all sorts of private interests: reelection, influence with colleagues, relations with the press, popular image, and place in the history books. Senators *may* be less interested than business executives in maximizing their private monetary income, but they're probably more interested on average in acquiring prestige and power.

The same kind of analysis applies to any employee of a government agency, whether it's a high appointed official on a regulatory commission or someone just starting a job at the lowest civil-service rank. However lofty, noble, or impartial the stated objectives of a government agency, its day-to-day activities will be the consequence of decisions made by ordinary mortals, subject to the pull and push of incentives

remarkably similar to those that operate in the private sector. Moreover, in recent years a special devotion to "the public interest" has been claimed for themselves by many executives in leading business corporations, eager to persuade us that the ultimate touchstone for their policies is not the maximization of net revenue but the fulfillment of their social responsibilities. We would be well advised to discount *all* the rhetoric about public versus private interests, and to look for the incentives that actually shape the decisions that people make.

Competition and Individualism

Some other common contrasts between the market and the government also grow more indistinct the longer we look at them. The market sector is often called the *competitive* sector. But there is competition in government, too, as every election year demonstrates. Within any government agency, competition for promotion exists among employees. Competition also occurs between government agencies vying for a larger share of appropriations. The two major political parties are continually competing. The executive branch competes with the legislative, members of Congress compete for committee assignments, even district judges compete with one another in the hope of an eventual appointment to a higher court. Do Supreme Court justices, holding appointments for life at the pinnacle of their profession, compete for reputation among editorial writers and law-school professors?

Sometimes we're told that *individualism* is the distinguishing characteristic of the market sector. But what constitutes "individualism"? Many of those who enter the market sector go to work for large corporations right after leaving school and continue as employees until retirement. Is there any significant difference between working in Baltimore as an employee of the Social Security Administration and working in Hartford as an employee of an insurance company? When Britain experimented after World War II with nationalizing, denationalizing, and renationalizing its steel industry, most of the employees (and lots of other people, too) had trouble discerning any difference. Some of the characters who frequent the halls of Congress seem far more individualistic (or at least more idiosyncratic) than the people who pass through the corridors of business.

Economic Theory and Government Action

Economic theory attempts to explain the workings of society on the assumption that all participants want to advance their own interests and try to do so in a rational way. The

marginal-cost/marginal-revenue rule that we introduced explicitly in Chapter 9, but have in fact been using throughout the book, is merely a formal expression of these assumptions: the way to advance one's interests is to expand each activity whose marginal revenue exceeds its marginal cost and to contract any activity whose marginal cost is greater than its marginal revenue. The economist does not assume, as we've pointed out before, that money or material goods are the only costs and revenues (or benefits) that consumers and producers care about, or that the interests people pursue are narrow and selfish ones. Economic theory can throw light on the social consequences of every kind of human interest.[1] Why shouldn't that apply to the human purposes and the social processes that control the course of government activities?

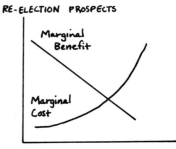

RE-ELECTION PROSPECTS

Marginal Benefit

Marginal Cost

NUMBER OF BABIES KISSED

Our answer is that it *does* apply. The principles of social interaction that guide production of *Time* or *Newsweek* are not as different from those that guide production of the *Federal Reserve Bulletin* as people commonly suppose. Governments as well as privately owned firms produce commodities and services. Governments, too, can do that only by obtaining productive resources whose opportunity cost is the value of what they would have produced in their next most valuable employment. Governments as well as privately owned firms therefore must bid for the resources they want and offer the owners of those resources adequate incentives. You'll want to note (we'll come back to it) that the government can use negative as well as positive incentives: the threat of imprisonment, for example, may be a major incentive as some people decide what portion of their income to offer the Internal Revenue Service each spring. United Way can't use that inducement. Governments even face the problem of marketing their output and of price searching, though monetary prices play a much smaller role in the distribution of government products. But there can be no doubt that demand curves exist for government-provided goods and that, since these goods are characteristically scarce, they must be rationed by means of some discriminatory criteria. And the people with a demand for government goods will consequently compete to satisfy those criteria, to pay the established price.

The main advantage of looking at government in this way is that it counters the tendency to think of government as a deus ex machina: a heaven-sent power that can resolve

---

1. An interest in chaos might be the one exception. In a society where people did not value rationality, but celebrated instead the rule of caprice, accident, and purposeless action, economic theory would have almost no predictive power. Its predictive power is correspondingly greatest in those areas of social life most marked by foresight and premeditated action.

difficulties as magically as a playwright does in the final act of every farce. It makes our expectations of government more realistic. It encourages us to ask about the conditions that enable government to act effectively in any given circumstance and not just to suppose that government always gets what it wants or catches what it chases. This way of looking at government also reminds us that the immediately preceding sentence was misleading in its suggestion that government is an "it"; for government is *many different people interacting on the basis of prevailing property rights.*

If you're wondering what property rights can possibly have to do with the behavior of government, you may have forgotten momentarily that economists use the concept of property rights to describe the rules of the game. Every participant in the processes of government, from voters through civil-service employees to the president, has certain expectations about what voters or civil servants or the president can and may do. Those expectations reflect *property rights.* Maybe it would help if we substituted for *property rights* the phrase *what people think they can get away with.* Unfortunately, that has connotations of conniving and unethical behavior that we don't intend at all. But the phrase does convey the force of the property-rights concept; the actions that people take will depend on their expectations about the consequences of those actions, on the anticipated marginal benefits and marginal costs to themselves of the decisions they're weighing. That's as true in the Senate Office Building as it is on the floor of the New York Stock Exchange. The key to understanding each of those worlds is a grasp of the very different property rights of senators and of stockbrokers.

The Right to Use Coercion

There is one significant difference between government and nongovernment that doesn't grow indistinct or disappear as we inspect it more carefully. *Government possesses a generally conceded and exclusive right to coerce adults.* The right is *generally* conceded, but not universally; thoroughgoing anarchists don't grant it, and neither do those who accept government in principle but reject as illegitimate the authority of the particular government under which they live. It's an *exclusive* right because, as we say, "people don't have the right to take the law into their own hands"; everyone is supposed to appeal to officers of government (police, judges, legislators) when coercion seems called for. And it's the right to coerce *adults* that uniquely distinguishes government, because parents are generally conceded the right to coerce children under certain circumstances.

What does it mean to coerce? We smuggled our definition of coercion into a discussion question at the end of Chapter 11. *To coerce means to induce cooperation by reducing people's options.* Coercion should be contrasted with the other way of obtaining cooperation from people, which is persuasion. *To persuade means to induce cooperation by offering people additional options.*

In a few cases we may not be able to agree whether particular actions constitute coercion or persuasion. These cases will often turn out to involve real or alleged deception, so that our disagreement turns on the issue of what people actually thought their options were when they were induced by others to cooperate. Or we might be disagreeing about the rights that we think people *ought* to have. But this definition will usually allow us to distinguish coercive from noncoercive efforts to influence the behavior of others. It is only to government that we grant the right to secure cooperation by withdrawing options, reducing people's freedom, taking away some of their rights.

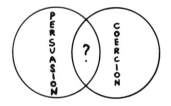

Coercion has a bad reputation, because most of us believe (or think we believe) that people should generally be allowed to do what they want to do. In addition, coercion implies authority, and many of us react with automatic hostility to claims of authority. But the traffic laws that tell us we must drive on the right and stop when the light turns red simultaneously coerce us *and* expand our freedom. The reason they expand our freedom is that they also coerce others. We all get where we're going faster and more safely, because we accept the coercion of traffic laws. This is the traditional defense of government and its right to coerce: we may all be able to achieve greater freedom (expanded options) if we all accept some limitations on our freedom (reduced options).

Is Government Necessary?

But do we have to use coercion? Couldn't we get equally good results by relying on voluntary cooperation? We have seen throughout this book that voluntary exchange is the principal mechanism of coordination in our society. Why couldn't voluntary exchange become the *only* means through which we induce cooperation? By asking this question seriously and pushing for an answer, we can gain some important insights into the capabilities and limitations of the various ways in which we try to get things done.

One way to get at the issue is to ask what would happen if there were no government at all in our society. What problems would arise? Would important tasks cease to be performed? Couldn't people resolve those problems and

accomplish those tasks either through individual action or by forming voluntary associations? A good example with which to begin sorting out the issues is the case of police protection. Would there be no police if there were no government? That can't be the case, since private police forces exist at the present time. But these forces supplement a basic, given level of government police protection, providing additional protection for those who want it and are willing to pay for it. Could we obtain that *basic* protection in the absence of government?

Excluding Nonpayers

Why not? If there were no government, people who wanted police protection could simply purchase it from private security agencies—much as those people do who aren't satisfied with the service that government provides now. Wouldn't that system even be more fair than the one we actually have? People with lots of property to protect and little time, inclination, or ability to protect it themselves would have to pay for the service. Those who own little property or are in a good position to guard it themselves wouldn't have to pay taxes for police protection that doesn't really benefit them. We make people pay for their own food, rather than providing it out of tax revenues, because we know that people want vastly different quantities and qualities. Why not use the same system for police protection?

The correct answer is *not* that police protection is a "basic necessity"; food is even more basic and necessary. The difference is that food can be supplied exclusively to those who pay for it and denied entirely to those who refuse to pay. And that's not altogether the case with police protection. The patrol officers whom my neighbors hire to guard their houses provide a measure of security also to my house, as a spillover benefit, when they patrol our street. Potential burglars won't realize that I haven't subscribed to the neighborhood security service and that they're consequently safe from apprehension if they break into my house. In fact, the burglars may *not* be altogether safe if they do that. The patrol officers might decide that they can most effectively protect their customers' property by arresting *all* the burglars they discover, regardless of whose property is being burglarized. That gives me protection for which I didn't pay.

In much the same way, fire fighters hired to protect my neighbors' houses might choose to put out a grass fire in my yard or a blaze in my attic just to keep it from spreading to their customers' property. And when they extinguish fires on their customers' property, they diminish the chance that the property of adjacent nonsubscribers will catch fire. In

Who will have an incentive to supply a good if people can obtain it without paying for it?

both cases someone who doesn't pay nonetheless acquires a benefit from production of the good. The key feature is the inability of the producers—the police officers or the fire fighters—to exclude nonpayers.

The Free-Rider Problem

When people can obtain a good whether they pay for it or not, they have less incentive to pay. They're tempted to become *free riders: people who accept benefits without paying their share of the cost of providing those benefits.* But if no one has an incentive to pay the costs, no one will have an incentive to provide the benefits. As a result, goods won't be produced, despite the fact that everyone values them more than the cost of producing them.

The free-rider concept describes one of the most frustrating problems in the study of social organization. It frustrates those who don't understand why the problem exists and who therefore keep insisting that it *ought* to go away:

"We can lick the energy problem if each of us will only. . . ."

"There would be no litter on our highways if each of us would only. . . ."

"If each of us studies the issues and goes to the polls on election day. . . ."

"If every nation would only renounce forever the use of force as a means of resolving international disagreements. . . ."

Those who plead so plaintively in all of these and dozens of similar cases recognize correctly that we could all gain "if each of us would only." They are frustrated by the persistent failure of people to do what would clearly and by everyone's admission make them all better off.

The free-rider problem frustrates economists, too, because economists encounter so much resistance when they try to persuade people that *each will not do what is in the interest of all unless it is in the interest of each.* People's actions are guided by the costs they expect to bear and the benefits they expect to receive *as a result of those actions.* If the benefits accruing to Jane Marcet will be exactly the same for all practical purposes whether or not she takes a particular action—but she will incur significant costs by taking it—she will not take the action.

If Jane is noble and generous, she will derive a great deal of benefit from helping others, while thinking lightly of the sacrifices she makes to do so. Consequently she will take some actions that others will not take. That must be stressed, because the free-rider concept definitely does not assert that people are completely selfish or that altruism plays no part in social life. Quite to the contrary, no society could

If all wheat farmers reduced their planting by 50 percent, all would earn a larger net revenue

But . . .

If all other wheat farmers reduce their planting by 50 percent, any one wheat farmer could make a fortune by increasing his planting by 50 percent.

What would you predict

continue to exist in which people were *completely* selfish. We asserted in Chapter 13—and will remind you again here—that some amount of genuine concern for the well-being of others is essential if any social cooperation at all is to occur. Neither markets nor governments could exist among people with no ability to empathize, to internalize at least some of what others experience.

Positive Externalities and Free Riders

In stressing the significance of the free-rider concept, the economist is insisting only that people have *limited* concepts of self-interest, that they do not by and large entertain the inner feelings of others, especially more distant others, with as much vividness and force as they experience costs and benefits that impinge on them more directly. The economist who calls attention to the free-rider problem is saying that positive externalities exist as well as negative ones, and that these externalities encourage people to behave as free riders. *Positive externalities are benefits that accrue to people other than those who created the benefits.* They raise this question: Will anyone have an adequate incentive to create those benefits, or will everyone wait to receive them as a spillover benefit from the actions of others?

Positive externalities or spillover benefits are probably even more widespread in modern societies than are spillover costs, the negative externalities that give rise to complaints about pollution. Homeowners who maintain beautiful lawns produce spillover benefits for neighbors and passers-by. People with engaging smiles distribute spillover benefits to everyone they encounter. Citizens who take the trouble to inform themselves on community issues improve the quality of public decisions and thereby benefit everyone. Moreover, ordinary producers and sellers regularly and as a matter of course provide benefits to customers considerably greater than what the customers are required to pay for them. Eliminating all spillover benefits would be as absurdly impossible as eliminating all pollution. Nonetheless, spillover benefits and the free-riding tendencies they encourage do create some serious social problems. Coercion through the agency of government is a way of dealing with these problems.

Transaction Costs and Coercion

We get a useful handle on the issue when we recognize that voluntary exchange always entails some *transaction costs*. These are simply *the costs of negotiating and monitoring agreements to*

exchange. Every commercial sale entails some transaction costs: buyer and seller must find each other, agree on what they're willing to offer and want to receive, and make reasonably sure that they're actually getting what they expected to get. Sellers in particular must incur transaction costs to be sure that nonpayers don't obtain the goods that they're supplying. Long-established business operations keep down transaction costs by reducing them to routine, thereby enabling all parties to derive larger net benefits from exchange. When transaction costs are so high, however, that they exceed the benefits from exchange, exchange won't occur and the potential benefits will be lost. Government can be viewed as an institution for reducing transaction costs through the use of coercion.

The amount of mutually advantageous exchange that occurs in a society is limited by transaction costs.

Law and Order

Let's take a look at some traditional functions of government to see how much this approach explains. We begin with the problem of "law and order." We can now summarize the argument of the last few pages: high transaction costs make it difficult to exclude nonpayers from the benefits of police patrols. To prevent free riders from destroying the incentive to supply police protection, government employs coercion. It supplies the service to everyone and pays for it with involuntary contributions called taxes.

A judicial system for resolving disputes that arise between citizens could perhaps be created through voluntary efforts somewhat more easily than a police force, as is suggested by the existence of numerous arbitration systems financed by voluntary efforts. But everyone benefits when the people occupying a common territory are all subject to the same system of laws and judicial rulings. Uniform and consistently enforced rules that are binding on all, whether or not they consent, make it much easier for everyone to plan with confidence. And the ability to plan confidently is what distinguishes a cooperating society from a chaotic mob. Since a system of laws and courts confers substantial benefits on people whether or not they choose to help pay for it and to be bound by it, societies use coercion to create and operate systems of justice.

National Defense

National defense is a very traditional function of government, and it provides the classic example of a benefit that can't be provided, except at prohibitive cost, exclusively to those who pay for it. Because free-rider problems would make it

How can a supplier of national defense make it available exclusively to those who have paid their defense subscription fee?

practically impossible to rely on voluntary contributions to finance a system of national defense, societies resort to coercion, collecting the funds through taxation.

Note carefully, however, because the point is easily overlooked, that government does not have to rely entirely on coercion to produce the good called national defense. And no government does. The taxes used to finance a military force are coercive levies. But when the funds are used to hire people for the armed forces and to purchase equipment from suppliers, government is relying on persuasion and voluntary cooperation, just as it does in supplying police officers and judges. This raises an interesting question. Why will a government sometimes use coercion to achieve its objectives when it would appear that persuasion would work just as well or even better? Why will a government choose to draft people into the armed forces (and onto juries) rather than rely on volunteers? Most people who work for government are persuaded, not compelled to do so. Why are some coerced? The dangers to which military personnel are subject cannot be the whole answer, since people are attracted into far more dangerous occupations without conscription. We'll suggest an explanation a little further on.

Roads and Schools

What about roads? Would we enjoy an adequate system of streets and highways if we didn't use coercion to finance them? Be careful; an adequate system doesn't necessarily mean the quantity and quality we now have. Roads are *over*supplied if the benefits from particular additions are less than the costs of making those additions, and that can surely occur. But is there any reason to expect a systematic *under*supply of streets and highways if their provision is left entirely to voluntary efforts? The transaction costs could be rather staggering if all streets and highways were owned and operated by people who had to rely entirely on tolls for the collection of revenue. The benefits, moreover, don't accrue exclusively to those who drive. People who live along a dusty gravel road receive benefits from the paving of that road even if they never drive. The experience of those who have built roads in remote areas or in private developments without using coercion suggest both that it can be done and that the costs of securing cooperation by exclusively voluntary means can be quite high.

What is the case for using coercion to finance education? The argument here is that people will acquire education only up to the point at which the marginal cost to themselves equals the marginal benefit to themselves. But education supposedly generates substantial externalities, benefits that

accrue to people other than the person acquiring the education. Thus everyone in a democracy benefits when citizens learn to read and to think. Because we don't take account of the benefits to others in deciding how much education to obtain, we obtain less than the optimal amount. By using taxes to subsidize education, the government lowers its cost to potential students and induces them to acquire more than they otherwise would. The question arises, as it does with roads, whether the use of coercion to prevent undersupply does not lead in practice to oversupply. We'll return to that question.

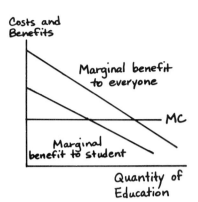

Income Redistribution

Another important category of government action is the provision of special benefits—money grants, food stamps, medical care, housing subsidies, and a variety of social services—to impoverished or disabled people. Why does this kind of activity require the use of coercion? Why don't we leave it to voluntary philanthropy, rather than compel people to contribute through the tax system? One part of the answer is that charity is subject to the free-rider problem. Assume that all citizens are charitably disposed and want to see more income made available to especially poor and unfortunate people. Although some citizens derive satisfaction from contributing to a charitable cause, most would prefer that problems be solved and suffering relieved at a minimum cost to themselves. They want to see poor people helped, but they also want to see others do the helping. And so they tend to behave like free riders. They hold back somewhat on their contributions in the hope that others will contribute enough to take care of the problem. But with everyone waiting for others to contribute, contributions fall short of the amount that everyone would prefer to see raised. Under such circumstances taxation can make people want to contribute more by assuring them that others are also doing their share.

The Regulation of Voluntary Exchange

What about the extensive list of government activities that fall under the category of regulation? Why do federal, state, and local governments regulate so many of the activities of citizens, using coercion to control the terms on which people may engage in voluntary exchange? Putting it in just that way— using coercion to control voluntary exchange—may prompt us to think a little harder and longer about all the things that government does in the name of regulation.

Transaction costs provide part of the answer. It would be very costly for all of us to carry our own scales to check the

accuracy of the ones that butchers use and our own gallon cans to be sure the gasoline pumps aren't cheating us. When physicians must be licensed and new drugs approved by the Food and Drug Administration before they can be marketed, buyers are spared the cost of evaluating goods whose quality most of them would be unable to assess for themselves—except at prohibitive costs. By compelling sellers to obtain certification, government agencies can enable us all to make satisfactory exchanges at lower cost. A substantial amount of government regulation can be viewed as coercion designed to reduce the cost of acquiring information.

The glaring flaw in this defense of regulation, however, is that it fails to account for the enthusiasm with which sellers so often support regulation. Those who have studied the matter know very well that the demand for government regulation of sellers more often originates with the sellers than with their customers. We saw in Chapter 10 why this occurs: sellers are eager to restrict competition, and government regulation in the name of consumer protection is a technique of proved effectiveness for eliminating competition. But why do the victims cooperate? Why does government employ coercion to promote special interests when it's supposed to be the responsibility of government to promote the public interest?

Government and the Public Interest

The basic answer suggested by economic theory brings us back in a surprising way to the problem with which we began this chapter. The coercive actions taken by government to compensate for the limitations inherent in purely voluntary cooperation are themselves subject to the same limitations. The reason for this is that coercion itself depends on voluntary cooperation. Persuasion always precedes coercion, because government will not act until particular people have been persuaded to act. Government is not the genie in Aladdin's lamp. Government is people interacting, paying attention to the expected costs and benefits of the alternatives that they perceive. The disconcerting part of all this is that the problems created by transaction costs, positive externalities, and free riders are particularly acute in the political life of democracies.

A surprising number of people assume without thinking about it that "government acts in the public interest." But does it really? Does it always do so? Why do we think so? Do citizens become more virtuous when they move from the line in the supermarket to the line at the polling place? Do people's characters change when they give up a post in

industry or academia to take a position with the government? Suppose we define the public interest as what everyone would want if everyone was adequately informed and impartial. Does economic theory have anything useful to say about the likelihood that government actions will proceed from adequate information and an impartial viewpoint?

Those whose decisions make up the sum of government actions will pay attention to the information actually available to them and the incentives that actually confront them. Economic theory predicts that this information and these incentives will tend to be both limited and biased.

Information and Democratic Governments

We can begin with citizen voters. None of us knows enough to cast an adequately intelligent vote. To persuade yourself that this is so, conduct a little mental experiment. Suppose you know that your vote, whether on a candidate or a ballot proposition, would determine the outcome of the election; your vote and your vote alone will decide the question. How much information would you gather before casting that crucial vote? A lot would depend, of course, on the importance of the office or the issue. But you would surely invest far more time and energy in acquiring information than you do when you're just one voter among 50 thousand or 50 million. As it is, most citizens, including intelligent, well-read, and public-spirited citizens, step into the polling place on election day equipped only with a lot of prejudices, a few hunches, some poorly tested bits of information, and vast areas of total ignorance. We do this because it's rational to do so! Given the actual importance of our one vote in 50 thousand or 50 million, it would be an almost unconscionable waste of time for us to learn enough to cast an adequately informed vote. The issue is not simply one of selfishness or lack of dedication to the well-being of society. A voter who wanted to make a personal sacrifice for the good of the commonwealth could do far more per hour, per dollar, or per calorie in social-service volunteer work than by gathering enough information to cast an adequately informed vote.

"But if everybody thought that way," goes the standard objection, "democracy wouldn't work." This objection is another instance of the argument that the free-rider phenomenon doesn't exist because the world would be a more satisfactory place if it did not exist. Those who are committed to democracy had better concern themselves with ways to make it work when citizen voters are uninformed and misinformed, and not pretend that voters have knowledge they obviously don't have.

Rational ignorance: when it's not worthwhile to learn.

Some defenders of democracy aren't overly discouraged by the incompetence of citizen voters. They rely on elected representatives to acquire the information that must be available if decisions are to be made in the public interest. Their confidence has a reasonable foundation in reality. Because the vote of each legislator has a far greater probability of affecting the outcome, because legislators can use the information they acquire to influence others in significant ways, because legislators are provided with staff and other information-gathering resources, because many people will have a strong interest in making relevant information available to legislators, because legislators' votes are monitored and must be defended—for all these reasons and more, elected representatives are far more likely to be adequately informed about the issues on which they vote than are ordinary citizens.

The Interests of Elected Officials

But even if we can assume that legislators' votes are adequately informed, are we entitled to assume that they will be votes in the public interest? Are elected representatives impartial? Another way of asking the same question is to ask whether they will always vote in the way that the information available to them tells them they ought to vote. Economic theory assumes that people act in their own interest, not that they act in the public interest. Sometimes it will be in a legislator's interest to pursue the public interest. But finding ways to produce such harmony is the major issue in the design of political institutions; we can't simply *assume* this advantageous concord without asking whether the institutions under which we live are likely to produce it. Because an interest in reelection is a common and healthy interest among most elected officials, we'll focus our analysis on this one particular private interest. Is an interest in being reelected likely to lead elected officials to vote and act in the public interest?

Let's begin by noticing how it limits their planning horizons. Elected officials can't afford to look too far ahead. Results must be available by the next election or the incumbent could be replaced by someone who offers better promises. We shall see in the last part of this book how an emphasis on the short run makes it difficult for governments to deal effectively with recessions and inflations. But the same will be true for any policy that requires current sacrifices for the sake of future benefits. Elected officials will tend to discount heavily the value of all future benefits that aren't expected until after the election. Their interest in reelection will thus keep them from fully using their own superior knowledge about the consequences of particular policies.

Paying $2000 one year from now for $1000 in benefits right now is worthwhile to someone who wouldn't otherwise be around one year from now.

In listing some of the reasons why legislators are likely to be well informed, we mentioned two that also explain why legislators will not always vote in the way that their information tells them they ought to vote. These were the last two reasons cited: many people have a strong interest in making relevant information available to legislators, and legislators' votes are monitored and must be defended. The problem is that the interest in providing information (or lobbying) and in holding legislators accountable for their actions is concentrated in special-interest groups. The positive externalities associated with the political process makes this almost inevitable.

The controversy over deregulation of the trucking industry nicely illustrates the problem. Regulation by the Interstate Commerce Commission over the years has produced wasteful practices and higher prices to shippers that ultimately show up as higher prices for just about everything we buy. But there are people who benefit from all this. By restricting competition, regulation has created privileged positions for the trucking firms that own operating rights and for members of the Teamsters Union. These groups expect deregulation to reduce their wealth substantially. They have therefore been extremely active in lobbying members of Congress, in making campaign contributions, and in threatening retaliation against elected officials who vote to "throw the trucking industry open to the chaos of competition."

The dollar benefits to the rest of us from lower transportation costs would almost surely be greater in the aggregate than the losses that the trucking firms and the drivers expect to suffer from deregulation. Nonetheless we don't see any significant amount of lobbying effort, campaign contributions, or demonstrations directed at getting Congress to vote *for* deregulation. The individual interest that each of us has in deregulation is simply not great enough to induce any of us to involve ourselves actively in the fight. As all of us, opponents and proponents of deregulation, consult our own personal marginal benefits and marginal costs, here is what occurs.

The few opponents who have much to lose invest vast resources in trying to influence the legislature. The many proponents with more to gain in total—but less to gain individually—invest nothing. Legislators respond to this sort of pressure, because a substantial number of them find that doing so serves their interest in being reelected. It seems rather futile to fault them for this; an ex-legislator with untarnished principles is not always a more effective public servant than a legislator who has bent a few principles to survive and fight another day. The fault lies with the externalities that prompt most of us to behave like free riders, hoping

that someone else will assume the costs of lobbying for the measures from which we would all benefit.

Positive Externalities and Government Policies

Our conclusion should come as no surprise. Government policies will tend to be dominated by special interests. Government will lean toward actions that harm many people just a little bit, rather than actions that displease a few people very much. Government policies will be guided not so much by the public interest as by an endless succession of extremely partial interests. This is why consumer interests win the oratorical contests, but producer interests control policy. The interests of producers are simply more concentrated, more sharply focused. Producers know that their action or inaction can make a significant difference to their own welfare, and so it's in their interest to act. But no individual consumer can expect more than a small benefit from political action, so none of them has an incentive to accept the costs.

Is this why the use of coercion to prevent an undersupply of roads often leads to an oversupply? The taxpayers' general interest in economy doesn't fare well when it goes head to head with a small group's intense interest in having a road or building a road. The same analysis applies to schooling. Those who produce schooling (the author's own vested interest, let it be noted) can make life difficult for legislators who try to save taxpayers money by reducing expenditures on education or research. Here is an explanation for the otherwise puzzling behavior of legislatures that approve larger and larger expenditures—even when every member favors reduced expenditures. There is no way to cut a budget without cutting specific projects. With every special interest organized to make certain that the cuts occur in someone else's project, expenditures cannot be reduced.

Why did we long have a military draft in this country, and what is the probability that Congress will restore it? Military conscription, as we noted earlier, extends the use of coercion into areas where persuasion is quite capable of securing the cooperation we want (at least in peacetime). The draft probably persisted as long as it did because the military establishment had a strong and sharply focused interest in maintaining a ready flow of personnel for the armed forces, whereas most of those who were adversely affected by the draft had a stronger incentive to find a personal escape route than to attack the whole system. It is interesting to note how many current advocates of reinstating the draft are now talking about *universal* conscription of young people for short-term service of some kind. Will this tactic (assuming that it

is a tactic) increase the number of those who are opposed to the draft? Or will it reduce the expected cost to each draftee below that critical point at which he or she would be willing to do political battle to prevent reestablishment of the draft?

What can we say about government actions to relieve poverty? We can predict that legislators will be slow to replace in-kind transfers with money transfers. Farmers benefit from the food-stamp program, the building trades benefit from housing subsidies, the medical-care industry expands with health-care assistance, teachers benefit from educational subsidies for the poor, and social workers know that giving money to the poor will never be as advantageous as hiring more members of the "helping professions." The political influence of these groups makes it easier for legislatures to support in-kind transfers to the poor than to support money transfers. There may be other and better grounds for rejecting money transfers, but this alternative would get more respectful attention in Congress if money were produced and sold by a money industry.

How Do People Identify the Public Interest?

None of this implies that farmers, hospital administrators, or social workers have *no* regard for the public interest. It implies only that they all have *some* regard for their own interests. And even those who work for government agencies charged specifically to protect the public interest define it with reference to their own special interests.

Consider, for example, a member of the Food and Drug Administration (FDA), responsible for preventing the introduction of new drugs without adequate testing. What is adequate testing? It's testing that makes sure we know all the side effects of a new drug before we allow it on the market. But we can *never* be sure. All we can do is acquire additional information and thus reduce the risk that someone will be killed or seriously harmed by an unanticipated side effect. How far should we reduce the risk? Not *too* far, because there are costs as well as benefits attached to additional testing. A major cost will be the lives lost and the suffering not relieved because the drug isn't available while it's being tested.

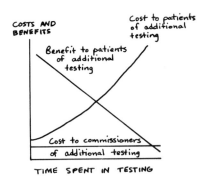

How will an FDA commissioner evaluate these two costs: the lives lost through premature introduction and the lives lost through excessive delay in introduction of new drugs? People will blame the FDA if an approved drug turns out to have disastrous side effects, and they will applaud the FDA if it refuses to approve a drug that subsequently turns out to have disastrous side effects in other countries. But almost no one condemns the FDA for lives lost while a drug is being

tested or applauds the FDA for cutting the testing period short in order to get a new drug on the market. The conclusion is obvious. FDA commissioners will find it in the public interest to test drugs beyond the point at which the marginal benefit equals the marginal cost to patients.

If all this is unsettling to those for whom it is an article of faith that the government takes care of the public interest, it may be time to question this article of faith. Perhaps it stems from the habit of equating "government" with "nation" and extending to the former the reverence felt for the latter. Or it may be a result of our belief that government is the last resort and therefore must be an effective resort, since we don't like to admit to any unsolvable problems. There's a popular bit of deductive reasoning that also leads toward this conclusion. It asserts that all social problems are the result of human behavior, that human behavior can be altered by law, and that government makes the laws, from which the argument concludes that government can solve all social problems.

Alexis de Tocqueville offered a more realistic view in *Democracy in America* (Book I, Chapter VIII): "There is no country in which everything can be provided for by the laws, or in which political institutions can prove a substitute for common sense and public morality."

Once Over Lightly

Economic theory assumes that the actions of government follow from the decisions of citizens and government officials who are paying attention to the marginal costs and marginal benefits to themselves of alternative courses of action.

The distinguishing characteristic of government is its generally conceded and exclusive right to use coercion. To coerce means to induce cooperation by reducing people's options. Voluntary cooperation relies exclusively on persuasion, which secures desired behavior by offering additional options.

Coercion is useful to the members of a society, because it can sometimes secure the production of goods that everyone values at more than the cost of supplying them, but which would not be supplied through purely voluntary cooperation.

A supply failure of this sort is likely to occur when there is no low-cost way of confining supply of a good to those who pay for it, or of preventing demanders from becoming free riders.

Coercion may be able to secure the supply of such goods by lowering transaction costs. These are deadweight costs incurred in the process of carrying through an exchange.

The traditional activities of government turn out upon examination to be largely actions aimed at reducing transaction costs and overcoming free-rider problems.

The coercive activities of government presuppose voluntary cooperation. Persuasion precedes coercion because, in the last analysis, citizens and government officials must be persuaded to employ coercion in particular ways. This implies that the limits on the effectiveness of voluntary cooperation that justify coercive action by government are limitations also on the effectiveness of the government's coercive action.

Positive externalities thoroughly permeate the political process in a democratic government. They make it unlikely that citizen voters will be adequately informed or that elected or appointed officials will consistently act in the way that the information available to them tells them they ought to act.

QUESTIONS FOR DISCUSSION

1. In what general, systematic way do the interests pursued by officials in government differ from the interests pursued by people in the private sector? Consider the following cases:
   (a) The president of a state-owned university and the president of a privately owned university.
   (b) A member of the U.S. House of Representatives who aspires to a seat in the Senate and a traveling sales representative for a large business corporation who wants a job as sales manager at one of the firm's plants.
   (c) A prominent political figure who wants to become president of the United States and a prominent actor who wants to receive an Academy Award.
   (d) An urban police officer and a uniformed guard employed by a private security firm.
   (e) A grant-awarding official in the Small Business Administration and a loan officer in a bank.
2. In each of the following examples, what are the significant differences between government-owned and nongovernment-owned enterprises? Why do you think the government owns the enterprises mentioned? What different forms does competition take in the case of government-owned enterprises? In what different ways do they operate because of their government ownership?
   (a) Investor-owned utilities and utilities owned by states or municipalities
   (b) State colleges and private colleges
   (c) City-owned intraurban bus companies and interurban bus companies like Greyhound and Trailways
   (d) Forest Service campgrounds and privately owned campgrounds
   (e) Public libraries and private bookstores

3. A frequent argument in support of government-produced goods is that they are vital to social welfare and therefore their provision cannot safely be left to the "whims" of the marketplace. Does this explain why parks and libraries are usually municipal services, whereas food and medical care are usually secured through the market? Can you suggest a better explanation to account for these cases?

4. A feature story in the *Wall Street Journal* of May 23, 1979, carries this headline: "Washington PR Staffs Dream Up Ways to Get Agencies' Stories Out."
    (a) How does a director of public affairs in a government agency differ from the director of advertising or public relations for a soap manufacturer?
    (b) Why do the departments of Defense, Transportation, Agriculture, and others of the federal government spend millions of dollars trying to influence public opinion? Isn't it true, at least in a democracy, that public opinion is supposed to control the actions of government agencies?

5. Should the managers of business corporations, in their official capacities, accept social responsibilities beyond the responsibility to increase the net income of the corporations which they run?
    (a) Do they have a moral obligation to go beyond what the law requires in order to advance such causes as race and gender equality, a clean environment, better public transportation, good government, and so on? Why or why not?
    (b) Who will pay the costs if corporation managers shoulder such responsibilities? Who will review their decisions to be sure that the decisions they make really are in the public interest?
    (c) Why might the president of a large corporation want to contribute $1 million of corporate funds to a hospital-building program in the city where the corporation is headquartered? What personal benefits and personal costs accrue to the president from such a gift?

6. Do you think that competition is more common or vigorous in capitalist countries than in socialist ones? Is competition more common or vigorous in wealthy countries than in poor ones?

7. Advocates of government regulation often make their case by attacking "unrestrained" or "unbridled" competition. Is competition *ever* "unrestrained"? What were some of the important restraints on competition that operated in the U.S. economy in the 19th century when, according to some accounts, competition was "unrestrained"?

8. Critics of government regulation often try to make a case for the "free" market. Are markets ever completely free? Free from what? Is a market "unfree" if participants operate under laws that prohibit the use of dishonest weights and measures? Laws that prohibit misleading advertising? That prohibit price increases which have not been approved by a government agency? Where do you draw the line between free markets and unfree or regulated markets? Why do you draw it where you do?

9. The graph below pretends to show the net revenue (during some time period) that the proprietor of a grocery store expects from stocking four categories of merchandise: milk and dairy products (M), canned and bottled staples (S), fresh produce (P), and frozen foods (F).
    (a) How many units of each will he want to stock?

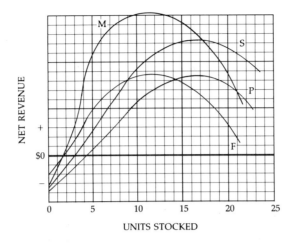

Figure 14A Expected net revenue of a hypothetical grocery store

(b) Now pretend that the four curves show the net satisfaction that the proprietor expects to receive from pursuing the four objectives of more money (M), enhanced status (S), greater personal power (P), and family well-being (F). How far will he pursue each goal?

(c) What general differences would you be inclined to expect between the "satisfaction curves" of a person in business and a person in government service, or running for public office, or in the ranks of the clergy, or teaching school, or working as a medical researcher?

10. The text warns about the dangers in speaking of government as an "it" that can be manipulated, like a tool, to do whatever we want done. Isn't it also misleading to use the word "we" the way it's used in the preceding sentence? Who are the "we" who want government to do this or that? Everyone? The majority? All informed and public-spirited citizens? Those who share my interests and my understanding of the situation? What do people mean when they say, "We must use government to control the effects of selfishness and greed"? Who is supposed to control whom in this vision of the way society works?

11. Guy Weyer is a former farmer turned suburban developer who built 50 houses on a 40-acre corner of his farm. He now rents these houses out.

(a) If one of Guy's tenants calls a meeting at which 26 of the 50 tenants vote to reduce the monthly rents by $100, is Guy morally or legally obligated to abide by their decision?

(b) If the 26 tenants simply withhold $100 of their monthly rent, does Guy have a moral and legal right to evict them?

(c) If the evicted tenants refuse to move, what moral and legal means are open to Guy to get them out?

(d) Suppose that the 26 tenants first form a local government, then reduce the rents by majority vote, and finally pass an ordinance prohibiting evictions. Would this make any difference in the answers you give to the questions above?

(e) What is the difference between a legitimate and an illegitimate govern-

ment or government decision? Is a democratic government one in which the majority rules? Are there any limits to what a majority may do in a democracy?

(f) The principle of majority rule requires a prior determination: majority of *whom?* Who ought to be entitled to a vote in matters such as those discussed above? Property owners exclusively? All residents over 18? Tenants, with one vote per house rather than one per resident? All adults in the county, with Guy Weyer's tenants forming just a small part of a much larger set of voters? What different consequences would be likely to emerge from these different ways of distributing voting rights?

(g) If you are incapable of imagining a legitimate distribution of voting rights other than one-vote-per-adult, consider the distribution of voting rights in a condominium association or a country club. What about the distribution of voting rights among those who own the stock of a corporation? Why do we observe these different ways of assigning voting rights?

12. Adam Smith assigned to the sovereign or commonwealth the duty of "erecting and maintaining those public institutions and those public works, which, though they may be in the highest degree advantageous to a great society, are, however, of such a nature, that the profit could never repay the expense to any individual or small number of individuals, and which it therefore cannot be expected that any individual or small number of individuals should erect or maintain." (*The Wealth of Nations,* Book V, Chapter I)

(a) How does this description of the goods that government should supply differ from the text's description of goods subject to the free-rider problem?

(b) Smith discusses four public institutions or works that at least partially satisfy his criterion: those "for the defence of the society . . . for the administration of justice . . . for facilitating the commerce of the society, and those for promoting the instruction of the people." How does Smith's assignment compare with the duties generally assigned to governments today? Is there any major duty of government that Smith overlooks?

13. The text discusses the problem of creating a police force for a community solely on the basis of voluntary cooperation. Isn't it the unwillingness of some people to cooperate on a strictly voluntary basis that makes a police force desirable in the first place? Aren't burglars and similar lawbreakers behaving as free riders?

14. Should the members of a volunteer fire department refuse to put out a fire in the home of someone who has refused to contribute to the fire-fighting service? (Assume that no property of subscribers is in danger.) What damage would they be doing by putting out the fire?

15. If everyone who uses public parks dislikes seeing litter on the ground, the parks won't necessarily be free of litter. Free-rider problems can produce litter which no one wants. The process by which this sometimes occurs can be presented in terms of what is called The Prisoners' Dilemma. (The name reflects the initial exposition of the dilemma, an exposition which used the example of two prisoners and a clever prosecutor.) The dilemma presented here assumes that each park user has the choice of either tossing litter on the ground or walking to a trash barrel to dispose of the litter. There are

many park users, however, so that one less act of littering will make no discernible difference. *Everyone* (or *almost* everyone) must walk to the trash barrel if the park is to be unlittered and attractive. The matrix below shows the results of the possible choice combinations, with the lower-left triangle in each possible outcome giving the results for each park user and the upper-right triangle the results for all other users.

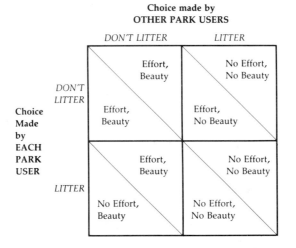

Figure 14B The park users' dilemma

(a) Each person who puts litter in the trash barrel is assured of bearing a cost, called effort; but whether this person will also receive the benefit of beauty depends on what all other users do. If each user aims at the maximum personal net advantage (benefit minus cost), the "society" may well end up in the southeast square. Why?

(b) If each user definitely and strongly preferred the northwest square to the southeast square, would that be sufficient to move the "society" to the northwest square? What would each user want to do, under our narrow assumptions, upon finding that the "society" had achieved the situation described in the northwest square? Assume that a single act of littering will not make a noticeable difference. How would this reproduce the less desirable situation described in the southeast square?

(c) How could "mutual coercion mutually agreed upon" produce the more desirable outcome of the northwest square?

(d) In the real world, why do people not always behave as this question assumes they all behave? Why will people with no fear of prosecution sometimes go to considerable "effort" to avoid littering even though they expect to obtain no "beauty" from it? An example might be a tourist leaving a national park campground.

(e) How many similar situations can you think of? Do they lead to the southeast square? If not, why don't they?

16. Nature Conservancy is the name of a national organization that tries to identify and then purchase endangered habitat in order to preserve it.

   (a) Nature Conservancy makes its purchases with funds that have been

donated by people who want endangered habitat preserved. How does the free-rider problem hinder Nature Conservancy's fund raising?

(b) Why is the free-rider problem less likely to hamper Nature Conservancy in obtaining gifts from corporations than from individuals?

(c) Nature Conservancy accepts gifts of land as well as money, including prime residential or business property. If you were running such an organization, how would you use commercially valuable urban property to promote the preservation of endangered rural areas?

17. Use the definitions of coercion and persuasion offered in the text to evaluate the following actions. In order to decide whether an option was added or subtracted, we must know what options people possess initially, or what their property rights are to begin with.

(a) A prospective employee with strong religious objections to working on Sunday is told he must consent to Sunday work if he wants the job. If he consents because he very much wants the job, has he been persuaded or coerced?

(b) Your employer says you will be fired if you smoke anywhere at all during working hours and so you reluctantly give up smoking from 9 to 12 and 1 to 5 on weekdays. Were you persuaded or coerced?

(c) You very courteously ask the student who lives just below you to please play his stereo at a lower volume from 7 to 10 in the evening when you're trying to study. He refuses on the grounds that he isn't playing it loud enough to prevent you from studying. So you stomp on the floor in the middle of the night when he's trying to sleep. He agrees after two weeks of this to adjust the volume as you requested. Was he persuaded or coerced?

(d) Are electricity users persuaded to pay more or coerced into paying more when their local electric utility raises its rates?

(e) You consider parking your car illegally in a loading zone but finally decide against it because you fear you'll be ticketed. Were you persuaded or coerced into finding another parking space?

(f) A homeowner offers to let you park on the street in a way that blocks his driveway if you agree to pay him $1. You pay and park. Were you persuaded or coerced?

(g) Are you being persuaded or coerced in your decision about how much to contribute at the office to the United Way if you know that the amount of each pledge will be posted on the bulletin board?

(h) Does the umpire in a baseball game secure cooperation among the players by persuasion or by coercion?

18. Does either persuasion or coercion enjoy any inherent advantages over the other as a way of inducing cooperation?

(a) People who are cooperating because they have been persuaded usually want to maintain the relationship. Those who have been coerced will typically be looking for ways to sever the relationship. What does this imply about the level of transaction costs that will be associated with cooperative endeavors in each case?

(b) Coercion can be used to deny people the opportunity to engage in voluntary cooperation. Does this occur? Why should anyone want to use coercion to prevent others from cooperating on a voluntary basis?

19. Is the free-rider problem a source exclusively of social *problems?* Doesn't the free-rider problem also prevent people from cooperating to take unfair advantage of others? Why do cartels generally break down unless they can enlist the support of government with its coercive powers?

20. "Of the 34,937 members in the cooperative eligible to vote, only 737 voted in the election of trustees, and 483 of these cast absentee ballots." Do these data indicate that the members don't support the cooperative? Do you think better trustees would be selected if more members voted?

21. Most automobile drivers probably exceed the legal speed limits somewhat when they think they can get away with it. Does this imply that they would vote for higher speed limits if given a chance?

22. Why do some people who drink alcoholic beverages vote in favor of legal prohibition?

23. Here is the opening sentence of a newspaper editorial lamenting the tiny turnout for a public hearing on improving the high schools in a large U.S. city: "Given the number of people who complain about public education, it's amazing how few attend meetings to tell the schools how to do better." Is it really surprising that many complain but few attend meetings?
    (a) What is the cost of complaining? What is the cost of attending a meeting?
    (b) What is the probability that a concerned citizen who spends an evening at a public hearing will actually be able to influence policies in a large urban school district?
    (c) The relative benefit-cost ratios of complaining and attending would seem to provide an adequate explanation for the facts lamented by the newspaper editorialist. But how can we explain the behavior of "activists," those few people who seem always willing to turn out for meetings on even the most inopportune occasions? Are there satisfactions other than that of actually affecting public policy that people can obtain through political participation?

24. Most parent-teacher associations have a hard time getting people to attend meetings and do other work for the associations.
    (a) Why does this not imply either that parents don't care about their children's education or that they don't think the PTA accomplishes anything?
    (b) Why is attendance usually better among teachers than among parents?
    (c) Why do a few parents choose to be very actively involved in the PTA?

25. Hospitals often find it not worth their while to hold down their costs, because reductions in costs produce lower reimbursement payments from government as well as a lower quality of patient care. A letter to the *Wall Street Journal* (February 24, 1982) complains about this attitude on the part of hospital administrators:

    > [E]very health care provider looks no further than his own check-
    > book. . . . If all providers would look to the size of the jar rather
    > than the one jelly bean they have plucked from it, there would
    > be bigger and better beans for everyone.

    How does this illustrate both the free-rider problem and the "if each of us would only" fallacy?

26. Largely in order to keep its streets free of traffic congestion, Singapore levies taxes on automobiles that raise their price about 150 percent.
    (a) Is it possible that car owners in Singapore are better off with the tax than they would be without it?
    (b) Assume that all car owners in Singapore believe that the benefit to themselves from reduced congestion due to the tax is worth more than the tax they must pay. Does it follow that each car owner will voluntarily pay the tax?

27. Each of the ten families on a suburban block is likely to have its own power lawn mower. Why don't families more often share a single lawn mower? Try to enumerate the principal transaction costs that stand in the way of such a cooperative arrangement.

28. It's difficult for entertainers to supply their services exclusively to those television viewers who are willing to pay for the entertainment.
    (a) How do entertainers nonetheless manage to secure payment for providing their services to television viewers? Think through the way in which the free-rider problem is handled in network television. To whom do entertainers sell their services? Through what sequence of transactions do viewers receive the entertainment? How is the free-rider problem handled at each stage?
    (b) Some homeowners today try to get cable-television programs without subscribing by picking up the signal from satellites, using their own receiving dishes. How does the use of scramblers and decoders by pay-television companies illustrate the acceptance of transaction costs to eliminate free riders?

29. If running laps around the football field improves the conditioning of athletes and makes them more effective players, why do so many players try to get away with running fewer laps than the coach orders? Who receives the benefits and who bears the cost of such conditioning activities? Are coaches likely to order their players to run a more-than-optimal number of laps?

30. When a government agency requires households or businesses to submit detailed reports on their activities, the costs are borne by those who must prepare the reports and the benefits (in the form of additional information) are received entirely by the agency.
    (a) How does this explain the expansion of government-required paperwork despite a general consensus that such paperwork is already excessive?
    (b) Do you think the requirements would decline if agencies were required to use funds from their budget allocations to compensate those who must submit the forms?
    (c) Should teachers be required to read and comment on all papers that they require their students to write?

31. If positive externalities create free-rider problems to the extent suggested in this chapter in the analysis of charitable programs, why do United Way campaigns work as well as they do in so many American cities? Are there elements of coercion in United Way fund drives, either in obtaining people to work on the campaign or in inducing people to contribute? What might be the advantages and disadvantages of having local government assume the welfare functions currently performed through the United Way?

32. Why do our courts require citizens who have been selected for jury duty to serve whether they want to or not? Couldn't courts obtain as many jurors as they require on a voluntary basis if they raised the fee for jury duty? Why don't we raise the fee, staff juries with volunteers, and stop imposing the heavy costs of jury duty on so many people who must abandon other valuable activities to do their "jury duty"? How do you suppose the composition of juries would be affected by such a move to a system of all-volunteer jurors? Is it legitimate to use coercion in this case because serving on a jury is every citizen's duty? If so, why don't we fine people who don't vote? Isn't voting a citizen's duty? Even better, why not fine people who fail a rigorous current affairs test *or* do not vote? That way we would coerce citizens into casting an informed vote. Or would we?

33. Should we have laws that require homeowners to insulate in order to save energy?
    (a) How will homeowners benefit from improved insulation? Should homeowners insulate if the cost to themselves of doing so exceeds the benefit to themselves?
    (b) How do others in a community benefit from the decision of some to insulate and thereby reduce their consumption of electricity? Do these spillover benefits justify a subsidy to encourage homeowners to insulate? Who would lobby for such a subsidy?

34. Would you agree that the U.S. Constitution describes the property rights of the president, members of Congress, and Supreme Court justices?
    (a) Why does the Constitution prohibit Congress from lowering the salaries of the president or of federal judges during their terms of office?
    (b) Are we likely to be governed better or worse during a president's first term than during the second? (The Constitution prohibits a third term.)
    (c) Would you expect more statesmanlike decisions from members of the House of Representatives, who must stand for reelection every two years, or from justices of the Supreme Court, who are appointed for life?

35. Do the decisions of people now living take any account of the demands of future generations for natural resources? Do these decisions take *adequate* account of the demands of future generations? Is government likely to take *better* account of the demands of future generations? Evaluate the contention that government must serve as the steward of natural resources for future generations.

36. The Constitution of the United States gives Congress the power to establish post offices.
    (a) Can you think of any reasons why the government should assume responsibility for providing a system of postal service? Were there better reasons in 1789 than there are today?
    (b) Congress has passed "private-express statutes" that give the Postal Service a legal monopoly over letter carrying. Why should the government prevent firms from competing with the United States Postal Service in the delivery of letters?
    (c) Who would be likely to put pressure on Congress to defeat any bill that was introduced to repeal the private-express statutes?

37. Could the problem of producer dominance in the legislative process be solved by creating a government agency charged with the task of representing consumers in legislative hearings?

38. You and your family enjoy camping in the national parks. In February, therefore, you urge your congressional representative to oppose a bill that would increase the fees for such camping during July and August. The following August you enter Teton National Park at 4:00 P.M. on a weekday and find that all the campsites are occupied.

    (a) Would you now like to see a higher schedule of camping fees? Why or why not?

    (b) Why are fees for the use of privately owned resources more likely to rise when demand increases than are fees for the use of government-owned resources?

39. By using the concepts of this chapter, can you explain the continuing use of violence (war) as a way of resolving disputes between nations?

40. In August 1985 the Federal Communications Commission stated that the Fairness Doctrine—a policy requiring broadcasters to air different views on controversial issues—no longer serves the public interest, because the number of television, radio, and cable-TV outlets has increased so dramatically since the policy was adopted in 1949. The FCC also said that it would nonetheless continue to enforce the doctrine because of Congress's "intense interest" in it.

    (a) Why would members of Congress support a policy that requires a federal government agency to monitor the views presented by broadcasters? Doesn't enforcement of the Fairness Doctrine violate the First Amendment to the Constitution?

    (b) Supporters of the doctrine claim that, because the number of licenses available is limited, licensees should be obligated to present all sides of controversial issues. Why doesn't this argument apply to daily newspapers, which are far more limited in number? (In 1983 there were 1,735 daily newspapers published in the United States and 8,807 commercial radio stations on the air.) How many sides does a controversial issue have?

    (c) Under the Fairness Doctrine, the FCC may require a station to provide free time for rebuttal to a group that claims an issue in which it is interested has not been fairly presented. Who benefits from such a policy? How are broadcasters likely to handle controversial issues if they know they might have to make free air time available to groups that claim the broadcasters' presentation wasn't fairly balanced?

    (d) Who do you suppose has encouraged Congress to have an "intense interest" in the Fairness Doctrine?

41. "Human rights must take precedence over property rights." Do you agree? Can you name one property right that is not the right of some humans? Can you name any human rights that are not property rights, as the term has been defined and used in the last four chapters?

42. Rights for anyone always imply corresponding obligations for someone else. Who must be induced to accept which obligations in order for you to have each of the following rights? The right to:

(a) attend college
(b) vote
(c) work
(d) sing in the church choir
(e) smoke cigarettes
(f) obtain medical care

43. Nine Chicago suburbs have passed ordinances designed to prevent racially integrated neighborhoods from becoming all black. The ordinances establish procedures for promoting purchases by whites and inhibiting purchases by blacks in neighborhoods that already contain more than a certain percentage of black homeowners. (The issues are briefly described in the *Wall Street Journal*, August 14, 1985.)

   (a) Do or should residents of an area have the right to encourage or discourage purchasers in order to achieve or maintain a racially integrated neighborhood? Do they thereby violate the rights of would-be sellers and purchasers who are prevented from arranging a mutually beneficial exchange because the purchaser is the wrong color?

   (b) Visualize a city whose population is 50 percent black and 50 percent white. Suppose further that no one objects to living next door to someone of the opposite color, but that they all object to having neighbors of the opposite color on both sides and will move if they find themselves in that position. Will a segregated or integrated housing pattern emerge under a system of voluntary exchange? Why? If integrated housing is considered a good thing, how could it be achieved under these circumstances?

   (c) It isn't as obvious but it's almost as inevitable that a severely segregated housing pattern will eventually evolve if the citizens of this city wait to move until their neighbors on *four* sides are of the opposite color. How could such a community give effect to the desire of each citizen to live in a racially integrated community?

Inflation, Recession, Unemployment: An Introduction

There is one responsibility of government that receives about as much attention these days from the press and public as all of the others put together: the responsibility of the federal government to prevent, cure, or otherwise control inflations and recessions. Except for an incidental mention, Chapter 14 ignored this responsibility in examining the functions of government. We'll make up for that omission now. The remainder of this book will be devoted almost entirely to the issue of aggregate economic fluctuations and government stabilization policies.

Why do we regard periods of inflation and recession as *problems*? Some readers will be thinking at this point that anyone who has to ask a question like that is too stupid to understand the answer. Inflation means a rise in the cost of living, and anything that makes it more costly for people to live is obviously a problem. As for recessions, they cause a loss of income and of jobs, and no one has to be told why both of those are problems. But matters are not that simple.

Dollar Prices and Real Costs

In the case of inflation, matters are not that way at all. *Inflation is not a rise in the cost of living. Inflation is basically a fall in the value or purchasing power of money.* Looking at it in another way, we can say that inflation is a rise in the money price of goods. You may even, if you wish, speak of inflation as a rise in the money cost of living. But the key word is *money*. A $2 hamburger this year really costs no more than a $1 hamburger last year if the cost of obtaining a dollar has been cut in half since last year.

The cost of obtaining anything is the value of what must be given up to obtain it. We get so into the habit of expressing the value of sacrificed opportunities in the common denominator of money that we sometimes forget to check on whether the value of the common denominator has changed. But that is precisely what inflation is. It's not an increase in the height of everything we're measuring—it's a decrease in the length of the yardstick that we're using to do our measuring.

Of course, everything is finally relative to everything else. It's logically possible to insist that money has maintained a constant value in recent years and everything else has gone up. But that would be as sensible as arguing that the price of a barrel of crude oil remained unchanged through the 1970s, while the value of everything else declined by about 75 percent. When we find oil prices moving relative to everything else, common sense tells us to look for the explanation in changes that have occurred in the conditions of supply or demand for oil—not for "everything else." When we see money prices moving relative to everything else, common sense ought to dictate the same course of inquiry.

Perhaps we would be more likely to see the essential link between money and inflation if we stopped to realize that *inflation simply could not occur in the absence of money.* If all exchanges occurred through barter, there would be absolutely no way in which we could experience inflation. You may have to think about it for a moment to convince yourself. But inflation is a logical impossibility in a society in which goods are exchanged directly for other goods without any use of money.

In a barter economy (where no money was used), it would be logically impossible for all prices to rise

Uncertainty About the Future Value of Money

If inflation does not actually raise the cost of living, why is it a problem? Why does everyone worry so much about it? *The problems that inflation creates are caused almost entirely by uncertainty.* It is not the fact that the value of money is falling that creates problems, but the fact that the future value of money cannot be predicted. A high but steady rate of inflation on which everyone could confidently depend would cause fewer problems than a lower but less predictable rate of inflation.

Deflation, which is *a rise in the value or purchasing power of money,* is just as much of a problem for society as is inflation, insofar as it also introduces uncertainty into the calculations of planners. The same is even true of disinflation, something experienced in the United States in 1982 and 1983. *Disinflation is a slowing down of the inflation rate;* it also creates serious

difficulties for those who fail to anticipate it correctly when making long-term plans.

The Real Costs of Inflation

Consider what happened to financial institutions that loaned money in 1965 on 15-year mortgages at a 6 percent annual interest rate, the standard rate in that year on mortgage loans for new homes. The lenders presumably expected a continuation of the inflation rate that they had experienced over the preceding decade, a rate of less than 2 percent per year. That would have left them with a 4 percent per year *real* return on their mortgage loans: the nominal rate of 6 percent minus the 2 percent per year decline in the value of money. But unexpected inflation played havoc with their expectations. From 1965 to 1980, the dollar declined in value an average of 6 percent per year. That left the lenders with a zero rate of return for the period, which was hardly enough to cover their costs. Lending institutions sustained large losses as a direct result of their failure to predict future changes in the value of money, and many went out of business.

When the value of money is expected to fall rapidly, it pays to take on debt. And anyone who wants to save had better be sure to put those savings into something whose dollar value will keep up with the inflation rate—something like real estate, for example. So when Americans concluded in the 1970s that inflation rates of 5 or even 10 percent per year were going to be the rule, not the exception, the demand to own real estate increased substantially. The purchase price of land and houses consequently rose. Mortgage rates on new homes also rose, to 10 percent in 1978 and on up to more than 15 percent in 1982. People were paying high prices for homes and financing them at high interest rates in the first few years of the 1980s because they had been experiencing 10 percent per year inflation and expected it to continue or even accelerate. But it did not. The inflation rate unexpectedly fell below 7 percent in 1982 and below 4 percent in 1983. Home buyers suddenly found that they had paid too much for the houses they owned and that, with their incomes no longer increasing by 10 or 15 percent per year, they could not keep up the monthly payments for which they had contracted.

The uncertainty about future prices that inflation generates leads to arbitrary redistributions of wealth, to costly efforts by people to protect themselves against losses in wealth, and—perhaps most serious of all—to mounting levels of resentment that can eventually cripple a society's capacity to maintain cooperation among its members.

Redistributions of Wealth

Inflation generates profits for some and losses for others because people fail to anticipate it correctly. Moreover, everyone isn't equally able to act appropriately once the truth about inflation comes to be known. Some sellers' prices are set for only short periods of time and can move up quickly in response to increased demand; examples are the prices of farm products and many of the raw materials used in industrial production. Others respond much less quickly to changed circumstances. Commercial and residential rents are usually set by contract and often cannot be changed for long periods. There are ways for landlords to compel reopenings of contracts in order to negotiate higher rentals, but these procedures entail additional costs to the landlord. Wages and salaries are typically established by agreements that are supposed to extend over longer periods of time. These agreements can also be renegotiated during the contract period, and some will even contain formal clauses calling for renegotiation if certain conditions change. Wages and salaries, however, tend to be less quickly responsive to changed conditions than are the prices of most goods.

Many prices cannot be raised quickly because to do so requires the consent of a regulatory body that may move with glacial speed: gas and electric utilities and telephone companies often complain of their inability to respond quickly enough to higher costs. Then there are those creditors who made long-term loans and can't raise the payments they receive for that service until the loan matures—which might be 25 years in the future. On the other hand, consider the happy position of the federal government, selling us national defense and a variety of social services and charging a price (the personal-income tax) that not only increases but increases at a progressive rate as we all spend and take in more money because the value of money has fallen. The net result of all this is that inflation redistributes income extensively and almost capriciously.

Prices that respond more slowly don't necessarily increase less; they just take longer to get where they're going. But that still means income is redistributed during the transitional period so that some people will have lost out even after they have caught up. The redistributive effects of inflation depend heavily on how rapidly the inflation occurs, because this affects the ability of different people to anticipate and adjust to it. From 1967 to 1973, for example, the consumer price index rose 41 percent, while the mean hourly wage of production workers in private industry rose 46 percent. So wages more than kept pace. But when the price level spurted up 16 percent from January 1973 to July 1974, the

People learn to protect themselves against slow, steady inflation

mean hourly wage increased only 12 percent, so that the real hourly wage declined.

These redistributions of wealth are hardly enough to account for the public's hostility toward inflation. The strength of the popular pressure on government to control inflation (or at least to seem to be controlling it) can be appreciated only if one understands why the beneficiaries of inflation so often join the victims in denouncing it. The principal reason is that they mistakenly think they are victims, too.

There is no better example than residential rents. At the outset of any period of rapid inflation, rents will lag well behind the rate of increase in other prices, including the "price" of labor as measured by average hourly wage rates. The result is that inflation redistributes wealth from landlords to tenants. But tenants don't realize this. They notice the increases in their rents. They don't notice that their rent is increasing at a lower percentage rate than the prices of everything else, including their own incomes. So they conclude they're being hurt by inflation, when in fact they're its beneficiaries.

Many of us are also inclined to exaggerate somewhat our own merit and the value of our contribution to the welfare of the world. So when we look back and notice that our annual income has gone up 120 percent over the last decade, we regard that as a 120 percent increase in the world's appreciation of our worth. When someone points out that the official index of consumer prices shows a 100 percent increase over the same period, we don't deflate that generous estimate of our own improvement. We still think we earned a 120 percent increase in our income, and we resent the fact that we have to pay twice as much nowadays for the things we buy.

Protection Costs

Illusion thus plays a major role in making inflation unpopular and creating pressure on governments to do something about it. But the costs of inflation to a society as a whole are not completely illusory. Imagine a situation in which the various state governments controlled the standards for weights and measures. Suppose that the only way to effect a shift to the metric system was to be sneaky about it—to expand the inch gradually until it measured 1/36 of a meter. So at periodic but unpredictable intervals over the next ten years, the officials of various states announced to their jurisdictions an official increase in the length of the inch—"never enough to notice," as they were fond of saying, but enough to increase the inch from its former length of 0.0254 meters to the desired length of 0.027⅞ meters.

Where would the costs of such a procedure show up? They would appear in resources devoted to guessing the timing and rate of changes and ensuring against the consequences of mistakes; in resources spent on translating measurements when goods produced in one state are used in another; in resources employed to fit tools conforming to older specifications to products made to newer specifications; in resources wasted on the correction of mistakes arising from the increased uncertainty and from the complexity of the coordinating task.

The real costs of inflation to a society are like the costs just described. We suggested a few paragraphs back that inflation is a change in the length of the measuring instrument. That doesn't mean inflation has no real costs. An elastic measuring instrument is a serious problem whenever decisions have to be coordinated over space and time. A large real cost of inflation is the effort and other resources that people devote to "beating" it. As evidence, thumb through a few of the unbelievable number of paperback books published in recent years telling people how to come out ahead or at least stay even during periods of inflation.

Inflation and Social Conflict

The most serious cost of inflation to a society such as ours, however, may be the damage it does to our resources of mutual trust and goodwill. We have tried to call your attention on several occasions to a fact that was well appreciated by Adam Smith, but which his modern successors in the economics profession too often slight. The cooperation that is the essence of society and of civilization presupposes a substantial amount of self-restraint on the part of its members, or a willingness to include the interests of others in the conception of one's own interests. If people come to believe that they're being defrauded, they will more readily throw off the constraints of ethics and do unto others what they think is being done unto them. When the illusory losses of inflation are added to the actual redistributions of wealth that inflation causes, the aggregate sense of injustice may rise to a critical level.

If people then organize into groups to secure a redress of their grievances through coercion, they feed the anger and resentment of others. School teachers striking in protest against salaries that don't keep pace with inflation add to citizen dissatisfaction with the school system and the taxes required to support it. The inflation that convinces tenants they are the victims of landlord exploitation—but which actually reduces the relative price of renting—creates low vacancy rates. This makes it appear that higher prices are producing less rental

housing. Meanwhile, the net revenue of landlords will be falling, bringing with it the predictable consequences for maintenance and the state of landlord-tenant feelings. Political demands become more strident when people believe they are being victimized, and the total of claims that groups start to insist on as their right climbs well above 100 percent of the society's output. These demands become concentrated on government because government is increasingly thought to have the duty and the power to set all things right. Elected officials will find themselves under pressure to do something, even if that something provides only short-term symptomatic relief and worsens the problem in the long run. Every action taken by government in response to mounting levels of citizen discontent creates a reason for doing more, either in response to the next interest group or to remedy the unanticipated problems caused by the last response. When the sum of the expectations by far exceeds the sum of what is available to satisfy them—and people begin using coercion to satisfy their expectations—something must give way. It could too easily be the consensus on which the society itself is founded.

What Happens in a Recession?

Recession is related to *recede,* which means to withdraw or retreat. A recession is a retreat from earlier rates of growth in the total output of the economy. By a general consent earned over many years, the National Bureau of Economic Research, a private, nonprofit research organization, has the privilege of deciding officially when a slowdown in growth has become a recession. But would every substantial slowdown in growth have to be a recession? Is perpetual growth the only possible norm?

That implication is avoided when we realize that *the costs of a recession are largely the costs of disappointed expectations.* The point is fundamental. If we lose sight of the relationship between recession and disappointment, we'll find ourselves unable to distinguish between unemployment and leisure, or between changes that leave people worse off than before and changes that add to human welfare. We may also miss seeing the crucial role that uncertainty plays in causing recessions and thereby conclude that recessions can be cured with remedies that are more likely to aggravate the disease.

If a recession were merely a slowdown in the rate of economic growth, recessions would be popular with advocates of zero economic growth and all those who think we should reduce our emphasis on the production of marketable goods. But recessions aren't popular with these groups or anyone

else, because they entail *unintended and therefore disruptive slowdowns* in the rate of economic growth. Bare statistics on aggregate output, like the data on gross national product that we'll be looking at in the next chapter, are incapable of revealing disappointed expectations. We may be able to infer widespread disappointment from such statistics, but aggregate data could truly measure a recession only if they could somehow measure the gaps between the output that people had counted on producing and what they finally decided to produce.

Producers' expectations are frustrated every day, of course. But every day some other producers are delighted to discover that events have turned out *better* than they had expected. A recession occurs when, for some reason, the number and depth of the disappointments increase, without any compensating increase in the quantity and quality of delightful surprises. Why that occurs and what can be done about it will be a major question in the chapters ahead.

We described the phenomenon of recession just now by referring to output or production. The costs and causes of recessions, however, may be better described in terms of income. It is the lost income that finally disappoints producers, and it is declining income that induces producers to cut back on the rate of output. The owners or managers of business firms count on selling some quantity of their product at some anticipated price. But when sales prove disappointing, inventories of unsold goods pile up, costs run ahead of revenues, and so production is slowed down or stopped altogether for a while. Net income is the criterion that guides these decisions.

When business firms reduce their rate of production below what they had intended earlier, they often lay workers off and thereby create unemployment. This is the problem that first comes to mind when we think about recessions: a rising rate of unemployment. But what exactly is the problem? Once again we must ask for patience from the reader who thinks the question is stupid because the answer is obvious. The answer is obvious only until we begin thinking about it carefully.

When Is Unemployment a Problem?

Recessions do indeed cause unemployment to increase. But it doesn't increase from zero, and it doesn't fall back to zero when the recession is over. Even in the year 1944, 1.2 percent of the labor force was classified as unemployed, at a time when one-sixth of the entire labor force was in the armed

forces, and people were being urged to leave school to take jobs, to come out of retirement, and to work six- or seven-day weeks. No one who lived through those labor-hungry years would believe that 1.2 percent of the labor force could not find jobs in 1944.

There is some amount of unemployment that no one worries about because it isn't a problem. How much is that? What is an acceptable unemployment rate? How can we distinguish problem unemployment from nonproblem unemployment? The distinction is important, because when unemployment reaches a "problem level," political pressure to do something about it begins to build. What the federal government does in response to these pressures will definitely have costs and may have other undesirable consequences, especially if unemployment is, in reality, not above the critical "problem level." But where is that level and how do we recognize it?

In some circles it is still common practice to duck the whole question by saying something like this: unemployment becomes a problem when it rises above the level of purely "frictional" unemployment. And "frictional" unemployment is the amount of unemployment that poses no problem because it represents ordinary labor-market turnover. This might be a satisfactory procedure if we had reason to believe that "ordinary labor-market turnover" was some identifiable constant over time. Quite to the contrary, however, we have excellent reasons for supposing that "ordinary labor-market turnover" is a variable, rather than a constant, and that it changes in response to a variety of factors that have shifted substantially in recent years.

What we would really like to do is find some way to distinguish clearly between those who are *unemployed* and those who are merely *not employed*. The extreme cases are easy to distinguish. Some people would do almost anything to find satisfactory employment, whereas there is almost nothing that would persuade others to accept a job. But did you spot the fudge factors in that preceding sentence? People who would describe themselves as "desperate" for work will nonetheless decline *some* job opportunities in the expectation of finding something better. And very few of those who say they "absolutely" don't want a job would decline *every* offer that might come their way. People who say they "can't find a job" mean they can't find a job at which they're willing to work. Those who say they "don't want to work" mean that they don't want to work at any job they can find. In some cases, the difference between those two situations isn't going to be discernible to an outside observer.

Employed, Not Employed, and Unemployed

The outside observers on whom we depend to make this distinction for us are some very highly trained employees of the U.S. government. The official data on U.S. unemployment are published by the Bureau of Labor Statistics (BLS), an agency in the U.S. Department of Labor. The source of the data is the *Current Population Survey,* a sample survey of households which the Bureau of Census conducts on behalf of the BLS. The sample consists of about 60,000 households, selected to represent the entire population and interviewed monthly. (The data are *not* derived, contrary to what many people think, from claims for unemployment compensation.)

In order to be included at all in the BLS report, a person must first be in *the noninstitutional population.* This is *the total of those who are 16 years of age or older, and not residing in an institution* such as a prison or a hospital.

Each person in the noninstitutional population is then classified as either employed, unemployed, or not in the labor force. Deciding who is employed presents no serious problems. But what is the distinction between someone who is *unemployed* and someone who is "not in the labor force" and therefore merely *not employed?* The BLS has developed precise criteria for distinguishing between these two groups and measures the size of each with considerable confidence. Measurement is not the problem. The problem is the significance of the distinction, especially in light of the highly diverse and changing costs to particular people of being "not in the labor force" or being officially unemployed.

Let's look more closely. To be classified in the household survey as unemployed, an individual must (1) be in the noninstitutional population; (2) have been without employment during the survey week; (3) have made specific efforts to find employment sometime during the preceding four weeks; and (4) be presently available for work. (Persons who are on layoff or are waiting to start a new job within 30 days are counted as unemployed without meeting the third criterion above, which requires that they be actively looking for employment.) The unemployed divided by the labor force yields the official unemployment rate, which makes the newspapers and the newscasts when the BLS publishes it each month.[1]

Details of this sort don't make very exciting reading. But it is crucial that we know what people must do or not do

[handwritten margin note:]
Total population
— under 16 or institutionalized
= noninstitutional population
— not in the labor force
= labor force
— employed
= unemployed

---

1. Data on the number of people employed or unemployed in any quarter or month are *seasonally adjusted* by the BLS. This means that they have been corrected to eliminate the effects of variations caused entirely by seasonal factors—the closing of schools in June, extra hiring in December, major holidays, and so on. Seasonal adjustment lets us detect trends that would otherwise be concealed or exaggerated by purely seasonal fluctuations.

in order to meet the BLS criteria for being unemployed. There is simply no way to understand the significance of unemployment or the nature of the problem it presents unless we know something about the cost of being unemployed to those who choose that status.

Labor-Market Decisions

Choose it? The notion that people choose to be unemployed seems at first to contradict the very concept of unemployment. But economic theory tries to explain *all* behavior as the consequence of choice. Insofar as people have no discernible or significant amount of choice in a situation, economic theory has nothing useful to say about their behavior. In assuming that unemployment results from the choices people make, we are not assuming that everyone has good choices, much less that unemployed people enjoy their condition. To choose simply means to select the best available alternative, on the basis of one's expectations regarding relative costs and benefits. The economic way of thinking urges us to explain changes in social phenomena, including changes in unemployment rates, as consequences of changes in perceived costs and benefits.

The BLS definition makes quite clear the specific choices that produce the status called "unemployed": (1) a decision to look actively for employment, and (2) a decision not to accept the employment opportunities offered. Both clearly are choices people make. The first decision stands at the fork that leads either to being unemployed or to being out of the labor force. The second decision marks the fork that leads to employment or to continued unemployment. For large numbers of people, the anticipated benefits and costs of particular decisions at those forks have changed considerably in recent years. As a result, particular unemployment rates don't mean what they meant 25 years ago or even ten years ago.

Unemployment Rates and Employment Rates

Table 15A summarizes labor force activity in the U.S. from 1950 through 1985. The unemployment rates for each year appear under "Unemployed" in the column headed "Percent of labor force." If you run your eye down that column, you will notice that the unemployment rate rises and falls. The sudden increases usually mark the appearance of recessions, while the subsequent (and slower) declines in the rate reflect recovery from the recessions.

The column reveals something else: a strong upward drift

Table 15A Employment status of the noninstitutional population 16 years and over, 1950 to 1985 (numbers in thousands)

Year	Noninstitutional population	Number in labor force	Percent of noninstitutional population in labor force	Labor force					Not in labor force	Employed as percent of noninstitutional population
				Employed			Unemployed			
				Total employed	Resident armed forces	Civilian employment	Number unemployed	Percent of labor force		
1950	106,164	63,377	59.7	60,087	1,169	58,918	3,288	5.2	42,787	56.6
1951	106,764	64,160	60.1	62,104	2,143	59,961	2,055	3.2	42,604	58.2
1952	107,617	64,524	60.0	62,636	2,386	60,250	1,883	2.9	43,093	58.2
1953	109,287	65,246	59.7	63,410	2,231	61,179	1,834	2.8	44,041	58.0
1954	110,463	65,785	59.6	62,251	2,142	60,109	3,532	5.4	44,678	56.4
1955	111,747	67,087	60.0	64,234	2,064	62,170	2,852	4.3	44,660	57.5
1956	112,919	68,517	60.7	65,764	1,965	63,799	2,750	4.0	44,402	58.2
1957	114,213	68,877	60.3	66,019	1,948	64,071	2,859	4.2	45,336	57.8
1958	115,574	69,486	60.1	64,883	1,847	63,036	4,602	6.6	46,088	56.1
1959	117,117	70,157	59.9	66,418	1,788	64,630	3,740	5.3	46,960	56.7
1960	119,106	71,489	60.0	67,639	1,861	65,778	3,852	5.4	47,617	56.8
1961	120,671	72,359	60.0	67,646	1,900	65,746	4,714	6.5	48,312	56.1
1962	122,214	72,675	59.5	68,763	2,061	66,702	3,911	5.4	49,539	56.3
1963	124,422	73,839	59.3	69,768	2,006	67,762	4,070	5.5	50,583	56.1
1964	126,503	75,109	59.4	71,323	2,018	69,305	3,786	5.0	51,394	56.4

Year										
1965	128,459	59.5	76,401	73,034	1,946	71,088	3,366	4.4	52,058	56.9
1966	130,180	59.8	77,892	75,017	2,122	72,895	2,875	3.7	52,288	57.6
1967	132,092	60.2	79,565	76,590	2,218	74,372	2,975	3.7	52,527	58.0
1968	134,281	60.3	80,990	78,173	2,253	75,920	2,817	3.5	53,291	58.2
1969	136,573	60.8	82,972	80,140	2,238	77,902	2,832	3.4	53,602	58.7
1970	139,203	61.0	84,889	80,796	2,118	78,678	4,093	4.8	54,315	58.0
1971	142,189	60.7	86,355	81,340	1,973	79,367	5,016	5.8	55,834	57.2
1972	145,939	60.9	88,847	83,966	1,813	82,153	4,882	5.5	57,091	57.5
1973	148,870	61.3	91,203	86,838	1,774	85,064	4,365	4.8	57,667	58.3
1974	151,841	61.7	93,670	88,515	1,721	86,794	5,156	5.5	58,171	58.3
1975	154,831	61.6	95,453	87,524	1,678	85,846	7,929	8.3	59,377	56.5
1976	157,818	62.0	97,826	90,420	1,668	88,752	7,406	7.6	59,991	57.3
1977	160,689	62.6	100,665	93,673	1,656	92,017	6,991	6.9	60,025	58.3
1978	163,541	63.5	103,882	97,679	1,631	96,048	6,202	6.0	59,659	59.8
1979	166,460	64.0	106,559	100,421	1,597	98,824	6,137	5.8	59,900	60.3
1980	169,349	64.1	108,544	100,907	1,604	99,303	7,637	7.0	60,806	59.6
1981	171,775	64.2	110,315	102,042	1,645	100,397	8,273	7.5	61,460	59.4
1982	173,939	64.3	111,872	101,194	1,668	99,526	10,678	9.5	62,067	58.2
1983	175,891	64.4	113,226	102,510	1,676	100,834	10,717	9.5	62,665	58.3
1984	178,080	64.7	115,241	106,702	1,697	105,005	8,539	7.4	62,839	59.9
1985	179,912	65.1	117,167	108,856	1,706	107,150	8,312	7.1	62,745	60.5
1986	182,293	65.6	119,540	111,303	1,706	109,597	8,237	6.9	62,753	61.1

Source: Bureau of Labor Statistics

in the unemployment rate since 1970. The 7.1 percent rate in 1985, which was *not* a recession year, was higher than the rate experienced in any year, including recession years, in the 1950s or 1960s. Why has this occurred? What's been happening since 1970? Why has the unemployment rate gotten "stuck" at such high levels in recent years?

A lot of answers commonly given to that question are demonstrably wrong. The rising unemployment rates of recent years can't be blamed on automation or foreign competition or any other factor that might have slowed down job creation, because jobs were in fact created in the U.S. economy even faster after 1970 than in the preceding two decades. The column labeled "Total employed" tells the story. From 1970 to 1985, the number of persons employed increased 35 percent, whereas in the fifteen years prior to 1970 total employment had increased by less than 25 percent.

The last column of the table reveals that the upward drift in the unemployment rate since 1970 has been accompanied by a significant rise in the *employment* rate. That's not the logical impossibility it appears to be. The employment rate compares employment with population. It shows that a higher percentage of working-age Americans were actually employed in 1985, when the unemployment rate was 7.1 percent, than had been employed in 1969, when the unemployment rate was only 3.4 percent. The basic reason for this surprising fact is that many more people *wanted* to work in 1985 than in 1969. The labor force participation rate, shown in the fourth column, jumped from 61 to 65 percent over the course of those fifteen years.

The principal cause, as you might suspect, was the decision of so many more women to enter the labor force. There was actually a decline in the rate of labor force participation by males between 1969 and 1985, but the flow of females into the labor force more than made up for it. Whereas 373 of every 1000 employed civilians in the U.S. were female in 1969, 441 of every 1000 were female in 1985.

The Unemployment Puzzle

The key question:
__Why__ do some people who say they want a job but who don't have one not make stronger efforts to find employment?

These data on employment ought to relieve any fears that the rising unemployment rate of recent years reflects some kind of breakdown in the economic system's capacity to create jobs. A puzzle nonetheless remains. Why are so many more job seekers today failing to find what they're looking for? Why has the percentage of those who want jobs but don't have them more than doubled since the 1960s? Some will suppose that the higher rate of labor force participation itself

supplies the answer: any time more are looking for something, a smaller percentage will succeed in finding it. But this belief reflects the common fallacy that jobs are scarce goods. They really are not. As long as our wants for producible goods remain unsatisfied, we should not run out of useful tasks for people to perform. A rise in the unemployment rate reflects not a growing scarcity of jobs but rather a change in the expected costs and benefits of looking for and accepting employment.

Costs and Decisions

We must beware of aggregation. Both the cost of taking a job and the cost of not taking one will differ considerably from one person to another, depending on such factors as skill, experience, age, family responsibilities, other sources of income, and even the values and attitudes of those whose opinions the person respects.

Consider the situation of teenagers living with their families. They often want jobs and may actively seek them in ways that qualify them for inclusion in the ranks of the officially unemployed. But if they're currently attending school, they are "presently available" for a very limited number of jobs. If they're on summer vacation, employers won't want to hire them for jobs that require a lot of training, so they aren't really "available" for these jobs either. If they're out of high school but trying to make up their minds about college, they'll be reluctant to accept any job that requires a commitment. Moreover, the job opportunities available to them will tend to be relatively unattractive, because employers don't want to pay much to teenagers, who tend to be unskilled and who quit before the employer has recovered the cost of training them.

But someone receiving free room and board from parents can afford to search for a long time, or to quit a job that proves unsatisfactory and start looking again. Any job will begin to seem unsatisfactory to teenagers who discover that they must work while their friends are partying. When we put all this together, we see that the cost of taking and keeping a job is high and rising for most teenagers, and that the cost of continuing to look is relatively low. Should we be either surprised or disturbed, then, to discover that the unemployment rate among people 16 to 19 years old was 18.6 percent in 1985?

Since lost income is usually the main cost of being unemployed, anything that promises to maintain people's incomes while they're not working is likely to increase the

unemployment rate. Thus the sizeable expansion since the 1960s in government welfare grants has undoubtedly contributed to the increase in unemployment.

Since the 1960s, we have offered unemployment insurance to more workers, extended the duration of benefits, and generally loosened the criteria for eligibility. Of course, this won't induce people with well paid and highly satisfying jobs to get themselves fired so they can start drawing unemployment compensation. At the margin, however, more generous unemployment benefits do make people less determined to hang on to current jobs and less eager to accept new ones, thus raising the unemployment rate. In Holland, where unemployment benefits replace, for extended periods, from 75 to 99 percent of the net income from working, and where eligibility criteria are not very strict, the unemployment rate in 1984 was 18 percent. The wonder is that it's not higher.

The rise since the 1960s in the number of multi-earner families must have had the same kind of effect. Inflation has aggravated this effect by boosting families into much higher income-tax brackets since the 1960s. When we add to this the impact of the higher social security tax on earnings, the financial incentive for a second earner to find a new job when an old one has been lost diminishes dramatically; it will sometimes even be negative until eligibility for unemployment compensation has been exhausted.

Expectations and Reality

Remember, too, that economic decisions depend on expectations. People enter the labor force because they *expect* to find satisfactory employment. If for some reason the expectations of many labor force entrants are unrealistically high, the result will be an increase in the unemployment rate. Suppose, for example, that more opportunities open up in the business world for women who want to enter management. These improved prospects will induce more women to enter or remain in the labor force. It's quite possible that the expectation of more and better career opportunities for women could pull so many additional women into the labor force that the female unemployment rate would actually rise. Unemployment would remain high until expectations adjusted to reality—or reality caught up with expectations.

Similarly, if recent college graduates or freshly minted lawyers hold exaggerated views about the value of their degrees in the labor market, the unemployment rate among them will rise. Steelworkers who are accustomed to wage rates about double the average of the wages usually paid in manufacturing will be slow to accept employment at lower

wages when the steel companies for which they've been working go out of business. They aren't very different from homeowners who refuse to believe that the house they are trying to sell won't move at the price they're asking; "for sale" signs consequently multiply and stay up longer in a declining real estate market.

A slowing in the rate of inflation will have a similar effect on the unemployment rate through the wedge that it opens between expected and actual wage offers. If a protracted period of high inflation has accustomed employees to large annual wage increases, they may find employers' wage offers inadequate once the inflation rate slows down. Employees who expect a higher wage than they are offered will more readily give up existing jobs and will prolong their searches for new jobs, which is going to raise the unemployment rate.

A Summing Up

We don't want to point out so many trees that you lose sight of the forest. The principal thesis we've been trying to establish is that unemployment is not simply something that happens *to* people, like being hit by lightning. In a recession, the demand for labor decreases, and this causes unemployment to rise. The recovery after a recession increases the demand for labor, and unemployment falls. But it doesn't follow from this that all unemployment is the result of an inadequate demand for labor. Unemployment rates are the product of complex decisions by both demanders and suppliers of labor, all of whom pay attention to the expected opportunity costs of their decisions to supply or to demand.

Moreover, the costs of unemployment don't fall with equal severity on every unemployed person and don't take the same form from one person to another. For some, the lost income is the principal cost of unemployment. For others, the cost of unemployment will be the loss of goods that they value even more highly than money income: a sense of contributing, a daily discipline, workplace associations, challenge and variety. For some people the sum of these costs will be crushing; for others the costs will be negligible; and for a few who receive unemployment compensation and live in families with more than one earner, the costs can even be negative.

There is no undifferentiated mass called *the unemployed*, upon whom the burdens of unemployment fall. There is no constant number above which unemployment first begins to be a problem. There is no single policy suitable for reducing all unemployment. There is no clear line that divides the unemployed from those who happen to be only "not em-

ployed." In the last analysis, the distinction between suffering unemployment and enjoying leisure can be made only by the person who calculates the relative net advantages of taking and of not taking a job.

None of these explanations of unemployment, however, tells us why recessions occur, pushing unemployment substantially higher for prolonged periods. We must turn our attention now to the causes and consequences of fluctuations in the overall or aggregate level of economic activity.

Once Over Lightly

Inflation is an increase in the average money price of goods. It is not an increase in the cost of living but a decrease in the purchasing power of money.

Inflation does impose real burdens on a society. It redistributes wealth, induces people to spend resources trying to anticipate its effects, and stimulates dissatisfaction and conflict among people who believe, rightly or wrongly, that they're being harmed by inflation. All of these are effects of the increased uncertainty that inflation introduces into people's estimates of future prices.

A recession is an unanticipated and disruptive slowdown in the rate of increase in total output and income.

Recessions add to unemployment by causing the demand for some goods—and hence for the labor of those who produce the goods—to fall short of expectations.

The level of unemployment depends on the supply of labor as well as the demand. The Bureau of Labor Statistics counts as unemployed all those who are not currently employed *and* are actively seeking employment. Both the decision to enter the labor force and the decision not to accept particular job offers will depend on people's estimates of the relative advantages of alternative opportunities.

Different unemployment rates for different population groups do not merely reflect differences in the demand for the labor services of the people in those groups. They also reflect variations in the cost to different people of searching for, accepting, and retaining employment.

Unemployment rates have been high in the 1970s and 1980s in comparison with unemployment rates in the 1950s and 1960s. But labor force participation rates and employment rates have also risen to record-high levels in the current decade.

Higher unemployment rates coupled with rising employment rates suggest that the expected benefits and costs both of entering the labor force and of remaining unemployed have been changing in recent years for many members of the noninstitutional population.

QUESTIONS FOR DISCUSSION

1. Was the "cost of living" in the United States higher or lower in 1985 than it had been in 1955?

   (a) The following data are adapted from the consumer price index:
   - The amount of food that could be purchased for a dollar in 1985 cost only 26¢ in 1955.
   - A dollar's worth of housing in 1985 could have been rented in 1955 for 32¢.
   - The clothing that a dollar bought in 1985 was available for 45¢ in 1955.
   - A dollar's worth of medical care in 1985 cost only 16¢ in 1955.

   Why do these data give us no answer to the question above?

   (b) Here are some additional data that might help you answer the question: the average hourly earnings of workers employed in the private sector outside of agriculture were about $1.70 in 1955 and $8.60 in 1985.

   (c) The data above suggest that one hour's wage of an average worker purchased considerably more food, shelter, and clothing in 1985 than it had done in 1955, but somewhat less medical care. Can you think of some good reasons for believing that the data on medical care are misleading? (Hint: The good that we are after when we purchase medical care is *health*. Did the medical services available in 1955 produce better health as effectively as medical services did in 1985?)

2. The text asserts that a society which did not make use of money but conducted all exchange by barter logically could not experience inflation. If you doubt this, ask yourself what form inflation could take in a bartering society. What would it mean to say that the average price of all goods in such a society had risen 10 percent?

3. The figure below compares the annual inflation rate in the U.S. from 1955

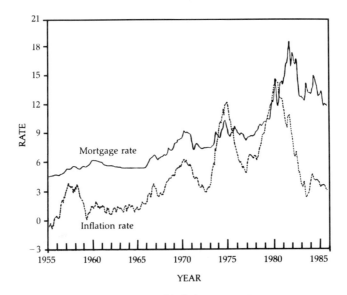

Figure 15A Mortgage rates and inflation rates

to 1985 with the average annual rate of return received by holders of home mortgages over this same period.

(a) What was the approximate real rate of return on mortgage loans in 1955? In 1970? In 1975? In 1985?

(b) How did the negative rate of return in 1975 and 1980 contribute to the very high rate of return after 1983?

(c) The inflation rate after 1983 fell to approximately what it had been from 1956 to 1958. Mortgage rates rose very little in response to the accelerated inflation of the late 1950s. Why were they so slow to fall in response to the disinflation of the early 1980s?

4. Numerous public-opinion surveys in the 1970s showed that the majority of Americans regarded inflation as a more serious threat than unemployment.

(a) Did this imply that the majority of Americans would rather be unemployed in a period of stable prices than employed in a time of rising prices?

(b) If the management of a firm allowed employees to vote on whether the firm should lay off 10 percent of the employees or reduce wage rates by 5 percent, how do you think they would vote? Do you think the outcome of the vote would depend on whether the employees knew in advance exactly who would be laid off?

5. If inflation redistributes income and wealth, there will be gainers as well as losers. Which classes and categories of people are most likely to gain and lose from an inflation? What difference does it make how well the inflation is anticipated?

6. Professor Plato received an annual salary of $12,000 in 1965 and $35,000 in 1985. The price level increased about 250 percent between 1965 and 1985.

(a) How did his real income change from 1965 to 1985?

(b) Is Professor Plato likely to think that his additional experience entitled him to a much larger salary in 1985?

(c) Do you think it was inflation or changed conditions of supply and demand that caused Professor Plato's real income to fall between 1965 and 1985?

(d) Professor Plato's college classmate, Rock Igneous, was also earning $12,000 a year in 1965, working as a mining engineer. In 1985 Rock's salary was $60,000. Why do you suppose that he fared so much better than Professor Plato in this inflationary period?

(e) Do you think it would have been easier or harder for the college to reduce Plato's salary from $12,000 to $10,000 in a period of stable prices than to raise it from $12,000 to $35,000 in a period when prices rose 250 percent? Why?

7. A letter to the editor of the *Wall Street Journal* (October 15, 1985) complained that it was "not only a fallacy but a fraud" for the Bureau of Labor Statistics to claim that the price level had risen only 3.5 percent during the past year. As evidence the writer cited the following price increases during the preceding twelve-month period: first-class postage, 20¢ to 22¢; the Sunday *New York Times*, $1 to $1.25; the *Wall Street Journal*, 40¢ to 50¢; "some" coinbox telephone calls, 10¢ to 25¢.

An accompanying letter told an opposite story: "The orange juice I buy is $1.99 a quart; a year ago it was $2.49. My 'jug wine' is $4.09, as opposed

to $4.49 a year ago. Instant coffee is $3.19, up from $2.99, but has been running a 30-cent coupon offer all summer."

Is it possible for the price level to rise at different rates for different people?

8. Why do you suppose it costs over 40 percent more to maintain a living standard in Oakland, California, than it costs to maintain a comparable standard in El Paso, Texas? Would it be correct to say that the cost of living is higher in Oakland?

9. A *Wall Street Journal* article of August 13, 1985, describes the effects of runaway inflation on daily life in Bolivia, where prices were rising at an annual rate of 8000 percent.

   (a) If prices rise by 18 percent per week, by what percentage will they increase in the course of a year? (You can use Table 11A to find the answer.)

   (b) What is the present value of one dollar in wages to be received at the end of a four-week pay period when inflation is running at a rate of 18 percent per week? (Use Table 11B.)

   (c) Why do you suppose that Bolivians try to convert their wages into either goods or U.S. dollars immediately upon receipt?

   (d) If peso prices for goods are rising in Bolivia while U.S. dollar prices being quoted for the same goods are stable, is Bolivia experiencing inflation or is it not? How does this example illustrate the point that inflation is a fall in the value of money?

   (e) The *Journal* quotes a Bolivian as saying, "We don't produce anything. We are all currency speculators." How can the people of a country survive if they are all currency speculators?

   (f) The same Bolivian commented: "People don't know what's good and bad anymore. We have become an amoral society." A prominent politician said: "We've learned you must be an idiot to do things by the rules." In what manner does runaway inflation undermine social morality?

10. In Switzerland, an unemployment rate of 1 percent has long been considered *high*. When recession hit Switzerland in the mid-1970s, the official unemployment rate stayed below 1 percent even when total manufacturing employment declined by more than 15 percent over a two-year period. How do you suppose the Swiss manage to maintain such a low unemployment rate even in the face of rapidly declining employment opportunities? (It may help you to know that about 10 percent of the Swiss population is made up of foreign workers, mostly Italians, Spanish, Portuguese, and Yugoslavs, who are not allowed to stay in Switzerland without jobs.)

11. Unemployment does not exist by definition in the Soviet Union, where any unemployment at all is held to be inconsistent with socialism. It is not just a matter of definition, however. There are so many jobs relative to workers that *Pravda,* the Communist Party newspaper, has in recent years urged the passage of laws that would prohibit job-quitting without adequate cause and would subject able-bodied workers to arrest if they are out of work for more than two weeks. How do you suppose the Soviet Union maintains a surplus of jobs while the United States seems to have a surplus of workers?

12. The unemployment rates in West Germany, France, and England were about

8 percent, 10 percent, and 13 percent respectively in 1985. Why do you think they were so much higher than in the U.S.S.R.?

13. Determine the missing numbers for the following set of imaginary U.S. data, using the definitions provided in the text:

Noninstitutional population	180,000,000
Resident armed forces	2,000,000
Civilian employment	106,000,000
Not in the labor force	64,000,000
Labor force	_____
Unemployed	_____
Unemployment rate	_____
Employment rate	_____

14. Can there be "overfull" employment?

    (a) Suppose that the vacancy rate on apartments in a large city is less than 1 percent. What undesirable consequences might be associated with such a full level of apartment employment? Would you enjoy moving to a city with such a low vacancy rate?

    (b) If you are driving on only 80 percent of the automobile tires you own, is the spare tire unemployed? Would you like to be driving with your tires at "full employment"? Across the Great Salt Lake Desert?

15. Jones is a tool and die maker earning $20 an hour. He is suddenly laid off.

    (a) He frequents employment agencies, reads want ads, and follows up leads on tool-and-die-making jobs for two weeks. Is he unemployed during this time, as the BLS measures unemployment?

    (b) At the end of two weeks he is offered a job driving a bread truck that pays $4.50 an hour. He turns it down. Is he unemployed?

    (c) He receives an offer of a job as a tool and die maker in a city 125 miles away. He turns it down because his teenage children don't want to change high schools. Is he unemployed?

    (d) After three months of searching, Jones becomes discouraged and quits looking. Is he unemployed?

16. A woman is laid off from her job and goes to work for herself (becomes self-employed) "producing" information about alternative job opportunities. How long she will remain self-employed in this way depends on her "productivity" (i.e., whether she is generating what she considers valuable information) and the opportunity cost of this self-employment (which she'll want to continue as long as her anticipated marginal revenue exceeds anticipated marginal cost). How will the duration of measured unemployment be affected by:

    (a) unemployment compensation?

    (b) food-stamp programs?

    (c) persistent rumors that many large firms are beginning to hire?

    (d) a spirit of confidence and optimism?

17. Should the hypothetical individuals who made each of the following statements be classified as unemployed or as not in the labor force? Which of them is voluntarily rather than involuntarily unemployed?

    (a) "I quit my job and I'm going to remain unemployed until I find a job that pays $1000 for 10 hours' work a week."

(b) "I was laid off last month. I had a great job as marketing consultant to a franchising chain. They paid me $1000 a week for about 10 hours of work. I'm going to keep looking until I find another job like that one."

(c) "I decided I could no longer be a part of the military-industrial complex, so I quit my job. I'm looking now for an engineer's position that doesn't require me to participate in murder, pollution, and mind-raping."

(d) "When they laid me off, I figured I could easily find another job in teaching. But now I don't care. I'll take any job at all that pays what I used to get."

(e) "I've been out of work for six months, and I'm pretty desperate. I'll do anything that's legal to get food for my family. But I have an invalid wife and five small children, so I can't take any job that pays less than $300 a week."

(f) "I could get any one of a dozen jobs tomorrow. But I don't want to. I'm eligible for three more months of unemployment compensation, so I'm just going to take it easy until the checks run out. Oh, if something really good turned up, I'd take it, of course."

(g) "I could get any one of a dozen jobs tomorrow. But I don't want to. I'm eligible for three more months of unemployment compensation, so I'm just going to spend my time really looking. I'm going to use those three months to find the very best job I can possibly get."

Aggregate Supply and Aggregate Demand

How do we measure changes in the value of money or the price level? How do we measure changes in the rate at which we are producing total output? And what do those measures tell us about the performance of the U.S. economy in recent years?

Gross National Product

The experience of the Great Depression in the 1930s gave encouragement to efforts that had begun around 1920 to compile reliable data on the overall performance of the U.S. economy. The best-known statistical series evolving out of these efforts is the national income and product accounts, compiled by the Bureau of Economic Analysis in the U.S. Department of Commerce. If you read only the front page of the daily newspaper, you will have encountered the gross national product. This is the most comprehensive item in the Department of Commerce accounts and the one most frequently cited. Some people watch the behavior of GNP, as it is familiarly known, with the intensity of children listening to the weather report on the morning of a picnic.

The gross national product is the market value of all the final goods produced in the entire country in the course of a year. Only the value of final goods is calculated in order to minimize overcounting. If the Bureau of Economic Analysis added the value of all the sheet metal to the value of all the automobiles produced in a year, it would have counted some of the sheet metal twice: once when it was sold by the steel companies to automobile manufacturers, and once more as a component

in the final price of the cars. To reduce the amount of such double counting, the value of intermediate goods is assumed to be incorporated into the market price of final goods.

Another way to think of and measure total output is to regard it as the sum of all the successive *value added* at each stage of the production process. In the case of bread, for example, it's the value added successively by the wheat farmer, the miller, the baker, the distributor, and the retailer as the loaf wends it way toward the customer's shopping cart. The price of the final good is then the summed value of all these successive contributions to output.

As the name of the accounts suggests, GNP can also be thought of and calculated as the value of the national income. The national income is the sum of all the payments made in the course of the production process to those who did the producing: the owners of labor, capital, and other resources. The value of the national output must necessarily equal the value of the national income, when properly calculated, because every dollar paid for output becomes income for someone. An apparent exception would be the amount of tax, such as sales tax, paid on a purchase. But this is income, too; it's income for government, which uses it to pay for the resources that government employs in the process of producing goods.

Another question might arise about unsold goods. They are part of the year's output, but since they aren't sold, they don't seem to generate income for anyone. This is handled in the accounts by assuming that the business firm that produced the goods also bought them. It surely had to pay to get them produced. And while it may not have intended to buy them itself, goods produced and not sold are indeed added, however reluctantly, to the inventories of the firm that produced them.

Thus we can actually measure GNP in *three* ways, all of which would yield the same total if we made no errors in counting: (1) the value added by each producer in the course of contributing to the year's total output of final goods; (2) the total income received, in the form of wages and salaries, interest, rent, and profits, by those who contributed the resources used to produce the year's total output; (3) the total purchases of final goods by households, business firms, and government, plus the purchases of foreigners in excess of what the foreigners sold us in return. When unsold goods are counted as additions to inventory and added to the total purchases of business firms, the sum of household, business, government, and (net) foreign expenditures on final goods must add up exactly to the total value of the goods produced.

Gross national product is

– the sum of all the value added by producers at each stage of the production process,

or

– the total income received by those producers,

or

– total purchases of newly produced final goods.

Some Limitations of National Income Accounting

Never make the mistake of confusing the gross national product with gross national well-being. The concept of GNP is based on so many conventions, with so many essentially arbitrary inclusions and omissions, that it should never be used to compare the well-being of different nations. The most it can do is indicate whether we're going faster or slowing down. And even there it gives misleading indications if we try to make comparisons over a long period of time.

Two examples may be enough to teach you caution. Among the services not counted by the Department of Commerce statisticians in the calculation of GNP are the services of the spouse who maintains the home. It is too difficult to evaluate these services, despite their enormous importance, so they are completely excluded from the accounts. But the value of hired housekeepers' service *can* be measured, by the payments made to obtain them; hence they do enter into the accounts. As a result, GNP will tend to decline as a direct consequence of marriages and increase with a rising divorce rate. It is doubtful that real welfare moves in the same direction. Also, as more women enter the labor force, the GNP expands by the amount of their contribution to total output, as measured by their earnings. Since there is no deduction, however, for the value of the work they are no longer doing at home, the increase in GNP exaggerates the increase in the value of total output—unless their housework had no value.

A second example to teach caution: when a coal-burning station generates electricity, its output enters GNP. When people are hired to clean and paint as a consequence of the sooty fallout from the generating plant, GNP rises once more. Overcounting obviously occurs in this case. It would make sense, if we were interested in welfare, to deduct the cost of the cleaning from the value of the electricity generated. If Chapter 13 did not put you sufficiently on guard, then be warned once more: the consequences for human welfare of particular economic decisions are not always what they seem at first glance. Systems for keeping score are useful, but they inevitably harbor deficiencies that must be kept in mind by those who use them. And the good life is far more (or is it far less?) than the simple sum of the values that enter into the national income and product accounts.

Nominal and Real Gross National Product

Can we use the gross national product to represent the total output of goods? We clearly cannot, because GNP is the

product of prices as well as quantities. Consider the decade of the 1970s, when the gross national product rose from one trillion to two and one-half trillion dollars. Only a small part of this represented an increase in the quantity of goods produced; most of it was a fictitious or purely nominal increase attributable to the rapid inflation that occurred in the 1970s.

The Bureau of Economic Analysis comes to our aid at this point by calculating for each period the value that GNP would have had if prices had remained unchanged. The technique they use is to figure the value of the current period's output in terms of the prices that obtained in an earlier year, chosen for reference purposes. The reference year is currently 1982. Let's see how the Bureau adjusts the nominal measure of GNP to arrive at a real measure of the quantity of goods produced.

Nominal GNP, or GNP in current dollars, was $2,508.2 billion in 1979. If all the goods produced in 1979 were valued at base-year prices, the prices that prevailed for those goods in 1982, the GNP would have been $3,192.4 billion.

1979 GNP :

$ 2,508 billion in 1979 prices
$ 3,192 billion in 1982 prices

1970 GNP :

$1,016 billion in 1970 prices
$2,416 billion in 1982 prices

$$2416 \overline{)3192} \quad 1.32$$

Nominal GNP in 1970 was $1,015.5 billion. Measured in the prices that those goods came to command in 1982, however, the value of 1970 GNP was $2,416.2 billion.

Now we can calculate the real increase in gross national product during the 1970s. Total output or the aggregate quantity of goods produced rose 32 percent from 1970 to 1979. That's far less than the almost 150 percent increase in nominal gross national product during the decade.

Real gross national product is the value of all final goods produced in a year stated in unchanging prices, specifically, the prices that held in the base year, which is presently 1982. It is our most comprehensive measure of changes in the rate at which goods are being produced.

The Implicit GNP Deflator

We also now have at hand a measure of changes in the overall price level or the value of money. Since nominal GNP was $2,508.2 billion and real GNP was $3,192.4 billion in 1979, the average price of GNP goods in 1979 must have been 78.6 percent of what they were in the base year of 1982. Nominal GNP divided by real GNP is the *implicit GNP deflator*. It is implicit in the definitions of real and nominal GNP. It is called the deflator because it can be used to deflate (or inflate) current-dollar calculations in order to arrive at a measure of real changes in output. It functions as a price index, with prices in the year 1982 set equal to 100 (percent).

$$\frac{\$ 2,508}{\$ 3,192} = .786$$

The GNP deflator is our most comprehensive measure of changes in the price level or the purchasing power of

money, and the one that was used in Chapter 15 to discuss
changing rates of inflation. It is not the best-known measure,
however. That distinction belongs to the consumer price
index, a measure of changes in the money price of goods that
enter into the budgets of typical urban consumers. The
Bureau of Labor Statistics surveys consumer prices each month
and publishes the results toward the end of the succeeding
month. The GNP deflator, by contrast, is much more difficult
to calculate, and only appears at quarterly intervals and
after a lengthy time lag. So while the GNP deflator is more
comprehensive, the consumer price index is more timely. It's
the index that makes the front page of newspapers each
month whenever there is substantial public concern about
inflation.

Recessions and Inflations Since 1950

Table 16A presents nominal gross national product, real gross
national product, and the implicit GNP deflator for each
year from 1950 to 1985. It also shows the percentage changes
from the preceding year for real GNP and the price level as
measured by the GNP deflator.

The recessions sustained by the U.S. economy since 1950
show up fairly clearly in the fourth column, as prolonged
slowdowns or actual declines in the rate of real GNP growth.
They aren't completely clear, because the National Bureau
of Economic Research has no hard criteria for infallibly distinguishing a recession from something slightly less serious.
There were officially designated recessions in each of the years
in which real GNP declined—1954, 1958, 1970, 1974-75, 1980,
and 1982; but the National Bureau also decided that a recession
occurred in 1960.

Another portrayal of the history of recessions in the
United States is provided in Figure 16A. This figure charts
quarterly rates of change in real GNP from 1950 to 1985. Real
GNP declined during each quarter in which the line dips
below the zero-change baseline.

Just below Figure 16A is Figure 16B, showing the official
BLS unemployment rates over the same period. Notice that
unemployment rises as a result of recessions, but with a lag; it
falls when the recovery occurs, but again with a distinct lag.
Moreover, the base level of unemployment to which the
economy returns afterward has tended to rise after each
recession, with the exception of the decade following the
1960-61 recession. And since 1970, as was pointed out in the
preceding chapter, the unemployment rate has been "sticking"
at levels that it never reached even in recessions during the
1950s and 1960s. Despite the strong economic recovery that

Table 16A Gross national product (in billions of dollars) and the price level, 1950 to 1985 (Minor inconsistencies are due to errors introduced by rounding.)

Year	Nominal gross national product	Real gross national product, in 1982 prices	Percentage change from preceding year	Implicit GNP deflator (1982 = 100)	Percentage change from preceding year
1950	288.3	1,203.7	8.5	23.9	2.0
1951	333.4	1,328.2	10.3	25.1	4.8
1952	351.6	1,380.0	3.9	25.5	1.5
1953	371.6	1,435.3	4.0	25.9	1.6
1954	372.5	1,416.2	−1.3	26.3	1.6
1955	405.9	1,494.9	5.6	27.2	3.2
1956	428.2	1,525.6	2.1	28.1	3.4
1957	451.0	1,551.1	1.7	29.1	3.6
1958	456.8	1,539.2	−.8	29.7	2.1
1959	495.8	1,629.1	5.8	30.4	2.4
1960	515.3	1,665.3	2.2	30.9	1.6·
1961	533.8	1,708.7	2.6	31.2	1.0
1962	574.6	1,799.4	5.3	31.9	2.2
1963	606.9	1,873.3	4.1	32.4	1.6
1964	649.8	1,973.3	5.3	32.9	1.5
1965	705.1	2,087.6	5.8	33.8	2.7
1966	772.0	2,208.3	5.8	35.0	3.6
1967	816.4	2,271.4	2.9	35.9	2.6
1968	892.7	2,365.6	4.1	37.7	5.0
1969	963.9	2,423.3	2.4	39.8	5.6
1970	1,015.5	2,416.2	−.3	42.0	5.5
1971	1,102.7	2,484.8	2.8	44.4	5.7
1972	1,212.8	2,608.5	5.0	46.5	4.7
1973	1,359.3	2,744.1	5.2	49.5	6.5
1974	1,472.8	2,729.3	−.5	54.0	9.1
1975	1,598.4	2,695.0	−1.3	59.3	9.8
1976	1,782.8	2,826.7	4.9	63.1	6.4
1977	1,990.5	2,958.6	4.7	67.3	6.7
1978	2,249.7	3,115.2	5.3	72.2	7.3
1979	2,508.2	3,192.4	2.5	78.6	8.9
1980	2,732.0	3,187.1	−.2	85.7	9.0
1981	3,052.6	3,248.8	1.9	94.0	9.7
1982	3,166.0	3,166.0	−2.5	100.0	6.4
1983	3,405.7	3,279.1	3.6	103.9	3.9
1984	3,765.0	3,489.9	6.4	107.9	3.8
1985	3,998.1	3,585.2	2.7	111.5	3.3
1986	4,206.1	3,675.0	2.5	114.5	2.7

Source: Bureau of Economic Analysis

took place in 1983 and 1984, the unemployment rate stayed stubbornly above 7 percent through most of 1985.

The last column in Table 16A shows that inflation also became a more serious problem in the 1970s than it had been in the preceding two decades. Inflation averaged about 2½ percent per year in the 1950s and 1960s. From 1970 to 1981, however, it ran at an average annual rate above 7 percent. The years 1974 and 1975 are especially disturbing. A severe

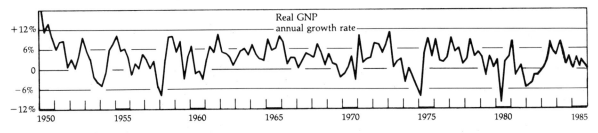

Figure 16A Quarterly changes in real gross national product (Source: Bureau of Economic Analysis)

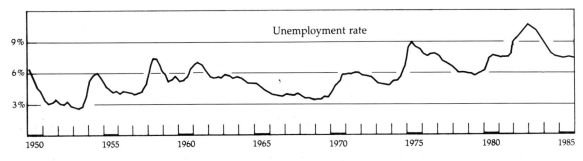

Figure 16B Unemployed as percent of labor force (Source: Bureau of Labor Statistics)

recession in those years produced sharply higher unemployment (see Figures 16A and 16B) while at the same time the price level was shooting up at rates unknown in the U.S. except in conjunction with major wars. The word began to spread in the 1970s, aided powerfully by television and newspaper commentators, that an unprecedented malady had seized the economy, one that economists were powerless to explain: recession coupled with inflation.

These rumors were incorrect. Inflation had occurred previously during recessions, most recently in the recessions of 1958 and 1960—though the inflation in those years had been considerably less rapid. Nor were economists completely at a loss for an explanation. On the other hand, some oversimplified notions about the causes of recession and inflation, notions that economists had helped create, were very definitely called into question by the experiences of the 1970s. The severe recession of 1974-75 at a time when prices were rising at a 10 percent annual rate made it abundantly clear that recession and inflation were not "opposites."

Aggregate Supply and Aggregate Demand: A Preliminary View

The idea that inflation and recession are opposites could readily occur to anyone who started thinking about these problems in terms of supply and demand. Suppose we use

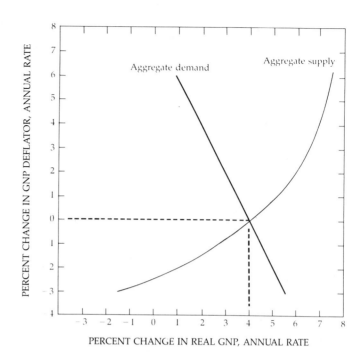

Figure 16C Hypothetical aggregate demand and supply curves for an economy with full employment and no inflation

real gross national product to represent the total quantity of goods (Q) and the GNP deflator to represent their average price (P). We could then draw an aggregate supply curve and an aggregate demand curve.

We don't really care about the *absolute* level of Q and P. What we're interested in is their rates of change. So in Figure 16C we have labeled the axes to show the *annual percentage change* in the price level and the *annual percentage change* in real GNP. The curves as drawn produce an "equilibrium" for the economy as a whole with a zero rate of change in the price level and with real GNP increasing at 4 percent per year. If we make the assumption that a 4 percent growth rate produces "full employment" (however defined), our hypothetical curves show an economy with full employment and no inflation.

Notice that inflation and recession are *not* opposites in this world; they would occur simultaneously if the aggregate supply curve shifted to the left. But perhaps the curves we have drawn tell a misleading story. Suppose that 4 percent is the maximum rate of growth in real GNP of which the economy is capable under existing conditions. Suppose further that prices and costs are rigid in the face of downward pressure and do not decline when demand decreases. Under

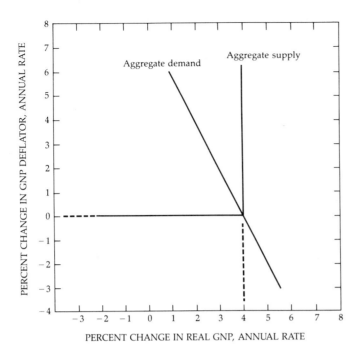

Figure 16D Hypothetical aggregate demand and supply curves, supply curve fixed: extreme case

such conditions, the aggregate supply curve might look like the one shown in Figure 16D. In such a world, *with the aggregate supply curve fixed*, any decrease in aggregate demand from the level shown on the graph will cause a recession, and any increase will cause inflation. Recession and inflation would be opposites in this case, one resulting from inadequate aggregate demand, the other from excessive aggregate demand. And we wouldn't expect to observe both of them at the same time.

The assumptions we used to construct the aggregate supply curve in Figure 16D are obviously too restrictive, however. There is no absolutely firm limit on the rate at which real GNP can grow. As Table 16A shows, it's capable of increasing, even for extended periods of time, at rates well above 4 percent. Suppose we assume that faster growth is possible, but that at higher growth rates "bottlenecks" develop, competition among producers starts to bid up the prices of scarce resources, and inflation begins. The faster the rate of growth, the higher will be the inflation rate. Let's further assume that, while costs and prices resist downward pressure below some "normal" level, they are not completely rigid in the face of declining aggregate demand. The result might be an aggregate supply curve something like the one

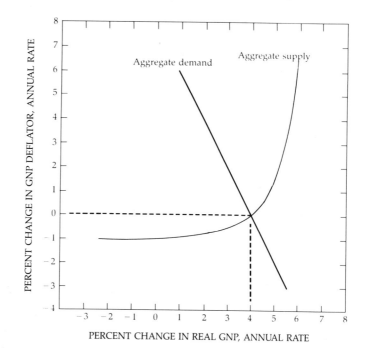

Figure 16E Hypothetical demand and supply curves, supply curve fixed: less extreme case

portrayed in Figure 16E. Under these conditions, recession and inflation would not be simple opposites. Higher levels of aggregate demand would begin to affect the price level even before a "full employment" rate of growth in real GNP had been attained. We are again assuming that the aggregate supply curve is something "given" and does not shift.

The aggregate supply curve of Figure 16E is drawn in a way that makes "full employment" without inflation a possibility. But this does not have to be the case. Suppose that the aggregate supply curve took the form shown in Figure 16F. There would then be *no* level of aggregate demand that could yield both "full employment" and zero inflation. To get the growth rate up to the "full employment" level, aggregate demand would have to increase by enough to raise the inflation rate to 5 percent per year. To eliminate inflation altogether, aggregate demand would have to fall to a level that produced only 1 percent annual growth in real output with, presumably, a substantial amount of unemployment.

Demand-Side Economics

The curves in Figure 16F summarize in a simplified way the relationship between inflation and unemployment that many, perhaps most, economists had come to assume by the 1960s.

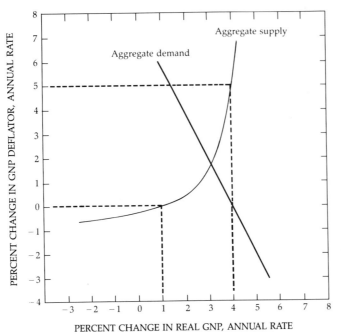

Figure 16F Hypothetical aggregate demand and supply curves, supply curve fixed: full employment and zero inflation mutually exclusive

They did not think of full employment with no inflation as a real option. The economy was insufficiently competitive, resources were not adequately mobile, and ignorance and uncertainties were too widespread to permit the maintenance of adequately high employment with *no* accompanying inflation. The task for policymakers, most economists seemed to think, was to choose an acceptable combination of unemployment and inflation and aim at that target *through the control of aggregate demand.*

Policymakers might also want to improve the menu of inflation-unemployment combinations presented to them by working a bit on the aggregate supply curve. This could be done by attacking cartels, dismantling government restrictions on domestic and international competition, expanding job-training systems, improving the flow of information, and generally trying to make resources more mobile. But this was a program for the long run, and it generally ranked low on the agendas of economists who concerned themselves with the problems of inflation, recession, and unemployment. They were for the most part demand-side economists, not supply siders—to use the terminology that came into prominence at the end of the 1970s. The dominant view was that high levels of employment with tolerable rates of inflation could be achieved through government control of aggregate

demand. How best to control aggregate demand was therefore the central issue for theorists and policymakers, at least until the 1970s.

The experiences of that decade—rapid inflation, coupled with a major recession and high unemployment rates—indicated that something was wrong with this way of thinking about the issues. Some economists began to suggest that it had been a mistake to apply the concepts of supply and demand to output as a whole and to the average level of prices.

Aggregate Supply and Aggregate Demand: Some Misgivings

The concept of a supply curve for any single good, such as soybeans, makes sense: we can conceive of farmers supplying larger quantities of soybeans in response to the expectation of a higher price for soybeans. Farmers will shift resources out of the production of other goods into the production of soybeans as the expected price of soybeans rises relative to other prices. But right there is the catch: *relative to other prices*. Farmers will want to grow more soybeans and less corn when the price of soybeans rises, *because* the price of corn has *not* risen. But if the price of *everything* rises, there is no obvious reason to expect anybody to do anything differently.

Recall that a rise in the price of everything simply means a fall in the value of money. Why would inflation, a fall in the value of money, prompt producers to supply more goods than before? It doesn't make much sense. At least it doesn't if the producers know what's going on. *But suppose they don't.* Suppose the producers mistakenly believe that only their own products have risen in price. In that case they will indeed want to supply more. But they will only want to do so for as long as they continue to misread the situation. When they discover that they were mistaken, that the price of the good they are supplying really has not gone up relative to other prices, they will want to correct their error and go back to producing the quantity they had previously been supplying.

The concept of aggregate demand is equally troubling when thought about carefully. A fall in the price of any single good will ordinarily cause an increase in the quantity demanded. Once again, however, it isn't clear that what is true for goods taken individually will be true for the aggregate of goods. If the price of everything falls, all that has happened is that the value of money has gone up. Why should that prompt people to increase their purchases? The concept of a

downward-sloping aggregate demand curve makes less sense than it might have seemed when we drew it. Aggregating in this manner may only conceal what is going on.

The Interdependence of Aggregate Supply and Demand

There is another difficulty that we have not considered: that aggregate supply and aggregate demand are dependent upon one another in a way that isn't true of supply curves and demand curves for individual goods. If improved technology lowers the cost of producing coal and so shifts the supply curve of coal to the right, we would not expect this to have any significant effect on the demand for coal. Similarly, we would expect a fall in the price of oil and natural gas to reduce the demand for coal, but not to have any noticeable impact on the supply curve. What makes supply and demand analysis a useful framework for thinking about the effects of changing circumstances is that factors influencing supply are largely distinct and independent from factors influencing demand. That obviously ceases to be the case when we start to talk about *aggregate* supply and demand.

As national income and product accounting reminds us, the total income available for the purchase of newly produced goods is always and necessarily equal to the value of those goods. We should therefore expect aggregate demand and aggregate supply to move together. More output means more income and hence, we could reasonably assume, more demand. Isn't it seriously misleading, then, to talk about the effects of changes in aggregate demand upon a fixed and unchanging aggregate supply curve, as we were doing just now? Most economists prior to the 1930s would have rejected any attempt to explain inflation and recession as the outcomes of an interaction between aggregate demand and aggregate supply, on the grounds that aggregate supply always creates an exactly equal aggregate demand.

This is an important truth, at least to begin with. It counters the strange but widespread and long-persistent fear that total output might increase *too fast*—too fast, that is, for total demand to keep up, so that the economic system collapses as a result of overproduction. Total income is always going to increase at precisely the same rate as total output, for the simple reason that they are the same phenomenon viewed from opposite sides.

That can be granted, however, without conceding that total *demand* will necessarily equal total output. What if people choose not to spend some of their income? Isn't the decision to save a portion of income received capable of reducing

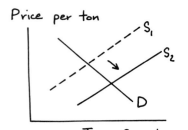

Price per ton

Tons of coal

Changes in the conditions of supply will have no significant effect on the demand curve for coal.

Total income = total output.

Total demand need not equal total income.

aggregate demand below the level of total output? And might this not cause overproduction and economic collapse?

The Original Supply-Side Economists

It all depends on what people do with the income they save. Except in the rare and unimportant case of misers and similar cranks, people invest what they save. That at least was the consensus view of the original supply-side economists, which included the great majority of economists up until the 1930s. People don't tuck their savings under their mattresses or into their cookie jars. They put their savings to work. If they themselves don't purchase capital goods with the income they save, then they purchase financial assets of some kind (bonds, stocks, savings accounts) and thereby turn their savings over to someone else who is going to purchase capital goods. Adam Smith put the doctrine concisely when he said: "What is annually saved is as regularly consumed as what is annually spent, and nearly in the same time too; but it is consumed by a different set of people."

Smith thought that people would have to be "perfectly crazy" (his term) not to invest everything they chose to save, at least where there was "tolerable security." The fear of overproduction or underconsumption was therefore ground-less. In the opinion of Smith and most of his successors, worrying that aggregate demand might be insufficient was evidence that one had not understood the basic working of economic systems. Overproduction was not a problem; the challenge was to increase production, so that people might be supplied with more of the "necessaries and conveniences" of life. Government's job in the economic system was not to stimulate demand but to preserve incentives, principally by maintaining the security of property. If this was done, people's natural desire to better their condition would lead them to produce, to save, to invest, and thereby to promote a continually rising rate of output. Consumption—the demand side—would take care of itself.

Where Do We Go From Here?

The Great Depression laid this optimistic belief firmly to rest. It became obvious in the 1930s that aggregate demand did *not* always "take care of itself." The result was the rise of new economic theories and policies concerned with the care and nurture of aggregate demand.

Demand-side economics flourished for many years, until the experiences of the 1970s revealed some of its more

glaring limitations. Then we saw a renewed interest in the contribution of supply-side factors to economic growth and price stability.

Where do we go from here? Back to basics. We had better begin by talking about that interesting social institution known as *money*.

Once Over Lightly

The gross national product is the market value of all the final goods produced in a year. It can be thought of either as the sum of all the value added by producers, as the total income earned by owners of productive resources, or as the sum of expenditures for new goods by households, business firms, government, and foreigners.

Gross national product in current dollars is the nominal GNP. Real GNP is calculated by determining what the value of nominal GNP would be if measured in the prices of a reference or base year.

Dividing nominal GNP for any year by real GNP yields a comprehensive price index known as the implicit GNP deflator. A better known though less comprehensive measure of price level changes is available monthly in the consumer price index.

Some economic analysts use aggregate supply curves and aggregate demand curves to think about the relationships between inflation and recession. Economists who employ these concepts often take aggregate supply to be "given" by the institutions and practices of the society. They then concentrate on controlling aggregate demand to achieve a preferred combination of price stability and employment from among those combinations that the supply curve makes possible.

Aggregate supply and aggregate demand are abstractions that may be too large to be useful. These aggregate concepts conceal interrelationships that are important for the understanding of inflation and recession.

If total income and total output are opposite sides of the same coin, as national income accounting explains, then aggregate supply and aggregate demand may be too interdependent to be useful analytical constructs.

The dominant view among economists prior to the 1930s was that aggregate demand will always be adequate, and that genuine economic problems represent malfunctions on the side of supply. The Great Depression of the 1930s provided persuasive evidence that aggregate demand could generate serious problems for an economic system and inaugurated an age of "demand-side" economics.

QUESTIONS FOR DISCUSSION

1. This question tries to make you think carefully about the relationship between income and output.
   (a) Can your personal income exceed the value of your personal output, at least for a limited time? How is this possible? Is it possible without gifts or loans from others?
   (b) Can the total income of all the members of a society, such as the United States, exceed the total value of all their output? How would this be possible?
   (c) If we learned that a particular society's total output had increased by 10 percent while its total income had increased by only 6 percent, what would we conclude must have happened?

2. How much do the following activities collectively contribute to the gross national product? Jack Lumber fells a tree and sells it for $10 to Saul Mill, who cuts it into boards that he sells for $25 to Lum Yard, who sells them at retail for $50 to Paul Thumbs, who uses them to build bookcases for his den that he thinks are lovely and that he wouldn't sell for less than $100. Be sure that you avoid double counting in making your calculations.

3. People who want to call attention to the huge size of certain business corporations will often compare the corporations' gross revenue from sales with the gross national product of some smaller nations. The implication is that the Exxon Corporation, for example, is bigger than Sweden in some relevant economic sense because its gross revenue exceeds Sweden's gross national product. Why is this a misleading comparison? If we added together the gross revenue of all business firms in the U.S., why would it be much larger than the U.S. gross national product? What must we subtract from a corporation's gross revenue to obtain the amount of its contribution to the gross national product?

4. List some ways in which increased inefficiency could cause GNP to rise. Are there any goods contributing to the total GNP whose rising output clearly reflects reduced welfare? What about home-security systems that protect against burglars?

5. If it could be shown that a rising GNP is associated with a rising level of anxiety, tension, and conflict in the population, would you favor deducting these psychological costs to obtain the true value of gross national product? How would you do so? How would you place a dollar value on increased anxiety?

6. Would you favor including the services of housewives in the calculation of gross national product? What arguments could be given for doing so? Are there any good reasons for continuing to exclude these services from the calculation of GNP? Do you think the exclusion reflects sexist attitudes, and that if more men were housekeepers, the Bureau of Economic Analysis would change its ways? Why doesn't the bureau count the value of a husband's work as a backyard barbecue chef, when it does count the very same sort of work done for pay by someone in a barbecued-rib outlet?

7. As an economy industrializes, a larger percentage of its population tends

to enter the labor force as conventionally measured. Fewer goods intended for use in the home are produced in the home, and a larger proportion of total product passes through the marketplace. What does this imply about the validity of GNP data in industrializing societies? Will estimates of per-capita income derived from GNP data tend to overstate or understate improvement over time?

8. To be certain that you understand the relationship between nominal GNP, real GNP, and the GNP deflator, fill in the following table.

Year	Nominal GNP	Real GNP	GNP Deflator
1	$3960 billion	$3600 billion	_____
2	_____	$3800 billion	115
3	$4800 billion	_____	120

9. You might want to familiarize yourself in a general way with the history of the U.S. economy in the post-World War II era, as it is summarized in Table 16A and Figures 16A and 16B.

(a) Nominal GNP increased almost 14-fold from 1950 to 1985. By how much did real GNP increase over this period?

(b) At which column in Table 16A would you look to find the years dominated by recessions? What years were they? Don't overlook 1960, which contained an official recession that might easily be missed; Figure 16A provides a more detailed and clearer picture. Which of the seven recessions since 1950—the National Bureau of Economic Research made a sometimes-disputed decision to count the 1980 and 1982 recessions separately instead of as a single, long recession—was the most severe?

(c) There was a great deal of public concern in early 1958 about the inflation that the nation had been experiencing for the previous three years, and some talk about the desirability of imposing price controls to stop it. In 1986, by contrast, there was enormous public satisfaction with our success in stopping inflation over the preceding three years. How would you explain these very different reactions to very similar inflation rates?

(d) Using Figures 16A and 16B, estimate how long it takes after the bottom of a recession is reached for the unemployment rate to hit its peak and start declining. About how long does it seem to take for the unemployment rate to fall back down after a recession has ended and recovery has begun?

10. You can test your understanding of the aggregate-supply/aggregate-demand analysis presented in Figures 16C–16F by thinking through the questions below.

(a) What could cause inflation with recession in the world of Figure 16C? How about deflation coupled with "boom" conditions or rapid economic growth?

(b) What could cause inflation with recession in Figure 16D? (Notice that the answer is the same as in Figure 16C. The key assumption in the accompanying text is that the aggregate supply curve is *fixed*. If we also assume in the world of Figure 16C that the aggregate supply curve does not change, but only the demand curve shifts, recession will always be accompanied by deflation.)

(c) In the world of Figure 16F, what approximate inflation rates are associated with growth rates of 1, 2, 3, and 4 percent? Suppose that the official unemployment rate is 5 percent when the annual growth rate of real GNP is 4 percent, and that the unemployment rate rises by 2 percentage points for each 1 percent decline in the growth rate. Construct a "menu" of inflation-unemployment combinations.

(d) Which "item" on the menu appeals most to you? Why?

11. Dee Raylor owns a fine bicycle that she enjoys riding on pleasant days. When someone last year offered to buy it for $300, Dee was tempted but finally decided not to sell. Then yesterday someone offered her $325. That was too tempting, and Dee plans to sell him the bike tomorrow.

(a) Did Dee make a sensible decision when she changed her mind?

(b) Unknown to Dee, who pays little attention to such things, the price level has increased more than 10 percent since last year. Does this information prompt you to reconsider the wisdom of Dee's decision? Is Dee at all likely to regret her decision to sell?

(c) How does this example help us understand why or under what circumstances a faster rate of inflation might produce a faster rate of economic growth?

The Supply of Money

Some economists believe that both inflation and recession are primarily caused by changes in the quantity of money held by the public, and that stabilizing the growth rate of the money stock is the most important contribution that government can make to stabilizing the economy. Other economists assign money a less dominant role in causing instability and propose a larger role for government in controlling inflation and recession. All would agree, however, that the monetary system is closely linked to the problems of inflation and recession. We must therefore find out what money is and how and why the quantity of money held by the public changes over time.

Money as a Unit of Accounting

You probably didn't even notice that we have come this far without discussing money. The previous chapters, after all, were full of dollar signs, and dollars are money. But the dollars referred to so far were simply conventional units for discussing values—a common denominator that enabled us to compare and add apples and oranges, convenient transportation and unpolluted air, goods in the hand and goods in the bush, the services of engineers and the gains from exchange.

One important function of money in a social system is to provide such a unit for accounting. We might have used any other common denominator, such as bread or human labor. We could have stated the values of gasoline and sugar in terms of the number of standard loaves for which a gallon of one and a pound of the other will exchange. Or we could have expressed the gross national product as the equivalent of so many hours of "average" labor time. But we're all

accustomed to thinking and talking about values in terms of dollars because we have had a lot of practice in translating the values of diverse commodities and services into dollar terms. Money functions effectively as a unit of accounting because of all the experience we've had with its more important function as a medium of exchange.

Money as a Medium of Exchange

A "medium of exchange" is just what the words say: a middle-thing used in the process of exchanging one good for another. The alternative to employing a medium of exchange is barter: exchanging the goods at our command directly for the goods we want to obtain. What do we use in the United States as our medium of exchange?

Most people who think about money think immediately of green pieces of paper, called Federal Reserve notes, and coins in various sizes and colors. Economists lump these all together and call it the currency component of the money supply. But what else do we use as a medium of exchange?

The most widely used medium of exchange is not currency but deposit credits in commercial banks, usually called checking accounts, but officially known as *demand deposits,* because they are deposits that can be withdrawn or transferred on demand.

Students often have trouble at first in seeing that demand deposits really are money. They themselves may handle all their transactions by means of currency, and when they receive a check, they cash it; that is, they obtain currency for the check and spend the currency. But student habits are in no way typical of the transaction procedures employed by business firms, government units, and households. The overwhelming majority of exchanges, measured in dollar value, employ demand deposits as the medium of exchange. Purchasers instruct their banks to transfer ownership of a portion of the purchasers' deposits to sellers: they write a check, in other words. Sellers typically deposit the checks rather than cash them, thereby instructing their own banks to collect the ownership whose transfer was ordered by the check writer. No currency at all changes hands. The bank in which the check is deposited makes an entry in its books; the bank on which the check is written makes an equal but opposite entry in its books.

It isn't hard to imagine a situation in which demand deposits are the only medium of exchange. As credit cards become more common, people will carry less currency and pay for more of their purchases with monthly checks. Couldn't all transactions be handled in this way? It would be possible,

even though inconvenient in some cases. But currency could disappear entirely without any reduction in our use of money as a medium of exchange.

Currency plus demand deposits. Is that all? Suppose someone asks, "How much money do you have?" You would calculate the currency in your possession. Having read this far you would then add the balance in your checking account. Should you also add what you have in your savings account? You can get it out quickly or transfer it to your checking account. It's available for spending, even though savings accounts can't be used directly as a medium of exchange. But then what of the deposit you have in a savings-and-loan institution? You could also convert that amount into "ready cash." And why not also the government bonds you own? They can be cashed too. How far shall we go in calculating how much money you have? Your automobile could also be converted into currency or a demand deposit. Is it therefore money?

Money as Liquidity

Notice what we've done now. We have shifted the definition of money from "the commonly employed medium of exchange" to "assets that can be exchanged in order to obtain other goods." But any asset at all, under the right circumstances, can be exchanged for other goods. Is every good therefore to be included in the money supply?

The distinguishing characteristic of money is its *liquidity*. Money is a liquid asset. The more liquid something is, the more moneylike it is. When an asset is completely liquid, it has attained the zenith of moneyness.

What do we mean by liquidity? *The liquidity of an asset refers to the cost of exchanging it for other assets.* An asset that can be exchanged for any other asset at a zero cost is a completely liquid asset. The Federal Reserve note in your wallet is an excellent example. It's an asset you can give in exchange for a great variety of other things you might want; sellers of every sort are willing to accept it without question *and without discounting it.* An asset that cannot be exchanged at all, because no one else would be willing to give anything in exchange for it, would be a completely illiquid asset. (Your toothbrush?) If you own a government savings bond, you can exchange it for other assets; but first you'll have to incur the cost of a trip to the bank where you exchange the bond for currency. So government savings bonds are liquid assets but they're not as liquid as Federal Reserve notes. Are they money? Just how liquid does an asset have to be to qualify as money? That turns out to be a difficult question on which competent people

We accept
Federal Reserve Notes
(eagerly)

No
Personal Toothbrushes
Accepted

disagree. In this world of continuous variables and every shade of gray, assets will rarely hit either end of the liquid-illiquid continuum. Most assets are somewhat liquid. The point to remember is that an asset becomes more moneylike as it becomes more liquid, as the cost of exchanging it for other assets approaches zero.

The concept of liquidity is important in the economist's way of looking at the world. To possess liquid assets is to have a greater range of choices, better opportunities, and hence more wealth. Your wealth, by which we mean the range of options available to you, will depend among other things on the precise forms in which you're currently holding the goods you own, or in the useful jargon of finance, on the *composition of your asset portfolio.* Suppose, for example, that you're in a strange city with a checkbook but no currency, and you're hungry. The restaurant signs "No Checks Accepted" establish that you are at the moment not as wealthy as you would be with $20 less in your checking account and a $20 bill in your wallet. You may also be driving an expensive sports car. But exchanging it for a meal (plus other assets) would almost certainly entail a substantial loss of wealth, because sports cars are not fully liquid assets.

How Money Creates Wealth

The advantages of using money rather than employing a barter system are enormous. The cost of exchanging would be far greater, and social wealth as a consequence far less, if there were no money to facilitate the process. In an economic system limited to barter, people would have to spend an inordinate amount of time searching for others with whom they could advantageously exchange. A violin maker would have to find a grocer, a haberdasher, an electrical utility, and a glue supplier, among many others, all willing to accept violins in return for the goods they sell. All that time devoted to searching would be time not available for violin making, and the production of violins would fall. Aware of the high costs of exchanging, people would increasingly try to produce goods for their own use, thus avoiding the necessity of searching out others from whom they can buy and to whom they can sell. Specialization would decline dramatically in a society confined to barter. And that means, of course, that people would lose the benefits that accrue from the systematic and widespread exploitation of comparative advantage. The evolution of some kind of money system in almost every known society, even when conditions were extremely unfavorable for it, is eloquent testimony to the advantages of having a generally accepted medium of exchange.

So the moneyness of particular assets is a matter of degree. How then are we going to define the money supply in the United States? The answer is: *somewhat arbitrarily*. There just is no completely satisfactory way to decide what should be counted in the money supply and what should be excluded. Some economists, known as monetarists, believe that changes in the rate at which the money supply grows make up the most important single factor causing recessions and inflations. Their contention is difficult to prove or disprove because they can't agree completely on what counts as money. That isn't because they're a disputatious lot. The appropriate definition of money is a function of financial institutions and social practices that evolve over time, usually very slowly, but sometimes with dramatic suddenness. You might even say that scholars can't agree on the best definition of money because the public, whose practices make something money, does not itself know what it will be using next year as a medium of exchange.

If we adhered strictly to the definition of money as the common medium of exchange, we would want to define the money supply in the United States as the total of currency in circulation plus checkable deposits (deposits at financial institutions that can be transferred by writing a check) plus travelers' checks. That's what we use to pay for almost all our transactions. To avoid double counting we must include only the currency that is in circulation, or outside the banking system. Thus when someone deposits a $20 bill in a checking account, the money supply doesn't change. The demand-deposit component rises by $20, but currency in circulation falls by $20. If we continued to count as money the currency now in the bank's possession, we would falsely conclude that deposits or withdrawals of currency from checking accounts change the quantity of the exchange medium held by the community. But they obviously don't; they change only the *form* in which it's held. After you've written a check for "cash," you have exactly as much money as before, and so does everyone else.

But do we want to define money strictly as that which actually functions as the common medium of exchange? What we're really after is insight into the determinants of total monetary expenditures for other goods. That will partially depend, as we shall see, on the amount of money people are holding relative to the quantities of other goods that they own or would like to acquire. The more money people possess, other things being equal, the more likely are they to surrender some portion of it in exchange for an alternate good when an attractive opportunity presents itself. Now it is quite clear that most people don't just look at their present stock of

The narrowly-defined money supply (M1): currency in circulation, checkable deposits, and travelers' checks

The broadly-defined money supply (M2): Currency in circulation, checkable deposits, travelers' checks, and non-checkable deposits

currency and demand deposits in deciding how much money they have. Savings held in commercial banks or in nonbank thrift institutions, such as savings-and-loan associations, would be regarded by most people as "available cash." So shouldn't we include these deposits in our working definition of the money supply?

The central bank of the United States, called the Federal Reserve, calculates the money supply in two principal ways and publishes the figures as M1 and M2. M1 attempts to measure the actual medium of exchange, and is therefore sometimes referred to as the *narrowly defined* money supply. M1 is the sum of currency in circulation, demand deposits, other checkable deposits, and travelers' checks. M2, the *broadly defined* money supply, is the sum of M1 plus savings deposits, time deposits in denominations of less than $100,000, money-market mutual-fund shares, and a couple of other relatively minor components that you don't even want to know about. M2 is an attempt to measure the stock of highly liquid assets that the public is holding.

Table 17A gives you some notion of the magnitude of each of these measures of the money stock. Since the quantity of money can and does fluctuate considerably from day to day, figures are usually expressed as averages over some period of time. The numbers are in billions of dollars and give the averages of daily figures in December of each year. Also shown is the percentage by which each measure of the money stock increased from the preceding year.

The stock of money, no matter in which of the two ways we measure it, has increased substantially since 1960. The average annual rate of increase from 1960 to 1985 was about 6 percent for M1 and 8.5 percent for M2. Moreover, the percentage rates of increase varied considerably, both between the two measures of the money stock and from year to year within each measure. Why? How has this come about? Where did all this additional money come from?

Commercial Bank Lending and the Creation of Money

The basic answer is that it came about through a net expansion of commercial bank loans. *The money stock increases when commercial banks make loans to their customers and decreases when customers repay the loans obtained from commercial banks.* That's the short of the story. The long of it is a bit more complicated but not really difficult to grasp.

Suppose your application for a loan of $500 from the First National Bank is approved. The lending officer will make out a deposit slip in your name for $500, initial it, and hand it to a teller who will then credit your checking account with

Table 17A Stock of money (in billions of dollars) and annual percentage increases

Year	M1	Percentage increase	M2	Percentage increase
1960	141.8	0.6%	312.3	4.9%
1961	146.5	3.3	335.5	7.4
1962	149.2	1.8	362.7	8.1
1963	154.7	3.7	393.2	8.4
1964	161.9	4.7	424.8	8.0
1965	169.5	4.7	459.4	8.1
1966	173.7	2.5	480.0	4.5
1967	185.1	6.6	524.3	9.2
1968	199.4	7.7	566.3	8.0
1969	205.8	3.2	589.5	4.1
1970	216.6	5.2	628.2	6.6
1971	230.8	6.6	712.8	13.5
1972	252.0	9.2	805.2	13.0
1973	265.9	5.5	861.0	6.9
1974	277.5	4.4	908.4	5.5
1975	291.1	4.9	1,023.1	12.6
1976	310.3	6.6	1,163.6	13.7
1977	335.3	8.1	1,286.6	10.6
1978	363.0	8.3	1,388.9	8.0
1979	389.0	7.2	1,497.9	7.8
1980	414.8	6.6	1,631.4	8.9
1981	441.8	6.5	1,794.4	10.0
1982	480.8	8.8	1,954.9	8.9
1983	528.0	9.8	2,188.8	12.0
1984	558.5	5.8	2,371.7	8.4
1985	626.3	12.1	2,564.1	8.1

Source: Board of Governors of the Federal Reserve System.

an additional $500. Demand deposits will have risen by $500. The money stock will be larger by that amount.

Where did the $500 come from? The bank *created* the $500 to lend you. Out of thin air? Not really. But the raw material isn't as important at this point as the fact that the bank really did create new money in making you a loan.

But what if you don't have a checking account at First National? Then the bank can open one and start you off with a $500 balance. But what if you don't want a demand deposit: you want the money? Slips! A demand deposit *is* money. You can use it to buy whatever it is you borrowed for. All right, but what if you decide to withdraw your $500 right away in $20 bills? Fine. The teller will accommodate you. The total of demand deposits will fall by $500, but the total of currency in circulation will increase by $500. The bank takes the currency from its vault, where it is *not* money, and gives it to you, whereupon it becomes currency held by the nonbank public or currency in circulation and hence *is* money.

COMMERCIAL BANK

ASSETS	LIABILITIES
+ Your $500 IOU	+ $500 Demand deposit

COMMERCIAL BANK

ASSETS	LIABILITIES
− $500 Currency from vault	− $500 Demand deposit

COMMERCIAL BANK

ASSETS	LIABILITIES
—Your $500 IOU +$500 Currency from your cookie jar	

COMMERCIAL BANK

ASSETS	LIABILITIES
—Your $500 IOU	—$500 Demand deposit

Does it all seem too simple? Why don't banks keep on doing that indefinitely? It seems just like having your own money machine in the basement. We'll see in a moment that banks are limited in their ability to make loans and thus add to the money stock. But first let's see how the stock of money is decreased.

One year later your note comes due. In the interim you've built up your money balance to be able to pay off the loan on time. You have $500 (plus the interest due, which we neglect for present purposes) either in your checking account or your cookie jar. If it's in the cookie jar, you turn it over to the bank on the due date and money in circulation drops by $500. Note again that currency counts as money when and only when it's held outside the banking system.

If, as is more likely, you have the $500 in your checking account, you write a check for that amount to the bank. The bank subtracts $500 from your demand-deposit balance. The money stock goes down by $500.

If you've grasped this simple process, you understand how money, defined as M1, is created and destroyed. Changes in the size of M2 are the consequence of the public's preferences regarding the form in which it wants to hold its stock of money assets. If you transferred the $500 you had borrowed out of your checking account and into a savings account at the bank where you borrowed, M1 would fall by $500. But M2 would be unchanged, because M2 includes everything in M1; the $500 contributes just as much to the total of M2 when it's in a checking account as when it's in the savings account. In short, commercial-bank lending increases M1. The public's desire to hold more or less of its assets in demand deposits or savings accounts will determine the different rates of growth between M1 and M2.

The Central Bank

But you must be wondering what has been left out. Surely private, commercial bankers can't create money without constraint. And you're right; they can't. First of all, the bankers must find people willing to borrow on the terms at which the banks are willing to lend. Second, each bank must operate within the constraint imposed by its reserves. That's the constraint which government authorities use in their efforts to exercise control over bank lending and hence over the process of money creation. Every bank is legally required to hold reserves in forms specified by law. A bank may make new loans, and thus create money, only when it has free reserves—that is, reserves greater than the minimum amount it's legally obligated to hold. And the Fed (the common

name for the managers of the Federal Reserve) has the power
to increase or decrease the reserves of the banking system.

401

The Supply of Money

The Federal Reserve is the central bank of the United
States, created by an act of Congress in 1913. Although
technically owned by the commercial banks that are its
members, the Fed is in practical fact a government agency. Its
board of governors in Washington is appointed by the
president of the United States, with the consent of the Senate.
And the board effectively controls the policies of the twelve
banks that make up the system. We seem to have twelve
central banks, but this is only an appearance, a legacy from
the days when much of the country harbored a populist
suspicion of Easterners, Wall Streeters, and men in striped
pants with cutaway coats. These suspicions were allayed
by scattering banks around the country. But the Fed has
actually been a single bank (with branches) at least since the
legislative changes enacted by Congress in the 1930s. The
power of any one of the twelve branch banks depends pretty
much on the amount of influence it's able to exert on policy
formation through its executive officers and research staff.

Many of the commercial banks in the United States are
not subject to all the rules of the Federal Reserve System.
Banks holding charters from the federal government have the
right to put the word "National" in their name and the
obligation to join the Federal Reserve System. But many banks
hold state government charters; they're permitted but not
required to join the system. We're going to simplify this account
by pretending that all banks are subject to the rules and
regulations of the Fed. Since the Fed indirectly but powerfully
influences the position of all banks and not just those subject
to its direct regulation, this assumption won't yield a seriously
misleading picture.

Bank Reserves as Constraints on Money Creation

Because of its power to fix legal reserve requirements for
member banks (within wide limits set by Congress) and its
power to expand or contract the dollar volume of reserves, the
Fed controls the lending activities of the commercial banking
system and thus the process of money creation. Reserve
requirements differ for savings deposits and demand deposits;
moreover, the legal reserve requirement on demand deposits
currently varies between 7 and 16¼ percent, depending on
the size of a particular bank's demand-deposit liabilities. (Note
that demand deposits are bank *liabilities:* your bank owes
you the amount in your checking account.) The Fed also
decides what may count as legal reserves—since 1960 it has
been the banks' vault cash plus the deposits the commercial

banks themselves have at the Federal Reserve Bank of their district. To see what all this has to do with changes in the money stock, we'll come in for a close-up look at the First National Bank of Anywhere.

Suppose that First National Bank is holding $10 million in vault cash, has $30 million on deposit with the Federal Reserve Bank, and is required by law to hold $38 million in reserves against its outstanding liabilities. That $38 million will be the sum and product of a lot of complex calculations involving different percentage reserve requirements for different liabilities. But we don't have to get into all the arithmetic, because it's irrelevant to our purposes. All we have to know is that First National Bank has $2 million in *excess reserves.* At least they're excess from the legal point of view. If First National has a reason of its own for holding $2 million more in reserves than it's legally required to hold, those won't really be excess reserves—any more than the amount in your checking account is an excess reserve because you aren't *legally* required to hold anything in your checking account.

But we're going to assume that First National has no desire to hold more reserves than the law says it must. So First National is indeed holding $2 million in excess reserves. Banks make use of excess reserves by lending them. First National can make new loans totaling $2 million if it can find acceptable borrowers. Let's assume it finds them and watch what happens as a result.

First National makes the loans by creating new demand deposits for its borrowers. The moment it does so, the stock of money increases by $2 million. All participants are happier than before. First National has additional income earning assets in the form of the borrowers' IOUs, and the borrowers have the money that they wanted badly enough to pay interest for it.

The story doesn't end here, however. The bank loans transformed $2 million of excess reserves into a $2 million addition to the stock of M1. But what will now happen to the $2 million in the checking accounts of the borrowers? Since people usually borrow in order to spend, we'll assume that's what these borrowers do, too. They write checks totaling $2 million.

The Dispersion of Excess Reserves

When the payees receive the checks, they deposit them in their own banks. Run the process through in your mind to convince yourself that no money is created or destroyed in this process. If borrower A writes a $100 check to the order of payee B, and B deposits that check in Second National Bank,

FIRST NATIONAL BANK

ASSETS	LIABILITIES
+$2 million in IOUs	+$2 million in demand deposits

Second National will add $100 to B's checking account and send the check to the Federal Reserve Bank for clearing. The Federal Reserve Bank will credit Second National with an additional $100 in its reserve account, will subtract $100 from the amount it has credited on its books to the reserve account of First National, and will send the check to First National. First National will subtract $100 from A's checking account. At the end of the process, the $100 of recently created money will be in B's checking account, and $100 of First National's excess reserves will have been added to the reserves of Second National.

But now Second National will have excess reserves! It acquired $100 in new liabilities and $100 in new reserves. But under our fractional reserve system, *at least* $83.75 of those new reserves will be excess reserves, because the *maximum* reserve requirement is 16¼ percent. So Second National will have an additional $83.75 or more to lend.

All around the commercial banking system, wherever the checks sent out by the borrowers are being deposited by payees, new additions are being made in this manner to the excess reserves of commercial banks. Some reserves will probably even find their way right back into First National, because some of the payees are almost certain to be depositors of First National Bank. All these new excess reserves permit further loans, which in turn create more M1. And when these further additions to the stock of M1 are spent by the borrowers and redeposited by payees, still more additions are made to the excess reserves of the commercial banking system.

The conclusion of the matter is this: *a dollar of original excess reserves can create several dollars in additional money* as banks use their excess reserves to acquire interest-paying assets. Exactly how many dollars of additional money will be generated from one additional dollar of excess reserves? We don't know. The ratio of new money to new reserves will depend on the legal reserve requirements in force, the size of the banks into which deposits move, the distribution of the deposits between member and nonmember banks of the Federal Reserve System, the public's preferences about the form in which it wants to hold new money, the lending policies and practices of banks, cash-management procedures of the federal government, the balance between exports and imports, and even the monetary policies of foreign central banks. The most important thing to know about this ratio may just be that it varies a good bit and is highly unpredictable, especially over short periods of time—such as a few months.

We know at least that the commercial banks can't continue indefinitely to create new money out of a given quantity of

new reserves. Additional lending creates additional liabilities against which reserves must be held, so that continual lending will eventually "use up" the excess reserves on which the lending was based. Moreover, the public will tend to withdraw larger quantities of money from the banking system as the stock of money increases, and every dollar of currency that moves into circulation reduces bank reserves by a dollar.

The discussion has been carried on in terms of excess reserves, additional loans, and more money. The process also works in reverse. When a bank's reserves fall below the legal minimum, it reduces its rate of new loans below the rate at which old loans are being repaid, in order to acquire the additional required reserves. If the entire banking system is doing this, the result is a net contraction of loans and hence a reduction in the money stock. Eventually, through the acquisition by the commercial banks of additional currency formerly in the hands of the public and the reduction of demand deposits as the public repays loans, the legal minimum reserve-to-deposit ratio will be reached. The process of contraction will stop.

It should be clear from all this that excess reserves plus a demand for bank loans on the part of eligible borrowers are the two factors jointly controlling the expansion of the money stock. The Fed can therefore influence the growth of the money stock either by changing the legal reserve requirements or by somehow changing the dollar volume of bank reserves. The latter is in fact the Fed's regular operating lever in money management.

The Tools Used by the Fed

How does the Fed actually go at the job of expanding or contracting the money supply? The most powerful tool and the one that sets the stage for the rest is the authority to establish legal reserve requirements. Changes in reserve requirements are generally viewed by Fed officials as a blunt weapon, not suitable for the delicate surgery that monetary management usually requires. They prefer to take the reserve requirements as the framework and alter the volume of reserves.

How is that done? The briefest explanation is that the Fed creates and destroys reserves in the same way that commercial banks create and destroy money: by extending and contracting loans.

The Fed can extend a loan to a commercial bank directly. It does so by crediting the bank's reserve account and taking in return the bank's IOU or someone else's IOU (a government

bond, for example) that happens to be in the bank's portfolio—just as a commercial bank lends to its customers by
creating a deposit balance in return for an IOU. The interest
rate at which such loans are made is called the *discount rate*.
It's a financial-page celebrity, because many people look
upon it as a sign of current Fed policy. It probably is more of
a symbol than a genuine rationing device, since the Fed is
selective about the banks to which it will lend. Official Fed
policy is to accommodate special circumstances, rather than
lend to any bank willing to pay the rate, and to behave
more like a Dutch uncle than a profit-seeking lender. But that's
what most people look for from a central bank.

The principal technique that the Fed employs is the
purchase and sale of United States government securities in
what are called *open market operations*. The Fed currently holds
a portfolio of government securities worth close to $200
billion. When it increases its holdings by purchasing securities
through dealers in government bonds, it writes checks for
the amount of the purchases on its own credit. These checks
are deposited in commercial banks. When the banks forward
the checks to their Federal Reserve Bank, they are credited
with additions to their reserve balances.

In short, the acquisition by the Federal Reserve Banks of
new earning assets, which is the same thing as the extension
of credit to someone, whether the government or banks,
increase commercial-bank reserves by that amount. And that,
as we have seen, enables commercial banks to increase their
own loans and thereby the money stock.

The entire process is reversible. The Fed can withdraw
credit from member banks or sell some of the government
securities already in its asset portfolio. This results in a
reduction of commercial-bank reserves. For example, when
the Fed sells a $1000 government bond, the bond winds up in
the hands of someone who pays the bond dealer with a
check. But the dealer in turn pays the Fed with a check, and
the amount of the check is deducted from the reserve
account of the bank on which it is drawn. That wipes out a
portion of the total reserves of the banking system.

Who Is Really in Charge?

Open market operations, as we said, are the principal working
tool of monetary management. A special committee, made
up of the seven members of the board of governors and five
of the twelve Reserve Bank presidents, sits as the Open
Market Committee and continuously determines the direction
of monetary policy. The question of the effectiveness with

FEDERAL RESERVE BANKS

ASSETS	LIABILITIES
+ Government bonds	+ Commercial bank reserves

COMMERCIAL BANKS

ASSETS	LIABILITIES
+ Reserve accounts	+ Demand deposits

which the Open Market Committee manages the money supply has long been debated by friends and critics of the Fed, among both economists and politicians.

There are two main questions. One is the determination of policy: Does the Fed set appropriate goals? Does it try to do what it ought to be doing? The other is the execution of policy: Does the Fed do an effective job of achieving the goals it sets for itself? The questions are related, of course, because intelligent policy formulation presupposes a realistic assessment of technical capabilities. The football coach who orders a passing strategy when his team is two touchdowns behind in the fourth quarter is making a poor policy decision if the quarterback has a rubber arm and all the receivers have butterfingers. Beware of textbook accounts which, like football plays on the blackboard, gloss over problems of execution and assume that the opposition isn't doing any planning of its own. It's a gross oversimplification to suppose that the Fed has a monetary brake and a monetary accelerator with which it adjusts the money stock as quickly and surely as you slow down and speed up your car in traffic. Monetary management may be more like driving a balky mule train that sometimes won't stop going even when firmly ordered to halt. To make matters worse, there's a bunch of bickering backseat drivers on the wagon, and some of them aren't above shouting their own instructions or even trying to grab the reins from the driver. We'll return to these problems in later chapters when we examine monetary policy.

Why Should Banks Hold Reserves?

Throughout our description of money and the banking system, we have treated reserves as constraints on the power of banks to make loans and thus to expand the money supply. That seems to have little or nothing to do with the concept of a reserve fund, something that can be drawn upon in an emergency. But legal reserves do not in fact perform a significant reserve function. The reserve requirement is today primarily a limitation on the ability of the commercial banking system to expand the money stock.

But isn't it necessary for the banks to hold reserves against the possibility of a "run" by depositors? If a lot of depositors suddenly lost confidence in a bank for some reason and tried to withdraw their deposits in currency, the bank would be unable to honor those withdrawals. And if that happened, the loss of confidence might spread to other banks and bring down a large part of the banking system.

There actually hasn't been a financial panic like that in the United States for over fifty years. The reason, however,

has little to do with the level of bank reserves. Bank customers no longer rush to withdraw their deposits on every rumor of financial trouble because their deposits are now insured by the Federal Deposit Insurance Corporation (FDIC). If a bank closes, for whatever reason, its depositors can expect reimbursement within a few days. Some critics argued when the FDIC was established in 1935 that the premiums it charged banks to insure their deposits were far too low, and that the FDIC would go broke trying to pay off depositors when banks closed their doors. But the very existence of the FDIC ended the phenomenon of bank runs; and in the absence of runs, banks no longer failed the way they formerly did. The FDIC premiums have thus proved more than adequate. And the institution of the FDIC may well be the single most stabilizing reform enacted in the 1930s.

Some credit must also go to improved Federal Reserve procedures since the 1930s. The Fed now understands clearly that it has the responsibility to provide short-term liquidity to the banking system, without regard to the amounts banks happen to be holding as reserves. Thus a bank today can meet any demand for currency, however large, by securing additional currency from the Fed. If the bank were to use up its entire reserve balance, the Federal Reserve Bank would simply lend the bank additional reserves, taking as collateral some of the IOUs in the asset portfolio of the borrowing bank. Banks are granted access to this "discount privilege" whenever they have a legitimate demand for additional reserves, and this has made the whole banking and monetary system more flexible in response to changing conditions as well as more resistant to crises and temporary dislocations.

What About Gold?

But hasn't something important still been left out of all this? If reserves aren't really reserves, what is it that provides backing for money? Doesn't money have to have some kind of backing? And where does gold fit into the picture?

The conviction that money must have "backing" if it is to have value raises an interesting question. What stands behind the backing to give it value? And behind the backing of the backing? But the whole set of questions is misdirected. In economics, value is the consequence of scarcity. And scarcity is the result of demand plus limited availability. It's clear enough why there exists a demand for money: it can be used to obtain all sorts of other things that people want, which is to say that it's accepted as a medium of exchange. The other part of the picture, limited availability, is taken care of, more or less effectively, by the monetary managers. No

"backing" is required. If this makes you nervous or causes you to doubt the value of your currency or checking account, you can easily shore up your faith by "selling" your money to others. You'll find that they're willing to take it and to give you other valuable assets in exchange.

The critical factor in preserving the value of money is limited availability and confidence that the supply will continue to be limited. Nature has made gold relatively rare. It's up to the Fed to keep Federal Reserve notes and demand deposits relatively rare. But many people have far more confidence in the reliability of nature than in the reliability of central banks and governments. That's why some intelligent and well-informed people would like to see us return to a genuine gold standard, under which currency could be exchanged for gold at some fixed ratio. It's not because they think that money must have backing, but because they distrust government money managers. If the government were required to maintain the convertibility of demand deposits into currency and currency into gold at predetermined exchange ratios, the limited availability of gold would severely restrict the power to increase the money stock.

As a matter of fact, governments are often tempted, especially in wartime, to create additional money as a way of financing expenditures without the painful necessity of openly levying taxes. And they haven't always resisted the temptation. The consequence has usually been inflation, a more concealed but hardly a more equitable way for the government to finance its expenditures. Urging a return to the gold standard would seem to be a counsel of despair, however. A government so irresponsible that it must be reined in by gold would be most unlikely to adopt a gold standard and even more unlikely to respond to the pressure of such a rein. The problem of irresponsible government is a weighty one; but it's hard to believe that the problem could be solved through a return to the gold standard. In any event, the United States seems unlikely to adopt the gold standard in the near future. We will probably have to be satisfied with making the present system work.

Once Over Lightly

Money is a social institution that increases wealth by lowering costs of exchange, thereby enabling people to specialize more fully in accordance with their own comparative advantages.

The moneyness of any asset is a matter of degree. An asset is money insofar as it is liquid. An asset is completely liquid when it can be exchanged for other goods at no cost. Whatever assets everyone freely accepts as a medium of exchange make up a society's stock of money.

In the United States today the stock of money is primarily the total of currency held outside the banking system plus the demand-deposit liabilities of commercial banks. But other assets, such as savings deposits, which can be converted into currency or demand deposits at negligible cost, also contribute to overall liquidity and are therefore included in more comprehensive measurements of the money stock.

The money stock increases or decreases primarily as commercial banks expand or contract their lending.

The managers of the Federal Reserve System have the responsibility for regulating the size of the money stock. The Fed does so by controlling bank lending through its power to set the legal ratio between commercial-bank liabilities and reserves and to expand or contract those reserves through loans to commercial banks and through open-market operations.

The idea that money must have "backing" to have value is not correct. Money must only be acceptable as a medium of exchange to have value. Limited availability is a necessary condition for continued acceptability of any functioning medium of exchange.

QUESTIONS FOR DISCUSSION

1. Do we ever use human labor rather than money as our "unit of accounting"? Have you ever encountered a comparison of international living standards which refers to the number of hours an average person must work in each country to earn the price of a loaf of bread, a pair of shoes, or a refrigerator? Why is this done?
2. Would your existence be more or less secure if we had a barter economy?
   (a) Why would we all be poorer if we had to rely entirely on barter to exchange goods?
   (b) Why might people's incomes fluctuate less in a society that did not use money?
   (c) Is a very poor family subject to 10 percent fluctuations in its income more or less secure than a wealthy family that experiences 50 percent fluctuations in its income?
   (d) We are much wealthier than we would be if our society did not use money, but our incomes are probably somewhat more uncertain than they would be if we relied entirely on barter. Can you think of any other important social consequences that emerge from the use of money?
3. Adam Smith complained in *The Wealth of Nations* that many people confused money with wealth. *Is* this a confusion?
   (a) Doesn't everyone's wealth increase when they acquire more money?
   (b) If any one person's wealth increases when he or she acquires more money, doesn't it follow logically that more money for everyone means more wealth for everyone?

(c) What would happen if the government of India tackled the problem of poverty by printing more rupees and distributing them generously to the poorest people in the country?

4. If someone asked how much money you have, how would you go about calculating the answer?

(a) Wouldn't you want to know why the person was asking? If you were out shopping and the other person wanted to borrow money from you to make a purchase, would you include the amount in your checking account as well as the currency in your wallet? When would you and when would you not? Is it ever appropriate to answer, "I have my credit card with me"?

(b) If you were to ask people how much money they have in the bank, most would probably not distinguish in answering between their checking-account and savings-account balances. Why might economists want to distinguish between the two? Why might this distinction have become less important in recent years as banks have made it easier for people to transfer deposits between savings accounts and checking accounts?

5. What is the value of *liquidity*?

6. Shares of common stock listed on a major exchange can be sold quickly—that is, exchanged for other assets. Is stock as liquid as money? Why might people hold part of their wealth in common stocks and part in money? Why might they shift the composition of their portfolios in order to hold more of one asset and less of the other?

7. People usually cannot spend the deposits they hold in commercial-bank savings accounts or savings-and-loan institutions without first withdrawing the funds—that is, converting them into currency or demand deposits. But since they're able to do that at almost no cost, these deposits are assets almost as liquid as checking-account balances.

(a) Would you expect total spending to be more closely correlated with M1 or with M2?

(b) Will your answer change if savings-and-loan institutions allow customers to pay bills through telephone transfers of their deposits to the accounts of others?

8. At any moment some already-printed Federal Reserve notes will be in (a) the wallets of the public, (b) the vaults and tills of commercial banks, (c) the vaults of Federal Reserve Banks. How does each enter into or otherwise affect the total money supply?

9. Commercial banks create money by extending loans. It's important that you see exactly why they can do this, and why money is ordinarily *not* created by the lending activities of other institutions.

(a) What is the advantage possessed by commercial banks that enables them to create money when they make loans? Credit unions and consumer credit companies do not have this advantage, and consequently do not create money when they extend loans to their customers. What do they lack that commercial banks have?

(b) Would you like to be able to make loans to your friends at will, simply by creating the money you lend them? You could help your friends, increase your popularity, and even earn a little interest if you could learn how to do this. What is the secret?

(c) Suppose everyone in town knows you, knows your signature, and trusts you completely. When a friend asks to borrow $10, you simply write a note saying, "I'll pay $10 to the holder of this note," sign it, and hand it to the friend. Will the friend be able to spend your note, that is, use it as money? Will the merchant who receives the note be able to spend it in turn, perhaps by giving it out in changing a $20 bill? Will you have succeeded in creating money?

(d) The narrowly defined money stock, or M1, is made up of Federal Reserve notes, checkable deposits, and travelers' checks. All of these are liabilities of trusted financial institutions. What does a person or institution have to do to be able to create money?

10. How does a withdrawal of currency from checking accounts affect the money stock? How does it affect a bank's reserves? How does it affect excess reserves? What effect might this withdrawal subsequently have on the money stock?

11. A good technique for getting a handle on the way in which commercial bank and central bank activities affect the stock of money is to trace the effects of their actions on assets and liabilities. The basic rule is that any change in assets must be matched by a corresponding change in liabilities or an offsetting change in other assets, so that total assets always equal total liabilities.

Set up four columns for yourself, with the headings given below, and trace through the effects of the actions described. The first one has been completed for you.

Federal Reserve Banks		Commercial Bank System	
Assets	Liabilities	Assets	Liabilities
(1) +$10,000 govt. bonds	(4) +$10,000 reserve account	(3) +$10,000 reserve account	(2) +$10,000 checking account

(a) Paying by means of check, a Federal Reserve Bank purchases $10,000 worth of government bonds from a member of the public, who deposits the check in a commercial bank, which then sends the check to the Federal Reserve Bank for credit to its reserve account.

(b) A commercial bank extends a $5000 loan to a customer.

(c) Customer uses a $5000 loan to pay for a new car, writing a check to a car dealer, who deposits the check in a commercial bank.

(d) A car dealer withdraws $2000 in currency from a commercial bank, which then obtains more currency from a Federal Reserve Bank by drawing down its reserve account.

12. Many people worry about the size of the national debt. Suppose the Federal Reserve Banks bought up all outstanding marketable securities, so that—in a sense—the government only owed the debt to itself. How could this be done? What would happen as a result?

13. You're the manager of a commercial bank and you want to increase your bank's free reserves. Perhaps you currently have *negative* excess reserves—in which case your bank is borrowing from the Fed and the Fed may be putting pressure on you to remove that debt. Or you may simply believe that your bank would be in a more advantageous position with a somewhat higher level of free reserves. What policies could you pursue to reach your

objective? What effects would these policies have on the banking and monetary system?

14. Why does the Fed use open-market operations as its principal tool of monetary management, rather than changes in legal-reserve requirements? What are the differences in the effects that each technique would have on individual banks, on the commercial banking system as a whole, and on the money supply?

15. Why might the Fed find it significantly easier to expand the money stock in a period of prosperity than in a period of recession? What must the Fed be able to do if it wants the quantity of money in the hands of the public to increase?

16. The narrowly defined money stock in the U.S. grew at an average annual rate of 4.1 percent during the 1960s, while nominal gross national product was growing at an average rate of 7.1 percent. In the 1970s, the growth rate of M1 was 6.7 percent per year and the growth rate of nominal GNP was 10.4 percent.

    (a) This question anticipates the analysis of the next two chapters—but do you think there is a causal connection between the higher growth rates of both M1 and nominal GNP in the 1970s?

    (b) In the 1960s real GNP increased at an average annual rate of 4.3 percent; in the 1970s, at the rate of 3.5 percent. Is a higher rate of growth in nominal GNP desirable if it doesn't produce faster growth in real GNP?

17. The table below shows the average annual growth rates in the stock of money, nominal GNP, and real GNP in the 1960s and in the 1970s for five major nations.

    (a) Are faster rates of money growth generally associated with faster rates of growth in nominal GNP?

    (b) Are faster rates of growth in nominal GNP generally associated with faster rates of growth in real GNP?

	1960s			1970s		
	Money Stock	Nominal GNP	Real GNP	Money Stock	Nominal GNP	Real GNP
Canada	6.1%	8.5%	5.5%	10.8%	13.2%	4.4%
France	10.6	10.2	5.8	11.6	13.5	3.9
Japan	18.1	16.6	11.1	15.3	13.0	4.9
United Kingdom	3.0	6.4	3.0	12.6	15.9	2.3
West Germany	7.3	7.8	4.6	10.0	8.4	2.9

18. If it is *not* essential that money have "backing" of some kind, why do so many people believe otherwise?

19. "Nature has made gold rare, but people have made it scarce." Explain.

20. Money gets a lot of attention but tends to have a bad press. Are the authors of the following statements talking about money as we have defined it? Or are they using money as a synonym or symbol for something else? What is that "something else" in each case where you conclude that money is not really the subject of discussion?

(a) "The love of money is the root of all evil." (Often misquoted as "Money is the root of all evil.")

(b) "Health is . . . a blessing that money cannot buy."

(c) "If this be not love, it is madness, and then it is pardonable. Nay, yet a more certain sign than all this: I give thee my money."

(d) "Wine maketh merry; but money answereth all things."

(e) "Words are the tokens current and accepted for conceits, as moneys are for values."

(f) "Money speaks sense in a language all nations understand."

(g) "Americans are too interested in money."

(h) "Protecting our natural environment is more important than making money."

Demand-Side Economics: Monetarist and Keynesian Perspectives

What happens when the quantity of money in the hands of the public increases—or decreases? Do people increase their spending as they acquire larger money balances? Do they reduce their spending when the quantity of money available to them declines? How quickly do they respond? And what difference does it all make? These are questions that *monetarists* are inclined to ask, because they maintain that changes in the quantity of money, through their effect on aggregate demand, are the principal cause of instability both in the price level and in total output.

Not all economists agree with that position. In the 1930s, largely as an outgrowth of ideas advanced by John Maynard Keynes, many economists adopted the view that aggregate demand could and did behave in a highly destabilizing manner without any prior change in the quantity of money. Keynesian economists consequently assigned much less importance than do monetarists to controlling the size of the money stock. They located the roots of instability elsewhere, and expected less by way of control or cure from those responsible for managing the money supply.

Both monetarists and Keynesians, it should be noted, lay primary stress on aggregate demand. Because they find the key to stability in the control of aggregate demand, we can group them together as *demand-side economists*. In this chapter, our aim is to clarify the principal points of agreement and disagreement among demand-side economists. We begin with the monetarists.

The Monetarist Perspective: The Demand for Money

The key proposition in the monetarist position is *stability in the demand for money.* The phrase "demand for money" strikes most people as a little odd when they first hear it. The demand for anything, such as raspberry jam, usually refers to the quantities people will want to purchase during a specified time period at various prices. At higher prices, people will shift toward substitutes for raspberry jam; at lower prices, they'll substitute raspberry jam more frequently for other goods. But what sense do those sentences make if we insert "money" in place of "raspberry jam"?

They make excellent and important sense if we remember two things: (1) money is not the same as income; and (2) although demand for raspberry jam is a demand to acquire and consume, the demand for money is a demand to *hold* an asset, not to "consume" it.

Distinguishing Stocks from Flows

You will never understand the important concept of the demand for money if you identify money with money income. *Money income is a flow,* and so must always be stated with reference to some time period: $4 per hour, $800 per month, $12,000 per year. But *money itself is a stock;* it is a certain amount in existence at some time. Because the size of the stock varies from day to day, we can measure it only with respect to some point in time. But it is *at a point* in time that we try to measure the size of a stock; we measure the size of a flow *during a period* of time.

Thus if an employee says, "I'm going in to see the boss this afternoon and demand more money," what is really meant is that he or she is going to insist on more money income: a larger flow of money per month. That is *not* what we're talking about here. The amount of money that people hold (as a stock) will usually be related closely to the amount of money income they receive regularly (as a flow). But it's certainly possible for one to go up while the other is going down.

The way to understand this is to think it through. How much money, defined as M1, are you currently holding? In other words, what is the sum of your checking-account balance and the currency plus coin that you have in your pocket, purse, billfold, and bureau drawer? Whatever it is, what must you do in order to increase or decrease this amount? To decrease it, you must exchange money for other assets (we'll assume you don't lose it or throw it away). These assets could be anything from food for immediate consumption to

shares of stock in AT&T. To increase the amount of M1 you're currently holding, you must give up other assets in exchange for currency or an addition to your checking-account balance (we'll rule out finding money or stealing it).

Now let's suppose you've been working 20 hours a week for $4 an hour. You've been exchanging 20 hours of your time each week for $80, yielding a money income of $80 per week. Then you decide to spend more time studying, so you cut your work hours to 15 per week and your income to $60 per week. If at the same time you reduce your expenditures by more than $20 per week (you eliminate a lot of recreation activities, let's say, in order to increase your study time), you will be adding to the stock of money you hold, even though your income has decreased.

It all seems too obvious to summarize. But we're going to use these basic relationships, and they should be clear in your mind. People add to the stock of money they hold, to their money balances, by reducing their expenditures below their income or by exchanging other assets for money. They reduce their money balances by raising their expenditures above their income or exchanging money for other assets.

Why Do People Hold Money Balances?

The demand for money, we said, is a demand to *hold* money, not to consume it. Money isn't unique in this respect. Lots of goods yield services by being held: fine art, shares of stock, and houses are examples. The demand for all of them should be understood, therefore, as a demand to hold the good in question, not to "use it up." It's clear how paintings, corporate stock, and houses yield services by being held or owned. But isn't it true that money provides a service only when it's spent?

It is *not* true. Money does provide services when it's spent, which is why people want to hold money in the first place. They're looking forward to the enjoyment of what they expect the money to buy them. But money also provides a service while it is being held. If it did not, no one would hold it, because holding money is costly. While holding money we're sacrificing the valuable current services that other goods would yield us if we bought them with the money: the interest on a government bond, the pleasure of a Woody Allen movie, a comfortable armchair in which to relax. Since present goods are more valuable than future goods, why don't people immediately spend their money income when they receive it and maintain their stock of money balances at zero? They obviously don't do this. And that implies, correctly,

Meat eaten per year is a flow. Meat in the freezer is a stock.

The stock can be increased by purchasing more than is eaten for a time.

The desire to hold more meat in the freezer does not necessarily imply a desire to eat more meat per year.

that holding money yields a valuable service, a service valuable enough in comparison with the cost of holding money to persuade people to hold those amounts that they do hold.

That service, quite simply, is flexibility. By holding money rather than some other asset, you increase your freedom to maneuver. You make it easier for yourself to buy what you want when you want it, to take advantage of opportunities that you don't know about yet, or to escape from an unexpected misfortune. Moreover, you make these things possible for yourself without the trouble and expense of first taking a trip to the bank or making a visit to your stockbroker. A synonym for flexibility is *liquidity,* a concept introduced in the preceding chapter to describe money. An asset that can be exchanged at any time at its full value for any other asset is a completely liquid asset. Money is, by definition, the most liquid asset in a society. The demand for money is the demand for liquidity.

Actual and Preferred Money Balances

M is the quantity of money supplied and the quantity being held.

Quantity actually held must equal M. Quantity public would prefer to hold may be greater or less than M.

Whatever the quantity of money the public *prefers* to hold, the quantity it *actually* holds will be the quantity supplied. This is a simple but important point to keep in mind. The size of the money stock at any time, however measured, will necessarily be equal to the quantity of money balances the public is holding at that time. But *actual money balances may not be equal to preferred money balances.* If the stock of money increased at a time when the public was satisfied with its current money holdings, some people would have to find themselves holding larger money balances than they preferred to hold. And so they would take steps to reduce their money balances back to the preferred level. If the money stock declined when people were holding their preferred amounts of money, they would try to raise their balances back up to the previous level. They would make these adjustments in the way we've already described, by changing the relationship between their incomes and their expenditures, or by changing the composition of their assets—exchanging corporate stock for money, perhaps, or money for government bonds.

When additional money is supplied to a public that is already holding the amount it prefers to hold, the public will attempt to exchange that additional money for other goods. This will increase the aggregate demand for goods other than money, including those newly produced goods that make up the gross national product. This increased demand will produce some combination of higher prices and larger output. Gross national product can thus be expected to increase in

response to an increase in demand for new goods that was prompted in turn by an increase in the quantity of money supplied to a public already holding its preferred amount of money balances. GNP will continue to rise in this way as long as spending for new goods keeps increasing. And spending will continue to increase as long as people are still holding more money than they want to hold.

Notice that the attempt by individuals to reduce their money holdings by increasing their expenditures adds to the money holdings of others; it doesn't reduce the money stock. The public's attempt to reduce its money balances can't succeed, because all the money that's supplied must be held by someone. What happens instead is that the attempt to reduce actual money balances to the level of preferred money balances causes total income to rise, until the public prefers to hold money balances equal to the quantity that has been supplied.

This way of putting it is somewhat misleading, because it suggests that people are *coerced* into holding the quantity of money that the monetary authorities, in conjunction with the banking system, supply. That's not true, of course. The money supply increases when commercial banks increase their loans. More loans mean people who *wanted to borrow* now have the ready money they were looking for. Surely they didn't borrow money and agree to pay interest on it in order to let that money sit idly in their bank accounts. They'll spend it, for whatever they had in mind when they borrowed.

Let's suppose it's a couple that borrowed in order to buy new living-room furniture. When they make the purchase, they transfer the amount that the bank had credited to their checking account to the owners of the furniture store. What do the furniture retailers do in turn? They *don't* say: "Drat! Here we were happily holding the quantity of money we preferred to hold. Then that inconsiderate couple stuck us with this extra money. Now we're going to have to waste our time figuring out a way to get rid of it. Do we know anybody we can dump it on?" Instead they say: "Great! We sold a couch and two chairs. Business is good. Our furniture inventory is down, however, so we'd better use this new money to replenish our stock." And so they (joyfully!) pass the money on to their suppliers, who accept it, also joyfully, and repeat the thinking of the furniture retailers.

The logic of it all is quite simple and really rather obvious once you think it through. More money produces more spending, which produces rising incomes until people become willing to hold that additional amount of money. At that point, GNP stops increasing. *The key assumption* that makes it

The attempt to exchange money for other assets increases nominal GNP.

The quantity of money the public wants to hold increases when nominal GNP increases.

Nominal GNP increases until the public is willing to hold the quantity of money supplied by the Fed.

all work is that *the quantity of money the public prefers to hold and will attempt to hold is some stable fraction of money income or expenditures.*

Why the Demand for Money May Change

Monetarists don't claim that the demand for money never changes. They readily admit that it will change in response to changing financial practices, such as greater use of credit cards or telephone transfer systems that make it easy to switch funds from one kind of bank deposit to another. But financial practices usually evolve somewhat slowly, as a result of which changes in the public's preferences with respect to money balances also occur slowly. That's still consistent with a *stable* demand for money.

Monetarists also don't claim that the quantity of money the public wants to hold is completely inelastic with respect to the rate of return on financial assets. If the rate of return one can obtain on safe and liquid financial assets rises, the opportunity cost of holding cash rather than some of these other assets goes up. And when the cost of holding money increases, people will want to hold somewhat less. It follows, then, that if the Fed brought down interest rates by making more credit available to commercial banks and the public, the quantity of money balances the public would want to hold would increase. Monetarists concede this. They simply don't believe that this is a major influence on the fraction of income and expenditures the public will want to hold in money balances. It doesn't invalidate their basic working assumption that the public wants to hold money balances equal to some stable fraction of nominal gross national product.

Monetarists certainly do not claim that the demand for money will remain stable in the face of any and all changes in the behavior of the monetary authorities. If a lot more money is suddenly supplied to the public, the value or purchasing power of money is eventually going to fall. People know that. At least many of them do. And when people expect the value of any asset they're holding to take a large tumble, they try to unload the asset before that happens. In short, people will become less willing to hold money balances when they anticipate an increase in the inflation rate. Conversely, they will want to hold larger balances if they decide the inflation rate is going to decrease significantly.

The implication of all this is that the public will try to hold money balances equal to some fairly stable fraction of nominal gross national product as long as those who control the supply of money behave in a moderate and responsible way. The monetarist thesis, in short, is that when there's

The demand for money depends upon its expected value.

If people expect its value to decline rapidly, they will not want to hold money.

trouble, it's the suppliers of money, not the demanders, who are at fault.

How Stable Is the Demand for Money?

How accurate is this thesis? That turns out to be one of the main issues separating monetarists from Keynesians. Unfortunately, it's not an easy question to settle. If the demand for money is basically stable, as monetarists aver, then aggregate demand will be stable as long as the monetary authorities prevent the money supply from behaving in a destabilizing fashion. The task of the monetary authorities then becomes to maintain a steady, modest, and predictable rate of growth in bank reserves and the money supply.

The villains in the monetarist drama are the suppliers of the money.

If, however, the demand for money is subject to sudden and sizable shifts, then the economy may be inherently unstable. Aggregate demand will be subject to large, unpredictable changes, and both the price level and real output are likely to bounce about in damaging ways. On this view the government may be called upon to exercise a substantial role in offsetting destabilizing changes in aggregate demand that originate in the private sector.

If we were to find that the money stock, however measured, is always the same fraction of nominal GNP, from month to month and year to year, the monetarist case would be pretty well established. We could safely assume that the demand for money is stable and we could begin looking elsewhere to find an explanation for observed fluctuations in the price level and in output. In actual fact, the measured ratio of the money stock to GNP has not been constant, over the short run or the long run. And in the 1930s, it rose suddenly and substantially, as aggregate spending collapsed, the price level fell, and real GNP tumbled. Was this rise in the demand for money the cause of the Great Depression?

The Great Depression

It was the Great Depression of the 1930s that decisively turned the attention of economists and policymakers toward the problem of aggregate demand. Half a century later, much of our thinking about recession, unemployment, and even inflation is still shaped by the experiences of the Great Depression. Anyone who lived through the 1930s will readily understand how the events of a single decade could have such an enduring impact.

For four successive years, beginning in 1930, real output and income declined. It declined by huge amounts: 9 percent in 1930, 8 percent in 1931, 14 percent in 1932, and another 2

percent in 1933. Compare that record with the performance of the U.S. economy since World War II as summarized in Table 16A. On only one occasion has total output declined in two successive years: it fell in 1974 and again in 1975. But the percentage declines were only 0.5 percent and 1.3 percent, almost unnoticeable by the standards of the Great Depression.

Moreover, a full recovery never occurred in the 1930s. In the three years after the 1974–75 recession, output increased by about 5 percent per year, quickly making up the ground lost during the recession. But six years after the trough of the Great Depression was finally reached in 1933, total output and income were only 1.5 percent above what they had been in 1929. With a larger population in 1939 than in 1929, that tiny increase in output and income over the decade was far below what would have been required just to restore pre-depression levels of prosperity. The per-capita after-tax income of Americans actually fell by 7 percent from 1929 to 1939. (It had fallen by almost 30 percent from 1929 to 1933.) The Great Depression even featured a recession within a depression, as real output and income dropped 4 percent from 1937 to 1938.

The most vividly remembered experience of those who lived through the 1930s, however, is the experience of massive, stubborn unemployment. If we leave out 1930, when unemployment was still growing, the unemployment rates of the 1930s averaged more than 19 percent. That is almost one out of every five members of the labor force. At the bottom of the recession, in 1933, 25 percent of the labor force was officially counted as unemployed.

The depth of the recession from 1929 to 1933 was unprecedented in U.S. history. Just as unsettling, however, was the persistent failure of the economy to recover fully after the decline ended. Economists had long known about recessions. They had even made some progress toward understanding why they occurred and what might be done to reduce their severity. But a basic assumption in all theorizing about recessions was that they were temporary disturbances. Recessions were the consequence of mistaken decisions based on misleading or erroneous expectations, and they quickly ran their course as those mistakes were corrected. When the corrections had been made, recovery was supposed to begin and carry total output and income to new heights. Recessions were viewed as temporary interruptions within an overall pattern of long-term growth. The experience of the 1930s raised grave doubts, for obvious reasons, about the adequacy of that analysis.

One man did so much to crystallize economists' rethinking of recessions during and after the 1930s that his name was attached to the "new economics" that emerged. John Maynard Keynes (rhymes with *gains*) was a British economist who lived from 1883 to 1946. He enjoyed a brilliant and diversified career as investor, editor, teacher, writer, government servant, and architect of systems for the reconstructing of international finance. But he is chiefly remembered today as the author of a book published at the beginning of 1936, entitled *The General Theory of Employment, Interest and Money.*

The General Theory, to give it the abbreviated title by which it's usually known, is by common agreement an obscure and badly organized book. "What *The General Theory* Means" was a topic for innumerable essays and symposia in the years immediately following its publication, evidence that its message was deemed important, but that no one quite knew what the essential message was. Books and articles about what Keynes *really* meant continue to appear today, half a century after the publication of *The General Theory.* But consensus at least exists on this much: Keynes believed that the traditional approach of economists to the question of recession came close to assuming the problem away, and that modern industrial economies such as those of Great Britain or the United States did not incline automatically toward full employment.

Order and Disorder in Economic Systems

One of the characteristics of economic theory about which Keynes had misgivings was its tendency to be *a theory of orderly coordination.* But if recessions resulted from a breakdown of the coordinative mechanism, no satisfactory explanation or remedy for recessions would be obtained from a theory which *assumed* that the mechanism was working adequately.

Traditional economic analysis looked on recessions as periods of temporary surplus, for that seems to be what we observe in a recession. Workers are unable to find jobs and products cannot be sold; the quantities of labor and produced goods being supplied are greater than the quantities currently demanded. The economist's ordinary solution to a surplus is a lower price. If workers can't find jobs, it's because they're holding out for a wage that's above their value to employers; at some lower wage all those who want work will be able to find it. If producers can't sell their entire output, it's again because they're asking too high a price; useful goods can always be sold at a sufficiently low price. It's a matter of supply and demand. A recession is simply a temporary disequili-

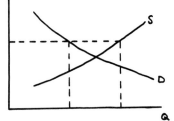

The traditional view:

a surplus indicates the price is too high.

brium. It will come to an end when prices and wages move to their equilibrium or market-clearing levels.

But how long will this take? It only happens instantaneously on the supply and demand graphs of economists. In the real world, market-clearing prices must be searched for, and that process may take weeks, months, or even longer. In the interim the world doesn't stand still. Unemployed workers reduce their spending because they're no longer receiving income, which further reduces the demand for goods. Producers who find themselves with unwanted additions to their inventories cut back production, laying off more workers and reducing the demand for the other goods they use as inputs. Might not an excess supply of labor and produced goods cause a downward spiral in income and demand before prices had fallen far enough to eliminate the surpluses? In that case, prices would have to fall still further to close the gap between supply and demand. Don't recessions, in fact, display just such a cumulative pattern of declining production, reduced income, further declines in production, and further reduced income?

The timeless equilibrium analysis of the traditional economics in which Keynes had been trained did not examine the groping process by which new equilibrium positions are found. It assumed, in effect, an instantaneous leap to a new equilibrium whenever an old equilibrium was disturbed. But if the causes of recessions are to be found in what happens while the economy is out of equilibrium, then the traditional analysis had indeed assumed the problem away.

The importance of expectations in shaping economic decisions also impressed Keynes very strongly. An emphasis on expectations meant an emphasis on the uncertainty of decision making, the frequency of mistakes, the need for time in which to adjust to unanticipated events, and the disorder of economic systems. None of this was captured in the timeless, orderly, errorless world of traditional equilibrium analysis. In *The General Theory* Keynes sought to explain the phenomenon of recession by taking into account the consequences of uncertainty and the processes of adjustment over time. That led him to focus on aggregate demand.

The Unstable Force: Investment Spending

The initiating cause of aggregate fluctuations in output and income, in the Keynesian framework, is a change in the desired rate of investment expenditure.

Recall what investment means. To invest is to purchase a good for the sake of the future income it is expected to yield. A business firm is investing, therefore, when it purchases

machinery, just as you would be investing if you purchased corporate stock. But we must distinguish between those two kinds of investment, because we're interested now in investment as a process of adding to the demand for new goods, for gross national product. Your purchase of corporate stock would merely be a transfer of financial assets. Even if you bought *new* stock, issued so that the corporation could purchase additional machinery, your surrender of money to acquire stock would be a financial transfer only. The real investment would occur when the new machinery was produced and sold to the corporation that you supplied with funds. Investment in this sense is one of the four components of total expenditures on gross national product—along with household consumption expenditures, government purchases of new commodities and services, and net exports.

Investment is extremely important for the understanding of recessions, in the Keynesian analysis, because investment spending is far less stable than consumption spending. There's no mystery about why that should be the case. It's usually easier to postpone the purchase of capital goods than to postpone the purchase of consumer goods. People are therefore likely to maintain consumption spending at a fairly steady rate, but to "bunch" investment spending at what they consider appropriate times. Moreover, the purchase of any good that's expected to yield its services over a long period of time entails additional uncertainty. Will the stream of services turn out to be as large as it's currently expected to be? Will some new method of securing these services appear soon and make this investment obsolete? Will a more opportune time come along later, perhaps a time when funds can be borrowed more cheaply or when capital-goods producers are offering lower prices? Continually changing conditions can act on the uncertain expectations of investors to produce waves of postponed or accelerated investment expenditures.

Are Fluctuations Self-Correcting?

There was nothing unusual in 1936 about focusing on investment decisions as the principal trigger of economic fluctuations. The big question was and still is: What happens next? *Does the economic system moderate or does it magnify the initial effects* of the change in investment expenditures? Most economists up to the time of Keynes believed that the economic system operated to check and reverse destabilizing decisions. Keynes found it more probable, at least in mature industrial economies, that the system would magnify disturbances and would demonstrate little capacity to generate a recovery from recessions. Which view is correct?

Almost anyone looking back from 1939 at the performance of the American economy over the previous decade would incline toward the Keynesian view. Whatever forces were supposed to arrest a decline in output and income certainly didn't seem to be working from 1929 to 1933. And if a recession was indeed a time for correcting mistakes, after which growth could resume again on a sounder basis, the payoff seemed terribly slow in coming.

Let's look at some of the stabilizing forces that were supposed to dampen recessions and initiate recoveries, then at Keynes's reasons for doubting their effectiveness. One such force was falling prices. Recessions had historically meant a falling price level, or a rising value for money. When people *expect* prices to fall, they become more eager to hold money. But once prices *have* fallen, the real value of the public's money balances is larger. Moreover, prices that have already fallen will be more widely expected to rise than to fall further. These two situations brought about by a recession—larger money holdings in terms of purchasing power and an increased expectation of rising prices—should prompt people to begin reducing their money balances by increasing their rate of expenditures above their incomes. This will bring about recovery.

If prices will fall, postpone purchases until goods are cheaper.

If prices have fallen, purchase now while goods are cheap.

But suppose the recession produces a sizable fall in output with very little change in prices? The public will still find its stock of money balances growing, relative to income and expenditures. At some point the public will decide it's holding all the money it wants to hold, in view of the lower gross national product, and will begin exchanging money for other goods. This will launch a recovery.

A decline in investment spending also implies less demand for loans, which in turn implies a decrease in the cost of borrowing. But as the cost of borrowing falls, the incentive to invest increases. Some investment projects that had been postponed will now be undertaken in response to better credit terms, and aggregate investment will revive. This will promote recovery.

The idle resources that begin to appear in a recession also provide opportunities for entrepreneurs who were waiting for the right location, favorable lease, or more advantageous terms from suppliers. Thus the recession itself encourages new initiatives, increased production, and additional investment. All of this works to slow down the decline in a recession and generate a recovery.

Keynesian Doubts

Keynes had reasons for suspecting that none of these countering forces might be sufficient, especially in a wealthy,

industrialized economy. To begin with, prices might not fall in response to decreased demand. The market power of larger sellers, the wage-fixing practices of labor unions, and the existence of long-term contracts all tend to put a floor under the existing level of prices. With prices rigid in a downward direction, decreases in aggregate demand would not raise the purchasing power of money. Decreases in demand would operate almost exclusively to reduce total output.

Another objection: although it is true that the public's money holdings increase when its expenditures decrease, that assumes other things remain equal. But they don't remain equal if income falls as fast as expenditures. And a reduction in total output entails a simultaneous reduction in total income, since people receive their income from the sale of what they produce.

If the stock of money doesn't change while gross national product is falling, the ratio between the public's cash balances and its income will rise, of course. But this doesn't necessarily mean the public will find itself holding larger money balances than it *prefers* to hold. Here is another Keynesian doubt: the demand for money might increase substantially because of the public's apprehension about the coming recession and the expectation that the value of money is going to increase.

The lower interest rates and other reduced costs that recessions usually bring in their wake do indeed tend to spur investment and production. But will their combined effect be enough to offset the gloomy expectations that recession creates? How much stimulus is a one-point reduction in the interest rate to entrepreneurs who fear that there will be no demand for their output?

Some of the most interesting passages in *The General Theory* present Keynes's thoughts (usually quite unsystematic) on the importance of expectations. It is expectations, as you know by now, that guide economic decisions. The relevant expectations will not be based exclusively on the decision makers' appraisals of their own particular prospects. Larger and more vague considerations will also enter in, such as the state of the economy, the political climate, the social milieu, and even (as Keynes suggests in one place) the nerves, hysteria, digestions, and reactions to the weather of potential investors.

Expectations and the state of confidence were especially important to Keynes's interpretation of the role that money played (or failed to play) in restraining a recession and promoting a recovery. Remember that the monetary authorities can increase the excess reserves of the banking system but cannot compel the commercial banks to extend loans and thereby turn those reserves into money. Moreover, the creation

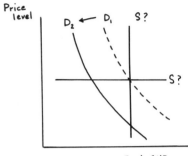

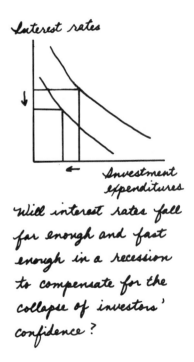

Will interest rates fall far enough and fast enough in a recession to compensate for the collapse of investors' confidence?

of a larger money stock will not produce an increase in spending if the public responds simply by building up its money balances.

In a recession, everyone tends to become more pessimistic and more cautious. Banks scrutinize potential borrowers more rigorously before extending loans and refuse to renew some loans that come due. Borrowers are less eager to apply for loans because short-term profit prospects seem unfavorable. People look for ways to increase their liquidity as a precautionary move. The expectation of declining prices also adds to the public's preference for holding money rather than assets whose value relative to money is likely to fall. In short, a recession can create a crisis of confidence that worsens the recession by prompting a sharp increase in the demand for money. The monetary authorities may find it difficult to satisfy this demand or to induce people to begin spending their idle balances. In these circumstances, efforts by the central bank to halt a recession or to spur a recovery will be like pushing on a string. "Pushing on a string" became, in fact, a common way of characterizing the impotence of monetary authorities in dealing with recessions.

The conclusions seemed rather clear to most observers by the end of the 1930s. Relatively small changes in demand can trigger substantial changes in output and employment. The cumulative interaction of expenditures, output, income, and expectations can transform minor disturbances into major disruptions, because the economic system does not contain stabilizing forces of sufficient strength. The adjustments of consumers, investors, and producers to changed circumstances don't necessarily push the economy back toward full employment when it begins to slip toward recession. On the contrary, the economy can settle down indefinitely at a rate of output far below capacity and with high unemployment.

The radical departure in the Keynesian way of looking at the world lies in the specific assumptions that were made, not always explicitly, by those who adopted the Keynesian framework. Almost all of these assumptions touch on the issue of *coordination*. Does the market economy transmit information smoothly and quickly enough to limit and dampen the effects of destabilizing decisions? Or does it aggravate the effects of such decisions by sending out signals that induce people to make things worse for others in an effort to make things better for themselves, with the eventual consequence that things are worse for almost everyone? The Keynesian attitude toward saving provides perhaps the best example of such a contrast in basic presuppositions.

Keynes himself liked to emphasize his theory's implications for the way we regard the act of saving. In the Keynesian perspective, saving is not the unmixed blessing that economists have traditionally assumed it to be. If intended investment falls, the attempt by savers to continue their current rate of saving will prevent consumption expenditure from picking up the slack. The result will be unsold goods, reduced output, and reduced incomes—until savers have been compelled by falling income to scale down their rate of saving to what investors want to spend. This comes close to reversing the traditional argument that high rates of saving are necessary to permit high rates of investment.

It has long been a fundamental tenet of economics that a nation's income and wealth grow roughly in proportion to the growth in its stock of capital. Investment is the process that adds to the capital stock. A higher rate of investment therefore means a faster rate of economic growth, a more rapid rise in national income, and a speedier improvement in living levels. But what determines the rate of investment? The classical answer was: the rate of saving. There is no way for a society to produce capital goods except by withdrawing some of its resources from the production of consumer goods. Those who save abstain from current consumption and either purchase capital goods themselves or turn their income over to others who purchase capital goods. Without saving there can be no investment. (If investment is financed by borrowing from abroad, foreigners must do the saving.) The incentive to save must therefore be preserved and extended, according to the classical argument; it is the root cause of social progress.

Keynes suspected that this line of reasoning might be altogether inapplicable to societies in advanced stages of economic growth. Economic growth, Keynes believed, had two effects that jointly made the practice of thrift an increasingly doubtful virtue. On the one hand, the accumulation of capital in the course of economic growth meant that the most profitable investment opportunities were steadily used up. Further additions to the capital stock had to go toward projects with lower expected rates of return for investors. The incentive to invest consequently tended to fall as economic growth proceeded.

On the other hand, the incentive to save tended to become stronger. Saving, Keynes maintained, depends primarily on income. People will tend to save more as their income rises and will in fact tend to save a higher proportion of their income as that income increases. Because economic growth

increases people's incomes, therefore, it increases the amounts that they desire to save relative to their income.

The implication is that in wealthy, industrialized economies the desire to save will be continually pushing out ahead of the desire to invest. But if people wish to save a larger amount than investors are willing to spend, the savers can't succeed. Their purpose will be frustrated by an insufficient aggregate demand, which will lead to lower output and higher unemployment, until the reduced incomes of savers finally persuade them to save no more than investors are willing to spend.

Demand-Side and Supply-Side Analysis

The classical argument on this issue has been revived in recent years under the title "supply-side economics," a title intended as a criticism of the Keynesian emphasis on aggregate demand. Both sides agree that higher real incomes and more employment opportunities depend on adequate rates of investment. But after that, they diverge. "Supply-siders" insist that the way to get increased investment spending is to enhance the incentive to save. Keynes, by contrast, argued that saving would take care of itself if only the level of investment spending could be maintained. And for that purpose, enhanced incentives to save were worse than useless. The solution lay in maintaining the demand for goods so that investors would want to purchase capital equipment.

From the Keynesian perspective, a chronic tendency toward insufficient demand, created by persistent efforts to save more than investors want to spend, might so damage the "state of confidence" that the aggregate desire to invest actually decreased. Here would be a strange outcome indeed, one that came to be known as the "paradox of thrift" among those who thought that the 1930s had shown it to be a genuine threat to prosperity. An increased desire to save so damages the incentive to invest that output and income fall below the level at which savers can even maintain their previously desired rate of saving. The attempt to save more results in less actual saving. The public would actually succeed in increasing the amount it saves if it determined to save less—and thus spent more.

This would not mean, it's important to note, that anyone can save more by spending more. And that's what counts. A household or business firm that wants to increase its rate of saving will not achieve that end by reducing its rate of saving. The paradox of thrift applies to the actions of savers and investors as a whole. But saving and investment decisions are not made by "wholes." They are made by persons who

Keynes: Demand will create supply.

"Supply-siders": Supply will create demand.

The traditional perspective:

INCOME

CONSUMPTION   SAVINGS

INVESTMENT

HIGHER OUTPUT AND INCOME

The Keynesian perspective:

INCOME

CONSUMPTION   SAVINGS

LESS DEMAND

LOWER OUTPUT AND INCOME

don't assume—and quite correctly don't assume—that their own actions will induce others to behave in the same way.

The Coordination Problem Once Again

That brings us back to the question of *coordination*. When you think about it for a moment, you realize that almost every single action within an economic system depends for its success on cooperative behavior on the part of other people. There's no earthly point to an author's struggling to explain Keynesian economics unless many, many other people completely unknown to him are going to cooperate later: editors, printers, sales representatives, postal clerks, professors, bookstores, and students, to mention just a few. Moreover, an author knows that his own efforts will not, by themselves, induce the required cooperation. Nonetheless, he sits at his desk struggling with words, when he would much rather be out playing tennis, because he believes that the system will work. The right people will somehow get the appropriate signals and the book will eventually be produced, marketed, and—here belief becomes hope—purchased in gratifying quantities.

Keynes feared that the system would *not* "work" when it came to the task of coordinating the decisions of savers and the decisions of investors. He feared that demand might be chronically insufficient in advanced industrial economies, with high levels of unemployment as the consequence. But he offered more than a gloomy diagnosis. He also offered suggestions for a cure. If the private sector was unwilling to invest enough to maintain full employment, government could take steps to close the gap.

That leads us to the consideration of monetary and fiscal policy, the topic for Chapter 19. In the course of the chapter, we will also examine the monetarists' "counterrevolution" and their case for the essential stability of the demand for money.

Once Over Lightly

Economists who emphasize the importance of controlling aggregate demand as a way of achieving high employment with price stability may be usefully divided into monetarists and Keynesians.

Monetarists claim that, because the demand for money is basically stable, the key to a stable economy is stability in the rate at which money is supplied to the economy.

Given a stable demand for money, increases in the quantity of money raise expenditures, and decreases in the quantity of money reduce expenditures.

These changes in expenditures cause changes in nominal gross national product and are the principal cause of fluctuations in output, employment, and the price level.

Keynesians point to the Great Depression as evidence that the economy is not inherently stable in the absence of disturbing changes in the money supply. In the Keynesian perspective, disturbances arise from the inherent instability of private-sector spending decisions, especially decisions affecting investment expenditures.

These disturbances are magnified by the functioning of markets, producing large cyclical swings in economic activity and the possibility of semipermanent economic collapse.

In the Keynesian view, aggregate demand may be chronically insufficient to maintain high levels of output and employment. In such circumstances, acts of saving will retard economic growth by removing some demand-side stimulus. This view directly contradicts the classical position, according to which aggregate demand is always adequate and saving accelerates economic growth by allowing further investment in productivity-enhancing capital goods.

QUESTIONS FOR DISCUSSION

1. Analogies must be used with care. But this one may help you visualize the major relationships between the two flows of income and of expenditures and the stock of money. Imagine a lake formed by a dammed-up river. Let the lake represent the stock of money someone is holding. The river above the lake represents income, the river below the lake represents expenditures.
   (a) What must be done to raise or to lower the lake level?
   (b) How could the lake level be raised, even though the flow above the lake is declining? How could the lake level be lowered, even though the flow above the lake is increasing?
   (c) If the dam operator anticipates a late-summer drought and wants to prevent the lake from falling below some desired level, what might be done during the spring?

2. What is the good that people want to obtain more of when they decide to increase the quantity of money they are going to hold?
   (a) What are the major factors you consider in deciding how large you want your stock of money balances to be? What sorts of events would induce you to increase or decrease your preferred stock of money balances?
   (b) What other assets function for you as partial substitutes for money balances?
   (c) What are some of the assets that business firms might choose to hold as partial substitutes for money balances?
   (d) Is a good credit rating an asset that someone might use as a substitute for money balances? Is that what people do when they start off on a

trip carrying little currency but a credit card with a large credit limit and a small current balance?

3. You want to buy a used sailboat if the right one comes along at the right price. You think you'll be able to get a better deal if you can offer the seller immediate cash. What are some good options for you to consider as alternatives to holding M1 while you're searching for the sailboat?

4. Some people think that consumers could stop inflation if they launched a consumer strike against higher prices.
   (a) What would happen to your stock of money balances if you decided to do your part in fighting inflation by reducing your expenditures?
   (b) How likely is it that large numbers of people will choose their preferred level of money balances by neglecting their personal interests and considering instead the contribution they might make to stopping inflation?
   (c) What would happen to the value of your stock of money balances if you did this and inflation continued?

5. Would money function as a medium of exchange if people were unwilling to hold it, even for very short periods of time? Is there any difference between a barter economy and an economy in which people hold no money balances?

6. What effect would you expect each of the following to have on the average size of the checking account balances that business firms and households want to hold?
   (a) An unusually high rate of expenditures is anticipated in the near future.
   (b) The rate of interest on savings accounts rises.
   (c) Banks offer to provide checking account services at no fee on accounts that maintain a $400 minimum balance during any month.
   (d) Banks pay interest on checking accounts.
   (e) The monetary authorities increase the quantity of money rapidly over an extended period of time and the public begins to anticipate a high rate of inflation.

7. We describe the demand for most goods by referring to prices and the number of units that would be demanded at those prices. But economists describe the demand for money by referring to the price (or cost) of holding money and *some percentage of income*.
   (a) Why is the quantity demanded expressed as a percentage in the case of money, rather than as a number of units?
   (b) Would you be willing to say that someone's demand for money had not changed if that person held the same quantity of dollars when his money income had doubled and the purchasing power of dollars had fallen 50 percent?

8. Suppose that every household and business firm decided to spend on Tuesday every dollar it was holding.
   (a) What would be the effect on the stock of money balances held on Wednesday by households and business firms?
   (b) What other effects would you predict from such a mass decision to unload money balances?
   (c) Suppose this decision resulted from a sudden conviction that money was going to be worthless by the end of the week. What do you think would happen?

9. Assume that the public wants to hold money balances, in the form of M1, equal to one-sixth of nominal gross national product.
   (a) How large will GNP have to be to persuade the public to hold $700 billion of M1?
   (b) If M1 rises by $10 billion, by how much will GNP have to rise to induce the public to hold this additional amount of money?
   (c) Will this increase in GNP mean greater prosperity?
10. Anyone who reads extensively in economic history will encounter periodic complaints from merchants about a *scarcity of money* in the hands of the public.
   (a) What observations by a merchant might prompt such a complaint?
   (b) What might cause a widespread increase in the incidence of such complaints from merchants?
   (c) Why do you suppose it is that so many merchants throughout history have associated an abundance of money with prosperity and a scarcity of it with hard times?
   (d) If more money in the possession of a particular merchant's customers will produce prosperity for that merchant, will more money in everyone's hands produce greater prosperity for all merchants?
11. What effect does inflation have on the value of people's money balances? What will happen if the monetary authorities, in an effort to maintain the real value of the public's money holdings, increase the stock of money when inflation occurs?
12. What caused the recession that began in the United States in 1929? Why did the decline continue for four years? Why did the decline occur at such a steep rate? Why did real output not regain its 1929 level until 1939? Why did the unemployment rate remain so extraordinarily high throughout the 1930s? Why has no recession or depression of even remotely comparable severity occurred since World War II? (Substantial disagreement still exists among economic theorists and economic historians on how these questions are to be answered. How one evaluates the long-run importance of Keynes's contribution to economic theory will depend largely on the answers given to these questions.)
13. Can an economy be in equilibrium if much of its industrial capacity is standing idle and a large percentage of its labor force is unemployed? Is that a question about fact or a disguised argument about the proper way to use the concept of equilibrium?
14. Suppose that consumer demand for the following goods turns out to be less than the producers anticipated, so that the goods already produced cannot all be sold at current prices. What consequences would you predict in the case of each good? Would prices or production levels be likely to fall first? How long will the sequence of adjustments take?
   (a) automobiles
   (b) beef cattle
   (c) secondary-school teachers
15. How long must a recession continue or a recovery be delayed before we're justified in assuming that recessions are not *temporary* disturbances?

16. If total expenditures on new goods fall below total income, so that aggregate saving increases, what happens to these savings?

17. Consumer expenditures on durable goods fluctuate far more from year to year than do consumer expenditures on nondurable commodities or on services. How does this support the contention that investment expenditures are less stable than consumption expenditures?

18. Do fluctuations in spending for particular goods necessarily cause fluctuations in the output of those goods? Do you think that production rates in the toy industry fluctuate as much as consumer expenditures for toys fluctuate? Under what circumstances can a smooth flow of production be reconciled with variations in expenditure on that output? When are reductions in expenditure most likely to cause production cutbacks and unemployment in a particular firm or industry?

19. The following questions all deal with the relationship between investment and interest rates.

    (a) How do interest rates affect investment spending?

    (b) How do higher interest rates affect residential construction?

    (c) "Shall we maintain production and allow our inventories of unsold goods to rise or should we shut down production until we've managed to sell off most of the finished goods now in the warehouses?" How might the level of interest rates enter into this decision?

    (d) An electric utility postpones construction of a new generating plant because the market price of its bonds is disappointingly low. How does this illustrate the relationship between investment and the interest rate?

    (e) A corporation plans to begin a huge capital expansion program, using proceeds from a sale of new stock. But common-stock prices decline and the firm postpones the stock sale and the investment program it was intended to finance. Does that have anything to do with interest rates?

    (f) "Higher interest rates don't deter any business firm that has a profitable use for the money. If we can make 30 percent on an investment, we're going to invest whether we can borrow at 3 percent or have to pay 12 percent." Evaluate this statement.

    (g) "The higher the interest rate I can get, the more I'm going to invest. Investment increases as interest rates rise." Is that right?

    (h) "Interest rates tend to be higher in booms than in recessions. But investment spending is usually greater in booms than in recessions. This implies that high interest rates encourage investment spending and low interest rates discourage it." Criticize that argument.

20. Does investment depend on saving? Can investment occur if there has been no saving? What are the real differences between the older view that investment could be maintained only by maintaining saving and Keynes's view that a high rate of investment might be a precondition for a high rate of saving?

21. Does the "paradox of thrift" imply that saving is an antisocial act and consumption an act that benefits society?

22. Congress cut tax rates substantially in 1964. A long period of rising output and falling unemployment followed. Did the tax cuts work by stimulating

consumer spending—the "demand-side" claim? Or did they work by offering investors better after-tax returns—the "supply-side" claim?

23. In the following passage from Adam Smith's *The Wealth of Nations*, the word *stock* refers either to a stock of goods or to a stock of money that can be used to acquire goods.

> In all countries where there is tolerable security, every man of common understanding will endeavor to employ whatever stock he can command, in procuring either present enjoyment or future profit. . . . A man must be perfectly crazy who, where there is tolerable security, does not employ all the stock which he commands [in one of these ways].

(a) Does this passage imply that all income will be either consumed or invested?

(b) Is this passage compatible with Keynes's analysis of the saving-investment relationship?

Fiscal and Monetary Policy

It all seems quite simple and straightforward when you first begin to think about it. Government can stop recessions and prevent inflations by using its power to affect the flow of total spending. Surely everyone agrees that government has that power. And if it has the power, it ought to use it. Why should people suffer from unemployment or rising prices when government knows how to prevent them?

It's all so clear and obvious *until* you begin thinking about it more carefully and concretely. Then uncertainties, problems, and contradictions start to appear and multiply rapidly, until in the end you may find yourself suspecting that government actually has very little power to prevent inflation or recession but an enormous capacity to create or aggravate these problems.

Aggregate-Demand Management

The topic of this chapter is *aggregate-demand management by government*. The government has two sets of tools with which it can affect aggregate demand: fiscal policy and monetary policy. Fiscal policy means budget policy. In the context of our discussion, *fiscal policy is policy aimed at controlling undesired changes in aggregate demand through planned changes in government expenditures and taxes.*

Monetary policy is policy aimed at controlling undesired fluctuations in aggregate demand through planned changes in commercial-bank reserves or legal reserve requirements, as explained in Chapter 17. It has only been within the last twenty-five years or so that monetary policy has achieved anything like equal status with fiscal policy in the thinking of economists. The impotence of monetary policy as a means of restoring prosperity seemed to many to have been adequately demon-

strated in the Great Depression, when the Fed pursued an "easy money" policy but could not stir a revival of bank lending and private spending. Keynesians and other critics of monetary policy argued that it was ineffective because the demand for money was unpredictable. Increases in the size of the money stock could be canceled out by simultaneous increases in the amount of money the public wanted to hold, perhaps in response to heightened misgivings about the future course of the economy that made people want to build up their reserves of liquid assets.

The power of fiscal policy, on the other hand, seemed to have been demonstrated by the "fiscal experiment" of 1940-44. After a decade of depression caused by low levels of consumer and investment spending and timid government responses, World War II practically compelled the government to run huge budget deficits. Government expenditures shot up much faster than taxes could be raised, and the economy revived spectacularly. Once they had been restored by a massive injection of government spending, consumption and investment were able to take up the slack when government expenditures fell sharply again after the war. That at least was the story Keynesians told.

Monetary policy inched its way back into esteem after World War II through a concurrence of events. One was the unexpected mildness of recessions in the postwar period and the persistence of inflation. Inflation was a problem against which monetary policy might be more effective than it supposedly was against recession. *Increases* in the money supply might be canceled out by increases in the demand for money; but that did not necessarily mean that *decreases* in the money supply would be equally ineffective. In the metaphor already mentioned, one could pull a balloon down with a string even though pushing on the string would not make it rise. As a practical matter, it was also much easier to tighten up on money growth when aggregate demand was expanding too rapidly than it was to get tax increases or spending reductions through Congress. So the monetary managers were able to practice their stabilization skills to some extent by trying to control inflation. These experiments in turn persuaded many observers that monetary policy, though perhaps impotent at the depth of a severe depression, might well be effective as an expansionary tool in *mild* recessions.

Meanwhile, however, economists who weren't satisfied with the Keynesian diagnosis and the prescriptions of fiscal policy were doing research on the critical question of the stability of the demand for money. They pointed out that the Fed had made enormous mistakes in the 1930s, first in allowing the banking system and the money supply to collapse

after 1929, then in failing to provide for a stable monetary expansion. Small wonder that consumer and investor confidence had collapsed, and that the public was inclined to build up liquid reserves in the 1930s whenever it got the chance.

Moreover, the demand for money was showing a great deal of stability in the years after World War II. The public was definitely not hoarding money in response to expansionary Fed policies and increased commercial-bank lending. On the contrary, the public seemed able and eager to use any new credit it could find. Private-sector borrowing grew faster than GNP, to finance business investment, residential construction, and consumer-goods purchases. Under these conditions, monetary policy might be a potent weapon even when used to expand aggregate demand. Monetarists even started to argue that it was fiscal policy rather than monetary policy that was powerless to affect aggregate demand.

Financing Deficits

Keep in mind that a deficit must be financed by borrowing. A federal-government deficit requires the Treasury to borrow the difference between government expenditures and government tax revenues. Where can the Treasury go when it wants to borrow?

One possibility, if it's permitted by law, is to borrow directly from the Federal Reserve. The Fed simply credits the Treasury with additional deposits in exchange for government securities. When the Treasury then spends those deposits, they flow into the bank accounts or currency holdings of defense contractors, welfare recipients, government employees, or whoever is on the receiving end of the expenditures. The money stock consequently increases.

From whom is the government borrowing when it runs a budget deficit?

These new deposits are also new reserves for the commercial banking system. Banks will therefore find their lending power increased. If they can locate eligible borrowers, the commercial banks will, by expanding their loans, create a further addition to the money stock.

It follows that the money stock could increase by the entire amount of the deficit even though the Fed directly financed only a portion of the deficit. A $50-billion deficit, for example, could be handled through some combination like a Fed purchase of $15 billion in new government securities and commercial-bank purchases of $35 billion. The Fed purchase, by supplying new reserves to the banking system, enables the commercial banks to acquire additional government securities by creating new demand deposits.

Will the lenders create the money they provide to finance the budget deficit?

That all looks suspiciously close to Treasury financing of government deficits through the creation of new money. If

Congress tries to prevent that by prohibiting the Fed from buying new Treasury securities, the Fed can simply buy old ones through its ordinary open-market operations. The effect will be, for all practical purposes, precisely the same: government securities will be added to the Fed's portfolio and additional reserves will flow into the commercial banking system. The only difference is that the Fed will be taking previously issued securities out of the portfolios of commercial banks, thereby enabling the banks to buy all the newly issued Treasury securities. That's a difference that doesn't make a difference. The effect is still to increase the stock of money by the amount of the government budget deficit.

The "Crowding-Out" Effects of Deficits

Is there then no way for the government to finance a deficit without increasing the stock of money in the process? There is a way. The Treasury must borrow neither from the Fed nor from commercial banks but from nonbank lenders. Instead of getting the banking system to create new money equal to the amount of its deficit, the Treasury must compete with other prospective borrowers for the available supply of loanable funds. But unless there are idle funds around, the Treasury is going to crowd out other borrowers when it goes this route. Interest rates will rise as the Treasury adds its demand to the private-sector demand for credit, and the higher price of credit will have the effect that higher prices always have. It will persuade some borrowers to give up their projects and withdraw from the credit market. The upshot is that the government's deficit spending will simply have displaced some private spending. Government expenditures will rise, but the sum of private-sector consumption and investment expenditures will fall by an equal amount, leaving no effect on aggregate demand. In a remarkable turnabout, it is fiscal policy rather than monetary policy that proves itself incapable of expanding aggregate demand. That at least is the story monetarists tell.

There's one other possibility, however. Suppose the public is holding large money balances because consumers and investors are fearful of the future and don't want to spend. People might be persuaded to exchange those balances for government securities. That would give the Treasury the money it wants without an increase in the money stock. More spending would then occur with no increase in the money supply, because the government would be spending previously idle balances that the public had been persuaded to exchange for government bonds.

But is that very likely except in a period of deep depression? Perhaps in the 1930s public confidence was so

Are there idle funds in the hands of the public that can be used to finance the budget deficit?

low that deficit spending could tap large idle money balances. But that doesn't seem to describe the situation at any time in the United States since World War II.

Links between Fiscal and Monetary Policy

The conclusion is a simple one. Deficit spending by the government affects the monetary sector. It results in some combination of an enlarged money stock and higher interest rates. Insofar as the Fed tries to prevent government expenditures from crowding out private expenditures by making more reserves available to the banking system when the Treasury is borrowing, it causes a growth in the money stock. If the Fed tries to prevent such an increase, it will force private borrowers to bid against the Treasury for the limited supply of credit. Fiscal policy is therefore inseparable from monetary policy.

Monetary policy, on the other hand, can be conducted independently of fiscal policy. Government spending uses money, but more money can be created and spent independently of any changes in the government budget. It doesn't follow, however, that fiscal policy cannot be a useful aid to monetary policy. Remember that the Fed doesn't control the size of the money stock directly. It can increase the available reserves of the banking system, but it can't force anyone to borrow and thereby convert free reserves into money. Government borrowing and expenditure is therefore one way to increase the money stock and to increase it rapidly. In a period of low confidence, when consumers and investors don't want to borrow, fiscal policy might be the only way to make monetary policy effective. The 1930s come immediately to mind.

All of this has some important implications. One is that the often vehement debates in recent years over the respective roles of fiscal and monetary policy in causing inflation might be largely debates over a nonissue. The federal government has been running very large deficits in recent years. To ask whether this causes inflation if the Fed does not simultaneously allow a rapid expansion in the money stock is a somewhat pointless question; an expansion of the money stock becomes almost inevitable when the federal government starts running $200 billion annual budget deficits.

The other important implication of our analysis is that the Keynesians might well have been correct in the 1930s without being correct today. Those who warned against government budget deficits in the 1930s on the grounds that the deficits would only crowd out private-sector spending and thereby delay the recovery seem rather absurd in retrospect. Of course, it is no less absurd to make policy for the 1980s on the

assumption that the times we're living in are basically like those of the 1930s.

The Necessity of Good Timing

Timing is absolutely crucial if aggregate-demand management is to be an effective stabilizing tool. But good timing proves extraordinarily difficult to achieve when it comes to fiscal or monetary policy, and for several reasons.

In the first place, we never know until long afterward whether aggregate demand was rising or falling. The economy doesn't come equipped with a speedometer that tells us how fast it's running at any moment. We find out what GNP is doing during the current quarter only at the end of the quarter. Even then the figures provided by the Bureau of Economic Analysis are highly tentative and subject to sizable revisions as more accurate data become available a month and more after the quarter has ended.

What's worse, even if we could know exactly where we are at any time, that wouldn't be enough. Those who conduct fiscal and monetary policy have to know where we're *going to be*, because today's action must aim at compensating for tomorrow's deficiency or excess. Stabilization policy is necessarily based on forecasting, and short-term economic forecasting, far from being an exact science, isn't even a respectable art.

Particularly troubling is our inability to predict how much time it will take for a fiscal or monetary policy action to have its effects. Estimates of the length of these lags range from a few months to several years, and diligent research efforts designed to nail down the time distribution of the effects haven't produced a workable consensus. The lags may even turn out to vary in ways we can't predict, in which case economists would be trying to measure something that actually has no standard length.

There are good reasons for supposing that the time lags between fiscal or monetary policy actions and their effects are not some constant that can be measured and then relied on. The effects of these actions will depend, after all, on how producers and consumers read their own uncertain individual futures. Government actions reduce some uncertainties, but they add others; they certainly don't enable people to start planning with complete confidence about what the future holds. Meanwhile the operating procedures of commercial banks, the payment practices of business firms, the perceptions of households and corporations with respect to the advantages of holding assets in one form or another, international monetary transactions, and even the public's efforts to

Time lags:

1. recognizing the problem

2. deciding exactly what to do

anticipate the effects of government actions will all play a part in determining the distribution over time of any policy's impact on total spending. These factors will be changing continuously. And they are especially likely to change in response to any improvement in our ability to forecast them! It is a case in which forecasts falsify themselves by altering the stock of information that had to be assumed in order to make the forecast. Here's a simple example: if we knew with confidence the pattern that some stock's market price would trace over the coming year, it wouldn't trace that pattern. This is the paradox with which sciences of human behavior must live. Predicting the future changes the future, because the people whose actions create the future read the predictions.

The Federal Budget as a Policy Tool

When we turn specifically to fiscal policy, an additional difficulty emerges. There is at least a touch of comedy in the belief that the federal government can use its budget as a stabilization tool when almost all observers agree that Congress no longer has effective control over the budget. The spending programs of the federal government are so many and so complex that no one can even begin to evaluate all of them for the purpose of determining annual appropriations. As a result, next year's budget begins by taking this year's budget for granted and adding on. Once a program gets in, it's almost impossible to dislodge, because its beneficiaries form a knowledgeable and determined lobby for its continuance, and no one on Capitol Hill has the time, energy, and interest to accumulate the evidence that could justify its removal.

3. from decision to impact

Fiscal policy is not something under the control of the Council of Economic Advisers. A change in government expenditures or in federal taxes requires action by the House of Representatives and then the Senate, with committee meetings before and often after, and a presidential signature at the end. That takes time—and timing, as we said, is crucial. The discussions will be complicated and prolonged by the fact that, even if Congress were to agree quickly on the desirability of a change in expenditures or taxes of a particular amount, it would still have to decide whose taxes will be changed and which expenditures. Conflicting interests will be involved as well as alternative theories about the expansionary or contractionary effects of particular actions. Is it better to cut the taxes of low-income people or to give tax credits for investment? Which will have a greater impact on employment? And are we talking about the long run or the short run? Meanwhile some members of Congress will certainly decide

that an important tax or expenditure bill provides an opportunity to eliminate the depletion allowance for oil producers, give a bonus to retired people on social security, prop up the housing industry through a special subsidy, or take a slap at multinational corporations—to mention only some of the concerns that managed to achieve expression in the March 1975 "antirecessionary" tax bill.

The more in a hurry Congress and the president are, the more likely they are to produce fiscal-policy actions that few competent and impartial observers will be able to defend. The imperative of haste tends to enhance the power of those who are willing to enforce their demands by threatening to block any action at all. But due deliberation, the careful assessment of alternatives, and the weighing of the probable short- and long-term outcomes may require so much time that the moment for action passes before any action is taken. The 1974-75 recession began late in 1973. Congress passed an antirecessionary tax-cut bill at the end of March, 1975. Even at that late date, the bill contained evidence of haste. And it came too late to counter the recession but just in time, perhaps, to help fuel the next round of inflation.

Advocates of stabilization through fiscal policy have long been aware of these difficulties. They know that the protracted discussions that precede any congressional action on taxes and expenditures could easily make fiscal policy unworkable: action might not be possible until the time for it has passed. They have consequently looked around for ways to speed up the process. One proposal recommended by some economists and urged by President John Kennedy was that Congress authorize unilateral action by the president. Appropriations for particular projects could be approved by Congress and then put on the shelf, to be taken off whenever the president and his advisers decided that the stimulus of increased government expenditures was called for. Congress could also authorize the president to increase or decrease tax rates within narrow limits when aggregate demand seemed excessive or inadequate.

If you're wondering why Congress never acted on such a "sensible" recommendation, think for a moment about the political power that a president would command if he could unilaterally determine the timing of tax decreases and the placement of expenditure projects. Congress isn't likely to grant that kind of power to any president, not even to a trusted president who is a member of the same political party as the majority in both houses of Congress. Some senators and representatives will be deterred by the constitutional principle of a balance of power among the branches of government, some by respect for Lord Acton's maxim that

absolute power corrupts absolutely. But all will know that such power in the hands of a president substantially diminishes their own power and influence. The conclusion, therefore, is that fiscal policy *at best* will continue to be a stabilization tool that doesn't become available until the appropriate time for its use has passed.

But isn't this negative verdict on fiscal policy inconsistent with the historical record? Hasn't fiscal policy actually been used effectively to fight recessions?

Stabilization versus Stimulus

The rather common belief that fiscal policy has proved its effectiveness as a stabilization tool seems to be based largely on a failure to distinguish between the ability to stabilize aggregate demand and the ability to change it. But stabilization requires more than the power to change aggregate demand; it presupposes the power to control it by fairly precise amounts and with close timing. We do have evidence that increased government spending with no increase in taxes, or reduced taxes with no reductions in government spending, can, under the right circumstances, stimulate total spending. World War II seems to be the clearest demonstration of fiscal policy's potency. The Great Depression finally ended when the federal government, responding to the imperatives of wartime, threw fiscal caution aside and began running huge deficits. Federal-government expenditures increased 105 percent from 1940 to 1941, by an additional 175 percent in 1942, and by yet another 50 percent in 1943. In 1944 federal-government expenditures, even after adjustment for changes in the price level, were six and one-half times what they had been in 1940. The federal budget deficit, measured in 1982 dollars, grew from about $5½ billion in 1940 to almost $340 billion in 1944.

The economy responded to this stimulus much as Keynesian analysis suggested that it would. Jolted out of the doldrums of the Great Depression by the massive fiscal stimulus of wartime expenditures, the economy produced almost as much real output in 1944 just for the government sector as it had produced for the combined private and government sectors in 1939. The total real output of the economy in 1944 was more than 75 percent greater than it had been in 1939.

In this colossal but undesigned test of fiscal policy's *stimulative* capabilities, there was no real test of its effectiveness for *stabilization* purposes. Nor could there be any such test until at least a majority in Congress and the president were persuaded to make the experiment. That situation certainly did

not exist before 1964. In that year Congress enacted and the president signed a tax-reduction bill that had been argued for largely on Keynesian grounds. Lower taxes without any accompanying reduction in federal-government expenditures were supposed to stimulate the economy and reduce the high unemployment rate that had developed and persisted since 1958.

Unemployment did decline after the tax cut. But even if we could be certain that it declined because the tax cut stimulated aggregate demand, we would once again have evidence for no more than the stimulative potential of fiscal policy. The economy was not in a recession in 1964 and consequently could not be pulled out of one by a compensatory federal budget deficit. The 1964 tax cut actually supports the point we're making, that fiscal policy cannot be used effectively to counter fluctuations in private spending because of the long time lags associated with its use. The Keynesian argument for a tax cut that culminated in the tax reduction of 1964 *began to be made in the recession of 1960.*

Nondiscretionary Fiscal Policy

We've been arguing that the federal government did not, in fact, use changes in tax rates or expenditures as a *stabilization* tool—at least not before the year 1964. We now want to suggest that the fiscal policy of the federal government after World War II may nonetheless have contributed significantly to economic stabilization. The second statement doesn't contradict the first, because a stabilizing fiscal policy doesn't necessarily require legislated changes in tax rates or expenditures. Fiscal policy can be automatic as well as discretionary. Only discretionary fiscal policy is incapacitated by the severe time lags associated with its use.

When an economic downturn begins, tax receipts fall automatically as corporate and personal incomes decline. Because the applicable rates on these two principal sources of federal revenue are progressive, taking a higher percentage of higher incomes, a decline in income actually leads to an even faster decline in taxes. The government also puts some additional income into the hands of the public during a recession whenever the economic decline leads to an automatic increase in unemployment compensation and welfare benefits. These automatic responses to a recession presumably function as stabilizers, dampening fluctuations in income and thereby reducing fluctuations in private spending.

Allowing budget deficits or surpluses to appear and deciding to do nothing about them is also fiscal policy. It must be distinguished from another view that was widely advo-

cated before the 1930s and the publication of Keynes's *General Theory*. The older position held that government should retrench in a recession, deliberately cutting its expenditures and increasing tax rates if necessary in order to preserve a balanced budget. Such a policy, if adopted, would be the exact reverse of what Keynes recommended. But it would be a discretionary fiscal policy, not an automatic one, and it would be subject as a result to the same problems of timing that make any discretionary fiscal policy an inappropriate instrument for stabilization.

Automatic fiscal policy was clearly at work, whether by design or by inadvertence, in the 1958 recession. The federal government's 1957 budget surplus of $5 billion (in 1982 dollars) turned into a $42-billion deficit in 1958. This happened not because Congress and the president chose to cut taxes or increase expenditures, but because federal tax receipts fell in response to the recession, while federal expenditures continued on their previously targeted course.

What contribution did this kind of passive fiscal policy make toward the relative stability of the economy in the years after World War II? We really have no good way of knowing. It can be argued that automatic fiscal policy is bound to increase stability, because it diminishes the impact that changes in investment expenditure have on the income of consumers. With consumer income buffered to some extent against fluctuations in output, the cumulative effect of destabilizing events is reduced. Automatic fiscal policy provides shock absorbers for the economy and may deserve part of the credit for the smoother "ride" of the years after World War II.

The Timing of Monetary Policy

Monetary policy does have one advantage over fiscal policy with respect to timing—unless it turns out to be a *dis*advantage. The monetary authorities aren't immune from the problems created by the fact that we can't predict the future accurately, don't know exactly where we are at the moment, and have no reliable information on the timing of the inevitable lags between policy actions and their ultimate effects on aggregate demand. But the Open Market Committee of the Fed can at least make quick decisions. Its members meet regularly and can confer by telephone between meetings. Moreover, being more insulated from political pressures than Congress or the executive branch, Fed officials can presumably do what they think the situation calls for without catering to the distracting demands of special interests.

But can we be sure that this is an advantage from the standpoint of stabilization? The speed with which the Open

449

Fiscal and Monetary Policy

Nondiscretionary fiscal policy: do not alter tax rates but let tax receipts fall in a recession.

Pre-Keynesian policy: raise tax rates in a recession to make up for falling receipts.

Keynesian policy: lower tax rates in a recession to expand the deficit.

Market Committee can act enables it also to make more frequent mistakes. Of course, it can quickly reverse direction when it learns it made an error. But sharp reversals of direction by an institution as powerful as the Open Market Committee can themselves be a destabilizing force.

Disagreement about the Conduct of Monetary Policy

The members of the Open Market Committee do not fully agree among themselves on the definition of a restrictive (tight) or expansionary (easy) monetary policy. The question of the proper target for monetary policy has been a controversial one for a long time. Monetarists hold that the monetary managers should pay attention exclusively to monetary aggregates: measures of the money stock such as M1, M2, or the total of currency in circulation plus commercial-bank reserves, known as the monetary base. The money supply is tight or easy according to the rate at which these aggregates are changing. Another view, to be discussed in the next chapter because it is associated with supply-side economists, is that movements in commodity prices are the appropriate measure of monetary tightness or ease. A third view, long advocated by Keynesians, is that the monetary managers should concentrate on interest rates, using some such measure as the federal funds rate, which is the rate of interest paid by commercial banks to borrow one another's reserves. This group holds that the money supply is tight or easy according to whether interest rates are high or low.

The disagreement between monetarists and Keynesians is complicated by the apparently widespread belief that interest rates reflect the scarcity of money, so that rates can be made to fall by increasing the money stock fast enough. We must think carefully about the relationship between monetary policy and interest rates if we are to avoid the error of assuming that high interest rates are conclusive evidence of tight money. When the Fed increases the stock of money, the demand remaining constant, elementary supply and demand analysis tells us that the price of money will fall. But interest is not the price of money! Interest rates can be thought of as the price of credit, but the price of money is the value of money or its purchasing power.

How *does* monetary policy affect interest rates? When the Fed increases bank reserves as part of an easier money policy, banks are enabled to expand their lending. Credit becomes easier to obtain and interest rates consequently tend to move downward. Easier money leads to lower interest rates—at least temporarily.

But we must push the analysis further. What happens to

the new money that is created when the Fed adds to bank reserves and the banks make additional loans? The increase in the stock of money will tend to increase aggregate demand. If the demand for credit from consumers, investors, and government expands when aggregate demand grows, that will tend to pull interest rates back up. The net effect after a longer period of time can't be predicted easily, because monetary policy finally influences both the supply and the demand for credit and pushes them both in the same direction.

Nominal versus Real Interest Rates

Most importantly, if the expansionary monetary policy leads to an excessive rate of increase in aggregate demand, prices will start to rise. And the expectation of rising prices will cause interest rates to rise. Why? Because if prices are expected to increase by 10 percent per year, lenders will demand an additional 10 percent in interest as compensation for the anticipated decrease in the value or purchasing power (the price) of money. And borrowers with the same expectations of inflation will consent to pay the additional 10 percent because they anticipate repaying the loan with depreciated dollars. The *nominal* interest rate—the rate quoted and charged, the *real* rate of interest plus the expected rate of inflation— will then exceed the real rate by 10 percent (or more, if interest income is taxable while interest payments are deductible items!).

The policy dilemma this poses for the Fed becomes exceptionally sharp when critics begin calling for a faster rate of growth in the money stock to get interest rates down. But will faster monetary growth lower or raise interest rates? If Fed watchers following the weekly reports on the money supply come to the conclusion that the Fed is pursuing an inflationary monetary policy, market interest rates may rise to reflect heightened inflationary expectations.

Popular Opinion and Interest Rates

The published reports of the Open Market Committee's policy directives in recent years reveal continuing uncertainty about the proper target at which to aim. But there is very little question about the target at which the general public looks in assessing monetary policy. It looks at interest rates. Moreover, the public looks primarily at nominal interest rates, the only interest rates that anyone publishes, and sees high interest rates as bad almost without qualification. High interest rates allegedly cause inflation (a rise in interest rates does push up the consumer price index) and recession (a rise in *real*

Effects of expansionary monetary policy:

1. *Increased supply of credit*

2. *(?) Increased demand for Credit (?)*

3. *Increased expenditure*

4. *(?) Accelerated inflation (?)*

5. *Higher nominal interest rates reflecting inflationary expectations*

interest rates does tend to reduce investment spending). High real interest rates also make it harder for homebuyers to obtain mortgages. (Rising nominal interest rates produce problems only when they bump against statutory ceilings on interest rates that make no allowance for the distinction between nominal and real rates.) High interest rates allegedly also "starve" the economy for credit, "choke off" expansion, "pinch" households and business firms, and perpetrate similar violence. The only people thought to benefit from high interest rates are bankers. And who loves bankers?

The majority of the public believes that the Fed *can* control interest rates and that it has an obligation to keep them at "reasonably" low levels. It can do this, supposedly, by expanding bank reserves whenever interest rates threaten to rise above some "reasonable" level. The upshot of it all is that the Fed runs into enormous public hostility if it tries to tighten its monetary policy at a time when the public is expecting fairly rapid inflation, because those expectations will produce high nominal interest rates that the public will regard as evidence of an excessively restrictive monetary policy. That's exactly what happened, for example, in the last half of 1979. Nominal interest rates were very high by historic standards in 1979, pulled up by the general expectation of rapid inflation in the immediate future. But newspaper articles and financial commentators rarely pointed out that a 12 percent interest rate when inflation was running at a 13 percent annual rate (as it did for a while in 1979) was a very low and in fact negative *real* rate of interest. Nor did they notice that M1 had been growing through the first three quarters of 1979 at a 10 percent annual rate, hardly evidence of a restrictive monetary policy.

The published policy directives of the Open Market Committee do little to clarify the situation. These directives regularly speak of maintaining the federal funds rate within some targeted range, as if the Fed had the power to set that rate independently of what was happening to nominal interest rates in the credit market. Remember, however, that the Fed exercises its influence on the federal funds rate, the interest rate at which banks exchange reserves, through buying and selling government bonds and thereby adding to or subtracting from commercial-bank reserves. If the federal funds rate is rising, it is because rising interest rates are inducing banks to bid more in order to obtain additional reserves that they can lend. To counter this movement, the Fed must supply additional reserves. But could the Fed have pumped large volumes of new reserves into the commercial banking system in mid-1979 without stirring expectations of still more rapid inflation and further stimulating the demand to borrow? No

action by the Fed can lower interest rates if that action increases the demand for federal funds by even more than it increases the supply.

This fundamental uncertainty about the effect that open market operations will have on interest rates is what has persuaded many economists, led by the monetarists, that the Fed should ignore interest rates and concentrate on monetary aggregates. The attempt to stabilize interest rates, these economists argue, causes the Fed to lose control over the growth rate of the money stock. And it is the rate at which the money stock grows that in the long run determines the rate at which total demand and hence the nominal gross national product will grow.

Is It Better to Have Tried and Failed?

It has become increasingly obvious in recent years that we don't have the knowledge that would be required to steer the economy on a steady course of full employment with price stability. But are we better off than we would have been if we hadn't tried? Most economists now agree that "fine-tuning" has been oversold, that we have been too optimistic about our ability to reduce fluctuations through aggregate-demand management. A smaller number go further: they argue that the attempt to stabilize has increased both unemployment and inflation.

How could this occur? The key element in the argument is the relationship between recessions and uncertainty. Recessions occur largely because mistakes are made and subsequently have to be corrected. It follows that anything which increases the probability of mistakes, of decisions based on a faulty anticipation of future events, will aggravate the recession problem. The question then becomes: Has the behavior of the federal budget and of the money supply in recent years made the future more predictable? Or has it increased the uncertainties confronting economic decision makers?

Stabilizing Factors

We can't jump from the fact that there have been no major recessions since the 1930s to the conclusion that the net effect of government stabilization efforts was greater stability. Other factors have been at work. In Chapter 17 we mentioned the importance of the Federal Deposit Insurance Corporation in eliminating the phenomenon of bank runs and also the supporting role of the Fed as the guarantor of short-run liquidity to the banking system. Between them they have

eliminated the panics that once swept regularly through the financial sector; and with financial panics a thing of the past, the economy has not again had to go through anything even remotely approaching the 25 percent contraction in the money stock experienced between 1929 and 1933.

Another stabilizing factor seems to have been the tendency for personal consumption expenditures after World War II to maintain their own steady rate of increase, with relative disregard for fluctuations in income. Some of this should probably be attributed to relatively high wealth levels, which enable people to maintain their spending during periods of temporarily reduced income. Some of it can also be credited, perhaps, to our system of progressive taxes on personal and corporate income that cushion income against fluctuations in gross national product. The fact that government transfer payments, such as unemployment compensation, move inversely to GNP has an added cushioning effect on aggregate consumption spending.

Destabilizing Factors

If personal-consumption expenditures have been a steady and stabilizing component of aggregate demand, investment expenditures have not. But did fiscal and monetary policy compensate for this instability, or were they a major *cause* of the instability? The construction component of investment is sensitive to monetary-policy shifts, and changing monetary policies do seem to have destabilized the building industry. What about the policy of shifting between tax surcharges to dampen inflation and special tax credits for investment spending to promote employment? Since there is usually considerable discretion about the timing of investment expenditures, couldn't government policy reversals be largely responsible for the large fluctuations from year to year in private investment? It's true that policymakers intended to reduce fluctuations through shifting tax policies; but it wouldn't be the only time a tax program hit something other than its target.

What have been the overall effects of government programs? Remember that an unanticipated change in the composition of spending will cause unemployment even though total spending doesn't change. When the government makes a decision to send people to the moon, to produce a particular military plane, to restrict oil imports, to subsidize a giant railroad system, to enforce high standards of job safety in industry, to become self-sufficient in energy, to encourage home ownership through government-subsidized loans, to enlarge steel-making capacity by granting special tax refunds

for investment—when the government does any of these things, it signals labor and other resources to move in specific directions. It tells people to change their places of residence, to acquire particular knowledge and skills, to sink resources into specific projects. *Any subsequent slackening of government intentions or shift in emphases announces that these resource movements were partly mistaken and thereby creates unemployment.* These changing signals from government may also trigger surges of investment spending by industries trying to make rapid adjustments to revised government policies. How sure can we be that private economic decisions are the unstable factor for which government decisions must compensate?

The Benefits and Costs of Aggregative Theories

It's difficult to discuss the problem of recession and unemployment without using large aggregates such as consumption expenditure, investment expenditure, government expenditure, tax revenues, total demand, national output, and national income. But there is an important sense in which these data conceal the very nature of the problem with which we're trying to deal. Total output is the sum of the outputs of several million firms producing different goods under constantly changing conditions, including conditions of both cost and demand that can change in different directions and at different rates for each separate firm. It is these differences and the uncertainties associated with them that produce the phenomenon of recession in the first place.

Remember that a recession is not a mere slowdown in the rate of economic growth. It is an unintended and therefore disruptive slowdown for a large number of producers (but never all producers!) who discover that their revenue expectations relative to their cost expectations were too optimistic. Recessions begin because imbalances have developed and accumulated over a period of time. Recessions can perhaps be measured with highly aggregative concepts. But they cannot be adequately understood or controlled without paying attention to the changing structure of costs and demand from one industry to another, one region of the country to another, and even one firm to another.

Attempting to counter recessions by stimulating aggregate demand assumes more uniformity and homogeneity within recessions than is actually the case. The enlarged demand must be a demand for the right goods if it's going to check the decline in output *in particular firms and industries,* which is the essence of the recession. It's true that in a recession most industries and perhaps most firms will experience disappointing revenue-cost outcomes. But they won't all

How will increased government spending on airplanes manufactured in Missouri affect unemployment among Oregon loggers?

do so, and among those who do encounter disappointment, the called-for adjustments will range from minor through major all the way to bankruptcy and reorganization. What can we expect to happen, then, if government responds to a recession by expanding aggregate demand?

Won't the result depend on how this policy affects the relative demand for the inputs and for the outputs of particular firms? Doesn't increased demand produce higher costs as well as higher revenues? Remember, too, that inputs are not some stockpile of perfectly substitutable resources that can quickly stop producing X and start producing Y when the demand for X goes down and the demand for Y goes up. Won't a policy of stimulating total demand in response to a recession make life easier for some firms but harder for others?

The massive economic breakdown of the Great Depression led to the construction of highly aggregative theories of economic fluctuations. That was certainly understandable. Only a highly aggregative theory is likely to suggest a cure sufficiently simple to be workable. And what was above all desired in the 1930s was a workable solution, something that could quickly be put into practice. Part of the tragedy of the Great Depression may have been the timidity that prevented national governments from taking the heroic measures to expand aggregate demand that the events of the 1930s seemed to require: 1929 to 1933 was no "normal" recession. Whatever the circumstances that produced or aggravated the long and deep decline into the depression of the 1930s, there was abundant evidence by 1933 that bold actions by government to stimulate recovery carried a low risk and a high potential benefit.

But if policymakers in the 1930s were guilty of failure to recognize an economic breakdown and to react appropriately, policymakers today may be guilty of responding in equally inappropriate ways by treating every recession as if it were a breakdown. The continuing confidence that many public officials and much of the electorate have in discretionary fiscal and monetary policy—despite the record of their performance—is hard to explain on any other grounds.

It wasn't until the mid-1960s that the United States acquired both a president and a majority in Congress who believed in the effectiveness and desirability of using discretionary fiscal policy along with monetary policy as stabilization techniques. Is the increased instability of the years since then a mere coincidence, to be blamed on external forces beyond the control of policymakers, such as the OPEC cartel and worldwide agricultural failures? That's certainly possible. And those who want to continue advocating discretionary aggregate-demand management, especially in response to recessions,

will find in those events a plausible explanation for the fact that increased use of these stabilizing techniques has been accompanied by increased instability. Whether you decide it's consequence or coincidence, the fact remains that our most rapid inflation and highest unemployment rates since World War II appeared *after* both major political parties had committed themselves to fine-tuning of the economy through aggregate-demand management.

Perhaps we have been traumatized by the experiences of the Great Depression into paying altogether too much attention to aggregate demand. What is there that might be done on the supply side to improve the performance of the economy? That will be the question running through Chapter 20.

Once Over Lightly

Fiscal policy and monetary policy are the principal techniques of aggregate-demand management available to officials of the federal government. Fiscal policy aims at controlling fluctuations in aggregate demand through compensatory budget deficits or surpluses. Monetary policy works toward the same goal through control over commercial-bank reserves and legal reserve requirements.

The Keynesian conviction that monetary policy was impotent, a conviction nurtured in the 1930s, gradually gave way after World War II to the realization that monetary policy was important in the control of inflation and might even have some capability of countering mild recessions.

Monetarists have tried to show not only that monetary policy is a powerful weapon, but also that the supposed effects of fiscal policy are actually the result of accompanying monetary policy.

Depending on the circumstances, government deficits might crowd out private spending rather than supplement it. In very different circumstances, such as a deep and prolonged depression in economic activity, government deficits might be a supplement necessary to make expansionary monetary policy effective.

Timing is crucial in any effective stabilization policy. The time lags that inevitably occur between the appearance and the recognition of a problem, the recognition and the decision to take a particular action, and the action and its ultimate effects combine to make aggregate-demand management less stabilizing in practice than on paper.

Attempts to stabilize aggregate demand through fiscal or monetary policy must entail accurate prediction if they are to be successful. But economic forecasting is an undeveloped

art. It is made especially hazardous by the fact that the people whose behavior is to be controlled try to anticipate and adjust for the controls.

The political delays inevitably associated with its use create especially acute timing problems for fiscal policy.

Although there is little evidence for the position that discretionary fiscal policy is an effective stabilization tool, a strong case can be made for its power to change aggregate demand under appropriate circumstances.

Nondiscretionary fiscal policy, operating through changes in taxes or government outlays that occur automatically in response to changing levels of output and income, may have contributed significantly to the post-World War II stability of the U.S. economy.

Monetary policy shares with discretionary fiscal policy a better-demonstrated capacity to change than to stabilize aggregate demand.

The successful conduct of monetary policy has been made more difficult by high-level disagreement on the proper targets for control: monetary aggregates, commodity prices, or interest rates.

Monetary expansion may lower interest rates by increasing the availability of credit; but the same policy may subsequently raise them by contributing to an increase in the demand for credit. Moreover, nominal interest rates will rise if monetary expansion creates expectations of more rapid inflation. These difficulties in the control of interest rates make interest-rate management an unreliable and even dangerous policy tool for the monetary managers to use.

There is no convincing evidence that government efforts since World War II to manipulate aggregate demand have actually resulted in lower unemployment rates and less inflation than we would have experienced in the absence of such efforts.

There is considerable evidence to suggest that activities of the federal government, including some of its stabilization efforts, have been seriously destabilizing in their consequences.

QUESTIONS FOR DISCUSSION

1. How does fiscal policy affect monetary policy?
    (a) Under what circumstances could the federal government run a large budget deficit without thereby producing an increase in the size of the money stock?
    (b) Suppose the Fed determined to run a "tight" monetary policy, allowing

no growth in commercial bank reserves, at a time when the federal government was trying to borrow to finance a large budget deficit. What would happen?

(c) Suppose the federal government began running a large budget surplus, and used the surplus to reduce the size of the national debt. Think through the effects this would be likely to have on the demand for loans from commercial banks. How might this affect the size of the money stock?

2. How will a large federal government budget deficit affect interest rates?

   (a) Assuming that interest rates are set by the demand for and supply of loanable funds, how could a large increase in federal government borrowing *not* produce higher interest rates?

   (b) Suppose the Fed tries to prevent the increased government demand for loanable funds from raising interest rates, by increasing the supply of loanable funds through an expansion of commercial bank loans. Will this Fed policy succeed in preventing interest rates from rising? At what point will the Fed's expansionary policy step up the inflation rate? How will the expectation of a higher rate of inflation cause interest rates to rise?

3. Suppose that the federal government begins to run a large budget deficit at a time when many productive resources are idle—factories are operating far below capacity in most industries, and there are surplus supplies of labor in almost every area of the economy.

   (a) How might the existence of all these idle resources prevent even a very large increase in government borrowing from leading to an increase in interest rates?

   (b) If you found part (a) hard to answer, ask yourself whether an expansionary monetary policy would be likely to cause inflation under the circumstances described. Remember that it is expectations of more rapid inflation that cause interest rates to rise when monetary policy becomes highly expansionary.

4. "An increase or decrease in government spending will usually entail an offsetting decrease or increase in private spending." Under what circumstances would you expect that statement to be true? Why? Under what circumstances would you expect that statement to be false? Why?

5. The late Senator Hubert Humphrey said shortly after the March 1975 tax cuts that "common sense" told him federal borrowing would not raise interest rates and crowd out private borrowers. "To a large extent this credit-market question takes care of itself," he said. "Private demands for credit go down when unemployment is high. This makes room in the credit market for government demand which goes up." Do you agree?

6. If Congress wants to use fiscal policy to counter recessions, should it cut taxes when the recession is a suspicion, when it's a widespread conviction, or when it's officially announced?

7. Assume that Congress and the president want to cut taxes by $5 billion to stimulate the economy in a period of recession. Does it matter whether they cut personal income taxes or corporate income taxes? Whether the cuts in

personal income taxes are concentrated among low-income groups or more widely distributed? What difference does it make and to whom does it make a difference?

8. During the depression of the 1930s, increases in federal-government expenditures were often accompanied by promises (threats?) of future tax increases to hold down the size of the budget deficit. Do you think this policy had any effect on investment spending? How does the prospect of higher tax rates in the future affect investment decisions?

9. Would you favor the proposal, mentioned in the text, to give the president authority to change tax rates or authorize expenditures on his own (within congressionally designated limits) as a way of making fiscal policy more flexible? Why or why not?

10. If tax cuts stimulate aggregate demand, is it possible that they also stimulate aggregate supply? How could a reduction in corporate or personal income-tax rates affect the supply curves of goods?

11. A budget is essentially a forecast: "This is what revenues are expected to be, this is what expenditures are expected to be."
    (a) How can uncertainty turn a balanced budget into an actual deficit or surplus?
    (b) Do Congress and the president have the ability to produce the relationship between government revenue and expenditures that they want to produce?
    (c) Would government be stabilizing or destabilizing the economy if Congress and the president made frequent changes in tax rates or in spending authorizations in an effort to keep the flow of government spending exactly equal to the flow of its tax receipts?
    (d) If the federal government ought to balance its budget, over what time period ought it to do so? Over what time period do households and business firms balance their budgets?

12. The text mentions three different criteria of a restrictive or expansionary monetary policy.
    (a) Keynesians tend to look at the level of interest rates for evidence on the tightness or ease of current monetary policy. How good an indicator is this? The prime rate (the basic interest rate banks charge their most secure customers) averaged 5.25 percent in 1972, 8 percent in 1973, and 10.8 percent in 1974. Was monetary policy restrictive or expansionary during these years? After falling to 6.8 percent in 1977, the prime rate rose to 9.1 percent, 12.7 percent, 15.3 percent, and 18.9 percent in the next four years. Was monetary policy restrictive from 1977 to 1981?
    (b) Monetarists maintain that the best test of monetary ease or tightness is the rate of growth in measures of the total stock of money. From 1972 to 1974, M1 grew by an annual average rate of 6.2 percent. From 1977 to 1981, M1 increased at an average annual rate of 7.3 percent. For comparison purposes, you might want to know that the average annual rate of increase in M1 over the two decades from 1965 to 1985 was about 6.7 percent. By the monetarist measure, does monetary policy from 1972-74 and 1977-81 look restrictive or expansionary?
    (c) Supply-side economists, whose views will be given more attention in

the next chapter, believe that the best test of monetary ease or tightness is what happens to prices. From 1972-74, the producer price index of finished goods rose at an average annual rate of 12.2 percent. Was monetary policy easy or tight by this measure? Before deciding definitely on your answer, you might want to note that 1973 and 1974 were the years in which OPEC first made its mark on petroleum prices. From 1977 to 1981, the average annual increase in the index of prices for finished producer goods was 10.4 percent.

(d) In 1985, the producer price index rose by 1.8 percent while M1 rose 11.9 percent and the prime rate fell from 10.5 to 9.5 percent. Was monetary policy expansionary or restrictive in 1985?

(e) A major reason that these various indicators seem to tell conflicting stories about the ease or tightness of monetary policy is that we are ignoring other relevant factors, such as the effect of expectations on interest rates, or the time lags between changes in the growth rate of monetary aggregates and price level effects. Economists can continue to hold a lot of conflicting opinions in this area because the relationships in which we're interested are not only complex and uncertain but probably also variable over time. When experts disagree, how should citizen-voters decide?

13. The real rate of interest *ex ante* (before the loan is made) is the market or nominal rate minus the *expected* rate of inflation. To the extent that expectations are wrong, the *ex post* (after-the-fact) real rate of interest will be higher or lower than the *ex ante* real rate. Why were *ex post* real interest rates so low in the 1970s and so high in the early 1980s?

14. Evaluate the following assertion: "When aggregate demand is greater than the aggregate capacity of the economy, we get inflation. When it is less, we get recession."

(a) Do firms ever lay off workers when the average price level is rising?

(b) Do firms ever raise their prices during a recession?

(c) How would we know whether the economy was operating at full capacity? Is the aggregate capacity of a single firm ever some definite quantity of output per time period? Think of the college you attend. What would be occurring if it was operating at 100 percent of capacity? Extend the question to an entire industry (e.g., the education industry). Then extend it again to the entire economy.

15. Is aggregate demand inadequate if there is a shortage of automotive mechanics and a surplus of secondary-school teachers? Can substantial unemployment exist at a time when listed job vacancies exceed total unemployment? Why will you find help-wanted ads in newspapers even during recessions?

16. "There is no danger that a government deficit will cause inflation when unemployment stands at 8 percent of the civilian labor force." Do you agree?

17. Suppose the unemployment rate is 8 percent, and economic statisticians tell the government that 2 of those 8 percentage points are a direct result of sharply reduced purchases of new automobiles. Discuss the advantages and disadvantages in such a situation of offering a tax rebate to purchasers of new automobiles equal to 10 percent of the manufacturers' suggested retail

price. Is a dollar of tax reduction offered in this way likely to reduce unemployment more than a dollar of personal income-tax reduction? Are the long-run effects on unemployment likely to be different from the short-run effects?

18. If the government decreased spending on highways by $5 billion and simultaneously increased spending on energy development by $5 billion, what effects, if any, would you predict on the level of unemployment?

19. "The basic cause of an excessively high unemployment rate is uncertainty." Explain whether you agree or disagree with that statement and why.

Supply-Side Perspectives

The conflict between supply-side and demand-side economics goes back at least to the 18th century, even though the terms only came into use in the 1970s. The predecessors of Adam Smith were largely demand-siders, concerned to maintain a flourishing demand for domestic production through policies that restricted foreign competition and kept a large quantity of money in circulation. Smith, by contrast, was a consistent supply-sider, concerned about incentives to producers, convinced that a nation would always have as much money as it could use, and persuaded that additional saving would automatically generate additional investment, never a deficiency of aggregate demand.

Supply-Side Economics: Its Varied Forms

The term "supply-side economics" was coined in the 1970s to describe a set of analyses and policy recommendations aimed at accelerating economic growth and employment through improving incentives to producers. A more favorable tax and regulatory environment for business was the principal recommendation of those who began to call themselves supply-side economists. In this chapter, however, we are going to use the term "supply-side economics" more broadly, to characterize in general those economic analyses that emphasize the ineffectiveness of demand management in bringing about high employment with price stability, and that recommend greater attention to factors on the supply side.

We shall find supply-side economists, as we are using the term, on both ends of the political spectrum. Some will claim that because markets do not work adequately, government must take a more active role in controlling prices and incomes if we are to have any chance of controlling both inflation

and recession. Others will argue almost the reverse: that markets work so well, they render aggregate demand management powerless to affect output and employment, and that the only way for the government to spur economic expansion is to improve the profit prospects of business firms.

The Popularity of Direct Controls

The general public has never had much trouble believing that inflation is the result of irresponsible behavior on the part of suppliers, whether of labor or products. The public looks for villains when things go wrong, and seems to find them in the business firms that announce price increases and the union leaders that call for wage hikes. An excessive rate of increase in demand is a force too abstract and impersonal to be a good candidate for villain, so that corporations and unions tend to be blamed for inflation even when wages and prices are clearly being pulled up by excess demand, not being pushed up by market power. That's why the imposition of wage and price controls during a period of inflation usually encounters an overwhelmingly favorable response from the public, at least initially.

The popularity of wage and price controls as a way of dealing with inflation makes it all the more urgent that the public understand the mechanisms of inflation. If wages and prices rise after the fiscal or monetary authorities have expanded aggregate demand faster than real output can keep up, or after some disaster (war, oil embargoes, crop failures) has reduced the level of real output, controls are worse than useless. For they suspend the rationing system through which scarce goods get allocated among competing claimants. This means that the goods will have to be allocated by other criteria: buyers will get in line early, cultivate contacts, try to negotiate special agreements, or offer illegal monetary inducements to get around the maximum price. The incentive to hoard goods will increase, because goods are undervalued at their legal prices and because buyers cannot be sure of obtaining supplies in the future. This further aggravates the scarcity.

Producers will have less incentive to expand output and maintain quality. Production will fall further as manufacturers find themselves unable to obtain particular inputs that have suddenly disappeared from suppliers' inventories; they may even have to suspend production and lay workers off. Export controls will be instituted to keep other countries from taking advantage of the controlled prices. Bartering will creep into the supply system, not only decreasing efficiency but also stirring up cries of inequity from those producers who have nothing of value to offer their suppliers. Items will

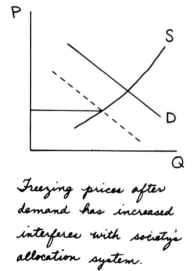

Freezing prices after demand has increased interferes with society's allocation system.

unexpectedly disappear from retail shelves—paper bags, shoe heels, plastic syringes, fertilizer—as shortages multiply and breed further shortages. Relative prices will not be able to change in response to changing relative scarcities, and so the structure of prices will start to give misleading signals to resource users. In short, suppression of the price system suspends the mechanism of economic coordination, leading to inequities, inefficiencies, and disruptions of production that only worsen the imbalance between demand and supply.

Imposing price controls in the face of an inflation caused by too many dollars chasing too few goods aggravates the problem by reducing the supply of goods and diminishing the incentive of demanders to economize in their use. And this is true whether the imbalance was caused by an excessive creation of dollars or a deficient creation of goods. Moreover, it diverts the attention of the public from the actual causes of the inflation and the proper remedies. Of course, a government whose fiscal and monetary policies have fueled an inflation will be only too happy to encourage the public's belief that private avarice is the root of the problem, that public-spirited self-restraint on the part of citizens is the ultimate answer, and that the rascals who have no public spirit must be controlled by law. Congress will rarely admit that its own spending habits are the cause of any ills, and presidents never locate the cause of inflation in their own earlier policies.

The wage and price controls of World War II are sometimes brought forward as evidence that controls can in fact be effective in preventing excess demand from pulling up prices. But this argument ignores some important facts. It overlooks the public's willingness to put up with shortages and tolerate inequities when they are viewed as temporary necessities. It overlooks the alternative rationing system created by the federal government during World War II to allocate scarce goods among competing claimants: the complex point system, the books of ration stamps, the special gasoline coupons, the priority allocations, and the army of controllers required to make the system work even as well as it did. It overlooks the role of wartime patriotism in securing the voluntary cooperation that kept the system functioning for several years, as well as the illegal and semilegal evasions that sometimes helped the system work by enabling people to circumvent it. And when the controls were removed, as they eventually had to be, the excess demand dammed up behind them poured out to raise prices 40 percent between 1945 and 1948.

Cost-Push Inflation? The Case of OPEC

It is worse than useless to impose price or wage controls when expansionary fiscal and monetary policies have created a

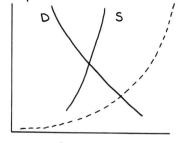

Price controls may be able to postpone price increases -- but at what cost?

Price per barrel

D   S

Barrels per day

demand for goods that can't be satisfied at prevailing prices. Suppressed inflation creates more inequities and inefficiencies than open inflation. But are inflations always the result of overly expansionary fiscal and monetary policies? Are all inflations caused by the pull of excessive demand? Are they never caused by pressure from the supply side? Is there no such thing as cost-push inflation?

It would be hard to convince any user of petroleum products that OPEC, for example, played no part in causing the U.S. inflation of the 1970s. The OPEC cartel used its market power to reduce the supply of oil and thereby raise the price of oil substantially to users. Oil and its products enter into the budgets of consumers, directly and indirectly, at innumerable points; every good's production cost was pushed up to some extent by the rise in energy costs. The only question, it would seem, is what portion of the price rises from 1973 to 1981 can be attributed to OPEC.

We said way back in Chapter 15 that inflation is a fall in the price of money, and that its causes must therefore be sought in the forces affecting the supply and demand for money. That's still true. If the supply of some good is reduced through the action of a cartel, or a drought, or a strike, or any other event, the relative price of that good will rise. The relative prices of goods that use it as an input will consequently also tend to rise. Since oil enters in some fashion as an input into the production of every good, it would then seem to follow that OPEC has the power to raise the relative prices of *all* goods and thus to cause inflation.

But that last sentence is nonsense. The *relative* prices of *all* goods cannot rise, because nothing would be left relative to which they could rise. An increase in the relative price of goods with large inputs of oil in their production processes logically entails a decrease in the relative price of goods with smaller inputs of oil in their production processes. To deny this would be like trying to see whether major-league baseball players are better today than they were a generation ago by checking on whether major-league clubs win a higher percentage of their games today than they did a generation ago.

Of course, the relative price of all goods *other than money* can rise; that's not a logical impossibility. And OPEC could conceivably be responsible for causing an increase in the price of everything *relative to money*. But don't you find it somewhat odd to focus entirely on oil and to ignore money altogether when the price of *everything* has changed *relative to money*?

Clear the cobwebs for yourself by thinking about the consequences of OPEC's actions in a world without money, where all trade is conducted by barter. OPEC's actions in

such a case would have compelled other countries to export more commodities and services per barrel of oil imported. Oil consumers would have had to choose between consuming less oil or sacrificing larger quantities of other goods. With the opportunity cost of acquiring a barrel of oil higher than before, producers would also look for ways to economize. They would produce relatively fewer of those goods that use lots of oil, thereby reducing the supply of these goods and causing an increase in their relative price. What would happen, in summary, is that the relative prices of goods that use lots of oil would rise, and the quantities of them produced and purchased would undergo a relative decline. This necessarily means that the relative prices of goods using very little oil would fall, while the quantities of these goods both produced and purchased would increase.

This is what actually happened after 1973. It happened in the United States in very clumsy and costly ways, because the U.S. government chose to interfere with the movements of relative prices by which these complex processes of reallocation are ordinarily guided. But much of this was camouflaged by changes in the value of money. We fail to see that the relative prices of some goods *fell* as a consequence of OPEC's successes, because our attention is riveted on the price of everything relative to money. The price of everything (or *almost* everything) relative to money has indeed risen substantially since 1973. But this occurred because the supply of money has increased faster than the demand for money.

From 1973 to 1980 (in the U.S.):

the price of heating fuel rose 170%

the price of clothing rose 40%

the consumer price index rose 85%

Supply-Side Shock and Demand-Side Response

Are we saying, then, that OPEC played no part in causing the U.S. or world inflation of the 1970s? Not at all. We are rather trying to find out exactly what that part might have been. And we're getting close. Suppose that the Fed had held the money supply constant between 1973 and 1980. What would have occurred? The most probable consequence would have been a sharp recession. The United States actually did have a recession that began right at the end of 1973 and continued into 1975. But if the Fed had followed a policy of no growth in the stock of money, or even of substantially slower growth, the recession would almost surely have been more severe.

The reason is that OPEC's actions necessitated large and rapid increases in the relative prices of petroleum-using products. That meant large and rapid *decreases* in the relative prices of other goods. But prices do not always change smoothly and quickly in response to altered conditions of supply and demand. Above all, they do not *fall* smoothly and quickly. The more immediate effect is accumulating invento-

ries, which lead to reduced orders, production cutbacks, and increased unemployment—to recession, in other words. This increased unemployment of labor and other resources continues until relative prices have adjusted to the new circumstances and resources have been reallocated.

The extensive shock that OPEC administered to the U.S. economy in 1973 undoubtedly contributed to the 1974-75 recession. Remember that recessions result from accumulated mistakes; in 1973 OPEC turned a lot of decisions very suddenly into mistakes. In 1973 OPEC unexpectedly compelled an extensive reallocation of resources in the United States, a reallocation that had to be directed by changes in relative prices. The Fed probably made those relative price adjustments easier and the reallocation process consequently quicker by increasing the stock of money. The increased stock of money permitted the necessary price adjustments to occur without any price having to fall in money terms, because all price adjustments could be upward. The goods whose relative prices were supposed to decrease simply rose, in money terms, less than the average. The Fed promoted inflation in response to OPEC's price increases; but it did so in an effort to counter the reduced output and employment caused by OPEC's unexpected success in cartelization.

Market Power, Unemployment, and Inflation

Here may be a major source of pressure on the Fed to pursue inflationary monetary policies. We gave so much space to the question of OPEC's role in the U.S. inflation of the 1970s because the issue illuminates a more general problem. Suppose that a significant number of wage rates are set by collective bargaining and that unions have the ability to obtain wage increases in excess of productivity increases. That would mean that unions (or some unions) can obtain for their members a wage that is above the value of the marginal worker's net contribution to the employer's revenue.

Employers adjust to such a situation by reducing the number of workers they hire. They may not actually lay anyone off; instead they will just refrain from replacing workers as they retire or quit. The result is a reduction in the number of jobs available and an increase in measured unemployment. It makes no difference if we assume that employers can raise their prices and recover the higher labor costs without reducing employment. At higher prices they won't be able to sell as much, and the reduced sales will eventually lead to employment cutbacks. Even if union members realize that higher wages will mean fewer jobs, a majority may vote for the wage increase in the belief that they themselves will be protected by seniority; they are risking the jobs of others.

Rising unemployment caused by this kind of market power puts the Fed under pressure to adopt an expansionary monetary policy. When it does so, prices rise generally. The rise in the price of everything else reduces the relative price of the good whose sales had fallen, its sales expand once more, and employment in that industry is restored. If employers lack the market power to pass the wage increase along to buyers, the increase in the price of all goods does the job for them. The real wage is consequently reduced, and employment is restored to its initial level. The upshot of the matter is that the use of excessive market power creates unemployment problems, and that to deal with the unemployment problems the Fed may be forced to cause inflation.

Many economists who believe that the key to a stable price level is monetary and fiscal restraint on the part of government have nonetheless come to the conclusion that it isn't enough to control aggregate demand. Labor and product markets may no longer function well enough to let fiscal and monetary policy be effective. If strong unions and business firms with substantial market power are able to raise wages and prices in the absence of any increase in demand, monetary and fiscal authorities may have to choose between causing unemployment by refusing to expand total demand or causing inflation by underwriting the wage and price increases.

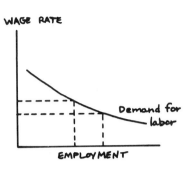

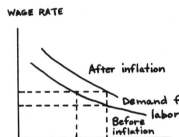

Supply-Side Controls

An alternative is for government to lay aside the tools of aggregate demand management and go after the supply-side forces that make price stability incompatible with the maintenance of high employment. If the problem is created by powerful unions, business firms selling in insufficiently competitive markets, and innumerable government regulations that tolerate, encourage, and even require practices that raise costs and reduce efficiency, the solution would appear to be structural reforms directed toward increasing competition and thereby making wages and prices more responsive to changing demand conditions.

Some economic analysts would carry such supply-side policies even further. Because they believe that organized interest groups today have the power simply to set the prices they choose for the goods or services they supply, without regard to the public interest, they want the government to assert an extensive control over economic decisions. In their view, inflation is the product of a struggle among such groups for a larger share of the gross national product. Unless the government establishes some kind of "incomes policy" to contain this struggle, it will face a perpetual choice between

expansionary fiscal-monetary policies that allow all parties to obtain what they demand, thus producing inflation, or non-inflationary fiscal-monetary policies that produce high unemployment and chronic stagnation.

If that line of argument is essentially correct and the processes of supply and demand are as thoroughly under the control of dominating interest groups as the advocates of "incomes policy" maintain, then this entire book has been much ado about very little. We are obviously not going to grant such a premise. Competition in something very much like its traditional sense is alive and well in the U.S. economy today, subject though it may be to frequent fractures and even occasional bouts of serious illness.

Moreover, if the situation were as serious as the advocates of "incomes policy" say it is, then their "solution" would be little more than wishful thinking. How could a democratic government, after all, create legislation to rein in interest groups that were themselves so firmly in control of the society and its economic life? It must be noted that governments have long been working actively to shore up the interest groups that they are now being called upon to put down or control. Is it realistic to expect them suddenly to reverse direction and begin undoing their own work? Even if markets were functioning in a wholly intolerable fashion, that fact would in no way demonstrate any capacity on the part of government to improve the situation. A moment's reflection even suggests that gross malfunctioning of the economy is very likely to be a result of failure on the part of government—failure to perform its essential function of clarifying and enforcing the rules of the game. We'll return to this theme in Chapter 22.

Expectations and Supply

The supply-side economics we have discussed so far grows out of the belief that markets do not work well enough to let demand-side policies be effective. Another version of supply-side economics takes just the opposite tack: markets work too well for demand-side policies to be effective.

Supply-side economists of this persuasion start off by asking why changes in aggregate demand should ever be expected to affect real output at all. People who make production and price decisions don't respond to *aggregate* demand. They pay attention to the demand for their own product. And they mostly learn about the demand for what they themselves are selling by watching their own sales. Automobile dealers, for example, don't increase their purchases from the factory or raise their selling prices because they

read that new-car sales are up 4 percent nationally, much less because they hear on the radio that M1 increased over the past four weeks at a 12 percent annual rate. They order more cars when sales deplete their inventories. They raise their prices (probably by reducing discounts, offering less for trade-ins, charging more for accessories) when they find that they can do so and still move cars in an acceptable volume.

Now if aggregate demand increases as a result, let us say, of expansionary monetary policy, automobile dealers will presumably get a share of the increased spending. Sales will improve and the dealers' inventories will decline. Prices may "firm" somewhat as dealers find they can sell cars without offering such generous trade-in allowances; but the principal effect at first is likely to be a greater volume of sales and so additional orders placed with the manufacturers. When the manufacturers respond by increasing production, real GNP will increase. An increase in the money supply will have caused an increase in output and employment.

Remember, however, that the automobile dealers were experiencing only their share of an economywide, general increase in spending. That means increased competition among buyers for resources of every sort. Won't that in turn cause a general increase in costs? The automobile dealers (and everyone else) may find to their dismay that business hasn't really improved. The increase in the money supply has merely produced a proportionate increase in the price level. Once everyone learns what has happened, sales and production will fall back to their original level.

The common belief that an increase in aggregate demand will lead to a permanent increase in output rests on the implicit assumption that producers are supplying less than they're willing to supply *at existing price and cost ratios.* It implies that suppliers aren't acting in their own best interest, that they're behaving irrationally.

Alternatively, it implies that suppliers are fooled by the increase in aggregate demand. A temporary spurt in production is quite likely in response to an increase in aggregate demand, as long as suppliers don't realize that what they're experiencing is a larger demand for everything and not just for what they themselves are selling. But they will eventually learn that their response was a mistake. When the mistake is recognized and corrected, the rate of real output will again decline and we'll be left with nothing but a higher price level.

The Phillips Curve: Use and Abuse

In 1958 an economist named A. W. Phillips published a study on "The Relationship between Unemployment and the Rate

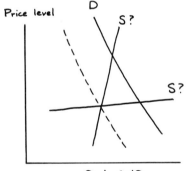

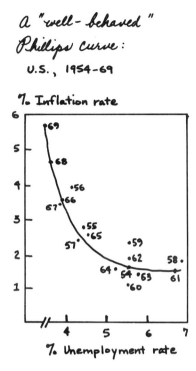

a "well-behaved"
Phillips curve:
u.s., 1954-69

% Inflation rate

% Unemployment rate

of Change of Money Wage Rates in the United Kingdom, 1861-1957" and invented the "Phillips curve." Phillips showed that there was a stable relationship during the period he studied between the unemployment rate and the rate at which the average money wage increased. Unemployment was greater when money wage rates were increasing more slowly, and fell in periods when money wage rates were rising rapidly. That seems thoroughly plausible. During periods of high demand for labor, employers will tend to bid up wage rates to obtain and keep the employees they want. In periods of high unemployment, employers will not have to bid so energetically for labor, and wage rates will increase less.

But the argument was subsequently extended to suggest that unemployment might be reduced by allowing an inflationary rate of increase in money wages and, by extension, in the average of all prices. The Phillips curve of this latter argument purports to show that there is a general trade-off between inflation and unemployment, so that less of one can be obtained by accepting more of the other. But the conclusion doesn't follow either from A. W. Phillips' data or from reflection on the causes of inflation and unemployment. And the notion that government policymakers can reduce the rate of unemployment by deliberately causing inflation is an extremely hazardous one.

It is probably true that prices and wages will be more likely to drift upward when the economy is close to "full" employment. The economic system always contains a great deal of internal movement: industries grow, others decline, firms rise and fall, new production techniques are introduced, the composition of demand changes, people enter and exit the labor force. Resources must therefore be attracted continuously into particular employments through the offer of acceptable employment terms. But employers and employees don't have perfect information. They must search for what they want and incur the costs of that search.

In a period of low unemployment, the cost of finding a new job will, on the average, be lower for employees than during a period of high unemployment. Employees will therefore be more ready to give up a job when they think the wage is unsatisfactory and begin searching for another. So employers will find it difficult to reduce wages.

Search costs for employers are higher in periods of full employment. And so employers will offer higher wages than they might otherwise be willing to offer in order to avoid making an extensive and costly search for the new employees they want and to reduce the risk of losing present employees, who would be expensive to replace.

The same argument applies to prices in product markets. When the economy is operating close to capacity, excess

supplies are generally hard to find, and buyers will pay higher prices rather than search for alternative sources of supply. In a period of high unemployment and substantial excess capacity, sellers will be shaving prices, because buyers are hard to find.

The identical conclusion emerges whichever way we look at it. "Full" employment fosters an upward creep in prices and wages; substantial unemployment and excess capacity encourages a downward drift in prices and wages.

The basic argument asserts that the direction of drift in price and wage movements is a response to tightness or slackness in markets. In other words, the level of employment is the cause and price-wage movement the effect. But we can't assume that because full employment causes inflation, inflation will bring about full employment. When there's a big crowd at the basketball game, the gymnasium temperature rises because of body heat; but the athletic department can't make a crowd come to watch a losing basketball team by overheating the gymnasium.

Reducing Unemployment by Illusion

Nonetheless, the policy of deliberately stepping up inflation probably would lower the unemployment rate—temporarily. People are unemployed because they don't find the job opportunities of which they're aware sufficiently attractive. A policy of deliberate inflation makes job opportunities *seem* more attractive by raising the money wage rate offers of employers. And this is how inflation might reduce unemployment. But the higher wage rate offers are only seemingly more attractive. As long as potential employees don't realize that the job opportunities they're now accepting are in reality no better than the opportunities they previously rejected, employment will indeed rise. But it will subsequently fall back down to its previous level when employees discover what's happening: that inflation is creating the illusion of more attractive wage offers. No permanent reduction in unemployment will have occurred, but the economy will be undergoing more rapid inflation.

A deliberate policy of pursuing lower unemployment by accepting a higher rate of inflation calls, then, for continuously increasing the inflation rate *so that workers always expect less than the actual rate of inflation.* In that way they can be made to overestimate continuously the real value of the money wages they're being offered. Or else the policy assumes that employees pay exclusive attention to money wage rates, never to real wage rates. This is a superficially plausible assumption, since we know that few employees consult the most recent changes in the consumer price index before deciding whether

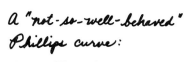

a "not-so-well-behaved"
Phillips curve:

U.S., 1970-81

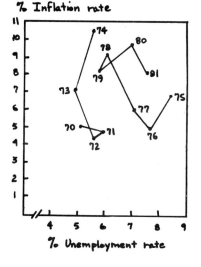

% Inflation rate

% Unemployment rate

a wage offer is adequate. They look at *money* wage rates, in other words. But they also learn after a while that their wages buy less and adjust their perception of the wage rate's real value. An extreme example will make the point. In 1960 workers stood in line for jobs in manufacturing offering $3 an hour. Manufacturers can find almost no one who will accept employment at that wage today. Employees do know, even if they've never heard of price indexes, that $3 is a much lower hourly wage today than it was a generation ago.

Policy cannot be constructed on the assumption that workers will be permanently fooled, for people learn from experience. And the simultaneous existence of high unemployment with very rapid inflation in the 1970s ought to be sufficient evidence that people have learned. When they begin to take continued inflation for granted, they no longer suffer from the illusion that money wages and real wages are the same thing.

But suppose a government tried this approach to the unemployment problem, found that it couldn't actually lower unemployment, and decided to abandon the policy. Suppose the government had been causing inflation by applying fiscal and monetary stimulus, and now it eases up. After a lag of some length, total spending will stop increasing so rapidly, and producers will be unable to sell at the prices they had anticipated; so inventories will mount, production will be curtailed, and unemployment will rise. Eventually sellers will learn not to expect such a rapid rise in prices. They will adjust downward the prices they ask and the prices they offer to pay for inputs, sales will revive, inventories will decline, production will start up again, and unemployment will fall. But that won't all happen within a week or even a month. The higher unemployment that will result from an attempt to slow down the rate of inflation will be temporary; but temporary can be a long time for those who are laid off.

What it all comes to is that government policies designed to raise output and lower unemployment by increasing aggregate demand will only work if they succeed in creating erroneous expectations on the part of the public. That probably occurred in the latter half of the 1960s. Expansionary fiscal and monetary policies raised output and lowered unemployment, because the public did not know what was happening and consistently underestimated the rate at which costs and prices were going to rise as a result of current policies. But eventually people figured out what was happening and adjusted both their expectations and their behavior. In the 1970s and early 1980s, even more expansionary aggregate-demand policies produced more rapid inflation, but accompanied this time by high rates of unemployment. Once the public

caught on, expansionary aggregate-demand policies produced little more than a faster rate of inflation.

Supply-Side Incentives

The aggregate supply curve implied by this analysis ceases to slope upward to the right and becomes vertical as soon as the public incorporates aggregate-demand policies themselves into its thinking and planning.

What policies can government adopt, then, to increase the rate of growth in real GNP and in employment? It must stick to supply-side policies: policies that improve the incentives perceived by those whose decisions might lead to more output and more jobs.

Supply-side economists of this persuasion have consequently laid great emphasis upon tax cuts that would increase the after-tax return to labor, innovation, saving, and investment. Some have even argued that total tax receipts might well rise as a result of a reduction in tax rates. This would happen if the lower rates gave such a boost to productive activity that the percentage increase in real GNP exceeded the percentage decline in the rate of taxation; the government would collect more revenue by taking a lower percentage of substantially higher corporate and personal incomes. A supplementary boost to tax revenues, of uncertain but potentially substantial size, would result if portions of the "underground economy" came to the surface as a consequence of lower tax rates. People now taking payment in cash and not reporting it on their tax forms might be induced by lower rates of taxation to pay more tax in return for less guilt and anxiety.

Higher tax revenues as a consequence of lower tax rates is a marvelous promise to anyone prepared to believe it. It was a promise doubly welcome in the late 1970s to those who were concerned not only about high rates of taxation but also about large and growing federal budget deficits.

A Digression on the National Debt

The size of the national debt is a topic that has long been able to arouse hysteria among a large percentage of otherwise thoughtful Americans. People wonder how we will ever pay it off, and while some worry about what might happen if we *cannot* pay it off, others worry about what will ensue if we *do* pay it off. Many probably worry simultaneously about both possibilities. The first step in thinking about the national debt, therefore, is to see exactly why it does not ever have to be paid off.

The individuals, households, banks, insurance companies, industrial corporations, nonprofit organizations, and government agencies, both in the U.S. and abroad, to whom the debt is owed are not holding government bonds because they feel sorry for this country. They regard government bonds as good investments. When they no longer do so, they sell what they own to someone else. If lots of people become less willing to hold government bonds, the price of the bonds will fall—just as happens when people become less willing to hold Edward Hopper paintings or urban real estate. As the market price of the bonds declines, the rate of return to someone who purchases them must rise. (Since the dollar return is a set amount, the rate of return always varies inversely with the price paid for the bond.) As the rate of return rises, people become more willing to hold government bonds. Since the U.S. government is not going to default on its debts—it could, if it had to, simply create new money to meet its obligations—there is some price at which people will be willing to hold all the bonds the government has issued.

What happens, however, when these bonds come due? Many of them have very short maturities. If you're seeking cause for alarm, ponder the fact that about 20 percent of the national debt is always due and payable less than one year from the present. This poses no problem, as it turns out. The Treasury Department simply sells new bonds to acquire the funds with which to pay off the old ones; it "rolls the debt over," as the expression goes. So long as the Treasury offers a high enough rate of return, it will be able to roll over as much debt as it cares to. And it can even add to its total indebtedness at the rate of $200 billion per year, as it began doing in the 1980s, if it is willing to provide lenders with a rate of return that is more attractive than what they can earn elsewhere, taking liquidity and security into account.

The Crowding-Out Problem

And right there is the most important problem created by the national debt. Treasury bond sales put the federal government into competition with every other potential borrower for the available flow of loanable funds. If the monetary authorities do not increase the flow by expanding the money stock, then the federal government is competing with households and businesses for the available flow of savings; and private sector borrowing and investment will be crowded out as a consequence. If the monetary authorities increase bank reserves to prevent such a "credit crunch," the result will be inflation. Crowding out will still occur; it's just that interest rates will now have to rise far enough to compensate for expected inflation as well as to squeeze out private-sector borrowers.

Thus a rapidly rising national debt is undesirable because it reflects large government budget deficits, which raise interest rates and crowd out private borrowing and investment.

Are Tax-Rate Hikes the Solution or the Problem?

Now the standard response to an objectionable deficit is a decrease in expenditures, an increase in revenue, or some combination of the two. Let's assume for purposes of argument that government expenditures cannot be reduced. (We'll see in Chapter 22 why that might be a realistic assumption.) How do we increase government revenues? By raising tax rates? Not necessarily. If the extremely optimistic version of the supply-side argument is correct, lower tax rates will generate larger revenues.

Suppose we agree, however, that this is too optimistic, and that higher tax rates will in fact increase total tax revenue. It doesn't follow that tax rates should be increased to close a deficit. In the first place, the long-run effect of a change in tax rates may be different from the short-run effect. If a 10 percent tax-rate reduction were to raise the annual growth rate of taxable income by 2 percent, the tax cut would be "paying for itself" within five years. In addition, it is surely not a national goal to maximize tax revenues. Deficits are undesirable because they have undesirable effects on the economy. The probable effects of cuts or hikes in tax rates must be set against the probable effects of deficits. An increase from 2 to 4 percent in the annual growth rate would produce a doubling of real output within 18 years. If such an increase in real growth could be obtained by accepting larger federal budget deficits, what reason would be left for objecting to larger deficits?

Of course, opponents of supply-side tax cuts argue that no such positive effect, or at least no positive effect of such dimensions, is going to follow from cutting tax rates at a time when the federal government's budget deficits are shattering records. They may be right; but it still would not follow that we ought to raise rather than lower tax rates. Remember that the deficit does its damage by sopping up too large a percentage of the flow of savings. The question arises, therefore, as to what effect higher or lower tax rates will have on the supply of savings as well as on the demand for them. It's true that the government's credit demands will shrink as it obtains more revenue from taxation. But how will this increase in tax revenue affect the supply of savings? If higher tax rates were to reduce the government deficit by $50 billion and private-sector saving by $100 billion, the tax increase would have aggravated rather than alleviated the crowding-out problem.

Further Complications

Some supply-side economists complain that their policies were denied an opportunity to prove themselves in the first years of the Reagan administration because the supply-side tax cuts were instituted too slowly, too cautiously, and with too many threats of reversal. The failure of Congress to demonstrate enthusiasm for tax-cutting policies darkened investor expectations and so dampened incentives.

Supply-siders also complain that the Fed sabotaged their program with an overly restrictive monetary policy. As evidence they cite the sudden and sharp disinflation of 1982 and 1983. Many economists of the supply-side persuasion have grave doubts about the basic monetarist aim, stability in the demand for money. They are consequently unwilling to trust the monetary policy preferred by the monetarists—namely, a steady and modest rate of growth in the money stock. If the demand for money were to rise significantly, for any of a number of possible reasons, a modest rate of money growth might be insufficient, they argue, to finance the combined spending plans of consumers, investors, and government. Supply-siders therefore want the Fed to keep its eye on commodity prices when setting monetary policy. Their argument is that the best definition of "enough and not too much" when it comes to monetary policy is whatever produces expectations of stable prices over the long run. They suggest commodity prices, and especially the price of gold, as the best available indicator of long-run price expectations. The Fed failed them, many supply-side economists claim, when it allowed the dollar price of gold to fall about 40 percent from 1980 to 1982. A larger supply of dollars would have prevented this huge and depressing decline in long-run price expectations.

There are so many possibilities to consider that it's easy to see why such a large number of fundamental issues remain unsettled. When there is so little consensus on the appropriate theoretical approach, it is hard to achieve agreement on issues of fact. And in the absence of agreement on the underlying facts, it is hard to decide which competing theoretical framework is most adequate. The truth is sometimes hard to discern even when everyone is pursuing a common objective. And that raises a still more troublesome question.

We have been assuming throughout our discussion of these matters that all parties share a common concern for price stability, economic growth, and low unemployment. No doubt they do. But those are not the only goals of citizens or government officials. We all entertain and pursue a variety of objectives, and we characteristically trade them off against one another on the basis of their anticipated costs and benefits.

When we introduce political factors into our discussion of stabilization policy, some serious new problems arise.

We shall consider some of these problems in Chapter 22. But first we must repair a major omission. The United States economy is linked with other economies through an extensive network of international exchange. We must therefore try to take the international setting into account before attempting any final conclusions.

Once Over Lightly

Many economists have become dissatisfied with the amount of attention given to demand in the search for the causes and cures of aggregate instability, and have begun urging more attention to supply-side forces and factors.

Price and wage increases initiated by groups with substantial market power could make it impossible to achieve high employment and price stability through the management of aggregate demand.

Do direct government controls on prices and wages or efforts by government to reduce the market power of powerful interest groups have the potential for securing high employment levels with low inflation rates? Anyone who thinks they do must explain how democratic governments will be able to impose and manage such programs.

Much of the popularity of demand-side economics stemmed from the belief that government-induced increases in aggregate demand would accelerate the rate of economic growth and cause employment to rise. This result is less likely if producers know what policies the government is following and are consequently not fooled into supposing that the increased demand they observe is a real increase in the demand for their products or services.

In the absence of illusion, some supply-side economists argue, increases in aggregate demand will produce nothing but inflation. They propose tax cuts and other policies to improve incentives to suppliers as more appropriate policies for stimulating economic growth.

The effect of reductions in tax rates on government revenues depends upon the extent to which the reductions stimulate effort, innovation, saving, investment, and thus the base on which the taxes are levied.

Whether tax cuts can be expected to increase or reduce government budget deficits (in the long run or the short run?), it should be noted that the deficits are significant largely to the extent to which they crowd out private-sector investment.

The national debt does not ever have to be "paid off." It can be and is "rolled over" as it matures.

Opponents of supply-side policies contend that the policies have been tried and found wanting; advocates say the policies have basically proved themselves despite their not having received a fair trial.

QUESTIONS FOR DISCUSSION

1. What is the difference between a cost-push and a demand-pull inflation?
   (a) The formal definitions are easy enough. But at what evidence could we look to decide whether a particular inflationary surge had been caused by increases in costs or by an overly rapid growth in demand?
   (b) What is wrong with this argument? "If we observe that wage rates have increased faster than productivity has increased during a period of inflation, we may reasonably conclude that wage increases have pushed up prices."
   (c) If union-won wage increases lead to an increase in unemployment and the Fed then expands the money supply in an effort to stimulate economic expansion and lower the unemployment rate, would any inflation that results be more accurately described as cost-push or demand-pull?

2. If OPEC was basically responsible for the surge of inflation that affected the United States between 1973 and 1981, the inflation rate ought to have been even higher during those years in nations more dependent on imported oil than the U.S. Here are the average annual rates of increase in the price level from 1973 to 1981 for the U.S. and six other countries.

	Annual Rate of Increase in Prices, 1973-81
United States	8.0%
United Kingdom	15.9
Switzerland	4.0
Mexico	22.6
Japan	6.5
Italy	17.7
Germany	4.6

   (a) Why do you suppose that Switzerland, Japan, and Germany had much lower inflation in these OPEC years than the United Kingdom, even though the United Kingdom was a major oil producer and the other three countries were not?
   (b) Here are the average annual rates of increase in the stock of money in the U.S. and the six other countries from 1973 to 1981.

	Annual Rate of Increase in Money Supply, 1973-81
United States	6.5%
United Kingdom	11.7
Switzerland	3.4

Mexico	28.8
Japan	8.7
Italy	17.4
Germany	7.8

If you wanted to guess how much inflation a particular nation had experienced from 1973 to 1981, and the only information you could obtain about the nation was *either* the degree of its dependence on imported oil *or* the rate of increase in its money supply, which would you prefer?

3. If a government allows the stock of money to grow at a 25 percent annual rate for several years and sets firm legal ceilings on prices, will inflation occur? What will happen if, at legally enforced prices, the quantity demanded of almost every good is substantially greater than the quantity supplied?

4. How does inflation ease the process of making relative price and wage adjustments?

(a) Supply and demand conditions in the market for college professors changed markedly from the 1960s to the 1970s. Is it easy for college administrators to lower salaries when supply increases and demand decreases?

(b) What reaction would you expect from professors who were told that market conditions call for a 7 percent reduction in their annual salary?

(c) What reaction would you expect from them if they were told that the budget will not allow for any salary increases this year—although the consumer price index has risen 14 percent since last year?

5. Is it possible to control inflation by having a panel of experts pass on all proposed wage or price increases?

(a) Should such panels include an equal number of business, labor, and consumer representatives?

(b) How will the members of the panel decide whether a particular increase is "justified" or not?

6. Is it unfair for money wage rates to rise more slowly than prices? Is it unfair for some money wage rates to rise faster and others more slowly than prices? Can you think of some wage and salary rates that ought to rise less rapidly than prices? On what basis would you answer this question?

7. "A teacher of chemistry should not be paid more than a teacher of history simply because the demand for chemistry teachers is greater relative to the supply. Teachers are not commodities. They are professional persons with family responsibilities who are providing essential public services." Do you agree with that statement? If a school district has a serious shortage of science teachers and is prohibited by law from raising wage rates, what can it do? Are there ways to make employment offers more attractive without increasing the official wage rate?

8. If it is true, as some advocates of "incomes policy" maintain, that powerful interest groups prevent the market from working adequately, won't those interest groups be powerful enough to prevent government from passing laws to control them?

9. Suppose the federal government and the Fed jointly announced a decision to double the money supply over the course of the coming year, beginning next week.

   (a) How would you expect this announcement to affect the planning and decisions of suppliers? Would you expect many of them to increase their production or their purchases in anticipation of larger sales? Would you expect many of them to increase their prices after hearing the announcement, without waiting for the money supply or total spending to increase?

   (b) Would you expect suppliers to behave differently if the federal government and the Fed pursued the same policy but did so without announcing it, and even tried to keep secret what they were doing as long as possible?

10. Why is the price level likely to be rising more rapidly when the unemployment rate is low than when it is high?

11. Suppose that a corporation opened a factory employing 5000 workers in a town of 10,000 people. Why would you expect to observe low unemployment, rising wage rates, and rising prices for locally produced goods such as housing and services? What is the causal connection in this case between the town's unemployment rate and its rate of inflation?

12. In the situation described in the preceding question, would you expect prices to start declining if the factory laid off half its labor force? What difference would it make whether the layoff was thought to be temporary or permanent? How much time would it take for a layoff to start bringing down the prices of housing and services in the town?

13. You decide to live in an apartment when you return to campus in the fall. Everyone tells you that apartments are extremely hard to find, so you arrive on campus to start searching a week before school begins.

    (a) If you find something you like but consider somewhat overpriced, are you likely to take it or to continue looking?

    (b) Is the owner likely to hold it for you for several days, while you continue your search, without a nonrefundable deposit?

    (c) How would the behavior of tenants and owners be different if recent construction had created a surplus of apartment units near the campus?

14. Can inflation reduce unemployment?

    (a) The "help wanted" column of an urban newspaper has been advertising for airport skycaps every day for the past six months. The only job requirements listed are a friendly attitude, a driver's license, and the ability to lift large suitcases. Does the continuous running of this advertisement for six months prove that all the truly unemployed people in the city lack either a friendly attitude, a driver's license, or physical strength?

    (b) How could the firm running this advertisement obtain all the qualified skycaps it wants, plus a pool of substitutes and eager apprentices?

    (c) How might a sudden, rapid surge of inflation provide this firm with all the applicants it wants?

    (d) When and why would the firm again find itself forced to advertise in the "help wanted" column?

15. Why is the aggregate-supply curve going to become more inelastic if the

public finds out that the government and the central bank are pursuing expansionary aggregate-demand policies in an attempt to increase the rate of growth in real GNP?

16. How large is the national debt of the United States?
    (a) The gross federal debt was about $2,100 billion in 1986. In 1946, as a result of wartime deficits, the debt was about $270 billion. Why is a simple comparison of these numbers seriously misleading?
    (b) If we state the 1946 debt in dollars of 1986 purchasing power, it becomes about $1,400 billion, or two-thirds the size of the 1986 debt. Is there anything still misleading about this comparison?
    (c) The 1946 debt was 128 percent of 1946 gross national product; the 1986 debt was about one-half of 1986 GNP. Is this the best way to compare the national debt in these two years?

17. The table below shows the size of the gross federal debt at the end of each fiscal year from 1977 to 1982, along with the net interest paid by the government in each year.

Year	Gross federal debt (billions of dollars)	Net interest paid (billions of dollars)
1977	709.1	28.5
1978	780.4	33.5
1979	833.8	40.7
1980	914.3	50.8
1981	1,003.9	66.7
1982	1,147.0	82.2

(a) Why did the interest paid increase almost 190 percent when the debt increased by only about 60 percent?
(b) If question (a) has you stumped, you might consider what happened to interest rates during this period. The average interest rate on 3-month loans to the government (90-day bills) was 5¼ percent in 1977 and 14 percent in 1981. Why did interest rates rise so spectacularly during this period?

18. Will government budget deficits grow or shrink in response to tax cuts? The numbers below are purely hypothetical and consequently provide no answer to that question. The exercise is designed to help you see why people disagree on the answer. Supply-siders forecast a 10 percent annual growth rate if taxes are reduced; non-supply-siders forecast only a 5 percent annual rate of growth. The numbers represent billions of dollars.

Year	Tax Rate	GNP: Supply-Siders' Forecast	GNP: Non-Supply-Siders' Forecast	Government Expenditures	Tax Revenue: Supply-Siders' Forecast	Tax Revenue: Non-Supply-Siders' Forecast
1	11%	$4,000	$4,000	$500	$440	$440
2	10	4,400	4,200	510	_____	_____
3	10	4,840	4,410	521	_____	_____
4	10	5,324	4,631	533	_____	_____

19. In 1985, gross private saving in the U.S. was about $700 billion: $130 billion in personal saving and $570 billion in saving by businesses. Gross private domestic investment was approximately $670 billion.

    (a) How did the federal government manage to finance a $200 billion deficit in 1985 when the private sector used all but $30 billion of what the public saved? If you have no idea, read part (b).

    (b) State and local governments ran budget surpluses of about $60 billion in 1985 and foreigners invested about $110 billion more in the U.S. in 1985 than Americans invested abroad. Can you now answer part (a)?

20. While American households were saving about $130 billion in 1985, they were spending almost $2,600 billion on durable goods, nondurable goods, and services. Suppose that the prospect of a higher after-tax return on income saved and invested induced the "average" household to reduce consumption expenditures by 5 percent. How large a contribution would this make to the alleviation of "crowding out" by the federal deficit?

National Policies and
International Exchange

The movement of goods and monetary payments across
national boundaries is both a problem and an opportunity for
government officials charged with stabilizing their domestic
economies. That's why this chapter on international exchange
comes before the concluding chapter on national policies for
dealing with recession and inflation.

Perhaps the insertion of this chapter *within* the chapters
on national policies can also serve as a reminder that
international economic policies are constructed by national
states. There is no "international government" today with the
will and the capacity to establish rules for the governance
of international exchange. We often hear that nationalism is
obsolete in the era of jet planes, rockets, space exploration,
satellite communication, and nuclear weapons. But that's the
statement of an ideal, not a description of reality. The
present reality is that any actual international economic order
will be produced by the interactions of people whose
allegiance is *not* to "the community of nations." And no
international economic system will get the support of a nation
unless that support is seen to be in the best interest of those
who control the nation's government.

Accounting for International Transactions

Balance-of-payments accounting provides a useful way to
begin thinking about the effects of international transactions
on national economies. In a simplified summary of a nation's
balance of payments, all transactions can be assigned to one
of five categories: exchange of merchandise, exchange of

services, investment income, transfers, or exchange of financial assets. Transactions in each category produce either payments *into* or payments *out of* the nation. Transactions generating payments into a nation are put in a credits column, while transactions generating payments out of the nation are assigned to a debits column.

The following imaginary statement of the U.S. balance of international payments will serve as an illustration.

	Credits	Amount in billions of dollars	Debits	Amount in billions of dollars
MERCHAN-DISE	Exports	$220	Imports	$335
SERVICES	Exports	80	Imports	75
INVESTMENT INCOME	From U.S. investments abroad	90	From foreign investments in U.S.	65
TRANSFERS	From foreigners to U.S.	5	To foreigners from U.S.	20
FINANCIAL ASSETS	Foreign acquisition of U.S. assets	95	U.S. acquisition of foreign assets	20
		TOTAL CREDITS: $490		TOTAL DEBITS: $515

The first row, exports and imports of merchandise, requires no explanation. In the second row, services include goods other than merchandise for which payment must be made, such as transportation, insurance, or the hotel accommodations of people traveling in foreign countries. Income from foreign investments is self-explanatory. Transfers are payments for services not currently being rendered, such as pension benefits or gifts. Financial assets include shares of stock, bonds, promissory notes, deposits in financial institutions, or even currency when it moves between nations.

While questions can be raised about where best to file particular kinds of transactions, every transaction that involves international payments can be fitted into one of these five categories. If the data gatherers who construct the balance of payments had a complete and accurate record of every international transaction, the sum of the items in the credits column would exactly equal the sum of the debits column. In our hypothetical example, the sums are not equal. The record keepers would consequently add the difference to the smaller total, label it "statistical discrepancy," and thereby *make credits equal debits* at $515 billion.

STATISTICAL DISCREPANCY: 25

TOTAL CREDITS: 515

They do this because every transaction has to be paid for in some fashion; the balance of payments must balance. Take the case of a gift, or what the data gatherers call a "unilateral transfer." How does a gift have to be paid for? Well, suppose that Hank Higgins, a resident of the United States, mails a $100 check to Eliza Doolittle in London as a token of his affection and esteem. U.S. debits rise by $100. But some item or items in the credit column must now rise by $100 to balance that increase in debits (unless, of course, some other item in the debits column declines to offset Hank's gift). If Eliza cashes Hank's check and gets five U.S. $20 bills, which she stuffs in her teapot, the U.S. has in effect exported financial assets: a foreigner (Eliza Doolittle) is now holding $100 worth of U.S. currency, the obligations of a Federal Reserve bank in the U.S. Without such a rise in the credits column (or decline somewhere in the debits column), there would be no way for Eliza to receive what Hank sent.

If Eliza pursues a more normal course and cashes Hank's gift for British pounds, then the bank at which she cashes the check will increase by $100 its holding of U.S. assets: a deposit credit in a U.S. bank. If the bank sells that deposit to a London importer of American merchandise, the financial asset will return to U.S. ownership when it's used to pay for $100 of merchandise exported to England. There will always be some transaction to offset Hank's gift, some increase in British wealth to match the decrease in Hank's wealth.

The easiest way to understand how the balance of payments remains in constant balance is to focus on that fifth row, which records exports and imports of financial assets. If the U.S.—households, business firms, and government— simultaneously exports a smaller value of merchandise and services than it imports, receives less income from foreign investments than it pays out on foreigners' investments in the U.S., and makes more transfers to foreigners than it receives, the fifth row *must* make up the difference. Otherwise there would be no way for all those transactions just described to occur.

How could Americans make the net payments to foreigners that all these transactions entail if there were no net increase in foreigners' holdings of U.S. financial assets? The answer is that they could not. If Americans want to import merchandise and services of greater value than they are currently exporting, they must in some manner obtain the means of payment to make up the difference. There are only three possibilities: income from foreign investments, gifts or some other kind of transfers from abroad, or loans from foreigners. What isn't

provided by investment income and transfers has to be supplied by loans from abroad. That means foreigners will have to acquire more IOUs from Americans and will then own a larger amount of U.S. financial assets.

Foreign Investment

There was a great deal of concern in the U.S. in the early 1980s, a concern often verging on hysteria, about the huge deficits in the U.S. balance of merchandise trade. The merchandise deficit wasn't being made up by the balance on services, investment income, or transfers, so that foreigners each year were increasing substantially their holdings of U.S. financial assets. A lot of people reacted to this as if foreigners were in a position to foreclose on our mortgage, and would surely do so if we did not reform our reckless and spendthrift ways. That's absurd. Foreigners were eagerly investing in the IOUs of Americans; they were doing so because they regarded investments in the U.S. as a better deal than other investments they could make. They liked our prospects, so they wanted to invest in our IOUs. They wanted to loan us money because they thought it would be profitable for themselves.

It was certainly profitable for us. The eagerness of foreigners to invest in the U.S. in the early 1980s substantially reduced the crowding-out effect of the federal government's huge budget deficits. Without their assistance, interest rates would have been higher and the U.S. capital stock would have grown more slowly.

To make all this possible, though, we had to import more merchandise and services than we were exporting. It's important to realize that merchandise and service exports and imports are no more "basic" than exports and imports of financial assets. All international transactions reflect decisions that people made because it seemed in their interest to do so. No particular set of transactions balances any other set. They fit together in a system of mutual determination, where the tail wags the dog as effectively as the dog wags the tail.

Foreigners were not "forced" to lend to us because we were importing more than we were exporting, anymore than we were "forced" to import more than we exported so that foreigners could invest in the U.S.

The Ambiguity of Disequilibrium

The balance of payments always and necessarily balances. You might be a bit surprised to hear that, since we're told so often that we must do this or cannot do that "because of the balance of payments." The implication is that the balance is precarious, and that we are in danger of disastrously losing our equilibrium. But if patriotism is the last refuge of a scoundrel, as Samuel Johnson suggested, the balance of payments is very often

the last refuge of Dr. Johnson's patriots. Special-interest groups looking for favors look also for a way to wrap themselves in the balance of payments.

What do people mean, then, when they talk about deficits or surpluses in the balance of payments? And why are they ever concerned about disequilibrium in the balance of payments if in fact it always balances? To understand this, we must first recognize that a deficit or a surplus is a discrepancy between what actually happened and what *someone wanted* to happen. That's always the meaning of a disequilibrium in the economic way of thinking, and you've encountered it before.

A disequilibrium price for wheat, for example, doesn't show up as a difference between actual sales and purchases (which are necessarily identical) but as a difference between the *intentions* of sellers and purchasers. The implication of a disequilibrium is that matters will not continue in this way because some people's intentions aren't being realized, and so adjustments are going to occur. It follows that we can't use the concept of equilibrium or disequilibrium unless we have a useful notion of who the people are whose plans are being frustrated.

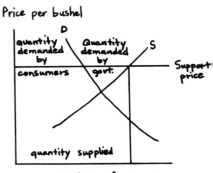

Those who complain about disequilibrium in the balance of payments never identify these people. That's not very surprising. The concept of a balance-of-payments disequilibrium is so extraordinarily ambiguous that we would probably be better off if we discarded the notion altogether. There are just too many intentions of too many different kinds entering into the aggregate of international transactions for anyone to assert that intended credits are larger or smaller than intended debits—which is the meaning of a disequilibrium. In general, the larger the universe to which we try to apply the equilibrium concept, the more vague and uncertain is its meaning—and the more likely is it to obscure rather than clarify the problems at which we're looking.

To claim that the U.S. balance of payments is in disequilibrium is really to claim that something undesired is occurring. But from whose point of view is this claim made? Didn't the importers want to purchase whatever they purchased? Didn't banks want to lend whatever they lent? Didn't governments, corporations, or individuals want to offer the gifts or grants they sent abroad? Who were the people for whom the results of international trade turned out to be inconsistent with what they had intended?

Which of the transactions in the balance of payments statement above was unintentional?

A simple little question should always be addressed to anyone who claims that the balance of payments is in deficit: "How do you know that?" The answer, if followed up properly, will tell you what the speaker disapproves of.

Suppose we find someone who is worried about what he calls "the deficit in the U.S. trade balance," and ask him how he knows we're running a deficit. He may point to the fact—and it *has* been a fact for a number of years now—that the United States annually imports more *merchandise*, in value terms, than it exports. The proper reply is to ask why he ignores exports of services and financial assets. Why ignore or slight or look suspiciously at these other transactions? Merchandise, services, and financial assets are *all* valuable to the people who receive them. They want them. They give up other goods of value to get them. By what criterion can some be set aside to create a surplus or deficit in the balance of payments?

Searching in Vain

Try thinking through an extreme case. Suppose that the Japanese government somehow managed to exclude all imports of both merchandise and services coming from the United States while continuing to export to the United States. It's clear that Japanese exporters would want to be paid. How would we be able to pay them? We might at first use our stocks of yen accumulated from earlier periods before we stopped exporting to Japan. After that we might use stocks of marks or pounds or francs earned by previous exporting to Germany, England, or France. When and if we had used up all our stocks of foreign currencies and our stock of gold and had sold off all our investments in other countries, would we be able to purchase any more goods from Japan? Perhaps. We could start paying in dollars. Would Japanese exporters be willing to accept dollars? Of what use would dollars be to Japanese exporters if they weren't allowed to purchase U.S. merchandise or services? If the Bank of Japan, the Japanese central bank, was willing to give the exporters yen for the dollars they received, those exporters would be perfectly willing to accept U.S. dollars in exchange for automobiles, television sets, and other exports.

Stop now and notice that at no point in the preceding paragraph was the U.S. balance of payments ever in deficit. Every Japanese export to the United States was paid for. Each debit in our balance of payments created by the imports was matched by a credit transaction in the form of financial assets moving from the United States to Japan. Why call such a situation a deficit?

Because we're losing financial assets? We are indeed, but why is that a deficit? One might better say that the Japanese are experiencing a deficit because they're losing automobiles and television sets.

Because this situation just can't continue forever? Perhaps it can't. It's even more certain that it *won't*. When the Bank of Japan gets tired of accumulating ever-larger dollar balances and stops buying dollars from Japanese exporters, then those exporters won't accept dollars in payment any longer and Americans will have to quit buying Japanese cars and television sets. But where in all of this is the *deficit?*

There's one other possibility. Our hypothetical friend who's so afraid of a balance-of-payments deficit might reply that the dollar is going to *depreciate* in the circumstances we've described, and that this depreciation would be evidence of the U.S. balance-of-payments deficit. Our search for the elusive meaning of a balance-of-payments disequilibrium has brought us to the important topic of exchange rates.

Foreign Exchange Rates and Purchasing-Power Parity

Foreign exchange rates, most simply, are relative prices that tie together *sets* of relative prices. The existing exchange rate between two currencies at any time will roughly express the relative purchasing power of the two currencies. If it takes 50 cents to buy a mark but only ½ cent to buy a Japanese yen, you can assume that 1 dollar, 2 marks, and 200 yen will all buy approximately the same amount of goods in the United States, Germany, and Japan respectively. Thus exchange rates, to begin with, adjust to create *purchasing-power parity* among national currencies.

The simplest way to see why this is so is to think about what will happen if it's *not* so. If 1 dollar exchanges for 200 yen, but 200 yen buy appreciably more goods in Japan than 1 dollar buys in the U.S., then dollar holders will want to buy yen with dollars in order to get more for their money. That increased demand for yen on the part of dollar holders will not be matched by an increased supply of yen, because yen holders will not be willing to give up 200 yen in return for just 1 dollar. The dollar price of the yen will consequently rise. Dollar holders will have to start offering $1.05 to obtain 200 yen. Viewing the same event from the other side, yen holders will now be able to purchase 1 dollar for about 190 yen.

Purchasing-power parity is only a first approximation, however, as we seek to find out why national currencies exchange for one another at the rates they do. Exchange rates can never exactly equate the purchasing power of two currencies because no two currencies will ever purchase exactly the same array of goods. Some goods, such as a vacation near Mt. Fujiyama, just aren't available for purchase with dollars in the United States or with marks in West Germany. Moreover, exchange rates are more responsive to the relative

prices of internationally traded goods (farm commodities, machinery, petroleum, automobiles) than to the relative prices of all goods, including those that are rarely exported or imported (housing, most services).

Expectations and Exchange Rates

More importantly, however, foreign exchange rates won't express the *current* purchasing power of currencies when their relative purchasing power is expected to change. A belief that the United States will experience more rapid inflation than Germany in the coming year is a belief that the German mark will lose less value than the U.S. dollar during the year. That belief increases the present demand for marks, relative to the demand for dollars, and causes the current value of the mark to rise relative to the value of the dollar. That explains a great deal that is otherwise inexplicable about movements in exchange rates.

Consider the complaints about the "overvalued dollar" that became chronic in the first half of the 1980s as the value of the U.S. dollar relative to most foreign currencies rose by more than 50 percent from 1980 to 1985. It's not hard to understand why some people were upset. A 50 percent appreciation in the foreign-exchange value of the dollar makes U.S. exports 50 percent more expensive to foreigners. That's not good news for American firms trying to sell in overseas markets. That 50 percent appreciation of the dollar simultaneously reduced the average price of foreign goods in the U.S. by one-third, a development not welcomed by U.S. firms selling in competition with imports. (It was pointed out less frequently and much less vociferously that those Americans who bought foreign goods at one-third lower prices benefited from doing so; the interests of consumers usually receive less attention than the complaints of producers.)

What caused this steep rise in the foreign-exchange value of the dollar? The first thing to notice is that the dollar had an extremely *low* value in 1980. All through the 1970s the value of the dollar had slid downward in the foreign-exchange markets, until in 1980 it stood at about 70 percent of its value in the 1960s.[1] So most of the appreciation after 1980 was merely a return of the dollar to its earlier value. The first question to ask, then, is why the dollar depreciated in the 1970s.

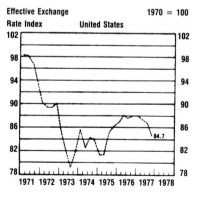

Effective Exchange Rate Index — United States — 1970 = 100

---

[1]These comparisons refer to the average value of the dollar relative to the currencies of the principal nations with which the U.S. trades, with the importance of each currency weighted, in calculation of the average, by the volume of trade with that country.

The Downs and Ups of the Dollar

The answer is the inflation that occurred in the U.S. in the 1970s. Prior to the 1970s, the U.S. was generally expected to run substantially lower inflation rates than other countries. We were expected to do this because we had in fact done so since World War II, and our political institutions seemed generally capable of resisting the inflationary pressures that besieged other governments. With the dollar expected to maintain its value better than most other currencies, foreigners chose to hold a substantial amount of wealth in dollar-denominated assets.

When the 1970s gradually revealed that the U.S. was not immune to inflation, and U.S. inflation rates climbed toward or even above those of other major economic powers, investors abandoned their confidence in the dollar. Since they expected it to lose value in the future, they became willing to hold dollars only when they could acquire them at a lower price. The value of the dollar in foreign exchange consequently declined, until it reached a level at which foreigners were willing to hold all the dollars supplied to them.

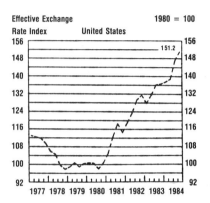

Then in 1980 evidence mounted that the U.S. was again going to bring its rate of inflation under control. The Fed had declared its determination to control the rate at which the stock of dollars would grow, and a new administration with conservative credentials prepared to take office vowing to end the spendthrift practices that had supposedly been responsible for the high inflation of the 1970s. It is expectations that control foreign exchange rates. The change in expectations raised the value of the dollar even before the U.S. inflation rate actually declined in 1982 and 1983.

There is more to the story than this, as there always is. In an introductory account, however, too many details will obscure the essential picture. And the essential point is that the desire by foreigners to hold dollars, relative to the quantity of dollars being supplied to them through the international transactions of Americans, determines the foreign-exchange value of the dollar. When foreigners increase their demand for dollars while other things remain equal, the dollar appreciates. They increase their demand for dollars when they conclude that the dollar is going to hold its value in the future better than they previously thought, or that investments in the U.S. are more attractive than they seemed to be earlier.

All of this causes foreign exchange rates to move up and down in ways that make international transactions riskier than they would otherwise be. Uncertainty of this kind makes it more difficult for producers to anticipate future demands for their product; even when they don't sell for export, they may have to compete with imported products whose prices

relative to their own can change suddenly and substantially due to an exchange rate movement. Costly mistakes are consequently made more often, and recessions, which are ultimately rooted in mistaken predictions, tend to become more frequent and more severe. It would be far better if exchange rates were fixed and stable.

The Bretton Woods System

It was largely in order to create a system of stable foreign exchange rates that the Western nations established the International Monetary Fund (IMF) after World War II. The IMF was supposed to assist any member nation whose currency was tending to depreciate and to advise on devaluation when it appeared that existing exchange rates seriously overstated the currency's value. With varying rates of economic growth from country to country and different rates of domestic inflation, exchange rates might have to be altered occasionally. But the objective of the Bretton Woods System (named after the town in New Hampshire where the international monetary agreements were negotiated in 1944) was fixed exchange rates. Each nation was supposed to buy and sell its currency in order to keep it pegged at the officially established rate of exchange. (Other currencies were pegged to the dollar, and the dollar was pegged to gold.) Out of all this, it was hoped, would develop an expansion of international trade.

The system wasn't a failure. International trade did expand under the Bretton Woods System, at roughly twice the rate of increase in domestic production. And the advantages of international specialization contributed substantially to rising levels of real income. But an international monetary system with fixed exchange rates is difficult to maintain among governments pursuing divergent domestic policies. Those policies inevitably produced different patterns of growth in industrial and agricultural production, different movements in the structure of relative prices between countries, different rates of inflation, and consequently large fluctuations in the international demand for different countries' currencies. To prevent depreciation or appreciation under these circumstances, governments were often required to intervene heavily and continuously in the foreign-exchange markets.

The governments whose currency was tending to appreciate had to buy foreign currencies. But they paid for foreign currencies with their own currencies, which meant that they were pumping additional money into their domestic economies and causing inflation. A noninflationary monetary policy was difficult if not impossible to pursue for a central bank required to keep its currency from rising in the foreign-

exchange markets. The currency would be tending to appreciate because it was undervalued at the fixed exchange rate, which usually meant that the central bank had been doing a better job than other central banks of holding down the rate of domestic inflation. What it all came to was that countries that controlled inflation through domestic policies were put under international pressure to accelerate their rate of inflation.

Governments whose currency was tending to depreciate, usually because of higher-than-average inflation rates, were required under the Bretton Woods System to purchase their own currency to keep its price from falling. But purchase it *with what?* The very situation that caused the depreciation, a high rate of inflation, made it difficult for that nation to sell enough goods to acquire enough foreign exchange to continue buying its own currency. Borrowing from the IMF could only be a stopgap measure. Without a change in the domestic policies that were producing the pressure for depreciation, devaluation was inevitable. Usually those policies consisted of government expenditures in excess of tax revenues, financed through the creation of new money, with inflation as the eventual result. When the IMF extended loans, it was always with the proviso that the government reduce its budget deficit and slow down its creation of new money. But this was largely empty counsel. The domestic pressures that were creating the budget deficits weren't going to disappear because the International Monetary Fund said that deficits were naughty.

Unplanned Consequences

Unfortunately, governments confronting a depreciating currency have another set of options. They can announce that their problems are the result of a "deficit in the balance of payments," and slap controls on imports to "reduce the deficit." A depreciating currency thus gives government officials a public-interest argument with which to camouflage their surrender to producer lobbies always interested in keeping out import competition. The United States government frequently played this game in the 1960s. At various times during that final decade of the Bretton Woods System, we raised the cost to American tourists of bringing back foreign merchandise, placed a tax on money borrowed by foreign corporations from U.S. sources, restricted foreign lending by U.S. banks, imposed first voluntary and later mandatory controls on direct investment abroad by U.S. corporations, recalled the dependents of American military personnel stationed overseas, threatened to impose quotas unless particular countries "voluntarily" curtailed their exports to us,

and in an endless variety of smaller ways tried to discourage imports and encourage exports. All this was done to "protect the dollar" against the balance-of-payments "deficits" that supposedly threatened the international monetary order. The irony is that we claimed to be doing all this in order to preserve the international monetary order and the system of free trade!

In 1971 the United States essentially abandoned its efforts to keep the dollar's value fixed in terms of gold, and other countries more or less reluctantly gave up their commitments to maintain a fixed rate of exchange between their currencies and the dollar. Exchange rates were turned loose and were allowed to *float*, as the jargon has it, in response to the changing expectations of suppliers and demanders. Some experts immediately announced the breakdown of the international monetary system and the onset of a world monetary crisis. Central bankers around the world called for emergency conferences to create a new system that would restore order before the flow of trade and exchange broke down in chaos.

Fixed or Floating Exchange Rates?

Outside of academic circles, and especially among the economists working for central banks, floating exchange rates were regarded as unworkable if desirable, and undesirable if workable. They would increase uncertainty for foreign traders and investors, it was argued. But they would also create additional uncertainty for domestic producers and investors, because a change in exchange rates could quickly and radically change the potential profitability of industries producing import-competitive goods, as well as goods that might be exported. Moreover, governments weren't likely to remain passive when a sudden depreciation in the currency of a major trading country led to an unexpected surge of imports or threatened established export markets. Governments would far more likely retaliate with trade and investment controls that could eventually lead to a breakdown of international exchange.

Nonetheless, the advocates of floating rates have generally had their way since 1971. This was more by default than by design: conflicting national interests simply prevented governments from agreeing on the structure of a new fixed-exchange-rate system. Most countries today don't allow their currencies to float freely, but try to keep them in some loose relationship with another major currency or set of currencies. A variety of limited international agreements, such as the European Monetary System that was launched in 1979, have aimed at reducing fluctuations in exchange rates—at least

Floating Foreign Exchange Rates
(currency units per U.S. dollar)

Country/currency	1983	1984	1985
1 Australia/dollar[1]	90.14	87.937	70.026
2 Austria/schilling	17.968	20.005	20.676
3 Belgium/franc	51.121	57.749	59.336
4 Brazil/cruzeiro	573.27	1841.50	6205.10
5 Canada/dollar	1.2325	1.2953	1.3658
6 China, P.R./yuan	1.9809	2.3308	2.9434
7 Denmark/krone	9.1483	10.354	10.598
8 Finland/markka	5.5636	6.007	6.1971
9 France/franc	7.6203	8.7355	8.9799
10 Germany/deutsche mark	2.5539	2.8454	2.9419
11 Greece/drachma	87.895	112.73	138.4
12 Hong Kong/dollar	7.2569	7.8188	7.7911
13 India/rupee	10.1040	11.348	12.332
14 Ireland/pound[1]	124.81	108.64	106.62
15 Italy/lira	1519.30	1756.10	1908.90
16 Japan/yen	237.55	237.45	238.47
17 Malaysia/ringgit	2.3204	2.3448	2.4806
18 Netherlands/guilder	2.8543	3.2083	3.3184
19 New Zealand/dollar[1]	66.790	57.837	49.752
20 Norway/krone	7.3012	8.1596	8.5933
21 Portugal/escudo	11.60	147.70	172.07
22 Singapore/dollar	2.1136	2.1325	2.2008
23 South Africa/rand[1]	89.85	69.534	45.57
24 South Korea/won	776.04	807.91	861.89
25 Spain/peseta	143.500	160.78	169.98
26 Sri Lanka/rupee	23.510	25.428	27.187
27 Sweden/krona	7.6717	8.2706	8.6031
28 Switzerland/franc	2.1006	2.3500	2.4551
29 Taiwan/dollar	n.a.	39.633	39.889
30 Thailand/baht	22.991	23.582	27.193
31 United Kingdom/pound[1]	151.59	133.66	129.74

[1]U.S. cents per currency unit

among countries that trade extensively with each other. And some small nations whose international trade is predominantly with a much larger economy have tried to maintain a rigidly fixed rate of exchange between their currency and the currency of the dominant trading partner. The system that has evolved since 1971 has its faults and its localized crises, but it does work. Floating exchange rates have not turned out to be the disaster that the central bankers forecast.

Perhaps the fairest judgment we can make is to say that the advocates of fixed foreign exchange rates and the advocates of floating rates are *both* correct. The ideal system is one of fixed exchange rates. Just try to imagine what would happen if the dollar had a different and constantly changing value in each of the fifty American states. Do you see how many additional costs and how much new uncertainty that would create for business firms? Our national wealth is in large part a consequence of the extensive specialization that we have been able to practice because low-cost, low-uncertainty trade was possible throughout our vast territory. Fixed exchange rates between the states—the dollar of a Maine film fan always exchanges for exactly one dollar of California-produced films—plays an enormous even if unappreciated part in facilitating that specialization and trade.

But the advocates of floating exchange rates are correct, too. The nations of the world are unlike the states of the United States in two critical ways: they are *not* prohibited by any constitution from restricting the free movement of merchandise, services, financial assets, and people across borders, and they *do* have the ability to run independent monetary policies. The governments of our states lack the power to create the conditions that would permit dollars in Alabama or Alaska to change in value relative to the dollars used in Hawaii and New Hampshire. The governments of nation-states have that power as well as political incentives to use it in ways that are almost inevitably going to cause the purchasing power of their currencies to change at divergent rates. Trying to maintain fixed exchange rates in a world of radically diverse national economic policies will almost certainly do more harm than good. It will encourage and sometimes even require governments to interfere with international trade, as the only way in which they can reconcile politically opportune domestic policies with predetermined foreign-exchange rates.

Private Interests, National Interests, Public Interests

All of this will suggest to some people that there is no longer *any* international economic order. That might be true for

those who equate order with legislated systems and international order with negotiated treaties. But it would not be true for those who see order simply in the continuation and extension of international exchange. It sometimes happens that we become so absorbed in our search for solutions that we forget what the problem was. Is it our goal that consumers, investors, producers, tourists, and bagpipe players—people, in short—be enabled to cooperate more freely across the barriers that national boundaries raise? Or is that the problem—namely, that people are engaging in international transactions that interfere with the goals of national governments?

It is certainly possible that the interests of the larger public might require some restrictions on international exchange. But a thoughtful person will wonder why the national interest seems so regularly to require that more be given away than is received in return; that jobs be preferred to goods; that efficient producers be hobbled to prevent them from using their advantage to the detriment of less-efficient producers; and that in general people be prevented from increasing their wealth by exchanging freely. The skeptic should be pardoned for concluding that the public interest may be something quite different from the national interest, at least as the national interest is usually defined by those who shape international economic policy.

Comparative Advantage under Attack

The principle of comparative advantage received its first explicit statement in the early nineteenth century as an explanation of the gains to be obtained from international trade. But the principle has never fared well in the area where it originated. "Everyone knows" that imports hurt domestic firms and destroy jobs, whereas exports generate profits for domestic producers and create additional jobs. Policies aimed at restricting imports and subsidizing exports have consequently had a strong political appeal for centuries, and never more so than when a recession is cutting into sales and adding to the level of unemployment.

The argument that imports destroy jobs has the seductive appeal of a half-truth. When Americans buy Japanese radios, they don't buy as many domestically made radios. An increase in radio imports can therefore lead to production cutbacks and layoffs in the domestic radio industry. So the owners and employees of radio-manufacturing firms have an obvious interest in restricting imports. And when they go to Congress to request taxes or quotas on radio imports, they have a handy slogan with which to claim that such protection is good for the country: it protects American jobs. But the argument is misleading.

In the first place, jobs are created by the production of export goods, as well as by the production of goods that compete with imports. And American firms can't continue indefinitely to sell abroad if foreigners aren't allowed to sell in the United States. Trade is a two-way street.

Moreover, jobs should not automatically be treated as goods. Some jobs no doubt are intrinsically satisfying and worth doing for themselves without regard to the commodities or services that result. But that's certainly rare. The justification for jobs generally is the income they provide for workers and the corresponding benefit to others in the form of useful goods. The "protect American jobs" argument ignores the gains in real income that come from specialization. If the Japanese can make better radios and sell them at lower prices than American manufacturers can, Americans ought to produce other products and buy their radios from Japan. The attempt to justify the protection of less-efficient producers on the grounds that this will preserve jobs runs quickly into absurdity. Why not push the argument further and produce domestically all the coffee we consume? American soil, climate, and geography are not as well suited for the production of coffee trees as are large areas of Brazil and Colombia. But think of all the jobs we could create by building and operating huge greenhouses in which we try to duplicate the favorable growing conditions in those countries! And why stop with goods currently imported? Think of how many new jobs we could create by outlawing the use of automated equipment in the telephone industry!

Producer Interests and the National Interest

For two centuries, economists have been arguing along these lines against the proponents of restrictions on imports, but not with great success. A French pamphleteer-economist named Frederic Bastiat (1801-1850) wrote a witty satire in 1845 in the form of a petition by the French candlemakers for protection against the unfair competition of the sun. Their request to the Chamber of Deputies for legislation that would protect the jobs of candlemakers by prohibiting windows brilliantly exposes the absurdity of protectionist logic. Bastiat's satire has been reprinted numerous times, but the arguments he ridiculed don't disappear.

Part of the explanation must be found in the resistance of special-interest groups to mere logic. People are readily persuaded by arguments in which they want to believe and have difficulty understanding arguments that run counter to their interests. More importantly, however, the political process almost guarantees that those who stand to benefit from restrictions on international trade will have a louder voice

in policy formation than will the larger group that stands to lose. Transaction costs prevent radio purchasers from organizing effectively to oppose domestic producers; and the foreign producers obviously have little influence on domestic policy. The externalities of the political process in a democracy make it almost certain that when government officials come to the point of choosing between the interests of American buyers of radios and American producers of radios, they will be surrounded by the clamor of producers but will hear almost nothing from consumers. Officials who wish to survive in their jobs pay attention to that kind of pressure.

A limited but legitimate argument for protection against imports can be constructed from the costs of change. The closing down of an industry unable to meet foreign competition entails losses for its owners and employees. The more narrowly specialized the displaced resources, the greater the losses. There may be a case for protection in such circumstances. Notice, however, that the argument can be applied to the case of an industry hurt by domestic competition as well as foreign. Domestic competitors have political influence, of course, and are therefore harder to exclude by special legislation. Nonetheless, if resources were attracted to an industry because of government restrictions on imports, it may be unfair to jerk that protection away suddenly. So there is a case for the maintenance of prior and long-continued restrictions on imports, or at least for their reduction at a slow rate. Equity considerations along with political realities may also suggest a policy of transitional subsidies, designed to reduce the loss to workers and owners or to help them find new opportunities. But this argument cannot be used to support the introduction of new or additional restrictions against imports.

There is no limit to the number of bad arguments that can be constructed in support of import restrictions, and it would be an exercise in futility to attempt to anticipate and refute each one. The fact that there is a kernel of validity in most such arguments complicates the task of their analysis. The valid reasoning must be winnowed from the chaff that surrounds it before the limitations of its applicability can be shown. Nothing would contribute more toward raising the quality of public discussion in this area than a firm grasp of the principle of comparative advantage.

The principle of comparative advantage shows why and how exchange creates wealth. It keeps insisting that the cost of a transaction is the value of what is given up and the benefit is the value of what is obtained, so that it is nonsense to claim that a country can grow wealthy by exporting more than it imports. The principle of comparative advantage undercuts the

claim that one country may be more efficient than another in the production of everything: the logical impossibility of that is apparent from the very definition of efficiency as a ratio between the value of what is produced and what is consequently not produced, between the goods obtained and the goods that had to be sacrificed because their production entails genuine opportunity costs. By focusing on the real factors involved in production and trade, the principle of comparative advantage dispels the confusion that so easily arises when trade policy is discussed exclusively in monetary terms.

Unfortunately, there are many parties who hope to gain from fostering this sort of confusion, because they know that they have no real chance to obtain the special-interest legislation they're after unless they can obscure what's going on. These are the people who invent deficits in the trade balance, who claim to find evidence for overvalued or undervalued exchange rates, and who regularly discover that their foreign competitors are engaging in unfair trade practices. In the world of political economy, such arguments have weight. That is the central problem for Chapter 22.

Once Over Lightly

The movement of goods across international boundaries can either frustrate or promote the domestic policies of national governments. Government stabilization policies have particularly close interconnections with international trade policies.

The total credits in a nation's balance of international payments must always exactly equal the total of its debits; any discrepancy reflects errors in record keeping.

A disequilibrium in the balance of payments implies that desired credits and debits (desired by whom?) are not equal. To assert that the balance of payments is in deficit is to imply that some credit items were unintended, or cannot be expected to continue, or should not have been allowed to occur. The assertion of a balance-of-payments disequilibrium is thus a complex policy judgment disguised as a simple statement of obvious fact.

Foreign exchange rates are prices that link the sets of relative prices existing in nations with separate currencies. The movement of these rates is an important factor in the coordination of international transactions and payments.

Exchange rates between national currencies reflect the forces of supply and demand, which are in turn guided by the relative domestic purchasing power of the currencies, modified by expectations with regard to the *future* value of holding various currencies or assets exchangeable for them.

Exchange rates can be set arbitrarily only by governments able to enforce arbitrary prohibitions on international exchange.

Fixed exchange rates promote trade and thus create wealth by reducing uncertainty. But fixed exchange rates between currencies presuppose coordinated domestic economic policies.

In a world of uncoordinated domestic economic policies, floating exchange rates probably produce less uncertainty and more trade than do fixed exchange rates, which in practice are frequently revised.

Most arguments in favor of restrictions on international trade ignore the fundamental principle of comparative advantage, a principle that has not fared well in the area of international trade against well-organized producer groups exploiting public ignorance and nationalist sentiments.

QUESTIONS FOR DISCUSSION

1. Suppose you established an accounting system to keep track of your personal "balance of payments" with your trading partners (i.e., everybody else).
   (a) If you "import" a new television set, you must "export" something else to pay for it. What would you have "exported" if you paid cash to the store at which you bought the set? If you traded in your old set and paid cash for the balance? If you wrote a check to cover the purchase? If you put the purchase on a bank credit card? If you simply promised the store owner that you would pay when you got some money this summer?
   (b) Could you have a balance of payments deficit or surplus?
   (c) How would you handle the transaction if your Uncle Miltie gave the set to you as a birthday present?
   (d) If you put a lot of large purchases on your bank credit card over several months while making only minimum payments on the account, are you running a deficit of any sort? Why isn't it proper to call it a deficit in your balance of payments? What will happen to prevent this deficit from continuing indefinitely?

2. An American sends $100 in the form of five crisp twenties as a gift to a relative in Vienna. This action counts as a debit in the U.S. balance of payments. Where does the balancing credit item appear as the following events unfold?
   (a) The Austrian relative exchanges the dollars for schillings at a Vienna bank. The bank holds the dollars, because it has customers who frequently want to buy dollars with schillings.
   (b) The Vienna bank sells the dollars to the Austrian central bank in exchange for schillings.
   (c) The Austrian central bank gives the dollars to the German central bank

in exchange for schillings that the German central bank had been holding.

(d) The German central bank sells the dollars to the Volkswagen Company in exchange for marks.

(e) The Volkswagen Company gives the dollars as expense money to a company executive who is taking a business trip to Pennsylvania. He spends them at a motel in Scranton.

(f) If the dollars had remained permanently in Europe, would this imply that the United States had a deficit in its balance of international payments?

3. Is it better for a country to export more merchandise and services than it imports, or to import more than it exports? If you're in doubt, ask the same question about a single household, such as yourself. Which is better for you: a surplus or a deficit in your personal exporting and importing of goods and services?

4. What are the consequences of heavy net investment in the U.S. by foreigners?

(a) Does this mean foreigners are obtaining control of our economy?

(b) What advantages does the U.S. receive from net investment by foreigners at a time when the federal government is running large budget deficits?

(c) If foreigners invest in U.S. agricultural land, do they acquire the power to control our food supply? If they buy stock in U.S. corporations, do they acquire the power to use these corporations in ways that run counter to the security interests of the United States?

(d) Who benefits and who loses if foreign nationals start acquiring large amounts of prime farming land in the Midwest? Who would want to see the price of such land raised and who would not?

5. Canadian firms trying to attract tourists from the United States will sometimes claim in their advertising that U.S. tourists can benefit from the low price of the Canadian dollar.

(a) Does the U.S. dollar buy more goods in Canada when one Canadian dollar exchanges for 75 U.S. cents than when one Canadian dollar exchanges for one U.S. dollar?

(b) If the exchange rate of one Canadian dollar for 75 U.S. cents reflects purchasing-power parity, how much should Americans expect to pay, in Canadian dollars, for a hotel room that would cost $30 in the U.S.? Why might hotel rooms cost considerably more or less than this even though the exchange rate reflects purchasing-power parity?

(c) Suppose you are a Canadian retailer of some sort, and you're interested in making as much money as possible from the tourist trade. Would it pay you to place this sign in your shop window: "U.S. dollars exchanged for $1.50 Canadian on all purchases"?

6. For many years Mexico maintained the price of its peso at 8 U.S. cents.

(a) Could Mexico have succeeded in doing this if the Mexican inflation rate had been much faster or slower than the U.S. inflation rate over a number of years?

(b) From 1963 to 1972, the rate of inflation in Mexico averaged 5 percent

per year; in the U.S., over the same period, the inflation rate averaged about 4 percent. From 1972 to 1975, however, the U.S. inflation rate ran at 8 percent while the rate in Mexico leaped to 17 percent. Was there any way the Mexican government could have maintained the 8 cents per peso exchange rate after 1975?

(c) After a series of devaluations, beginning in 1976, the Mexican government in 1982 abandoned all attempts to fix the rate of exchange between pesos and dollars. Throughout this period the supply of pesos was growing at annual rates in the vicinity of 30 percent. The peso tumbled steeply when the "peg" was abandoned. For a few months thereafter, Americans found Mexican goods remarkably cheap. Why did Mexican goods become major bargains for Americans in 1982? Why didn't the bargain prices last very long?

7. What do people mean when they say that a currency is *overvalued?* The U.S. dollar, for example, was said by many to be overvalued relative to the yen in 1985 when one dollar was exchanging for 250 yen.

(a) If people think the dollar is worth less than the price it's currently commanding in the foreign exchange markets, how can they profit from this knowledge? What will happen to them if they turn out to be wrong?

(b) What is the test of whether they are right or wrong? Where do we look to discover the true value of one currency relative to others?

8. In 1986 the Japanese began complaining that the yen was overvalued, at a time when a dollar could be purchased for 160 yen.

(a) On what grounds do you suppose the Japanese were making their complaint?

(b) If the yen is overvalued relative to the dollar, must the dollar necessarily be undervalued relative to the yen?

9. What do you suppose happened to the price of Japanese cars in the U.S. when the yen appreciated in 1985 and 1986 from 250 to 160 per dollar?

10. How do large changes in foreign exchange rates, such as the sharp swing from 1985 to 1986 in the dollar-yen exchange rate, affect business firms engaging in extensive international exchange? Who puts political pressure on a government, and what do they ask for, when that government's currency appreciates substantially?

11. From 1980 to 1985, the U.S. dollar appreciated over 50 percent relative to the weighted average of other currencies. How did this affect the following groups?

(a) Americans interested in buying foreign automobiles

(b) Americans interested in buying U.S.-made automobiles

(c) American automobile manufacturers and their employees

(d) Americans planning foreign travel

(e) Americans operating businesses that cater extensively to foreign tourists

(f) American firms that export extensively

(g) American firms that manufacture items with a lot of imported materials and parts

(h) American firms that fit both of the two preceding descriptions

12. Under a system of fixed exchange rates, every nation must experience approximately the same rate of inflation as every other.

(a) Why is this so?

(b) How can a country determined to have both a low inflation rate and a fixed rate of exchange between its own and other nations' currencies go about achieving these two objectives if other countries choose high inflation rates?

13. "Floating exchange rates free a nation to pursue the domestic policies it prefers." Is that true?

14. What is the difference between exchange rates that are free to fluctuate in response to conditions of supply and demand, and exchange rates that are fixed but are periodically altered in accordance with changed conditions of supply and demand?

15. Why can't one country have a comparative advantage over another country in the production of everything if the first country has excellent natural resources, a huge capital stock, a highly skilled labor force, and ingenious technicians and managers, while the second country is poor in all four areas?

16. What evidence exists to support the view that Japan has a comparative advantage with respect to the United States in the production of small automobiles? How would you account for this comparative advantage? How would you explain the fact that the United States in general seems to have a comparative advantage in the production of large automobiles but a comparative disadvantage in the production of smaller ones?

17. How does the theory of "free riders" help explain the generally greater legislative influence of producers than of consumers?

18. Estimates published in 1972 predicted that the Concorde SST, the French and British supersonic commercial plane, would not repay its development costs, would create environmental problems, and would not generate sufficient additional revenue to cover the associated costs for the airlines that purchased them. These were essentially the objections that led to cancellation of government financing for an American supersonic commercial plane. A counterargument in both cases was that these planes would provide many additional jobs, help the balance of payments, and prevent other countries from gaining an advantage. How would you evaluate these counterarguments?

19. Everyone will agree that *some* policies that would create more jobs for Americans are nonetheless not in the national interest. For example, no one recommends that we build highways without using heavy machinery, even though many more jobs would be created if highways were built entirely with hand tools. When is the job-creation argument actually used? Are there any circumstances in which it's a defensible argument?

20. In order to take advantage of lower production costs, a Massachusetts textile manufacturer builds a factory in North Carolina, and a United States television-manufacturing firm opens an assembly plant in Mexico.

(a) In what ways is the action by the television firm different from the action by the textile firm?

(b) Is either action contrary to the national interest?

(c) Is either action likely to encounter effective political opposition?

Inflation, Recession, and Political Economy

If all the interrelationships that we've been discussing since Chapter 15 were clearly and confidently understood, so that economists could explain cause and effect as precisely as chemists do in their laboratories, government stabilization policies might be set in the public interest. But the theories of economists in this area are much less precise and far more subject to debate than are the theories of chemists. That leaves considerable room for policymakers to talk persuasively about the public interest while actually responding to the pressure of much narrower interests. The net result of such policies could well be less stability rather than more.

The Political Setting

Government is not like Aladdin's marvelous genie, who always obeyed commands and always succeeded in accomplishing what he was told to do. The agencies of government, for all their power and importance, are staffed entirely by human beings. Moreover, even if government is "of the people, by the people, for the people," in Abraham Lincoln's immortal phrase, government is not necessarily going to do what the majority wants. As Chapter 14 tried to show, the policies of government will reflect the interests of those people who are in a position to extract benefits for themselves from the political process at low cost. Government may be unable to prevent inflation or moderate recessions because the people in control of government policies don't actually want to. This is not to suggest that any policymaker prefers inflation to price stability, or frequent and deep recessions to steady levels

Government officials have short time horizons.

Government officials pay attention to those who are paying attention to them.

of production and employment. It suggests only that policy-makers may not find it in their interest to do what must be done if periods of recession and inflation are to be avoided.

The economic theory of government predicts that elected and appointed officials will pay attention to their own interests in choosing policies and carrying them out. Elected officials, with their gaze fixed on the next election, will prefer policies that pay benefits before election day and don't present their costs until after the voters have made their choice. Policies with short-term benefits and long-term costs thus have a strong advantage under the democratic political process. That fact has serious implications for the conduct of stabilization policies.

Moreover, appointed as well as elected officials won't weigh each citizen's interests equally in making their decisions. They'll be partial to the pressures and pleadings of those who make their preferences known precisely, and who care enough to monitor the decisions that government officials finally make. The squeaking wheel gets the grease. Few sugar consumers know or care very strongly how their legislative representative votes on a bill to raise sugar support prices or exclude sugar imports; but you can be certain that U.S. sugar producers know and care, and that your legislator in turn knows and cares who knows and cares—and who doesn't and isn't paying attention. That is also going to make it more difficult for government to stabilize the economy, for reasons we shall explore.

Time Horizons and the Sequence of Effects

When we look carefully at the way in which changes in fiscal and monetary policy are likely to affect economic activity, we discover how important are the time horizons of those who construct such policy.

Suppose that the government finances an increase in its expenditures by borrowing from commercial banks, thereby increasing the money supply. This will increase the aggregate demand for newly produced goods. We cannot be sure how the resulting effect on GNP will be distributed between larger output and higher prices; but we do have good grounds for believing that any effect on output and employment will appear *before* the effect on prices. The reason is that sellers interpret increased sales as an increased *relative* demand for what they are selling, and consequently try to expand output. It takes more time for all these efforts to manifest themselves as an increased demand for resources generally, and to produce an increase in costs and prices. So the "good stuff" arrives first: a rise in real GNP and a fall in the unemployment rate.

The "bad stuff," a higher rate of inflation, is delayed. If politicians are contemplating an imminent election—and in the United States every member of the House of Representatives is on average only one year from the next election—the temptation will be strong to pursue short-run "good stuff" and let someone else worry later about the "bad stuff."

Contractionary policies will also produce their effects on output and employment more quickly than they affect the rate of change in the price level. In this case, however, the "bad stuff" arrives before the "good stuff." Any attempt to lower the rate of inflation by narrowing the government deficit and reducing the growth rate of the money supply will threaten to produce increased inventories and hence reduced output and employment. The disinflationary impact will be delayed until the reduced demand for resources has had a chance to exert downward pressure on costs and prices. In short, an attempt to slow down the inflation rate by initiating less-expansionary fiscal and monetary policies is very likely to produce a recession before it succeeds in its aim of reducing inflation.

Destabilization through Stabilization Policies

What predictions follow? Elected officials will be quick to approve expansionary fiscal and monetary policies, opting for expansion whenever they are in doubt. This course will further commend itself to them because expansionary fiscal and monetary policies would generally be attractive to voters even if they had no effect at all on aggregate demand. Lower taxes and increased expenditures on behalf of interested parties make good campaign material for incumbents. Increased monetary ease tends to lower interest rates, at least momentarily; and that is also looked upon approvingly by voters.

Contractionary policies by contrast inflict pain. Higher taxes and reduced expenditures will antagonize voters, as will any higher interest rates that result from tightening the supply of credit. Unless economic decision makers understand exactly what is going on and immediately lower their prices when aggregate demand falls, contractionary policies will produce a business slump and a rise in unemployment. The ensuing complaints will be listened to attentively by those who are contemplating an imminent election. They will be sorely tempted to withdraw the painful medicine and substitute the soothing tonic of expansionary policies.

All of this suggests that democratic political processes will tend to produce jerky aggregate-demand policies with a bias toward expansion. When expansionary policies produce

Changes in aggregate demand affect output and employment before they affect prices.

(eventually) an intolerable rate of inflation, the contractionary brakes will be applied. Unless disinflation comes quickly, however, the resulting recession and unemployment will create pressure to let up on the brakes and step once more on the accelerator. Such "go-stop-go" policies make the future more uncertain and result in more mistakes, which are the basic underlying cause of recessions. More frequent and severe recessions along with a rising rate of inflation could easily become the standard pattern in democratically governed societies.

Deficits Unlimited

Governments that must pay attention to popular opinion have long been tempted to spend more than they collect in taxes. You don't have to study economics to learn that it's easier for a legislator to support tax reductions than tax increases, and to support enlarged expenditures rather than reduced expenditures. As a result, even if every member of the legislature wanted a budget surplus, a surplus wouldn't necessarily emerge. While a large majority of voters may want a decrease in government expenditures, they will also want increased expenditures, or at least no reductions, for the tiny part of the total budget that constitutes their own sliver of the pie. And when that particular sliver is being sliced, each little special-interest group lets the legislators know that a cut at this point will have repercussions on campaign contributions and votes. There's no way to reduce the total budget while expanding each individual item in it. That's why government expenditures rise even though each and every legislator wants them to decline.

Reducing expenditures means reducing some people's benefits

If this analysis is to account for chronic government budget deficits, however, it has to explain why state and local governments don't produce such deficits, and why the federal government didn't regularly do so before 1970.

First of all, state and local governments differ from the federal government in one crucial respect. Only the federal government has control over the ultimate means for the payment of debts. State and local governments are like you: they can't borrow, and so can't run deficits, unless they can convince potential lenders that today's deficit is a temporary shortfall that will be compensated for by a surplus tomorrow. Chronic, persistent deficits are ruled out by the fact that lenders won't extend credit to a government unless they believe that government will be able to repay its debts in full and on time. This fact imposes no constraint on the federal government, however, because lenders know that the federal government can always *create* the money it needs to meet

Creditors love to lend to anyone who can create the means of repayment.

its obligations. Although money creation of this sort means that lenders will be repaid in dollars of decreased value, it also means that all creditors, not just creditors of the federal government, will be repaid in depreciated currency. Consequently no one worries about lending to the federal government.

That might explain why the federal government runs continuous and growing budget deficits if we could also explain why the federal government did *not* run chronic deficits before 1970. The answer may be the strong public prejudice against government deficits, a prejudice that used to view such deficits as immoral, evidence of an irresponsible failure on the part of government to live within its means. Moral convictions that are strongly and widely held do operate as an effective check on legislators, especially when a majority of the legislators themselves adhere to that moral conviction.

That brings us to the last link in the chain of explanation. Americans are no longer as firmly persuaded as they once were that deficits are immoral. The public today vaguely "knows" that a budget deficit can be a means for promoting prosperity. The lesson supposedly taught by Keynesian analysis was that budgets don't have to be balanced from year to year; they need only to be balanced over the course of the business cycle, with surpluses in periods of prosperity making up for deficits in periods of slump. This new doctrine was widely used to argue that deficits in the 1960s and 1970s were good for the economy, and that anyone insisting on a balanced federal budget just did not understand "modern economics." Most people are willing to be convinced of something they would like to be true.

Deficits aren't "immoral" if they are policy tools.

The trouble with this new doctrine is that its effect is to permit perennial deficits. There is no fiscal period that can be identified with "the course of the business cycle." As a result, the surplus that is supposed to balance the deficit never has to be budgeted; it can always be promised for next year or the year after. With the last effective pressure toward a balanced budget thereby eliminated, the bias of the democratic political process takes over and produces a long and perhaps endless succession of deficits. As the deficit years continue and the national debt increases but the sky does not fall, the conviction that the government's budget really ought to be balanced is bound to lose its hold.

The Political Economy of Monetary Policy

We've been paying attention primarily to fiscal policy in the course of arguing that government demand-management policies are likely to be go-stop-go with an expansionary bias.

What about monetary policy? Couldn't the monetary authorities refuse to finance government deficits? Suppose that the Fed allowed the money stock to grow by only 4 percent per year. What would happen? Could large and continuing government budget deficits lead to inflation if the monetary authorities withheld their cooperation? And in the absence of accelerating inflation, disruptive changes in policy direction could be less frequent.

These are particularly important questions because the monetary managers are not subject to the political pressures that constrain elected officials. The people who created the Federal Reserve System in 1913 were aware that popular politics exerts pressure on governments to pursue inflationary policies, and so they put control of the monetary system in the hands of an independent agency of the federal government. Members of the Board of Governors are appointed by law for fourteen-year terms, so that they can act independently of Congress and the administration. What would happen if the Fed exercised its statutory independence to the extent of directly opposing the government's fiscal policies?

The Fed would lose in an all-out confrontation, because Congress can, finally, take away the independence that it has granted. On the other hand, Congress would be reluctant to take such dramatic steps or to precipitate a public debate in which members of Congress might be seen as advocates of inflation. So the Fed probably could, up to a point, pursue monetary policies designed to neutralize the impact of federal deficits. Nonetheless, it is doubtful that the Fed would persist for very long in any such policy. The reasons are rooted in uncertainties about the way in which monetary policy works, in the mounting public hostility toward the Fed that such a course would almost surely nurture, and perhaps also in the bureaucratic conservatism that almost inevitably dominates a central bank.

We can at least be sure of this: it will be politically difficult for the Fed to counter inflationary fiscal policies until the public acquires a better understanding of interest rates—how they function to allocate scarce resources among competing claimants and between present and future; how inflationary expectations raise nominal but not real interest rates; how monetary policy actually influences interest rates; and how limited is the ability of the monetary authorities to control interest rates. We can also be sure that no effective campaign to educate the public on the significance of interest rates will be possible as long as disagreement on the subject exists even among high-ranking officials in the Federal Reserve System.

Why is it, someone might be wondering at this point, that Fed officials have so much trouble deciding at what targets

they ought to aim and how best to hit them? Can't they learn from experience? The Federal Reserve has extensive freedom to experiment and enormous resources in people, money, and data with which to carry out experiments on the effectiveness of monetary policy procedures. Moreover, the system's managers have possessed roughly their present powers for more than thirty-five years now. Why haven't they learned more than they claim to know about the conduct of monetary policy? Is it possible that the Fed suffers from a severe case of bureaucratic inertia?

A vast and powerful organization, insulated from competitive pressures and from effective political control, could easily develop a strong interest in maintaining the status quo. Monetary policy in this country might be a bit of a muddle because the nation's monetary authorities like it that way. It makes them the managers and guardians of important and mysterious processes that no one fully understands.

Discretion and Rules

There is considerable evidence that the use of discretionary fiscal and monetary policy to stabilize the economy has actually increased its instability, at least since the late 1960s. This judgment, which cannot be conclusively demonstrated, will be strenuously resisted by those who want to believe that we do possess the knowledge and skills required to achieve milder recessions and greater price stability through aggregate-demand management. The fact that stabilization policy obviously failed in the 1970s won't discourage anyone who thinks it failed only because the right people weren't in charge. But institutions should not be evaluated on the assumption that angels will run them. It is far more likely that government policies will be controlled by politicians than by angels, and that monetary and especially fiscal policies will be formulated in the same political context that produces decisions on import tariffs, flood-control projects, and the location of military bases.

The alternative to discretionary fiscal and monetary policies is not *no* policy but policy based on firm commitments to known rules. Sometimes this is called *automatic* or *nondiscretionary* fiscal and monetary policy. But there is actually nothing automatic about adhering to clearly enunciated rules, and continuing to do so in the face of strong temptations to relax the rules is certainly a discretionary act. The issue is not whether discretion is better than the absence of discretion. The question, rather, is whether anyone can in fact increase the stability of the economy by deliberately moving the government budget between surplus and deficit and deliberately changing bank reserves or reserve requirements. The

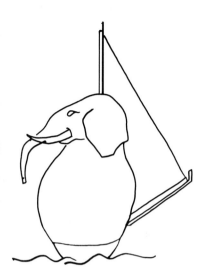

alternative view is that efforts to stabilize in these ways will actually be destabilizing, because no one has the knowledge and other capabilities, technical and political, to manipulate aggregate demand with the necesssary precision. A sufficiently graceful elephant could stabilize a sailboat in rough weather by shifting its weight with delicacy and perfect timing. But the sailing companions of an elephant without these gifts would probably prefer that it remain quietly in the center of the boat.

Those economists who believe that fiscal and monetary policies have aggravated recession and fostered inflation over the last two decades offer two recommendations. With respect to fiscal policy, they want the level of expenditures determined without reference to stabilization imperatives, and tax rates set so as to balance the budget over a normal period. In recessions tax receipts will fall and the budget will be in deficit. In a period of boom or when a recovery is well along, tax receipts will be high and will generate a surplus. These recurring deficits and surpluses will function as self-regulating governors, dampening oscillations in the economy. Any additional discretionary-policy actions are more likely to aggravate than to reduce instability, because discretionary actions are hard to time appropriately and because anticipation of them creates additional uncertainty for private decision makers.

The critics of discretionary demand management also want monetary policy to enunciate a course and stick to it. They want the Fed to maintain a steady hand on the stock of money, either holding it constant or allowing it to increase by some definite, known, uniform, and moderate rate, perhaps one equal to the long-term average growth rate of real output. There are automatic monetary stabilizers as well as automatic fiscal stabilizers in the economic system. A boom will eventually run against rising interest rates and credit rationing if the monetary managers don't feed the boom by pumping new reserves into the banking system. And during a period of economic decline, lending terms will tend to improve as the demand for credit slackens, thus encouraging some potential investors. More management than this, as in the case of fiscal policy, is much more likely to increase than to diminish instability.

Who Is at the Controls?

The drive for a constitutional amendment to require a balanced federal budget rests basically on the belief that political control of the economy must itself be subject to control. That's an important insight. But if such an amendment were to be enacted and ratified, balancing the budget would still be

a difficult task. Achieving an annual balance between expenditures and receipts might well produce some highly destabilizing actions on the part of the federal government. And in the last analysis, it wouldn't prevent the timing and allocation of transfer payments, government purchases, or tax-law changes in ways that destabilize the economy but improve the reelection prospects of incumbents.

Although we mustn't expect mortals to be angels, we also mustn't expect miracles from formulas. The Greek physicist Archimedes supposedly said that he could move the earth itself if given one firm spot on which to stand. The thought of such an Archimedean vantage point is alluring to those who worry about economic problems. "There *has* to be a solution. If the economy doesn't work properly, we'll have the government fix it. If the government doesn't work properly, we'll amend the Constitution. If we can't get the Constitution amended, we'll launch a vast educational campaign. If education doesn't work, we'll transform the whole school system. . . ." There just isn't any firm spot on which an Archimedes can set his fulcrum and lever society into the proper position.

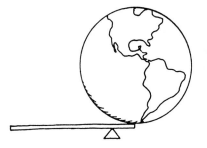

The functioning of the economy, along with the functioning of government and every other social institution, depends finally on our mutual ability to secure cooperation. We noted on the first page of Chapter 1 how difficult it is for most of us even to recognize the many extraordinary ways in which we successfully cooperate every day. As with an automobile engine, it is only failure that attracts our attention. When the engine is performing well, we don't think about it; we give our attention to the scenery or the road ahead. But because we don't look at our mechanisms of social coordination when they're functioning well, we often fail to discover either how they work or how dependent we are on their continued smooth performance. And we often conclude erroneously that some simple bit of tinkering will make them function even better.

Wealthy, industrialized economic systems have always experienced periodic fluctuations in production and employment. Is instability an inherent characteristic of an economic system operating without government intervention? That's very probably the case. But how much instability will exist in the absence of government intervention to stabilize aggregate demand? How deep will recessions be? How much time will ordinarily elapse before recovery begins? What will be the costs of recessions? On whom will they fall? Those are important questions.

But so are these. How much instability will exist in the *presence* of government intervention to stabilize aggregate

demand? Does anyone really know enough to compensate for fluctuations in private spending? Who will actually be in charge? What interests will guide their decisions? How often will long-term stability be sacrificed for the sake of a short-term performance that improves reelection prospects?

All of these are in large part questions about how well market systems work. How smoothly and quickly do prices adjust to changing conditions of demand or supply? How smoothly and quickly do resources move about in response to the new information that changing prices present? While we can hope that continuing empirical and theoretical inquiry will improve our understanding of these matters, big-picture questions of this sort are notoriously hard to answer to everyone's satisfaction. Fact and fancy, logic and longing get mixed up with each other in the course of such inquiries. Our judgments about what is possible are subtly colored by our visions of what is desirable.

We would probably find it easier to agree on how the economy works if we were all agreed on how we *want* the economy to work. In the absence of such a consensus, however, we might just have to go on discussing the issues without ever being certain that we have found the best solutions.

Once Over Lightly

Government stabilization policies are controlled not by impartial—much less omniscient—experts, but by political processes. Those who make policy do so in the light of their own interests and in response to the incentives they perceive.

Stabilization policies in a democratic society are significantly affected by the relatively short time horizons of government officials, who will be under pressure to ignore the long-run costs of programs that produce short-run benefits.

An unanticipated change in the rate of growth of aggregate demand will affect output and employment before it affects costs and prices. The benefits therefore precede the costs when policy takes an expansionary turn, but the costs precede the benefits when policy turns contractionary. Political officials looking toward imminent elections will consequently find expansionary policies in their interest and contractionary policies contrary to their interest. This will tend to produce go-stop-go policies with an inflationary bias.

The democratic political process also tends to produce chronic federal-government budget deficits which in turn put pressure on the monetary authorities to expand the money supply.

Because the federal government ultimately controls the means of payment, it can always borrow successfully. In the

absence of any overriding imperative to achieve a long-run budget balance, democratic political processes may produce an indefinite sequence of budget deficits.

Political pressures on the Fed make the control of inflation through monetary policy a difficult task. Effective monetary policy has also been made more difficult by the inability or unwillingness of the monetary managers to improve the techniques of monetary control.

Government might make its greatest contribution to economic stability by trying to do less. Government policies that were more stable and predictable would introduce less uncertainty into the economic system.

The argument between advocates of discretionary stabilization policy and those who want policy to be governed by fixed rules known in advance turns largely on the issue of how equitably and efficiently markets work.

QUESTIONS FOR DISCUSSION

1. Unanticipated changes in the growth rate of aggregate demand tend to affect production and employment *before* they affect prices.
   (a) Why do the output and employment effects tend to precede the price effects?
   (b) Why does this give elected officials an incentive both to approve expansionary policies and not to persist in contractionary policies?
   (c) Why would a president serving a second term and hence ineligible for reelection still be under pressure to pursue policies with quick benefits and deferred costs? Who would apply the pressure?
2. If the members of Congress genuinely believe that large government budget deficits are a threat to prosperity, why don't they reduce the deficits?
3. Suppose a member of Congress votes against a bill to allocate $100 million in taxpayers' money to an irrigation canal that will provide about $10 million in benefits to a few hundred ranchers. Why might this action cause the legislator a net loss in both votes and campaign contributions?
4. Why do so many members of Congress believe that the federal government should subsidize local projects, such as improvements in bus or subway systems in major cities?
   (a) Who would benefit from construction of a subway system in a large city?
   (b) Can you think of a *public interest* argument for having taxpayers across the country pay for a local subway system?
   (c) If you knew that your taxes were going to go up $10 a year in order to finance a subway in some distant city, would you write a letter of protest to your legislator?
   (d) If your city was being considered for a large federal grant to subsidize an improvement in the local public transportation system, would you expect your local government officials to go to Washington and lobby

actively for it? Would you expect your congressional representatives to support it? Would you form a more favorable opinion of local officials and congressional representatives if your city proved successful in its grant application?

5. If you favor reduced government expenditures, do you also favor reducing government financial assistance to programs that benefit you?

6. New York City teetered on the edge of bankruptcy some years ago because it had accumulated large debts through deficit spending and seemed unable either to raise taxes or to cut expenditures sufficiently to balance its budget. Lenders refused to extend additional credit unless the federal government guaranteed that it would pay New York City's debts in the event of a default.

   (a) How did New York City get into such a situation?

   (b) Of what use to lenders was a federal-government guarantee when the federal government was in fact running much larger deficits than New York City and had even poorer prospects for balancing its budget?

   (c) What consequences would you predict if the federal government committed itself to paying off all creditors who might otherwise be hurt through the financial default of municipal or state governments?

7. In every year throughout the 1970s and the first half of the 1980s, the combined budgets of state and local governments showed a surplus, whereas the federal-government budget was in deficit. How would you account for this dramatic difference?

8. Voters who don't want their taxes increased impose obvious constraints on any democratic government's ability to raise additional revenue. But there are other constraints as well.

   (a) How can people legally avoid a state income or sales tax?

   (b) Voters don't seem to be terribly hostile toward increased taxes on business. Why can't state and local governments collect all the revenue they want simply by raising taxes on businesses?

   (c) Why don't these constraints bind the federal government as effectively as they bind state and local governments?

9. When a state or city government starts borrowing to finance current expenditures (as distinct from capital expenditures for highways, schools, public buildings, and the like), its bond rating usually falls. A lower bond rating indicates a riskier investment.

   (a) Why does the bond rating fall?

   (b) What will happen to the price of bonds whose rating is lowered?

   (c) What does this do to the cost of borrowing?

   (d) How does this constrain state and local governments from borrowing to finance current expenditures?

   (e) What must a state or local government do if it is determined not to borrow to finance current expenditures?

   (f) Why doesn't any of this happen to the federal government when it finances current expenditures through borrowing rather than taxation?

10. When a corporation successfully sells additional bonds or a new issue of common stock, it goes deeply into debt.

    (a) Is this evidence that the corporation is failing or that it's succeeding?

    (b) How well or poorly does an analogy from the area of business indebtedness apply to questions of government indebtedness?

(c) Suppose the government borrows to construct a dam. How is such borrowing similar to or different from business borrowing for investment?

11. Do you think that people who "live beyond their means" display a character flaw? What about a government that fails to confine its expenditures to the amount of its tax receipts?

12. Suppose the Treasury borrowed $20 billion in September of the presidential election year in order to increase the benefits to be paid on October 1 to recipients of social-security benefits, welfare grants, and unemployment-compensation. What would be the effects on the money supply? On consumer spending in October? On the unemployment rate? On the price level? On the election? When would you expect these various effects?

13. The Federal Reserve was created to be an independent agency of the federal government—independent, that is, of the immediate political pressures that are felt by elected officials and appointed officials whom the elected officials can demote or discharge.
    (a) Is it "undemocratic" to have an organization as powerful as the Fed that isn't answerable to the voters?
    (b) If Fed officials had to answer to elected officials, would that make them answerable to the voters?
    (c) Under which of these three circumstances do you think it is most likely and under which do you think it is least likely that monetary policy would promote the public interest: the present system; a system under which presidents could dismiss Fed officials the way they can now dismiss cabinet members; a referendum system under which the Fed's policies would have to be periodically approved by a majority vote of the electorate?

14. How independent is the independent Fed? Fed officials and Treasury officials regularly cooperate to smooth the financing and refinancing activities of the federal government as it borrows the vast sums required to cover current deficits and refund the huge national debt.
    (a) Don't people who work cooperatively usually come to see their problems in similar or at least compatible ways? Isn't the Fed more likely to conclude that a particular monetary policy is the best policy if it also happens to ease the financing problems of the Treasury?
    (b) The Treasury would like to keep down the costs of its borrowing and refunding. How could the Fed help achieve this laudable objective?
    (c) If the Fed tries to provide enough reserves to the banking system to make sure that borrowing costs don't rise during large Treasury borrowing operations, what must it do? Why might a succession of such cooperative moves by the Fed eventually cause interest rates and Treasury borrowing costs to rise steeply?

15. Would you expect to find a relationship between an informed person's attitude toward attempts at fine-tuning and his or her reactions to the following judgments? Explain why.
    (a) "Fiscal and monetary managers have better information than business decision makers because they have access to statistical data on the overall performance of the economy and don't have to concern themselves with details."

(b) "The government must establish procedures for national economic planning if we are to avoid the kinds of economic crises experienced in the 1970s."

(c) "The market does not work as it used to. Competition no longer sets prices or allocates resources in the U.S. economy. Most of that is done by organized interest groups with substantial market power."

(d) "The U.S. economy displays an absurd social imbalance. Privately purchased goods are produced in abundance while public-sector goods such as education must be content with the leavings."

(e) "Power tends to corrupt, and absolute power corrupts absolutely."

The Limitations of Economics

The possibility of civilization depends largely on how well societies work. What does the economic way of thinking reveal about the working of society? Is there anything of importance that it conceals?

If you can bring yourself to return to the first chapter of this book, you will find a brief discussion of the biases of economic theory. You might want to read that section again, now that you've completed the book. Are those really biases? Or are they something more like useful working hypotheses?

What Economists Know

The economic way of thinking employs such concepts as demand, opportunity cost, marginal effects, and comparative advantage to order familiar phenomena. The economist knows very little about the real world that is not better known by business executives, artisans, engineers, and others who make things happen. What economists do know is *how things fit together*. The concepts of economics enable us to make better sense out of what we observe, to think more consistently and coherently about a wide range of complex social interactions.

This turns out in practice to be a largely negative kind of knowledge about mostly impersonal transactions. The economic way of thinking, as you may have noticed, contributes relatively little to our understanding of relationships within the family or other small groups where people can know one another well enough to cooperate on a personal basis. Economics mostly explains how cooperation occurs among people who don't know one another at all, but who nonetheless manage to work together with extraordinary effectiveness. Perhaps you also detected, as you read through the chapters

of this book, a greater emphasis on what *should not* be done than on what *should* be done. But negative conclusions are important. The economist Frank Knight used to defend the heavily negative character of economic reasoning with a quotation: "It ain't ignorance that does the most damage; it's knowin' so derned much that ain't so."

Too many people "know" how to solve pressing social problems. Their mental picture of the economic universe is a simple one, in which intentions can easily be realized and the only obstacle to a better society is therefore a lack of good intentions. But social actions have consequences that run far beyond those that can be easily predicted or foreseen. Restricting textile imports into the United States, for example, does, for the present at least, protect the jobs and income of textile producers; that's clear enough. But it takes a tutored eye to notice that this will shift even more income away from other Americans, by raising textile prices, reducing American export opportunities, and in general inhibiting the exploitation of comparative advantage. Again, it is easy to see that rent controls hold down the money payments that tenants must make to landlords. But how many advocates of such controls are aware of the alternative payments that tenants will have to make, of the new forms of discrimination that will replace discrimination on the basis of money price, and of the short- and long-run effects on the supply of rental housing?

Nonetheless, people easily become impatient with those who warn against the inadvisability of actions that will make matters worse without proposing solutions of their own. And in a society such as ours, accustomed to the almost miraculous accomplishments of science and technology, the demand for "doing something" tends to exceed by a wide margin the supply of genuine solutions to social problems. We have probably erred in assuming that social problems can be handled in the same way that we manage technological problems. We admit that conflicting interests create hard problems for social policymakers. But we still underestimate the difficulties in the way of bringing about planned social change, largely because we underestimate the complexity of social systems, of the networks of interaction through which behavior is coordinated in a society and people are induced to cooperate in the achievement of their goals.

Perhaps that's why economic theory often treats proposals for reform of the economic system so unkindly. It's not that economists are themselves uninterested in reform, much less that they're the paid lackeys of the privileged classes. But economic theory, by revealing the interdependence of decisions, calls attention to the unexamined consequences of

proposals for change. "It won't work out that way" is the economist's standard response to many well-intentioned policy proposals. Realism is not necessarily conservatism, but it often looks quite similar. And there is a sense in which knowledge does promote conservatism. Even physicists have been accused of hopeless conservatism by would-be inventors of perpetual-motion machines.

Beyond Mere Economics

John Maynard Keynes once proposed a toast to economists, "the keepers of the possibility of civilization." The *possibility* of civilization—that is all. The efficient allocation of resources enlarges the realm of possibility, but it does not by itself guarantee the progress of civilization. A well-coordinated and smoothly functioning society gives individuals more opportunity to choose; it does not guarantee that they will choose well. The economic way of thinking, especially in a democracy, is an important preliminary. But it is no more than that.

Economists are for the most part prepared to admit that the concepts they employ sometimes distort the reality they study. And they are willing to submit their analysis and conclusions to the test of rational criticism. But some point of view is indispensable to any inquiry, in the physical sciences as well as the social sciences. If the economic way of thinking sometimes leads to distortions, to misplaced emphasis, or even to outright error, the appropriate corrective is rational criticism. The application of that corrective has frequently altered the conclusions of economics in the past. It will probably continue to do so in the future.

Index

Acton, Lord, 446–47, 524 (question 15)
Adelman, M.A., 221 (question 28)
adjudication and pollution reduction, 294–97
administered prices, 161, 169
advertising, 152–53, 211–12
aggregate-demand management, 439 ff., 512–18
aggregate supply and aggregate demand, 379–87
aggregative theories, benefits and costs of, 363, 384–85, 455–57
alternative economic systems, 54–55, 108–09
Anderson, Terry, 88 (question 34)
annuities, 242–46
"antitrust" policy, 210–13
Archimedes, 519
automatic versus discretionary policy, 448–49, 517–18
automation, fear of, 265–66

Baden, John, 310 (question 19)
balanced-budget constitutional amendment, 518–19
balance of international payments, 489–95
Bastiat, Frederic, 503
bias in economic theory, 7–11, 527–29
bond prices and interest rates, 228, 478
Bretton Woods System, 498–50
Browning, Edgar K., 270

capital, 226–259
cartels, 203–04
caveat emptor, 150
caveat venditor, 150
Clayton Act, 211–12
closed shop and union shop, 279 (question 18)
coercion, 256 (question 37), 322 ff.
"command and control" approach to pollution reduction, 298–300
Commodity Credit Corporation, 79
comparable worth, 280–83 (questions 29–34)
comparative advantage, 126–29, 131–32, 303, 502–05
competiton and government policies, 201 ff.
competition and scarcity, 71–79
competition as a process, 213, 320
competition between sellers and between buyers, 267–68

concentration ratios, 173–74 (question 10)
conglomerate mergers, 211
consumer price index, 377
cooperation and coordination, 1–3, 5–6, 67 ff., 82–83, 423–24, 431, 519–20, 528
cost-push inflation, 467–72
"crowding-out" effect, 442–43, 478–79
currency component of the money supply, 394

David, Paul, 88 (question 30)
deadweight costs, 74
deficits, government budget, 441–43, 477–79, 514–15, 518–19
deflation, 350
demand, concept of, 18, 21 (note)
    law of, 19, 263
        price elasticity of, 29–34, 163, 165–66, 191–92
        quantity demanded versus, 21–24
demand deposits, 394–95, 397 ff.
demand-side economics, 382–84, 386–87, 415 ff.
democracy, economics of, 330–36, 511–20
Devons, Ely, ix–x
discounting future amounts, 240–47
discount rate, 405
discretionary versus automatic policy, 448–49, 517–18
discrimination and scarcity, 72–73
disinflation, 350–51
draft, military, 51–53, 328, 334–35
Dutch auction, 199 (question 18)

ecology and economics, 287
economic way of thinking, 4–13, 527–29
efficiency, 119–21, 129–31
employment and unemployment, 356–66
employment rate, 360–62
Environmental Protection Agency, 139 (question 30), 303–04
equilibrium concept, 424, 426–28, 492–93
Erving, Julius, 126
ethics and economics, 232–33, 235–36, 292–93, 301–02, 326, 336, 354
European Monetary System, 500

exchange, 122–23, 125–29
excluding nonpayers, 324–25
externalities, 288, 326

family incomes in the United States, 269–71
Federal Aviation Administration, 80
Federal Communications Commission, 86 (question 21), 239–40, 346 (question 40)
Federal Deposit Insurance Corporation, 407, 453
federal funds rate, 450–452
Federal Reserve System, 401 *ff.*, 516–17
Federal Trade Commission, 211–12, 221 (question 27)
Federal Trade Commission Act, 211
"fine-tuning," 453
fiscal policy, 439 *ff.*, 512–18
fixed versus floating exchange rates, 500–01
flow versus stock concepts, 416–17
Food and Drug Administration, 158 (questions 21–23), 335–36
foreign exchange rates, 495–501
free riders, 325 *ff.*, 503–04
"frictional" unemployment, 357
futures (contracts), 148, 156–57 (questions 14, 16)

General Theory of Employment, Interest and Money, The, 423, 427
gold, 407–08, 498–500
government, economic analysis of, 319 *ff.*, 445–47, 511–20
Great Depression, 386, 421–22, 426, 456–57
gross national product, 373–76

hedgers, 148
Hobbes, Thomas, 3
Hopper, Edward, 478
horizontal mergers, 211
human capital, 259–60, 262–63
Hume, David, 312 (question 29)

impersonal transactions, 316 (question 40), 527
implicit GNP deflator, 376
income and wealth, 274–75 (question 1)
income distribution, 257 *ff.*, 329
incomes policy, 471–72
inflation, 20–21, 349–55, 378–79, 467–71, 473–77, 498–99
information, scarcity of, 141 *ff.*
interest rates, 225–28, 240–47, 450–53, 516
International Monetary Fund, 498–99
international trade and exchange, 489 *ff.*
Interstate Commerce Commission, 206, 251 (question 18), 333
investment, 100–01, 262–63, 424–25, 429–30

Johnson, Samuel, 492
joint costs, 207–08
just price, 64 (question 24)
justice, systems of, 327

Kennedy, John, 446
Keynes, John Maynard, 4, 415, 423–31, 529
Keynesian perspective, 421–31, 439–40, 443–44, 515
Knight, Frank, 223, 528
Kuhn, Thomas S., 9

labor force, 358–59
labor unions, 268
Lave, Charles, 87–88 (question 30), 138 (question 29)
Leacock, Stephen, 287
legal reserve requirements, 400–01, 404, 406–07
legislation and pollution reduction, 297–98
"licenses to pollute," 301–02
lifetime income profiles, 262–63
Lincoln, Abraham, 511
liquidity, 395–96, 417–18
Little, I.M.D., 10–11

McInnis, Noel, x
malpractice suits, 151–52
marginal adjustments, 5–6
marginal analysis, 93–94
marginal cost, 96–98
marginal revenue, 182–85, 187
marginal tax rate, 272
market power, 163, 176 (question 18)
market processes, social interaction interpreted as, 8, 144–45, 319–22
markup theory of pricing, 179–80, 192–93
"material" wealth, 121–22
medium of exchange, 394
mergers, 211
methodological individualism, 7–8, 17
middlemen, 142–44
minimum-wage legislation, 263–65
Molière, 33
monetarism and monetarist perspective, 415–21, 440–41, 517–18
monetary policy, 400–06, 428, 439 *ff.*, 469–71, 473, 480, 512–18
money, 350, 393 *ff.*
    central bank control of, 400–09. *See also* monetary policy
    creation of, 398–404
    demand for, 416–21, 426–27
    functions of, 393–95
    measures of, 397–98
    value of, 20–21, 349–55, 378–79
monopoly, 161–65
Mother Teresa, 12 (question 2)

National Bureau of Economic Research, 355
National Collegiate Athletic Association (NCAA), 86 (question 23)
national debt, 477–79
national defense, 327–28
national income and product accounts, 373–79
negotiation and pollution reduction, 293–94, 302–03
nominal versus real gross national product, 375–76
nominal versus real interest rates, 351, 451
nominal versus real wage rates, 475–76
nondiscretionary fiscal and monetary policy, 448–49, 517–18
noninstitutional population, 358

objective ("real") costs, 50–51
oligopoly, 169–70, 203
Open Market Committee, 405–06, 449–53
open market operations, 405

opportunity cost, 45 *ff.*, 123–28, 224–25
"optimal" resource allocation, 166–69

"paradox of thirft," 430
persuasion (versus coercion), 256 (question 37), 322–23, 342 (questions 17–18)
Phillips, A. W., 473
Phillips curve, 473–77
pollution, 287 *ff*
post hoc ergo propter hoc fallacy, 11
predatory pricing, 206–10
present values. *See* discounting future amounts
presuppositions of economic theory, 7–8
prices as coordinating signals, 68–69, 75–77, 82–83, 144–45
price controls, 69–79, 466–67, 471–72. *See also* rent controls
price discrimination, 185–92, 202
price searching, theory of, 179 *ff.*
price takers and price searchers, 165–66
prisoners' dilemma, 340–41 (question 15)
productive services, 258, 263–67
profit, 223 *ff.*
property rights, 53–54, 81–82, 130–31, 233–36, 240, 260–62, 288 *ff.*, 322. *See also* rules of the game
purchasing-power parity of foreign exchange, 495

rational expectations and aggregate supply, 384, 472–73, 476–77
rational ignorance, 331
rationality postulate in economic theory, 8, 321
rationing and scarcity, 72
Reagan administration, 480
real versus nominal gross national product, 375–76
real versus nominal interest rates, 351, 451
real versus nominal wage rates, 475–76
recession, 355–56, 453, 455–56
regulation of voluntary exchange, 329–30
Rembrandt, 129
rent controls, 63–64 (questions 22–23), 77–79, 85–86 (question 19), 105–06, 112 (question 5), 117 (question 28), 175 (question 17), 352–53, 354–55
resale-price-maintenance laws, 206
restrictions on competition, 163–64, 203–06, 237, 239–40
rights and obligations, 36 (questions 5–6), 261–62, 346–47 (question 42)
roads, government provision of, 328
rules of the game, 8–9, 12–13 (questions 3–6), 53–54, 72–73, 76, 82, 131, 181, 233, 240, 260–62, 271–73, 322, 518–19. *See also* property rights.

saving and investment, 385–86, 429–31
scarcity, 71–72
Schofer, Joseph L., 33
schools, government provision of, 328–29
seasonal adjustments, 358
Securities and Exchange Commission, 159 (question 26)
selfish behavior, 4–5, 25
selling short, 147
Sherman Act, 206, 210–13
shortage, 71, 73–74
Smith, Adam, 4, 31, 174 (question 16), 232, 340 (question 12), 354, 386, 409 (question 3), 436 (question 23), 465
speculation, 147–50, 235
spillover costs and benefits, 288, 326
Stigler, George, 213
stock versus flow concepts, 416–17
Stroup, Richard, 310 (question 19)
sunk costs, 94–96, 100–02
supply, 45 *ff.*, 93 *ff.*
  price elasticity of, 70
supply and demand, 67 *ff.*, *passim*
supply and marginal opportunity cost, 46–48, 61 (question 10), 89 (question 36), 96–98, 106–08
supply-side economics, 386–87, 430, 465 *ff.*
surplus, 79–80, 423–24

tax rate reductions and economic growth, 477, 479
taxes and pollution reduction, 300–301
teaching economics, vii–xii
time lags in aggregate-demand management, 444–50
time preference, 227, 332, 512–13
Tocqueville, Alexis de, 336
trade. *See* exchange, international trade and exchange
transaction costs, 326–27, 504
transfer payments, 257, 335, 490

Ubinas, Luis, 254 (question 27)
uncertainty, 18, 141 *ff.*, 229–40
unemployment, 356–66, 377–79, 474–77
unemployment rate, 358, 360–61

valuations and efficiency, 120–21, 129–31, 185, 304
vertical mergers, 211

wage and price controls, 466–67, 471–72
Wayland, Francis, 60 (question 2)
Wenders, Wim, 45
"windfall" profits, 232–36
Wriston, Walter, 159 (question 27)

exchange, 122–23, 125–29
excluding nonpayers, 324–25
externalities, 288, 326

family incomes in the United States, 269–71
Federal Aviation Administration, 80
Federal Communications Commission, 86 (question 21),
    239–40, 346 (question 40)
Federal Deposit Insurance Corporation, 407, 453
federal funds rate, 450–452
Federal Reserve System, 401 *ff.*, 516–17
Federal Trade Commission, 211–12, 221 (question 27)
Federal Trade Commission Act, 211
"fine-tuning," 453
fiscal policy, 439 *ff.*, 512–18
fixed versus floating exchange rates, 500–01
flow versus stock concepts, 416–17
Food and Drug Administration, 158 (questions 21–23), 335–
    36
foreign exchange rates, 495–501
free riders, 325 *ff.*, 503–04
"frictional" unemployment, 357
futures (contracts), 148, 156–57 (questions 14, 16)

General Theory of Employment, Interest and Money, The, 423,
    427
gold, 407–08, 498–500
government, economic analysis of, 319 *ff.*, 445–47, 511–20
Great Depression, 386, 421–22, 426, 456–57
gross national product, 373–76

hedgers, 148
Hobbes, Thomas, 3
Hopper, Edward, 478
horizontal mergers, 211
human capital, 259–60, 262–63
Hume, David, 312 (question 29)

impersonal transactions, 316 (question 40), 527
implicit GNP deflator, 376
income and wealth, 274–75 (question 1)
income distribution, 257 *ff.*, 329
incomes policy, 471–72
inflation, 20–21, 349–55, 378–79, 467–71, 473–77, 498–99
information, scarcity of, 141 *ff.*
interest rates, 225–28, 240–47, 450–53, 516
International Monetary Fund, 498–99
international trade and exchange, 489 *ff.*
Interstate Commerce Commission, 206, 251 (question 18),
    333
investment, 100–01, 262–63, 424–25, 429–30

Johnson, Samuel, 492
joint costs, 207–08
just price, 64 (question 24)
justice, systems of, 327

Kennedy, John, 446
Keynes, John Maynard, 4, 415, 423–31, 529
Keynesian perspective, 421–31, 439–40, 443–44, 515
Knight, Frank, 223, 528
Kuhn, Thomas S., 9

labor force, 358–59
labor unions, 268
Lave, Charles, 87–88 (question 30), 138 (question 29)
Leacock, Stephen, 287
legal reserve requirements, 400–01, 404, 406–07
legislation and pollution reduction, 297–98
"licenses to pollute," 301–02
lifetime income profiles, 262–63
Lincoln, Abraham, 511
liquidity, 395–96, 417–18
Little, I.M.D., 10–11

McInnis, Noel, x
malpractice suits, 151–52
marginal adjustments, 5–6
marginal analysis, 93–94
marginal cost, 96–98
marginal revenue, 182–85, 187
marginal tax rate, 272
market power, 163, 176 (question 18)
market processes, social interaction interpreted as, 8, 144–
    45, 319–22
markup theory of pricing, 179–80, 192–93
"material" wealth, 121–22
medium of exchange, 394
mergers, 211
methodological individualism, 7–8, 17
middlemen, 142–44
minimum-wage legislation, 263–65
Molière, 33
monetarism and monetarist perspective, 415–21, 440–41,
    517–18
monetary policy, 400–06, 428, 439 *ff.*, 469–71, 473, 480, 512–
    18
money, 350, 393 *ff.*
    central bank control of, 400–09. *See also* monetary policy
    creation of, 398–404
    demand for, 416–21, 426–27
    functions of, 393–95
    measures of, 397–98
    value of, 20–21, 349–55, 378–79
monopoly, 161–65
Mother Teresa, 12 (question 2)

National Bureau of Economic Research, 355
National Collegiate Athletic Association (NCAA), 86 (ques-
    tion 23)
national debt, 477–79
national defense, 327–28
national income and product accounts, 373–79
negotiation and pollution reduction, 293–94, 302–03
nominal versus real gross national product, 375–76
nominal versus real interest rates, 351, 451
nominal versus real wage rates, 475–76
nondiscretionary fiscal and monetary policy, 448–49, 517–
    18
noninstitutional population, 358

objective ("real") costs, 50–51
oligopoly, 169–70, 203
Open Market Committee, 405–06, 449–53
open market operations, 405

opportunity cost, 45 *ff.*, 123–28, 224–25
"optimal" resource allocation, 166–69

"paradox of thirft," 430
persuasion (versus coercion), 256 (question 37), 322–23, 342 (questions 17–18)
Phillips, A. W., 473
Phillips curve, 473–77
pollution, 287 *ff*
post hoc ergo propter hoc fallacy, 11
predatory pricing, 206–10
present values. *See* discounting future amounts
presuppositions of economic theory, 7–8
prices as coordinating signals, 68–69, 75–77, 82–83, 144–45
price controls, 69–79, 466–67, 471–72. *See also* rent controls
price discrimination, 185–92, 202
price searching, theory of, 179 *ff.*
price takers and price searchers, 165–66
prisoners' dilemma, 340–41 (question 15)
productive services, 258, 263–67
profit, 223 *ff.*
property rights, 53–54, 81–82, 130–31, 233–36, 240, 260–62, 288 *ff.*, 322. *See also* rules of the game
purchasing-power parity of foreign exchange, 495

rational expectations and aggregate supply, 384, 472–73, 476–77
rational ignorance, 331
rationality postulate in economic theory, 8, 321
rationing and scarcity, 72
Reagan administration, 480
real versus nominal gross national product, 375–76
real versus nominal interest rates, 351, 451
real versus nominal wage rates, 475–76
recession, 355–56, 453, 455–56
regulation of voluntary exchange, 329–30
Rembrandt, 129
rent controls, 63–64 (questions 22–23), 77–79, 85–86 (question 19), 105–06, 112 (question 5), 117 (question 28), 175 (question 17), 352–53, 354–55
resale-price-maintenance laws, 206
restrictions on competition, 163–64, 203–06, 237, 239–40
rights and obligations, 36 (questions 5–6), 261–62, 346–47 (question 42)
roads, government provision of, 328
rules of the game, 8–9, 12–13 (questions 3–6), 53–54, 72–73, 76, 82, 131, 181, 233, 240, 260–62, 271–73, 322, 518–19. *See also* property rights.

saving and investment, 385–86, 429–31
scarcity, 71–72
Schofer, Joseph L., 33
schools, government provision of, 328–29
seasonal adjustments, 358
Securities and Exchange Commission, 159 (question 26)
selfish behavior, 4–5, 25
selling short, 147
Sherman Act, 206, 210–13
shortage, 71, 73–74
Smith, Adam, 4, 31, 174 (question 16), 232, 340 (question 12), 354, 386, 409 (question 3), 436 (question 23), 465
speculation, 147–50, 235
spillover costs and benefits, 288, 326
Stigler, George, 213
stock versus flow concepts, 416–17
Stroup, Richard, 310 (question 19)
sunk costs, 94–96, 100–02
supply, 45 *ff.*, 93 *ff.*
    price elasticity of, 70
supply and demand, 67 *ff.*, *passim*
supply and marginal opportunity cost, 46–48, 61 (question 10), 89 (question 36), 96–98, 106–08
supply-side economics, 386–87, 430, 465 *ff.*
surplus, 79–80, 423–24

tax rate reductions and economic growth, 477, 479
taxes and pollution reduction, 300–301
teaching economics, vii–xii
time lags in aggregate-demand management, 444–50
time preference, 227, 332, 512–13
Tocqueville, Alexis de, 336
trade. *See* exchange, international trade and exchange
transaction costs, 326–27, 504
transfer payments, 257, 335, 490

Ubinas, Luis, 254 (question 27)
uncertainty, 18, 141 *ff.*, 229–40
unemployment, 356–66, 377–79, 474–77
unemployment rate, 358, 360–61

valuations and efficiency, 120–21, 129–31, 185, 304
vertical mergers, 211

wage and price controls, 466–67, 471–72
Wayland, Francis, 60 (question 2)
Wenders, Wim, 45
"windfall" profits, 232–36
Wriston, Walter, 159 (question 27)

CONTENTS

INTRODUCTION
USING THIS STUDY GUIDE EFFECTIVELY   v

CHAPTER 1
TEACHERS, TEACHING, AND EDUCATIONAL PSYCHOLOGY   1

CHAPTER 2
THE MIND AT WORK: COGNITIVE DEVELOPMENT AND LANGUAGE   13

CHAPTER 3
PERSONAL, SOCIAL, AND MORAL DEVELOPMENT   27

CHAPTER 4
INDIVIDUAL VARIATIONS   40

CHAPTER 5
LEARNING: BEHAVIORAL VIEWS   51

CHAPTER 6
APPLICATIONS OF BEHAVIORAL APPROACHES   64

CHAPTER 7
LEARNING: COGNITIVE VIEWS   75

CHAPTER 8
THE COGNITIVE PERSPECTIVE AND TEACHING PRACTICE   84

CHAPTER 9
MOTIVATION IN THE CLASSROOM   95

CHAPTER 10
CLASSROOM MANAGEMENT AND COMMUNICATION   106

CHAPTER 11
SETTING OBJECTIVES AND PLANNING   116

CHAPTER 12
EFFECTIVE TEACHING   128

CHAPTER 13
TEACHING EXCEPTIONAL STUDENTS   137

CHAPTER 14
USING STANDARDIZED TESTS IN TEACHING   148

CHAPTER 15
CLASSROOM EVALUATION AND GRADING   160

EPILOGUE : TEACHING AND
LEARNING IN THE COMPUTER AGE   173

APPENDIX A
UNDERSTANDING THE STANDARD DEVIATION   180

ANSWERS   187

INTRODUCTION

USING THIS STUDY GUIDE EFFECTIVELY

We have designed this *Study Guide* to enhance your understanding and enjoyment of *Educational Psychology* . In addition, we believe that the information presented in the text and reviewed in this *Study Guide* provides a firm foundation for becoming an effective teacher. As you will learn when you read *Educational Psychology* , the creative problem-solving and decision-making skills so necessary for excellent teaching are based upon a thorough knowledge of many basic facts, concepts, and principles. Teaching, like medicine or architecture, is both a science and an art. While you will have to bring your own creativity and judgment to teaching to develop your own artistic style, creative teaching is more likely if you have an understanding of the scientific basis of teaching.

LEARNING FROM A TEXTBOOK

Educational psychologists are interested in how people learn and how to improve the teaching/learning process. Over the years there have been many suggestions about how to understand and remember what you read. One of the most enduring systems is the SQ3R (**survey, question, read, recite, review**) approach developed by F. P. Robinson (1961). This and similar systems have proved effective with many types of students (Sargent, Huus and Andersen, 1970). A more recent variation is called PQ4R (Thomas and Robinson, 1972). In this system the extra **R** is for **reflection**. The phases are preview, question, read, reflect, recite, review. If you were applying the PQ4R method to study this text, you would do the following:

Preview: Begin with a survey of your entire text. Use these questions, adapted from Sargent et al. (1970) to preview *Educational Psychology*, 3rd Edition.

1. What is the title of your book?
2. When was it published?
3. Why should you notice the date of publication?
4. What study guides do you find in your book?
5. Where is the table of contents?
    a. How many main topics are discussed in this book?
    b. Are subtopics listed in this book?
6. Where is the index? Practice using the index to find answers to questions. For example, find the section that compares "expository teaching" with "discovery learning."
7. Where is the glossary?
    a. Why is it a good study habit to use the glossary in a book?
    b. If a book does not have a glossary, what reference do you need to use?
8. Does your book have a preface or introduction?
    a. What does the preface usually tell you?
    b. When do you need the preface?
9. Does your book have a bibliography?
    a. Where is the bibliography located?
    b. How does a bibliography help you?

In addition, each chapter of the text should be previewed before you attempt a detailed reading. In surveying the chapter you should read the chapter title, overview, and objectives, the headings and sub-headings, the summary and perhaps initial sentences of the major sections. The *Study Guide* will be useful to you during this survey stage. The chapter outlines and objectives presented in the Guide provide an excellent preview of the chapters. Previewing each of these parts of the textbook and the *Study Guide* will allow you to set more specific purposes that will guide you in reading the material. Some purposes might be to determine the main idea, identify details, evaluate the material, or determine the authors' prejudices and goals in writing the passage.

Question : Create questions about each major section related to your purposes. One way is to turn the headings and sub-headings into questions. If you are beginning to use this method of reading, it often is helpful to write down brief questions as they come to mind.

Read : At last! The questions you have formulated can be answered through reading. You should pay attention to the main ideas, supporting details, and other data in keeping with your purposes. You may have to adjust your reading speed to suit the difficulty of the material and your purpose for reading.

Reflect : While you are reading, try to think of examples or create images of the material. Make connections between what you are reading and what you already know.

Recite : After reading each section, sit back and think about your initial purposes and questions. Can you answer the questions without looking at the book? In doing this, your mind has a second chance to connect what you have read with what you already know. If your mind is blank after reading the section, it may have been too difficult to read comfortably or you may have been daydreaming. Reciting helps you monitor your understanding and tells you when to reread before moving on to the next section. Reciting should take place after each headed section, but might be required more often in reading difficult material.

Review : Effective review helps limit forgetting and incorporates new material more permanently into your memory. As study progresses, review should be cumulative, including the sections and chapters you read previously. Rereading is one form of review, but trying to answer key questions without referring to the book is the best way to review. Wrong answers can direct you to areas that need more study, particularly before an exam.

USING THE STUDY GUIDE

For each chapter in the textbook you will find six different types of learning aids in this *Study Guide*. These include a chapter outline, chapter objectives, key concepts, applications, discussions situations, and multiple choice questions.

Chapter Overviews . These outlines give reference points for organizing and locating information and for developing your own notes on the chapter contents. In addition, you can see how different ideas and concepts are related when you read through the outlines. This part of the *Study Guide* should be included in your initial **survey** if you use the PQ4R approach.

Chapter Objectives . While the overview at the beginning of each chapter of the text lists five to six main objectives, you will find more detailed objectives in this *Study Guide*. These objectives describe the major information and skills you should gain from the chapter. They serve to focus your attention for studying and should also be **surveyed** before you begin reading the textbook chapter.

Key Concepts . In order to review what you have read and test your understanding, you should complete the key concepts section without looking back at the textbook. The questions are in the form of a matching exercise. You will be given the major concepts from the chapter and asked to complete sentences with these concepts.

Multiple - Choice Questions. In order to review the material in the text and test your knowledge under conditions similar to those you might experience during an exam, you can complete the multiple choice questions. These questions call for factual information, comprehension of key concepts and principles, application of principles, and analysis of problem situations. Use the mistakes you make in answering these questions to guide your study. The page number containing the information in the text is given for each multiple choice question. This will help you locate the information rapidly.

Application and *Discussion Questions*. An intellectual understanding of the key concepts, while basic to learning educational psychology, is only the beginning. You must be able to apply these concepts to solve problems that teachers face. The application and discussion section provides a bridge from an intellectual understanding of the text to a recognition of the principles in action. In completing these exercises you will be translating theory into practice in common situations. These activities can be completed by individuals or discussed in groups. The situations present real-life classroom problems that can be solved using ideas and information from the text. In considering these you will have the opportunity to link past learning with newly acquired information by approaching the situations from different viewpoints. If you discuss the problems with others in your class, you will see how these other students, your future colleagues in the teaching profession, approach the problems. Your instructor might use the situations for small group discussion, asking each group to report its analysis of the problem and solution to the entire class.

A note of thanks to **F. A. Davis** for consideration during the writing of this *Study Guide*.

A special thanks to **Patricia Cullum**, Memphis State University, for her careful assistance in the preparation and design of this *Study Guide*.

We thank **Otto Benavides** and The Center of Excellence in Teacher Education, Memphis State University, for support of this project.

We hope you find educational psychology interesting and useful, both now and as you continue your career in teaching. If you have any suggestions to improve this guide or the textbook, please write to us at:

Jane F. Davis and Todd M. Davis
c/o Woolfolk, *Educational Psychology,* 3rd Edition
College Division
Prentice-Hall, Inc.
Englewood Cliffs, NJ 07632

REFERENCES

Robinson, F.P. *Effective Study* . New York: Harper and Brothers, 1946.

Sargent, E., Huus, H., & Andersen, O. *How to Read a Book* . Newark, Delaware: International Reading Association, 1970.

Thomas, E.L., and Robinson, H.A. *Improving Reading in Every Class* : *A Sourcebook for Teachers* . Boston: Allyn and Bacon, 1972.

CHAPTER 1

TEACHERS, TEACHING, AND EDUCATIONAL PSYCHOLOGY

CHAPTER OVERVIEW

I.   Teaching: An Art, a Science, and a Lot of Work
    A. The many roles of a teacher
        1. Instructional expert
        2. Motivator
        3. Manager
        4. Leader
        5. Counselor
        6. Environmental engineer
        7. Model
    B. Advantages and Disadvantages of a Career in Teaching
        1. Disadvantages
            a. routine paperwork - busywork
            b. unlavish salaries
            c. isolation
            d. sources of stress leading to burnout
        2. Advantages
            a. opportunity to make a difference
            b. summer vacation time
            c. instructional and classroom management autonomy
            d. relationships with students and colleagues
    C. Major Concerns of Beginning Teachers
        1. Three stages of psychological development of teachers
        2. Reality Shock - discipline, motivation, frustration

II.   Social Issues Affecting Teachers Today
    A. Criticisms and Commissions
    B. Teacher Quality
        1. Academic abilities
        2. Quality of teacher training
    C. Accountability

D. Mainstreaming
E. New Technology/Old Curriculum
F. Future of the Job Market
G. Changes in the Family

III. Role of Educational Psychology
    A. Definitions
        1. Education
        2. Psychology
        3. Educational psychology
    B. Need for a Scientific Approach
        1. Not just common sense
        2. Using research to solve classroom problems
        3. Theories for teaching

IV. Major Areas of Study: The Contents of This Book
    A. Orderly Progression
        1. Teacher's point of view
        2. The student: human development
        3. The learning process
        4. Organizing and managing a classroom
        5. Effective instruction
        6. Evaluation of student learning
    B. Putting the Book to Work
        1. Questions educational psychology can help you answer
        2. Solutions to questions

CHAPTER OBJECTIVES

1. Discuss teaching as an art and/or science.
2. Describe the seven major roles a teacher assumes.
3. Explain the advantages of a career in teaching.
4. Explain the disadvantages of a career in teaching.
5. Describe some of the problems and concerns of teachers.
6. Discuss seven major issues that affect teachers today.
7. Describe the role of educational psychology in education.
8. Differentiate the term "educational psychology" from "education" and "psychology."
9. Identify two types of research methods used in education.
10. Identify ways in which research and theory may help teachers.
11. Become acquainted with the organization of the textbook.

KEY TERMS AND CONCEPTS

Fill in the blanks of the following statements with the letters preceeding the terms and concepts listed below.

a. classroom management
b. minimum competency test
c. mainstreaming
d. educational psychology
e. random
f. Principles
g. education
h. accountability
i. PL 94-142

j. correlated
k. theories
l. cause-and-effect relationships
m. observation
n. laws
o. psychology
p. model
q. scientific
r. stress

1. In many states, a requirement for high school graduation or passing from one grade to the next, is the achievement of an adequate score on a _____ .

2. The process by which society transmits its knowledge and values to new members is known as _____ .

3. A term that describes the maintenance of a healthy learning environment which is relatively free of disruptions and behavior problems is called _____ .

4. Established relationships between two or more factors are _____ .

5. When each subject in a research study has an equal and independent chance of being in the sample, the researcher is using a _____ sample.

6. Principles that stand the test of time and repeated investigations, become _____ of human functioning.

7. Merely describing what is happing in a classroom is known as _____ .

8. The study of human behavior, mental processes, development, and learning is known as _____ .

9. The movement to place students with special learning needs into the regular classroom whenever possible instead of segregating them into special classes is called _____ .

3

10. When two events are likely to appear together, although not necessarily in a causal relationship, we say that those two things are _____ .

11. Attempts to explain entire processes, such as cognitive development, and provide a framework for developing creative solutions to unique problems are known as _____ .

12. Experimentation involves manipulating the environment in order to identify _____ .

13. The field concerned with understanding and improving the teaching/learning process are known as _____ .

14. The notion that teachers and schools should be held responsible for what students learn is the main idea behind the _____ movement.

15. The law that requires public schools to provide an appropriate free education for every young person, regardless of handicap is _____ .

16. Knowledge about the processes of learning and teaching, including the rules that govern the relations between a teacher's actions and students' responses, comprise the _____ aspects of teaching.

17. Mrs. Jones demonstrated the proper way to deliver a speech to an audience. This is an example of a teacher acting in the role of a ___ .

18. Teachers indicate that large classes, lack of teaching materials, increasing discipline problems, and few or no breaks are the major sources of _____ .

MULTIPLE CHOICE QUESTIONS

These questions cover the social issues that affect teachers. Respond by selecting the letter of the appropriate answer. The number of the page in the text that contains the information cited in the question appears at the end of each stem.

1. A general theme running through the criticisms of liberal reformers Holt, Illich, Kozol, and Postman is that (pg. 14)

   a. private schools are less effective than public schools.
   b. schools stifle real learning and creativity.
   c. schools are skewed toward minorities and the disadvantaged.
   d. there is insufficient emphasis on the basics of academics.

2.   "Almost every student can learn material taught in schools if he is given enough time and the right instruction." This statement is an assumption of those involved in _____ . (pg. 17)

       a.   accountability
       b.   achievement testing
       c.   mainstreaming
       d.   technological instruction

3.   The idea that teachers are responsible for the lack of learning of students in their classroom has fostered (pg. 15)

       a.   a lowering of academic standards.
       b.   flight of academically talented teachers from classrooms.
       c.   a growth in teacher assessment programs.
       d.   an increase in the private school population.

4.   Teaching students with special needs in the regular classroom is known as (pg. 18)

       a.   accountability
       b.   minimal educational standards
       c.   mainstreaming
       d.   resource teaching

5.   In 1984, students in U.S. elementary and secondary schools had approximately _____ computers available to them. (pg. 19)

       a.   100,000
       b.   245,000
       c.   300,000
       d.   350,000

6.   It is estimated that ___ million children come home from school to an empty household each day. (pg. 20)

       a.   10
       b.   15
       c.   20
       d.   25

7.   What percent of children born in 1976 will spend some part of their lives with a single parent before they turn 18? (pg. 20)

       a.   25%
       b.   35%
       c.   45%
       d.   55%

APPLICATION AND DISCUSSION QUESTIONS

1. In this chapter, seven roles of the teacher were discussed. For each of these roles, list 3 characteristics that teachers should possess to fulfill that particular role. After listing these characteristics, assess your own strengths and weaknesses in relation to each of these characteristics.

2. Correlational and experimental research were discussed in this chapter. For each of the studies described below, indicate whether it is an *experimental* or *correlational* study.

    a. It is known that some classes of students seem to achieve and others do not. The teachers of the classes of students who are achieving are observed to determine how their teaching strategies are alike.

    b. Three groups of children are given different types of computer training to determine which type of computer training is most effective in teaching wordprocessing skills.

    c. Fine motor skill tests are given to a group of boys and girls to determine if there is a relationship between sex and fine motor dexterity.

    d. Two groups of athletes begin a fitness program. To determine the impact of nutrition, one group is given explicit instructions regarding their nutrition while the other is advised to continue eating their regular diet.

3. Imagine yourself in a classroom in which several handicapped students have been mainstreamed. Cite some of the positive aspects of this situation and the problems which the situation may cause.

4. The accountability movement shows no sign of wanning. Imagine yourself being held accountable for whether or not the students in your class learn what you are trying to teach. If they are not learning, you will probably not get a raise, and may even be fired. Cite some of the desirable and undesirable side effects which you think may occur as a result of the accountability movement.

5. How Vulnerable Are You to *Stress?*

    The following test was developed by Psychologists Lyle H. Miller and Alma Dell Smith at Boston University Medical Center. The test indicates your vulnerability to stress. Score each item from 1 (almost always) to 5 (never), according to how much of the time each statement applies to you.

    _____ 1.   I eat at least one hot, balanced meal a day.

    _____ 2.   I get seven to eight hours sleep at least four nights a week.

_____ 3. I give and receive affection regularly.

_____ 4. I have at least one relative within 50 miles on whom I can rely.

_____ 5. I exercise to the point of perspiration at least twice a week.

_____ 6. I smoke less than half a pack of cigarettes a day.

_____ 7. I take fewer than five alcoholic drinks a week.

_____ 8. I am the appropriate weight for my height.

_____ 9. I have an income adequate to meet basic expenses.

_____ 10. I get strength from my religious beliefs.

_____ 11. I regularly attend club or social activities.

_____ 12. I have a network of friends and acquaintances.

_____ 13. I have one or more friends to confide in about personal matters.

_____ 14. I am in good health (including eyesight, hearing, teeth).

_____ 15. I am able to speak openly about my feelings when angry or worried.

_____ 16. I have regular conversations with the people I live with about domestic problems, e.g., chores, money, and daily living issues.

_____ 17. I do something for fun at least once a week.

_____ 18. I am able to organize my time effectively.

_____ 19. I drink fewer than three cups of coffee (or tea or cola drinks) a day.

_____ 20. I take quiet time for myself during the day.

_____ TOTAL

To get your score, add up the figures and subtract 20. Any number over 30 indicates a vulnerability to *stress*. You are seriously vulnerable if your score is between 50 and 75, and extremely vulnerable if it is over 75.

APPENDIX

RESEARCH IN EDUCATIONAL PSYCHOLOGY

APPENDIX OVERVIEW

I. Asking and Answering Questions
   A. Forming a research question
   B. Choosing variables and selecting measurement techniques
   C. Stating a hypothesis and choosing an approach
      1. A descriptive approach
      2. An experimental approach

II. Is the Research Valid?
   A. Dual payoff of being able to evaluate research studies
   B. Eight questions for evaluation of a research experiment

III. A Sample Study: The Effect of Student Expectations
   A. Essential data
   B. Judging validity

APPENDIX OBJECTIVES

1. Describe four methods which can be used to measure variables.
2. Distinguish between correlation and experimental approaches.
3. Judge the validity of a research study by using the Guidelines found in your text for evaluating a research study.
4. Propose a study to answer a question from your own teaching.

8

KEY TERMS

Fill in the blanks in the following sentences with the letters preceding the concepts listed below.

a. variable
b. self-report
c. direct observation
d. test
e. teacher rating
f. peer rating
g. subjects
h. hypothesis

i. correlation
j. independent variable
k. dependent variable
l. control group
m. Hawthorne effect
n. abstract
o. confederate

1. An educated guess about the relationship between two variables is a/an _____ .

2. Any characteristic of a person or the environment that can change under different conditions or distinguishes one person from another is called a/an _____ .

3. In a causal relationship, the variable which we assume causes the change is called the _____ and the variable which changes is the _____ .

4. At the beginning of a research article you will find a/an _____ which is a brief summary of the article.

5. In an experimental study, the subjects which are not manipulated form the _____ .

6. There are **three** basic approaches to the measurement of variables. These are: _____ (using people watching classroom situations to do the assessment), _____ (directly questioning participants about themselves), and _____ (asking teachers or students to do the assessment of others).

7. Sometimes a researcher will make use of an assistant, or _____ , who pretends to be one of the subjects.

8. Because there is a general tendency for large objects to weigh more, there is a/an _____ between size and weight.

9. Changes which occur simply because subjects are given special attention are said to be examples of the _____ .

10. The participants in a study whose behavior is being measured are called _____ .

MULTIPLE CHOICE QUESTIONS

1. At the end of a class, each student is asked how many times he raised his hand to answer a question. The measurement technique being employed is (p. 35)

    a. peer rating.
    b. self-report.
    c. direct observation.
    d. primary sample.

2. A study using the descriptive approach has noted a relationship between the color of the classroom walls and student absenteeism. This study allows a teacher to (p. 37)

    a. make a prediction.
    b. infer a negative relation.
    c. infer a causal relation.
    d. isolate variables.

3. Experimenters need baseline data for comparison, so they must test what happens when the independent variable is not manipulated at all. To do this they use (p. 38)

    a. control groups.
    b. dependent variables.
    c. random classifications.
    d. unbiased measuring systems.

4. An experimental study finds positive results in an entirely new area of inquiry. Its hypothesis has been (p. 36)

    a. verified.
    b. founded.
    c. supported.
    d. proved.

5. Subjects should be assigned to experimental groups on a random basis because this increases the likelihood that (p. 38)

    a. the groups will be the same size.
    b. no subject's hurt feelings will skew the result.
    c. the causal relationship will appear.
    d. the groups will be very similar.

6. When the results of a study are probably due to more than just chance, the researcher calls them (p. 41)

   a. statistically insignificant.
   b. statistically significant.
   c. nonrandom.
   d. corrected for correlation.

7. When the subjects react to the novelty of an experimental situation rather than to the manipulated variables, they demonstrate (p. 40)

   a. experimental feedback.
   b. inappropriate responses.
   c. the Hawthorne effect.
   d. random interference.

8. If a study has been repeated and the same results found, it has been (p. 41)

   a. replicated.
   b. confirmed.
   c. proved.
   d. verified.

9. At the beginning of a published study there is a brief summary of the study's design and results. This is called a/an (p. 41)

   a. digest.
   b. abstract.
   c. artifact.
   d. summary.

APPLICATION AND DISCUSSION QUESTIONS

1. Locate one of the following journals in the periodical section of your library. Read and evaluate the article listed according to the questions and Guidelines provided in the Appendix: Research in Educational Psychology following Chapter 1 in your textbook.

   Anderson, R.C., Pichert, J.W., and Shirey, L.L. "Effects of the Reader's Schema at Different Points in Time," *Journal of Educational Psychology*, 1983, *75*, 271-280.

   Woolfolk, R.L., and Woolfolk, A.E. "Modifying the Effect of the Behavior Modification Label," *Behavior Therapy*, 1979, *4*, 575-578.

Weinstein, C., and Woolfolk, A.E. "The Classroom Setting as a Nonverbal Source of Expectations About Teachers," *Journal of Environmental Psychology*, 1981, *1*, 117-129.

Bettencourt, E.M., Gillet, M.H., Gall, M.D., and Hull, R.E. "Effects of Teacher Enthusiasm Training on Student On-Task Behavior and Achievement," *American Educational Research Journal*, 1983, *20*, 435-450.

Chaikin, A., Sigler, E., and Derlega, V. "Nonverbal Mediators of Teacher Expectancy Effects," *Journal of Personality and Social Psychology*, 1974, *30*, 144-149.

Anderson, L., Evertson, C.M., and Brophy, J.E. "An Experimental Study of Effective Teaching in First-Grade Reading Groups," *Elementary School Journal*, 1979, *79*, 193-222.

McKinney, C.W., Larkins, A.G., Ford, M.J., and Davis, J.C., III. "The Effectiveness of Three Methods of Teaching Social Studies Concepts to Fourth-Grade Students: An Aptitude-Treatment Interaction Study," *American Educational Research Journal*, 1983, *20*, 663-670.

2. The Hawthorne effect can occur in research studies but it can also happen in the classroom. Explain some circumstances under which the Hawthorne effect might occur in a class you are teaching.

3. Describe a study you would like to do in your teaching field. Specifically indicate

   a. question to be studied
   b. variables
   c. sample
   d. descriptive or experimental method

CHAPTER 2

THE MIND AT WORK:
COGNITIVE DEVELOPMENT AND LANGUAGE

CHAPTER OVERVIEW

I. Development: Toward a General Definition
    A. Definition of development
    B. Aspects of development
    C. Influences on development
    D. General developmental principles

II. Comprehensive Theory About Thinking: The Work of Piaget
    A. Readiness and thinking
    B. Making sense of the world
        1. Influences on development
            a. maturation
            b. activity
            c. social transmission
            d. equilibration
        2. Organization
        3. Adaptation
            a. assimilation
            b. accommodation
            c. equilibration
    C. Four stages of cognitive development
        1. Sensorimotor stage
        2. Preoperational stage
        3. Concrete operations stage
        4. Formal operations stage

III. Piaget's Theory: Implications and Limitations
    A. Determining cognitive abilities
    B. Choosing teaching strategies
    C. Speeding up cognitive development: Pro and con
    D. Vygotsky's zone of proximal development

IV. Information Processing
    A. Attention
       1. Controlling attention
       2. Fitting attention to the task
       3. Planning
       4. Monitoring
    B. Memory and metacognitive abilities

V. Development of Language
    A. Stages in the process
       1. One-word stage
          a. holophrases
          b. overgeneralization
       2. Two-word stage or telegraphic speech
       3. Overregularization

IV. Dialect: Variations Within Languages

V. Teaching and Language
    A. Teaching strategies
       1. Be sensitive to stereotypes regarding dialects
       2. Repeat Instructions, paraphrase or give examples
       3. Focus on ideas expressed
       4. Read aloud
       5. One-to-one interaction with adults
    B. Metalinguistic awareness

CHAPTER OBJECTIVES

1. Define development.
2. Name four aspects of development
3. Name two major influences on development
4. List the three general principles of cognitive development
5. Give three criticisms of Piaget's research method.
6. Discuss the relationship between readiness and thinking.
7. Explain the four influences on development.

8. Describe the process involved in organizational changes, i.e., how more complex schemes develop.
9. Explain the processes involved in adaptation: assimilation and accommodation.
10. Explain the concept of equilibration and its function in adaptation.
11. Describe the activities of a child in the sensorimotor stage.
12. Explain the concept of object permanence.
13. Describe the activities of a child in the preoperational stage.
14. Define the following concepts:
    a. operations
    b. one-way logic
    c. reversible thinking
    d. conservation
    e. decentering
    f. collective monologue
15. Discuss four guidelines that should be followed when teaching the preoperational child.
16. Describe the activities of a child in the concrete operations stage.
17. Define the following concepts:
    a. identity
    b. compensation
    c. classification
    d. seriation
18. Discuss four guidelines which should be followed when teaching the concrete operational child.
19. Describe the activities of a person in the formal operations stage.
20. Explain adolescent egocentrism.
21. Discuss four guidelines that should be followed when teaching the formal operational person.
22. Discuss, from the viewpoint of teachers, five implications for Piaget's theory of cognitive development.
23. Give the pro and con arguments for accelerating cognitive development.
24. Explain Vygotsky's zone of proximal development.
25. Define information processing.
26. Describe Flavell's four aspects of attention.
27. Explain Case's procedures for instruction based on the information processing theory of cognitive development.
28. Define metacognition.
29. Explain the one-word stage of language development.
30. Explain the two-word stage of language development and telegraphic speech.
31. Describe overregularization.
32. Define dialect.
33. Give two examples of dialect variations and problems in the classroom that may be related to these dialects.
34. Discuss five teaching strategies that may be used to enhance language development.
35. Define metalinguistic awareness.

KEY TERMS AND CONCEPTS

Fill in the blanks of the following statements with the letters preceeding the terms and concepts listed below. For clarity, they are grouped according to topic.

General Development Concepts

a. development
b. physical development
c. personal development

d. social development
e. cognitive development
f. maturation

1. Changes in the way an individual relates to other people and society is the concern of ____ .

2. The increasing complexity of the mental process of thinking and problem solving is called ____ .

3. Changes in personality due primarily to environmental influences are included in ____.

4. Change that occurs naturally and spontaneously and is to a large extent genetically determined is ____ .

5. The change that occurs in the body structure as one gets older is called ____ .

6. Changes that occur in orderly ways between conception and death and remain for a reasonably long time are categorized under the term ____ .

Piagetian Concepts

a. adaptation
b. assimilation
c. accommodation
d. schemes
e. organizational changes
f. equilibration
g. disequilibrium
h. operations
i. sensorimotor
j. preoperational
k. concrete operational
l. collective monologue
m. proximal development

n. formal operational
o. object permanence
p. goal-directed actions
q. one-way logic
r. conservation
s. decentration
t. reversibility
u. identity
v. compensation
w. seriation
x. classification
y. egocentrism
z. scaffolding

1. The ability to focus on one or more characteristics when grouping objects is referred to as _____ .

2. The mental ability to think back through an operation from the end to the beginning is _____ .

3. A process in which one tries to make sense of and come to terms with the environment is _____ .

4. Organized systems of actions or thoughts that allow us to represent mentally the objects and events in our world are called _____ .

5. In searching for balance in our thinking, actual changes in cognition take place through the process of _____ .

6. Actions that are mentally rather than physically carried out and which may be reversed are _____ .

7. Using existing schemes to make sense of events in the world is the process of _____ .

8. The integration of simple units of learning to form more complicated and sophisticated structures of thought and behavior is _____ .

9. Arranging objects in sequential order according to one aspect, i.e., size is _____ .

10. To understand a situation, one sometimes changes or expands upon existing knowledge through the process of _____ .

11. In Piagetian terms, deliberate activity toward a goal is called _____.

12. When one encounters a stimulus that cannot be accounted for or satisfactorily responded to by using previously existing knowledge, one enters the uncomfortable state of _____ .

13. Children become able to think logically, but need visible materials to aid their thinking processes when they are in the _____ stage of cognitive development.

14. Growth occurs primarily in the refinement of the senses and body movement in the _____ stage of cognitive development.

15. The time of "childhood logic" before the development and mastery of logical operations is termed the _____ stage of cognitive development.

16. Students are able to think abstractly and deal with hypothetical questions in the _____ stage of cognitive development.

17. "Changes or alterations in one dimension can be offset by changes in another dimension" is the principle of _____ .

18. When a child recognizes that an object still exists even though it is not in sight, he has developed _____ .

19. The principle that some properties of an object remain constant even though other properties may vary refers to _____ .

20. If a child understands that an object remains the same if nothing is added or taken away, even though the object may change its form, she has mastered the concept of _____ .

21. The inability to take another person's point of view is termed _____ .

22. When a person is unable to carry out a task calling for reversible thinking, we say he is using _____ .

23. The ability to focus on more than one aspect of a situation at the same time is known as _____ .

24. The form of speech in which children in a group talk but do not really interact or communicate is termed _____ .

25. The middle point where a child cannot solve the problem alone but can be more successful under adult guidance is the zone of _____ .

26. Assistance in which people serve as guides for children to enable them to eventually solve problems on their own is called _____ .

Information Processing and Language Development

a. information processing
b. controlling
c. metacognition
d. holophrases
e. overgeneralization
f. telegraphic
g. planning

h. semantics
i. overregularization
j. dialect
k. metalinguistic
l. one-word
m. two-word
n. monitoring

1. Children sometimes apply rules of speaking in situations in which the application is incorrect. For example, "I goed to the zoo yesterday and ate lots of popcorns." This incorrect application is called _____ .

2. A young child who calls all small animals "doggies" is demonstrating _____ .

3. A child who states "Up!" and means "Mommy please pick me up and take me with you" is probably in the _____ stage of language development.

4. Variations of standard languages, spoken by particular ethnic or social groups, and which have logic and rules are termed _____ .

5. The study of how humans perceive, comprehend, and remember information they gain from the world around them is called _____ .

6. When a child is able to focus upon a task and ignore irrelevant details, we say he has become adept at _____ his attention.

7. When children decide they are using the wrong strategy in attending to a task and change their approach, we say they are _____ their attention.

8. The term used to indicate that children have the ability to anticipate the need to pay better attention is called _____ .

9. People's awareness of their own cognitive abilities and how those abilities work is termed _____ .

10. In examining language construction, we often look at not only the structure, but the meaning or _____ of what has been said.

11. Speech in which only the words that carry the most meaning are included and the nonessential details are left out is called _____ .

12. Single words which are used to express complex ideas or whole phrases are termed _____ .

13. When children begin to understand language and explicitly how it works, we say they have begun to develop _____ awareness.

14. When a child says "Daddy read" and means "Daddy pick me up and read me my book," the child is in the _____ stage of language development.

Multiple Choice Questions

For the following questions, circle the correct response. Once you have reviewed the answers at the end of the chapter, study your text for the items you missed. Each item is keyed to the text to help you find the information more easily. The page number appears in parentheses following the stem of the question.

1. The term generally used to describe changes in the body is ____ development. (p. 49)

    a. cognitive
    b. personal
    c. physical
    d. social

2. Changes in the way an individual relates to others are generally called ____ development. (p. 49)

    a. cognitive
    b. personal
    c. physical
    d. social

3. Piaget would agree with which of the statements below? (p. 51)

    a. Adult thought is about the same as children's thought.
    b. Environmental influences are most important in development.
    c. Some skills are more easily learned at age 16 than at age 9.
    d. There is no limitation on the kinds of things a child can learn.

4. When environmental changes lead to changes in behavior, we call the process ____ . (p. 52)

    a. adaptation
    b. assimilation
    c. goal directed action
    d. external modification

5. Piaget labeled "taking in" stimuli or fitting a new idea into the existing cognitive organization as ____ . (p. 53)

    a. accommodation
    b. assimilation
    c. conservation
    d. decentration

6. When we modify our existing cognitive structure to encompass a new idea or new data, the process is called ____ . (p. 53)

    a. accommodation
    b. assimilation
    d. adaptation
    e. centration

7. Willie's mother took his stuffed rabbit away and Willie could no longer see his toy. Willie did not look for his toy; it was as if the toy had ceased to exist. According to Piaget, Willie is in the _____ stage of cognitive development. (p. 56)

    a. concrete operational
    b. formal operational
    c. preoperational
    d. sensorimotor

8. In Piaget's terminology, operations are actions carried out (p. 57)

    a. egocentrically.
    b. mentally rather than physically.
    c. reversibly.
    d. with a goal in mind.

9. The statement "Knowledge based on bodily activity," refers to which stage? (p. 56)

    a. concrete operational
    b. formal operational
    c. preoperational
    d. sensorimotor

10. When children see the world only from their own viewpoint, we say they are displaying _____ thought. (p. 59)

    a. assimilation
    b. egocentric
    c. goal-directed
    d. hypothetical

11. Classification and seriation develop during the _____ stage of cognitive development. (p. 61)

    a. concrete operational
    b. formal operational
    c. preoperational
    d. sensorimotor

12. Conservation refers to the child's ability to recognize that (p. 58)

    a. abstract thought is necessary to complete many tasks
    b. materials may be grouped according to specific characteristics
    c. objects do not change just because their appearance changes
    d. toys may be placed in various orders according to appearance

13. A year ago, Johnny would have used a trial and error approach to putting a puzzle together. Now he is able to work out some parts of the puzzle "in his head" before he actually moves the puzzle pieces. Johnny has entered the ___ stage of cognitive development. (p. 63)

    a. concrete operational
    b. formal operational
    c. preoperational
    d. sensorimotor

14. According to Piaget, cognitive development proceeds through invariant stages. This means that: (p. 55)

    a. All people proceed through stages at the same rate.
    b. Bright persons can skip one or more stages.
    c. Everyone proceeds through the stages in the same order.
    d. The sequences of stages varies from one culture to another.

15. Bruce can arrange blocks according to their size, largest to smallest. He has attained the operation of ____ . (p. 61)

    a. causality
    b. classification
    c. decentering
    d. seriation

16. Ms. Brown entered her classroom to find all the children chattering, but no one seemed to be talking to or interacting with anyone else. Ms. Brown was observing ____ in her classroom. (p. 59)

    a. assimilating language
    b. collective monologue
    c. metalinguistic awareness
    d. telegraphic speech

17. The mental structures that people are continually reorganizing into systems for interacting with the world are called ____ . (p. 53)

    a. adaptations
    b. cognitive formats
    c. schemes
    d. transferences

18. The search for balance in one's thinking is termed _____ . (p. 54)

a. adaptation
b. concentration
c. equilibration
d. organization

19. Tara refuses to go to the football game on Friday night. She thinks the haircut she had Friday afternoon looks terrible and is sure that everyone in the stadium will laugh at her. Tara is demonstrating the characteristic of_____ . (p. 64)

a. abstract cognition
b. adolescent egocentrism
c. metaphorical thinking
d. schematic assimilation

20. Claire tells her mother that she wants to drink from the taller glass rather than the shorter glass because the tall glass has more juice. When shown that, in fact, both glasses contain the same amount of liquid, Claire continues to insist that the tall glass has more juice. Claire is demonstrating that she has not yet acquired the principle of _____ . (p. 58)

a. classification
b. conservation
c. seriation
d. transformation

21. Little Hamilton cries when his favorite Teddy bear is taken away and he looks frantically about for it. Hamilton has developed _____. (p. 56)

a. conservation strategies
b. decentering
c. object permanence
d. seriation abilities

22. Researchers in information processing have suggested that children seem to have more limited short-term memories because. (p. 73)

a. children are unable to monitor their memories.
b. memory traces fade more quickly in children
c. they must devote part of their working memory to basic operations
d. youngsters are more easily distracted from the material.

23. Children's speech that contains only essential words, such as "go store" or "want cookie" is called_____ . (p. 75)

    a. dialectic
    b. holophrastic
    c. metalinguistic
    d. telegraphic

24. Sarah has spent a lot of time at the stables with her big sister and calls all large animals that she sees, "horsie". Sarah is engaging in _____ in her speech. (p. 75)

    a. catagorical errors
    b. holophrastic phrases
    c. overgeneralization
    d. overregularization

25. The monitoring of one's own thinking and thinking of others is called _____ . (p. 73)

    a. cognitive organization
    b. developmental analysis
    c metacognition
    d. social transmission

26. Most children have mastered the basics of their own native language by the age of _____ years. (p. 77)

    a. 2
    b. 4
    c. 6
    d. 9

27. Robert says, "Poppa ride" and his father understands that Robert wants him to pick him up and carry him on his shoulders down to the lake to feed the ducks. Robert's sentence was short, but the _____ were much more complex. (p. 75)

    a. associations
    b. holophrases
    c. overgeneralizations
    d. semantics

APPLICATION AND DISCUSSION QUESTIONS

1. What Piagetian stage of cognitive development is indicated in the following situations? Give the characteristic that is illustrated in each example.

a. From a group of objects, Wanda chooses a straw, a pencil, and a ruler to form a group of "things that go together" because they are all long and skinny.

   Stage_____ Characteristic _____

b. Bill puts the straw and glass together because you use a straw to drink out of a glass.

   Stage_____ Characteristic _____

c. Susan puts the pencil and ruler together because they are both made out of wood.

   Stage_____ Characteristic _____

d. A student is able to discuss the question, What would the world be like if John F. Kennedy had not been assassinated?

   Stage_____ Characteristic _____

e. Terry can now enjoy playing "peek a boo."

   Stage_____ Characteristic _____

f. When given 3 kinds of lettuce, 3 kinds of cheese, and 3 kinds of vegetables, Louise can make 27 kinds of salads.

   Stage_____ Characteristic _____

g. Child showing an egg timer to a friend: "Then you turn it upside down and get your three minutes back."

   Stage_____ Characteristic _____

h. If Hamilton wants a his rattle, he can reach for it and pick it up.

   Stage_____ Characteristic _____

i. Janice is able to solve the problem: "If A is greater than X and X is greater than Z, but Z is less than C which is less than X, what is the order of the letters?

   Stage_____ Characteristic _____

j. Ralph is able to help stuff envelopes: He folds the papers, puts them in the envelope, closes the envelope, licks the stamp and puts the stamp on the envelope.

   Stage_____ Characteristic _____

2. Teaching the child who is in the preoperational stage of cognitive development is a challenge! Remembering the characteristics of the preoperational stage, explain how you might go about teaching a child in this stage a) to pop popcorn and give each person in the class a portion and b) the idea of sharing one's toys.

3. By the time a child reaches the concrete operational stage of cognitive development, they have some operations and strategies that they are able to employ. Considering these new skills, explain how you might go about teaching a child in this stage a) a history lesson about the American Revolution and b) the importance of the four food groups to nutrition.

4. Suppose you were teaching the concept of "prejudice" to a third grade class and to a twelfth grade class. How and why would your presentations and expectations differ?

5. Equilibration could be considered as a Piagetian term roughly equivalent to the more common concept of motivation. According to Piaget's concept of equilibration, how would you go about motivating a student?

6. You have been assigned to teach 10th grade science. These students are just beginning to use formal operations. What strategies will you keep in mind when forming your lesson plans?

CHAPTER 3

PERSONAL, SOCIAL, AND MORAL DEVELOPMENT

CHAPTER OVERVIEW

I. A Comprehensive Theory: The Work of Erikson
    A. Tasks and Stages Throughout Life
    B. Infancy; Trust v. Mistrust
    C. The Toddler: Autonomy v. Shame and Doubt
    D. Early Childhood: Initiative v. Guilt
    E. Elementary and Middle School Years: Industry v. Inferiority
    F. Adolescence: The Search for Identity
    G. Beyond the School Years: Intimacy, Generativity, and Integrity

II. Issues in the Early Years
    A. Sex-Role Development
    B. The Impact of Day Care
    C. Friendships in Childhood

III. Issues Affecting Adolescents
    A. Physical Development in Adolescence
    B. Sexual Maturity

IV. Understanding Ourselves and Others
    A. Self-Concepts: Origins and Influences
    B. The Self and Others
    C. Moral Development

V. Education for Emotional Growth
    A. What Do Teachers Think?
    B. How Do Teachers Encourage Personal Growth?

CHAPTER OBJECTIVES

1. State the general characteristics of Erikson's theory of personal development.
2. Name Erikson's eight developmental crises.
3. Describe the environmental conditions that encourage positive resolution of the Erikson's first through fifth developmental stages.
4. Identify the role parents may play in children's sex role development.
5. Discuss the impact schools may have upon the development of children's sex roles.
6. Describe procedures that may be useful in helping teachers prevent sexism in teaching.
7. Explain the impact day care may have upon children's personal, social, and intellectual development.
8. Identify levels of friendships in childhood.
9. Describe the effects of early and late maturation on adolescents.
10. Explain procedures that may be used in the classroom to deal with physical differences in students.
11. Define self-concept.
12. Discuss the origins of and influences on self-concept.
13. List specific ways in which teachers can encourage the development of a positive self-concept.
14. Trace the development of a child's concept of other people.
15. Define empathy.
16. Describe how empathy develops in children.
17. Identify Kohlberg's six stages of moral development.
18. Explain the basis of moral development at each of Kohlberg's stages.
19. Distinguish between moral judgment and moral behavior.
20. Describe strategies teachers may use to encourage moral development.
21. Explain the problems and criticisms associated with Kohlberg's theory of moral development.
22. List strategies a teacher may use to avoid cheating in the classroom.
23. Define aggression.
24. Define assertiveness.
25. Describe some of the effects violence on TV may have on children's behavior.
26. Discuss teachers' positions on the importance of personal growth and ways in which they encourage its development.

KEY TERMS AND CONCEPTS

Fill in the blanks of the following statements with the letters preceeding the terms and concepts listed below.

a. psychosocial
b. trust
c. initiative
d. identity
e. identity achievement
f. moratorium
g. affective
h. empathy
i. preconventional
j. generativity
k. moral dilemmas
l. aggression

m. developmental crisis
n. autonomy
o. industry
p. self-concept
q. forclosure
r. academic
s. social cognition
t. sexually mature
u. gender identity
v. prosocial
w. conventional
x. post conventional
y. assertiveness

1. How a person views himself or herself academically, emotionally, socially, and physically may be called a person's _____ .

2. Erikson's _____ theory of personal development stresses the importance of achieving positive resolutions to developmental crises that individuals encounter at different stages in the life cycle.

3. Kohlberg's stages of moral judgment are based on the reasoning a person gives for making a decision in response to _____ .

4. Children who are willing to work hard tend to become adults who are well-adjusted and successful. They have positively resolved the developmental crisis of _____ .

5. The thoughts and ideas people have about their social world, i.e., their understanding of other people, are known as _____ .

6. An adolescent who is in the midst of experimenting with different life styles and examining her values is in an identity status called _____ .

7. Caring for the needs of future generations is a main concern of the developmental stage of _____ .

8. By helping students see each other's point of view, teachers can help students develop _____ .

9. When a subject is able to consider the underlying, individual values that may be involved in a decision, he may be said to be in the ____ level of moral development.

10. Self-concept based on how well a student performs in scholastic areas is called ____ self-concept.

11. Programs that are concerned with the emotional growth of children are known as ____ education.

12. Behaviors that are of benefit to society, such as cooperation and concern for others, are generally referred to as ____ behaviors.

13. An adolescent who is "going to be a lawyer just like my Dad" may be in the ____ identity status unless she has considered many different alternatives and made a conscious choice in which case it is ____ .

14. A specific conflict whose resolution prepares the individual for the next stage is known as ____ .

15. According to Erikson, a baby will develop a sense of ____ if his basic needs for food and care are met with comforting regularity.

16. Young children who are beginning to carry out goal-directed behavior and developing physical and mental abilities to allow them some control over their lives are striving toward ____ .

17. When a subject is able to look beyond the immediate personal consequences and consider the views, and approval of others, we say she is in the ____ level of moral development.

18. An eagerness to engage in productive work and seeing the relationship between perseverance and the pleasure of a job completed is called ____ .

19. The search for the answer to the complex question of "Who am I" is known as ____ .

20. In Kohlberg's theory, the level in which judgment is based solely on a person's own needs and perceptions is called ____ .

21. Learning what it means to be a male or female in our society is something contributes to our ____ .

22. Adolescents who are physically and hormonally equipped for sexual relationships are said to be ____ .

23. Violent behavior is called ____, whereas affirming or maintaining a legitimate right is known as ____ .

MULTIPLE CHOICE QUESTIONS

1. Erikson's theory of development is best described as a _____ theory. (p. 87)

   a. cognitive development
   b. psychoanalytic
   c. psychosocial
   d. socioeconomic

2. In the child's earliest months, parental closeness and responsiveness contribute to the child's sense of (p. 88)

   a. autonomy
   b. industry
   c. initiative
   d. trust

3. The way that children resolve the autonomy vs. doubt crisis influences their later sense of (p. 90)

   a. attachment to the family.
   b. confidence in their own abilities
   c. cooperation in groups.
   d. evaluation of new ideas.

4. Studies indicate that mothers interact with babies differently than fathers. The differences may influence the development of (p. 97)

   a. attachment to the family.
   b. attitudes toward authority.
   c. gender identity.
   d. trust or mistrust of parents.

5. Allowing preschool children to perform adult-like tasks and accepting their efforts is one way to encourage (p. 91)

   a. identity.
   b. industry.
   c. initiative.
   d. intimacy.

6. Friendships among preschoolers may form and dissolve quickly depending on acts of "niceness" or "meanness." This is probably because preschoolers (p. 100)

    a. become angry very quickly and without reason.
    b. have little sense of friends having stable characteristics.
    c. have a stronger attachment to their parents than their peers.
    d. seem to be prone to forget past actions.

7. Susan, age 7, is beginning to attempt longer projects and to see them through. She also seems to enjoy this product work. Erikson would call this a sense of (p. 91)

    a. identity.
    b. industry.
    c. inferiority.
    d. initiative.

8. The composite of feelings, attitudes, and ideas that people hold about themselves is generally called (p. 104)

    a. gender identity
    b. intimacy.
    c. self-concept.
    d. social role.

9. Ralph, a college student, has changed his major three times and is continuing to take lots of courses trying to decide what career path he will follow. Ralph may be said to be Marcia's ____ identity status. (p. 119)

    a. foreclosure
    b. identity diffusion
    c. identity achievement
    d. moratorium

10. Susan has decided that she wants to be just like her mother, get a college degree in teaching and teach first grade. Susan may be said to be in Marcia's ____ status of identity. (p. 119)

    a. foreclosure
    b. identity diffusion
    c. identity achievement
    d. moratorium

11. Hamilton has considered numerous careers and after much discussion with professionals and a lot of soul searching, he has decided to become a lawyer. Hamilton may be said to be in Marcia's ____ status of identity. (p. 119)

   a. foreclosure
   b. identity diffusion
   c. identity achievement
   d. moratorium

12. Juanita just seems to be drifting around in deciding on a career choice. She isn't really considering any alternatives, nor does she appear particularly concerned about her future. Juanita may be said to be in Marcia's ____ status of identity. (p. 119)

   a. foreclosure
   b. identity diffusion
   c. identity achievement
   d. moratorium

13. Mr. McLin is trying to avoid stereotyped sex roles in his class. When he needs a computer-oriented student to run some computer programs, he asks for (p. 98)

   a. students who have their own computers at home.
   b. students who have experience playing video games.
   c. volunteers to assist him in running the programs.
   d. male students as they know more about computers.

14. According to Erikson, adolescence is characterized by which of the following psychosocial stages of development? (p. 93)

   a. autonomy vs. shame
   b. indentity vs. role confusion
   c. initiative vs. inferiority
   d. intimacy vs. isolation

15. In Erikson's broader terminology, generativity refers to the (p. 96)

   a. acceptance of mortality.
   b. desire to procreate.
   c. growth of self-understanding
   d. maintenance of the world.

16. Paul has never developed a clear sense of his own identity. He has the feeling that other people's personalities overwhelm his own. It will probably be very difficult for him to achieve (p. 96)

    a. integrity.
    b. intimacy
    c. self-initiative
    d. sexual relations

17. Social cognition refers to the ways children conceptualize (p. 107)

    a. other people and their thoughts and emotions.
    b. individuals responsibilities under the law.
    c. the historical continuum of mankind.
    d. their own roles in society.

18. According to Erikson, the elderly face the stage of (p. 97)

    a. generativity vs. self-absorption
    b. integrity vs. depair.
    c. intimacy vs. isolation
    d. initiative vs. shame

19. Discipline based on threats and punishment is likely to instill morality based on (p. 114)

    a. appreciation of natural outcomes.
    b. a firm sense of right and wrong.
    c. a fear of getting caught.
    d. traditional standards of behavior.

20. Kohlberg evaluated moral reasoning by studying responses to (p. 109)

    a. actual recorded events.
    b. moral dilemmas.
    c. rules and proscriptions.
    d. threats of punishment.

21. When a person's moral development is at the preconventional level, the most important moral criteria are (p. 111)

    a. direct personal results of an action.
    b. intuitive feelings of right and wrong.
    c. principles underlying an action.
    d. statements of laws.

22. The postconventional level of moral reasoning requires (p. 111)

    a. logical consequences.
    b. formal operations.
    c. extensive training
    d. deep insight.

23. One procedure suggested for helping students achieve higher levels of moral reasoning is (p. 112)

    a. emphasizing the student's sense of right and wrong.
    b. enforcing strict discipline
    c. holding discussions of moral dilemmas.
    d. teaching a firm understanding of social theory.

24. Bandura showed that after children watch other children hit others and behave in a violent way, they tend to (p. 113)

    a. become more aggressive.
    b. interact less frequently.
    c. tolerate less aggression among their peers.
    d. view others as more assertive.

25. "Plus-one matching" in a discussion of moral issues refers to (p. 116)

    a. discussion of the rights of third parties.
    b. finding a middle road to students' arguments.
    c. presenting arguments one stage above the student's stage.
    d. putting students in pairs so they may discuss dilemmas.

26. A teacher who was fostering traditional and sexually stereotyped roles would probably do which of the following: (p. 98)

    a. Ask for volunteers from the class to bring refreshments
    b. Encourage girls to be the secretary of the class
    c. Request that someone offer to carry boxes to the basement
    d. Review textbooks to avoid sexist views

27. Girls are, on the average, taller and heavier than boys their same age when they are between the ages of _____. (p. 101)

    a. 6 and 8
    b. 9 and 10
    c. 11 and 14
    d. 15 and 18

28. Little Judy will not cross the street because she knows if she does her mother will make her sit in the corner for an hour. Little Judy is operating in the _____ stage of moral development. (p. 110)

   a. conventional
   b. moral conventional
   c. postconventional
   d. preconventional

29. Critics of affective education believe that schools should (p. 115)

   a. encourage students to determine their own values.
   b. stick to cognitive goals and leave values to the family.
   c. teach morality to students in all grades.
   d. use values clarification strategies in the classroom.

APPLICATION AND DISCUSSION QUESTIONS

1. The following scenario is a Kohlbergian moral dilemma. Classify the responses that follow the dilemma according to Kohlberg's stages of moral development.

Sharon is a student in a math class. She has not been doing very well in math class and is considering cheating on an upcoming math test. Should she cheat on the exam?

   a. Yes, because if she cheats and does well on the test, her parents will think she is a good daughter and will be proud of her.

   b. No, because if she gets caught she will be punished severely.

   c. No, because cheating is against all the rules of the school.

   d. No, because cheating is unfair to all the other individuals in the class. A person should complete their own work.

   e. Yes, because if she cheats and gets a good grade on the test, her parents will probably reward her by letting her go to a movie.

2. The positive resolution of a developmental crisis is based on consistent experiences which encourage and support such a resolution. Match the following types of experiences with the crisis in which they would have the MOST impact. Also indicate whether the experience would support a positive or negative resolution to the crisis.

Crisis	Resolution
A. Trust vs. mistrust	+ Positive Resolution
B. Autonomy vs. shame and doubt	− Negative Resolution
C. Initiative vs. guilt	
D. Industry vs. inferiority	
E. Identity vs. role diffusion	

a. When a student finally completes a complex and involved science project, the teacher criticizes him for taking so much time.

b. The baby sitter bangs loud pots together and the baby cries with fear. She continues to do this so that the baby will not be afraid of loud noises.

c. When the baby is hungry and cries, his nanny feeds him even though it has not been two hours since his last feeding.

d. When a student wants to pour water in a clay bowl, which he has made, the teacher lets him because she tries to let students carry out their own ideas.

e. Little Susan wants to feed herself, but her mother, annoyed by the mess her daughter creates, insists on feeding the child herself.

f. Students in Mrs. Jones class decide to sell candy to make money for the local muscular dystrophy association. Mrs. Jones praises the children for this project, even though it will mean considerable work for her.

g. Mrs. Ross purchases tennis shoes with velcro closings rather than shoe laces so that her children may take their shoes off and put them on themselves.

h. Mr. Shumard allows his seniors in government class the opportunity to discuss not only the current events of the day, but also their views and opinions regarding those current events.

i. Claire built a boat out of cardboard and wood. When Claire decided to sail her boat, the Big Dipper, in the lake, her parents gave the launching of her boat the same fanfare and attention that they gave to the launching of the model boat that her father built.

j. Mrs. Clark, the 11th grade English teacher, is all business. She believes that classroom time should be spent on lessons and not on discussion of students "ideas." Therefore, her class time is spent telling the students the appropriate interpretations of the plays and poems.

3. The following excerpts were written by college students about past experiences that they felt influenced their self-concepts. After reading the excerpts, discuss the following questions:

a.   How did other people contribute to each person's self-concept?

b.   What effect did the experience have on the resolution of the person's developmental crisis at that time? Are the two related?

c.   Do you think the criticisms were magnified because they were given in front of other people?

d.   How could you have handled the situations more sensitively?

e.   Do you remember any school experiences that had an effect on your self-concept or developmental crisis?

Exerpt 1   My mother worked mornings as a maid and went to nursing school in the evenings. I stayed in the evenings with a teenaged babysitter who lived with her parents. Her father called me "Cluck" whenever he had a chance. He always made me cry calling me "Cluck," which to me was another name for stupid.

In the third grade I got sick and was out of school for a couple of weeks. When I returned, everyone knew their multiplication table but me. The teacher gave me a list of the tables to learn but didn't explain the concept or anything. At the babysitter's I couldn't learn them for worrying about being left in the room alone with her father, he kept calling me "Cluck" and, made me keep crying.

The next day students were lined up with the teacher asking the multiplication facts. He asked me one I didn't know. I felt so stupid that I started to cry and he fussed at me. And back to the babysitter's with him calling me "Cluck" all night and me crying. I became afraid of math, felt stupid, and just didn't enjoy going to that class.

Maybe if I had been able to talk to somebody about what was bothering me back when I was small, things would be different for me now.

Exerpt 2   In the seventh grade I had an art teacher who took a real interest in me. Without me knowing he took some of my work and displayed it at a local contest. In the meantime I moved, and a few months later, I received a package in the mail which contained a first-prize award from the contest. This man went through all the trouble of finding my new address and sending the award just for me! I guess I was just lucky, but I've had some great people as teachers in my time!

Exerpt 3   When I was in sixth grade I had an experience I'll never forget. I hope, as a future teacher I'll never make the mistake of openly criticizing a student.

It was dress rehearsal for the annual school Christmas program, which consisted of numerous Christmas songs and a choral reading. Many parents and teachers had come to watch, so the auditorium was almost full. As we came walking down the aisle, singing some Christmas song, our teacher suddenly stops us and says, "Those of us not blessed with beautiful voices, <u>Marcia</u>, please don't sing so loud."

I was crushed to say the least! I realize I've never been able to sing like Olivia Newton-John but . . . . The color red zoomed to my face and for the remainder of the rehearsal and the actual show I never sang; I faked it. To this day, I rarely sing in public. Whoever said, "music is a universal language," if only those with beautiful voices may speak?

4. In many lessons, both cognitive and affective goals are important. Below are listed several topics. How would you integrate cognitive and affective goals into your lessons about these topics?

    a.   The increase in the legal drinking age from 18 to 21 years of age.

    b.   Apartheid in the country of South Africa

    c.   Columbus's voyage to America

    d.   The explosion of the NASA shuttle that killed 7 astronauts

    e.   The growing hispanic population in Miami and the need for education in that city to be bilingual

    f.   Proper nutrition: The basic food groups, reduction in fats

    g.   The growing number of working mothers in America: Their jobs and their families

CHAPTER 4

INDIVIDUAL VARIATIONS

CHAPTER OVERVIEW

I. The Origin of Differences
   A. Hereditary Factors
   B. Environmental Factors
      1. Socioeconomic Differences
      2. Cultural Differences
      3. Child-Rearing Practices
      4. Birth Order
      5. Divorce
      6. Working Mothers
      7. Latchkey Children
      8. Child Abuse
   C. Current Views: A Complicated Interaction

II. Individual Differences in Intelligence
   A. What Does Intelligence Mean?
      1. Intelligence: One Ability or Many?
      2. Components View of Intelligence
   B. How is Intelligence Measured?
      1. Binet and Simon
      2. Weschler Scales
   C. What Does an IQ Score Mean?
   D. Intelligence: Nature or Nuture?
   E. Improving Intelligence
   F. Gender and Mental Abilities
   G. Age and Mental Abilities
   H. Ability Grouping

III. Creativity
   A. Assessing Creativity
      1. Divergent Thinking
      2. Convergent Thinking
   B. Creativity in the Classroom

IV. Variations in Cognitive Style
   A. Field Dependence and Field Independence
   B. Impulsive and Reflective Styles

CHAPTER OBJECTIVES

1. Explain the concept of heritability in human development.
2. Define heritability ratio.
3. Describe the role of the different environmental factors (SES, culture, child-rearing practices, birth order, divorce, working mothers, latchkey children, child abuse) in the development of individual similarities and differences.
4. Define: SES, culture, birth order, latchkey children
5. Discuss the ways in which children affect the adults in their environment and the implications of these effects.
6. Define intelligence.
7. Explain Spearman's and Guilford's theories of intelligence.
8. Explain the components view of intelligence.
9. Trace the development of intelligence tests (Binet, Weschler)
10. Define mental age and the concept of intelligence quotient.
11. Know the formula for calculating an intelligence quotient.
12. Describe some of the reasons group intelligence tests may be unreliable.
13. Explain the meaning of an IQ.
14. Define polygenetic.
15. Explain some procedures which have been used to try to improve children's intelligence.
16. Discuss some of the guidelines that should be followed when interpreting IQ scores.
17. Discuss the relationship between gender and mental abilities.
18. Describe the relationship between age and mental abilities.
19. Define longitudinal study.
20. Define fluid intelligence and crystallized intelligence.
21. Describe two methods of ability grouping.
22. Define creativity.
23. Describe some of the procedures that may be used in assessing creativity.
24. Define divergent thinking and convergent thinking.
25. Define brainstorming and explain how this procedure may be used.
26. Define: cognitive style, field-dependent, field-independent, impulsive, reflexive, self-instruction.
28. Describe the learning characteristics of field-dependent and field-independent students.

KEY TERMS

a. child abuse
b. polygenetic inheritance
c. field-independent
d. socioeconomic status (SES)
e. primary mental abilities
f. mental age
g. components
h. IQ
i. longitudinal study
j. fluid intelligence
k. cognitive styles
l. creativity
m. reflective

n. culture
o. heritability ratio
p. field-dependent
q. intelligence
r. convergent thinking
s. faces of intellect
t. latchkey
u. deviation IQ
v. brainstorming
w. crystallized intelligence
x. divergent thinking
y. impulsive

1. A strategy used to develop creative thinking in which ideas are generated but not evaluated until all possible suggestions have been made is termed _____ .

2. A method used to assess creativity in which students are asked questions to test their ability to think of many different ideas is called _____ .

3. Variations among families in wealth, power, and prestige are referred to as _____ .

4. The proportion of the variation among individuals in a particular characteristic that is due to genetic differences is called _____ .

5. Guilford proposes multiple cognitive abilities: mental operations, types of content, and different products. This theory indicates three _____ .

6. Originally, _____ was computed by comparing the mental age score of a person to his actual chronological age. This concept has been replaced by the ___ which is determined by how much better or worse than average the person did on the intelligence test.

7. When a teacher assures students that originality and uniqueness will be appreciated and accepted rather than evaluated and rejected, that teacher is probably going to encourage _____ .

8. Binet and Simon devised a system of scoring tests by which a child's _____ was determined by the number of items completed at different levels.

9. The ability to adapt, cope successfully and deal effectively with the world is linked to the concept of _____ .

10. Field-independence/dependence and impulsivity/reflectivity are two examples of _____ .

11. When the same people are assessed repeatedly over a period of time, the researcher is said to be carrying out a _____ .

12. When many genes influence a particular characteristic, the phenomenon is called _____ .

13. Mental abilities that develop without formal training are called _____ .

14. Mental abilities that are valued and taught directly by the culture are called _____ .

15. A parent who was harshly disciplined as a child and who has unrealistic expectations for his or her child is at a greater risk of committing _____ .

16. A total life style, the rules, expectations, attitudes, beliefs, and values that guide behavior in a particular group of people, is called _____ .

17. Students who need help in learning to pick out important features and ignore irrevelant details, have a _____ cognitive style.

18. Thurstone insisted that there is not just one but several _____ .

19. Children without adult supervision for some part of the day are termed _____ children.

20. In an information processing view, basic problem solving processes underlying intelligence are termed _____ .

21. The act of narrowing possibilities to the one, single answer is _____ .

22. The cognitive style in which a child responds very quickly but often inaccurately is called _____ .

23. The cognitive style in which a child responds slowly, carefully, and accurately is called _____ .

1. The heritability ratio for human intelligence is (p. 125)

    a. between .45 and .55.
    b. between .65 and .75.
    c. disputed among researchers.
    d. impossible to calculate.

2. All of the following are true of SES **except** (p. 126)

    a. income information alone is an effective measure of SES.
    b. high SES has a positive correlation with test achievement.
    c. high SES parents tend to have higher levels of education.
    d. SES is usually divided into three different levels.

3. If the heritability ratio for dyslexia among boys is .40 and Ralph has dyslexia, then it is safe to say that (p. 125)

    a. about 40% of Ralph's male children will be dyslexic.
    b. environmental factors have played a part in Ralph's dyslexia.
    c. Ralph's condition would be the same no matter what his environs.
    d. Ralph's dyslexia is 40% due to heredity.

4. According to current research (cited in your text), the correlation between achievement and socioeconomic status is approximately (p. 126)

    a. .30 in grade 1
    b. .45 in grade 2
    c. .50 in grade 6
    d. .85 in grade 8

5. With regard to diversity of culture in school, there is increasing interest in (p. 127)

    a. isolating the various cultures.
    b. leveling differences in America's cultural "melting pot."
    c. preserving and valuing cultural differences.
    d. raising the lower cultures to match the higher.

6. As compared to females, male children of divorce tend to show (p. 130)

    a. fewer problems.
    b. more acceptance of stepparents.
    c. more difficulties.
    d. quicker adjustment.

7.   Mrs. Brown is firm with her children regarding the appropriate behavior in their home, but she also provides a consistent and loving atmosphere. Mrs. Brown may be said to be using a _____ style of parenting. (p. 129)

   a.   authoritative
   b.   authoritarian
   c.   permissive
   d.   laisse faire

8.   Mrs. White, while she loves her children, makes few demands upon her them, has few rules, and avoids punishments. She may be said to be using a _____ style of parenting. (p. 129)

   a.   authoritative
   b.   authoritarian
   c.   permissive
   d.   laisse faire

9.   Mr. and Mrs. Trepp's children are unhappy, low achievers and have not learned how to be self-reliant. It is very likely that these children were raised in a _____ home. (p. 129)

   a.   authoritative
   b.   authoritarian
   c.   permissive
   d.   laisse faire

10.   There is some evidence that some children who are abused are (p. 133)

   a.   better adjusted than their peers.
   b.   usually early maturers, and thus bigger than their peers.
   c.   passive, easy going, and quiet.
   d.   tempermentally difficult to discipline and control.

11.   Guilford divided cognitive abilities into three categories he called (p. 137)

   a.   faces of intellect.
   b.   intelligence levels.
   c.   intellective types.
   d.   categories of intelligence.

12.   Binet originally developed a test for the (p. 138)

   a.   early identification of gifted children.
   b.   diagnosis of learning disabilities.
   c.   identification of children who would need help in school.
   d.   placement of children in vocational classes.

13. The original idea of IQ has been replaced by the concept of (p. 139)

    a. average IQ
    b. derived IQ
    c. deviation IQ
    d. normative IQ

14. The idea that, underlying all mental functions, there is an intellect composed of a general factor (g) is attributed to (p. 136)

    a. Binet
    b. Cattell
    c. Guilford
    d. Spearman

15. Individual intelligence tests are more reliable than group tests for all the following reasons **except:** (p. 140)

    a. they are less open to distractions.
    b. the testee is more likely to be motivated by individual attention.
    c. they require more reading and writing skills.
    d. they are more likely to yield an accurate picture of skills.

16. "Intelligence is a current state of affairs, affected by past experiences and open to future changes." The importance of this statement for teachers is that (p. 143)

    a. IQ is directly related to class performance.
    b. students of varying SES levels may have the same IQs.
    c. the IQs of students can be improved.
    d. twins reared apart will have similar IQs.

17. The more closely two persons are related the (p. 142)

    a. greater the heritability ratio.
    b. higher the correlation of their IQs.
    c. more important the role of the environment.
    d. stronger the variation one will find in IQs.

18. It has been found that IQs of children from lower SES homes may be raised with intensive educational and health care. The unfortunate outcome of this treatment is the (p. 143)

    a. children are unable to relate to their other family members.
    b. IQ gains seem to fade in later grades.
    c. participants develop behavioral problems in school.
    d. students lose school motivation and aspirations.

19. One basic reason why general intelligence tests find no sex differences in mental abilities is (p. 145)

    a. differences in abilities disappear before intelligence is testable.
    b. the differences between males and females are all physical.
    c. there are no measurable differences in abilities between the sexes.
    d. tests are designed to minimize sex differences.

20. Which of the following is a well-documented difference in abilities between male and female school-aged children? (p. 146)

    a. boys excel in verbal ability
    b. girls perform better at visual and spatial tasks
    c. girls have poorer retention of facts
    d. boys excel at mathematical tasks

21. Which of the following is an example of the use of fluid intelligence? (p. 147)

    a. adjusting the thermostat on an air conditioner
    b. behaving in an appropriate manner at a costume party
    c. being able to translate English to Spanish
    d. reasoning through a practical problem

22. Which of the following statements is TRUE concerning ability grouping? (p. 148)

    a. Children should remain in the same ability group for the entire term.
    b. The teacher should encourage comparisons among the groups to spark competition.
    c. Members from the various ability groups should remain separate from the other groups.
    d. The number of groups should be kept small, two or three at most.

23. The most basic idea of creativity, that can be applied to any area of interest, is (p. 150)

    a. analytic ability
    b. divergency
    c. newness
    d. flexibility

24. Which of the following is an example of a question requiring divergent thinking? (p. 150)

    a. What are the main agricultural resources of Colombia, S.A.?
    b. Describe the possible structural configurations of a chair.
    c. Explain the mechanical workings of a microcomputer.
    d. Define the term "sextant" and use it in a sentence.

25. The relationship between IQ and creativity might best be described as: (p. 150)

    a. average intelligence is necessary for creativity
    b. creativity and intelligence are actually unrelated
    c. creativity is always present in those of high intelligence
    d. high IQ correlates with high creativity

26. When one generates as many ideas as possible without evaluating them, one is engaging in the process of (p. 151)

    a. brainstorming.
    b. convergent thinking.
    c. field-independent activity.
    d. impulsive cognition.

27. As a teacher who wants to foster creativity in the classroom, you should **avoid** which of the following? (p. 153)

    a. accept and encourage divergent thinking.
    b. emphasize that everyone is capable of creativity.
    c. encourage students to look to you for evaluation.
    d. tolerate dissent and disagreement of opinions.

28. Field-dependent individuals tend to be superior when it comes to (p. 155)

    a. handling criticism and corrective comments
    b. providing their own structures and goals
    c. remembering social information and interactions.
    d. reorganizing situations presenting to them.

29. Ralph always finishes a test before his peers, is the first one to raise his hand when a question is asked, and often begins writing his essay assignments before the teacher has completed the instructions. It is safe to say that Ralph probably has a (an) _____ cognitive style. (p. 155)

    a. analytical
    b. impulsive
    c. reflective
    d. self-instructed

30. Rebecca is a child with a reflective cognitive style. She often tends to continue working on a project well beyond the necessary requirements. In considering her best interests, it would probably be wise for her teacher to (p. 155)

    a. criticize Rebecca for being so very slow and tedious
    b. encourage her to continue working on the project
    c. leave the decision of stopping or starting another project completely up to Ann
    d. suggest she stop working on the project and begin something else

APPLICATION AND DISCUSSION QUESTIONS

1.   In this chapter, three basic discipline styles were discussed. Below you will find situations and the parent's response to the situation. Classify the parent's responses according to the discipline style they illustrate: 1. authoritative; 2. authoritarian; 3. permissive.

Situation 1: Child comes home late from school and the parent says...

a.   "You were supposed to come straight home from school every day. I don't want to hear any excuses. Furthermore, you are grounded for the weekend and if I hear any complaining, the grounding will be expanded to next weekend too.

b.   "You were supposed to come straight home from school. I need to know where you are so I won't worry. Do you understand why I might worry when I don't know where you are? You must stay in the house for the rest of the day.

c.   "You're supposed to come straight home from school. Where in the world have you been? I'd rather this didn't happen again. I need to go out to the grocery store and to run some errands.

Situation 2: Child asks for more money and the parent says...

a.   "Are you asking me for money again? What happened to your allowance? Money doesn't grown on trees. Here is $5.00, but this is the last time I am doing this. You should learn to spend your money more carefully.

b.   "No, I'm not giving you any more money. If you're stupid enough to spend all your money on those awful records and those mindless video games, you'll have to go without. Are you ever going to learn how to handle money? Maybe you'd be more careful if you had less money to spend."

c.   "I'm sorry you don't have money to go to the show, but you don't get your allowance until Monday. Maybe you can see it next week. By the way, you might be able to earn a little extra money by doing some odd jobs for Mrs. Hale. Perhaps we should sit down and try to work out a budget for your allowance so you'd know where it is going."

Situation 3: Child wants a cookie before dinner and the parent says...

a.   "Don't eat any cookies now -- you'll spoil your appetite and won't want to eat any of this good meal I'm cooking. Oh, all right, you can have just one, but don't ask for any more."

b.   "You can't have any cookies to eat before dinner because they'll fill you up and you won't be hungry for the food that is good for you. Now, if I hear any more whining about cookies, you will go to bed without any cookies or dinner.

c. "You know you are not allowed to have any cookies before dinner. How many times do we need to discuss this? Now go in and watch TV while I finish preparing dinner."

2. Student performance and self-esteem are greatly influenced by teacher attitude and expectations, which are often influenced by racial and class stereotypes. Teachers may have attitudes that prevent them from dealing effectively with minority students. To increase your awareness of your own attitudes and feelings, complete the following statements as if you were a classroom teacher. How would your attitude affect your behavior toward a minority student?

a. When I have to discipline a child of another race, I feel _____.

b. When I am about to have a conference with a parent of another race I feel _____.

c. When I hear racial name-calling by students, I _____.

d. When two children of different races are fighting, I _____.

e. When I fail a minority student, I _____.

f. The prospect of making a visit to the home of a student of another race makes me feel _____.

g. When I see interracial socializing and dating in my classroom, I _____.

3. If you knew that **heredity** was the **major factor** in determining a child's intelligence, would that fact have any effect on your teaching behaviors?

4. In today's society, many children experience the divorce of their parents. Describe some of the things a classroom teacher can do to help a child weather a divorce.

5. Explain some of the guidelines a teacher should keep in mind when interpreting IQ scores.

6. You have been asked to develop reading ability groups in your third grade class. Explain how you would go about developing these groups and the conditions you would try to meet.

7. As a teacher who wants to foster creativity in the classroom, describe five things you would do to enhance creativity in the class.

CHAPTER 5

LEARNING: BEHAVIORAL VIEWS

CHAPTER OVERVIEW

I. Learning: Toward a General Definition
   A. Behavioral and Cognitive Views
   B. Learning Is Not Always What It Seems

II. Contiguity: Learning Through Simple Associations

III. Classical Conditioning: Pairing Automatic Responses with New Stimuli
   A. Pavlov's Dilemma and Discovery
   B. Examples of Classical Conditions: Desirable and Undesirable
   C. Generalization, Discrimination, and Extinction
   D. Classroom Applications

IV. Operant Conditioning: Trying New Responses
   A. The Work of Thorndike and Skinner
   B. The ABCs of Operant Conditioning
   C. Controlling the Consequences
   D. Reinforcement Schedules
   E. Controlling the Antecedents

V. Learning by Observing Others
   A. Elements of Observational Learning
   B. Classroom Applications of Observational Learning

VI. Applying the Principles: Behavioral Technology
   A. Programmed Instruction
   B. Keller Plan

1. Define learning.
2. Name the major aspects of behavioral learning theories, cognitive learning theories, and social cognitive theory.
3. Define and give an example:
   a. contiguity
   b. stimulus
   c. response
4. The terms below are used in explaining classical conditioning. Define each term and provide an overall example using all the terms:
   a. unconditioned stimulus
   b. unconditioned response
   c. conditioned stimulus
   d. conditioned response
5. Diagram an example of classical conditioning.
6. Explain desirable and undesirable instances of classical conditioning
7. Define and provide an example of each of the following:
   a. generalization
   b. discrimination
   c. extinction
8. Define operant conditioning.
9. Know the names of Edward Thorndike and B.F. Skinner as men who played major roles in developing the knowledge of operant conditioning.
10. Explain the law of effect and provide an example.
11. Describe a Skinner box.
12. Define: behavior, operant, antecedent, consequence.
13. Explain the basic principle of operant conditioning.
14. Consequences may take four forms: define and provide an example for each:
   a. positive reinforcement
   b. negative reinforcement
   c. presentation punishment
   d. removal punishment
15. Define continuous and intermittent reinforcement.
16. State when continuous and intermittent reinforcement should be used.
17. Explain the four schedules of reinforcement and know the effects of each:
   a. fixed ratio
   b. variable ratio
   c. fixed interval
   d. variable ratio
18. Describe the controlling of antecedents.
19. Define and provide an example of cueing.
20. Define observational learning.
21. Know that Albert Bandura is responsible for much of what we know about modeling and observational learning.

22. Explain Bandura's classic study of aggression.
23. Explain the four elements of observational learning:
    a. attention
    b. retention
    c. production
    d. motivation or reinforcement
24. Describe the five effects of observational learning:
    a. teaching new behaviors
    b. encouraging already learned behaviors
    c. strengthening or weakening inhibitions
    d. directing attention
    e. arousing emotion
25. Explain the ripple effect.
26. Apply Skinner's four guidelines for using behavioral principles in the classroom.
27. Define programmed instruction, frames, linear programs and branching programs.
28. Describe the benefits of programmed instruction.
29. Explain the Keller Plan or PSI.

KEY TERMS

General Learning & Classical Conditioning Terms

a. conditioned response
b. unconditioned stimulus
c. conditioned stimulus
d. learning
e. classical conditioning
f. contiguity
g. neobehaviorist

h. extinction
i. behaviorism
j. generalization
k. cognitivism
l. discrimination
m. stimulus

1. When a person interacts with the environment and a change occurs, for better or worse, deliberate or unintentional, we can say that _____ has occurred.

2. When an emotional or physiological response is elicited by a previously neutral stimulus, learning by _____ has occurred.

3. Learning by _____ occurs when two events repeatedly happen together and thus become associated.

4. A person learns not to respond to a conditioned stimulus because it is not followed repeatedly by the unconditioned stimulus. This process is referred to as _____ .

5. A person has the same responses to stimuli which are similar to the stimulus originally producing the response. This process is referred to as _____ .

6. When a person responds differently to stimuli that are similar the process is called _____ .

7. Any occurrence or event in the environment that may or may not cause a response is called a _____ .

8. The view of learning that learning is an internal process that cannot be observed directly is called _____ .

9. The view of learning that focuses on observable behaviors and states that learning is a change in behavior is called _____ .

10. Both internal events and observable behaviors are included in the study of learning from a _____ view of learning.

11. When he first visited the dentist, Marg actually enjoyed the trip since he liked the people in the office. But after having several painful fillings, she began to feel tense as soon as the dentist turned on the light to examine his teeth. According to classical conditioning, the pain from the drilling is the _____ . The light is the _____ . The feeling of tension is the _____ .

Operant Conditioning Terms

a.	reinforcer	i.	antecedent cues
b.	variable ratio	j.	Skinner box
c.	behaviors	k.	continuous
d.	fixed interval	l.	contingent
e.	punisher	m.	law of effect
f.	removal	n.	negatively
g.	operants	o.	intermittent
h.	positive reienforcement	p.	operant conditioning

1. Anything that increases the probability of a behavior occurring again is called a _____ .

2. Any observable and therefore describable actions are called _____ .

3. Any consequence that decreases the probability of a behavior occurring again is called a _____ .

4. Deliberate actions are called _____ .

5. Clues that are reminders of the probable consequences of certain behaviors are _____ .

6. Mrs. Brown wants to strengthen a new behavior and therefore she reinforces the behavior each time it occurs. She is using a _____ schedule of reinforcement.

7. "Any behavior followed by a satisfying state will be repeated in a similar situation." This statement defines the _____ .

8. When one reinforces a behavior frequently, but not every time, one is using _____ reinforcement.

9. An aversive stimulus is present, but you do something to get rid of that aversive stimulus. In getting rid of the aversive stimulus, your behavior has been _____ reinforced.

10. When a reward is dependent upon the emitting of a behavior, we say that the reward is _____ on the behavior.

11. Learning in which voluntary behavior is strengthened or weakened by consequences or antecedents is called _____ .

12. A cagelike apparatus used by Skinner to study learning is the _____ .

13. Strengthening behavior by presenting a desired stimulus after the behavior is called _____ .

14. When a person looses something pleasant or desirable as a result of a behavior, he has received a _____ punishment.

15. A person is reinforced after every five minutes. He is on a _____ schedule of reinforcement.

16. A person is reinforced after the 5th correct response, then after the 3rd, then after the 10th, and then after the 2nd and so on. He is on a _____ schedule of reinforcement.

Observation and Behavioral Technology

a. obervational learning
b. reinforced
c. social learning theory
d. immediate
e. ripple effect

f. linear program
g. programmed instruction
h. branching program
i. PSI

1. A person observes another person perform actions and experience consequences, and then does the same thing. We can say that _____ has taken place.

2. Albert Bandura is the name most associated with ____ .

3. When student inhibitions are strengthened or weakened by observing the consequences that result after another student performs the inhibited behavior, ___ has occurred.

4. A set of self-teaching instructional materials featuring self-pacing and immediate feedback is called ____ .

5. An approach to individualizing instruction that does not require special materials or computers and is also known as the Keller Plan is called ____ .

6. A form of programmed instruction in which the student selects a multiple choice response and that response determines which frame appears next is called a ____ .

7. The form of programmed instruction in which the student moves through a fixed sequence of frames designed to keep errors at a minimum is called a ____ .

8. A major advantage to programmed instruction is that it provides ____ feedback to students.

9. Even if a student acquires a new behavior through modeling, he is unlikely to persist in that behavior if it is not ____ .

MULTIPLE CHOICE QUESTIONS

1. Thorndike, Watson, and Skinner limited their analyses of learning to "behavior." They reasoned that only behavior is (p. 165)

    a. internal.
    b. modifiable.
    c. observable.
    d. responsive.

2. Whenever two stimuli occur together repeatedly they will become associated. Later the presence of one of the stimuli will trigger the memory of the other. This is the principle of (p. 168)

    a. contiguity.
    b. observation.
    c. paired association.
    d. stimulus-response.

3. In classical conditioning, the conditioned stimulus and the unconditioned stimulus must be (p. 168)

   a. equal to each other.
   b. in opposition to each other.
   c. learned prior to the conditioning.
   d. paired with each other.

4. Sam had looked forward to beginning kindergarten, however, he had an unfortunate experience his first day of school. As he walked into his class, the fire alarm system malfunctioned, sounding a loud alarm that frightened him. Sam developed an extreme fear of going to school. Sam's fear of school is best explained by (p. 170)

   a. classical conditioning.
   b. cognitive learning.
   c. operant conditioning.
   d. social learning.

5. The theorist most often associated with operant conditioning is (p. 175)

   a. Pavlov.
   b. Skinner.
   c. Thorndike.
   d. Watson.

6. A third grade teacher becomes aware that her students respond very positively to smiles. In attempting to operantly condition hand raising, her best approach would be to (p. 176)

   a. frown or show no expression when students do not raise their hands.
   b. smile at each student after she raises her hand.
   c. smile at specific students to encourage hand raising.
   d. smile more often at the entire class throughout the day.

7. Mary trained her dog to sit down when she gives him the command "sit." She has noticed however, that her dog also sits when she says "git," or "bit" or "hit." This example illustrates the principle of (p. 171)

   a. generalized reinforcement.
   b. secondary response.
   c. stimulus generalization.
   d. vicarious reinforcement.

8. An individual's ability to respond differently in the presence of different stimuli is called (p. 171)

   a. generalized reinforcement.
   b. negative reinforcement.
   c. stimulus discrimination.
   d. stimulus generalization.

9. Many of the principles of behaviorism were studied using a cagelike laboratory apparatus commonly called a (p. 175)

   a. Behavioristic chamber.
   b. Reinforcement container.
   c. Skinner box.
   d. Test gridiron.

10. Demerits, spankings, and harsh words and frowns are examples of (p. 178)

    a. aversive reinforcement.
    b. negative reinforcement.
    c. presentation punishment.
    d. removal punishment.

11. Joe likes to shoot mechanical ducks at the Alabama State Fair. Even though Joe's accuracy does not improve as he shoots, he notices that he wins a prize after shooting continuously for 15 to 18 minutes. Joe was winning on which types of reinforcement schedule? (p. 179)

    a. fixed interval
    b. fixed ratio
    c. variable interval
    d. variable ratio

12. A migrant worker is paid $0.58 for every three boxes of oranges he packs. This worker is on which types of reinforcement schedule? (p. 179)

    a. fixed interval
    b. fixed ratio
    c. variable interval
    d. variable ratio

13. A slot machine is programmed to pay $100.00 to the first quarter inserted between the 2000th and 3000th quarter. This slot machine is reinforcing the player on a _____ schedule. (p. 179)

    a. fixed interval
    b. fixed ratio
    c. variable interval
    d. variable ratio

14. A father was able to motivate his son to learn the multiplication facts by telling him he would not have to participate in nightly drills once he had mastered the tables. This is an example of the use of _____ reinforcement. (p. 177)

    a. intrinsic
    b. negative
    c. positive
    d. secondary

15. Once the appropriate behavior has been established, the cue may be (p. 181)

    a. faded or made indirect.
    b. harmful to further performance.
    c. used to elicit new behavior.
    d. viewed negatively by the learner.

16. Ratio schedules are more effective than interval schedules in producing (p. 179)

    a. long-lasting results.
    b. speed of performance.
    c. trials of new behaviors.
    d. variations in the quality of response.

17. Harry, the most popular student in your class, made "funny faces" at you while you were writing on the blackboard. Because your back was turned, he did not get caught. The other students who saw this are likely to try this behavior in the future. This is an example of (p. 186)

    a. discrimination.
    b. generalization
    c positive reinforcement.
    d. ripple effect.

18. A client at the local mental hospital failed to clean his room properly. Points were subtracted from his reinforcement sheet. The loss of the points is an example of (p. 178)

   a. extinction.
   b. negative reinforcement.
   c. removal punishment.
   d. shaping.

19. Little Robbie sees his father pound on the coke machine when the machine does not give him the coke. Several days later when the machine that dispenses candies does not give Robbie his candy, Robbie hits the machine. We can say that Robbie is _____ his father's behavior. (p. 183)

   a. conditioning
   b. imitating
   c. reinforcing
   d. stimulating

20. John watches Betty cheat on a test and get a grade of "A." The next time John takes a test, he decided to cheat to also earn an "A." We can say that cheating was _____ reinforced. (p. 186)

   a. negatively
   b. positively
   c. secondarily
   d. vicariously

21. Claire observes that her best friend, Betty, is reprimanded for talking without raising her hand. Claire decides that she will not talk unless she has raised her hand and the teacher calls on her. We can say that the observation has _____ Claire's inhibition to talk out of turn. (p. 186)

   a. punished
   b. strengthened
   c. weakened
   d. stopped

22. Programmed instruction is characteristically designed for (p. 188)

   a. mathematical topics.
   b. self-teaching.
   c. use with mechanical teaching aids.
   d. younger children.

23. A distinctive feature of linear programs is that students must (p. 189)

    a. create their own answers.
    b. choose among several answers given.
    c. finish the program to get the right answers.
    d. repeat frames they answered incorrectly.

24. In programmed instruction, a small step containing a bit of information and at least one question is a (p. 189)

    a. cue.
    b. frame.
    c. linear step.
    d. programmed text.

25. A major attribute of the Keller Plan is (p. 191)

    a. failure to master one unit before moving on to the next.
    b. frequent testing.
    c. low levels of mastery.
    d. totally independent activities.

26. Programmed instruction that uses multiple-choice programming and sends students to various frames depending upon their response is called a ____ program. (p. 189)

    a. branching
    b. linear
    c. mastery
    d. processing

DISCUSSION AND APPLICATION QUESTIONS

1. Fill in the diagrams of classical conditioning and operant conditioning with behaviors or feelings from the following situations. For each, note how the two types of conditioning are related.

SITUATION: A child was climbing into the seat of a grocery basket and accidentally fell and scratched her leg. She started crying because she was scared and hurt. Her mother hugged her and gave her a box of cookies so she would stop crying.

CLASSICAL CONDITIONING MODEL

_____   *leads to*   _____
unconditioned stimulus   unconditioned response

61

_____ *leads to* _____
(potential) conditioned stimulus   conditioned response

OPERANT CONDITIONING MODEL

_____ *leads to* _____ *leads to* _____antecedent
    behavior   consequence

SITUATION: Henry's Dad often plays "tickle" with Henry. At first, Dad would actually tickle Henry, but now all he has to do is wiggle his fingers around Henry's body and Henry bursts into peals of giggles and laughter. At the end of the game, Henry's Dad gives Henry a big hug and a kiss.

CLASSICAL CONDITIONING MODEL

_____ *leads to* _____
unconditioned stimulus   unconditioned response

_____ *leads to* _____
(potential) conditioned stimulus   conditioned response

OPERANT CONDITIONING MODEL

_____ *leads to* _____ *leads to* _____antecedent
    behavior   consequence

2. A student in your class frequently complains of an upset stomach shortly after the school day begins. Using the classical conditioning model, how would you explain this situation and how would you deal with it?

3. What cues or prompts would you give to elicit the following behaviors?
    a. The class looks at you in order to hear you give directions.
    b. The class opens their books to the assigned page when the bell rings.
    c. The class gives you their full attention when you are making an important point in the lesson.
    d. A student remembers to walk from his desk to the door when class is over.

4. In your English class the students' reading levels range from third grade to tenth grade. How can you use the principles of programmed instruction to cope with this problem?

5. If you were going to write a programmed instructional activity for the subject matter you teach, what kind of program would you use, branching or linear, and why?

6. Describe classroom situations in which you would use each of the following techniques:

   a. positive reinforcement
   b. negative reinforcement
   c. presentation punishment
   d. removal punishment
   e. extinction

CHAPTER 6

APPLICATIONS OF BEHAVIORAL APPROACHES

CHAPTER OVERVIEW

I. Focusing on Positive Behavior
  A. Reinforcing with Teacher Attention
  B. Alternatives to Behavior Problems
  C. Selecting the Best Reinforcers

II. Developing New Behaviors
  A. Cueing and Prompting
  B. Modeling
  C. Shaping

III. Coping with Undesirable Behavior
  A. Negative Reinforcement
  B. Satiation
  C. Punishment

IV. Special Programs for Classroom Management
  A. Group Consequences
  B. Token Reinforcement Programs
  C. Contingency Contract Programs

V. Self-Management
  A. Approaches to Self-Management
  B. Teaching Self-Management

VI. Problems and Issues
  A. Ethical Issues
  B. Criticisms of Behavioral Methods

CHAPTER OBJECTIVES

1. Describe how teachers use and misuse attention and praise to reinforce student behavior.
2. Explain five guidelines for using praise appropriately.
3. Define positive practice.
4. Explain the purpose of positive practice and describe how it may be used effectively.
5. Describe two methods of selecting effective reinforcers.
6. Explain the use of the Premack principle and provide an example.
7. Explain three guidelines for stressing the positive in the classroom.
8. Define and provide examples of the use of cueing.
9. Define and provide examples of the use of modeling.
10. Define and provide examples of the use of shaping.
11. List the four methods of using shaping that were described by Krumboltz and Krumboltz (1972).
12. Explain three guidelines for developing new behaviors.
13. Describe and provide examples of the use of negative reinforcement.
14. Describe and provide examples of the use of satiation.
15. Three types of punishment have proved useful: reprimands, response cost and isolation. Explain the use of each and provide examples.
16. Discuss some of the cautions one should keep in mind when using punishment.
17. Explain four guidelines for the use of punishment.
18. Describe the use of group consequences and some of the cautions one should keep in mind.
19. Define token reinforcement program.
20. Identify procedures used in token reinforcement programs.
21. Explain five guidelines for the use of token reinforcement programs.
22. Define contingency contract program.
23. Identify procedures used in contingency contract programs.
24. Write a contingency contract.
25. Define self-management.
26. List the four aspects of self-management.
27. Describe some programs that have taught self-management.
28. List four guidelines for the use of self-management programs.
29. Discuss the ethical issues related to the use of behavior management strategies.
30. Discuss criticisms of behavioral methods.

KEY TERMS

Fill in the blanks in the following sentences with the letters preceeding the concepts listed below.

a. Premack principle
b. reprimands
c. self-management
d. satiation
e. contingency contact
f. shaping
g. punishment
h. cue

i. response cost
j. time-out
k. positive practice
l. teacher attention
m. prompt
n. ignore
o. negative reinforcement
p. token economy

1. When one reinforces a low-frequency behavior with a high frequency behavior, but the less preferred behavior must occur first, one is using the _____.

2. Loud, public corrections of student misbehavior are much less effective than soft, private _____ .

3. When a person sets his own goals, evaluates his performance, and provides his own reinforcement, ___ has occurred.

4. The procedure that requires that a student continue an undesirable behavior until he tires of doing it is called _____ .

5. A written agreement between a student and a teacher specifying what the student must do to earn a particular reward is a _____ .

6. Rewarding each step leading toward the final behavior is called _____.

7. The strategy that is used to supppress behavior and that also tends to be accompanied by negative side effects is _____ .

8. A stimulus that lets an individual know that a behavior or set of behaviors will be reinforced is a _____ .

9. Losing a privilege, money, tokens, or a desirable object because of inappropriate behavior is called _____ .

10. The behavioral technique which assumes the classroom is a desirable place to be and therefore, removes misbehaving children from the classroom for a short period of time is called _____ .

11. When a class made too much noise going from the room to the cafeteria, the teacher had them go back to the room and start again. This is called _____ .

12. If students are not responding to a cue, a teacher can make the cue more effective by following it with a _____.

13. To minimize disruptive behavior, it is necessary for a teacher to both reward appropriate behaviors and _____ inappropriate behaviors.

14. When a behavior ends an unpleasant situation or removes an unpleasant stimulus, the likelihood of the behavior occuring again increases. This is the principle of _____ .

15. A reinforcement system that uses chips or points which at the end of a period of time may be exchanged for tangible objects or special activities is termed _____ .

MULTIPLE CHOICE QUESTIONS

1. Mrs. Brown has always used a loud, stern voice to stop undesirable behavior in her first graders. But the "stern voice" only seems to make Robbie talk out of turn more frequently. For Robbie, the "stern voice" is apparently a (p. 214)

   a. cue.
   b. model.
   c. prompt.
   d. reinforcer.

2. Studies of teachers' verbal behavior show that teachers voice more (p. 200)

   a. approval than reinforcement.
   b disapproval than approval.
   c. encouragement than praise.
   d. praise than reprimands.

3. Discouraging a negative behavior without encouraging a positive alternative runs the risk that students will (p. 210)

   a. not respond to the discouragement and ignore the teacher.
   b. react emotionally and poorly to classroom situations.
   c. replace the negative behavior with another unwanted one.
   d. think they are being unfairly criticized and withdraw.

4. Correcting mistakes quickly and then practicing the correct response is called (p. 202)

   a. attention to alternatives.
   b. positive practice.
   c. Premack principle.
   d. repetition reinforcement.

5. Mr. Brinkley told his class that anyone who made an A on five out of six weekly tests would be excused from the final exam. He is using _____ reinforcement. (p. 205)

   a. negative
   b. positive
   c. secondary
   d. vicarious

6. High frequency behavior can be an effective reinforcer for low frequency behavior. This statement describes the (p. 203)

   a. frequency reinforcer method.
   b. Premack principle.
   c. prompting procedure.
   d. satiation strategy.

7. In developing new behaviors, cueing and modeling are usually attempted before shaping because shaping (p. 207)

   a. does not work with all students.
   b. has only temporary effects.
   c. is much less precise and effective.
   d. requires much more time.

8. Cueing is appropriate for bringing about only those behaviors that students (p. 204)

   a. are already capable of performing.
   b. find pleasant or intrinsically rewarding.
   c. frequently perform on their own.
   d. realize consist of simple responses.

9. Ms. Alexander, one of the remedial mathematics teachers, realizes her students have all had a history of bad experiences with math and tries hard to reward every improvement. She is following a process called (p. 207)

   a. cueing.
   b. modeling.
   c. saturating.
   d. shaping.

10. In using negative reinforcement, Krumboltz and Krumboltz (1972) suggest that it is important to (p. 210)

a. be stern and firm.
b. be consistent and thorough.
c. keep control of the aversive stimulus.
d. maintain the unpleasantness a sufficient length of time.

11. Punishment is not very effective in ____ behaviors. (p. 211)

a. controlling.
b. developing.
c. modifying.
d. suppressing.

12. Johnny enjoys making faces at other children to make them laugh. After inviting him to the front of the class to make faces for a full 15 minutes, the teacher notes that Johnny no longer makes faces. This illustrates (p. 210)

a. modeling.
b. punishment.
c. response cost.
d. satiation.

13. The behavioral term for social isolation is (p. 212)

a. response cost.
b. solitary confinement.
c. removal punishment.
d. time out.

14. Which of the following is a potential side effect of punishment? (p. 213)

a. attendance rates improve.
b. higher levels of aggression.
c. increased cheating.
d. neutral feelings toward school.

15. In which of the following situations is punishment necessary? (p. 211)

a. One student's misbehavior is being initiated by others in the class.
b. Positive behaviors occur too seldom for effective reinforcement.
c. Students know the correct behavior but frequently act otherwise.
d. Students seem unable to behave correctly in the class.

16. Which of the following is a fringe benefit of a token reinforcement system? (p. 216)

    a. students are given little sense of control.
    b. students learn that rewards must be earned.
    c. the system itself takes a substantial amount of time.
    d. the system is easily varied to fit specific situations.

17. Students gain experience in negotiation and in setting reasonable goals when they participate in (p. 216)

    a. group responsibility systems.
    b. self-management systems.
    c. setting up contingency contracts.
    d. token reinforcement systems.

18. When an individual sets his own goals and reinforces himself for attaining these goals, the individual is practicing (p. 221)

    a. cueing.
    b. satiation.
    c. self-management.
    d. vicarious conditioning.

19. Bobby nags his teacher, Mrs. Daily, in an attempt to coax her into allowing him to deliver messages to the principal. Mrs. Daily gives in each time to escape Bobby's nagging. Mrs. Daily is being (p. 209)

    a. negatively reinforced.
    b. positively reinforced.
    c. punished.
    d. shaped.

20. Johnny has developed a habit of tapping his pencil on the desk top. It is distracting to the entire class. The moment Johnny ceases tapping, however brief the silence the teacher, praises Johnny for not being disruptive and allowing a moment of silence. The teacher is utilizing (p. 200)

    a. modeling.
    b. punishment.
    c. reasoning.
    d. reinforcement.

21. Mark is easily upset in class and frequently cries, drops his books, and is generally disruptive. The school psychologist advises the teacher to direct Mark to go to a private area of the classroom and remain there for 10 minutes each time he becomes upset. The school psychologist has recommended the technique of (p. 212)

    a. punishment.
    b. response cost.
    c. satiation.
    d. social isolation.

22. Mr. Jones is teaching Susan to play tennis. He reinforces each successive approximation of her correctly holding the racket. He is employing the technique of (p. 207)

    a. negative reinforcement.
    b. repetition.
    c. shaping.
    d. stimulus generalization.

23. Matthew misbehaved in class and the teacher told him that he would not be allowed to go to recess. "Not going to recess" is an example of the employment of (p. 212)

    a. negative reinforcement.
    b. presentation punishment
    c. response cost.
    d. time-out.

24. Externally imposed reward systems seem particularly appropriate for students who (p. 199)

    a. are self-motivated.
    b. lack interest in the subject.
    c. like the topic being discussed.
    d. learn rapidly and easily.

25. Research has shown that students can learn to increase their attention spans if they are given (p. 223)

    a. adequate reinforcement.
    b. external evaluation.
    c. good models to observe.
    d. specific strategies to employ.

26. Student self-recording and self-evaluation in a reinforcement program should be accompanied by (p. 223)

    a. cross-checks with other students.
    b. frequent examinations.
    c. intermittent checking by the teacher.
    d. large changes in behavior.

27. After being knocked down by a large dog, your son became very fearful of all dogs. To cope with this problem, you reward him for saying "dog," then for looking at pictures of dogs, then for walking to within 10 feet of a dog, then for watching while you pet a dog, etc. This illustrates the procedure called (p. 207)

    a. extinction
    b. negative reinforcement.
    c. satiation.
    d. shaping.

APPLICATION AND DISCUSSION QUESTIONS

1. Listed below are five scenarios. For each, determine an appropriate behavioral procedure or procedures to use to help solve the problem. In addition, indicate what you would anticipate happening when you use the strategy.

SCENARIO #1

Jim, a fourth grader, would much rather carve desks than do his assignments. His carvings are not random but involve a definite design--a complete circle with tiny circles surrounding it. His carving tools consist of pens, pencils, rulers, and compasses. Year after year, Jim produces a new masterpiece. The school can no longer afford to allow Jim to carve desks.

Design a strategy to eliminate the carving behavior. Explain what you anticipate happening with the strategy.

SCENARIO #2

Mr. Horatio Stevens is a second grade teacher at Green Elementary School. He has only been teaching for a few weeks and is having problems. He has a class of 25 overeager children who consistently blurt and yell out their answers instead of waiting and raising their hands. He finds the blurting out disruptive and it is difficult to respond to each student. He is pleased with their eagerness but needs a calmer setting.

Design a strategy to help Mr. Stevens. Explain what you anticipate happening with the strategy.

SCENARIO #3

Polly is very adept at mimicking her teacher's idiosyncrasies, for example, hand gestures and facial expression, and this behavior is being reinforced by Ms. Garcia's tirades and the applause reaction of classmates. The more Ms. Garcia has lectured Polly about her behavior, the greater the frequency and exaggeration of the mimicking behavior.

Design a strategy to aid this situation. Explain what you anticipate happening with the strategy.

SCENARIO #4

Jim, a 13-year-old boy, was transferred from Berry School to Tampa County School. His passivity and lack of assertiveness have pervaded all aspects of his classroom adjustment, and are especially noticable in gym class. He seems interested in but afraid of athletic activities, as evidenced by his hovering on the fringe of the action. The teacher's attempts to involve him directly have been met with stubborn resistance by Jim.

Design a strategy to help Jim. Explain what you think will happen.

SCENARIO #5

Toni flusters and irritates her teacher by playing the role of the "dumb, slow student." Toni constantly asks questions to which the answers are evident. For example, after the teacher had given the pages of an assignment out loud, and written them on the board, Toni asked what pages the assignment was on.

She also manipulated her teacher to give her a negative, flustered response by pretending not to be able to do an assignment in which she has been previously successful. This behavior was exemplified by her reading assignment. Toni was called upon to read some words, she read them very well, and the teacher praised her reading. The other students did not do nearly as well so for the next day's assignment the class was to study the words and to be able to read them correctly. The next day, when Toni was called to read the same words, she faltered and pretended that she could not read the words. The teacher knowing that she knew the words, became irritated with her and reassigned them as homework.

Design a strategy to help this situation. Explain what you think will happen.

2. Laura never completes assignments for her social studies class. Design a contingency contract between Laura and her teacher which addresses completion of assignments.

3. Read the following situation. Identify in the situation the following techniques: positive reinforcement, satiation, punishment, negative reinforcement, and modeling.

Situation: Several times a week, attendants dragged Charlie down the hall to one of his classes as the boy screamed and buckled his knees. On several of these occasions, the boy threw himself on the floor in front of a classroom door. A crowd of staff members inevitably gathered around him. The group usually watched and commented as the boy sat or lay on the floor, kicking and screaming. Some members of the group hypothesized that such behavior seemed to appear after the boy was teased or frustrated.

Observing one such situation that occurred before her class, the teacher asked the attendant to put the boy in the classroom at his desk and leave the room. Then she closed the door. The boy sat at his desk, kicking and screaming; the teacher proceeded to her desk and worked there, ignoring Charlie. After 2 or 3 minutes, the boy, crying softly, looked up at the teacher. Then she announced that she would be ready to work with him as soon as he indicated that he was ready to work. He continued to cry and scream with diminishing loudness for the next 4 or 5 minutes. Finally, he lifted his head and stated that he was ready. Immediately, the teacher looked up at him, smiled, went to his desk, and said, "Good. Now let's get to work." The boy worked quietly and cooperatively with the teacher for the remainder of the class period.

Situation taken from Zimmerman, E., and Zimmerman, J. "The Alteration of Behavior in a Special Classroom Situation." In K.D. O'Leary and S.G. O'Leary, Classroom Management. Elmsford, N.Y.: Pergamon Press, Inc., 1972.

Reprinted from Journal of the Experimental Analysis of Behavior, 1962, 5 (1), pp. 59-60.

CHAPTER 7

LEARNING: COGNITIVE VIEWS

CHAPTER OVERVIEW

I. Elements of the Cognitive Perspective

II. The Information Processing Model of Learning
    A. Sensory Register
    B. Influence of Perception
    C. Role of Attention
    D. Short-Term Memory
    E. Long-Term Memory
    F. Schemata

III. Remembering and Forgetting
    A. Why Do People Forget?
    B. How Do People Remember?
    C. Stategies for Helping Students Remember

IV. Learning About Learning: Metacognitive Abilities
    A. Strategy Instruction
    B. Metacognition and Reading

CHAPTER OBJECTIVES

1. Describe learning and the function of internal and external events according to the cognitive viewpoint
2. Diagram the information processing model.

3. Define receptors and sensory register.
4. Explain how the sensory register works.
5. Define perception.
6. List two influences on perception and identify the principles of Gestalt, Pragnanz, and figure ground.
7. Explain feature analysis, bottom-up processing and top-down processing.
8. Describe the role of attention in perception in learning.
9. List some suggestions that might aid teachers in focusing attention.
10. Define short term memory and explain its characteristics.
11. Explain the process of rehearsal.
12. Define chunking.
13. Define long term memory and explain its characteristics.
14. Describe semantic and episodic memory.
15. Explain a propositional network.
16. Define schema and explain why it is the "key unit of the comprehension process."
17. List six guidelines for applying the ideas of information processing theorists.
18. Explain why people forget information in short-term and long-term memory.
19. Define retroactive interference and proactive interference.
20. Explain the role of reconstruction in memory.
21. Explain what happens in the "tip-of-the-tongue phenomenon."
22. Define elaboration.
23. Three elements of processing improve retrieval: elaboration, organization, and context. Explain these elements.
24. Describe strategies for helping students remember information learned by rote memorization.
25. Describe strategies for helping students remember meaningful material: mnemonics, peg-type mnemonics, loci method, peg-type method, chain method, keyword method.
26. Identify some metacognitive abilities and discuss their relationship to a student's age and ability level.
27. Explain some possible comprehension failures and possible remedies.

KEY TERMS

Fill in the blanks in the following sentences with the letters preceding the concepts listed below.

a. interference
b. top-down processing
c. elaboration
d. long-term memory
e. propositional network
f. schemata
g. meaningful
h. perception

t. linking system
u. metacognition
v. feature analysis
w. rehearsed
x. receptors
y. Gestalt
z. short-term memory
aa. massed practice

i. Pragnanz
j. mnemonics
k. figure-ground
l. retroactive
m. bottom-up processing
n. chunking
o. decoding
p. sensory register
q. pegword
r. distributed practice
s. levels of processing theory

bb. story grammar
cc. tip-of-the-tongue phenomenon
dd. serial-position effect
ee. relearning
ff. episodic memory
gg. loci method
hh. key word method
ii. semantic memory
jj. proactive interference

1. One of the most critical aspects of learning is the transformation of information so it can become a part of _____ .

2. An interconnected set of concepts and relationships is called _____ .

3. If a person can make many associations with information, that information is considered to be _____ .

4. A basic principle of Gestalt theory in which people reorganize stimuli so that they are more simple and complete is called _____ .

5. A basic principle of Gestalt theory in which people focus on a basic figure with other stimuli becoming less important is called _____ .

6. The art of memory or connecting new information with previously existing knowledge is the purpose of _____ .

7. The process by which we take in sights, sounds, smells, and give meaning to them is called _____ .

8. Patterns or guides used to understand an event are _____ .

9. One factor needed to transfer information from short-term to long-term memory, a factor that involves adding meaning to new information is _____ .

10. One type of perception that is based on context is called _____ , in which patterns are recognized through the context of the situation.

11. Information is lost from short-term memory because of _____ from new information.

12. Translating the printed word into speech is called _____ .

13. Patterns of neural activitiy produced when stimuli reach the receptors are registered by the _____ for a brief period of time.

14. Information that is completely analyzed, associated, and organized will be remembered over long periods of time is the major idea of the _____ .

15. Knowledge about your own cognitive processes and products is referred to as _____ .

16. Information in short-term memory only can remain about 20 seconds unless it is _____ , or it is repeated until it is no longer needed.

17. One explanation for how we recognize patterns and give meaning to sensory events is called _____ ,which suggests we try to recognize a new stimulus by searching for its basic elements.

18. Using visual images to tie each item on a list to the next item is called a _____ .

19. Studying for short intervals over a long period of time is called _____.

20. Combining small bits of information into fewer larger bits which can help short term memory retain more information is called _____ .

21. Analyzing basic elements and combining them into meaningful patterns is called _____ .

22. The interference of new information with the memory of old information it is called _____ interference.

23. The interference of old information with the memory of new information it is called _____ interference.

24. Parts of the human body that receive sensory information are called _____ .

25. A German word which means pattern or whole is _____ .

26. The part of long-term memory that holds information associated with particular times and places is known as _____ .

27. The part of long-term memory that holds general knowledge unconnected to time or place is called _____ .

28. The sense of being about to recall something or "near retrieval" is _____ .

29. Breaking a list of rote items into shorter bits is called _____ .

30. Remembering the beginning and end but not the middle of the list is called the _____ .

31. Practice for a single extended time is _____ .

32. Filling in the gaps and encoding more completely material that is not totally familiar is _____ .

33. A mnemonic method which associates items with specific places is called _____ .

34. A mnemonic method which associates items with cue words is _____ .

35. A mnemonic method in which one associates new words or concepts with similiar sounding cue words is _____ .

36. Typical structures or organizations for stories are called _____ .

37. The name for your working memory that holds a limited amount of information briefly is _____ .

MULTIPLE CHOICE QUESTIONS

1. Cognitive views of learning differ from behavioral views in that the emphasis is placed on (p. 235)

   a. internal structure and thinking.
   b. learning rather than simply rewards.
   c. long-term rather than short-term retention.
   d. the environmental consequences of behavior.

2. Cognitive theorists assert that learning is the result of (p. 234)

   a. an inflow of new information from stimuli.
   b. attempts to make sense of the world.
   c. practice of rewarded behavior.
   d. stored associations between stimulus and response.

3. A parent immediately picks out his child's face in the summer camp picture but doesn't notice the face of his brother's child. This is an example of the Gestalt principle of (p. 239)

   a. closure.
   b. figure ground.
   c. Pragnanz.
   d. similarity.

4. Top-down processing is distinguished by its reliance on a (an) (p. 240)

   a. assembly of elements into a meaningful pattern.
   b. downward scanning of the eyes.
   c. search for familiar features or elements.
   d. understanding of the context of a situation.

5. A proposition is the smallest unit of information that can be (p. 246)

    a. associated with a specific meaning.
    b. held in the memory.
    c. judged true or false.
    d. remembered.

6. An interconnected set of concepts and relationships is called (p. 245)

    a. dual code theory of memory.
    b. propositional network.
    c. short-term memory.
    d. metacognition.

7. We organize our experience into meaningful systems by reference to patterns or structures called (p. 247)

    a. features.
    b. networks.
    c. propositions.
    d. schemata.

8. Neural activity generated when stimuli reach any of the receptors is briefly recorded in (p. 236)

    a. sensory input channels.
    b. sensory register.
    c. short term memory
    d. temporary storage.

9. Which of the following is a **true** statement regarding long-term memory? (p. 244)

    a. It has a limited capacity.
    b. Information enters it relatively quickly.
    c. Information in it is transient.
    d. Retrieval from it depends on organization.

10. Research has shown that the capacity of the short-term memory is limited to about _____ chunks. (p. 243)

    a. 2 - 4
    b. 5 - 9
    c. 11 - 12
    d. 13 - 15

11. Some cognitive researchers suggest that information is drawn out of long-term memory by (p. 251)

    a. elaboration.
    b. interface.
    c. reconstruction.
    d. rehearsal.

12. Samantha cannot remember the Spanish words she learned three days ago. She remembers only those she learned last night. The inability to remember the words she learned three days ago is probably due to _____ from learning the new words last night. (p. 250)

    a. proactive interference.
    b. reconstruction.
    c. retroactive interference.
    d. time decay.

13. Using unexpected events, changing the environment, moving and gesturing, and arousing curiosity with questions are all ways to (p. 241)

    a. focus attention.
    b. improve recall.
    c. integrate old and new material.
    d. elaborate previously learned information.

14. Before giving a lesson on the fruit "oranges," the teacher reviews related material in the previous lesson on "citrus fruits." Her purpose is probably to help students (p. 248)

    a. bring prior learning into their working memories.
    b. clarify the purpose of the lesson.
    c. distinguish new material from old.
    d. focus their attention before going into new material.

15. Dr. Brown needed to pick up a pen, an eraser, pencils, scissors, and ink from the office supply store. To aid his memory he thought of the word PEPSI. This is an example of using (p. 256)

    a. acronyms.
    b. chunking.
    c. imagery.
    d. loci.

16. Mnemonics are most useful when the materials to be memorized are (p. 254)

    a. extensive and not meaningful.
    b. limited and meaningful.
    c. linked to a network.
    d. difficult to rehearse.

17. Dr. Beach used to be a typical "absent-minded professor." However he found he could remember the things his wife asked him to pick up at the grocery store by imagining the items he needed placed on his desk, bookshelf, and file cabinet. His mnemonic device is called (p.256)

    a. chunking.
    b. keyword method
    c. linking system.
    d. loci method.

18. With the the serial-position effect, when a list of similar items is memorized the _____ are more easily remembered. (p. 254)

    a. beginning items
    b. ending items
    c. first and last items
    d. items in the middle

19. Breaking a list into segments to be memorized is called (p. 254)

    a. distributed practice.
    b. fragmented studying.
    c. part learning.
    d. reconstruction.

20. The tip-of-the-tongue phenomenom is probably due to partial _____ of information. (p. 251)

    a. processing
    b. reconstruction
    c. perception
    d. abstraction

APPLICATION AND DISCUSSION QUESTIONS

1. For the following situations, name the encoding process used in each:

    a. In order to help remember the symbol for the number "eight," the teacher makes a snowman out of the figure 8 while telling a story about the snowman with 8 buttons who lives for 8 days.

    b. To remember that Bismarck is the capital of North Dakota, a student imagines making N.D. on a biscuit.

    c. To help students remember how to spell "separate," the teacher says, "There is *a rat* in separate."

    d. A student lists the products of Alabama so that the first letters spell CAPS for (cotton, apples, paper products, and soybeans),

    e. Columbus sailed the ocean blue in fourteen hundred and ninety-two.

    f. To remember a grocery list, Mrs. Tarent imagines cheese on her TV, limes on the sofa, milk on the table, beans in the wicker basket and tomatoes on the stove.

    g. The teacher uses a time-line to show the major events before, during and after the Vietnam War.

    h. Students are asked to compare their present home chores with chores they might have if they lived during the Civil War times.

2. The class assignment is to learn the steps that Jimmy Carter took to end the hostage crisis. How can you present this information so that students can remember it more easily?

3. Montessori taught the sounds of letters through the use of sandpaper letters. Children traced the letters with their fingertips while saying the sound. Why is this a good approach to use?

4. A junior high teacher occasionally brings out a puppet and carries on a dialogue about an important point in a lesson. What purpose does the puppet serve and why is it effective? Can you think of other ways to achieve this purpose?

CHAPTER 8

THE COGNITIVE PERSPECTIVE AND TEACHING PRACTICE

CHAPTER OVERVIEW

I. Learning Outcomes: Gagne'

II. Learning Through Discovery: Bruner
   A. Discovery in Action

III. Reception Learning: Ausubel
   A. Advance Organizers
   B. Making the Most of Expository Organizers

IV. Teaching and Learning About Concepts
   A. How We Understand Our World
   B. Views of Concept Learning
   C. Strategies for Teaching

V. Problem Solving
   A. Understanding and Representing the Problem
   B. Selecting the Approach
   C. Executing the Plan
   D. Evaluating the Results
   E. Effective Problem Solving; What Do the Experts Do?

VI. Study Skills
   A. PQR4
   B. Underlining and Note Taking

VII. Teaching for Transfer
   A. Positive and Negative Transfer
   B. Specific and General Transfer

C. Teaching for Positive Transfer: Principles

VIII. Teaching Thinking
    A. Improving Thinking

██

CHAPTER OBJECTIVES

1. Define Gagne's five categories of learning outcomes: attitudes, motor skills, verbal information, intellectual skills and cognitive strategies.
2. According to Bruner, explain the following terms:
   a. structure
   b. inductive reasoning
   c. coding system
   d. eg-rule method
   e. intuitive thinking
   f. discovery learning
   g. guided discovery
3. Discuss four guidelines that should be followed when applying Bruner's ideas to the classroom.
4. According to Ausubel, explain the following terms:
   a. meaningful verbal learning
   b. expository teaching
   c. subsumer
   d. rule-eg method
5. Define advance organizer and explain the function of an advance organizer.
6. State the characteristics and appropriate applications of comparative organizers and expository organizers.
7. Describe the characteristics of expository teaching and give examples of its application.
8. Discuss four guidelines that should be followed when applying Ausubel's ideas to the classroom.
9. Define the term "concept" and explain how concepts help us understand our world.
10. Explain the two views of concept learning: defining attributes and prototypes.
11. Discuss the four components of a lesson in teaching concepts.
12. Explain overgeneralization and undergeneralization as they relate to the teaching and learning of concepts.
13. Define the term "problem solving."
14. Describe the steps involved in problem solving.
15. Name the factors that interfere with problem solving and the factors that facilitate problem solving.

16. Define the following problem solving-related terms:
   a. functional fixedness
   b. response set
   c. insight
   d. algorithm
   e. heuristic
   f. means-end analysis
17. Differentiate declarative and procedural knowledge and describe their relationship to expert problem-solving.
18. Describe the differences between novice and expert problem solvers.
19. Discuss five guidelines which may be followed in encouraging problem solving in the classroom.
20. Explain the study skill method of PQ4R.
21. List suggestions for marking textbooks.
22. Discuss six guidelines which may be followed in using appropriate study skills and learning strategies.
23. Define the following "transfer" terms and provide an example of each:
   a. positive transfer
   b. negative transfer
   c. general transfer
   d. specific transfer
24. Give the principles involved in teaching for positive transfer.
25. Discuss the concept of "overlearning."
26. Discuss the teaching of critical thinking skills.

KEY TERMS

Fill in the blanks in the following sentences with the letters preceding the concepts listed below.

a. concepts
b. algorithm
c. intuitive thinking
d. heuristic
e. subsumer
f. means-end analysis
g. eg-rule method
h. insight
i. rule-eg method
j. linguistic comprehension
k. attitudes
l. problem solving
m. procedural
n. overgeneralization
o. declarative

r. verbal information
s. discovery learning
t. advance organizer
u. prototype
v. activate
w. overlearning
x. meaningful verbal learning
y. functional fixedness
z. guided discovery
aa. expository teaching
bb. inductive reasoning
cc. transfer
dd. defining attribute
ee. concepts
ff. negative

p. undergeneralization
q. response set

gg. coding system
hh. discrimination
ii. cognitive strategies
jj. structure

1.   Abstractions that allow us to group events or ideas into meaningful units based on similarities are called _____ .

2.   Teachers should encourage students to make their guesses based on incomplete information and then check out their guesses more systematically when they wish students to develop _____ .

3.   According to Bruner, the fundamental framework of ideas is _____ .

4.   Teaching concepts in which examples are presented first and students try to derive the general concept is called the _____ .

5.   Teaching concepts in which a general definition is stated before examples are given is called the _____ .

6.   According to Gagne', from positive and negative experiences and modeling we probably learn _____ .

7.   Cognitive strategies for problem solving are _____ knowledge.

8.   Basic information is _____ knowledge.

9.   A step by step procedure for solving a problem which if implemented correctly, is guaranteed to accomplish its intention is called a(an) _____ .

10. To link new material with what the student already knows and help him make sense of the upcoming lesson, Ausubel suggests beginning a lesson with a(an) _____ .

11. When practice no longer leads to improvement, _____ has occurred.

12. The inability to use things in new ways is termed _____ .

13. The predisposition to respond to a problem in a certain way is termed _____ .

14. The belief that students learn best when they find out for themselves fundamental ideas and relationships is a cornerstone of _____ .

15. The best representative of a category is termed a/an _____ .

16. When a teacher presents concepts, principles, and ideas to students in an organized and meaningful way, she is using _____ .

17. When something previously learned facilitates or interferes with current learning, we say that _____ has occurred.

18. We are able to organize much information into categories through the use of _____ .

19. The arrangement of categories from most general to most specific comprises a(an) _____ .

20. The use of acronyms to remember a list of words and the use of analogies in problem solving are examples of _____ .

21. Another name for the facts, names, and definitions included in a lesson is _____ .

22. The intellectual skill that requires a student to distinguish among objects of symbols is called _____ .

23. If the ability to drive a manual shift car interferes with learning to drive an automatic drive car, this is called _____ transfer.

24. The quality, "cannot move on its own," is a _____ for the concept, "non-living."

25. Formulating general principles based on knowledge of examples and details is known as _____ .

26. An adaptation of discovery learning in which the teacher provides some direction is called _____ .

27. Verbal information, ideas and relationships among ideas are all encompassed under the term _____ .

28. Comparative organizers _____ or, bring from long term memory into working memory, already existing schemata.

29. Exclusion of some true memory from a category and thus limiting a concept is called _____ .

30. The inclusion of nonmembers of a catetory and thus overextending a concept is known as _____ .

31. Formulating new answers or going beyond the simple application of previously learned rules to create a solution is called _____ .

32. When a child understands the meaning of sentences, we say he has _____ .

33. The sudden realization of a solution is called _____ .

34. In _____ the problem is divided into a number of subproblems and then a means of solving each is figured out.

35. A general strategy used in attempting to solve problems and has a reasonable chance of succeeding is termed a _____ .

36. The general concept at the top of a coding system is the _____ .

MULTIPLE CHOICE QUESTIONS

1. Attitudes are probably learned through positive and negative experiences and (p. 272)

    a. discussion.
    b. intuitive recognition.
    c. modeling.
    d. reasoning.

2. The two components of motor skills are (p. 272)

    a. coordination and action.
    b. practice and feedback.
    c. purpose and performance.
    d. rule and muscle movement.

3. It would be impossible for us to deal with all of the items and events of our lives on an individual basis, so we group them together into categories called _____ . (p. 281)

    a. concepts.
    b. forms.
    c. ideas.
    d. sets.

4. Which of the following is a defining attribute for the concept "bird?" (p. 282)

    a. building nests
    b. eating insects
    c. growth of feathers
    d. territorial vocalizations

5. According to critics of the traditional view of concept acquisition, we learn about concepts first by (p. 282)

    a. collecting defining attributes.
    b. making discriminations from more general ideas.
    c. reference to prototype.
    d. refining an abstract schema.

6. Bruner's approach to instruction stresses providing examples of the subject matter and allowing students to (p. 274)

    a. discover the structure for themselves.
    b. examine the relevant details.
    c. find other examples on their own.
    d. learn particular facts about the subject.

7. Relationships among concepts may be better understood when they are placed in a (p. 274)

    a. coding system.
    b. context of verbal information.
    c. deductive framework.
    d. value perspective.

8. Many traditional teaching practices have the effect of punishing wrong answers and rewarding only the single correct one. This has the unfortunate effect of discouraging (p. 275)

    a. appreciation of structure.
    b. deductive approaches
    c. intuitive thinking.
    d. retention of detail.

9. Ms. Alexander prefers that her students use discovery learning rather than reception learning. Ms. Alexander is probably interested in her students (p. 275)

    a. gaining extrinsic rewards from learning.
    b. listening to her explain the relationships between concepts.
    c. independently organizing the material into its final form.
    d. working in small groups to determine the contribution of each student.

10. Ausubel's approach stresses giving students organized, sequenced, and finished information, because he thinks the most useable information will be learned by (p. 277)

    a. concept formation.
    b. discovery.
    c. induction.
    d. reception.

11. Ausubel believes meaningful learning and retention can be maximized by presenting ideas that are general and inclusive prior to the lesson material. The presentation of totally new ideas in this manner refers to Ausubel's concept of (p. 278)

    a. correlative subsumption.
    b. dissociability.
    c. expository organizers.
    d. need state.

12. Ausubel calls the general concept which stands at the top of a coding system the (p. 277)

    a. categorizer.
    b. organizer.
    c. subject header.
    d. subsumer.

13. Ms. Van Dyke explains the general theory of behaviorism and then provides specific examples to clarify her explanation. She is using which of the following procedures? (p. 277)

    a. eg-rule method
    b. discovery learning
    c. rule-eg method
    d. advance organizers

14. Students must learn new material and distinguish it from the old, and therefore Ausubel's approach (p. 280)

    a. ends with a summary of the current lesson and a comparison with the last.
    b. is careful never to overlap lesson plans.
    c. presents examples separately from nonexamples.
    d. stresses both similarities and differences.

15. When routine or automatic responses do not fit the current situation it is an occasion for (p. 283)

    a. advance organizers.
    b. deductive reasoning.
    c. discovery approaches.
    d. problem solving.

16. Which of the following is **not** useful when one is trying to solve a problem? (p. 287)

    a. analogical thinking
    b. flexibility
    c. functional fixedness
    d. verbalizing

17. Dr. Smith has been making Ralph stand in the corner as punishment for his outbursts in class. But Ralph's outbursts are growing more frequent. The problem has her stumped. "Why won't he respond to punishment?" she thinks. The problem is **Dr. Smith's** (p. 287)

a. inductive approach.
b. lack of transfer.
c. response set.
d. role as enforcer.

18. Which of the following is **not** a characteristic of an effective problem solver? (p. 292)

a. disregard of familiar ideas
b. persistence
c. store of well-organized prior knowledge
d. systematic approach to problem solving

19. George is trying to design and build his own airplane, but he keeps running into insolvable problems. Fred, his next-door neighbor, is a professional engineer. Fred will wander over to George's drawing board, look for a moment, then suggest three possible solutions. Which of the following is **not** a likely reason why Fred is better at these tasks? (p. 284)

a. Fred is more familiar with patterns of engineering solutions.
b. Fred is more motivated to find the answers.
c. Fred's knowledge is organized around principles instead of details.
d. George is burdened by misinformation and apprehension.

20. Story problems of the "Susan had two computer disks and obtained three more" type are important in developing schemata for (p. 289)

a. diagramming problems.
b. practicing the step-by-step nature of computation.
c. translating verbal problems into mathematical expressions
d. understanding the basic concepts of mathematics.

APPLICATION AND DISCUSSION QUESTIONS

1. In the following lesson presentation, identify the principles (listed below) the teacher uses to help the class remember the information more easily. In addition, suggest any ways to improve the lesson.

Principles: a. advance organizer; b. subsumer diagram; c. categorization; d. rehearsal and practice; e. relating to what the student already knows; f. organization; g. application of principles

Lesson Presentation *...The bell rings and the teacher walks in front of her desk, stands and waits for the class to quiet.*

"Today we are going to study three classes of the animal kingdom which together account for the majority of the animals in the world. At the end of the period, I will give you a diagram of three animals that represent each class and ask you to label the parts that identify the animal as a member of a certain class or phylum."

"The three classes we are going to study are named Mollusk, Arthropod, and Chordate. Each class is called a phylum." *...The teacher turns to the board, writes the name of each phylum across the board in bold print, and underlines each.*

"What are some common animals that you can name?" *...Class names several animals with which they are familiar. "* O.K. Let's consider a fish, a lizard, and a rabbit, which are all Chordates. How are they alike? *...She elicits common characteristics and adds essentials ones that may not be mentioned. She goes through the same process with the other phyla. At the end of the discussion there is an outline on the board of the three phyla, their characteristics, and some examples of each.*

"Now I am going to show you some pictures of animals and see if you can classify them according to the phylum to which they belong." *...She shows the class several pictures, they identify essential characteristics according to the outline, and she places the pictures on the chalk tray under their proper phylum .*

"Are there any questions?" *...pause...* "We will be using this information later in the course, so you should have a copy of this chart in your notes. I will give you the animal diagrams to label and I expect them to be completed by tomorrow. You may work together quietly if you wish."

2.   Explain the possible sources of difficulty in solving each of the problems below:

a.   Johnny was hit by a car when he was crossing the street. Luckily, his father was passing by and rushed him to the hospital, where he was taken to the operating room. The surgeon came in and said, "I can't operate on this boy. He's my son." How can this be?

b.   How can two people stand on a single sheet of newspaper so that they can't possibly touch each other? (No, you can't tear the newspaper)

c. Without lifting your pencil, draw through all nine dots using only four straight lines.

3. One day a second-grade student asks you if Alabama is in New York. What concepts are unclear to him? How would you answer him? What activity or materials could you use to clarify the concepts for him?

4. You are teaching a unit on Indian tribes and their different houses, clothing, food, tools, etc. One way to present the information would be to fill in a chart showing the names of the tribes, their occupations, skills, food, etc. Another way is to go beyond just the facts and teach for transfer.

    How would you teach the unit so that positive transfer would occur when, for example, the students later study a unit on the culture of a foreign country? (**Hint:** What principles would you teach?)

5. A teacher decided to do a unit on important numbers as a way for her class to learn their own telephone numbers, their addresses, birth dates, an emergency phone number, etc.

    What transfer would you expect to take place?

    What advice would you give the teacher?

    Can you deduce a general teaching principle from this situation?

CHAPTER 9

MOTIVATION IN THE CLASSROOM

CHAPTER OVERVIEW

I. What is Motivation?
    A. Behavioral Views of Motivation
    B. Cognitive View of Motivation
    C. Humanistic Views of Motivation

II. The Learning Process: Influences on Motivation
    A. Attitudes Toward Learning
    B. Meeting Students' Needs
    C. What Does Achievement Theory Mean for Teachers?
    D. Tapping Interests and Arousing Curiosity
    E. Maintaining a Positive Emotional Climate
    F. Reinforcement and Fostering a Sense of Competence

III. Teacher Expectations
    A. Two Kinds of Expectation Effects
    B. Sources of Expectations
    C. Teacher Behavior and Student Reactions

IV. Anxiety in the Classroom
    A. Individual Differences in Anxiety
    B. Coping with Anxiety

CHAPTER OBJECTIVES

1. Define motivation.
2. Describe the behavioristic view of motivation.
3. Define extrinsic motivation.
4. Describe the cognitive view of motivation.
5. Define intrinsic motivation.
6. Explain attribution theory.
7. Define locus of control.
8. Describe characteristics of external and internal locus of control.
9. Define learned helplessness and provide some examples.
10. Describe the humanistic approach to motivation.
11. Define humanistic psychology.
12. Explain the concept of "need" from the humanistic viewpoint.
13. Identify and provide examples of deficiency needs and being needs.
14. Describe the criticism and uses of Maslow's Hierarchy of Needs.
15. Explain achievement motivation and resultant motivation.
16. Describe the relationship between achievement motivation and self worth.
17. Discuss some methods of encouraging motivation during the learning process and give a brief description of how to implement each method.
18. Explain cooperative, competitive and individualistic goal structures.
19. Explain the system designed by Robert Slavin called Student Teams-Achievement Divisions (STAD)
20. Describe a special motivation program developed by deCharms.
21. State the appropriate uses of extrinsic reinforcement for motivation.
22. Explain the phenomenon of the self-fulling prophecy and the sustaining expectation effect.
23. Identify sources of teacher expectations.
24. Discuss the ways in which teachers may behave differently toward students and communicate their expectations to the students.
25. Identify methods which may be used to avoid the negative effects of teacher expectations.
26. Define anxiety.
27. Identify the relationship of anxiety to academic performance and ways in which teachers can help anxious students.

KEY TERMS

a. resultant motivation
b. self-fulfilling prophecy
c. STAD
d. humanistic psychology

l. extrinsic motivation
m. attribution theory
n. need
o. goal structure

e. motivation
f. being
g. anxiety
h. pawns
i. intrinsic motivation
j. hierarchy
k. learned helplessness

p. achievement motivation
q. locus of control
r. sustaining expectation effect
s. deficiency
t. self-actualization
u. self-efficacy
v. individual learning expecatation
w. origins

1. If a person's need to achieve in a particular situation is greater than the need to avoid failure, the overall tendency or _____ will be to take the risk and try to achieve.

2. A specific system that uses cooperative goal structures is the _____ . This results in students feeling more involved in their work and more liked by classmates, having better attitudes toward other races, and learning more.

3. "An experience of general uneasiness, a sense of foreboding, a feeling of tension" is called _____ .

4. "The absence of anything a person requires, or thinks he requires, for his overall well-being" is called a _____ .

5. Factors that energize and direct behavior toward a goal are called _____ .

6. "Where people locate responsibility for successes and failures--inside or outside themselves" --is referred to by the term _____ .

7. The result of external events, such as rewards or punishments, is _____ .

8. The need for achievement and the need to avoid failure are the bases for the _____ theory by Atkinson and McClelland.

9. The sense that one is doomed to fail, based on past experiences is known as _____ .

10. DeCharms calls people who feel powerless and think they have no control over their fate, _____ .

11. The result of internal events, such as satisfaction of curiosity, is _____ .

12. The label given to the interpersonal factor that describes the ways people relate to others involved in accomplishing the same goal is _____ .

13. When a prediction causes the expected results to happen, we call this phenomenon a _____ .

14. The theory of motivation that is concerned with the causes a person gives for his success or failure and emphasizes the notion of individual perception is _____ .

15. A term used by Maslow to indicate the highest level of personal growth the realization of personal potential is _____ .

16. The branch of psychology concerned with the total person and the fulfillment of the individual's positive potential is referred to as _____ .

17. A score that is based on previous work and represents the student's average level of performance is called _____ .

18. Maslow's four lower level needs that must be satisfied before other needs may be pursued are called the _____ needs.

19. The needs of intellectual achievement, aesthetic appreciation and self-actualization are termed the _____ needs.

20. Maslow suggested that human needs are arranged in a _____ .

21. Problems may arise when students show some improvement but teachers do not alter their expectations to take into account the improvement. This is called a _____ .

22. Belief about personal competence in a particular situation is known as _____ .

23. Those who take responsibility for setting and reaching their own goals are known as _____ .

MULTIPLE CHOICE QUESTIONS

1. Grades, gold stars, and treats that are not part of the learning situation itself are called _____ motivation.

   a. artificial
   b. extrinsic
   c. intrinsic
   d. spurious

2. In classroom settings, attribution theory explains motivation as an attempt to

   a. duplicate strategies that were previously effective.
   b. extend personal control and power.
   c. maximize reward from peers and teachers.
   d. understand the causes of success or failure.

3. Jeff is apathetic and resigned to failure. He makes poor marks in school and is not inclined to seek help. He is typical of students who attribute their failures to causes that are

   a. external, stable, and uncontrollable.
   b. external, unstable, and controllable.
   c. internal, stable, and uncontrollable.
   d. internal, unstable, and controllable.

4. Francis believes that he can master all the skills and strategies necessary to win the spontaneous speaking debate. We would say that Francis has a strong sense of

   a. extrinsic motivation.
   b. individual learning expectation.
   c. self-actualization.
   d. self-efficacy.

5. Mrs. Jones has failed to notice that Juanita has dramatically improved her spoken English from broken words and sentences to smooth fluency. As a result of her failure to note this change, Mrs. Jones continues to respond to Juanita and treat her as if her English is poor. Mrs. Jones is demonstrating the

   a. use of extrinsic motivation.
   b. self-fulfilling prophecy.
   c. attribution theory.
   d. sustaining expectation effect.

6. The expression, "If at first you don't succeed, try, try again." is an appropriate slogan for people

   a. equal in achievement motivation and fear of failure.
   b. higher in achievement motivation than fear of failure.
   c. lacking both achievement motivation and fear of failure.
   d. more fearful of failure than motivated to achieve.

7. The need for achievement is partially offset by a fear of failure, leaving

   a. apathy.
   b. low self-esteem
   c. deficiency needs
   d. resultant motivation

8. In deCharm's observations, students who are in control of their own achievement are called

   a. actualizers.
   b. achievers
   c. origins.
   d. self-motivators

9. Defensive underachieving and defensive goal setting are behaviors employed by _____ students to protect their self-esteem.

   a. failure-avoiding
   b. risk-taking
   c. self-actualized
   d. success-oriented

10. Peter is a failure-avoiding student. This student adopts a coping strategy of not studying and non-participation in class. As Peter's teacher you should:

    a. give easy tests so Peter can succeed.
    b. make the classroom severly competitive.
    c. never reveal objectives to Peter.
    d. stress that success depends on effort.

11. Systematic reinforcement is appropriate for students who have a

    a. high need for achievement.
    b. history of success in similar tasks.
    c. poor academic self-concept.
    d. well-prepared homework assignment.

12. When a teacher's expectations lead to a student achievement that conforms to those expectations, the effect is called

    a. cooperative goal structuring.
    b. personal causation.
    c. proactive feedback.
    d. self-fulfilling prophecy.

13. In the STAD system, cooperative groups are determined by

    a. alphabetical order.
    b. mixing abilities, sexes, and ethnic backgrounds.
    c. random selection.
    d. tests of student ability.

14. Ms. Gibbons does not expect much of Sally. She thinks Sally just is not very bright. In classroom interactions she is likely to give Sally

    a. easier questions and less time to answer.
    b. more praise for correct answers.
    c. greater encouragement to succeed.
    d. verbal prompts and cues to the correct answer.

15. Research has shown that teachers are likely to alter their expectations of student performance

    a. as soon as their expectations are disconfirmed.
    b. only after repeated disconfirmations.
    c. when expected high achievers perform poorly.
    d. where other teachers express expectations.

16. Jim has failed so often at school and feels so inadequate that he has decided that nothing he does really matters. He thinks that it won't make any difference if he studies or not because he is doomed to failure. Jim is a victim of

    a. intrinsic motivators.
    b. poor goal structures.
    c. an internal locus of control.
    d. learned helplessness.

17. Anxious students are at an advantage when

    a. doing simple, well-practiced tasks.
    b. performing in competitive situations.
    c. responding to standardized tests.
    d. taking tests over difficult material.

18. Anxious students are likely to select goals that are

    a. dictated by social pressure.
    b. extremely difficult or very easy.
    c. long-term in nature.
    d. of moderate difficulty.

19. The curiosity of younger children can most easily be stimulated by

    a. humerous slogans and quotations.
    b. logical puzzles and games.
    c. things to be manipulated and explored.
    d. thought-provoking questions.

20. You ask your students to imagine they are stranded on a desert island. Then you ask them to list the five things they would most like to have with them to improve their chances of survival. This assignment may increase motivation by

   a. individualizing instruction.
   b. presenting an insolvable problem.
   c. stimulating curiosity.
   d. using appropriate goal structures.

21. Which of the following goal structures has been found superior in teaching complex learning and problem solving?

   a. competitive.
   b. cooperative
   c. individualistic
   d. ranked

22. Mrs. Brown was told by another teacher that Johnny was a "slow student and very disruptive in class." By the third day of school, Johnny had been placed in the lowest reading and math groups and been sent to the principal's office 4 times. Johnny may indeed be appropriately placed, but he may also be a victim of a/the _____ .

   a. low level of aspiration.
   b. self-fulfilling prophecy.
   c. fear of failure.
   d. poor self image.

23. Which of the following statements would apply to someone with an **external** locus of control?

   a. I studied hard and made an "A."
   b. I'm sure I can do it if I try hard enough.
   c. The reason I made a good grade is because the test was easy.
   d. I want to work hard to improve my skills in typing.

24. Which of the following statements would apply to someone with an **internal** locus of control?

   a. It sure was lucky that Mrs. Brown asked us those questions.
   b. I will study hard and earn a good grade on the next test.
   c. There is no way I can make a good grade.
   d. There's nothing I can do about it...I'll just have to wait and see.

APPLICATION AND DISCUSSION QUESTIONS

1. Match the statements below with the appropriate view of **motivation**:

1. Behavioral view (extrinsic motivation)
2. Cognitive view (intrinsic motivation)
3. Humanistic view (Maslow's need hierarchy)
4. Need for achievement
5. Need to avoid failure
6. Attributing success/failure to internal or stable causes
7. Attributing success/failure to internal or unstable causes
8. Attributing success/failure to external-stable causes
9. Attributing success/failure to external-unstable causes
10. Social Learning view (importance of attainable goals)

❈❈❈❈❈❈❈❈❈❈❈❈❈❈❈❈❈❈

a. "If at first I don't succeed, I'll try again." (This student likes challenges and doesn't need excessive praise or encouragement.)

b. "I'm going to stay home tonight and work on my science project. it's interesting and I've got an idea I want to try out."

c. "That's the last time I'm going to a concert the night before a test. I did <u>awful</u>!"

d. "The teacher will let me be first in line if I work quietly during reading period."

e. "If at first I don't succeed, I quit." (This student likes safe situations where he'll probably succeed and needs recognition of successes.)

f. "I know I'm dumb in math, and I don't even want to try anymore."

g. "I want to finish the week's assignment by Thursday because I get to do what I want in Friday's class if I've completed my work."

h. "Mrs. Burns grades too hard. Last year she flunked half her class. And she never answers your questions. I know I'm going to fail."

i. "I just can't concentrate on the lesson because I know at lunch nobody is going to want to sit with me."

j. "Last night Brian called and somehow we started talking about the English assignment and it turned out I was all confused. I would have made an F for sure if I hadn't talked to him."

2.   Listed below are ten ways to encourage students to feel more like "origins" instead of "pawns" and to take personal responsibility for their actions. Match the teacher statements to the method they illustrate.

To encourage students to feel more like **origins**:

1.   Draw the connection between a student's behavior and its consequences.
2.   Solicit and incorporate students' opinions in classroom discussion.
3.   Give choices rather than orders.
4.   Encourage student input when working out a contract.
5.   Indicate to a student that you are listening to his or her ideas, preferences, problems, etc.
6.   Call attention to improvement that the student has made.
7.   Let a student live with the consequences of his or her decisions, yet point out that a different decision would have had a different result.
8.   Praise a student when he or she fulfills a responsibility.
9.   Provide opportunities for students to be responsible.
10.   Incorporate student comments into the lesson.

Teacher Statements

a.   "Would you rather work on your reading or math during study period.?"

b.   "I will lend you this book over the weekend, and I trust you to return it to me before school on Monday."

c.   "When you finish this assignment, how do you want to reward yourself?"

d.   "You were listening carefully to my explanation of the assignment, so you did it exactly right."

e.   "Your handwriting in this paper is so much easier to read than the one you handed in last week. I appreciate your effort."

f.   "Ira, that was an interesting comment you made. Can anyone respond to what Ira said?"

g.   "Thank you for returning the book. I'll remember that you do what you say you'll do."

h.   "Francis got mad at you because you poked him with your pencil. If you want to be friends with him, you should ask him to listen to a record with you."

i.   "Class, we need to decide which games you want to play during P.E. this week."

j.   "These things you're saying make me think it really bothers you to get up and talk in front of the class."

3.   One teaching strategy with a cooperative goal structure is the "jigsaw" method of learning. In this method the class is divided into small groups and each member of a group is given a different piece of information. They must teach each other so that all members of the group will know all the information in order to achieve a goal.

What are the benefits of this strategy...

...for classes with different ability levels?
...for withdrawn students?
...for students low in self-esteem?
...for classes divided into cliques or segregated groups?
...for encouraging leadership?
...for group responsibility for monitoring its members?

4.   There is a student in your class who seems very discouraged. He doesn't cause any trouble; as a matter of fact, he is rather quiet. However, he is not doing very well academically because of his listlessness and lack of interest.

How would you encourage him to be motivated through the use of ...

...extrinsic motivation?

...intrinsic motivation?

...Maslow's hierarchy?

...achievement theory?

...attribution theory?

...social learning theory?

CHAPTER 10

CLASSROOM MANAGEMENT AND COMMUNICATION

CHAPTER OVERVIEW

I.   Classrooms Need Managers
     A. The Ecology of Classrooms
     B. The Goals of Classroom Management

II. Planning for Good Management
     A. A Look Back
     B. Some Research Results
     C. Rules and Procedures Required
     D. Getting Started: The First Weeks of Class

III. Maintaining Effective Management: Motivation and Prevention
     A. Encouraging Engagement
     B. Prevention Is the Best Medicine
     C. Special Problems with Secondary Students

IV. The Need for Communication
     A. Communication and Metacommunication
     B. Diagnosis: Whose Problem Is It?
     C. Counseling: The Student's Problem
     D. Confrontation and Assertive Discipline

CHAPTER OBJECTIVES

1. Explain the use of the term "ecology" in association with classrooms.
2. Identify characteristics of classrooms that affect the students regardless of how they are organized for learning or what educational philosophy is being used.
3. Discuss the need for cooperation in the classroom.
4. List the age-related management needs that have been identified by Brophy and Evertson (1978).
5. Discuss the three major reasons why classroom management is important.
6. Define the following terms:
   a. allocated time
   b. engaged time
   c. participation structures
7. Explain the terms "procedures" and "rules" as they relate to classroom discipline.
8. Discuss five guidelines for establishing class procedures.
9. Write five rules for the elementary school and justify your choice of these rules.
10. Write five rules for the secondary school and justify your choice of these rules.
11. Describe characteristics and behaviors of effective managers (teachers) for elementary students.
12. Describe characteristics and behaviors of effective managers (teachers) for secondary students.
13. Discuss the manner in which the format of a lesson affects student involvement.
14. Explain the term "withitness."
15. Discuss four guidelines for encouraging student responsibility.
16. Explain timing errors and target errors and how effective managers deal with these problems.
17. Discuss the use of overlapping and group focus in classroom management.
18. Describe procedures that a teacher may use in movement management.
19. Identify the special problems teachers may have in managing secondary students.
20. Define the term "metacommunication."
21. Discuss the idea of Thomas Gordon (1974) that "the key to good teacher-student relationships is determining why you are troubled by a particular behavior and whose problem it is."
22. Explain the procedure of empathetic listening.
23. List the components of active listening.
24. Explain the use of "I messages."
25. Describe the major components of Lee and Marlene Canter's (1976) method of assertive discipline.
26. Once "I" messages and assertive responses have failed and the student persists in misbehaving, the teacher has three methods for resolving the conflict. Discuss these three methods of resolving the conflict between the teacher and student.

KEY TERMS

Fill in the blanks in the following sentences with the letters preceeding the concepts listed below.

a. procedures
b. rules
c. withitness
d. overlapping
e. group focus
f. movement management
g. allocated
h. participation structures

i. engaged
j. norms
k. metacommunication
l. empathetic listening
m. "I" messages
n. assertive discipline

1. The hidden or underlying communication, the implicit message received in an interaction is _____ .

2. A/an _____ is used in confrontation and consists of three parts: What the other person is doing, its effect on you, and how it makes you feel.

3. Group _____ are standards that are implicitly agreed upon by the group members.

4. In order to smoothly accomplish routine activities in the classroom, students must learn _____ .

5. Being successful in _____ means that the teacher can supervise several different activities at the same time.

6. Reflecting to a person what you heard him say and the emotions and meaning you think are implicit in his communication involves _____ ; it is used when the other person owns the problem.

7. Smooth transitions, appropriate lesson pace, and variety are characteristic of effective _____ .

8. _____ should make clear to students the expected behaviors and forbidden actions in the class.

9. Teachers who deal with problems by clearly stating their expectations and following through with established consequences are using _____ .

10. Teachers who continually monitor the classroom and effectively stop minor disruptions have what Kounin calls _____ .

11. The goal of _____ is to keep each student involved in appropriate group activities.

12. According to Kelley, trying to hear the student and avoiding jumping in too quickly with advice or criticism is an example of _____ .

13. Time set aside for learning is termed _____ time.

14. Time spent actively learning is termed _____ time.

15. Rules defining how to participate in different activities are _____ .

MULTIPLE CHOICE QUESTIONS

1. Allowable student choices should be made more clear-cut and structured when (p. 352)

   a. one of the assignment goals is to teach self-discipline.
   b. the students are young children.
   c. efficiency of learning is not a factor.
   d. students become rebellious in class.

2. Your text suggests taking all of the following factors into account when developing plans for your class **except** (p. 356)

   a. individual variations among students.
   b. methods for motivating students toward course objectives.
   c. setting clear rules and consequences.
   d. student expectations of proper classroom procedures.

3. Class rules specify (p. 357)

   a. how to accomplish classroom activities.
   b. expected and forbidden actions.
   c. punishments and rewards that will be used.
   d. punishable offenses.

4. Which of the following is **not** an example of rules for secondary school classes mentioned by your text? (p. 359)

   a. keep your appearance neat and tidy
   b. bring all needed materials to class
   c. obtain permission before leaving your seat
   d. respect and be polite to all people

5. At the beginning of the school year, effective managers will (p. 361)

    a. use shorter work cycles.
    b. explain and review rules.
    c. provide many extrinsic rewards.
    d. expect stricter behavior standards.

6. On the first day of class, praise and positive statements should be (p. 362)

    a. directed toward the most cooperative individual students.
    b. used sparingly to instill discipline.
    c. given to each member as he responds to roll call.
    d. directed toward the group as a whole.

7. Mrs. Black's lesson plan for the first day of her 4th grade science class is devoted completely to learning the students' names and lecturing them on scientific nomenclature. She runs the risk that (p. 362)

    a. her students' first impression will be that the class is boring.
    b. many students will be rebellious.
    c. anxiety may be increased among many students.
    d. the material will be forgotten because the setting is new.

8. Greg was trying to pass Bill a note, but Bill kept his eyes on his work and thought, "Why does Greg do this to me? Mrs. Peeper will spot him for sure. She never misses anything. Boy, you'd think she could read minds." Mrs. Peeper could be described as (p. 364)

    a. an evaluating teacher.
    b. wary.
    c. withit.
    d. a good movement manager.

9. To encourage student responsibility, you should do which of the following? (p. 365)

    a. make basic work requirements clear.
    b. Communicate the specifics of assignments.
    c. Monitor work in progress.
    d. Give academic feedback at least every two weeks.

10. The ability to keep track of and supervise several activities at the same time is called (p. 366)

    a. group focus.
    b. movement management.
    c. overlapping.
    d. withitness.

11. One of the best ways to avoid discipline problems is to (p. 366)

    a. have a comprehensive set of rules.
    b. make sure the classroom is a pleasant environment.
    c. keep the group focused on productive learning.
    d. isolate troublemakers from the rest of the class.

12. Experimental studies of primary classes indicate that it is very important for teachers of young children to (p. 354)

    a. make gradual, fluid transitions in the material.
    b. hold reading groups for brief periods only.
    c. clearly direct the students' attention.
    d. give them well-ordered ideas to assimilate.

13. When effective secondary school teachers are faced with students who continually break the same rules, they (p. 368)

    a. grow increasingly more critical of the behavior.
    b. try to catch the students before the rule is broken.
    c. slowly increase the consequences of rule-breaking for that student.
    d. secure at least a promise of better performance.

14. Metacommunication is (p. 369)

    a. a summary of a person's words.
    b. an underlying or hidden message.
    c. the cooperative solution to a problem.
    d. communication without specific content.

15. Active (or empathetic) listening should be used by the teacher when (p. 371)

    a. the student owns the problem.
    b. the teacher owns the problem.
    c. the communication is confused.
    d. personal conflicts are involved.

16. Mr. Matthew had just assigned a "nature walk" to some of his students when he realized that the directions he gave them were rather involved. What should he have done to make sure they understood? (p. 370)

    a. repeat the assignment again more slowly
    b. ask them to write out the assignment directions
    c. ask them whether or not they understand
    d. ask them to paraphrase the assignment

17. All of the following are components of empathetic listening **except** (p. 371)

    a. attending to both verbal and nonverbal messages.
    b. accounting for all the stimuli surrounding the speaker.
    c. differentiating between emotional and intellectual content.
    d. making inferences regarding the speaker's feelings.

18. Telling a student what he or she is doing, and how it affects the teacher and the teacher's feelings is (p. 372)

    a. empathetic communication.
    b. owning the problem.
    c. dynamic communication.
    d. sending an "I-message."

19. A clear, firm, unhostile responsive style is characteristic of _____ discipline. (p. 372)

    a. aggressive
    b. assertive
    c. group focused
    d. extrinsic

20. Mrs. Jones seems to always be talking to Jody and Ruth. The rest of the class is often left to do independent work while she attends to these two students. Mrs. Jones is failing to maintain a (an) (p. 363)

    a. group focus.
    b. movement management flow.
    c. empathetic classroom.
    d. assertive disciplinary action.

21. A teacher who gives too many directions and creates a slowdown and wastes time in starting a new activitiy is not practicing _____ properly. (p. 367)

    a. group focus
    b. movement management
    c. overlapping
    d. withitness

22. One of the important goals of classroom management is to expand the number of minutes available for learning. The time available for learning is known as _____ time. (p. 353)

    a. allocated
    b. classroom
    c. engaged
    d. teaching/learning

23. Time on task or time spent actively attending to specific learning tasks is called ____ time. (p. 354)

    a. allocated
    b. classroom
    c. engaged
    d. teaching/learning

24. Rules defining who can talk, what they can talk about, and when, to whom, and how long they can talk are called ____ . (p. 354)

    a. classroom rules
    b. interaction guidlines
    c. participation structures
    d. speaking norms

APPLICATION AND DISCUSSION QUESTIONS

1. You have learned several ways to prevent problems from occurring in the classroom. In "Practices That Encourage a **Disruptive** Classroom"* these preventive principles are considered in **reverse**. Match each practice with the principle that it violates.

Preventive Principles

    a. have clear learning objectives.
    b. use positive reinforcement to encourage positive behavior.
    c. assign work at the student's ability level.
    d. motivate students.
    e. be an effective classroom manager.

Practices That Encourage a **Disruptive** Classroom

____ 1. Begin class late. Idle time encourages restlessness.

____ 2. Teach to the middle one-third of the class. Those who are bored or frustrated with the lesson will find other ways to keep themselves occupied.

____ 3. Provide failure experiences. Students who continuously experience failure will become discouraged and are likely to become hostile.

____ 4. Present totally spontaneous rather than planned lessons. Conduct activities on the spur of the moment even though you don't have the materials and equipment you need.

_____ 5. Be inconsistent. When a student breaks a class rule, let your reaction depend on how you're feeling that day.

_____ 6. Pay attention to disruptive students. Ignore students who are engaged in academic activities; after all, that's what they're supposed to be doing.

_____ 7. Don't bother to keep your cool. A good argument can disrupt the entire class. A calm reaction only promotes a healthy learning environment.

_____ 8. Get really absorbed in teaching a small group of students. Don't pay attention to the rest of the class until a major disruption occurs.

2. In the following situations, first decide who owns the problem and then respond appropriately with active listening or an I-message. Active listening paraphrases the other person's message and includes the feeling communicated. An I-message states what the other person is doing, its effect on you, and how you feel about it.

   1. Student: "You always blame me every time something goes wrong in the classroom. I know you don't like me and I don't like you either."

      Who owns the problem? _____

      Response: _____

   2. A student tells you that his dog got run over by a car last night and is at the veterinary hospital now.

      Who owns the problem? _____

      Response: _____

   3. An "A" student suddenly starts making bad grades on his tests and assignments.

      Who owns the problem? _____

      Response: _____

   4. A teacher continually complains about a certain student when she's in the teachers' lounge.

      Who owns the problem? _____

      Response: _____

5. A student persists in daydreaming and being disinterested in class, and your efforts to motivate him seem to have no effect.

   Who owns the problem? _____

   Response: _____

6. Several pages are torn from the books in the readers' corner.

   Who owns the problem? _____

   Response: _____

3. You are planning for the first week of class and have prepared some interesting, well-organized, and detailed lesson plans. As to teaching the subject matter, you feel well-prepared. What are some other areas you should give attention to in order to develop a smoothly functioning classroom?

4. It is often difficult for a teacher to find time to listen attentively to a student, but listening to another person can have many positive results. Think of a situation in which someone has really listened to you. What kind of feelings did you have about the other person? How can listening be a way of preventing/handling classroom problems?

5. What are some factors that you like or dislike about groups of which you are a member?

---

*Adapted from Stainback, S.B. & Stainback, W.C. Classroom Discipline. Springfield, Il.: Charles C. Thomas, 1974, p. 37.

CHAPTER 11

SETTING OBJECTIVES AND PLANNING

CHAPTER OVERVIEW

I.   Teacher Planning

II.   Objectives for Learning
    A. The Value of Objectives
    B. Kinds of Objectives
    C. Criticisms
    D. In Summary: What Are the Advantages?

III. Task Analysis
    A. The Basic Method
    B. An Example of Task Analysis

IV.   Taxonomies
    A. The Cognitive Domain
    B. The Affective Domain
    C. The Psychomotor Domain
    D. The Big Picture: Course Objectives

V.   Basic Formats For Teaching
    A. Recitation and Questioning
    B. Lecturing and Explaining
    C. Group Discussion
    D. Seatwork and Homework
    E. Individualized Instruction

VI.   Settings for Achieving Objectives
    A. Interest-Area Arrangements
    B. Personal Territories

CHAPTER OBJECTIVES

1. Researchers have studied teacher planning. Describe some of the characteristics of teacher planning that the researchers found from interviewing teachers.
2. Define "instructional objective."
3. Name the benefits of communicating learning objectives to students.
4. Compare and contrast general, specific, and behavioral objectives. Write an example of each.
5. Define the term "operationalize."
6. Identify the three components of Mager's behavioral objective and write several examples.
7. Explain Gronlund's combined system of writing objectives.
8. Discuss the major criticisms of writing objectives.
9. Discuss the advantages of writing objectives.
10. Explain three guidelines for writing instructional objectives.
11. Describe the process and benefits of task analysis.
12. Define "taxonomy."
13. List the six basic objectives in Bloom's taxonomy of the cognitive domain.
14. Explain the use of cognitive objectives for evaluation.
15. List the six basic objectives in Bloom's taxonomy of the affective domain.
16. Explain why assessing affectives objectives may be helpful.
17. List the six basic objectives in Bloom's taxonomy of the psychomotor domain.
18. Discuss methods of evaluating psychomotor objectives.
19. Describe the use of a behavior-content matrix in planning objectives for an entire unit.
20. Discuss the processes and important points involved in these teaching formats: recitation and questioning, lecturing and explaining, group discussion, seatwork, and individualized instruction.
21. Define "anticipatory set."
22. Explain seven guidelines for leading class discussions.
23. Define two kinds of spatial organization and identify the situations for which each is best suited.
24. Describe how teachers may design interest areas that match their objectives.
25. Discuss how physical setting may influence teaching and learning in classrooms organized by territories.
26. Define "action zone."

Fill in the blanks in the following sentences with the letters preceding the concepts listed below.

a. instructional objectives
b. operationalized
c. anticipatory set
d. task analysis
e. taxonomy
f. cognitive domain
g. affective domain
h. psychomotor domain
i. knowledge
j. essay test
k. behavior-content matrix
l. recitation
m. divergent thinking

n. individualized instruction
o. analysis
p. synthesis
q. environment-behavior
r. action zone
s. characterization by value
t. perceptual skills
u. skilled movements
v. checklist
w. seatwork

1. The effects of the physical classroom setting on behavior are studied in _____ research.

2. The unobservable changes usually found in general objectives need to be _____ into more specific objectives which are defined in terms that can be measured.

3. The approach to teaching that is comprised of structure (setting a framework), solicitation (asking questions), and reaction (praising, correcting, and expanding) is called _____ .

4. In order to benefit from independent _____, students must be kept actively involved in the assignment so that the time is not wasted.

5. The type of test most appropriate for measuring synthesis- and evaluation-level objectives is the _____ .

6. The area of the room in which the most teacher-student interaction occurs is called the _____ .

7. Objectives for intellectual skills are found in the taxonomy for the _____ ; objectives for attitudes and emotional growth are in the _____ ; objectives for movement and motor skills are in the _____ .

8. An interested, receptive frame of mind in students is termed _____ .

9. The definition of the final performance requirement and identification of underlying subskills and subprocesses is called _____ .

10. In developing a set of objectives for an entire unit or course, it is very useful to use a/an _____ .

11. The essence of _____ is not that students work individually but that their work has been planned to meet their individual needs and abilities.

12. The use of _____ increases student achievement by helping students focus on important information and provides a basis for fair evaluation procedures.

13. A/an _____ is a classification system.

14. To answer questions that have many possible answers _____ is required.

15. Remembering, but not necessarily understanding, is at the _____ level of Bloom's taxonomy.

16. Breaking something down into its component parts is at the _____ level of Bloom's taxonomy.

17. Creating or generating a unique solution would be classified as a _____ level skill by Bloom.

18. Once a person is firmly committed and acts according to a new value, he is operating at the _____ level of the affective domain.

19. The translation of stimuli received through the senses into appropriate movements is at the taxonomic level called _____ .

20. Pitchers in baseball have a variety of different pitches. Each pitch is an example of the taxonomic level called _____ .

21. Performance outcomes can be measured by an instrument that includes the measurable dimensions and space for judgment statements. This instrument is called a _____ .

MULTIPLE CHOICE QUESTIONS

1. Your text defines an instructional objective as a (p. 383)

   a. broad and generalized description of instructional intent.
   b. clear and unambiguous description of instructional intent.
   c. specific listing of intended changes in behavior.
   d. summary of course content and intended activities.

2. Research indicates that announced instructional objectives increase learning (p. 384)

    a. only when the objectives are repeated periodically.
    b. in all common classroom situations.
    c. when instructional activities are less organized and structured.
    d. when instructional activities are more organized and structured.

3. Instructional objectives can improve communication by (p. 384)

    a. setting up broad headings for class activities.
    b. making the teacher's actions consistent.
    c. using "work image" to aid comprehension.
    d. clarifying the teacher's ambiguous purposes and messages.

4. Behaviorists tend to write objectives that include the words (p. 386)

    a. "understand" and "appreciate."
    b. "list" and "identify."
    c. "citizenship" and "character."
    d. "less" and "more."

5. When unobservable objectives are defined in terms that can be measured they have been (p. 386)

    a. realized.
    b. operationalized.
    c. specified.
    d. expressed.

6. In Mager's behavioral view, which of the following is **not** part of a good objective (p. 387)

    a. a list of conditions under which the behavior will occur.
    b. a statement of the intended behavior's value to the student.
    c. a set of criteria for acceptable performance.
    d. a verb phrase describing the intended behavior.

7. Which of the following best describes Gronlund's system for writing cognitive objectives? (p. 387)

    a. specific goal and conditions of performance
    b. specific goal and criteria for evaluation
    c. general purpose and specific learning activities
    d. general purpose and examples of achievement

8. Critics of instructional objectives point out that precise objectives used year after year may cause the curriculum to (p. 388)

    a. become predictable.
    b. stagnate.
    c. shrink.
    d. allow laziness.

9. Teachers who use instructional objectives should (p. 390)

    a. decide on activities before setting objectives.
    b. make sure tests are related to the objectives.
    c. use "magic" phrases to impress students of the objectives' importance.
    d. exclude objectives whose outcomes cannot be specified.

10. The basic procedure of task analysis is (p. 390)

    a. the restating of objectives in measurable terms.
    b. sythesizing objectives into a cohesive whole.
    c. breaking skills and processes into subskills and subprocesses.
    d. projecting the end result of a certain activity.

11. Benjamin Bloom developed a classifications system of educational objectives which he called (p. 392)

    a. logical domains.
    b. the awareness scale.
    c. levels of processing.
    d. a taxonomy.

12. It is a good idea to consider Bloom's three domains separately because (p.392)

    a. the behaviors in each domain only occur separately.
    b. schools do not give enough stress to cognitive changes.
    c. behavioral concerns do not overlap those in other domains.
    d. this accentuates the affective and psychomotor areas.

13. Putting parts of different ideas together to create something new occurs in what category of objectives? (p. 393)

    a. evaluation
    b. synthesis
    c. psychomotor
    d. affective

14. The ability to shuffle cards falls into what category of Bloom's classification system? (p. 395)

    a. psychomotor
    b. behavioral
    c. knowledge
    d. manipulative

15. Frances set an objective that her class should learn the names of the various types of clouds. She should measure this learning with (p. 393)

    a. evaluative discussion.
    b. an objective test.
    c. an essay test.
    d. a written assignment.

16. For as long as Jim could remember, he loved physics. He took apart the radio and made steam rockets in his elementary years and read library books on subatomic particles in his high school years. Jim can hardly wait to get into college so he can study physics at his own speed. His level in the affective domain of objectives is (p. 394)

    a. responding.
    b. characterization by value.
    c. valuing.
    d. evaluation.

17. Evaluations of affective objectives (p. 394)

    a. are easily verified.
    b. should not be graded.
    c. are useful as periodic measures of progress.
    d. should be kept private.

18. In the lowest level of objectives in the psychomotor domain, actions are (p. 395)

    a. highly practiced.
    b. patterns of movements designed to fill a purpose.
    c. involuntary.
    d. attempts to communicate.

19. Checklists and rating scales are most useful in measuring _____ objectives. (p. 396)

    a. creative
    b. affective
    c. psychomotor
    d. cognitive

20. A behavior-content matrix is an aid in developing (p. 396)

    a. teaching formats for course objectives.
    b. specific objectives for broad areas of course material.
    c. evaluation guides for affective objectives.
    d. expressive body movements.

21. Questions are called convergent when they have (p. 398)

    a. only one right answer.
    b. several right answers.
    c. their own answer.
    d. no generally accepted answer.

22. The best pattern of questions for high-ability students seems to be (p. 400)

    a. fast pace, many correct answers, and frequent reviews.
    b. fast pace, few correct answers, and little encouragement or discussion.
    c. knowledge- and comprehension-level questions and no pauses.
    d. high-level questions only with much discussion.

23. All of the following are disadvantages of the lecture method of instruction **except** (p. 401)

    a. it is a poor way to introduce new topics.
    b. some students may have trouble listening for more than a few minutes at a time.
    c. it does not allow for different paces in student learning.
    d. it puts students in a passive role.

24. All of the following are disadvantages of the group discussion format **except** (p. 403)

    a. some students may be anxious and have difficulty participating.
    b. the students must have a common background of knowledge.
    c. students have little chance to ask for clarification or more information.
    d. it is unwieldy in large groups.

25. Individualized instruction is characterized by the fact that (p. 405)

    a. students work with lesson plans designed for their own needs.
    b. students work alone.
    c. one teacher works with one student.
    d. students use lesson plans suitable for no one else.

26. In the traditionally arranged classroom, students' desks are positioned according to a principle of (p. 408)

 a. spatial function.
 b. shared workspace.
 c. territoriality.
 d. autonomy.

27. In Musgrave's terminology, seating arrangements that are semipermanent and suitable for a wide range of learning situations are called (p. 410)

 a. normal floor plans.
 b. traditional layouts.
 c. home-base formations.
 d. special formations.

APPLICATION AND DISCUSSION QUESTIONS

1. Indicate whether the following instructional objectives are **general or specific**, and if they are in the **cognitive, affective,** or **psychomotor** domain.

Kind of Objective	Domain		
_____	_____	1.	Given a diagram of a skeleton, the student will identify at least 12 major bones.
_____	_____	2.	The student will learn to be responsible in the classroom.
_____	_____	3.	The student will write the letters "o," "a," and "c" three times each so that they are well-rounded and touch both writing lines.
_____	_____	4.	The student will value the effort that people have made in order to overcome their hardships or handicaps.
_____	_____	5.	The student will improve his visual-motor coordination.

124

_____   _____   6.   The student will distinguish between
                        well-written and poorly written
                        instructional objectives.

_____   _____   7.   The student will develop good study
                        habits.

2.   Identify the level in the cognitive domain -- knowledge, comprehension, application,
      analysis, synthesis, or evaluation -- of the following objectives:

_____   1.   The student will identify those elements in
                      Columbus's background that led to his eventual
                      voyage.

_____   2.   The student will describe the difficulties
                      encountered by Columbus on his voyage.

_____   3.   On a world map the student will draw the
                      routes of Columbus's attempts to sail around
                      the world.

_____   4.   The student will argue the pros and cons of the
                      effects of Columbus's discovery on Spain and on
                      the New World.

_____   5.   The student will recall the names of the three
                      ships on which Columbus sailed.

_____   6.   The student will compare Columbus's voyage to
                      America with the first astronaut's trip to the
                      moon.

3.   Classify the following questions according to Bloom's taxonomy.

      a.   knowledge   d.   analysis
      b.   comprehension   e.   synthesis
      c.   application   f.   evaluation

____   1.   What were some causes of the oil shortage?

____   2.   From what countries does the United States import oil?

____   3.   Why is it so difficult to substitute other sources of power for oil?

____   4.   In what ways is oil used?

____   5.   What might happen if other countries refused to sell oil to the United
             States?

_____ 6. Give an example of how our daily lives are affected by the availability of oil.

4. Write a behavioral objective for each of the following learning experiences. Use Mager's three parts of a behavioral objective.

    a. The students have been given the definition and examples of a noun.
    b. The librarian has given the class a tour and instructions on the use of the library.
    c. The students have watched a film on "The Water Cycle."
    d. The students have been shown how to convert fractions to decimals.
    e. The students have heard a lecture on the uses of imagery in literature.

5. A second-grade child is having difficulty in spelling (i.e., writing down words which the teacher dictates).

    Do a task analysis of this situation to identify the possible sources of his difficulty. How would you go about determining the exact source of the problem? Be specific.

6. What are some attitudes and values you want students to develop in your subject area? Are goals in the affective domain more difficult to identify than goals in the cognitive domain? If so, why? Are there ways to include psychomotor objectives in your teaching area?

7. A beginning English literature teacher is having trouble in organizing her class for the semester.

    What guidance could you give this teacher?
    What procedure could the teacher use to clarify the goals and direction of the course?

8. You have decided you want to use the group discussion method of teaching, so you begin by asking several higher-level questions, such as, "What do you think can be done to reduce the energy consumption in this country?" However, you get very little response and soon the discussion dies. One reaction you might have is to decide that your class doesn't like discussion or that they don't have sufficient verbal ability to engage in discussion. Another reaction you could have is to examine your lesson structure and your own behavior.

    What are some reasons the class might not respond and what remedies would you recommend? (Consider your past responses to student contributions: for example, evaluation or use of student ideas, their basic knowledge of the subject, their cognitive level, the pace of teacher questioning and length of wait time for answers, teacher domination of discussion, etc.)

9. What suggestions would you make for improving the kindergarten room arrangement shown on the next page?

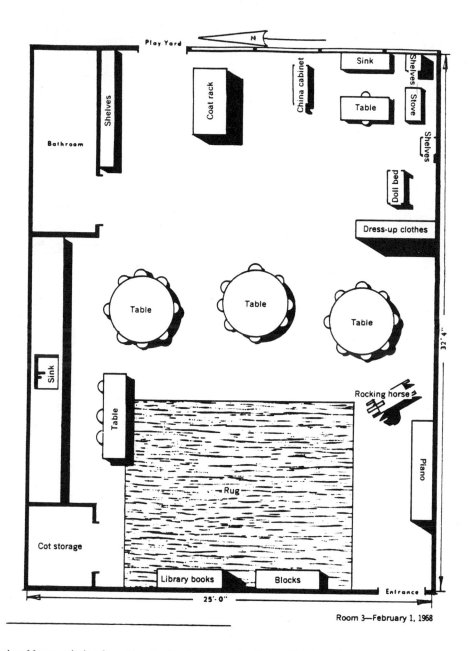

Room 3—February 1, 1968

Reprinted by permission from <u>Planning Environments for Young Children: Physical Space</u> by E. Prescott, S. Kritchevsky, and L. Walling. Copyright © 1969, 1977. National Association for the Education of Young Children, 1834 Connecticut Avenue N.W., Washington, D.C. 20009

CHAPTER 12

EFFECTIVE TEACHING

CHAPTER OVERVIEW

I. The Search for the Keys to Success
    A. Do Teachers Make a Difference
    B. Methods for Studying Effective Teaching
    C. An Example of a Research Program
    D. Characteristics of Effective Teachers

II. Meanwhile What's Happening with the Students?
    A. Academic Tasks

III. Effective Teaching for Different Subjects
    A. Basic Skills: Direct Instruction
    B. Beyond the Basics

IV. Effective Teaching with Different Students
    A. Different Strategies for Younger and Older Students
    B. Students with Different Aptitudes

V. Integrating Ideas about Effective Teaching
    A. A Second-Grade Class That Works
    B. A Fifth-Grade Class That Works
    C. A Secondary Class That Works
    D. Teacher Effectiveness: Conclusions

CHAPTER OBJECTIVES

1. Identify some teacher characteristics studied in research and explain in general terms how these characteristics can affect student learning.
2. Explain six guidelines for effective teaching.
3. Explain some of the limitations of research on teacher characteristics.
4. Discuss the relationship between teaching strategies and student learning.
5. List the four general categories of academic tasks as suggested by Doyle (1983).
6. Explain how tasks may be characterized by:
   a. risk involved
   b. ambiguity
   c. cognitive operation
7. Discuss the limitations that should be considered when applying the findings of effective teaching research.
8. Explain direct instruction/active teaching/explicit teaching.
9. List the six teaching functions based on the research on effective instruction (Rosenshine & Stevens, 1986).
10. Describe Hunter's Mastery Teaching Program.
11. Describe Good and Grouws's Missouri Mathematics Program.
12. Discuss different strategies that may be appropriate for effective teaching for younger and older students.
13. Discuss different strategies that may be appropriate for effective teaching for students with different aptitudes.
14. Explain aptitude-treatment interaction and higher order interactions and provide examples of each.
15. Explain approaches that may be helpful in teaching low achievers.
16. Describe approaches that may be helpful in teaching high achievers.
17. Demonstrate a lesson presentation to high ability students; to low ability students.
18. Explain seven guidelines for organizing instruction.

░░

KEY TERMS

Fill in the blanks in the following sentences with the letters preceding the concepts listed below.

a. correlation
b. high inference characteristics
c. comprehension tasks
d. direct instruction
e. active teaching

h. systematic
i. memory tasks
j. consistent
k. routine or procedural
l. prior knowledge

f. aptitude-treatment interaction
g. higher-order interaction

m. ability
n. opinion tasks
o. knowledge

1. Tasks that require students to go a step beyond the information given or to choose the best among many approaches are called _____ .

2. Characteristics that are difficult to define objectively are termed _____ .

3. The fact that teaching methods that work well with nonanxious students do not work so well with highly anxious students is an example of a/an _____ .

4. In the upper grades, as more teacher explanation and lecture are used to convey information, teacher _____ becomes increasingly important.

5. Because it involves more than two variables a/an _____ is difficult to interpret.

6. To refer to a teaching approach that is related to improved student learning , Tom Good uses the term _____ .

7. Researchers look for a/an _____ between two factors such as teaching method and student achievement even though they cannot be sure that there is a cause-and-effect relationship.

8. Presenting lessons at a quick pace allowing many student responses, is one suggestion of _____ .

9. Teachers at both the secondary and elementary school levels who are consistent and _____ in their teaching tend to maintain better morale in their classrooms than disorganized teachers.

10. Tasks that simply require students to recognize or reproduce information they have encountered before, as in matching states and capitals, are called _____ .

11. One reason it is difficult to identify particular teacher behaviors related to student learning is that teachers are not _____ in their actions over time.

12. Tasks that involve using an algorithm to solve a problem; that is, if the students apply the procedure correctly, they will get the right answer, are called _____ .

13. Students with little _____ need much more of a direct instruction approach.

14. In ATI research, the term _____ refers not to a theoretical notion of potential but instead to readiness for instruction.

15. Tasks that ask students to state a preference, such as which color is their favorite, are termed _____ .

MULTIPLE CHOICE QUESTIONS

1. The famous studies that linked student achievement not with teacher influence but with social class and student ability are based only on (p. 419)

    a. small sample groups.
    b. isolated experiments.
    c. general correlations.
    d. observations of low SES teachers.

2. Greg knew his subject cold and he was conversant in all the newest principles of instruction and learning. He walked into his fourth grade class confident that all his students would become prizewinners. In fact, his class turned out to rank a little below average, proof of the maxim that knowledge (p. 422)

    a. comes only through experience.
    b. does not translate to student ability.
    c. is necessary but not sufficient for effective teaching.
    d. is unrelated to teacher effectiveness.

3. In addition to its correlation to student learning, teacher clarity and organization seem to be related to (p. 422)

    a. student ability levels.
    b. simplicity of subject matter.
    c. teacher promotions.
    d. student morale.

4. To make sure you are presenting a lesson clearly, you should do all of the following **except** (p. 423)

    a. signal transitions between topics clearly.
    b. do written work yourself to identify possible problems.
    c. build checkpoints into the lesson plan.
    d. avoid any pauses in presenting the material.

5. To keep lessons clear and organized you should avoid all the following **except** (p. 423)

    a. "not very"
    b. "sort of"
    c. "somehow"
    d. "significant"

6. Qualities of a teacher's performance that are difficult to define objectively are called (p. 424)

   a. random factors.
   b. insignificant variables.
   c. affective characteristics.
   d. high-inference characteristics.

7. Teacher warmth and enthusiasm are found to be (p. 424)

   a. positively correlated to student learning.
   b. negatively correlated to student learning.
   c. impossible to operationalize.
   d. unrelated to student involvement.

8. Which of the following lists if characteristics best describes direct instruction? (p. 430)

   a. teacher is leader, objectives are general, atmosphere is relaxed
   b. teacher is leader, objectives are specific, atmosphere is busy
   c. teacher is leader, objectives are specific, atmosphere is relaxed
   d. students lead, objectives are general, atmosphere is busy

9. Psychologists generally agree that direct instruction is an effective system for teaching (p. 430)

   a. problem-solving.
   b. creativity.
   c. abstract thinking.
   d. basic skills.

10. Classroom discussion, lectures, and independent learning are likely to be helpful (p. 435)

    a. at all grade levels.
    b. only above the third or fourth grades.
    c. only in high school and above.
    d. only in reaching affective goals.

11. Effective strategies in the early grades involve all of the following **except** (p. 435)

    a. periodic chances to discuss the material.
    b. drill and more drill.
    c. structured presentations of new material.
    d. speedy individual feedback.

12. Which of the following is an example of aptitude-treatment interaction? (p. 436)

    a. all the second graders are confused by long lectures.
    b. Frank needs drill but his classmate John responds better to discussion.
    c. higher ability students move through material more quickly.
    d. younger students need a nurturing atmosphere.

13. In a three-way interaction study of ATIs, Peterson and colleagues found that the type of instruction used had a large effect on (p. 436)

    a. anxious students.
    b. high-ability students.
    c. high-ability anxious students.
    d. low-ability anxious students.

14. The clear implication of ATI research is that teachers should (p. 437)

    a. try a new approach if the students are having difficulty.
    b. select the approach that best suits all the students.
    c. give extra attention to low-ability anxious students.
    d. try to characterize each of their students before planning lessons.

15. In ATI research, "ability" is generally thought of as (p. 437)

    a. the results of standardized tests.
    b. readiness to profit from instruction.
    c. general intelligence.
    d. previous training and instruction.

16. Successful teachers of low-ability students vary the standard classroom format by (p. 438)

    a. using more individualized, self-paced instruction.
    b. using more seatwork and less drill.
    c. using shorter cycles of presentation and practice work.
    d. maintaining a stricter behavior standard.

17. Low-ability students should be given all of the following **except** (p. 438)

    a. questions that have a high rate of right answers.
    b. work and supervision in group settings.
    c. games, artwork, and interest centers.
    d. specific praise for good performance.

18. In general, high-ability students benefit most from (p. 440)

    a. a nurturant learning atmosphere.
    b. a mix of factual and higher-level questions.
    c. a fast pace with little emphasis on correcting errors.
    d. highly-structured lesson plans.

19. In teaching mathematics to a fifth grade class, your text discourages (p. 442)

    a. putting individual students to work on their own.
    b. changing lesson plans to use unexpected events.
    c. asking many questions and correcting many answers.
    d. giving students reasons for their assignments.

20. Which of the following is **true** about effective teaching methods in secondary classes? (p. 444)

    a. There are many patterns for different ages and subjects.
    b. They are more heavily structured in science and mathematics.
    c. They emphasize learning at the group level.
    d. They use more stimuli to focus attention.

21. In organizing your instruction you should do all of the following **except:** (p. 442)

    a. Avoid the use of unexpected events as vehicles for teaching.
    b. Balance cognitive and affective objectives.
    c. Be flexible: if one approach does not work, try another.
    d. Vary the amount of structure to fit the needs of the students.

22. Open, inquiry-type approaches seem to be more effective with high school students in all but one of the following areas; identify the area in which open, inquiry -type approaches are **not** as effective. (p. 445)

    a. abstract problem solving
    b. affective development
    c. basic subjects
    d. creative endeavors

23. Which of the following students listed below needs a supportive atmosphere, a great deal of structure, and lessons broken up into small doses of presentation and seatwork? (p. 445)

    a. high ability
    b. creative
    c. low ability
    d. secondary

24. One clear implication of ATI research is that teachers (p. 437)

  a. should be diligent in returning papers rapidly.
  b. must be flexible and willing to try a new approach if one is not working well.
  c. should use direct instruction most of the time.
  d. who are the most knowledgeable in their subject matter are the most successful.

25. Which of the following is **not** a characteristic of a learning task? (p. 427)

  a. ambiguity
  b. level of risk
  c. materials
  d. operation

APPLICATION AND DISCUSSION QUESTIONS

1. Different instructional strategies are often more effective for some students than others. Check the instructional strategies that are likely to be effective and put an X for those which are especially inappropriate for the different types of students.

TYPE OF STUDENT

INSTRUCTIONAL STRATEGIES	2nd grader	9th grader	High ability	Low ability	Anxious
Questions:					
Challenging					
Good chance for success					
Factual					
Higher level					
Structure:					
High					
Low					
Reinforcement:					
Much					
Little					

Type of instruction:
    Direct instruction   _____
    Discussion   _____
    Lecture   _____
    Independent   _____
    Individualized   _____

Other:
    Concrete materials   _____
    Rapid feedback   _____
    Clear objectives   _____
    Drill and repetition   _____
    Organized lessons   _____
    Clear explanations   _____

2.   One characterisic of effective teachers as compared to ineffective teachers is that they provide more feedback for inappropriate behavior.

    Does this characteristic conflict with the behavior management principle of ignoring inappropriate behavior? Justify your answer.

3.   You are teaching a tenth-grade science class, and there are four students in your class who read three grade levels below the reading level of your text. You also have a student who has cerebral palsy and one who is visually impaired.

    What are some ways you can modify the lessons to fit the needs of these students?

4.   It is time for English in your fifth-grade class. As you ask the class to get out their English books, you hear the class's habitual response of moans accompanied by pained expressions on their faces. After school you decide to deal with the situation rather than ignoring or excusing it, so you start by brainstorming all the possible reasons why the class might dislike English.

    What ideas do you list?

5.   You have been asked to speak to new teachers about effective teaching. What are some of the guidelines you would discuss with them? Provide examples for your guidelines.

6.   You are beginning a new school year and want to organize your instruction and teaching activities. Discuss some of the points you would keep in mind as you complete this task.

CHAPTER 13

TEACHING EXCEPTIONAL STUDENTS

CHAPTER OVERVIEW

I.   What Does It Mean to Be Exceptional?
   A. What's in a Name?: Cautions in the Use of Labels
   B. Beyond the Labels: Teaching Students

II. Students with Learning Problems
   A. Physical and Health Problems: Orothopedic Handicaps, Epilepsy, Cerebral Palsy
   B. Impaired Vision or Hearing
   C. Communication Disorders
   D. Behavior Disorders
   E. Specific Learning Disabilities: What's Wrong When Nothing is Wrong?
   F. Mental Retardation

III. Mainstreaming
   A. Public Law 94-142
   B. Making the Programs Work

IV. Resources for Mainstreaming

V.   Students with Special Abilities: The Gifted
   A. Who Are the Gifted?
   B. Recognizing Gifted Students
   C. Teaching the Gifted

VI. Multicultural and Bilingual Education
   A. Making Multicultural Education Work
   B. Bilingual Education

1. Define the term "exceptional."
2. Identify the potential problems in using specific labels to categorize students.
3. Discuss the disagreement concerned with teaching to strengths and weaknesses and its resolution.
4. Define "orthopedic devices" and provide some examples.
5. Explain the disorder epilepsy and discuss some of the problems students with epilepsy may have in the classroom.
6. Describe the condition of cerebral palsy and spasticity and the difficulties the condition may present in school.
7. Discuss adjustment and self-concept for students who are physically handicapped.
8. Describe the activities of speech reading, sign language, and finger spelling.
9. Explain the debate regarding whether oral or manual approaches are better for children with hearing impairments.
10. Explain nine guidelines for teaching the hearing-impaired student.
11. Define the terms low vision and educationally blind.
12. Identify some of the behaviors that students who have difficulty seeing may present.
13. Define the following speech-related terms:
    a. speech impairment
    b. articulation disorder
    c. stuttering
    d. voicing problem
14. Identify the four types of language disorders.
15. Explain five guidelines for helping the student who stutters.
16. State the four categories of behavior disorders identified by Quay (1979).
17. Define hyperactivity and describe the characteristics of a hyperactive child.
18. Explain why a suicide threat or suicide attempt should be taken very seriously.
19. Define the term "specific learning disability."
20. Explain six guidelines for helping students with learning disabilities.
21. Define "mental retardation."
22. Identify, as specified by the AAMD, the three key factors in mental retardation.
23. Discuss the causes of mental retardation.
24. Define Down syndrome.
25. Discuss the learning goals of mentally retarded students and the impact of their presence on a regular classroom.
26. Describe the developmental characteristics of mentally retarded individuals.
27. Explain twelve guidelines for teaching retarded students.
28. Explain the purpose and provisions of Public Law 94-142 and describe ways in which it is implemented.
29. Explain the concept of "least restrictive placement" and discuss the problems associated with the concept.
30. Describe an individualized education program and list the points which must be covered in an IEP.
31. Describe the purpose and activities of a resource room.

32. Describe how you might recognize and teach a gifted student in your class.
33. Explain five guidelines for teaching gifted students.
34. State the goal of multicultural education and some conditions and approaches for its implementation.
35. Explain the two contrasting teaching approaches for children who do not speak English as a first language.

KEY TERMS

Fill in the blanks in the following sentences with the letters preceding the concepts listed below.

a. specific learning disability
b. orthopedic devices
c. epilepsy
d. cerebral palsy
e. spasticity
f. speech reading
g. sign language
h. finger spelling
i. low vision
j. educationally blind
k. speech impairment
l. articulation disorders
m. voicing problems

n. gifted students
o. hyperactive
p. mental retardation
q. Down's syndrome
r. least restrictive placement
s. individualized educational program
t. resource room
u. multicultural education
v. cultural pluralism
w. native language approach

1. One cause of mental retardation is ____ that can be detected early in pregnancy through amniocentesis.

2. Mild vision problems can be corrected with glasses; students with ____ may need only large-print readers to remain in the regular classroom; the ____ student must have Braille materials, recordings, or readers to provide information.

3. Two types of ____ are grand mal, characterized by uncontrolled jerking movements, and petit mal, characterized by a temporary loss of contact with the environment.

4. The most common forms of ____ are stuttering, ____ (substitution or omission of sounds), and ____ (speaking with an inappropriate pitch, quality, loudness, or flexibility).

5. A/an ____ must include the student's present achievement level, instructional goals, services provided, degree of participation in the regular school program, and evaluation procedures.

6. Many physically handicapped children can participate in a normal school program with the aid of _____ such as braces or wheelchairs.

7. According to the concept of _____, students should be assigned to the most normal program possible and moved up to a more integrated program as soon as appropriate.

8. Damage to the brain and central nervous system can result in _____ which may affect only movement but frequently is accompanied by secondary handicapping conditions. The most common form is characterized by _____ (involuntary muscle contractions).

9. The concept of _____ rejects the ideas of the "melting pot" and the existence of separate cultures; it endorses a society that values diversity, or _____ .

10. An example of the oral approach to teaching the hearing-impaired is _____; manual approaches include _____ and _____ .

11. There are two types of _____ . One type excels in academic tasks and the other is above average in solving problems in new and effective ways.

12. A disorder in one or more of the basic psychological processes involved in understanding or using language, spoken or written, which may manifest itself in an imperfect ability to listen, think, speak, read, write, spell, or to do mathematical calculations is termed _____ .

13. Students who are mainstreamed may spend part of the day in a regular classroom and part in a _____ working with a specially trained teacher.

14. Many _____ children receive stimulant medication which may have several negative side effects.

15. One approach to bilingual education is the _____ which uses a student's first language for instruction while he is learning the majority language.

16. Intellectual functioning, adaptive behavior, and age of onset must all be considered in the identification of _____ .

MULTIPLE CHOICE QUESTIONS

1. For many years, special education used a disease model which focused on (p. 453)

   a. medication and therapy.
   b. finding a cure.
   c. prevention and treatment.
   d. diagnosis and classification.

2. When teachers and parents set expectations for achievement based on a label and not on the individual's abilities the child is being (p. 453)

    a. segregated.
    b. dehumanized.
    c. underrated.
    d. stigmatized.

3. All of the following are true of the labels placed on exceptional students **except** (p. 452)

    a. they can be assigned with great accuracy.
    b. they can determine teacher expectations.
    c. they can protect the students from the misunderstanding of their classmates.
    d. they can provide guidelines for seeking information.

4. The best way to prevent exceptional students, their peers, and their teachers from forming negative attitudes about them is to (p. 454)

    a. segregate them from normal students.
    b. ignore their differences.
    c. help the students learn and change their behavior.
    d. place them in the middle of the activities in class.

5. Grand mal epilepsy is characterized by (p. 456)

    a. slow degeneration of sight and hearing.
    b. a temporary loss of contact with the outside world.
    c. uncontrolled jerking movements for brief periods.
    d. total loss of fine motor control.

6. Zeke is having an epileptic seizure on the first day of class. His teacher should (p. 456)

    a. move hard objects away and calmly explain to the other children.
    b. put something hard between his teeth to protect his tongue.
    c. try to restrain Zeke's movements and ask other students to help.
    d. immediately call a doctor.

7. Spasticity is the general term for (p. 457)

    a. temporary loss of contact with the outside world.
    b. spontaneous firings of neurons in the brain.
    c. cerebral palsy.
    d. involuntary contraction of muscles.

8. When teaching hearing impaired students it is important for the teacher to (p. 459)

   a. speak loudly and distinctly.
   b. make sure the student can see the teacher's face.
   c. allow the student to ask classmates to repeat instructions.
   d. supplement their words with expressive hand gestures.

9. Janice holds her head at an odd angle in class. She often misunderstands the assignments written on the board, and she holds her books very close to her face while reading. Janice's teacher should be aware of the possibility that Janice is (p. 460)

   a. emotionally disturbed.
   b. visually impaired.
   c. dyslexic.
   d. mildly retarded.

10. A first-grade student has difficulty speaking loud enough to be heard in class. This student may have a/an (p. 461)

    a. hearing impairment.
    b. articulation disorder.
    c. voicing problem.
    d. emotional problem.

11. To help a student who stutters, a teacher should (p. 462)

    a. give special opportunities to recite on good days.
    b. excuse the student from embarrassing classroom responsibilities.
    c. correct the speech whenever possible.
    d. excuse the student from assignments where the stuttering interferes.

12. Hyperactive children experience all of the following difficulties **except** (p. 464)

    a. difficulty responding appropriately.
    b. the inability to work steadily toward goals.
    c. a fixation on a specific word or item.
    d. the frequent inability to control their behaviors on command.

13. Problems with the acquisition and use of language that may show up as difficulty with reading, writing, reasoning, or math are termed ____ (p. 465)

    a. single-sense impairments.
    b. focused impairments.
    c. monoclinical disfunctions.
    d. specific learning disabilities.

14. Almost every definition of mental retardation includes the idea that mentally retarded individuals (p. 466)

    a. have IQ scores below 75.
    b. are functionally immature.
    c. cannot adapt adequately to their environment.
    d. have limited verbal abilities.

15. Students who have limited verbal abilities but who are capable in social situations and have adequate adaptive behavior are (p. 468)

    a. not mentally retarded.
    b. mildly mentally retarded.
    c. educable retardates.
    d. trainable retardates.

16. When younger children who are mildly retarded are placed in regular classes, they are likely to (p. 468)

    a. be more successful in making and keeping friends.
    b. be less isolated thatn when they are kept in special classes.
    c. be more easily accepted by their nonretarded classmates.
    d. experience some gains in academic achievement.

17. Under PL 94-142, an IEP must be updated (p. 471)

    a. every semester.
    b. quarterly.
    c. yearly.
    d. every five years.

18. Classrooms with special materials and equipment that are staffed by specially trained instructors are called (p. 473)

    a. exceptional instruction rooms.
    b. alternate education rooms.
    c. crisis centers.
    d. resource rooms.

19. Students who excel in situations that require the application of information and the creation of new solutions to problems are said to have (p. 475)

    a. high IQs.
    b. academic giftedness.
    c. analytic giftedness.
    d. creative/productive giftedness.

20. The best single predictor of academically gifted students is (p. 476)

    a. teacher observation.
    b. performance on first grade tasks.
    c. observational by experts.
    d. the individual IQ test.

21. Upper Crust University is attempting to make placement decisions for its incoming freshmen, a group with a very mixed cultural background. What tests could the administration use to pick out gifted students missed by the IQ tests? (p. 477)

    a. reports of motivation and persistence
    b. reports of social abilities
    c. tests of creativity
    d. tests of reading comprehension

22. In dealing with gifted students, you should do all of the following **except** (p. 478)

    a. focus on problem-solving, divergent thinking, and long-term projects.
    b. use immediate and concrete rewards as reinforcers.
    c. involve students in planning their own curriculum.
    d. allow time for independent work and privacy.

23. The concept of multicultural education rejects the notion of assimilating other cultures and advocates (p. 479)

    a. protecting American cultural values.
    b. the segregation of cultures.
    c. the American melting pot.
    d. cultural pluralism.

24. The native language approach to multicultural education believes that a country's official language should be taught (p. 481)

    a. gradually, as appropriate.
    b. immediately by the most direct method.
    c. immediately so it can be used as the medium of instruction.
    d. through reading before it is used in speaking.

25. Studies in multilingual education have found that (p. 481)

    a. bilingual students progress as quickly as their single language counterparts.
    b. programs in bilingual instruction show immediate student gains.
    c. students should be taught to speak a second language before learning to read it.
    d. bilingual instruction retards the development of the primary language.

APPLICATION AND DISCUSSION QUESTIONS

1. Match the category of exceptionality with the behavior that could indicate its presence.

   a. gifted and talented
   b. physical/health problems
   c. visual impairment
   d. hearing impairment

   e. communication disorder
   f. behavior disorder
   g. specific learning disability
   h. mental retardation

   _____ 1. A student behaves in one of two extremes: he is either loud, hostile, and disruptive or he is subdued, withdrawn, and uncommunicative.

   _____ 2. A student often turns one ear toward the speaker and seems intent on looking at the speaker's face.

   _____ 3. A student is at the top of the class academically and is a leader in the class because of his advanced social development.

   _____ 4. A student seldom speaks in class, and when he does, he speaks jerkily in very short phrases or sentences.

   _____ 5. A child seems to daydream frequently, and at times he "blanks out" or "spaces out" of what is happening in the classroom.

   _____ 6. A student seems quite bright when answering questions orally, but writing is a very tedious task for him and he writes slowly and poorly.

   _____ 7. A student starts reading his assignment, but after a few minutes he begins clowning around or says how dumb the story is or exhibits some other behavior which allows him to avoid reading.

   _____ 8. This student is a very low achiever in all areas and frequently acts like a much younger child in social situations.

2. Read the language sample and accompanying explanation. Respond to the questions.

Delayed Verbal Development

Teacher: "Sam, what is your favorite thing to do on a weekend?"

Sam: "Ride my minibike."
      "What color is it?"
      "Red."
      "Where do you ride it?"
      "In the field."

145

"Tell me more."

"That's all."

"It must break down sometimes; how do you fix it?"

"Take the engine out."

"Then what do you do?"

"Fix it."

This language sample was taken when Sam was conversing alone with his teacher. It is apparent that Sam is uncomfortable when urged to speak; he does not contribute spontaneously and does not elaborate. When you take into consideration that Sam is 12 years old and talking to a familiar person about a subject he is interested in and knowledgeable about, then you realize the extent of the problem.

Sam is an extremely reserved, cooperative sixth grader who is struggling with reading. Perhaps because he has never posed a behavioral problem, his previous teachers have not taken note of Sam's sparse verbalizations. Although he is seeing the remedial reading teacher, he has never been referred to supplementary help in language. He scored at the 2.0 level on the California Achievement Test, Lower Primary, Form W, in September. When he reads, Sam makes numerous substitutions, particularly on basic words. He tends to substitute words such as "house" for "home." In both reading and speaking, Sam omits words or distorts the order of words, uses incorrect tenses, and makes errors of syntax.

Sam has an expressive language problem. He is unable to plan and organize words for the expression of ideas in complete sentences. This in turn contributes to the reading problem.

Performance Objective

Sam will generate sentences that include more descriptive language in the form of adjectives and adverbs.

What are some learning activities you could plan in order for Sam to achieve the performance objective?

How could you encourage Sam to talk more so that his confidence in speaking will increase?

3. Today many exceptional children are mainstreamed into the regular classroom for part of the day. Describe what kinds of accommodations in your classroom you might make for each of the exceptional children listed below:

a. Susan is a visually impaired student. Her sight problem can be overcome if she wears her glasses.

b. Trudy is an epileptic and has petit mal seizures frequently.

c. Christina has the condition of cerebral palsy, is in a wheelchair and has some spasiticity.

d. Herman is a severly hearing impaired student.

e. Becky stutters whenever she is asked to speak in class.

f. Ralph is extremely anxious, withdrawn and shy and is said to have an anxiety-withdrawal disorder.

g. Johnny is a hyperactive child - always out of his seat, lacks attention to the lessons and is impulsive in responding.

h. Tom has a specific learning disability and is unable to think and write at the same time. He has difficulty taking notes and writing anything spontaneously from his head.

i. Jim is considered a gifted student and often appears bored in your class.

CHAPTER 14

USING STANDARDIZED TESTS IN TEACHING

CHAPTER OVERVIEW

I. Measurement and Evaluation
   A. Norm-Referenced Tests
   B. Criterion-Referenced Tests

II. What Do Test Scores Mean?
   A. Basic Concepts
   B. Types of Scores
   C. Interpreting Test Scores

III. Standardized Tests
   A. Achievement Tests: What Has the Student Learned?
   B. Diagnostic Tests: What Are the Student's Strengths and Weaknesses?
   C. Aptitude Tests: How Well Will the Student Do in the Future?

IV. Current Issues in Standardized Testing
   A. The Role of Testing
   B. Advantages in Taking Tests: Fair and Unfair

CHAPTER OBJECTIVES

1. Differentiate measurement and evaluation and describe the relationship between them.
2. Define norm-referenced testing and criterion-referenced testing.
3. Give the uses and limitations of norm-referenced tests and criterion-referenced tests.

4. Define the following terms:
   a. standardized test
   b. norming sample
   c. frequency distribution
   d. central tendency
   e. mean
   f. median
   g. mode
   h. standard deviation
   i. normal distribution
   j. histogram
5. Understand the computation procedures for the following:
   a. mean
   b. median
   c. mode
   d. standard deviation
   e. z-score
   f. T score
6. Be able to interpret and give the advantages and limitations of the following scores:
   a. percentile rank scores
   b. grade-equivalent scores
   c. z-scores
   d. T scores
   e. stanine scores
7. Explain the concept of reliability.
8. Define true score and explain its relationship to standard error of measurement.
9. Explain the use of a confidence interval.
10. Explain the concept of validity.
11. Discuss five guidelines which may be followed to increase the reliability and validity of a test.
12. Discuss the use of achievement tests.
13. Describe how you might use information from a norm-referenced achievement test.
14. Explain the purpose of diagnostic tests and list some frequently used diagnostic tests.
15. Define aptitude test and explain the purpose of a scholastic aptitude test.
16. Discuss the relationship between IQ and scholastic aptitude.
17. Explain the purpose of vocational aptitude and vocational interest tests.
18. Discuss the use of minimum competency tests.
19. Explain the "truth-in-testing" law which went into effect in New York on January 1, 1980.
20. State the sources of test bias and identify attempts that have been made to ensure the fair use of tests.
21. Define "culture-fair/culture-free tests."
22. Explain the reasons for and consequences of the Larry P. v. Riles case in California.
23. List ways to prepare students to take tests.
24. Discuss some new approaches that have emerged to deal with common testing problems and identify the difficulties with the new approaches.
25. Define "curriculum-based assessment."

Fill in the blanks in the following sentences with the letters preceding the concepts listed below.

a.	evaluation	s.	z-scores
b.	measurement	t.	T-scores
c.	norm-referenced testing	u.	stanine scores
d.	criterion-referenced testing	v.	validity
e.	standardized tests	w.	curriculum based assessment
f.	norming sample	x.	minimum competency tests
g.	frequency distribution	y.	reliability
h.	histogram	z.	true score
i.	mean	aa.	standard error of measurement
j.	central tendency	bb.	confidence interval
k.	median	cc.	achievement tests
l.	mode	dd.	diagnostic tests
m.	bimodal distribution	ee.	aptitude tests
n.	standard deviation	ff.	vocational interest tests
o.	variability	gg.	culture-free tests
p.	normal distribution		
q.	percentile rank scores		
r.	grade-equivalent scores		

1. _____ are obtained from different norming samples for each grade level and different forms of the test are often used at different grade levels.

2. _____ have a specific procedure for administration, scoring, and resporting the scores; they have been given to a _____ which serves as a comparison group.

3. A test has _____ if it measures what it is supposed to measure.

4. Three measures of _____ are the _____, which is the arithmetic average score; the _____, which is the most frequent score, and the _____, which is the middle score of a group of scores.

5. _____ identify specific problems that are interfering with learning; _____ measure how much a student has learned; _____ predict how well a student will learn in the future.

6. A test has _____ if it is consistent in its measurement on repeated administrations.

7. A system for testing based on mastery of curriculum objectives is termed _____ .

8. A/an _____ shows the number of people who receive each score on a test.

9. _____ have attempted to eliminate cultural bias in tests but have not been successful.

10. Standard scores are based upon the standard deviation and may be reported as _____, which tell how many standard deviations above or below the average a score is; _____, which eliminate negative numbers; or _____, which are less precise than the other standard scores.

11. _____ compares a person's score with those of other people; _____ compares a person's score with a fixed standard of performance.

12. A/an _____ indicates the spread of scores around the mean; it reflects the _____ of a group of scores.

13. The _____ or "standard error band" of a score is the student's score plus or minus the _____ of the test.

14. _____ involves judgments and is based on information from a variety of sources, one of which can be _____, which gives a numerical value to observations or characteristics.

15. There is no method of finding an absolutely accurate or _____; however, the more accurate or reliable a test is, the smaller standard error of measurement it will have.

16. _____ compare raw scores and tell the percentage of students in the norming sample who scored at or below a particular raw score.

17. Tests asking students to choose what activities they prefer are called _____ .

18. In a/an _____, the mean, median, and mode are all the same point.

19. Tests which measure competence in reading, writing and arithmetic and are required for graduation from high school are termed _____ .

MULTIPLE CHOICE QUESTIONS

1. An evaluation is made by (p. 488)

   a. comparing criteria with measured values.
   b. analyzing material to establish criteria.
   c. comparing information to criteria and then making judgments.
   d. turning raw data into numbers.

2. Before being allowed to solo in an airplane, a student pilot must pass a medical exam that shows her vision to be no worse than 20/40 when corrected. This is a (p. 490)

    a. statistical norm.
    b. raw score.
    c. norm-referenced test.
    d. criterion-referenced test.

3. Norm-referenced tests would be appropriate in all of the following situations **except** (p. 489)

    a. comparing gereral abilities in English or American history.
    b. assessing the range of abilities in a large group.
    c. measuring mastery of addition and subtraction.
    d. selecting candidates when only a few openings are available.

4. When teachers wish to measure a range of different abilities instead of progress toward a specific objective they should use (p. 490)

    a. criterion-referenced tests.
    b. norm-referenced tests.
    c. non-objective tests.
    d. essay tests.

5. In order to accurately reflect a student's ranking, a standardized test must be (p. 504)

    a. designed to fit specific objectives.
    b. given right after the student has studied the material.
    c. given under controlled standard conditions.
    d. scored by an objective observer.

6. When scores are totaled and the total divided by the number of scores, the result is a (p. 492)

    a. deviation.
    b. mode.
    c. median.
    d. mean.

7. The mode is the (p. 493)

    a. score that occurs most oftern
    b. number of people making the average score.
    c. arithmetic average.
    d. midpoint in the range of scores.

8.   On Miss Furr's histogram of the class frequency distribution, the two highest bars both show twenty students at their respective scores. This is a (p. 493)

    a.   split average.
    b.   bimedial distribution.
    c.   bimodal distribution.
    d.   distribution without central tendency.

9.   Which of the following best describes the standard deviation. It is a measure of (p. 493)

    a.   the distance between the median and the extremes.
    b.   how well the students met the tested objective.
    c.   the spread of scores around the mean.
    d.   the slope of the bell curve at the mean.

10.   In a perfect normal distribution (p. 495)

    a.   the mean, median, and mode are all at the same point.
    b.   the standard deviation is .50.
    c.   the z score is 0.
    d.   the tails are at the median points.

11.   In a normal distribution, approximately what percent of scores fall more than two standard deviations from the mean? (p. 495)

    a.   1.0
    b.   2.5
    c.   5.0
    d.   7.5

12.   Grade equivalent scores should be avoided because they (p. 497)

    a.   are unreliable measures.
    b.   are easily misinterpreted.
    c.   give no criterion for evaluation.
    d.   may change drastically from year to year.

13.   The CEEB has a mean of 500 and a standard deviation of 100. Paul has a CEEB score of 400. This gives him a stanine score of (p. 498)

    a.   1
    b.   2
    c.   3
    d.   4

14. Fay's z score on the test is +1.45. Her stanine score is (p. 498)

    a. 6.45
    b. 7
    c. 7.5
    d. 8

15. One of the advantages of stanine scores is that they (p. 498)

    a. encourage teachers and parents to think in general terms.
    b. give a more precise reflection of the student's abilities.
    c. grow linearly with percentile rank.
    d. are more stable from year to year.

16. Fred made a 103 and Frank made a 96 on a test with a confidence interval of 4. This means that (p. 501)

    a. Frank's true score is higher than Fred's.
    b. testing error might account for the difference in their scores.
    c. their true scores are the same.
    d. the test is very unreliable.

17. When profiles and test printouts on achievement tests are used to determine a child's strengths and weaknesses, the test is being used for (p. 507)

    a. observer corroboration.
    b. aptitude purposes.
    c. a measure of cognitive ability.
    d. diagnostic purposes.

18. Which of the following is not true of diagnostic tests? They are (p. 507)

    a. given by highly trained specialists.
    b. usually given to groups of students.
    c. given to find weaknesses in learning processes.
    d. generally aimed at younger students.

19. IQ scores can be considered a standard score with (p. 508)

    a. a mean of 90 to 110 and a confidence interval of 15.
    b. a mean of 90 to 110 and a standard deviation of 30.
    c. a mean of 100 and a standard deviation of 30.
    d. a mean of 100 and a standard deviation of 15.

20. It is most accurate to say that IQ tests measure (p. 508)

    a. current functioning.
    b. overall ability.
    c. general intelligence.
    d. specific achievement.

21. Which test would be most beneficial to a student wanting to know more about his attitudes relevant to career decisions? (p. 510)

    a. ACT
    b. SAT
    c. WISC-R
    d. DAT

22. In the past, a large number of minority students were inappropriately classified as mentally retarded because (p. 571)

    a. standard tests were invalid for them.
    b. standard tests were unreliable for them.
    c. their test scores were interpreted incorrectly.
    d. they could not understand test instructions.

23. In 1983, The National Commission on Excellence in Education placed the rate of functional illiteracy among teenagers in the U.S. at

    a.   6 percent.
    b. 13 percent.
    c. 18 percent.
    d. 20 percent.

24. The court case which indicated that 20 percent of black seniors and only 2 percent of white seniors in Florida were denied diplomas on the basis of minimum competency tests was: (p. 512)

    a. Larry P. v. Riles
    b. Debra P. v. Turlington
    c. Diana v. State Board of Education
    d. Birdie Mae Davis v. Mobile Board of Education

25. Truth-in testing laws may have all the following disadvantages **except** (p. 512)

    a. assessment procedures for minority students may be impaired.
    b. the costs of testing programs may increase.
    c. some of the most effective questions may be made public and therefore useless.
    d. it will be more difficult for researchers to compare results across studies.

26. Fernando was born in Cuba and raised in Miami in an Hispanic bilingual community. When he takes a standardized test he is likely to be at a disadvantage for all the following reasons **except** (p. 513)

   a. Fernando may be less at ease and therfore less verbal.
   b. the tests more often reward middle-class values.
   c. standardized tests are poor predictors of achievement for minorities.
   d. the questions tend to center on facts and experiences from the dominant culture.

27. Which of the following is known to be effective in improving standardized test scores? (p. 514)

   a. drills of vocabulary words
   b. familiarity with the test-taking procedures
   c. practice in quick computation
   d. mnemonic memory aids

APPLICATION AND DISCUSSION QUESTIONS

1. Below are several categories of questions. Respond to each as directed.

A. Match the specific test with its type:

   a. IQ test   d. aptitude test
   b. achievement test   e. interest test
   c. diagnostic test

   ____ 1. WISC-R   ____ 5. Stanford-Binet
   ____ 2. Iowa Test of Basic Skills   ____ 6. Woodcock-Johnson
                                                   Psycho-Educational Battery
   ____ 3. Detroit Test of Learning   ____ 7. Kuder Preference Record
           Aptitude
   ____ 4. SAT

B. Match the type of test which would be most appropriate in the following situations:

   a. IQ test   c. diagnostic test
   b. achievement test   d. aptitude test

   ____ 1. The teacher wants to know how her biology class performs in comparison with the classes in other high schools.

_____ 2. A student is being evaluated to determine if he should be placed in a class for the mentally retarded.

_____ 3. A teacher needs to predict which eighth-grade students would be likely to succeed in a freshman algebra class and which should take ninth-grade math.

_____ 4. A third-grade student is having difficulty in reading and the teacher wants to know the specific skills in which he needs remedial help.

C. Match the following test items with the type of test on which they would probably appear:

a. individual IQ test   d. diagnostic test
b. group IQ test   e. aptitude test
c. achievement test

_____ 1. Tester: "I'm going to say two words and you tell me if they begin with the same sound or with different sounds."

_____ 2. White is to snow as green is to _____ .

Flower   Grass   Winter   Summer

_____ 3. Draw a sketch of these familiar objects:

house, fork, book, tree, table, lamp.

_____ 4. Punctuate the following sentence:

Im glad to meet you said Mrs Clay

_____ 5. Tester: "What should you do if you find a jar that has fallen and broken in a grocery store?"

D. Indicate whether the following statements refer to a criterion-referenced test (CRT) or a norm-referenced test (NRT) .

_____ 1. The purpose of the test is to discriminate among the students.

_____ 2. A student must pass an eighth-grade reading and math test before he can graduate from high school.

_____ 3. Students may retake similar tests over the same material until they pass 80% of the test items.

_____ 4. The school wants to select a group of individuals to be in a class for gifted students.

2. The following questions pertain to the interpretation of test scores. Respond as indicated.

   a. Find the mean, median, and mode for the following group of scores: 3, 3, 4, 6, 10, 21, 30.

      Mean = _____   Median = _____   Mode = _____

      Which measure most *accurately* reflects the central tendency of the scores?

   b. A reading test has a mean of 30 and a standard deviation of 5. A math test has a mean of 50 and a standard deviation of 8. Johnny made a raw score of 37 on the reading test and 56 on the math test. Did he perform better in math or reading (**Hint** : Draw a normal distribution curve for the reading test and for the math test and locate Johnny's scores on the curves.)

   c. Two English classes took the same test. Class A had a mean of 50 and a standard deviation of 3. Class B had a mean of 50 and a standard deviation of 8. Which class is probably grouped according to ability?

   d. A high school with 1200 students is placing students with an IQ score of 130 and above in an accelerated class. Assuming a normal school population, approximately how many students will be assigned to the accelerated class?

   e. A math achievement test has a mean of 60, a standard deviation of 8, and a standard error of measurement of 3. Alice made a raw score of 72. What is the confidence interval in which her true score probably falls? _____ What is her percentile rank? _____; stanine score: _____; z-score: _____; T-score: _____. Most students (68%) had a raw score between _____ and _____ .

3. A superintendent of schools administered a standardized math test to all seventh-grade pupils in his system. He found that the **median** score of the pupils in one of the classes was seriously below the norm and criticized the teacher for this fact. The teacher wants to raise the median on the next test. She feels (correctly) that the best chance of doing so rests upon her concentrating her instructional efforts on just a certain few of her students.

   On which of the students should she concentrate her efforts and why?

4. A third-grade pupil has an IQ score (from a group intelligence test) of 83 and a grade equivalent score in reading of 4.7 in October.

--Is this student an "overachiever" or an "underachiever"?

--Do you think his IQ score is valid?

--Does it make any difference whether the score is valid or not?

--What may be the effect of his IQ score being recorded in his cumulative folder?

CHAPTER 15

CLASSROOM EVALUATION AND GRADING

CHAPTER OVERVIEW

I.   Classroom Evaluation and Testing
   A. Two Uses of Tests
   B. Objective Testing
   C. Essay Testing

II. Planning a Measurement Program
   A. Planning Evaluation
   B. Cautions: Being Fair

III. Effects of Grades and Grading on Students
   A. The Effect of High Grades
   B. The Effect of Low Grades
   C. Effects of Feedback

IV. Grading and Reporting: Nuts and Bolts
   A. Criterion-Referenced versus Norm-Referenced Grading
   B. Preparing Report Cards
   C. The Point System
   D. Percentage Grading
   E. The Contract System
   F. The Mastery Approach
   G. Grading on Effort and Improvement

V.   Beyond Grading: Communication

160

CHAPTER OBJECTIVES

1. Distinguish between formative and summative measurement of achievement.
2. Define the terms "pretest" and "diagnostic test."
3. Explain the use of data-based instruction.
4. Name the four formats of objective testing and explain the use of the term "objective."
5. Define the terms "stem" and "distractor."
6. Apply the guidelines for writing objective test items in writing items.
7. Apply the proper procedures for constructing and scoring essay items.
8. Compare the advantages and limitations of essay tests and objective tests.
9. Discuss planning evaluation and the use of a behavior-content matrix.
10. Identify factors that tend to influence teacher grades.
11. Discuss how grades may be influenced by the "halo effect."
12. Name the three factors that determine the effect of a grade upon a student.
13. Describe the effects of high grades, low grades, and feedback upon students.
14. Discuss the idea of "working for a grade vs. working to learn."
15. Explain five guidelines for minimizing the detrimental effects of grading.
16. Contrast criterion-referenced and norm-referenced grading.
17. Explain the concept of "grading on the curve."
18. Explain the process of preparing report cards.
19. Describe the following grading systems:
    a. point system
    b. percentage grading.
    c. contract system
    d. mastery approach
    e. individual learning expectation
    f. dual marking system
20. Discuss some guidelines that would apply to using any grading system.
21. Explain the value and purpose of student conferences and parent conferences.
22. Describe the guidelines for a successful parent-teacher conference.

KEY TERMS

Fill in the blanks in the following sentences with the letters preceding the concepts listed below.

a. formative measurement
b. pretest
c. diagnostic test
d. summative measurement
e. objective tests
f. stem

j. individual learning expectation
k. norm-referenced grading
l. grading on the curve
m. percentage grading
n. contract system
o. revise option

g. distractors
h. halo effect
i. criterion-referenced grading

p. mastery learning
q. dual marking system
r. holistic scoring
s. data-based instruction

1. Tests that have very reliable scoring procedures are called _____ .

2. _____ reflects a student's standing in comparison with others in the class.

3. The basic assumption of _____ is that every student is capable of achieving most of the course objectives if given enough time and the proper instruction.

4. _____ occurs before or during instruction for the purpose of guiding or forming educational plans.

5. A/an _____ is a form of grade notation that recognizes both achievement and effort.

6. Multiple-choice items consist of two parts: The _____, which is the part that asks the question, and the choices or alternatives that follow.

7. In order to determine what a student already knows, a teacher may wish to employ a/an _____ .

8. _____ is a form of norm-referenced grading in which students are graded in relation to the average level of performance for the class.

9. A cooperative, bright student who happens to hand in a poor paper might still receive a good grade because of a positive _____ .

10. _____ occurs at the end of an instructional unit for the purpose of assessing the students' final level of achievement.

11. The wrong answers among the alternatives in a multiple-choice question are called _____ and should be plausible in order to be chosen by students who have only a partial understanding of the subject.

12. _____ indicates how much a student has learned and tends to motivate students to achieve since everyone has a chance to get a high grade.

13. A/an _____ specifies the work required for a particular grade; quality control can be a problem with this approach to grading.

14. A/an _____ may be given in order to identify areas of instruction that need reteaching.

15. Grading students with respect to achievement of a set of specified objectives is known as _____ .

16. Your school district uses the following system: A = 90 to 100, B = 80 to 89, C = 70 to 79, D = 60 to 69, F = below 60. This is an example of _____ .

17. In the contract system, allowing students whose work is unsatisfactory to improve their work but penalizing them for not getting it right the first time is called a/an _____ .

18. A method using daily probes of specific skill mastery is termed _____ .

19. The evaluation of a piece of written work as a whole, without separate grades for individual elements is called _____ .

20. The grading system in which students earn improvement points on tests or assignments for scoring above their personal base or average score, or for making a perfect score, is termed _____ .

MULTIPLE CHOICE QUESTIONS

1. Tests which are used to guide the course of instruction rather than establish a student's grade are called (p. 525)

   a. formative.
   b. objective.
   c. evaluative.
   d. summative.

2. The concept of divergent evolution is a bit tricky, so Ms. Wallace gives her biology class a twenty-minute test halfway through the unit to "test the waters." She is giving a (p. 525)

   a. summative test.
   b. directive test.
   c. diagnostic test.
   d. pretest.

3. Objective tests are so named because their answers (p. 526)

   a. fit specific course goals.
   b. require a particular viewpoint.
   c. are not subjective.
   d. refer to specific objects.

4. Multiple-choice questions can test higher-level objectives by (p. 526)

    a. testing more than one problem at a time.
    b. focusing on subtle details.
    c. using plausible distractors.
    d. adding novel content.

5. The most difficult part of using objective tests is (p. 527)

    a. grading the test.
    b. writing the test.
    c. defending the correct answers.
    d. selecting appropriate test material.

6. On the fifth multiple-choice question, 23 people chose the wrong answer and 4 people chose the right answer. The teacher should (p. 527)

    a. use the question in following years.
    b. review the material the question covers.
    c. call it an extra credit question.
    d. discard the question.

7. When you write multiple-choice questions you should **avoid** all of the following **except** (p. 528-529)

    a. stems that present a single problem.
    b. stems that use negative language.
    c. categorical words like "never" or "all."
    d. using "all of the above."

8. The best solution to the problem that essays sample a limited content area is use (p. 530)

    a. one or two essay items with several objective items.
    b. several essays to cover more area.
    c. essays only for short units.
    d. essays only for diagnostic purposes.

9. Some research indicates that college instructors give higher grades to essays that are (p. 530)

    a. short.
    b. wordy.
    c. direct.
    d. disorganized.

10. To improve your consistency in grading essay tests it is a good idea to (p. 531)

    a. have another knowledgeable teacher check you for bias.
    b. read each answer at least twice.
    c. shuffle the papers before you read any.
    d. read all the responses to one question before moving to the next.

11. Trevor wrote the final exam in educational psychology and then realized that he had written 15 questions dealing with parents (a minor topic) and only two on testing (a major topic) . He could have avoided this problem by planning the test with (p. 532)

    a. the help of other instructors.
    b. a behavior-content matrix.
    c. a prepared outline.
    d. more essay and fewer objective elements.

12. Teachers are more likely to give higher grades to students whose achievements they attribute to (p. 534)

    a. ability.
    b. effort.
    c. past learning.
    d. uncontrollable factors.

13. Mr. Burns is not particularly fond of Jimmy. The boy has dirty fingernails and loud clothes. And besides, he's just plain lazy. Jimmy is likely to get lower grades because of (p. 534)

    a. the friction effect.
    b. the halo effect.
    c. his uncooperative attitude.
    d. the smog effect.

14. All of the following are likely to influence the effect of a grade on a student's motivation **except** (p. 535)

    a. the grades of the other students in class.
    b. the student's attribution of cause for the grade.
    c. the student's expectation for the grades.
    d. the grades the student usually gets.

15. High achievers tend to be more reinforced by good grades and are therefore likely to (p. 535)

    a. conform to the teacher's views on assignments.
    b. give creative answers.
    c. appreciate high standards.
    d. see the connection between work and improvement.

16. High grades tend to be positive reinforcers for students who are (p. 535)

    a. lower in ability.
    b. accustomed to high marks.
    c. creative.
    d. nonconforming.

17. Students who typically receive Cs and Ds are likely to see grades as (p. 535)

    a. trivial.
    b. rewards.
    c. punishments.
    d. arbitrary.

18. Feedback is most helpful to students when it tells them (p. 537)

    a. when they are wrong.
    b. why they are wrong.
    c. if they are right.
    d. how this performance compares with their past performance.

19. Student errors on objective tests are generally caused by (p. 538)

    a. guessing.
    b. illogical thinking.
    c. misconceptions and incomplete knowledge.
    d. complete ignorance.

20. Written comments on students' work should be (p. 539)

    a. general and long.
    b. short and standardized.
    c. encouraging and personalized.
    d. detailed and specific.

21. "This is not an easy course," said Mr. Toleb. "It is possible for all of you to fail." The course grading system will be (p. 542)

    a. criterion-referenced.
    b. norm-referenced.
    c. formative.
    d. objective.

22. Traditional norm-referenced grading systems are most appropriate for (p. 542)

    a. determining which students have met the instructional objectives.
    b. diagnosing weaknesses and strengths in student learning.
    c. grouping students for instruction, college admission, and employment.
    d. deciding when students are ready to advance to new material.

23. Natural gaps in the range of scores are used as boundaries between grades in (p. 544)

    a. criterion-referenced systems.
    b. adjusted norm-referenced systems.
    c. two-thirds Cs systems.
    d. percentage grading systems.

24. "In this district, scores of 93 to 100 will earn As and scores below 75 will be Fs." The district has a (p. 547)

    a. point system.
    b. criterion-referenced system.
    c. percentage grading system.
    d. norm-referenced system.

25. On the first day of class, Ms. McLendon announces that to achieve an A, a student must turn in three written book reports plus the work required for a B. She is using a (p. 548)

    a. percentage grading system.
    b. contract system.
    c. point system.
    d. quantity system.

26. One advantage of the contract system is that it (p. 548)

    a. simplifies the task of separating good from poor work
    b. increases reliability as all students perform the same tasks.
    c. reduces student anxiety about grades.
    d. emphasizes quality of work over quantity.

27. In mastery learning students may improve their grades by (p. 549)

    a. going through a unit again and taking another form of unit test.
    b. going through a larger number of units.
    c. finishing units within specified time limits.
    d. turning in specified extra work.

28. In Clements' dual marking system, grades are based on both (p. 550)

    a. conduct and aptitude.
    b. effort and aptitude.
    c. effort and achievement.
    d. aptitude and achievement.

29. The Buckley Amendment of 1974 provides that (p. 555)

    a. certain information in school records must be kept confidential.
    b. parents may review and challenge material in their children's school records.
    c. no federal monies may be used for aptitude testing of minorities.
    d. placement tests given to minorities must be culture-fair.

30. Julia has divided her class's assignments into relative importance. The midterm for instance, is worth 30 percent of the total grade. Next she assigns points to her students' performances on those assignments. A+ on the midterm equals 30 points, A equals 27, B equals 25, and so on. This is called (p. 546)

    a. percentage grading.
    b. grade translation.
    c. evaluation weighting.
    d. the point system.

APPLICATION AND DISCUSSION QUESTIONS

1. Identify the faults in the following multiple-choice items. Rewrite the item so that it is satisfactory.

    1. The word "gordo" in Spanish means

        a. thin.
        b. underweight.
        c. skinny.
        d. fat.

        FAULT :
        REWRITE :

2. A spider is an

   a. marsupial.
   b. arachnid.
   c. vertebrate.
   d. chordate.

   FAULT :
   REWRITE :

3. Tennis courts that will require the least maintenance than any other tennis court is the tennis court which

   a. is made of grass.
   b. is made of clay.
   c. is made of lakold.
   d. is made of Rubico.

   FAULT :
   REWRITE :

4. The development of the self-concept is not principally influenced by

   a. parents.
   b. peers.
   c. growth rate.
   d. physical appearance.

   FAULT :
   REWRITE :

5. "Culture-fair" tests are

   a. always reliable.
   b. always valid.
   c. power tests.
   d. usually nonverbal in order to offset cultural differences in language.

   FAULT :
   REWRITE :

2. Rewrite the following essay items so that they are more precise and students will understand what information is desired by the instructor.

   a. Write about the World's Fair.

      REWRITE :

   b. What do you think about changing the legal driving age from 16 to 21 years of age?

      REWRITE :

   c. Compare Switzerland and Holland.

      REWRITE :

   d. What is a good computer?

      REWRITE :

   e. What did the character in the play do?

      REWRITE :

3. Indicate whether an objective test or an essay test would be more appropriate for these purposes:

   _____ 1. To test the students' knowledge of the terminology used in lab experiments.

   _____ 2. The test must be given and graded in the 2 days before the end of the 6-week grading period.

   _____ 3. To test the students' ability to present a logical argument.

   _____ 4. To balance subjective judgments with a highly reliable measure.

   _____ 5. To test student understanding of a few major principles.

4. You have a student who made poor grades last year but so far this year he seems to be trying to do better. You are grading one of his written reports and are trying to decide whether he deserves a C+ or a B-.

   What factors might influence you to give the lower grade?
   What factors would influence you to give the higher grade?
   If you gave the lower grade, how could you offset its discouraging effect?

5. You are using a contract system in one of your classes. One of the requirements for and A is "to write a book report." However, some students are reporting on books that you think they read last year and some are handing in short, superficial reports.

How can you structure the contract system so that the students will do a better quality of work?

6. Review the test scores below and respond to the questions which follow:

Test 1 : 56 50 48 48 45 40 39 37 35 33 31 30 30 28 27 25 23 22 20 17 15

Test 2 : 95 91 88 86 84 79 77 75 74 71 70 67 66 65 63 62 59 56 50 49 45

Assuming that the course grade is based on these two tests, what **grades** should **Jay** and **Judy** receive?

Student	Test 1	Test 2	Grade
Jay	30	79	----
Judy	39	70	----

How can you justify your assignment of grades?

7. *These are brief descriptions of seven children, each of whom went home last month with a "D" on his report card in English. Read the description of each child and then indicate whether or not you think this child should receive a "D" for the reasons given. Circle YES if you think the child should receive a "D" and circle NO if you think he should not receive a "D." Compare your responses with those of others in your class.

A. John is just not very bright. He tries hard but barely has enough ability to get by in school.   YES   NO

B. Fred is bright enough, but he is lazy. He knows when he has done enough to earn a "D," and then he quits working.   YES   NO

C. Walter is bright, but he has a language handicap because he comes from a home in which the English language is not spoken. He barely earns a "D" but should do much better when he learns the language.   YES   NO

D. Jean is probably a "C" student in English, but he is such a discipline problem that his teacher is not inclined to give him the benefit of any doubt, so he receives a "D."   YES   NO

E. Mac does "A" or "B" work when he is in school, but he is absent so much of the time that he barely makes a "D."   YES   NO

F. Steve does "B" or "C" work in the English literature part of the course, but his composition is atrocious, so his marks average out at a "D".   YES   NO

G. Ben is doing far below passing work in English, but he flunked the course last year, and we see no point in failing him more than once in the same thing.   YES   NO

---

*Adapted from Harris, B.M., Bessent, E.W., and McIntyre, K.E., *Inservice Education: A Guide to Better Practice*, Prentice-Hall, 1969.

EPILOGUE : TEACHING AND
LEARNING IN THE COMPUTER AGE

CHAPTER OVERVIEW

I.   Computer Literacy: What Is It?
     A. Approaches and Availability
     B. Components and Functions: Hardware

II. Putting Computers to Work in Today's Classrooms
     A. The Origins and Basics of Computer-Based Education
     B. Computers as Tutors: CBI and Its Software
     C. Advantages of CBI
     D. Limitations of CBI
     E. What the Research Shows

III. Computers as Instructional Tools
     A. Word Processing
     B. Data Processing
     C. Computer-Managed Instruction

IV. Computers as Tutees: Programming

V.   What the Future Holds

CHAPTER OBJECTIVES

1. Discuss the meaning of "computer literacy."
2. Discuss the origins and basics of computer-based education or CBE.
3. Define microchip and microcomputer.
4. Describe a time-sharing system and a stand-alone unit.

5. Identify and tell the function of the following computer components:
    a. monitor
    b. hardward
    c. peripherals
    d. disk drive
    e. disk
    f. printer
    g. hard copy
    h. modem
6. Define the terms "kilobyte" and "byte."
7. Define "CBI" and "software."
8. Describe the use of CBI for the following:
    a. drill and practice
    b. tutorial
    c. simulations
    d. instructional games
9. List the advantages and limitations of CBI.
10. Discuss the research findings regarding the effectiveness of CBI.
11. Explain the uses of computers as instructional tools. Specifically in the areas of:
    a. word processing
    b. data processing
    c. computer-managed instruction
12. Identify guidelines for selecting microcomputer hardware and software.
13. List characteristics and uses of each of the following computer languages:
    a. BASIC
    b. Pascal
    c. LOGO
14. Discuss the benefits and limitations of computers.

KEY TERMS

Fill in the blanks in the following sentences with the letters preceding the concepts listed below.

a. microcomputer	k. software
b. BASIC	l. stand-alone unit
c. computer literacy	m. timesharing system
d. CBE	n. CBI
e. CMI	o. disk drive
f. hardcopy	p. disk
g. chip (microchip)	q. word processing
h. hardware	r. modem

174

i. monitor
j. peripherals

s. downtime
t. kilobytes (K)
u. data bases
v. Pascal
w. LOGO

1. A computer-based education system in which students have separate terminals that are connected to a main computer is called a/an ____ .

2. The programs that tell the computer what to do, called ____, are usually stored on a ____ or tape cassette.

3. ____ is an acronym for one of the easiest computer languages to learn. It uses simple English words and common mathematical expressions.

4. The direct application of the computer to teaching is known as ____ .

5. In ____ , the computer is used for record keeping, testing, scheduling, and other management and supervision functions.

6. A/an ____ such as those sold by Apple, Texas Instruments, Radio Shack, and others, is an example of a/an ____ which is similar to a terminal but is capable of storing and processing information by itself.

7. ____ is a broad term that refers to the general educational applications of the computer.

8. The physical equipment that goes into a compter such as mechanical and electronic devices is called ____; accessory devices such as printers and keyboards are called ____ .

9. A/an ____ is a small piece of silicon that can hold thousands of electronic circuits and made possible the size and weight reduction of computers.

10. Three of the most useful peripherals are the keyboard, the ____ which allows information to be stored outsdide the computer's memory, and the ____ which displays information from the computer.

11. A/an ____ uses regular phone lines to transmit information between computers.

12. The size of a computer's memory is expressed in ____ (equal to 1024 characters).

13. One of the disadvantages of a timesharing system is that during ____ when the main computer is not operating, students are unable to operate the terminals.

14. Information printed out on paper by a computer printer is known as ____ .

15. The information in the computer is stored in and retrieved from data files called _____ .

16. The computer language designed to facilitate the construction of highly structured and readable programs and also helps beginning students to develop good programming habits is called _____ .

17. A programming language for very young children that emphasizes discovery learning is called _____ .

18. Knowledge of the computer's basic operations and its potential and limitations is the concept of _____ .

19. Electronically creating and editing text on a monitor is known as _____ .

MULTIPLE CHOICE QUESTIONS

1. Widescale use of computers in homes and classrooms is made possible by the advent of small, relatively inexpensive systems called (p. 562)

   a. microcomputers.
   b. game machines.
   c. metacalculators.
   d. single chip devices.

2. The first general purpose computer, built in 1946 at the University of Pennsylvania, took an enormous amount of power and space because it relied on (p. 561)

   a. transistors.
   b. macrochips.
   c. mechanical linkages.
   d. vacuum tubes.

3. Computer-based education, or CBE, was first used for training (p. 561)

   a. upper-level mathematicians.
   b. personnel in the computer industry.
   c. high school students.
   d. preschoolers.

4. Computer-based education was found to be a natural way of presenting (p. 562)

   a. physical concepts.
   b. programmed instruction.
   c. reinforcers and punishers.
   d. new material to high-ability students.

5. In CMI systems the computer is used for (p. 572)

    a. recordkeeping, scheduling, and resource management.
    b. giving instant reinforcement for right answers.
    c. presenting instructional material.
    d. presenting lessons, feedback, and evaluations.

6. Many independent terminals communicate with a centralized computer and with each other in systems that use (p. 562)

    a. participatory monitors.
    b. time-sharing.
    c. group access.
    d. stand-alone units.

7. When a terminal is self-contained and needs access to no other computer it is called a (p. 562)

    a. calculator.
    b. time-share.
    c. stand-alone unit.
    d. basic computer.

8. All of the following are examples of computer hardware **except** (p. 563)

    a. language.
    b. peripheral.
    c. modem.
    d. disk drive.

9. Computers can communicate directly with other computers by the use of compatible (p. 564)

    a. modems.
    b. printers.
    c. disks.
    d. microchips.

10. Some computer games place the player in fantasy situations where they face problems not solvable in conventional ways. The player must obtain information from the computer and employ it in imaginative ways to reach his goal. Such games teach (p. 561)

    a. self-pacing.
    b. analytical skills.
    c. divergent thinking.
    d. meaningful information.

11. All of the following are disadvantages of CAI **except** (p. 567)

    a. many students find it awkward for reading text.
    b. there is not enough hardware for widespread use.
    c. it is limited to relatively simple learning levels.
    d. often there is no appropriate software available.

12. Research shows that CBI is generally associated with all of the following **except** (p. 570)

    a. improvements in long-term retention.
    b. moderate improvements in learning.
    c. reductions in instructional time.
    d. more positive student attitudes.

13. In evaluating comparisons of CBI with traditional methods, teachers should remember that the results may be skewed by (p. 571)

    a. instructors hoping to lighten their workloads.
    b. computer manufacturers.
    c. self-interested programmers.
    d. the Hawthorne effect.

14. A program in which a student pilot practices take-offs, landings, and other exercises is termed a _____ . (p. 565)

    a. drill and practice.
    b. instructional game.
    c. simulation.
    d. tutorial.

15. Martha is behind her peers in subtraction. She would probably benefit from repeated practice of the math facts and thus would likely use which of the following types of programs? (p. 565)

    a. drill and practice.
    b. instructional game.
    c. simulation.
    d. tutorial.

16. Susan has difficulty with her handwriting. In English, her class is now composing themes and doing a lot of creative writing. Susan would probably benefit from (p. 571)

    a. drill and practice.
    b. instructional games.
    c. word processing.
    d. data processing.

17. In selecting microcomputer hardware and software, you should do all of the following **except:** (p. 573)

    a. Evaluate how well available types and brands of hardware fit your needs.
    b. Avoid free software that is available as it is often of poor quality.
    c. Keep apprised of the latest-quality software available.
    d. Check catalogs sold in bookstores.

18. All of the following are limitations of computers except: (p. 575)

    a. lack of flexibility and creativity
    b. inappropriateness for presenting extensive amounts of text
    c. independence of the quality of software available
    d. lack of human qualities and inability to provide support

APPLICATION AND DISCUSSION QUESTIONS

1. What are your own thoughts, attitudes, fears, etc. about interacting with a computer?

2. Do you think computer programming should become a part of teacher education curriculum? Do you think **you** need to learn more about computers?

3. There are a many sources where you can learn more about computers and computer programming. Name several.

4. CBI provides four basic types of instruction: drill and practice, tutorial, simulation and instructional games. Discuss how you might use each of these in your teaching area. What are some advantages and difficulties that you might encounter in the use of each?

5. You have been given $5000.00 by your principal to purchase a microcomputer and software for your instructional needs. What steps would you go through in making your purchase?

APPENDIX A

UNDERSTANDING THE STANDARD DEVIATION

As the textbook described, knowing the standard deviation of a set of scores gives you a significant amount of information about the performance of the group tested, especially if the scores are normally distributed. We will review how to determine the standard deviation and give you practice with two methods for calculating it.

CALCULATING THE STANDARD DEVIATION

Below are a few symbols that you need to know to understand the formula for the standard deviation:

X is the symbol for any "score."

$\bar{X}$ is the symbol for the "mean" of all the Xs or scores.

N is the total "number" of scores.

Σ means "sum of."

$(\ )^2$ means "squared" or multiplied by itself.

$\sqrt{}$ means "square root."

As explained in Chapter 14, the standard deviation is calculated by following six steps:

1. Calculate the mean (written as $\bar{X}$) of the scores.

2. Subtract the mean from each of the scores.

   This is written as $(X - \bar{X})$.

3. Square each difference (multiply each difference by itself).

   This is written $(X - \bar{X})^2$.

4. Add all the squared differences.

   This is written $\Sigma (X - \bar{X})^2$.

5. Divide this total by the number of scores. This is written

$$\frac{\Sigma (X - \bar{X})^2}{N}$$

6. Find the square root. This is written as:

$$\sqrt{\frac{\Sigma (X - \bar{X})^2}{N}}$$

and is the formula for calculating the standard deviation.

EXAMPLE USING THE COMPLETE STANDARD DEVIATION FORMULA

Below is an example of using the formula. Follow each step as it is explained.

FIGURE A-1

Students' Points Earned on Five Assignments

Student	Test 1 20% 20 points	Test 2 20% 20 points	Unit Test 30% 30 points	Homework 15% 15 points	Project 15% 15 points	Totals
Amy	10	12	16	6	7	____
Bert	12	10	14	7	6	____
Cathy	20	19	30	15	13	____
Doug	18	20	25	15	15	____
Ed	6	5	12	4	10	____
Frieda	10	12	18	10	9	____
Grace	13	11	22	11	10	____
Herbert	7	9	12	5	6	____
Isaac	14	16	26	12	12	____
Joan	20	18	28	10	15	____
Keith	19	20	25	11	12	____
Linda	14	12	20	13	9	____
Melody	15	13	24	8	10	____
Ned	8	7	12	8	6	____
Olivia	11	12	16	9	10	____
Peter	7	8	11	4	8	____
	____	____	____	____	____	

We can use the standard deviation formula to calculate the standard deviation for the students' scores on the Unit Test as follows:

1. Calculate the mean (written as $\overline{X}$) for the scores.

$$\overline{X} = \frac{\text{total of scores}}{\text{number of scores}} = \frac{311}{16} = 19.44$$

182

2. Subtract the mean from each individual score, written as $(X - \overline{X})$.

We will use 19 as the mean to avoid working with decimals.

16 - 19 = -3	26 - 19 = 7
14 - 19 = -5	28 - 19 = 9
30 - 19 = 11	25 - 19 = 6
25 - 19 = 6	20 - 19 = 1
12 - 19 = -7	24 - 19 = 5
18 - 19 = -1	12 - 19 = -7
22 - 19 = 3	16 - 19 = -3
12 - 19 = -7	11 - 19 = -8

3. Square each resulting difference, written as $(X - \overline{X})^2$

$(-3)^2 =$	9	$(7)^2 =$	49
$(-5)^2 =$	25	$(9)^2 =$	81
$(11)^2 =$	121	$(6)^2 =$	36
$(6)^2 =$	36	$(1)^2 =$	1
$(-7)^2 =$	49	$(5)^2 =$	25
$(-1)^2 =$	1	$(-7)^2 =$	49
$(3)^2 =$	9	$(3)^2 =$	9
$(-7)^2 =$	49	$(-8)^2 =$	64

4. Add all these square numbers together, written as $\Sigma (X - \overline{X})^2$.

9	49
25	81
121	36
36	1
49	25
1	49
9	9
49	64
	___
	613

5. Divide the total by the number of scores, written as $\dfrac{\Sigma (X - \overline{X})}{N}$.

$$\frac{613}{16} = 38.31$$

183

6. Find the square root, written as

$$\sqrt{\frac{\Sigma\,(X - \bar{X})^2}{N}}$$

38.31 = **6.19** = standard deviation

(If we had done an exact calculation using 19.44 as the mean, we would have found a standard deviation of 6.37.)

Practice Problems

1. Calculate the mean and standard deviation of Test 1 in Figure A-1. (answer: mean = 12.75, standard deviation = 4.71)

2. Calculate the mean and standard deviation of Test 2 in Figure A-1. (answer: mean = 12.75, standard deviation = 4.65)

3. Calculate the mean and standard deviation of the homework scores. (answer: mean = 9.25, standard deviation = 3.53)

4. Calculate the mean and standard deviation of the project scores. (answer: mean = 9.88, standard deviation = 2.94)

A SHORT FORMULA FOR CALCULATING THE STANDARD DEVIATION

A very accurate shortcut method for calculating standard deviations was developed by Diedrich (1964). The steps in using this method are:

1. List all the scores in order from highest to lowest.

2. Add together the top 1/6 of the students' scores (e.g., the top 4 scores in a class of 24).

3. Add the bottom 1/6 of the scores.

4. Subtract the total of the bottom 1/6 from the total of the top 1/6.

5. Divide the difference by 1/2 the total number of scores.

The formula is:

$$\text{standard deviation} = \frac{\text{sum of top 1/6 scores - sum of bottom 1/6 scores}}{\text{1/2 the number of scores}}$$

Now let's use this simplified formula to calulate the standard deviation for that same Unit Test in Figure A-1.

Example of Using Shortcut Formula

1. List all the scores in order from lowest to highest.

1.	30	9.	18
2.	28	10.	16
3.	26	11.	16
4.	25	12.	14
5.	25	13.	12
6.	24	14.	12
7.	22	15.	12
8.	20	16.	11

2. Add together the top 1/6 of the scores. One sixth of 16 is approximately 3.

    30
    28
    26
    ──
    84

3. Add together the bottom 1/6 of the scores.

    12
    12
    11
    ──
    35

4. Subtract the bottom 1/6 from the top 1/6 and divide by 1/2 the number of scores.

    $$\frac{84 - 35}{8} = \mathbf{6.13} = \text{standard deviation}$$

Compare the standard deviation found with the simplified formula to the standard deviation found using the exact formula.

Practice Problems

1. Using the shortcut formula*, calculate the standard deviation for
   (a) test 1....................   (answer = 4.88)

   (b) test 2....................   (answer = 4.88)

   (c) homework scores......   (answer = 3.75)

   (d) project...................   (answer = 3.13)

   (*Use three scores as 1/6 of 16.)

2. Compare the standard deviations found using the shortcut formula with the standard deviations calculated using the complete formula.

References

Diedrich, P.D. *Short-cut Statistics for Teacher-made Tests* .

Princeton, N.J.: Educational Testing Service, 1964.

Appendix A by Anita E. Woolfolk.

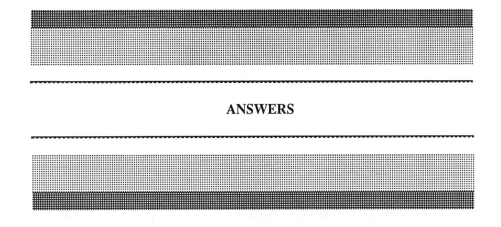

ANSWERS

The answers to the key terms, multiple choice, and some of the application/discussion questions for each chapter are listed below and on subsequent pages.

CHAPTER 1

Key Terms

1.	b	10.	j
2.	g	11.	k
3.	a	12.	l
4.	f	13.	d
5.	e	14.	h
6.	n	15.	i
7.	m	16.	q
8.	o	17.	p
9.	c	18.	r

Multiple Choice Questions

1.	d
2.	a
3.	c
4.	c
5.	d
6.	b
7.	c

Application/Discussion Questions

2. a. correlational
    b. experimental
    c. correlational
    d. experimental

APPENDIX A

Key Terms

1.	h	6.	c,d,b,e,f	1.	b	6.	b
2.	a	7.	p	2.	a	7.	c
3.	j,k	8.	i	3.	a	8.	a
4.	o	9.	m	4.	c	9.	b
5.	l	10.	g	5.	d		

CHAPTER 2

Key Terms

General Development Terms

1. d
2. e
3. c
4. f
5. b
6. a

Piagetian Terms

1.	x	14.	i
2.	t	15.	j
3.	a	16.	n
4.	d	17.	v
5.	f	18.	o
6.	h	19.	u
7.	b	20	r
8.	e	21.	v
9.	w	22.	q
10.	c	23.	s
11.	p	24.	l
12.	g	25.	m
13.	k	26.	z

Information Processing and Language Development Terms

1.	i	8.	g
2.	e	9.	c
3.	l	10.	h
4.	j	11.	f
5.	a	12.	d
6.	b	13.	k
7.	n	14.	m

Multiple Choice Questions

1.	c	15.	d
2.	d	16.	b
3.	c	17.	c
4.	a	18.	c
5.	b	19.	b
6.	a	20.	b
7.	d	21.	c
8.	b	22.	c
9.	d	23.	d
10.	b	24.	c
11.	a	25.	c
12.	c	26.	c
13.	a	27.	d
14.	c		

Application and Discussion Questions

1a.	Late Preoperational	Perceptual Feature
1b.	Early Preoperational	Functional Relationship
1c.	Concrete Operations	Common Elements
1d.	Formal Operations	Hypothetical Reasoning
1e.	Sensorimotor	Object Permanence
1f.	Formal Operations	Combinatorial
1g.	Preoperational	Childhood logic
1h.	Sensorimotor	Goal directed actions
1i.	Formal Operations	Hypothetical Reasoning
1j .	Concrete Operations	Seriation

CHAPTER 3

Key Terms

1.	p	13.	q, e
2.	a	14.	m
3.	k	15.	b
4.	o	16.	n
5.	s	17.	w
6.	f	18.	c
7.	j	19.	d
8.	h	20.	i
9.	x	21.	u

Multiple Choice Questions

1.	c	16.	b
2.	d	17.	a
3.	b	18.	a
4.	c	19.	c
5.	c	20.	b
6.	b	21.	a
7.	b	22.	b
8.	c	23.	c
9.	d	24.	a

10.	r	22.	t
11.	g	23	l,y
12.	v		

10.	a	25.	c
11.	c	26.	b
12.	b	27.	b
13.	c	28.	d
14.	b	29.	b
15.	d		

Application/Discussion Questions

1. a. 2
   b. 1
   c. 2
   d. 3
   e. 1

CHAPTER 4

Key Terms

1.	v	15.	a
2.	x	16.	n
3.	d	17.	p
4.	o	18.	e
5.	s	19.	t
6.	h, u	20.	g
7.	l	21.	r
8.	f	22.	y
9.	q	23.	m
10.	k		
11.	i		
12.	b		
13.	j		
14.	w		

Multiple Choice Questions

1.	c	16.	c
2.	a	17.	b
3.	b	18.	b
4.	c	19.	d
5.	c	20.	d
6.	c	21.	d
7.	a	22.	d
8.	c	23.	c
9.	b	24.	b
10.	d	25.	a
11.	a	26.	a
12.	c	27.	c
13.	c	28.	c
14.	d	29.	b
15.	c	30.	d

Application/Discussion Questions

Situation 1		Situation 2		Situation 3	
a.	2	a.	3	a.	3
b.	1	b.	2	b.	1
c.	3	c.	1	c.	2

CHAPTER 5

Key Terms

Classical Conditioning	Operant Conditioning	Observational Learning and Programmed Instruction
1. d	1. a	1. a
2. e	2. c	2. c
3. f	3. e	3. e
4. h	4. g	4. g
5. j	5. i	5. i
6. l	6. k	6. h
7. m	7. m	7. f
8. k	8. o	8. d
9. i	9. n	9. b
10. g	10. l	
11. b,c,a	11. p	
	12. j	
	13. h	
	14. f	
	15. d	
	16. b	

Multiple Choice Questions

1.	c	15.	a
2.	a	16.	b
3.	d	17.	d
4.	a	18.	c
5.	b	19.	b
6.	b	20.	d
7.	c	21.	b
8.	c	22.	b
9.	c	23.	a
10.	c	24.	b
11.	c	25.	b
12.	b	26.	a
13.	b	27.	a
14.	b		

CHAPTER 6

Key Terms

1.	a	9.	i
2.	b	10.	j
3.	c	11.	k
4.	d	12.	m
5.	e	13.	n
6.	f	14.	o
7.	g	15.	p
8.	h		

Multiple Choice Questions

1.	d	16.	b
2.	b	17.	c
3.	c	18.	c
4.	b	19.	a
5.	a	20.	d
6.	b	21.	d
7.	d	22.	c
8.	a	23.	c
9.	d	24.	b
10.	b	25.	d
11.	b	26.	c
12.	d	27.	d
13.	d		
14.	b		
15.	b		

CHAPTER 7

Key Terms

1.	d	19.	r
2.	e	20.	n
3.	g	21.	m
4.	i	22.	l
5.	k	23.	jj

Multiple Choice Questions

1.	a	12.	c
2.	b	13.	a
3.	b	14.	a
4.	d	15.	a
5.	c	16.	a

6.	j	24.	x		6.	b	17.	d
7.	h	25.	y		7.	d	18.	c
8.	f	26.	ff		8.	b	19.	c
9.	c	27.	ii		9.	d	20.	b
10.	b	28.	cc		10.	b		
11.	a	29.	hh		11.	c		
12.	o	30.	dd					
13.	p	31.	aa					
14.	s	32.	ee					
15.	u	33.	gg					
16.	w	34.	q					
17.	v	35.	hh					
18.	t	36.	bb					
		37.	z					

CHAPTER 8

Key Terms

1.	a or ee	18.	ee or a
2.	c	19.	gg
3.	jj	20.	ii
4.	g	21.	r
5.	i	22.	hh
6.	k	23.	ff
7.	m	24.	dd
8.	o	25.	bb
9.	b	26.	z
10.	t	27.	x
11.	w	28.	v
12.	y	29.	p
13.	q	30.	n
14.	s	31.	l
15.	u	32.	j
16.	aa	33.	h
17.	cc	34.	f
		35.	d
		36.	e

Multiple Choice Questions

1.	c	11.	c
2.	d	12.	d
3.	a	13.	c
4.	c	14.	d
5.	c	15.	d
6.	a	16.	c
7.	a	17.	c
8.	c	18.	a
9.	c	19.	b
10.	d	20.	c

CHAPTER 9

Key Terms

1.	a	13.	b
2.	c	14.	m
3.	g	15.	t
4.	n	16.	d
5.	e	17.	v
6.	q	18.	s
7.	l	19.	f
8.	p	20.	j
9.	k	21.	r
10.	h	22.	u
11.	i	23.	w
12.	o		

Multiple Choice Questions

1.	b	13.	d
2.	d	14.	a
3.	c	15.	b
4.	d	16.	d
5.	d	17.	a
6.	b	18.	b
7.	d	19.	c
8.	c	20.	c
9.	a	21.	b
10.	d	22.	b
11.	c	23.	c
12.	d	24.	b

CHAPTER 10

Key Terms

1.	k
2.	m
3.	j
4.	a
5.	d
6.	l
7.	f
8.	b
9.	n
10.	c
11.	e
12.	l
13.	g
14.	i
15.	h

Multiple Choice Questions

1.	b	13.	b
2.	d	14.	b
3.	b	15.	a
4.	a	16.	d
5.	b	17.	b
6.	d	18.	d
7.	a	19.	a
8.	c	20.	a
9.	d	21.	b
10.	c	22.	a
11.	c	23.	c
12.	c	24.	c

CHAPTER 11

Key Terms

1.	s	11.	p
2.	b	12.	a
3.	l	13.	e
4.	o	14.	n
5.	j	15.	i
6.	t	16.	q
7.	f,g,h	17.	r
8.	c	18.	w
9.	d	19.	x
10.	k	20.	y
		21.	z

Multiple Choice Questions

1.	b	14.	a
2.	c	15.	b
3.	d	16.	b
4.	b	17.	b
5.	b	18.	c
6.	b	19.	c
7.	d	20.	b
8.	b	21.	a
9.	b	22.	b
10.	c	23.	a
11.	d	24.	c
12.	d	25.	a
13.	b	26.	c
		27.	c

CHAPTER 12

Key Terms

1.	c	9.	h
2.	b	10.	i
3.	f	11.	j
4.	o	12.	k
5.	g	13.	l
6.	e	14.	m
7.	a	15.	n
8.	d		

Multiple Choice Questions

1.	c	14.	a
2.	c	15.	b
3.	d	16.	c
4.	d	17.	c
5.	d	18.	b
6.	d	19.	a
7.	a	20.	a
8.	b	21.	a
9.	d	22.	c
10.	b	23.	c
11.	a	24.	b
12.	b	25.	c
13.	d		

CHAPTER 13

Key Terms

1.	q	9.	u,v
2.	i,j	10.	f,g,h
3.	c	11.	n
4.	k,l,m	12.	a
5.	s	13.	t
6.	b	14.	o
7.	r	15.	w
8.	d,e	16.	p

Multiple Choice Questions

1.	d	13.	d
2.	d	14.	c
3.	a	15.	a
4.	c	16.	d
5.	c	17.	c
6.	a	18.	d
7.	d	19.	d
8.	b	20.	d
9.	b	21.	c
10.	c	22.	b
11.	a	23.	d
12.	c	24.	a
		25.	c

CHAPTER 14

Key Terms

1.	r	11.	c,d
2.	e,f	12.	n,o
3.	v	13.	bb,aa
4.	j,i,l,k	14.	a,b
5.	dd,cc,ee	15.	z
6.	y	16.	q
7.	w	17.	ff
8.	g	18.	p
9.	gg	19.	x
10.	s,t,u		

Multiple Choice Questions

1.	c	8.	c
2.	d	9.	c
3.	c	10.	a
4.	b	11.	b
5.	c	12.	b
6.	d	13.	c
7.	a	14.	d
		15.	a

Application and Discussion Questions

1. A.		1. B.		1. C.		1. D.	
1.	a	1.	b	1.	d	1.	NRT
2.	b	2.	a	2.	b	2.	CRT
3.	c	3.	a	3.	e	3.	CRT
4.	d	4.	c	4.	c	4.	NRT
5.	a			5.	a		

6. c

7. e

2. Mean = 11
   Median = 6
   Mode = 3

3. Reading raw score of 37 = + 1.4 S.D.
   Math raw score of 56 = + .8 S.D.

4. Class A because there is less variability in the scores

5. Confidence Interval = 69 - 75
   Percentile Rank = 93
   z-score = 1.5
   T score = 65
   Stanine score = 8
   Raw score = between 52 and 68

CHAPTER 15

Key Terms

1.	e	11.	g
2.	k	12.	i
3.	p	13.	n
4.	a	14.	c
5.	q	15.	i
6.	f	16.	m
7.	b	17.	o
8.	l	18.	s
9.	h	19.	r
10.	d	20.	j

Multiple Choice Questions

1.	a	16.	b
2.	c	17.	c
3.	c	18.	b
4.	d	19.	c
5.	b	20.	c
6.	d	21.	a
7.	a	22.	c
8.	a	23.	b
9.	b	24.	c
10.	d	25.	b
11.	b	26.	c
12.	b	27.	a
13.	b	28.	c
14.	a	29.	b
15.	a	30.	d

Key Terms

1.	m	11.	r
2.	k,p	12.	t
3.	b	13.	s
4.	n	14.	f
5.	e	15.	u
6.	a,l	16.	v
7.	d	17.	w
8.	h,j	18.	c
9.	g	19.	q
10.	o,i		

Multiple Choice Questions

1.	a	10.	c
2.	d	11.	c
3.	b	12.	a
4.	b	13.	d
5.	a	14.	c
6.	b	15.	a
7.	c	16.	c
8.	a	17.	b
9.	a	18.	c